THE BIENNIAL READER

THE BIENNIAL READER

EDITED BY

ELENA FILIPOVIC · MARIEKE VAN HAL · SOLVEIG ØVSTEBØ

BERGEN KUNSTHALL

HATJE CANTZ

Editors: Elena Filipovic, Marieke van Hal, and Solveig Øvstebø
Editorial Assistant: Helene A. Lazaridis
Copyediting: Krystina Stermole
Graphic Design and Typesetting: Grandpeople, www.grandpeople.org
Commission: City of Bergen, Department of Culture, Church Affairs, and Sports
Production: Solveig Øvstebø, Bergen Kunsthall, and Angelika Hartmann, Hatje Cantz
Reproductions: Weyhing digital, Ostfildern
Paper: Munken Print White, 100 g/m^2
Printing and Binding: fgb · freiburger graphische betriebe

Published by:

Bergen Kunsthall
Rasmus Meyers allé 5
5015 Bergen
Norway

T: +47 55 55 93 10
F: +47 55 55 93 19
www.kunsthall.no

and

Hatje Cantz Verlag
Zeppelinstrasse 32
73760 Ostfildern
Germany

T: +49 711 4405-200
F: +49 711 4405-220
www.hatjecantz.com

This book was made possible by the generous funding of the City of Bergen.

BERGEN KOMMUNE

With support from: Arts Council Norway, Fritt Ord, Hordaland County Council, and Mondriaan Stichting

NORSK KULTURRÅD
Arts Council Norway
FRITT ORD
HORDALAND FYLKESKOMMUNE
Mondriaan Stichting (Mondriaan Foundation)

Hatje Cantz books are available internationally at selected bookstores. For more information about our distribution partners, please visit our website at www.hatjecantz.com.

ISBN 978-3-7757-2610-8

Printed in Germany

If it can be said that for more than a century museum and gallery exhibitions have largely been "the *medium through which most art becomes known,"* then it is the* biennial exhibition *that has arguably since proved to be* the *medium through which most contemporary art comes to be known.*

*Reesa Greenberg, Bruce W. Ferguson, and Sandy Nairne, "Introduction," in idem (eds.), *Thinking about Exhibitions* (London and New York, 1996), p. 2

CONTENTS

HISTORIES, PRECEDENTS, AND ORIGINS

WHAT IS A BIENNIAL? POTENTIALS, FUNCTIONS, AND IDEALS

THE CURATORIAL

RETHINKING BIENNIALS: MODELS AND FORMATS

THE POLITICS OF A GLOBAL ART WORLD

FOREWORD

THIS publication has its origins in the Bergen City Council's interest in establishing a biennial of contemporary art in Bergen, Norway. Well aware of both the rewards and the problematic realities of founding a new biennial, the City of Bergen agreed, at the encouragement of the Bergen Kunsthall, to begin the planning process with a careful reflection on the biennial phenomenon and its implications. It was thanks to this exceptional open-mindedness that the City of Bergen, rather than immediately succumbing to the seductive power this exhibition format can have, gave the Bergen Kunsthall the task of organizing the Bergen Biennial Conference of 2009. This international conference and think tank's study and discussion of the status of the biennial as an exhibition model offered an ideal context for debate about the plans for a Bergen Biennial.

To conceive this conference, which developed into one of the most extensive discussions about biennials to date, I solicited the collaboration of Elena Filipovic and Marieke van Hal, both scholars and professionals in the field of biennial research. Together, we wanted to create a platform where crucial aspects of the phenomenon of the perennial exhibition could be discussed. Thirty-three professionals from all over the world, as well as an audience that was both local and international, thus came together with a shared purpose: to take an uncompromising look at the potentials and problems of the production and presentation of contemporary art in the large-scale exhibition format. The incredible debate that ensued prompted intense and vivid exchanges among the leading historians, curators, critics, scholars, and artists involved in biennial-making today.

For this occasion we were also fortunate to have the possibility of exhibiting the Arquivo Histórico Wanda Svevo (Wanda Svevo Historical Archive) on international biennials that was conceived as part of the twenty-eighth São Paulo Biennial and constitutes the world's most comprehensive documentary resource on biennials. Making this archive available for consultation during the conference was an important part of our approach to this project, which saw research as a crucial starting point. We can say the same about the international "Call for Biennial Knowledge" issued prior to the conference, which provided us with valuable source material to draw upon in the process of conceiving both the conference and what later became this book, *The Biennial Reader*. Our research and the "Call for Biennial Knowledge" also confirmed what at first seemed quite unimaginable: that there were virtually no extensive publications devoted to the history and theorization of the perennial exhibition phenomenon.

The City of Bergen's plan included producing a publication, which was initially envisioned as a printed version of the conference proceedings. However, the research carried out in preparation for the conference revealed that there was a lamentable paucity of material on biennials, and this convinced us all of the need for a more profound publication about the biennial phenomenon, one that would serve not only the City of Bergen, but also the broader international art world. In the light of this, the City of Bergen showed incredible determination, flexibility, and courage in letting us develop our project one step further with the publication of *The Biennial Reader*. The book is an anthology that pays homage to some of the best essays written on the subject of biennials, ones that have shaped scholarship and curating and have opened up the possibility for continued debate today, but also incorporates new contributions, some of which are derived from lectures given at the Bergen Biennial Conference. *The Biennial Reader* is also supplemented by a booklet presenting reviews of the various sessions of the conference.

Although it is still uncertain if Bergen will one day host a biennial of its own, the knowledge gleaned from the conference's three-day symposium and from this publication will hopefully inspire further research and stimulate the kind of debate and artistic and curatorial development that would be essential in launching a Bergen biennial.

I would like to thank all of the authors who contributed to this publication and all of those who participated in the 2009 conference for their important contributions to this project. I would also like to express my thanks to the staff of the Bergen Kunsthall, which has demonstrated remarkable know-how and dedication during the organization of the Bergen Biennial Conference and the preparation of *The Biennial Reader.*

Last but not least, I would like to thank my fellow editors, Marieke van Hal and Elena Filipovic, for an enriching collaboration and the City of Bergen for making this publication possible.

Solveig Øvstebø

Director
Bergen Kunsthall

BIENNIALOGY

12

Elena Filipovic, Marieke van Hal, and Solveig Øvstebø

FOR some skeptics the word biennial has come to signify nothing more than an overblown symptom of spectacular event culture, the result of some of the most specious transformations of the world in the age of late capitalism—in short, a Western typology whose proliferation has infiltrated even the most far-reaching parts of the world, where such events are little more than entertaining or commercially driven showcases designed to feed an ever-expanding tourist industry (in other words, something not far removed from the art fair or Disneyland). Pernicious not only in its imported form, the biennial is taken to be equally dangerous to the development of serious art, which can hardly be made to thrive in what Peter Schjeldahl famously and damningly reduced to "festivalism."[1] For others, the biennial is a critical site of experimentation in exhibition-making, offering artists, curators, and spectators a vital alternative to museums and other similar institutions whose institutional inertias do not allow them to respond with immediacy and flexibility to contemporary art's developments. Some even see the biennial form as being full of redemptive and even utopian possibility, or as a testament to a paradigm shift: a platform—like perhaps no other art institution before it—for grappling with such issues as politics, race, ethics, identity, globalization, and postcolonialism in art-making and -showing today. And while being emphatically *also* an exhibition (at least it has been thus far), the biennial's supporters often understand it as being "neither exclusively nor even primarily a space of spectacular display," as curator and writer Ranjit Hoskote posits in his essay in this volume, but rather as "a discursive environment: a theater that allows for the staging of arguments, speculations, and investigations concerning the nature of our shared, diversely veined, and demanding contemporary condition."[2] And between the contradictory positions of either malaise or rapture, and cynicism or critical embrace lie questions about what a biennial *can* or *should be.*

What, however, *is* a biennial? Over the years, the term has been used to refer to a vast landscape of different exhibition projects, with no source agreeing on their total number (currently thought to be somewhere between one hundred and two hundred around the world). The first to carry the title was the Venice Biennial, begun in 1895, but it wasn't until a half century later, when the São Paulo Biennial was founded in 1951, that the term "biennial" was used again to label such an art event.[3] The now-defunct Paris Biennial followed in 1959, with the Sydney Biennial formed more than a decade later in 1973.[4] Others were established in the decades that followed, but the "proliferation" we now attribute to the biennial was slow and, in many ways, mirrored the transformations of the art world at large (the rise of the art fair, the vast increase in the number of art journals, the creation of curating courses, and more widespread general interest in contemporary art, etc.). The Havana Biennial and Istanbul Biennial, for instance, both particularly remarkable for the catalyzing effect they had in sparking debate about the so-called periphery, were founded in 1984 and 1987 respectively. And it would take until the nineteen-nineties, when an exponential expansion of the genre occurred with the launching of more than a dozen new biennials, for the term to become the household name with which we are now familiar.[5] Moscow, Liverpool, Taipei, Bucharest, Lyon, Johannesburg, Sharjah, Berlin: these are just some of the many cities that have appended "Biennial" to their names over the years to announce their own versions of a contemporary art event that generally recurs every two years (though not always, as financial, political, or other practical circumstances and local desires sometimes have gotten in the way of this).[6] Other related events, such as Manifesta (European Biennial of Contemporary Art), the Mercosul Biennial, or the Biennial of the End of the World, have paired the term with more evocative descriptions of their regional or other focuses.[7] And for many, "biennial" refers less to a specific periodicity (namely, an art event produced biannually, as its etymology suggests) than to a type or model of large-scale, perennial, international manifestation that has become so common in the landscape of exhibition-making today. Often grandiose in scale, sometimes dispersed across several locations in a city, at times locally embedded through site-specific commissions while being global in ambition, and often involving discursive components such as symposia, extensive publications, or even accompanying journals alongside a group show featuring, for the most part, a panoramic view of a new generation of artists, "the biennial" has become shorthand for many wildly different recurring exhibitions of contemporary art, including triennials and even Documenta, which occurs every five years.[8]

The project of *The Biennial Reader* is based on the premise that this potentially contradictory thing called "the biennial" must not remain unexamined, all the more so precisely because its relevance and critical currency are so profoundly contested. However, instead of being a collection of cursory arguments for or against it, or perceiving its proliferation as a problem in itself, which merely shuts down discussion, this publication brings together a wide range of opinionated texts that, although coming from different generational, cultural, and historical positions, seriously tackle the concept of the biennial as cultural object. The essays gathered here are written by curators, artists, critics, and scholars, both established and emerging, who critically examine the biennial's conceptual, institutional, aesthetic, and political reasons for being, its way of speaking to us over time, and its potential for continued relevance, if relevance there is to be. For to dismiss the biennial because of its shortcomings would be to fail to take into account a platform that has undeniably given rise to some of the most engaged debates and thought-provoking artworks of our time. For instance, Hans Haacke's *Germania,* composed of the shattered interior of the German Pavilion at the 1993 Venice Biennial (fig. 1), is but one example of how an artwork commissioned for and seen in a "mega-exhibition" left us with an indelible experience and prompted widespread critical reflection on issues such as nation, history, politics, and memory. And there are others: Tania Bruguera's *The Burden of Guilt* produced for the 1997 Havana Biennial, Steve McQueen's *Western Deep* for Documenta 11 in 2002, Song Dong's *Waste Not* at the 2005 Gwangju Biennial, and Mladen Stilinovic's "poor" paintings at the 2009 Istanbul Biennial, to name just a few. In addition to the experience of encountering individual artworks, in these exhibitions there is also the experience of the way a particular staging of works of art in space and time creates relationships between viewers and objects, between one object and another, and between all of these elements and space, architecture, and cultural and institutional history—all of which has made us look and think differently. Indeed, as art critic Thomas McEvilley once posited so beautifully, "A sensitive exhibition defines a certain moment, embodying attitudes and, often, changes of attitude that reveal, if only by the anxieties they create, the direction in which culture is moving."[9] To attempt to understand biennials, then, is to attempt to understand something crucial about our culture today.

If it can be said that for more than a century museum and gallery exhibitions have largely been "*the* medium through which most art becomes known,"[10] then it is the *biennial exhibition* that has arguably since proved to be *the* medium through which most contemporary art comes to be known. And this is the case, no matter what one's position on or opinion about it may be. Indeed, biennials have become, in the span of just a few decades, one of the most vital and visible sites for contemporary art and the production, distribution, and generation of public discourse around it. This shift demands a revision of how we think about not only the way in which art is being conceived and received today, but also the way in which its history can be written. Art history has long been built on an analysis of individual, autonomous artworks (open any art history book and you will see this), yet, as scholars have recognized in recent years, the writing of that history should also involve the analysis of the site or context in which the artwork first gains public visibility.[11] It can also be argued that the history of contemporary art must be written through, with, and alongside an understanding of the biennial *in particular,* because to take into account the armatures for art's presentation today means, increasingly, to attend to the history and specificity of the large-scale, perennial exhibitions of our contemporary period.[12]

What might provocatively be called a "biennialogy" is thus called for. The suffix "ology" usually connotes the study of something in a systematic, rigorous way in order to generate a body of knowledge. A "biennialogy," we thought, would argue for the possibilities—indeed the necessity—of treating this contemporary phenomenon as a serious subject of study. Doing this felt necessary, because despite the number of symposia, lectures, and debates that biennials have inspired, little sustained critical assessment of the phenomenon—in all its specificities and implications—has yet been carried out. Already in 2003, curator Carlos Basualdo pointed out that while a rather profuse bibliography on the museum existed by then, not a single publication had been devoted to the subject of large-scale exhibitions. Shortly after, art historian Charlotte Bydler published her doctoral dissertation, *The Global Art World, Inc.*, the first in-depth study analyzing the development of biennials in relation to globalization.[13] However, the broad expansion of the biennial landscape worldwide has still, surprisingly, hardly changed the situation since. Apart from a number of now-seminal essays scattered across various journals and books (many of which are collected and republished in the present volume), publications that have actually focused on the biennial in a sustained way remain rare.[14] It is within this context that this anthology aims to critically locate, historicize, and even trouble and reformulate "the biennial," and, in the process, be able to critically assess its past, its potential for continued relevance, and its future.

So, why might all this matter? This publication argues that exhibitions in general, and biennial exhibitions specifically and increasingly, are central sites for understanding the artwork of today. If we are to believe Jacques Derrida, there is no "hors-texte," no *outside* the text that is not also in some way *also the text,* which is to say that it is impossible to completely separate the words on a page from the fact that they are on a page, and that the page is published in a certain way, in a certain context, by a certain journal (for instance, with left or right leanings, etc.).[15] These conditions are integral to our understanding of that text, just as they are to our understanding of the artwork. Although one might consider the work of art an autonomous thing that articulates a meaning that unquestionably inheres in itself, it would be naïve (and even dangerous) to ignore the ideological and aesthetic impact of the context, dramaturgy, and discursive armatures that bring an artwork into public view. This is because the frame around the artwork—geopolitical, institutional, discursive, and spatial—is never neutral, but instead administers readings and interpretations. This does not, however, suggest that the meaning of the artwork is the *result* of the exhibition, nor does it advocate (as some have) thinking of the curator as a co-author of the artwork.[16] It does not even plead for the consideration of the container as being more important than what is contained, but only that the container, too, should not be assumed to be negligible, innocent, or disinterested. Instead, artworks, at their best, define positions that can contribute to, as much as resolutely resist, the exhibition frames within which we place them. They can, quite simply, undo the very arguments or classificatory systems thought to contain them. For a work of art—and herein lies its incredible power and complexity—*can construct the exhibition as much as it can be constructed by it.* This is no less true of the way that artworks operate in relation to the increasing number of biennials, so, following the global shifts of ideologies, power, and empire that have faced the world in the last few decades, the need to examine this prevalent exhibitionary site of the construction (and potential resistance) of aesthetic, political, and intellectual meaning presents itself with all the more urgency today.

This publication thus reads the claimed theoretical, political, and other ambitions of mega-exhibitions against the grain of the realities they actually generate. In the volume's attempt to bring together new research by both celebrated and emerging scholars as a means of addressing a major contemporary phenomenon, it also seemed important to gather preexisting texts written about biennials over the last five decades in order to acknowledge the slow but increasing development of the biennial as an object of study over time. These seminal essays range from the late critic and curator Lawrence Alloway's 1969 description of the radical transformations of the Venice Biennial in 1968 (just at the moment when so much in the world was changing) to artist Daniel Buren's 1972 "Exhibition of an Exhibition," a critical response to Harald Szeemann's watershed Documenta 5 and its cult of the curator, and from founder of the Havana Biennial Gerardo Mosquera's 1992 denunciation of Eurocentrism and what he called the "Marco Polo Syndrome" to Michael Brenson's 1998 proclamation of the beginning of "The Curator's Moment." These and the other historic essays reprinted in the present volume, many of which are now out of print or difficult to find, contribute to a broader understanding of what we call "the biennial" today. Whether classic or newly written, all of the texts in this volume seek provisional answers to the questions haunting our contemporary moment, and we hope they will spark the kind of debate that can fuel further study.

To locate the potential significance of the biennial, we thought it was important to begin by speaking of the histories and exhibitionary precedents that made it possible, but even these origins are the subject of some dispute: Do they lie in the Crystal Palace, that commercial and architectural feat of 1851 so elegantly written about by Donald Preziosi and Marian Pastor Roces in 2001 and 2005, respectively? Is the Venice Biennial (itself a product of the nineteenth-century *expositions universelles*) indeed the true "mother" of the genre, as art historian Caroline A. Jones argues in her new essay in this volume? In her telling, a model of nation-building and the display of cultural patrimony undergird the biennial's genealogy. Or is the Havana Biennial, the first fully international, globally concerned, and discursively backed biennial launched in 1984, the true model for the proliferation of biennials that would follow in its wake, as Rafal Niemojewski suggests in an essay in this book that emerges from his extensive doctoral research on the topic? Together, these texts not only articulate a multiplicity of possible precedents for the biennial, but also reveal the stakes of such myths of origin.

Can one even speak of a singular origin or history of "the biennial" when the various examples that would seem to fit the category are spread all over the world and when the cultural, financial, and ideological differences between them are so vast? The fact is that the founding stories of individual biennials must also be told, because despite their emphatically global ambitions, many large-scale recurrent exhibitions were made possible, or even necessary and urgent, because of decisive "local" events and issues. In the case of Documenta, it was Germany's postwar reconstruction; for the Johannesburg Biennial, it was the end of apartheid; for Manifesta, the fall of the Berlin Wall was claimed as a conceptual point of reference; for the Havana Biennial, it was the crucially felt need to offer an alternative position to the Western/American domination of the art world; in the case of the Gwangju Biennial, South Korea's turn to democracy after years of repressive military dictatorships was claimed as its reason for coming into being; for the Riwaq Biennial, the event's motivation was to generate an international dialogue in Palestine about the political circumstances of occupation and isolation; Prospect, for its part, was an urban renewal project for New Orleans sparked by the need to respond to the devastation left behind by a hurricane; and the Luanda Triennial was supposed to be about the cultural enrichment and empowerment of a population recovering from years of war... And the list could go on. Besides perceived social, political, economic, or even ecological needs (each of which differently impacts the tenor or scope of the resulting project), how much of what biennials have become, in the aspirations of many of them to represent cultures other than those of the West and to reflect a truly international art world, is the result of an entirely different kind of genealogy? For instance, might one instead trace them back to another exhibition, *Les Magiciens de la Terre,* which, however flawed, arguably changed the parameters of biennials around the world?[17] We thought it was important that this volume provide a sampling of these vexed histories and multiple genealogies (and for each one included there are several others that, sadly, had to be left out for reasons of space), because in them one understands how each individual biennial—and indeed "the biennial," as an overarching genre or type—might still be coming to terms with its own historical development.

In a 2003 essay reprinted in this volume, Carlos Basualdo called the biennial a fundamentally "unstable institution" whose identity can perhaps best be defined, *ex negativo,* in contrast with the more established, self-possessed, permanently fixed, and symbolically weighty institution of the museum. Expanding on this notion of instability, Maria Hlavajova suggests in the new essay she contributed to this book that "the identity of the biennial must necessarily be unstable, always in flux, and difficult to articulate in terms of continuity or as something more than just the sum of its editions over time." She then goes on to say that we should first "remind ourselves that speaking about '*the* biennial' is an impossible task, as no single form representing this entire hybrid field of cultural endeavor exists." This gives rise to a curious paradox: the biennial *cannot be fully defined* and yet, as we argue, *must* be studied; while it may evade easy definition, we nonetheless need to understand it in order to make sense of the conditions and development of contemporary art.

Complicating this paradox is perhaps yet another question that poses itself: after exploring what the biennial is and has been, how can we determine what the biennial *can yet be?* Again and again contributors to this volume counter prevailing doubts about *whether* "to biennial" at all (or any more) with an altogether different query: *how* and *what* should we biennial today?[18] In the process, different models of institutions are discussed. For while the large-scale exhibition has been compared to such structures as the art fair and even the Olympics, the one institutional body it has most frequently been discussed in relation—or rather in contrast—to is the museum. The utopian promise of the biennial was that while the museum (that Enlightenment institution par excellence) was the place for authoritative pronouncements, classification, canonization, and preservation, the biennial's raison d'être was to provide a site for experimentation, contingency, testing, ambiguity, and inquiry. So, did biennials live up to that potential? And if they did, in what context and in response to what impulses did they develop? For we must remember that the traditional art institution has long been understood as being conventional in form, slow in its workings, and endowed with monumentally stable architectures full of supposedly neutral spaces, all of which is burdened by inflexible systems of accountability (at least this was the idea of the museum against which many biennials originally positioned themselves); on the other side of this idea of the institution stands a rapacious market that answers to a consumptive logic of supply and demand connected to confirmed values. Challenging both, the examples of what was called a "new institutionalism" that emerged in the nineteen nineties (in response to many of the same forces with which biennials grappled) demonstrated not only that the art institution itself could change, but also that the biennial would have to as well in order to continue to be relevant.[19] Thus while biennials might have been, at certain points in recent history, the experimental cousins of more established art institutions, their seemingly more stable counterparts (not only museums, but also art centers, *Kunsthallen,* etc.) arguably—and unsurprisingly—evolved as well, thereby causing the distance between the two to shift at times.[20] And along the way, despite its institutional-critical pretensions, the biennial itself might have become one more bonafide institution of the art world just like any other.

It is undeniable that the legacy and impact of the "dematerialization" of the art object in the nineteen-sixties in combination with the overwhelming transformations of the political, social, and aesthetic economy of our globalized, postcolonial, post-history millennium has in many ways led artists to produce artworks in a different way than they did half a century ago (when, for instance, the first biennial outside of Venice was being inaugurated). And while one could argue that the development of the biennial accompanied the historical shift in art-making from the "genius artist," who made auratic and autonomous art (meant for the museum), to the altogether different ambitions that artists and art production pursue today (not to mention, simply, the changes in artists' ways of working since as recently as the nineteen-nineties), the questions we might ask are: Did biennials in some way change the nature or tenor of the art being made, or, conversely, are biennials the direct product and development of art?[21] And how can we assess the direction, causes, and merits of such developments? After grappling with these (admittedly potentially unanswerable) questions, we commissioned essays that ventured a variety of tentative responses, including curators Bruce W. Ferguson and Milena M. Hoegsberg's exploration of how shifts in art practice may have impacted the turn towards discursivity in exhibition-making, Maria Hlavajova's discussion of the way the cultural function of biennials and art institutions like museums and art centers impact one another and interrelate, and writer Jan Verwoert's fable about "biennial art," a term that essentially reflects the politics of the tendentious discourse that named it. Along with these newly commissioned texts, we have also reprinted a 2005 essay by Elena Filipovic, who argues that despite their critical ambitions, many biennials rely on an unspoken fidelity to some of the most doggedly traditional and Western display constructs—most notably, the museal "white cube." Together, these essays propose that the very format of the biennial exhibition, even if it replicates known models or even if it is immaterial, has repercussions for the way art and other non-biennial exhibitions are made, shown, addressed, and discussed; in short, *the question of the biennial's format matters.*

Invariably, from these considerations emerge questions concerning the figure who has moved, following the rapid transformations of the art world, from being a *faiseur d'expositions* (in French) or an *Ausstellungsmacher* (in German)—in other words, an "exhibition-maker" (part intellectual, part impresario, as opposed to a museum collection's caretaker/civil servant)—in the nineteen-sixties to being the "curator" or even the "author" of the exhibition. The rise of the "independent curator," for instance, cannot be separated from the proliferation of biennials, as several texts in this volume are quick to point out.[22] Expanding on their respective doctoral research on biennials, Federica Martini and Vittoria Martini look closely in their new collaborative essay at the evolution of the curator as auteur (the descendent of the ur-curator-auteur, Harald Szeemann, if ever there was one). For their part, the theorist-artist-curators of the Raqs Media Collective have written a new essay that reflects on the place of the biennial as a critical public sphere and the curatorial responsibility it thus requires. Alongside these, we have reprinted Paul O'Neill's 2007 essay discussing the "curatorial turn" that has shifted the central role of the curator from "practice to discourse." John Clark's essay, excerpted from his forthcoming book on Asian biennials, takes a different tack, suggesting that biennials not only impact the development of art, but also, paradoxically, are less a site privileging the presentation of those artworks than the locus "through which curators themselves are circulated and try to achieve their own further circulation." If doubts linger about the biennial's relationship to art itself, theorist Simon Sheikh reminds us in his 2009 essay that "biennials are not only part of the present, but also always . . . an investment in the future: a statement about art." Thus, if a direct investigation or interpretation of specific art objects (of the kind already found in art history) seems to be lacking in this volume, it is not because our interrogation of the biennial proposes a hierarchy of importance in which the biennial or the curator might surpass the artwork or the artist. Rather, it seemed to us that exposing the site of art's public presentation and the motivations of its organizers might help us understand better if, how, and to what extent biennials impact the way we perceive, and ultimately historicize, art today.

Because the biennial is, at its core, a global phenomenon that has played a crucial role in the dissemination of art from all over the world, the suggestion that contemporary art history should be written alongside a consideration of the biennial thus necessarily also hopes to prompt the writing of a properly global art history.[23] In our research we were interested in gathering critical writing from as wide a cultural and geographic spectrum as possible, so that the discourse on biennials presented in this volume might reflect something of the truly expansive reach of the exhibitions themselves. To strive to achieve this, we translated a number of texts so as to highlight some of the analytical thinking on biennials emerging from beyond the literature available in English. As one example, we have included a translated excerpt from Yacouba Konaté's book on the history of the Dak'Art Biennial and how it has functioned as a mechanism for creating an alternative history of art and Pan-Africanism. Vinicius Spricigo's chapter from his doctoral dissertation on the São Paulo Biennial and the historical and conceptual underpinnings of its twenty-eighth edition—nicknamed by some "the void biennial"—is another. Oliver Marchart's 2008 book about the last three editions of Documenta—which explores not only the inherent politics of any such large-scale perennial exhibition, but also the ways each edition of an event might respond to and build upon (or undo) the ideological or aesthetic positions of its predecessor—has also been included here in an abridged and translated form. Making these remarkable resources more widely available was one of our ways of attempting to confront the multiplicity of cultural positions that lies at the very heart of the biennial.

In this volume, discussions about specific biennials also appear, and they often also reveal a great deal about larger, shared issues in the genre. Through an in-depth discussion of the seventh Gwangju Biennial, Ranjit Hoskote describes a biennial typology he calls the "biennial of resistance," one that has emerged from transitional societies and examples of which include the São Paulo Biennial, the India Triennial, the Havana Biennial, the Asia-Pacific Triennial, the Gwangju Biennial, the Johannesburg Biennial, and the never-realized Delhi Biennial. Two of these very examples are examined in greater detail in both art historian Sabine Marschall's 1999 essay on the now-defunct Johannesburg Biennial and Gerardo Mosquera's new discussion of the utopian idealism that underlay the founding of the Havana Biennial, whose mission was to be the first biennial platform for the "Third World." Providing concrete examples, these essays also mark what Hoskote calls "a cumulative counterpoint to the Venice Biennial as the universal template for the biennial as form and medium" and reveal that there is "a substantial non- and perhaps even counter-Venetian history of the biennial form that has yet to be narrated."

The promulgation of counter-narratives and experimentation with counter-models for exhibition-making remains the utopian promise of the biennial in the age of globalization. But how should we understand the term "globalization" to which the biennial is said to be now intimately linked? Is the so-called globalization of the cultural sphere of the last few decades a development towards greater inclusivity of artistic practices beyond (Western) modernity or, on the contrary, does it represent the promotion of a (decidedly Western) hegemony for art, exhibition models, curators, and audiences? In other words, in the biennial's celebration of globalization, does it prove to be a truly inclusive, transnational, multicultural, "counter-hegemonic" project, as Okwui Enwezor contends? Or is the biennial, as George Baker argues, a mere consolidation of dominant bourgeois culture that is both "archaically nationalistic and explicitly occidentalist," especially in its championing of globalization, which shows itself, in fact, to be "a process of Westernization, not its critique"? Juxtaposing two compelling but dissenting positions on the claims of the biennial, we have reprinted Enwezor's landmark essay "Mega-Exhibitions and the Antinomies of a Transnational Global Form" and Baker's percussive response to it, "The Globalization of the False: A Response to Okwui Enwezor," which takes up a position against Enwezor's fundamental claims and those of many other advocates of the biennial.[24] Contributing to our understanding of the contested stakes of the biennial, these two texts as well as others in this volume underscore something we have tried to bring together throughout the book: they highlight the dissenting opinions and as-yet-unanswered questions that haunt the biennial. They also testify to our desire that *The Biennial Reader* attempt to fill the lacunae in the history of large-scale exhibitions without effacing either side of the debate that still rages today about their significance to our contemporaneity.

This essay began with a paradox: although the biennial cannot be precisely or absolutely defined, it nonetheless demands that we examine it. Throughout this essay and the anthology it introduces we have therefore argued for the importance of taking the biennial seriously, all the while embracing the possibility that the phenomenon would remain something essentially amorphous, contradictory, and even contested. And, as we have posited, nothing less than the future of art history depends on it. The entire thrust of this assemblage of texts is thus meant to invert the logic that proposes that either an artwork or an exhibition can be isolated from the larger pressures, contexts, frameworks, and constructs that perforce determine the ways in which they speak to their publics. For while the intellectual, aesthetic, and ideological object we call “the biennial” might well be considered inspiring or absurd, radical or retrograde, it nevertheless matters as an instrument that helps us to make sense of our contemporary culture. As such, taking the biennial as a central subject of study generates a prism through which to look at the broader art world (if not the world as a whole), because what we can learn from biennials informs us about all the things that biennials depend upon, react to, and ineluctably impact: art, artists, audiences, curating, and art institutions, but also cultural policy, the market, the public sphere, specific locales, tourism, and city branding. And yet we would also like to suggest that there is no ultimate closure to be derived from the subject we set out to examine. Instead, the various readings of the biennial proffered here counter the notion that neat lineages can be drawn, or that unequivocal motivations or trajectories can be confirmed; thus, our call for the creation of a biennialogy, rather than being rigidly empirical and teleological, might usefully prompt more questions than definitive answers. In the end, we felt that the promise and greatest potential of biennials could lie in their capacity to be experimental forms whose contours are capable of continual change and which, in changing, can both question and reinvent themselves and the histories they participate in writing. This book aspires to be a catalyst in this process. ●

1

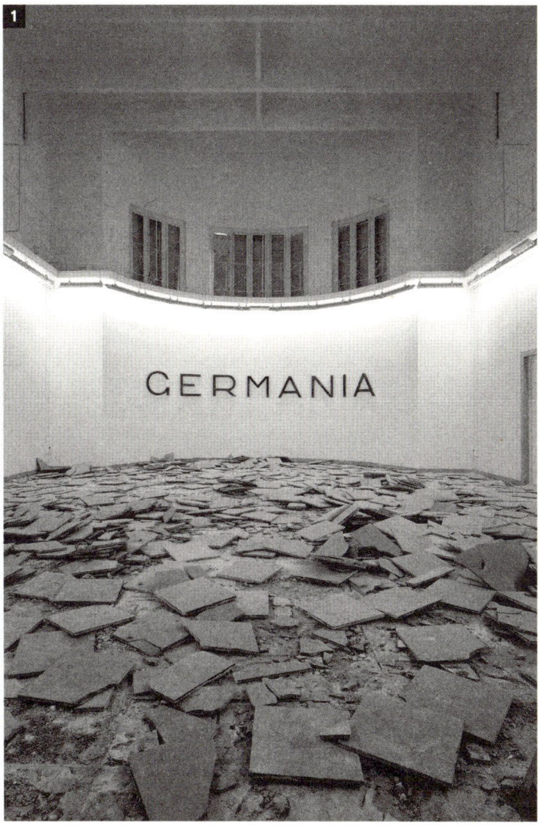

1 Hans Haacke, *Germania*, Venice Biennial, 1993.

NOTES

1 Peter Schjeldahl, "Festivalism: Oceans of Fun at the Venice Biennale," *The New Yorker* (July 5, 1999), pp. 85–86.

2 Confirming this, Maria Hlavajova states: "We now know that it is undeniable that the exhibition format *is* the primary vehicle on which biennials rest, but let's acknowledge for the time being that the radically diverse projects that take place under this label, hand in hand with the expanded field of contemporary curating, involve not only production and display but also, and progressively even more importantly, the production of discourse and the distribution of knowledge. And who says that biennials need to be exhibitions at all?" See her essay in this volume.

3 One exception to this is the Whitney Biennial, founded in 1932, although initially it took on the term to mean not the frequency of the exhibition but the purview of the art it represented: in 1932 it was as annual exhibition that featured a panorama of the production of art in America over the preceding two years. In 1973, it became a properly biannual event and then, only in very recent years, an international one.

4 The founding of several other large-scale recurring contemporary art events, although not properly speaking biannual, could also help sketch a picture of the landscape in which the creation of new biennials emerged. Some of the most influential examples from the period before the wide proliferation of the biennial include: the Carnegie International, founded in 1896 in Pittsburgh as a yearly survey exhibition, became a biennial event renamed the Pittsburgh International in 1950 and then a triennial event in 1955, only to return finally to its original name and more anthological format in 1982, with shows occurring approximately every three years; Documenta, founded in 1955 in Kassel, began as a one-off major survey show lasting a hundred days, but then went on to recur, with only one exception, every four years between 1955 and 1972, finally taking on its current quinquennial or once-every-five-years format after Harald Szeemann's 1972 edition and retaining the hundred-day format; and the India Triennial, founded in 1968 in New Delhi and from the start imagined as an event that would recur every three years.

NOTES

5 To give a somewhat schematic impression of the evolution of the art world in the nineteen-nineties, here is a list of some of the world's biennials and when they were launched: 1991: Lyon Biennial; 1992: Dak'Art Biennial; 1993: Asia-Pacific Triennial, Sharjah Biennial, and Vento Sul Biennial; 1994: Shanghai Biennial; 1995: Gwangju Biennial, Johannesburg Biennial, São Tomé e Príncipe Biennial, and SITE Santa Fe Biennial; 1996: Manifesta (European Biennial of Contemporary Art); 1997: Mercosul Biennial and Periferic; 1998: Berlin Biennial, Busan Biennial, Momentum (Nordic Biennial), Montreal Biennial, and Taipei Biennial; 1999: Caribbean Biennial, Fukuoka Asian Art Triennial, and Liverpool Biennial; 2000: Echigo-Tsumari Art Triennial and Scape Biennial; 2001: Auckland Triennial, Göteborg Biennial, Tirana Biennial, Valencia Biennial, and Yokohama Triennial. In this same time period, various curatorial courses that attempted to devise a specific theoretical and practical framework for independent curating were founded so that the profession of the curator became more articulated. Some of most well-known in the West include: Le Magasin, Grenoble (established in 1987); Royal College of Art, London (1992); De Appel, Amsterdam (1994); Bard College, New York (1994); and Goldsmiths College, London (1996).

6 Throughout this volume we have, as a matter of practicality and consistency, opted to use the English spelling "biennial" to refer to each of the biennials discussed regardless of their linguistic differences or official or semiofficial spellings. We are aware that, at times, conceptual positions are revealed in the decision of a particular biennial to use the spelling "biennale" (thereby suggesting a connection to the Italian precedent, the "Venice Biennale"), "biennial" (thereby employing an English, and hence potentially more international-sounding, spelling), or even "bienal," etc. However, there was often a lack of consistency in the spellings used in the printed matter about the various biennials around the world, so an "official" version of their names could not always be accurately determined. Also, in the cases of several biennials, their official name has changed since their foundation, so it would have been difficult to refer to them with consistency throughout the book.

7 "Mercosul," a compressed form of *Mercado Comum do Sul*, or Southern Common Market, takes its name from the 1991 free-trade agreement pertaining to the region including Argentina, Brazil, Paraguay, and Uruguay. The Biennial of the End of the World, on the other hand, uses its title to suggest the cultural and ideological implications of geographic isolation, pursuing the explicit mission of "pondering at the end of the world what other world is possible."

8 Technically speaking, Documenta would seem to have little reason for being included in the category of "biennials," but in the course of our research we were surprised by how many essays, reviews, and indeed how many professionals regularly use the term "biennial" to refer to Documenta. We have done the same here not so much to perpetuate inaccuracy, but rather to signal a cultural fact and help us better examine the kinship that exists between various large-scale perennial exhibitions.

9 Thomas McEvilley, "The Global Issue," *Artforum,* 28 (1990), p. 20.

10 Reesa Greenberg, Bruce W. Ferguson, and Sandy Nairne, "Introduction," in idem (eds.), *Thinking about Exhibitions* (London, 1996), p. 2.

11 Brian O' Doherty's essays, first published in *Artforum* in 1976 and then later collected in *Inside the White Cube: The Ideology of the Gallery Space* (Santa Monica, 1986), spoke presciently and unabashedly about the exhibition as both a historical phenomenon and an ideological device. Other early publications on specific historical exhibitions include Bruce Altshuler's *The Avant-Garde in Exhibition: New Art in the 20th Century* (New York, 1994) and Mary Anne Staniszewski's *The Power of Display: A History of Exhibition Installation at the Museum of Modern Art* (Cambridge [MA], 1998). Even Greenberg, Ferguson, and Nairne's *Thinking about Exhibitions* (London, 1996), now just over a decade old, remains a landmark for being a collection of essays dedicated not so much to an institution or site (for instance, the museum or the *Wunderkammer*) but to the exhibition *as such.* More recently, Hans Ulrich Obrist has attempted to respond to the aporias concerning the history of exhibition-making with a series of interviews with groundbreaking curators in his *A Brief History of Curating* (Zurich, 2009). And, although it does not actually address the biennial, Bruce Altshuler's *Salon to Biennial: Exhibitions that Made Art History, Volume I: 1863–1959* (London, 2008) suggests in its title alone that great exhibitions over the last century and a half might be responsible for "making" art history. As Maria Hlavajova importantly points out in her contribution to this volume, "the history of exhibitions as it stands in the theoretical discourse today is, in fact, relatively separate from that of biennials (or even "biennial exhibitions"), with only occasional points of intersection." It is precisely this state of affairs that *The Biennial Reader* is attempting to address.

12 Writing with regard to Documenta in 1992, Walter Grasskamp first called for recognition of the central place held by that particular mega-exhibition in the production of postwar art history. At the time, however, when exhibitions were not yet seriously considered valid objects of critical study, his call must have seemed like a polemical proposition. To some, even ours will seem so today. See Grasskamp, "For Example, *Documenta,* Or, How Is Art History Produced?" in Greenberg, Ferguson, and Nairne 1996 (see note 10), pp. 67–78.

13 Charlotte Bydler's dissertation, *The Global Art World, Inc.: On the Globalization of Contemporary Art* (Uppsala, 2004), contextualized the biennial precisely in relation to the dissemination of information and increased access to travel (the Internet, low-cost airlines, etc.) and the shifts in power that globalization prompted to create the polyphony of centers in which we are living today. Although it was published, it enjoyed such a limited distribution that, despite the pioneering nature of its research, we felt it important to include a significant excerpt from the book in this volume.

14 These include Barbara Vanderlinden and Elena Filipovic's edited volume entitled *The Manifesta Decade: Debates on Contemporary Art Exhibitions and Biennials in Post-Wall Europe* (Cambridge [MA], 2005) and special issues of journals devoted to the subject, such as: Jorinde Seijdel and Liesbeth Melis (eds.), "The Art Biennial as a Global Phenomenon: Strategies in Neo-Political Times," special issue, *Open* 16 (March 2009); and Marieke van Hal, Viktor Misiano, and Igor Zabel (eds.), "Biennials," special issue, *MJ–Manifesta Journal* 2 (Winter 2003–Spring 2004).

15 Jacques Derrida, *Of Grammatology* (Baltimore, 1998).

16 Examples include Boris Groys' "Multiple Authorship" (in Vanderlinden and Filipovic 2005 [see note 14]) and Michelle White and Nato Thompson's "Curator as Producer" (in *Art Lies,* no. 59 [Fall 2008]), two of the more explicit

NOTES

declarations of the curator as the artist's equal coproducer of the art object. With them, boundless other slightly less explicit statements that argue for the artist-function of the curator have pushed the debate in that direction. The condemnation of that tendency came as early as 1972 with Daniel Buren's "Exhibition of an Exhibition" (reprinted in this volume), in which he claimed: "More and more, the subject of an exhibition tends not to be the display of artworks, but more the exhibition of the exhibition as a work of art." For a further discussion of the larger debate, see Paul O'Neill's essay in this volume.

17 *Magiciens de la Terre* (1989), curated by Jean-Hubert Martin and conceived as a replacement of the format of the traditional Paris Biennial, was spread between the Musée national d'art moderne (Centre Georges Pompidou) and the Grande Halle of Parc de la Villette in Paris. Martin's show explicitly attempted to confront the ethnocentric, colonialist mentality largely perpetuated in exhibition-making, most glaringly in *"Primitivism" in 20th Century Art: Affinity of the Tribal and the Modern,* held at the Museum of Modern Art, New York, just five years prior. It proposed a "fully international" art exhibition that included one hundred artists from around the world, fifty from the so-called centers of the world (the U.S. and Western Europe) and fifty from the "margins" (Africa, Latin America, Asia, and Australia), and displayed them without any sense of hierarchy. Although the resulting exhibition is still largely considered problematic and deeply flawed, and thus is hardly thought of as something to be repeated as such, it nonetheless incited widespread debate about the terms and parameters of artistic selection in exhibition-making and has come to be seen as both a landmark in the history of exhibitions and as a model to which many biennials have explicitly or implicitly responded.

18 Different rephrasings of the question "To biennial or not to biennial?" that served as a leitmotif of the 2009 Bergen Biennial Conference were proffered by several participants at the conference and most directly by Maria Hlavajova (see her essay in this volume).

19 A term borrowed from sociology and economics, "new institutionalism" referred to the transformation of art institutions that began in the nineties, often at the initiative of curators who were themselves also actively involved in organizing biennials (so that the question of who influenced whom is not a one way street in either direction). The special issue of *Verksted* entitled "New Institutionalism," edited by Jonas Ekeberg, synthesized the debate and contributed to its wider dissemination; see *Verksted,* no. 1 (2003). See also Nina Möntmann (ed.), *Art and Its Institutions* (London, 2006), and Alex Farquharson, "Bureau de Change," *Frieze,* no. 101 (September 2006).

20 Jens Hoffmann asks: "Is there any site then that remains for alternative approaches to curating? At this point in time no major museum dares to present such controversial and inspiring group shows such as *Black Male* (1991), curated by Thelma Golden, *Cities on the Move* (1997), curated by Hou Hanru and Hans Ulrich Obrist, *Places with a Past* (1993), curated by Mary Jane Jacob, and *This Is a Show and a Show Is Many Things* (1994), curated by Bart de Baere. Intellectually and politically ambitious exhibitions have been moved out of the major museums." See Hoffmann, "A Certain Tendency in Curating," in Paul O'Neill (ed.), *Curating Subjects* (Amsterdam and London, 2007), p. 141.

21 To some extent this was already the direction in which Harald Szeemann was pointing when he wrote: "About 1960, artists began to work for the museum in the same sense that they created works knowing in advance that they would be shown exclusively in the museum. However, even in the sixties, artists were already beginning to become allergic to the idea of cooperating with museums, seeking to escape from the static atmosphere of the museum by organizing their happenings and concerns. Today, in 1971, their preoccupations have a more social aim. Artists are no longer interested in getting into the museum, but want to conduct their activities on a wider stage, for example the municipality." Szeemann, "Problems of the Museum of Contemporary Art in the West: Exchange of Views of a Group of Experts," *Museum* 24, no. 1 (1972), pp. 5–32, cited in Bruce W. Ferguson, Reesa Greenberg, and Sandy Nairne, "Mapping International Exhibitions," in *On Taking a Normal Situation . . .* (Antwerp, 1993). Another view, posited by Okwui Enwezor in this volume, concentrates rather on shifts in size and spectacularity, arguing that the "anxiety of anonymity . . . and dramatic expansion of . . . mega-exhibitions require mega-objects."

22 About a decade into the "moment" of the independent curator (à la Michael Brenson), a series of publications that treated the redefinition of curatorial practice and the rise of a new generation (and, it was posited, new *kind*) of curator emerged, including: Mika Hannula (ed.), *Stopping the Process: Contemporary Views on Art and Exhibitions* (Helsinki, 1998); Gavin Wade (ed.), *Curating in the 21st Century* (Walsall and Wolverhampton, 2000); Carin Kuoni (ed.), *Words of Wisdom: A Curator's Vade Mecum on Contemporary Art* (New York, 2001); Carolee Thea (ed.), *Foci: Interviews with Ten International Curators* (New York, 2001); Paula Marincola and Robert Storr (eds.), *Curating Now: Imaginative Practice, Public Responsibility* (Philadelphia, 2001); Susan Hiller and Sarah Martin (eds.), *The Producers: Contemporary Curators in Conversation,* vols. 1–5 (Gateshead, 2000–02).

23 That art history has long been and still astonishingly continues to be an emphatically Western, white, male, exclusive affair is made evident simply by looking through the most prominent publications on art history over time (which also happen to be the most relied upon in art history courses today), from H. W. Janson's sweepingly Eurocentric *History of Art: The Western Tradition* (its subtitle announcing art history itself as a "Western tradition," especially as no other tradition was offered as an equal or parallel supplement to this one), first published by Harry Abrams in 1962 and currently in its eighth edition, to the more recent but still resolutely Euro-American-focused *Art since 1900* (Rosalind Krauss, Hal Foster, et al. [eds.]; London, 2004).

24 Enwezor's text first appeared in German as "Grossausstellungen und die Antinomien einer transnationalen globalen Form" (in Gottfried Boehm and Horst Bredekamp [eds.], *Berliner Thyssen Vorlesung zur Ikonologie der Gegenwart,* no. 1 [2002]), and was then published in translation as "Mega-Exhibitions and the Antinomies of a Transnational Global Form" in a special issue of *MJ–Manifesta Journal* edited by Marieke van Hal, Viktor Misiano, and Igor Zabel (vol. 2 [Winter 2003–Spring 2004], pp. 6–31). It was then subsequently republished in a slightly modified form in *Documents* in 2004 (vol. 23, pp. 2–19) along with George Baker's response to it. It is the 2004 *Documents* version that we have reprinted in this volume.

HISTORIES, PRECEDENTS, AND ORIGINS

THE CRYSTALLINE VEIL AND THE PHALLOMORPHIC IMAGINARY (2001)

Donald Preziosi

I want to begin with the opening stanzas of a rather remarkable poem published anonymously in 1852 and entitled *Recollections and Tales of the Crystal Palace* (fig. 1). It begins:

> *Now sing the CRYSTAL PALACE!—theme sublime,*
> *That shall astound the world throughout all time!*
> *Aid me. Ye Muses! Aid! Your seat is here!*
> *Ye murmuring fountains, charm my listening ear!*
> *Fair sculptured forms, whose classic beauty bears*
> *The spirit back to Rome's enchanted years,*
> *Lend to my strains the power of art divine,*
> *And let your soul poetic breathe in mine!*
> *Lo! As I roam o'er this unequalled spot,*
> *Earth and its drearier scenes are all forgot;*
> *The mighty minds that with resistless will,*
> *Raised the fair temple, seem to haunt it still!*
> *A solemn glory shines along these aisles,*
> *And in the violet-tinted distance, smiles;*
> *And Peace, with dove-like pinions, seems to brood*
> *Above this swarming, countless multitude.*
> [. . .]
> *Yet shall this crystal pile—this mighty plan,*
> *An influence wield upon the mind of man,*
> *Free as itself, as wondrous and as vast,*
> *And lasting still—whilst time itself shall last.*
> *No narrow views—no rights exclusive, bar*
> *This brilliant scene—nor its enchantments mar!*
> *The prince and serf, the peasant and the peer,*
> *Alike may revel in the beauties here;*
> *Alike must feel how feeble and how small,*
> *Each man alone—how great, how glorious all!*
> *And in this fairy world of labor, see*
> *A type of what the actual world should be.*[1]

This is but the smallest fraction of what was a poem of epic proportions—it was 150 pages long—by an unidentified woman author who in the same year (1852) also published the second edition of her popular book *Belgravia, A Poem,* itself of great length. Her Crystal Palace poem was divided into six parts, devoted, respectively, to (1) an overview of the half year of the Exhibition from its opening on May 1, 1851, to its closing on October 15 of the same year; (2) morning in the Crystal Palace (with the "joyous arrival" of the Queen, who in fact visited virtually every other day the building was open); (3) a discourse on the great building's resemblance to even greater natural edifices of ice—icebergs—seen by Arctic mariners; (4) the lamentation of a mother for a daughter lost in the crowds and (apparently) finally recovered; (5) a description of the progress of two anonymous persons through the Exhibition during a single day; finally closing (6) with a meditation on "the ties that exist between a great Author and those of his Readers who appreciate his works."

I've called this essay "The Crystalline Veil and the Phallomorphic Imaginary," and my aim in doing so was to call attention to what I'll be referring to as the "optics" and spatial logic of this extraordinary building, and to the ways in which the Crystal Palace was the lucent embodiment and epistemological Summa of the principles of modern order and identity themselves—principles that at the same time served to found the practices of art history and museology as we know them today. I cannot emphasize too strongly how fundamental and essential this remarkable artifact was to so many facets of what we have come to recognize as our modernity over the past century and a half.

I'm aware that these are strong claims; in order to sketch even the outline of a justification we shall need to look closely at what this blindingly brilliant object both revealed and veiled. Accordingly, I will be delving into what I might call for the moment (and explain as we go along) the "orthopsychic" construction of subjects in representation. This will entail questions of vision and blindness, the modern gaze, desire, narcissism, and the problem of what does or does not lie "behind" representation, as well as the question of why any of this should matter for practices that we might still avidly desire to be simple and straightforward, namely, art history, art criticism, and museology. So I'll begin with some reflections on the latter, and work my way back through the sentence I just read. The Crystal Palace will occupy a double position in all of this, constituting both the object of our interest, and what in fact has already founded and determined that interest. We'll be speaking both *in and of* that "theme sublime," as our poet calls it.

It has been customary for some time to believe that artworks are historically significant phenomena, and that art itself has a "history," the astute delineation of which would provide us with significant insights into the (presumably parallel or complementary) histories of individuals and of peoples—insights which, and not least of all, may be legible as providing lessons for our own time. The modern institutions of art history and museology are of course grounded in this enabling assumption, one of whose several corollaries has been that changes in form are taken to *correspond* (in any of a variety of direct or indirect ways) to changes in beliefs, attitudes, mentalities, or intentions, or to changes in social, political, or cultural conditions. This has long been (by which I do mean to suggest that it has its own history) a virtually irresistible fiction, and it has been one of the cornerstones of the edifice of the modernity that we have built ourselves into, whose exits have yet to lead elsewhere but to other, identical spaces.[2]

There was no more brilliant stage upon which this was delineated, demonstrated, and factualized than the *Great Exhibition of the Arts and Manufactures of All Nations* at the Crystal Palace in London in 1851.[3] This most radically translucent—and simultaneously stubbornly opaque—of nineteenth-century constructions may well have been our modernity's most *unsurpassable* artifact. It was the lucent embodiment and semiological *summa* of the principle of modern order itself: infinitely expandable, scaleness, anonymous; transparently and stylelessly abstract. A "mighty plan," and a "type of what the actual world should be" that is in fact "lasting still," everywhere in us and around us. The very diagram of the modern Symbolic Order, it was, again in the words of the poem, "as wondrous and as vast" as "the mind of man" itself. I shall argue that we ourselves are no less the products and effects of this extraordinary object.

Simply put, the Crystal Palace offered—as Freud was later to say of psychoanalysis[4]—an "impartial instrument, like the infinitesimal calculus" for making legible both the differences and similarities, and the cognitive, aesthetic, and (consequently) ethical hierarchies amongst peoples by means of their juxtaposed and plainly seen products and effects. All the world "'neath one roof," in a single room: at once the modern apotheosis of the *Wunderkammer,* in which objects were catalysts for a fraternal intercourse bent toward making conversational sense of a jumble of things.[5] As the ideal horizon and logical fulfillment of the arcades of London, Paris, and other European and American cities, the Crystal Palace was the *system* of modern museology (and art historicism) as such, stripped to the skin. A dream from which we have yet to awaken.

I would contend that modern museology and art history cannot be appreciated or substantially understood apart from this "impartial instrument," this "father's feast." A feast, moreover, that was itself haunted by the presence of the greatest patriarch of them all, Victoria, who was herself present (as a sort of permanent strolling exhibit) virtually every other day of the building's 165-day *in situ* existence, and the mortal representative of that "great First Cause" seen behind all the "wonders wrought" here in this "common home"—the projective *Urbild* or *Umwelt* ("one Heaven above—one Earth beneath") of a British Imperial Imaginary; this "fair temple" whose "classic beauty bears / The spirit back to Rome's enchanted years." In seeing Victoria seeing, a whole world learned what and how to see. Victoria, in short, ostensified the spectator as consumer.

The modern disciplinary practices of art history and museology are among the more powerful *effects* of this "mighty plan," and its indispensable *mode d'emploi.* Art history was and remains the ghost *in* that crystalline machine, as it perpetually carries the memory of this "Muses' seat" as *its* innermost *fixation.* The blinding quiddity of this "crystal pile," whose image is permanently imprinted, eidetically, on the art historical gaze, was bourgeois modernity's *stade du miroir,* its mirror stage. It is also the Unconscious of every museum in the world; every museum's imaginary lost origin and the image of an ideal plenitude, containing all things no less than all peoples.

The Crystal Palace's grand and "styleless" system was replicated in countless expositions, museums, and city plans created throughout Europe and the European dominated and influenced world (rapidly becoming, in the nineteenth century, coterminous with the world as such). Its exhibitionary order was the ideal horizon and the blueprint of patriarchal colonialism; the epistemological technology of Orientalism as such.[6] It was the laboratory table upon which all things and peoples could be objectively and poignantly compared and contrasted in a uniform and perfect light, and phylogenetically and ontogenetically ranked. All this in relation to a Europe that had been learning to stage itself as the eyes and ears of the world; as the brain of the earth's body. The Crystal Palace—whose "bright visions" and "brilliant scene" were so profusely celebrated in the 150-page paean of 1852 whose opening stanzas I quoted before—was the paradigm of the loom of modernity on which sexuality, capitalism, and art have come to be woven tightly together into a sturdy, enduring fabric which has in fact hardly frayed since (or which, like something from Disney's *Fantasia,* seems uncannily to weave itself back together after the occasional critical rip).

The enterprise of the modern discipline of art history prefigured by Winckelmann, Kant, and Hegel was fully and lucidly *figured* in the 1851 *Great Exhibition*—itself a *phallomorphic imaginary* for rendering visible Europe's Others.[7] This visibility is both the proof and condition of the presence of the Other, whose existence is thereby guaranteed by its exhibitionary *representation*—which in effect precludes recognition of the Other's difference in favor of its phallocentric makeup: a covering up of difference by a uniform visibility which de-Others others and domesticates all difference. This universal lucidity (what our poem calls this "common home" and "father's feast") is thus a transparency which is opaque; a *crystalline veil.* The dream of a totally transparent society is the *hijab* of Europe's modernity.

Most importantly, the Crystal Palace grounded and gave substance to an Art History as a practice of the self, of the self's commodification, demonstrating that the "history" of art was a supremely practical business. Its erasure of difference (this "abstraction") in favor of a "universal" and uniform "*fairy world* of labor" endows everything (as the effective condition of its visibility in modernity) with a phallicized, commodified, and fetishized value, making it evident that at the core of modernity is precisely the *conflation* of aesthetics, ethics, and sexuality in the *commodity.*

It is perhaps fitting that (despite its own material descendants on other sites, and even the incorporation of some of its actual physical members into these other "crystal palaces") the Crystal Palace was a momentary, six-month phenomenon: a brief and blinding flash in mid-century that revealed, as would the quick shine of a torch in the night, an unexpected and uncanny landscape. The flash has remained imprinted on the European optic nerve now for well over a century; the uncanny landscape revealed is, in Walter Benjamin's words, capitalism: that catastrophic "new dream sleep [that] fell over Europe."[8]

I've again evoked the name of Walter Benjamin—a reflex that has recently been customary amongst contemporary art historians searching for yet another "hindsight-father" whose writings might be scoured to clarify or highlight the underlying conditions of our modernity. But I'd like to suggest now an opposite tack and situate Benjamin's work, and in particular his "Arcades Project" and his "Theses on the Concept of History," as the effects of, and as impossible without presupposing, the Crystal Palace itself. This is not, as I hope to make clear as we proceed, a putting of a cart before the horse, or a misconstruing of cause and effect: I really *do* mean to say that rather than using Benjamin to understand or "read" phenomena such as the arcades or the Crystal Palace itself, more will be gained by reversing this: reading Benjamin—and by what I take to be a justifiable extension, art history and museology themselves—through the Crystal Palace.

What I want to do, in other words, is to seriously "think with" the Crystal Palace: rather than rereading art history through the optic of Benjamin, it may be more useful to reread Benjamin through the optic of that nineteenth-century museology (whose most lucid European epitome was the Crystal Palace) of which his own quasi-messianic practice (at one with the art historicism of his time) was the product.

In an 1868 essay, the linguist Michel Bréal wrote that, in standing before a picture,

> *Our eyes think they perceive contrasts of light and shade, on a canvas lit all over by the same light. They see depths, where everything is on the same plane. If we approach a few steps, the lines we thought we recognized break up and disappear, and in place of differently illuminated objects we find only layers of color congealed on the canvas and trails of brightly colored dots, adjacent to one another but not joined up. But as soon as we step back again, our sight, yielding to long habit, blends the colors, distributes the light, puts the features together again, and recognizes the work of the artist.*[9]

What is being constructed here as well in this perfectly commonplace observation, one of scores one can find in the literature of many fields, is the subject itself as an economy of vision; as an instrument for making sense of things in its discovery of a point of resolution and legibility. What I'd like to call an "ortho-psychic" subject; a self whose agency is a product of spatial alignments and positioning. A "putting things in perspective," as we say.[10]

The masses of objects in a museum or exhibition came to be understood as analogous to the gobs of color and the abstract dots and dashes described by Breal as on a painted canvas. Only by taking up a proper (orthopsychic) "perspective" and distance may these bits and pieces be seen as joining up to create the image, the figure, the physiognomy, of the character or mentality of a person, people, or period. It is precisely the pursuit of such a *perspectival position* that constitutes the modern discipline of art history as *an epistemology of the gaze* for the modern subject; as constituting that subject. At the same time, in resolving ambiguities—that is, in appearing to do so—the subject instantiates the fiction that what is in fact the nothingness "behind" any "representation" is *something.* The result historically was an instrumental technology for fabricating genealogies of value, character, race, spirit, or mentality through the mediating fictions of style, intention, authorship, and reflection: what we call with disingenuous modesty "art history."

It was the Crystal Palace that powerfully put all this in the proper scale and perspective *for all to see,* in the same place and at the same time. In so doing, this supreme taxonomic and comparative instrument was arguably the first fully realized modernist institution: a real astrolabe of Enlightenment. It was in fact the historical realization and the implicit ideal, the Ur-form and *Gesamtkunstwerk,* of what Benjamin's *Passagenwerk* was aiming to evoke in bits and pieces from the Parisian arcades (and also the Paris 1937 Exposition). Benjamin, however, quoting another verse about the Crystal Palace, saw the latter as an Ur-form of the Paris Exposition's "Pavilion of Solidarity,"[11] and never in fact addressed the Great Exhibition in any substantive way. What makes Benjamin's *Passagenwerk* so frustrating is not its fragmentary nature as such but rather the absence of that which each and every arcade implied and presupposed, even *avant le lettre;* namely, the Crystal Palace.

As I've said before, the key metaphorical conundrum, the central obsession, of modernity is that the *form* of your work is (and should properly be *legible as*) the *figure* of your truth. This is in fact built upon what I referred to in an earlier lecture as a secular theologism, the modernist continuation and obverse of centuries of Christian practices of the self, wherein one's (good) "works" were an index and direct reflection of the worthiness of one's soul. As if by a materialist masquerade of Christian piety, every art historical object comes to be framed as an object-*lesson,* and a window into the spirit of a time, place, person, or people. Art history, as a key facet of the nineteenth-century enterprise of historicism, was designed quite pragmatically to render the visible legible; to reveal and reconstitute what lay "within" or "behind" objects. The entire theory of mimesis or representation is based on this supposition.

During the middle of the nineteenth century, museological and art historical, theoretical, and critical practices were becoming interlinked sites for the manufacture of the present, in fact a "presence" that constituted Europe in its relation to all possible Others—that "modernity," that co-option of all possible ethnocentrisms, that has since come to cover the planet through its extensions, imitations and recapitulations everywhere. Art history is no less a factory for the production of the fictions that make up the load-bearing walls of that modernity—the phantasms of ethnicity, race, gender, nation, sex, indigeneity, class, all grounded and enabled by the keystone fiction of "art" itself—art as "representation."

Art history has since its origins been the site of a modern semiotic and epistemological problem and paradox, one born out of a powerfully enabling set of assumptions: that the art object's visibility is a function of its legibility as a *symptom* of everything and anything that could be plausibly adduced as contributing to its appearance and morphology. A symptom of lack; of what is absent and lacking, in short. It became eminently reasonable to believe that the astute delineation of formal or stylistic genealogical relationships among artworks would provide significant insights into the (presumably parallel, complementary, or homologous) histories of individuals and peoples. The modern institutions of art history and museology are of course founded upon this enabling assumption, wherein changes in form (or a lack thereof) are taken to correspond to and reflect or embody changes (or a lack of change) in beliefs, attitudes, mentalities, or intentions, or to changes (or not) in social, political, or cultural conditions. An assumption which simultaneously projects the effects of a science of palpable causes and effects and derails any effective fixities of causality—as our poet displaced causality onto "Mind" or "Soul."

Simply put, the artwork (and perforce any palpable cultural artifact, object, or practice) is taken to bear a relationship of resemblance (a metaphorical—and hence substitutional—relationship) as well as a part-to-whole relation (a synecdochal—and hence metonymic or juxtapositional—connection; an index) to its circumstances of production. This situation—this *synecdochal metaphoricity*—is precisely that of the *pantograph,* that horizontal, scissorlike artistic implement by which one can scale up an image from a smaller to a larger size (or vice versa), thus retaining all the picture's features and qualities at an expanded size. As a *pantographic* enterprise, the analytic practice of the historian or critic may be justly said to comprise the projection of the figure of the object onto a larger "screen" or horizon of the social, cultural, historical, ethnic, racial, national, etc. In this regard, the artwork is a homuncular entity, whose *finality* is the horizon of its ideal, projected fullness.

Such metaphorical instruments may aid us in appreciating a deeper truth: the fact that "art" and "history" are *coconstructed* artifacts of the great enterprise of modernity; interdependent epistemological technologies linked to a larger matrix of practices and institutions, which for lack of a better term I might call *museography* (itself, then, a species of pantography, which in turn is a dimension of allegory). Since the late eighteenth century, these coimplicative practices have functioned to render an object-domain called "the past" synoptically visible so that it might operate in and upon (whilst at the same time distancing itself from) "the present"; so that this present might be seen as the demonstrable *product* of a specifically delineated past; and so that the past so staged might be framed and illuminated as an object of genealogical *desire* in its own right, configured as that from which a properly socialized and disciplined modern subject (the citizen of the nation-state) might learn to desire descent (or, conversely, might learn to abhor and learn how to reject). In the most basic terms, "art history" is a mode of staging and envisioning thought—about nations, individuals, ethnicities, races, genders, and classes, *on behalf of* social agendas or political desires projective of that *other* dimension of the present, that obverse of the past and its complementary fiction, "the future." No art, no "history"; and, to look the other way across the pantograph, no history, no "art."

The Crystal Palace simultaneously made this legerdemain perfectly visible and completely opaque.

Art history is thus also a pantographic instrument for the evocation and connection of two Imaginaries; for unceasingly shunting an insatiable desire for wholeness between two temporal poles—two Edenic realms of integrity (where might be projected, for example, a concordance or *commensurability* between the subject and its objects; where Adam and Eve had no need for knowing the names of things, and where in the ultimate future our souls and bodies are reunited). In other words, an originary past and the future horizon of its imaginary rebirth, resolution, or reconstitution: that which the past is imagined to desire as *its* fulfillment; as if through the agency of us in the present—orthopsychic subjects—who work to bring "it" about—when in fact it is we who are brought about, who are founded "in" that "it."

My contention is that everything art history has been for the past two centuries follows from this psycho-theological dreamwork, and an appreciation of it is necessary to understanding the history of art history both institutionally, as a professional, academic discipline, and more widely, as a component part of correlative institutions and practices (including, minimally, art criticism, history-writing, aesthetic philosophy, art-making, tourism, urbanism, museology, and the heritage industry). In the long run, the very "looseness" of the organization of this overall museographical matrix, the opportunistic adaptability of its component practices, and the refracted echoes of one practice in another or others, have proven especially effective in naturalizing the very idea of "art" as a kind of innate and "universal" human phenomenon, with variable but concordant manifestations from one society to another. Once again, this is, as our poet called it (blessed as she tells us with a "living soul that soars above and contemplates the whole"), a condition of the very visibility of Others in modernity's "common home" and "father's feast."

All of which has served to legitimize the principal function of art and art history for modernity as a powerful instrument, measure, and frame for staging the social, cognitive, and ethical *teleologies* of all peoples: narrative emplotments linking past and future, origins and ends. The principal *disciplinary* function of this "museography" over the past two centuries has thus been the *coproduction of modern subjects and objects*—and by extension the naturalization of an entire nexus of dyadic concepts resonating with and framing many facets of modern life. Since concepts of the object within the horizons of the Western metaphysical tradition are invariably deponent, being linked indissolubly to coconstructed framings and articulations of the subject, any attempt to understand art history's institutions necessarily entails a certain stereoptical attention to the ways in which this dyadic opposition has functioned in and for the history of art history. But it's more than a question of any simple or direct envisioning, as we'll see shortly.

Understanding the larger social enterprise of modernity—and, perforce, modernity's core problematic, namely, *the orchestration of orderly, describable, and predictable relations between subjects and between subjects and objects* (the topologist's haunt)—is essential to any attempt to appreciate what art history was all about. In saying "was," I don't mean that art history is now "over," but rather that it was *always already impossible;* always grounded in a fiction that is itself tied to the fictions at the heart of the fabrication and maintenance of the self. Even in its perpetuation and contemporary indispensability: we live, in modernity, *in and as* that impossibility. Such a project also entails turning art history and its avatars "inside out," so to speak, so as to delineate the kinds of subjects that art historical objects produce; the kinds of "readers" that artifacts evoke.

As already suggested, art history arose historically as one of a series of practices and institutions aimed at addressing the central problem of modernity: namely, the nature and status of the individual as a subject of newly evolving forms of community and fraternity.[12] This problem came to be expressed on two broad fronts—synchronically, and diachronically. The art history of the late-nineteenth-century Viennese art historian and curator Alois Riegl occupied a significant juncture in the playing out of this problem, and his theory of art and of art's history constituted an attempt to articulate a kind of organic historicism capable of addressing both facets of this problem.

For Riegl, a "universal history" aligning together the stylistic features that might be seen at a given time and place (in everything from churches to tchotchkes) was to be the "culminating point of all art historical research."[13] The will to form (*Kunstwollen*) is something that must be shown to be manifested in all aspects of the social and cultural milieu of a time and place. The formational principle of a *Kunstwollen* is imagined to be imposed with equal force and immediacy in every facet of the material culture of a time, place, and people. In this immanentist organicism, Riegl was of course prefigured by Hegel; but he diverged from the Hegelian Romantic tradition that constituted so much of art historical theory and practice in the nineteenth century (and that provided the template for academic practice in Europe and America) in two respects. First, in his thesis that in principle all styles are of equal value—a consequence of his position that the significance of an object is a function of the standpoint of the observer. And secondly, in his articulation of an historicism without a teleology—a notion of the consistency and necessity of artistic development, in which any conflict between (as the twentieth-century French art historian Henri Focillon was to put it) "the timely, the premature, and the superseded,"[14] is not resolved in favor of unilinear progress, as in Hegel's evolution of "world Spirit" toward ever more perfect manifestations in cultural form (for Hegel, in fact, in the forms and formats of worship in north German Protestant Christianity).

For Hegel, the systems and structures of a culture had proximate sources—what he called "national geniuses" or *Volksgeister*—individuals who were in effect mouthpieces of the deeper source, the unfolding world Spirit. History becomes a genealogy of that Spirit as its "effects" are manifested "in" the objects produced by societies through their national geniuses. Heinrich Wölfflin's "anonymous art history," or an art history without names, elaborated in the first two decades of the twentieth century, consisted of a genealogy of certain *aprioristic* aesthetic categories, such as "seeing," in a manner that was perfectly consistent with Hegelian historicism.

Alois Riegl's aims—though no less historicist and essentialist than those of his near contemporary Heinrich Wölfflin, or his progenitor Hegel—were somewhat more modest, in that for him art's history was a history of solutions to aesthetic and material problems. In this, as the social historian of art Arnold Hauser rightly observed half a century ago,[15] the work of art became an "illustration" of formal problems. The evolution of styles consists of "questions to be decided." What art historians were thought to be faced with, then, were solutions; "answers" to questions or problems which it is then necessary to reconstruct. Art history, for Riegl, was fundamentally a *pantographic practice of double-writing or double inscription,* in which the art object (in Riegl's case, literally any material cultural formation, from saltcellars to cities) is the occasion, the catalyst, for the larger and greater articulation (the *Wollen*), which is imagined to "pervade" equally every cultural artifact at a given time and place. *The object is the answer,* and the art historian was charged with reconstituting the answer's question.

In this regard, Riegl's art history was completely consistent with the historicist project of modernity just briefly sketched out, representing a minor inflection of the immanentist Romanticism of the Hegelian tradition. Yet ultimately, Riegl is a less interesting and original thinker than Hegel, or his own contemporary, the great French philosopher, historian, and art historian Hippolyte Taine—the person Nietszche regarded as the greatest nineteenth-century historian. Taine's history of art, seen as an evolution of *mentalities* which were manifested as a complex and dynamic triangulation of what he called race, force, and moment, was elaborated in a series of lectures at the Ecole des Beaux-Arts starting in 1865. In this system, which he regarded as part of a larger study of what he called in his lectures "problems in psychological mechanics," the full significance of any artifact was a function of its relationship to its entire cultural context. The central concepts of Ferdinand de Saussure's new linguistics and semiology at the beginning of the twentieth century were taken from Taine's lectures (which Saussure attended as a student in Paris), and thus it is of no small interest that at the heart of modern language theory is a series of semiotic principles and metaphors taken from nineteenth-century art history. (I discussed this in some detail in *Rethinking Art History.*)[16]

Now I'd like to focus more directly on this extraordinary artifice and address some of the themes I've been raising—those of the constitution of the modern subject, of representation and its (im)possibilities, and the questions of desire, narcissism, vision, blindness, and the gaze. What I'm about to say is implied in what I've already been saying. And also, as will have become evident, in the great poem we've been attending to here. Listen to these final words of the poem:

Long did I wander through that fairy place
By quiet paths I oft had learnt to trace,
Dwelling on beauteous forms, familiar grown,
Yet finding still fresh marvels, all unknown—
Till faint at last with gazing, I began
To turn from Man's unequalled works—to Man
Then on a quiet bench I sat—and found
Food for fresh thought in all that passed around:
Seeking—no hard nor thankless task—to trace
The Soul's unuttered thoughts on every face!
In many a soft dilating eye, I saw
Joy mixed with wonder—eagerness with awe!
While sterner men, with philosophic thought,
Mused on what labor, led by Mind, had wrought,
And giddy fair ones gazed, but heeded less
The works of Art around them, than the dress;
Finding in gay capote, Parisian shawl,
Or lace-trimmed robe, more powerful charms than all.[17]

One of the things continually marked in our poem is a certain dualism; a clear distinction made between things seen (as effects) and the forces, minds, and spirits taken as preexistent causes. Not causes as in the particularities of authorship or manufacture that would be commonplace in twentieth-century art historical practice, namely, that this beautiful sculpture or textile may have been Belgian or Chinese, or the work of a particular master, but rather that each and every thing was a product of "Benignant power[s] of mind [also italicized]," and that in each and every thing could be seen "the *great First Cause.*" Another constant theme is the power attributed to "beauty"—by which one can properly understand all that the Great Exhibition had on offer (all those things that "light man here and direct him higher")—to affect character and behavior, since as she says, that in "Partak[ing] with joy of all that varied store," "How wide so'er their home—uncouth their name, / Or wild their nature, *here* [and the word is italicized in the poem] they feel the same." It didn't matter that you came from some outlandish place or climate: *here* everybody's "bosoms beat with rapture."

And all this was not only a "father's feast" (Prince Albert's, in this case—in which Victoria was more than simply a gracious hostess to her international guests), but a "common home." This was indeed, as she tells us, "a fairy world of labor," and one moreover where everyone could "see / A type of what the actual world should be." A world as real as Disneyland—and as deadly. Victoria in effect served as a roving or traveling eye, ostensifying a browsing, restless vision, one that in fact seemed to mask the artifice of the whole charade. Her royal progress was followed by scores of visitors bent on seeing what she saw and admired.

Our poet ends on what might be taken as a sad note, where she contrasts the reactions and musings of "sterner men" with "giddy fair ones," the former musing on "what labor, led by *Mind* [again italicized] had wrought," the latter finding in what people were wearing ("lace-trimmed robes"; "Parisian shawls") "more powerful *charms* [my italics] than all." Yet the sadness of the poet's realization of what some visitors were paying more attention to should not distract us from seeing a fundamental complementarity here between the two reactions to the spectacle: "Mind" and "charm" stand in the same relationship to their material effects—beautiful works of art and fashionable clothing. This points up not so much a contrast between art and commodity as a *parallel:* both are framed as commodities, the distinction between the artwork and the shawl being one of quality and ostensible functionality. What the Great Exhibition wrought, in other words, was the bringing of all artifacts into mutual alignment within the same frame or system, and, in a complementary fashion, the alignment of the individual citizen—what I've been calling the modern "orthopsychic subject"—into a proper position and relationship not simply "to" but *at the center of and within* this world of artifice: the point of resolution. The interchangeablity of subjects and objects in the imaginary space, the abstract stage, of the commodity.[18]

This point might be clarified by thinking with a famous optical illusion that played a prominent role in mid-twentieth-century theories of perception. It was invented by the psychologist and ophthalmologist Adalbert Ames in the nineteen-forties, and has since come to be known as an "Ames Room" (fig. 2). It was an odd arranging together in real space of a variety of full-size trapezoidal forms which, when photographed or looked at through a pinhole, gave the illusion of a normal cube or room, except for the fact that two figures of the same size could be made to seem of radically different size (as you see in the illustration of an Ames Room with identical twins)—a conundrum or impossible scene. In fact, it was the room and its parts that were deliberately skewed: all the walls and furniture were actually fragments of things splayed out in such a way as to make it appear that the two figures were standing next to each other, when in fact the one on the left was quite far away and behind the other. Figure 3 shows how the Room is constructed: because of the skewed angle you are looking from (and the fact that you're only using one eye in looking), what you see is the imaginary cubic space (indicated by dotted lines).

What I'm suggesting we imagine here, in looking at the Great Exhibition, is that this great mass and jumble of things presents to its visitors a challenge to sense; a challenge to make sense of this hitherto unimaginable diversity; to find or invent a "perspective" on the whole so that objects could be made to "stay and lie orderly." To take up a perspective—like the viewer looking into an Ames Room or like the viewer of a painting in Michel Bréal's essay quoted at the beginning of this talk who finds the observation point which transforms the gobs of color into the outlines of a figure or a landscape. To become, in short, a "correct(ed)-" or "*ortho*"-psychic subject. In all this, Victoria herself as Imperial Browser shows the way.

Or a *genius loci;* a "spirit of [a] place" or a perspectival point of resolution. Our poet in effect gives voice to all of this and in that respect was a most astute observer of this great spectacle, this "Muses' seat," as she put it, that she was hardly by any means alone in firmly believing that it "shall *astound* [my italics] the world throughout all time." The Great Exhibition, as an "impartial instrument, like the infinitesimal calculus," as Freud said half a century later of psychoanalysis, in fact *crystallized* and put into its proper place an Imperial fantasy-world or imaginary geography of all peoples and products, with the modern citizen-consumer, the orthopsychic subject—*at and as* its (imaginary) center. This phallomorphic and orientalist machinery, this epistemological technology, transformed difference and otherness into stylistic variation and exoticism, blanketing over other realities into a "fairy world" of seemingly endless flavors of the same ice cream. Geography as pantography.

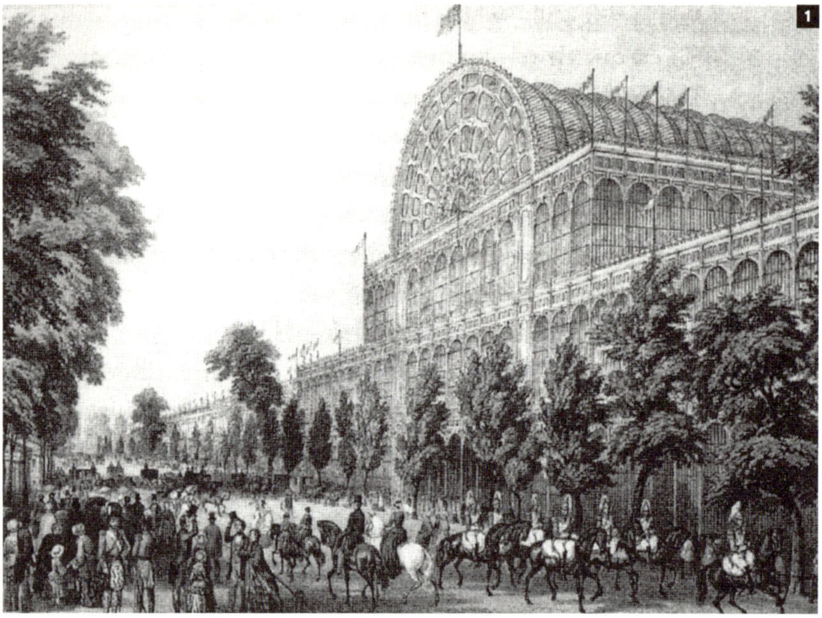

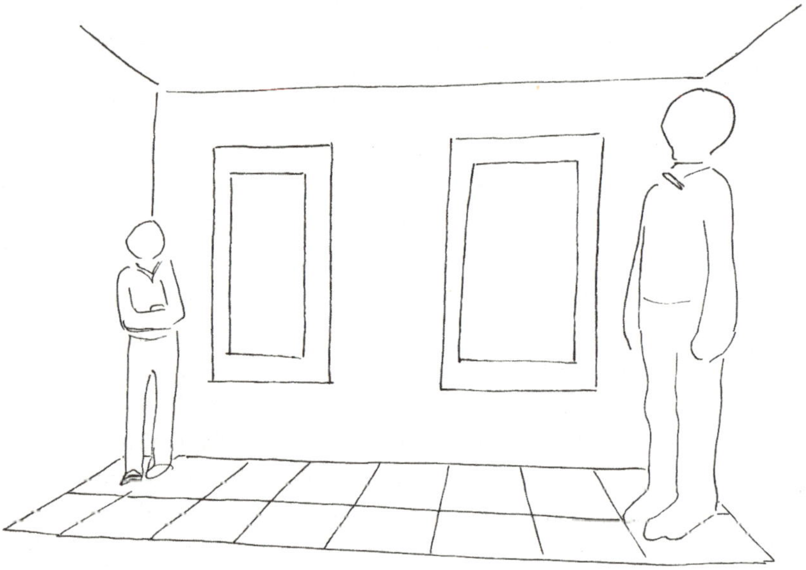

1 Exterior of the Crystal Palace.

2 A view into an actual Ames Room.

3

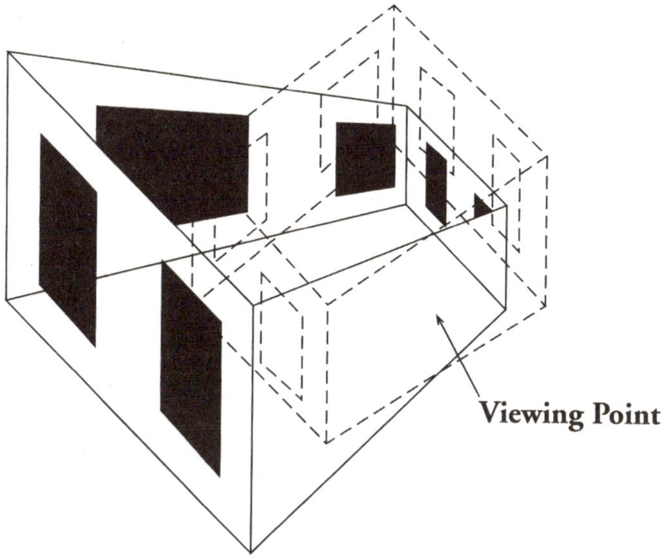

4

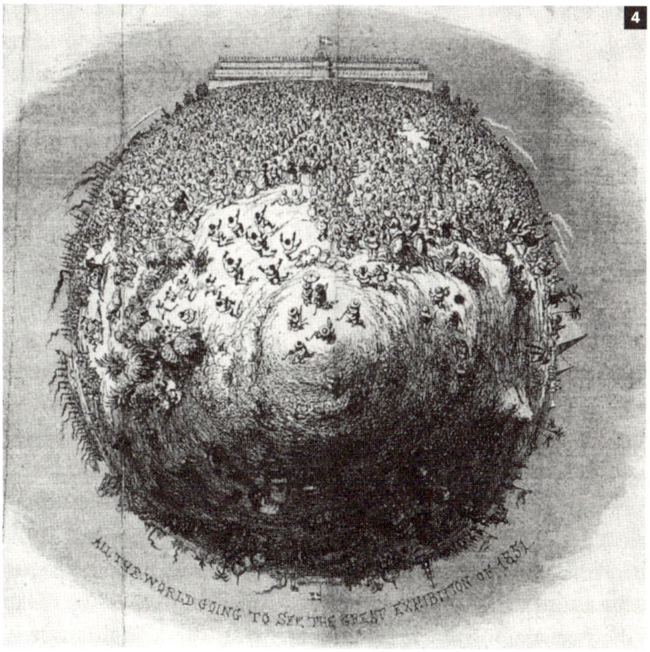

3 Actual construction of an Ames Room.

4 Lithograph by George Cruickshank showing the Crystal Palace on top of the world.

The world was indeed astounded, stunned, by this astonishing artifice and its endlessly proliferating progeny: hypnotized and paralyzed by the parallax created therein. Although the Great Exhibition itself was closed and everything vacated from the Crystal Palace while the organizers, including Prince Albert, decided what to do with the building, it remained in place and empty for about a year, prior to its being dismantled and rebuilt in slightly altered and enlarged form at Sydenham. During its quiescence and prior to being moved away, the empty building became a destination for countless visitors who, as during the time the Exhibition was open, came to marvel at the extraordinary building itself. What the many thousands of visitors saw was in effect the bare skeleton of a brilliant taxonomic machine, the system of modern order and classificatory logic as such: an experimental laboratory or an abstract stage on which any thing could be shown and compared to any other thing. The Crystal Palace, this great dazzling and frozen iceberg of a theory of order was as mesmerizing empty as it was when full. Modernity's methodology, sketched out and inscribed in glass and iron.

The Crystal Palace worked because it was grounded in and was the epitome of nineteenth-century historicism; in a new and rapidly embraced rhetoric of "art" as historical; where art gave form to and distinguished between past and present, and which the Great Exhibition demonstrated was the most effective vocabulary or *medium* for imagining nation, empire, ethnicity, and identity in a manner that neutralized otherness whilst simultaneously fetishizing differences as but "stylistic" variations of the same. It was what I've been calling "phallomorphic" in that its logic was not unlike that of the little boy in Freud who, discovering that his sister lacked a "part" that he possessed, concluded that she was but a deponent "he." Museology has been the Crystal Palace's afterlife, and, along with art history and criticism, constitutes the dreamwork we as orthopsychic subjects in and for modernity endlessly practice, *both* as sterner minds and as giddy-minded shoppers or fashion junkies. And we show few signs of wanting to relinquish being haunted not only by things but by the Crystal Palace and its effects.

We've never left this building. An engraving of 1851 by Cruickshank (fig. 4) sums up all of this quite succinctly and economically, showing the Crystal Palace astride the globe of the world (London, we may imagine, is at the top of the world), absorbing all peoples and their products, shown arriving from every point on the planet by boat, train, cart, and by foot. ●

NOTES

This essay is a slightly revised version of Chapter 3 in: Donald Preziosi, *Brain of the Earth's Body: Art, Museums, and the Phantasms of Modernity* (Minneapolis and London, 2003).

1 Anonymous, *Recollections and Tales of the Crystal Palace* (1852), pp. 3–6. This remarkable 150-page poem by the unidentified authoress of *Belgravia, A Poem,* 2nd ed. (1852), is divided into six parts, devoted, respectively, to an overview of the year of the Exhibition from its opening on May 1 to its autumn close, morning in the Crystal Palace (with the joyous arrival of the Queen), a discussion of the building's resemblance to great edifices of ice seen by Arctic mariners, the lamentation of a mother for her daughter lost in the crowds, a description of the progress of two anonymous persons through the Exhibition one day, closing with a discussion of "the ties that exist between a great Author and those of his Readers who appreciate his works" (p. 137). See the excerpt quoted at the end of this essay. The Crystal Palace opened May 1, 1851, and closed October 12, 165 days later.

2 These issues are taken up at length in my *The Art of Art History: A Critical Anthology* (Oxford and New York, 1998), especially in the essay "The Art of Art History," pp. 507–25.

3 A useful introduction to the building and to a good sample of the recent literature is John McKean, *Crystal Palace* (London, 1994). The present essay is in part a synopsis of Chapter 3, "The Crystalline Veil and the Phallomorphic Imaginary," of my *Brain of the Earth's Body: Art, Museums, and the Phantasms of Modernity* (Minneapolis, 2003), pp. 92–115.

4 Sigmund Freud, *The Standard Edition of the Complete Psychological Works,* ed. James Strachey (London, 1953–74), vol. XXI, p. 36.

5 See Tony Bennett, "Pedagogic Objects, Clean Eyes, and Popular Instruction: On Sensory Regimes and Museum Didactics," *Configurations* 6, no. 3 (1998), pp. 345–71, and Paula Findlen, *Possessing Nature: Museums, Collecting, and Scientific Culture in Early Modern Italy* (Berkeley, 1994), pp. 100–109.

6 On the history of art as an inescapably orientalist enterprise, see my *The Art of Art History* cited above.

7 My perspectives here are indebted to the work of, and to work in the wake of, Luce Irigaray. See the special issue of *Diacritics* (28, no. 1 [Spring 1998]) devoted to her work, and especially the article by Anne-Emmanuelle Berger, "The Newly Veiled Woman: Irigaray, Specularity, and the Islamic Veil," pp. 93–119, and see also Luce Irigaray, "The Blind Spot of an Old Dream of Symmetry," in idem, *Speculum of the Other Woman*, trans. Gillian C. Gill (Ithaca, 1985), pp. 41–68.

8 Walter Benjamin, *Gesammelte Schriften,* ed. Rolf Tiedemann and Hermann Schweppenhausen, with the collaboration of Theodor W. Adorno and Gerschom Scholem (Frankfurt am Main, 1972–), vol. V: *Das Passagen-Werk,* ed. Rolf Tiedemann (1982), p. 494 (K 1a,8).

9 Michel Bréal, "Les idées latentes du langage," *Mélanges de mythologie et de linguistique* (1887), p. 321. Regarding affinities between late nineteenth-century linguistic and art historical theories (and theoreticians), see Donald Preziosi, *Rethinking Art History: Meditations on Coy Science* (New Haven, 1989), pp. 80–121.

10 Among many useful introductions to Lacanian psychoanalytic theory, one of the more lucid for our purposes is Joan Copjec's *Read My Desire: Lacan Against the Historicists* (Cambridge [MA], 1994), and in particular Chapter 2, "The Orthopsychic Subject: Film Theory and the Reception of Lacan," pp. 15–38, and Chapter 8, "Sex and the Euthanasia of Reason," pp. 201–36.

11 Cited in Susan Buck-Morss, *The Dialectics of Seeing: Walter Benjamin and the Arcades Project* (Cambridge [MA], 1989), p. 324 and n. 137.

12 On relationships between the origins of the modern museum movement in the late eighteenth century and European freemasonry, particularly in Britain and France, see Preziosi 2003 (see note 3), Chapter 2: "The Astrolabe of the Enlightenment," pp. 63–91.

13 Alois Riegl, "Kunstgeschichte und Universalgeschichte" [1898], in *Gesammelte Aufsaetze* (Augsburg, 1929), p. 7.

14 Henri Focillon, *Vie des formes,* 3rd ed. (Paris, 1947), pp. 82–83.

15 Arnold Hauser, *The Philosophy of Art History* (New York, 1959), p. 162.

16 See Preziosi 1989 (see note 9), pp. 88–90, 115–16.

17 *Recollections and Tales* (see note 1), pp. 34–35.

18 My use of the term "orthopsychic" is indebted to the work of Joan Copjec; see Copjec 1994 (see note 10).

CRYSTAL PALACE EXHIBITIONS (2005)

50

Marian Pastor Roces

> *Besides the spearlike gaze of relentless semiosis, the other weapon Columbus carried with him was Minerva's gorgon-bossed shield of mimesis. This, commonly imagined in the Renaissance as made of crystal and reflective like a mirror, was a device for stopping natives in their tracks and making them wonder who the actors were—themselves or the reflections.*
>
> Paul Carter, *The Lie of the Land*

SPECTERS IN MIRRORS

IN the second half of the nineteenth century, a world at once overt and chimerical was conjured at the universal expositions by their imperial inventors. Natives from everywhere were stopped in their tracks, wonderstruck, for they were spectators but also, clearly though phantasmically, actors. Minerva's crystal shield of mimesis is an astonishing machine. In its reappearance as the Crystal Palace as the industrial revolution got underway, the shield secured clarity of vision by bedazzlement. It is the same shield that plays with our reflections in our turn-of-the-millennium international art events. It plays with—and finally annuls—time and space as inherited from the Enlightenment. Confoundingly, the Crystal Palace mirrors its future and its spatial dilation in today's global art shows, which glint with endless spectral reflections of nineteenth-century imperialism (fig. 1).

Queen Victoria herself was bedazzled, and understood this magic experience, with its discrete layers of private anxiety and affection, as inherent to imperial purpose. She wrote effusively in her diary on the opening day of the very first universal exposition, in London in 1851, for which the original Crystal Palace was built:

> *The Park presented a wonderful spectacle, crowds streaming through it—carriages and troops passing, quite like the Coronation and for me the same anxiety... I never saw Hyde Park look as it did, being filled with crowds as far as the eye could reach... The sun shone and gleamed upon the gigantic edifice, upon which the flags of every nation was flying... The sight as we came to the centre... facing the beautiful crystal fountain, was magic and impressive... My beloved husband, the creator of this peace festival "uniting the industry and art of all nations of the earth," all this was indeed moving, and a day to live for ever. God bless my dearest Albert, and my dear Country, which has shown itself so great today.... Albert left my side and at the head of the Commissioners... read the Report to me... and I read a short answer... After this the Archbishop of Canterbury offered up a short and appropriate prayer, followed by the singing of Handel's Hallelujah chorus, during which time the Chinese Mandarin came forward and made the obeisance. This concluded, the Procession of great length began, which was beautifully arranged, the prescribed order being exactly adhered to.*[1]

In addition to being reflective, Minerva's shield is the Gorgon's face. Equally reflective are the monarch's words, which crystallize the power to stun. To produce unity globally, movement is curated, "the prescribed order . . . exactly adhered to," and accidents tabooed. "Peace" is in this manner a stillness, which is realized within a finely produced state of stupefaction. "The viewer's mystical sense of being carried to a higher realm is calculated; it means, in effect, experiencing the no-place of seeing all places in terms of a single formal key," writes spatial historian Paul Carter, who sees the reiteration of the colonizer's vision in the twentieth-century aesthetics of formal structure.[2] In both the imperial vision and high modernism, what is of value is "the composition as a whole rather than in its particulars... it still at bottom insists on grasping the object as a whole, in a single glance."[3]

That particular single glance, cast "as far as the eye could reach," projects toward the outer limits of what is possible to be perceived or known at all. Thus the success of the Crystal Palace as a sign of modern ambition: it materialized the glance as architecture. The transparent edifice produced the no-space of seeing all places, contrived to contain the uncontainable outside.

Perhaps it is the spatial turn in postmodernism that makes the crystal-palace form such grim (if not baleful) reading, as this essay does read it. Certainly the phantom links between the universal expositions and the current biennials and triennials are fleshed out, as it were, only thinly—caricature-like and emptied of fulsome menace—in temporal terms, as lineage. Not so, when they are regarded as similarly rarefied loci where an aristocratic few exercise the will to order plurality on a vast scale. Even if we grant the shift toward global art events as an attempt to outstare the colonizer's gaze, there are bedeviling risks of paralysis in spaces of contest that mirror the spaces created by the forces contested. Time, then, offers the assurance of safe distance and a guarantee of liberating epistemological change. That which is consigned to the past is rendered curiously unthreatening today.

It is with a bravura shaped by historical distance (which plots space diachronically as well) that, for instance, Rosa Martínez, curator of two of the newest biennials, in Santa Fe and Istanbul, avers that "We are reinventing the biennial today. New biennials have arisen on the periphery. Havana, Johannesburg, and Istanbul are introducing new approaches that question the nineteenth-century model of the Venice Biennale."[4] Articulating faith in historical progress, in this case tracked along an emancipatory trajectory, Martínez speaks of emergence: "New biennials have arisen from the will to exorcise political traumas, . . . to create new spaces for art in the Third World."[5] Such reversals can only be proposed within an obdurately linear history, which has a precise medial axis for folding. That median is verbalized offhand as a "center" in the explanation provided by curator Germano Celant for his departure, in the forty-seventh Venice Biennial, from the thematic exhibition modality in favor of the flipping of time conveyed by the title of his effort, *Future Present Past:* "The past is my future and my future is my past; these two meet at the center, which is the present."[6] That privileged present is still the sphere of the modern subject (persisting atemporally in postmodernity), so given to inventive ways of coupling a receding past with a future that thrusts forward in search of a target.

Liberation from myriad griefs is one such target, the express aim of most of the current mega-exhibitions. "The ideal biennial is a profoundly political and spiritual event. It contemplates the present with a desire to transform it," concludes Martínez, who then cites Arthur Danto for his description of the biennial as "a glimpse of a transnational utopia."[7] Then again, because the Crystal Palace events were likewise glimpses of a kind of transnational utopia, one wonders if hope is an apparition. The universal expositions, too, were ideal events in a profoundly political and spiritual sense. Thus the suspicion and the worry arising from the synchronic view.

The spaces produced in the nineteenth century for the global diffusion of capitalist power may have closed off the reinvention of those same spaces for social justice. As a single spatial form that reasserts its controlling power even as it is perpetually replicated, the world exposition, in its very dimensions, annuls any new spaces that are shaped transformatively.

Danto bracketed the young Johannesburg Biennial of 1993 with the concurrent edition of the oldest biennial, that of Venice. Taking up the title of the Venice event, *Punti dell'arte,* he briefly undertook a poetics of mapping: "The [Venice] exhibition was to serve precisely the purposes of a compass: it was to orient the viewer to the artistic geography of the Biennale, and then to that of the world itself—so a map within a map." He continued: "A compass does not define the center of the world, after all: it orients the user wherever the user stands." Then he observed: "So far as I can tell, Johannesburg was not one of the cardinal points on [Venice Biennial curator] Bonito Oliva's compass."[8] He spotted a lacuna in the biennial's liberal, humanist encompassing of the earth.

Danto's pithy observation may very well be the necessary provocation alerting the erstwhile native, who is drawn into international art events, to the mystifying force of mimesis. It is hard to avoid being transfixed; perhaps it can be done only by cultivating a wariness of the too-overt and overly celebrated democratized space, or by detecting equally telling lacunae. Such urgencies, of course, make for baffling wanderings. To head off into the politics of centers and margins leads into domains where time and space are each in turn imprisoned in binary formulae. To keep retracking art history with a gusto for politically valuable nuance leads paradoxically to the tight, long space of genealogy. The tightness leaves little room for any description of the blurring of every period idea in that sequence of radicalism—in other words, for any description of a mess of ideas, differently chaotic in different places, that often cancel one another out.

The movement can be only into messy digressions. Nonetheless, this peripeteia will at least be like prowling, or stalking. The Crystal Palace expositions were constructions of vastness, and so are their replications today. Vastness—the grand integrities that are the spatial form of dominance—is perhaps vulnerable only to the unruly minutiae encountered in stalking about the crystal palace of mimesis.

THE PRODUCTION OF CITY

REM Koolhaas writes:

The inspiring example of London's International Exhibiton, held in 1851 in the Crystal Palace, triggers Manhattan's ambition. Two years later, it has organized its own fair, staking a claim for its superiority, in almost every respect, over all other American cities. At this time, the city hardly extends north of 42nd Street—apart from the omnipresent Grid. Except near Wall Street it looks almost rural: single houses scattered on the grass-covered blocks. The fair, implanted on what will become Bryant Park, is marked by two colossal structures that completely overwhelm their surroundings, introducing a new scale into the island's skyline, which they dominate easily. The first is a vision of London's Crystal Palace [fig. 2].[9]

Already a spatial discourse on the global in its prehistory and in its textual formulations as *universal*, the Crystal Palace expositions hothoused nothing less than the modern city, the spectacular space that materializes the power to command constructions of the global. The international art exhibitions of the last century have in large part performed the same imperative. Through the 2000 Shanghai Biennial, entitled *The Spirit of Shanghai*, for instance, the organizers set a course for this city to be the "Venice of the East." As in Shanghai, the international art events organized in Gwangju, Pontevedra, Lyon, and Rotterdam are understood as assertions of metropolitan wherewithal, aimed at having these cities shed their secondary status within their respective countries.

In the case of the august Documenta, which does not articulate itself in terms of Kassel's economic and architectural growth, the exhibition is nonetheless framed by the city's historical and cultural position in German and European history.[10] Since 1959, Documenta has also been "organized by a limited liability company, the asso-

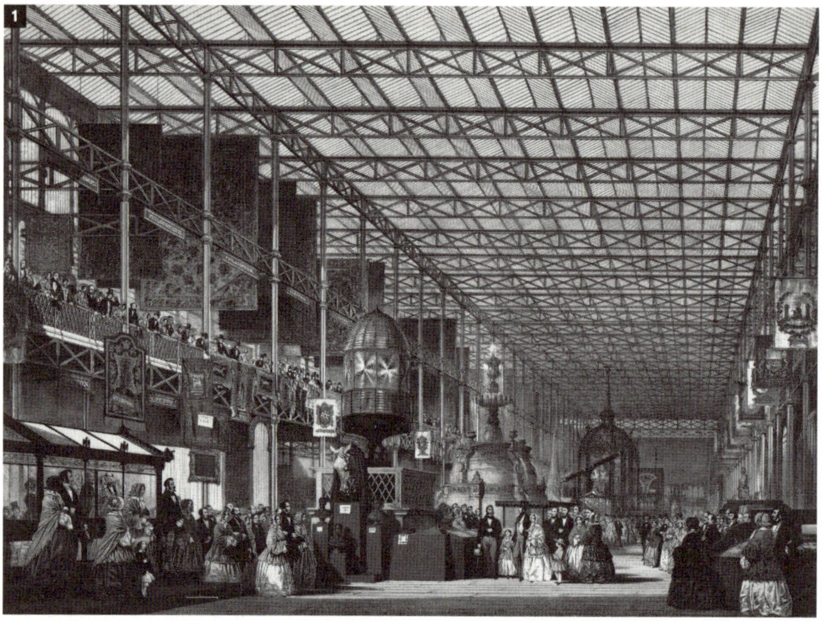

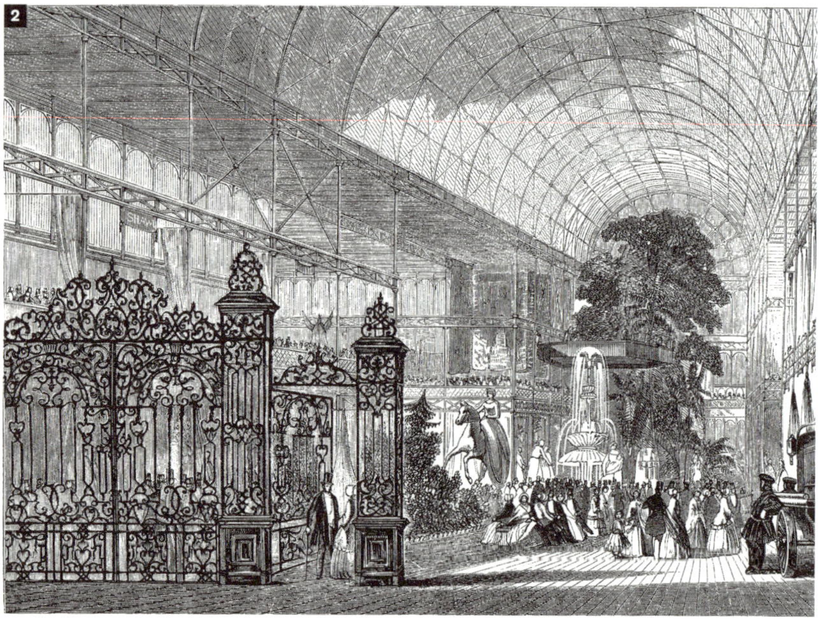

1 "Crystal Palace Interior," in *The Art Journal Illustrated Catalogue: The Industry of All Nations, 1851* (1851), p. xvii.

2 "The British Nave," in *Dickinson's Comprehensive Pictures of the Great Exhibition of 1851* (1854), plate 3.

ciates being the City of Kassel and the State of Hess."[11] The regrettably short-lived Johannesburg Biennial succumbed to city politics. It was dependent for funding on a specific metropolitan cluster, and the issue was, ironically, about which of the four clusters birthed by the Biennial itself would foot the bill.[12]

City-centric hubris was evident in the mid nineteenth century, even though the political intent underpinning the expositions was typically articulated as national pride and imperial capacity—the power, that is to say, to orchestrate worldwide harmony. A placard at the first Crystal Palace exposition declared its statement of purpose: "The Strengthening of the Bonds of Peace and Friendship Among All Nations of the Earth." It was, nonetheless, the resonant notion of "capital"—the capital idea, capitals of columns, capital letters, capitalism, and imperial and national capital cities—that focused the claims of superiority. The expositions, magniloquent celebrations of capitalism, were for and about the metaphysical dimensions of the capital, meaning the national and imperial realm at its control center. The materials on display were organized around the triumphalism of the city/realm, as when, for example, paintings and sculptures from twenty-eight nations were exhibited at the second universal exposition, in Paris in 1855, in what constituted the first international art exhibition.

All curatorial enterprise subsumes parts into the whole. The large-scale effort, of course, makes the distance dramatic between micro and macro. At the universal expositions, individual exhibits are indeed minutiae of the big picture. Because the titanic domain is the city itself, it is the spatial experience of urban renewal that was, and is, made to speak most extravagantly to the spectator. The direct impact of the first universal expositions on the built environments of their host cities, London and Paris, assured the persistence, throughout the last century and a half, of "exposition" as shorthand for urban modernization.

As was the case in London, the second Paris universal exposition was forthright about the relationships between architecture, urban design, art, industry, and money. Addressing lack of space as plans were being considered, Napoléon III suggested a grid "with national sections along one axis and exhibition categories along the other."[13] The prince's plans were realized in 1867 in Frédéric LePlay's great oval exhibition hall, built at the Champ de Mars. As it turned out, according to Patricia Mainardi, the centering of power of capital within the power of place was quite literally realized:

Within, exhibitions were organized in concentric ovals, heavy industry being the outermost ring, the fine arts being near the center (and thus taking up less space). Paul Mantz wrote: "Material things occupy the first ring and, with each circle crossed, you approach the spiritual." This lovely symbolism was ruined however. Perhaps in a moment of supreme honesty, the Imperial Commission revealed its true spirit by placing in the innermost circle, at the heart of the Exposition, a display of money.[14]

So far as art is concerned, the decision to go with small private works rather than large public ones, and to hold retrospective exhibitions for major artists at the 1855 exposition, served to uphold the Romantic individual. The ideology "emphasizing individual self-referential development—the concept of progress defined in aesthetic terms—has proved to be the principal Modernist tool for understanding art apart from its social and political milieu,"[15] writes Mainardi, tuning up what has become the standard account of the birth of the modern. She contributes a significant refinement to that account by providing the direct link between the universal expositions and subsequent international art exhibitions.[16]

The literal diminution of the art object at that pivotal moment, as art itself compacted around the modern bourgeois subject, was at the same time the enlargement of the promise of social change vested in capitalism and expressed in urban renewal. Extraordinary social significance was vested in change; the more sweeping, the more passionately charged. This passion persists in contemporary art practice, and its register is turned up very high indeed during the biennials and triennials. It persists despite and because of the failure of capitalism and modern aesthetics to live up to their promise of social justice, because the bourgeois domestication of art to the task of maintaining critical pressure in relation to onerous power, cast as the onerous past, remains an enduring aspect of modern subjectivity. The mythos that the world exposition space holds radical possibilities continues to be compelling. It pertains to no less than the structural shape of the modern subject, particularly as this form of life is sustained and validated in city-building work that itself preserves and reiterates the heroic aspirations of its nineteenth-century precedent.

The kind of utopian agenda that provides strong reasons for the holding of international exhibitions today tends to be expressed in a vocabulary reminiscent of the Romantic imagination. The references to reinvention, crossing over, discovery, looking beyond, and redefinition in Martínez's explanation of her curatorial approach to the Santa Fe Biennial may or may not accurately represent the collective political timbre of the works exhibited, but they do envelop them in a heroic light: "The title of the biennial is 'Looking for a Place,' because we have to reinvent the places occupied by art, beyond the limitations of disciplines, cross over the museum walls, discover the implications in the separation of public and private spaces, and redefine the politics of exploitation.... Art must contribute to make the world a more habitable place."[17] A more habitable place was similarly claimed at the 2000 Shanghai Biennial, expressed as a struggle with the ruling powers of the People's Republic of China:

> *The third Shanghai Biennale... will go down in Chinese art history as marking a new chapter in the re-entry of contemporary Chinese art [in]to its homeland.... Not only is it the first time that leading international contemporary artists have been invited to participate in an event initiated by Chinese organizers... but it is the first time for works by contemporary Chinese artists to be given official blessing to enter the hallowed halls of a national art museum.*[18]

The city/realm of distinction, globally valid, is produced even where the project is to deconstruct the Romantic rhetoric of utopian dreaming. The Gwangju Visual Media Academy, represented with works at the Gwangju Biennial, draws discursive power from a specific moment of political violence, which allows the positive re-creation of this city vis-à-vis a negative state.[19] Allan Smith, curator of the inaugural Auckland Triennial, creates a seamless weave of the intent to place Auckland on the world art map and the postmodern aspiration to reconsider the myths that determine the mapping of the world: "The working thesis of *Bright Paradise* is that New Zealand is peculiarly well suited as a place from which to speculate on the disturbing beauty of artificial paradises and the fateful allure of utopian desire." Smith puts faith in how "such speculations uncover metaphors of our contemporary world caught between an exhilarating desire for experience, information, on one hand, and a powerful sense of our having corrupted history and destroyed any oceanic sublime or paradise on the other."[20]

Utopia appears no more endlessly malleable than in these events—but not necessarily as the postmodern strategy posited by Fredric Jameson, which requires incessant modification to address the quicksilver manipulations wreaked by power in the age of transnational capitalism,[21] nor in the way Hal Foster argues the possible recuperation of the political force of an insistently transmuting and returning avant-garde. For Foster, "There is this fundamental stake in art and academy: the preservation, in an administered, affirmative culture, of spaces of critical debate and alternative vision."[22] It is in this way that there is cause for doggedness. Indeed, the prowler's alertness—to the operations of utopian imaginings that are too comfortably assimilable to what remains a nineteenth-century technology of representation—is indispensable. The universal exposition, the ur-form of capitalist cultural infrastructure, conceived to be an alternative space in the first place, may be expected to literally corner the market on alternatives. And utopia, institutionalized in the city as produced in the nineteenth century, may be expected to dazzle as it shields the powers that be.

The Havana Biennial was the first instance in which an alternative vision of the biennial was institutionalized. Taking up a locus of resistance to the spatial politics of the world exposition, it was also the one biennial that projected a parallel world (the Third) rather than the city/realm. (It did not, and could not, have the ambition to renew Havana architecturally, or economically, or politically.) Curator and critic Gerardo Mosquera sketched the difficult terrain of its intent:

> *The idea behind the Biennial was always to introduce artists who work outside of the main centers. It was meant to facilitate horizontal relations, which doesn't exclude North–South relations. However, this wasn't supposed to come as an attempt at legitimization by the mainstream, but rather to facilitate an equal relationship upon the inclusion in the mainstream mechanisms, which is something completely different. There's a difference between trying to be an active presence in these circles and letting oneself be subordinated. It's important how the Biennial deals with this problem, so that it doesn't end up a shop window for critics and curators from the centers—a kind of "scouting for Third World talent."*[23]

That it has become such a window, however, is not necessarily its undoing. Since it formed itself as an alternative biennial, the idea of an alternative art market does not present itself. Nonetheless, it presents itself with an instructively oxymoronic charge. For there is no alternative to the market; the market is a unified field. Which leads to the principal difficulty: is there really, in tautological and practical terms, an alternative biennial?

Regret has been expressed about the softening of the Havana Biennial's rhetoric as it engages art-world realpolitik. For Rachel Weiss, at the time, the Havana "organizers have proved that a convincing global position can be developed from outside the usual circles of power; their task now, one fears, is to defend their achievement from its own success well enough to preserve its voice and distinctness—a problem of middle age."[24] But if this biennial were to be considered only in terms of a career path to security, which is to say, as a temporal track, the spatial dimensions of its politics of contestation recede from view.

The synchronic repetition of the crystal-palace exposition form locates the essentially historical question the Havana Biennial experience begs. A point of departure may be a refreshed appreciation for the originality of Havana's political location in the world of world expositions—but not only in that it is a site/sign of the domains of the Other. More importantly, Havana was outside a planetary network of cities recreated during the second half of the nineteenth and first half of the twentieth centuries, specifically in relation to the architectural, artistic, and technological efforts given expression during the expositions. Realizing the organic and machinistic metaphoric conventions that framed modernity, the universal expositions were the factories—the hothouses—of this network of cities; but they were *merely* the factories and hothouses. It was, and is, the network itself that shaped and styled itself as international. The unconnected place, Havana, connected itself to this network even as it thought to oppose it. But the world exposition form is a production and supply node, and it maintains linkage more than it contradicts. The opposition constructed by the Havana Biennial is not that of without/within; the network rearranged itself to accommodate a productive bilateral symmetry. The Havana Biennial can therefore properly claim to be an alternative biennial, and that indeed there is such a thing, but one that provides symmetrical beauty, and fresh creative labor (from without), *within* the network.

Havana remains outside the realm of physically altering cityscapes (though it may be destined for scenographic delight in the global scheme of things). In this location, at that time, there remained hope in rupture, because the city itself obliged art-making to fall into and widen the cracks, instead of elevating it in the service of visions of global ascendancy. (It is for this reason that the demise of the Johannesburg Biennial occasioned regret.) That this is not also the case in Gwangju, Taipei, Shanghai, Fukuoka, Yokohama, and the host of other newly "crystal-palaced" cities is due to their surfaces, which are metaplinths for art, capital, histories of monolithic power, and global ambition. Given that East/West is a coarse and bankrupt scenographic divide that has obscured the labyrinthine lines of difference in the world, the victim side of the politics of alterity is only claimed implausibly in the arena of competition of cities. A response is sought, for instance, by René Block:

> *Charged with the task of selecting twenty artists from Africa and Europe for the 3rd Biennale in Gwangju, I recall the embittered remarks of the South African artist, curator and critic, Kendell Geers, which he wrote for the catalogue of the Fellbach Triennial in 1998: "Traditionally, the exhibitions are staged in a 'white cube,' somewhere in a major European or American art centre, and typically with the 'exchange' flowing in just the one direction: into the 'white cube' gallery, which—as we all know—can house anything imaginable. . . . Placing non-Western work into this setting has nothing to do with dialogue or exchange, but rather with a restoration of the colonial power structure. The non-Western work is expected to behave as the guest it is and respect the rules of its hosts regardless of how condescending or racist they are." Yet already at this stage we can conclude that this gathering of twenty artists from Northern Europe, South Africa and the Orient at the Gwangju Biennale will have fulfilled at least one of Kendell Geers' aspirations. All the submitted works will be exhibited in a non-Western context. They all will respect the rules of their Asian hosts. And perhaps it will be possible, by virtue of the equidistance to Europe, Africa and the Orient, to view these works from diverse perspectives. The presentation on "neutral" Asian ground will serve to highlight the common cultural roots but also the substantive differences in their artists' works.*[25]

But the rules of their Asian hosts may have more in common with those of the Western hosts of international art events than can be comfortably acknowledged. The key players at the hothouses share a common culture, and transit and live together in abstract modern space. It is for this reason that any spatialized account of modern art, architecture, and city planning reads like an album of friends. Though industrial capitalism was realized differently in England and France, Richard Sennett points out that, nonetheless, "from capital to capital, such differences were not as extreme as differences from nation to nation."[26]

Today's international elite is distinguished, more than anything else, by the speed of their travel to absorb the world. It exists in the same rapid-transit space as that which was home to the nineteenth-century cosmopolitans. In both cases their elite status and transnational resources are assured by a savoir faire with communication technology. It is disingenuous for this elite to appeal to geography-based cultural difference, without reflecting on the hostility to difference ordering their aesthetics of mobility and speed; to profit from the gains of radical art and activism; and to displace attention from themselves in the critique of power. It is precisely their culture and interests that maintain the modern construction of the global. A strong contrary position is called for whenever blind spots are offered that may occlude the operations of power, including the power of organizing international art events. Hence, one takes exception to a suggestion offered by Okwui Enwezor, artistic director of Documenta 11, in connection with his earlier effort at the Johannesburg Biennial, when he said that such work "should ultimately lead to a focus on the artworks themselves, and not on the trials and problems of the people trying to organize these events."[27] For to point out that the trials and problems of the organizers are precisely the site to be watched most stringently and engaged by progressive critics is to press the progressive curators, Enwezor among them, to lay aside Minerva's shield.

Foster gives a valuable glimpse of the power infrastructure vis-à-vis which critical effort must persist, citing both Mandel, to whom "the postindustrial signals not the supercession of industrialization so much as its extensions," and Jameson, to whom "the postmodern announces not the end of modernization so much as its apogee."[28] The postindustrial and the postmodern invoked in recent international exhibitions are then the object, not the subject, of critical engagement. This is not lost on most commentators, for instance, Hazel Friedman, who writes of *Africus* in Johannesburg: "Biennales . . . constitute a microcosm of power relations in the real world. They have their centralized cores of high visibility and their undeveloped, neglected cultural peripheries; their skyscrapers and squatter shacks, city councilors and serfs."[29] Given this space, artists respond by resisting or performing to expectations, often simultaneously. The activity of hothousing ideas for cities has often been taken up literally, and with compelling subtlety, by many artists.

How artists maintain subtlety, let alone reflexivity, in the hothouse requires another extended discussion. However, participants in today's crystal-palace events do understand, or sense, that a grave disjunction exists between the minutely layered, minutely differentiated spaces of radical contestation, where it really hurts, and the colossal spaces celebrating the radical, where it really effervesces. The effervescence raises the temperature in the crystal palace, but one finds that the temperature must be so well calibrated that the experience is curiously pleasant, and the exotica on display so useful to the status quo. As proof of that invigorating heat, perhaps the most riveting example is the online introductory text for *Cities on the Move,* curated by Hans Ulrich Obrist and Hou Hanru. The following section is verily Victorian:

> *Asian cities are becoming new key points in the "network" of global cities which are the very central forces influencing, controlling and even dictating the new world order. In the meantime, the urban spaces are being fast expanded. The political, economic and cultural authorities also share a long-term vision of modernization. In spite of the search for typically modernist symbols such as the tallest skyscrapers, they also conceive projects and strategies to develop the future industry represented by new technologies. In many cities, new areas are planned and developed to become "Asian Silicon Valleys." The Malaysian Multimedia Super Corridor (planned by Kisho Kurokawa), among others, is the most mediated example, while most of the computers in the global market are produced in Taiwan, Malaysia, Korea, Singapore and China. What is also remarkable is that the most advanced telecommunication technologies have become a natural aspect of everyday life in Asian urban societies. Mobil [sic] phone[s], Internet and video games are not only trendy gadgets for young people to show off, but indispensable "survival kits" for the urban inhabitants ... As a natural part of the "success story," the pressure of the growth of international travels makes all cities invest in new commuting infrastructures.*[30]

History, modern to postmodern, lies. It converts its readers to the arousals of change where stasis is everywhere. It has, among other confidence tricks, promoted the construction of the last century and a half as a *long* time, time in which change in the structures of domination has been supposedly well under way. What *is* well under way is the work of radicalizing the understanding that things are not all right in the world. Such work benefits from any realization that the nineteenth century is not such a long time ago. The Crystal Palace exposition is inherent in a spatial order that, because it is architecturally imposed on the earth, does not disappear quickly, certainly not to make room for dissent beyond the confines of clearly marked hothouses. ●

NOTES

Previously published in: Gerardo Mosquera and Jean Fisher (eds.), *Over Here: International Perspectives on Art and Culture* (Cambridge [MA] and London, 2005), pp. 234–50.

1 Among other sources of the quotation, see Christopher Hibbert, *Queen Victoria in Her Letters and Journals* (Gloucestershire, 2000), pp. 84–85.

2 Paul Carter, *The Lie of the Land* (London, 1996), p. 133.

3 Ibid., p. 132.

4 Rosa Martínez interviewed by Carlos Basualdo, "Launching Site," *Artforum* (Summer 1999); consulted online at http://www.findarticles.com/cf_o/mo268/10_37/55015163/p1/article.jhtml.

5 Ibid.

6 Germano Celant, formerly available at http://dialnsa.edu/iat97/Venice/FPP/index.html.

7 Martínez interviewed by Basualdo (see note 4).

8 Arthur Danto, "Mapping the Art World," originally published in the "Essays" link of the Official Internet Archive of Africus '95, Johannesburg Biennial, formerly available at http://sunsite.wites.ac.za/biennale/essays/danto.html.

9 Rem Koolhaas, *Delirious New York* (Rotterdam, 1994), p. 23.

10 See Catherine David, paper presented at the "Art and Theory" conference, Mumbai, convened by the Mohile-Parikh Art Centre in 1998.

11 According to information provided on the Documenta Web site, "The documenta und Museum Fridericianum Veranstaltungs-GmbH is a non-profit organization owned and financed by the City of Kassel and the State of Hesse"; see http://www.documenta.de/kontakt.html?&L=1.

12 See Brenda Atkinson, "Behind the Biennale Blues," *Electronic Mail and Guardian*, December 11, 1997, formerly available at http://www.chico.mweb.co.za/mg/art/reviews/97dec/11dec-biennale.html.

13 Patricia Mainardi, *Art and Politics of the Second Empire: The Universal Expositions of 1855 and 1867* (New Haven, 1987) p. 131.

14 Ibid.

15 Ibid., p. 196.

16 Ibid., p. 197.

17 Martínez interviewed by Carlos Basualdo (see note 4).

18 Introduction to the Shanghai Biennial catalogue, consulted online at http://www.sh-artmuseum.org.cn/double/msg2000/e-jihua.htm.

19 See references to "Kwangju of May" and "the life of the martyr, Yoon Sang-won" in the Arts and Human Rights section of the Gwangju Biennial Web site, http://www.gwangju-biennale.org/last-biennale/2000/english/sspeci-artartist34.htm. See also Frank Hoffmann, "Monoculture and Its Discontents," *Art in America* (November 2000), pp. 71–79.

20 Allan Smith, introduction to *Bright Paradise, the First Auckland Triennial*, exh. cat. Auckland, Auckland Art Gallery (Auckland, 2001), p. 5.

21 Fredric Jameson, *The Cultural Turn: Selected Writings on the Postmodern, 1983–1998* (London and New York, 1998).

22 Hal Foster, *The Return of the Real: The Avant-Garde at the End of the Century* (Cambridge [MA], 1996), p. xvii.

23 Gerardo Mosquera interviewed by Gerhard Haupt, "Sixth Biennial of Havana," available online at http://www.universes-in-universe.de/car/havanna/opinion/e_mosqu.htm.

24 Rachel Weiss, "The Sixth Havana Biennial," *Art Nexus*, no. 26 (October–December 1997), available online at http://www.universes-in-universe.de/artnexus/no26/weiss_eng2.htm.

25 René Block, "Commissioner's Concept," Gwangju Biennial, 2000, formerly available at http://www.gwangju-biennale.org/last-biennale/2000/english/mainex-concept-eu.thm.

26 Richard Sennett, *The Fall of Public Man* (New York, 1997), p. 138.

27 Okwui Enwezor, quoted in Brenda Atkinson, "The Art Show of the Year," Johannesburg Biennial update, *Electronic Mail and Guardian*, August 14, 1997, formerly available at http://www.chico.mweb.co.za/mg/reviews/97aug/14aug-biennale.html.

28 Foster 1996 (see note 22), p. 218.

29 Hazel Friedman, "The Curator as God," *Electronic Mail and Guardian*, October 9, 1997, formerly available at http://server.mg.co.za/mg/art/reviews/97oct/90c-biennale2.html.

30 Hou Hanru and Hans Ulrich Obrist, introduction to the exhibition *Cities on the Move* (Bangkok), consulted online at http://www.art4d.com/bangkokonthemove/2542/city/index_1.html.

BIENNIAL CULTURE: A LONGER HISTORY

66

Caroline A. Jones

INTRODUCTION

THE Venice Biennial was just opening its doors in 1895 when a strident pamphlet began circulating in Paris: *Pas d'Exposition en 1900!* This wildly successful opposition from the province of Nancy targeted the French Assembly, where funds for the 1900 exposition had to be provided and decisions made.[1] (We know the exposition did happen, but probably not before back-room deals were cut, since there was another exposition mounted in Nancy in 1909.) But a young law student, H. Georges Berger, decided in his 1901 *thèse* for the Université de Paris that the politicking, the debates, and the expositions should all stop. He began by clarifying the two positions that had raged in the chamber of deputies. The opponents claimed:

> *The Expos* [are] *active agents of this bad politics that one calls internationalism* [and] *cosmopolitanism, which* [make] *a country lose its originality, its proper character, rendering it feeble because it becomes less coherent and placing it at the mercy of its neighbors, who, better advised or stronger, have conserved intact the traditions that are most often instrumental to the grandeur of nations.*[2]

But liberal proponents just as fervently desired the kind of international exchange the expos represented (fig. 1):

> *A city such as Paris, is it not made to be admired*[?] *Should it surround itself with a veritable Great Wall of China? Should it enclose itself like the sacred cities of Islamism?... No, we don't live in a cloister, behind grillwork barriers, and an influx of foreigners should not terrorize us.*[3]

This 1901 publication with its Orientalist specters concluded that both pro and con arguments were outmoded. The *expositions universelles* had done their job. If initially they had an indispensable didactic character that countered xenophobic protectionism and fostered free trade, in the new century they merely seemed agglomerations of trivial or embarrassing attractions. So Berger endorsed the suggestion of one senator who called for permanent institutions to replace the periodic expos—*musées généraux* and *musées commerciaux*—freeing regions to conduct smaller, trade specific events showing only art or only industry.[4] Seemingly unaware that the first biennial in Venice had pioneered this very thing, the young law student concluded in favor of "those many partial expositions of all imaginable types that are organizing themselves in many places—to the exclusion of the great international solemnities having the pretension of being universal."[5] Now we may ask whether the trade-specific substitutes for those "great international solemnities" are themselves still useful. An analysis of biennial culture, and its history, may give us a clue.

STAKES AND ASSERTIONS

LET me set out some of the stakes and assertions undergirding my history from the present. First, I share the view that the contemporary art biennial is deeply connected to the vast international expositions of the nineteenth century (which, in turn, developed from the national trade fairs of the late eighteenth century). Granting the continuities among these exhibitionary forms suggests shared structures and functions, thereby propelling the larger thesis of my paper: when we can look beyond claims to futurity or assertions of contemporaneity, we can begin to see the historical connections linking biennials to world's fairs, tourism, and spectacular urbanism, with implications for the efficacy and purpose of these exhibitions for the present.

Second, I argue that the biennial form is an enduring one—adaptable to surprising shifts in the art world, while capable of ensuring just as many continuities. If installation and video are the genres of the new millennium, then biennials are their regulating salon. We can debate the ethics or benefits of these types of exhibitions, but demonstrably the existing art world cannot live without them. Some estimate there are 100, others 200; some say they have passed their peak, and some argue for their necessary expansion.[6] They have been facilitated by supranational sources of funding (EU, Baltic, UNESCO, Africalia) as well as national agencies (German Federal Cultural Foundation, French Ministry of Culture, British Council, Japan Foundation); such funders see the benefit of the biennials' discursive reach. Likewise, corporations (Illy, Sonatel, Nivea, Tecno, Generali, BMW, Audi, Hitachi) provide funds and services in exchange for a small logo in the catalogue, a place at the opening, and a diffuse association with highbrow cultural exchange. Since I assert that these quintessentially "contemporary" assemblies are structurally indebted to perennial international exhibitions of the past, I will propose that many of the features of those earlier world pictures are replicated or implied in the present (among them: presumptive universality, goals of knowledge production, ties to tourism, implications for urban infrastructure, regulation of international art-world trade routes, rehabilitation—through the cosmopolitan city—of previously restrictive or totalitarian regimes, and openings for multinational capital investment and new geopolitical ambitions, all in paradoxical conjunction with local political purposes). At the same time, I want to propose that the proliferation of the biennial format has itself stimulated certain key aesthetic shifts that correspond to subjectivities crucial to the present. From a discourse of movable objects established by a newly secular art world during the Renaissance and then carried over into the nineteenth-century fairs and early-twentieth-century biennials, art in the new millennium has increasingly come to embrace *experience*—whether unknowingly echoing earlier displays or knowingly critiquing them. In sum, biennial culture is a shorthand term I use to designate the contemporary appetite for *art as experience*—and biennials are the event structures where this taste has been cultivated, and its aesthetic codified and defined.

Being an art historian rather than a social scientist, I am primarily concerned about the fate of *art and artists* in biennial culture, and the situation of the subject constructed by the work of art. The dominance of installation art and the simultaneous rise of biennials need to be examined as conjoint phenomena—mutually reinforcing and linked to specific geopolitical and aesthetic conditions. This leads to my second assertion: while there are many recurring exhibitions that do not use the word "biennial" in their title, it seems clear to me that as we begin to write their history, whether they call themselves "Manifesta," "Documenta," "Guangzhou" / "Baltic Triennial," or otherwise, all such events form themselves against the backdrop of the ur-biennial, *la Biennale di Venezia*. While I acknowledge the compelling argument made by Rafal Niemojewski that the Third World biennials (particularly in Havana and Istanbul) set up a new model for biennials in the late nineteen-eighties—primarily through their charged site-specific localism—I focus on the shared structures from the past that determine so much of our present.[7] Far from privileging the contemporary biennials as exceptional, I might even want to suggest that their proliferation post 1990 is a *second* wave, one that echoes the earlier international epoch of the nineteen-fifties and -sixties in which numerous biennials established themselves (first that of São Paulo, but quickly those of Paris, Tokyo, and even Sydney by 1973), not all of which survived. We have not yet recovered *this* history of internationalism, battered as it was by the recessions, oil shortages, and world re-orderings of the late sixties; we would do well to recall that checkered past as we attend to the global biennials of today.

Few of the critics or proponents of contemporary biennials are willing to dig into their collective historical background or epistemic effects. Critics berate the biennial structure as being either a bad way to present art (too haphazard, too market-driven) or a miserable way to see it (too crowded, too superficial). Proponents praise the utopianism of biennials, which they believe has achieved what the French celebrate as *mondialisation* (in distinction to commerce-driven globalization), moving toward new transnational subjectivities that dislocate center and periphery.[8] Yet the form itself is seen as little more than a contemporary container for existing works of art. I argue instead that *because* of their long links to event structures, tourism, and apparatuses of knowledge production, biennials have produced and participated in a more enduring epistemic shift. Beginning in the world's fairs and gradually transforming the art world, this shift forces an acknowledgment that the placement of an art object within a world picture determines the significance of both the picture and the object. The central question then becomes: what are the conditions of possibility for the global work of art?[9] And more specifically, in the structures of world expositions leading up to the biennial form, what were the prerequisites such that a work of art could be said to have *international* (now global) purchase, and how does the contemporary aesthetics of experience propel this same claim?

This leads to the codification of my third assertion: ideologies of universal signification need to be unpacked. We are no longer talking about artworks as fixed bearers of a meaning that can be shipped around and then translated using an internal code. Rather, the moment a work is inserted into a world's fair or international biennial it should be understood as *always already translated,* yet only in order to speak of *difference itself.*[10] This holds even for the first biennials and the world's expositions that sired them. Although ideologically constructed as autonomous art objects moved into the setting of the fair in order to allow the dispassionate evaluation of comparative excellence, the truth is that meanings were often determined by the world pictures in which artworks were situated. In the past few decades, that determination has become an active site for artists' explicit strategies and a dialogical constituent of the work of art.

REPETITION AND DIFFERENCE

THE shift I am chronicling here is certainly related to Nicolas Bourriaud's unfairly maligned post-Bourdieu formulation of relational aesthetics:

> *Nowadays, the word "art" seems to be no more than a semantic leftover of [an earlier] narrative, whose more accurate definition would read as follows: Art is an activity consisting in producing relationships with the world with the help of signs, forms, actions and objects.*[11]

But what I am asserting is that this "leftover" narrative of art as object was destabilized long ago—it is the theorization of relationality that has only belatedly been understood as an artistic tactic. What I want to modify in Bourriaud's formulation is that the shift to "actions" should include those of the viewer as commonly as those of the artist, and these relations have a very long history. It is the viewer who must make sense of the world picture, in my argument, and as long as we are talking about biennials, we are talking about world pictures rather than imaginarily isolated objects (or even the autonomous anti-objects of installations, videos, and performative artworks).

Daniel Birnbaum echoed this way of thinking in his 2009 statement for the fifty-third Venice Biennial: "A work of art is more than an object, more than a commodity. It . . . must be seen as a way of 'making a world.' A few signs marked on paper, a barely touched canvas, or a vast installation can amount to different ways of world-making."[12] But while Birnbaum picks up on the time-honored trope of the artwork *as* a world, I am arguing something else: that the artwork is inserted *into* (in order to complete) a picture of *the* world, and this has consequences we must examine.[13] Most crucially, I want to historicize Bourriaud's theory *and* Birnbaum's curation so that these influential ideas can themselves be seen as markers of the historical shift I am tracing—evidence of the moment at which they became not only possible but necessary positionings of the contemporary subject as molded and produced by biennial culture. In sum: rather than works of art I want to interrogate how art *works* in circuits that were once international and are now global in their systematism.

Why is biennial culture so embarrassed about its history? And why are the parallels with the nineteenth century's groaning spectacles so frequently assumed but so little elaborated upon? Because they are foundational, and foundations do not like to be revealed. The ontogeny of the biennial emerged from the ontology of the grand expositionary form. The biennial came into being as a trade-specific miniature of, *and antidote to,* the exhausted and over-analyzed world's fair. The Venetians' future-oriented idea was to focus purely on art, which had long been the easiest mode of exchange within the cosmopolitan trading cultures that nineteenth-century Venice in particular was keen to reinvent.

The repetition built into the biennial must be leveraged by linking it to an ever-renewing present and future; in this way difference is promised, if not always secured. Rosa Martínez's statement for the 2005 Biennial in Venice is typical of the positioning of biennials exclusively for the future:

> *A biennial . . . looks beyond the present and into the future. . . . Biennials are the most advanced arena for this expanded field precisely because they do not function like museums. Museums are temples for the preservation of memory. . . . Biennials are a context for the exploration and questioning . . . of the present.*[14]

Biennials' perpetual construction of their futurity is rooted, of course, in the very "preservation of memory" that Martínez abjures. As Deleuze argued in *Repetition and Difference,* the recurring holiday that "differentiates" itself from the routine of passing days is constituted as such *only in repetition.*[15] The storming of the Bastille is not yet Bastille Day—likewise, it is only in repetition that a biennial can be a biennial. While the concept of a *recurring* fair was not explicit in the first international *grandes expositions* (such as that of 1851 in London, for example), their roots in previous recurring national fairs were soon revealed and a rhythm was quickly established (especially in French practice, where the *grandes expositions* occurred regularly every eleven years).

It is astonishing but true that what we hold to be biennials' most rudimentary characteristics—that such exhibitions are international and recurring—only slowly took shape in the planning of what is acknowledged as the world's first art biennial.[16] In documents from the earliest deliberations among Venetian town councilors in 1893, there is an intention of "perpetuity" but only a passing indication that the institution being established (and annually funded) was to present a *repeating* exhibition ("ad ogni biennio").[17] And as late as 1894 it was still assumed this would be a *national* show (modeled on the national exposition of Italian art that had been mounted in

1887, also in Venice's Giardini).[18] The change to an international scope was recognized by the town council on March 30, 1894, when councilors voted that this biennial event would be "Nazionale ed Internazionale." Vagueness remained endemic, however; while it is perhaps only an accident of graphic design, the first exposition's poster merely announced "1895, Esposizione Internazionale d'Arte della Città di Venezia," which was corrected in the later posters and catalogue to "*Prima* Esposizione Internazionale."[19]

In the summary of poet and mayor Riccardo Selvatico aired in that town council meeting held in St. Mark's Square on April 19, 1893, the founders (Selvatico along with politician Antonio Fradeletto and philosopher Giovanni Bordiga) proposed that the city create an "institution of public utility and benefit" with the intention to "recall perpetually" the "twenty-fifth wedding anniversary of the Italian King and Queen"—Umberto and Margherita of Savoia. Thus repetition-as-commemoration was inserted at the heart of the putatively future-oriented event, glancingly determined to be biennial. Administrators at the meeting agreed with the blatant flattery of the commemoration,[20] but married the patriotic royalist goal to their pragmatic hopes for a future "benefiting the reputation [of] and . . . creating an art market" for the city.[21] In two years of planning, the repeating structure was confirmed, a committee of Venetian artists and politicians was formed to counsel the mayor's office on the best form for the exposition, and finally the opening show was postponed to 1895 to allow for it to be fully *inter*national.[22]

The future of that internationalism was promised by a cycle of repetition (honoring a past event), by the recurrent excitement generated by medals and prizes (familiar from the world's fairs), and by the vision of a new art market (also continuing the commerce that the *grandes expositions* explicitly waged). Such claims for futurity must always be placed in relation to a past, usually apostrophized as "the museum." In the case of Venice, the "museum" was Venice itself. The perceived decadence of the museum-city had been festering ever since Napoleon's takeover (and art extraction) a century before—hopefully to be reversed by biennial culture. But while the museal entombment of Venice was to be combated by the intended dynamism of biennial practices (event, prizes, market), the two were in fact united through touristic devices such as the guidebook, the camera, the municipal map, urban transportation, and signage systems. The importance of such practices had been established by the Grand Tour, extended by the great fairs, and then carried directly over to the biennial, as indicated by early posters, which often depict the guidebook-toting art-lover consulting her authoritative text (fig. 2). But even as they are linked by tourism, biennial practices need to be discursively distinguished from "museum culture." The museal desires a stable consistency that produces unique and sustained relations to the local. The biennial, despite its manifestly repetitive nature, was intended to instantiate the freshly renewing and unprecedented. Relations to the local in biennials are foundationally insecure and productively dynamic, a staging reflected in the wonderfully witty 2005 Venice Biennial poster showing bemused tourists in decidedly non-Venetian settings consulting their map in search of the grounds of that year's Biennial (fig. 3).

STRUCTURES, CONTINUITIES, ECONOMIES

THE parallels I am outlining here can be drawn among centuries of recurring exhibitionary forms, but need to be parsed for their significance in the present. Some suggest structural relations that endure over time; others reveal punctuating events and ruptures that establish new traditions on the historical continuum. Take the Arsenale and Corderie (or "rope-making factory") in Venice, for example. When successive curators of the Venice Biennial pushed to open the former military and industrial buildings behind the Giardini in the nineteen-eighties, that initiative formed one moment of origin for today's expanded urban biennials. The gesture was also part of the shift to experience, in that standard art spaces (heavily decorated nineteenth-century galleries slowly mutating into twentieth-century white cubes) were blasted open in such military-industrial architectures, allowing the proliferation of experimental and open-ended forums rather than forms.[23] The *Aperto* function set in place by Harald Szeemann and his collaborators (Achille Bonito Oliva and Agnes Kohlmeyer) for the 1980 Venice Biennial paired the rough space of the postindustrial with the emerging attributes of the postmodern: youthful experiments in process yielded uneven but dynamic experiences for the visitor, and objects gave way to environments and performative provocations.[24]

Often set in cities grappling with the history of totalitarian regimes, post-nineteen-eighties biennials such as those in Johannesburg, Gwangju, Istanbul, or Havana deploy the art experience to frame and aestheticize aging urban facilities (whether schools, military depots, industrial plants, or religious establishments) that were never "public" in quite this way before. At the same time, infusions of biennial culture produce a potential future for these buildings (most often military-industrial in origin), exorcising a sometimes painful past by de-localizing sites and introducing nonlocal visitors. I take as exemplary this quote from the press release for the 2005 International Istanbul Biennal: "[Curators Charles] Esche and [Vasif] Kortun will not be using any of the historic monuments located in the historical peninsula, preferring to work in sites that have a more common reference to post-industrialisation, the physical legacy of modernity and the shift to a consumer economy."[25]

Thus we may compare Venice's Corderie to an Istanbul tobacco warehouse, while acknowledging shared desires to position Third World cities as postindustrial (though they may never have been fully industrialized in the first place). Again, it is not the viewing of discrete art objects that the latter-day biennials will offer, but experiences of an expanded urban situation. Investigating and understanding the significance of such urban geographies is a necessary task.

Even in Venice, the significance of claiming the Giardini for the first biennial exposition was overdetermined. Napoleon's 1797 "liberation" of Venetians from the "tyranny" of the world's oldest republic had been accompanied by the invading commander's magnanimous gesture of creating a public garden out of the fields and churchyards of the island's eastern end by clearing an area of its other uses and naming it the *Giardini pubblici.* When the founders of the biennial chose this same physical site—used also for the national exposition of 1887 (awarded to Venice in 1883 by the Eighth Artistic Congress in Rome)—they confirmed a resounding nationalist gesture, seizing this charged terrain and effecting "the most decisive change for the area since Napoleon's original decree in 1807."[26] Venice, the former republican city-state capable of snubbing Rome's authority for 500 years but humiliatingly conquered by the French at the turn of the nineteenth century, could now demonstrate its importance to the young nation of Italy. Venice would not be staged within the Veneto as one town among many, but would continue to perform its old ostentatious role. As a portal to the world, it could both be a leading component of the nation-state (thereby flattering its king) and assert its time-honored international identity as a cosmopolitan center of the liberal arts and free speech. In this we see the pattern of so many other biennials: São Paulo founded its biennial (and modern art museum) in 1951 to assert an identity within the nation (competing with Rio) as well as to turn a capital-friendly face to Cold War America through its embrace of "Rockefeller artists" endorsed by New York's Museum of Modern Art; Havana, its former cosmopolitanism on hold due to Cold War ostracism and Soviet patronage alike, emerged as a prefiguration of Gorbachev's glasnost and perestroika to represent Latin America and the Third World more generally with what was assertively proclaimed a "*Havana* biennial" in 1984; likewise the *Istanbul* (not Turkish) biennial was founded in 1987, a post-apartheid *Johannesburg* (definitely not South African) biennial was inaugurated in the year of the first free elections (1994), and a swath of regional biennials were begun in post-Tiananmen China.

As these patterns reveal, the biennial is an enlightenment project that secures a kind of nationalism in the very act of transcending it.[27] The founding of a biennial pledges to renew knowledge perpetually, stakes a claim for the cosmopolitan urban center to rejoin a wider international community (the common phrase is "put our city [back] on the map"), and makes a pedagogical promise to visitors to bring them the world (in the form of an encyclopedic and renewing art exhibition). But if they are marked by this originary episteme, the biennials of the world are no longer dominated by the Euro-American version of enlightenment. Indeed, an invocation of "enlightenment" may seem perverse when we consider the recent proliferation of the exhibitionary form in party-state systems (China) or autocracies (United Arab Emirates). But I would argue that these are anomalies that prove the rule, with the rule being an invitation tendered by a locality to a global art world for an event that might, through the force of culture and discourse, balance geopolitics and leverage military risks. The rule combines local pride with "city branding" in order to attract both nationals and foreigners whose patronage might replace extraction-based economies with a future of tourism (or, in Tour-famous Venice, update existing tourism with an art market).[28] The rule sees education in art, imagining this benefit will be appreciated by a local population and will pay off in the "creative industries" to come. To the extent that these activities continue to follow the energies of the Enlightenment (which I maintain they do, even outside the militarized democracies of the West), we might need to recall that the Enlightenment took many forms. Take that modeled by Frederick the Great, whose provincial monarchic military accomplishments were paralleled by his eagerness to join a world of cultural possibilities wider than those presented by Prussia's largely feudal agricultural economy. Would Voltaire's tenure at Frederick's Sans-Souci in Potsdam be analogous to the international curator building an art world for the Emirates' Sharjah?

To put it bluntly, biennials and world's fairs conduct politics by other means. But my paraphrasing of Carl von Clausewitz's famous statement about war is only to emphasize that these events stage themselves as pacifist alternatives and engagements that aim to make war less likely. In this respect, biennials are no different than sporting competitions and diplomatic exchanges that sublimate military desires. Indeed, the modern Olympic games were invented at exactly the same moment as the Venice Biennial in 1894, when the French aristocrat Baron Pierre de Coubertin got seventy-nine delegates from nine nations to meet together in Paris (fig. 4). The Comité Internationale Olympique was formed, and in a brilliant stroke of internationalism the Greek-born Parisian Demetrius Vikelas was selected to be its first president, with Athens as its first venue. Some have argued that Coubertin was aware of the recurring exhibition form established by artists' associations in Germany (the Berliner Kunstverein, for example, rather than the then ineffectual French state salons), which fused in his mind with the ancient Greek model of recurring athletic festivals to produce an argument for the rehabilitation of the games. Not incidental in all this was the French defeat in the Franco-Prussian war, which Coubertin blamed on the lapse of athletic vigor in the French nation. Like the Biennial, international competition was imagined as a way of both sharpening national skills and neutralizing the risk that national mettle would be tested in war. As Coubertin stated in 1892: "Let us export our oarsmen, our runners, our fencers to other lands. That is the true Free Trade of the future; and the day it is introduced into Europe the cause of Peace will have received a new and strong ally."[29]

This all may seem utopian, but recall that French senators had complained that the whole territory of Luxembourg had been lost while the nation was fussing over *grandes expositions*, a development some would praise as a sublimation of aggressive expansion.[30] What is statistically striking is the sheer number of these events offered during the period of Europe's most competitive industrialization, expansion, and colonization. Determining whether the expositions helped avoid conflict or accelerated the onset of the First World War, however, is beyond the scope of this essay.

Given the complexity of such interlocking objectives undergirding fairs and biennials, can we at least identify the social practices that constitute their culture? I have proposed examining the aesthetics of experience, with its hints of pilgrimage and tourism, as a first approach. These rituals were already in place when *la Biennale* opened in 1895, a preexisting set of economies that had witnessed the replacement of the Grand Tour by universal expositions, Crystal Palaces, and world's fairs complete with imported natives, industrial innovations, exotic goods, and package tours.[31] In this far longer history, we can follow the city's transformation in the nineteenth century from attractive assemblage of utilitarian and historic buildings to explicitly arranged spectacle, with the physical conversion of once useful sites into aesthetic and touristic domains—key structural components of what has become "biennial culture." I have suggested that some elements were innovations in the longer tradition of mounting exhibitions in public gardens—new patterns linking Venice's Corderie, the Berlin Biennial's converted margarine factory, or Istanbul's tobacco warehouse. But already in the world's fairs that produced the template for biennial culture we can locate recurring forms of urbanism, particularly in the mother lode of recurring expositionary spectacle: Paris, France.

Why was the military training ground of the Champ de Mars, for example, the logical site for a century of ever-more-space-hungry Parisian *grandes expositions?* Because as soon as the French Revolution produced the possibility of civic control for this military territory, it was requisitioned as the highly symbolic site for revolutionary fêtes and republican guard parades. As soon as there were citizens to be molded, this site was appropriated for rituals of mass subjectivation. Like Napoleon's Giardini in Venice, the park planned for the people of the French republic still harbored a remnant of its military function (an *École militaire* that can still be seen in operation at the end of the Champ de Mars, which is comparable to the military installations that still skirt the Venetian Arsenale). It was the Venetians who took the rue des Nations concept of the 1889 (and 1900) Exposition in Paris and allowed it to become incrementally permanent in their Giardini, committing the logical error of populating Napoleon's urban garden (and site of military spectacle) with pavilions that fixed spatial relations in a world picture doomed to anachronism (fig. 5). But if this initiative confused recurring with permanent, inviting dereliction and neglect in the biennial's off seasons, the pavilion structure also proved enormously generative in the aesthetics of experience that has become explicit in contemporary art.

The confusion between permanent and recurring is understandable given the legacy of the world's fairs, where selected buildings had sometimes been constructed to be permanent (or later declared so, as with Eiffel's tower). Indeed, the universal expos would leave their mark on countless cities and create the modern field of urban planning—in fact, this was often the covert or explicit aim of the exposition to begin with. Paris in particular utilized the eleven-year rhythm of recurring expositions to accomplish major infrastructural development: several bridges across the Seine, the creation of new avenues, the building of a metro, railway extensions, and sewage improvements—all accomplished with the allocation of state funds and the flow of international capital that came with the fairs. London built a commuter railway when it relocated the Crystal Palace to Sydenham; Chicago developed a city plan for its waterfront; San Francisco and St. Louis got museums. In Venice, it was the Fascist administrators of the biennial in the nineteen-thirties who pushed for a train connection to the mainland and expanded the franchise of the "Venice Biennial" to include the glamorous medium of film in a biennial cinema festival that was to alternate with the exhibitions of art.[32]

This impetus for urban development and city branding is an obvious continuity between the *grandes expositions* and the biennials. Another is these exhibitions' role in fostering the various (national, regional, and local) economies in which art, and artists, circulate. We like to forget, for example, that the roots of all of these exhibitionary forms lay in *market* fairs, in the first instance the French Convention's decision to sponsor a national fair in Paris after the Revolution.[33] Conceived by the Marquis d'Avèze, commissioner of the three former Royal Manufactories—the Sèvres porcelain plant, the Gobelins tapestry works, and the Savonneries carpet factory—the national fair was seen as a way to move inventory internally at a time when the other European countries had blockaded French ports. This first entirely national fair was so successful that the government decided to repeat it. As Minister François de Neufchâteau put it in 1798, "Our manufactures are the arsenals which will supply us with the weapons most fatal to British power."[34] As late as 1900, world's fairs exhibitors didn't ship all those things back—goods were tendered to those who had paid for them at the fair, with the organizers getting a commission on every exhibit that sold. As we've seen, the Venice Biennial established itself at its origin as a market—and functioned that way, with sales yielding commissions to finance the exhibition until activists in the nineteen-sixties declared such commerce anathema to art.

SUBJECTS, INFRASTRUCTURES, CULTURES

WE have begun to clarify the sets of values and cultural practices inculcated by such large-scale international exhibitions. Seeded by the event of the fair, these practices could involve impressive diplomatic events, scholarly conferences (in fact, the form was invented at the *grandes expositions*), spectacular images, celebrated works of art, collectible objects—the literally materialized "memories" that are souvenirs—as well as new experiences (and thus new subjectivities) for the middle class. The label "tourist" is far too simple—it collapses distinct demographic categories that could range, in the case of the 1900 Paris Exposition Universelle, from provincial Frenchmen to foreign heads of state; industrialists or engineers checking out the competition at the Palace of Transportation, the Palace of Machines, or the Palace of Chemical Industries; children trailing behind their suffragist mothers at the education conference; or even the young Picasso coming with friends from Barcelona to see the exposition, thereby clinching their collective decision to move to Paris a few years later. Photographic album souvenirs could have been acquired by the culture-seeking businessman/diplomat, the traveling Boston historian Henry Adams, or conceivably even a Dahomeyan villager living in the "Colonies et pays de protectorats" display. Crucial to understanding the impact of such events is that attendance surpassed the population of the French nation. The repeating surges of exhibition architecture and engineering turned Paris into modernity's "société du spectacle." We see in the architectural iconography of the fairs a persistent thrust to make of the city a spectacle, and to provide spaces in which that urban panorama could be consumed.

That aesthetic of festive industrial urbanism bled seamlessly into the postindustrial aesthetic of today (fig. 6). Take the case of the Palais de Tokyo, where the city of Paris sponsored its first modern art museum and then in 2002 began to solicit an internationally renewing contemporary art scene—a site for something very much like "biennial culture." It's worth remembering that the Palais is a remnant of one of the successive *grandes expositions*—in this case, the 1937 World's Fair. Architectural critics praising Lacaton & Vassal's 2002 renovations describe the liberation of this building from the shards of a decaying proto-Fascist past to an entirely experiential "future." A critic commenting on the renovation offers an extraordinary metaphor of just what that new experience *is* for visitors in the renovated world's fair building: "[The architects'] vision of social space is pervasive, inspired, partly, by the Djemaa El-Fnaa market square of Marrakesh—a space of movement and change, constantly formed and reformed by the 'whim of its actors.'"[35]

Of course, I want to emphasize the exceptional conjunction of an inspiring Moroccan market with a formerly imperial French exhibitionary space, not too far from the Café Maroc that refreshed visitors to the 1900 Exposition. These are the "coincidences" that reveal the extensive and surviving armatures of world pictures: the categories of exotic amusement that were confected by the French empire for its citizens and visitors to the Exposition Universelle in 1900 became sublimated into colonial outposts at the world's fair of 1937 only to return again as the marketing of difference, offered within the perpetually renewing aesthetics of experience for twenty-first-century subjects of biennial culture.

NATIONS, ARTISTS, SHIFTS

THESE continuities between past and present are not seamless, nor do they unfold in some ideal uninterrupted fashion. Indeed, the twentieth century witnessed the dramatic shift with which I began, when the energies of the world's fairs were appropriated by the trade-specific biennial form. But the shared presumption of the exhibitionary structures themselves, from the expositions universelles to today's "platforms" of experience, is that the (modern, Western) artist would both represent his tribe and become transcendently *international.* This fundamental paradox spans the nineteenth century's adoption of Jozef Israëls as "the Dutch Millet" (wielding the then-international style of French Realism in order to speak of low-country particularity) and the twenty-first century's hunger for polemical pavilions (from Yung Ho Chang's decaying bamboo structure of 2005 for China to Sandi Hilal and Alessandro Petti's "Stateless Nation" pavilion for Palestine in 2003). Generated deep within modernism and its geopolitics, the cosmopolitan mark(et)ing of difference continues today.[36]

PAVILIONS, AESTHETICS, EXPERIENCE

I HAVE argued that a vast historical arc links the search for world pictures and experience in the Grand Tour with the great expositions that industrialized that legacy for everyone. National pavilions and biennials only made manifest the earlier formulae by which the artist would become "representative," demanding that objects and artists transmit national or ethnic meaning even while insisting that they use international styles to do so. Art history has produced a narrative of artistic developments after the Second World War that leads away from objects altogether, and I have speculated that some part of that development owes its force to the increasingly experiential nature of biennial culture. Recurring international exhibitions had established robust links between tourism and art, fostering the seductive marketing of experience that fuels contemporary biennial culture today.

I have proposed that it is no coincidence that the codification of installation art in the nineteen-nineties came at the same cultural moment as the increase in global biennials and the problematization of national pavilions. Such major transformations are never simple in their causes. But I argue that the shift to experience seeded by an embodied and material installation art has been codified by recurring exhibitionary forms in an unacknowledged canon of biennial culture—while posing itself in dynamic relation with the spectacle that is the enduring legacy of the massive international exhibition. That is, if "experience" is forwarded to counteract spectacle, it necessarily also enters the spectacular frame of the urban setting in which the biennial contextualizes itself: experience embedded within an urban spectacle that is itself mobilized as a tourist experience, all further staged within a larger world picture that "the X Biennial" always invokes.

Despite this circularity, the aesthetic of experience is not inherently totalizing. Discursively, its claims to counter-spectacle are linked to the liberation from national pavilions, or at the least to a thorough critique of them. This briefer history identifies Hans Haacke's noteworthy smashing of the German Pavilion's floor in 1993 as one of its inaugural moments. The experiential aesthetic, on this account, began with this violent antivisual gesture: the experience was visually "empty" but acoustically rich, as ambient sounds of visitors' feet were heard crunching over shards of marble brought from buildings Hitler had renovated in 1937 (Haacke's intervention explicitly performs "politics by other means"). Apotheoses of antispectacular experience may include Tino Sehgal's contribution to that same German pavilion in the 2007 Biennial, where gallery attendants sang to visitors: "Tino Sehgal! Tino Sehgal! It's so contemporary, contemporary!" As the sponsors' Web site describes it, Sehgal is "assembling meaning through directing people rather than creating objects."[37] If we understand the national pavilion to be a set piece of architecture, then Haacke was indeed initiating its ruination, and Sehgal announcing its obsolescence. But if we understand the national pavilion as a concept, an ideology, and a funding structure, the longer and more complicated history unfolds.

So although more contemporary biennials such as those of Istanbul or Guangzhou claim that Venice's creaky national pavilion system is obsolete (a position that São Paulo took in establishing the world's second biennial already in 1951), the truth is that the pavilion component of biennial culture in Venice has proved useful. Pavilions have allowed the problematization of both spectacle and the ethnic state, because artists of established cultural capital (such as Haacke) are allowed free rein to deploy their experiential aesthetics within them. Until the curtain closes on the larger theater of nations and geopolitics, biennials and national pavilions will continue to have conceptual and political roles to play.

This is where I leave you with a final provocation from my own politics of biennial culture. I want to be honest in admitting that I think biennials are an excellent way to pursue "politics by other means." I'd rather have a reformulation of the abandoned 1978 Baghdad Biennial (although without the Shah's tortured Westernism this time) than war in Iraq. Usually we are required to accept biennials as the salve after violence, not as its alternative. Yung Ho Chang's dissolving bamboo pavilion for Venice is a perfect emblem in this respect. Undercutting the harsh edge of Chinese imperialism, the architect deployed traditional Third World building materials in a fragile but sophisticated algorithmic progression—as if computer-aided design were made of sticks and string. We need concepts of nation to make sense of a "Chinese pavilion," yet our long-term desires for the world picture have entered a new phase in which the very terms "nation," "internationalism," and "global exhibition" must be subjected to permanent critique. There is no better place for that critique than the

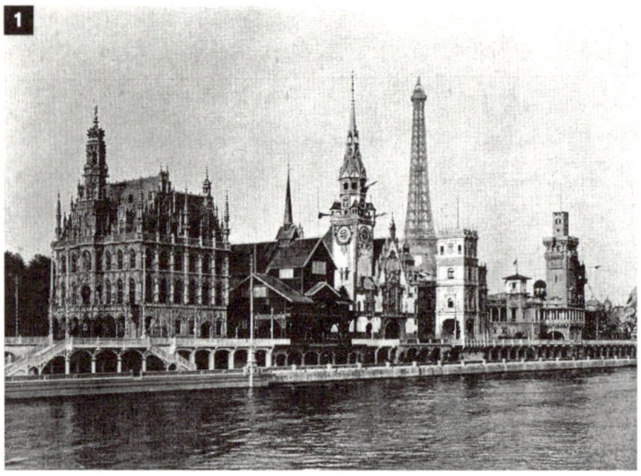

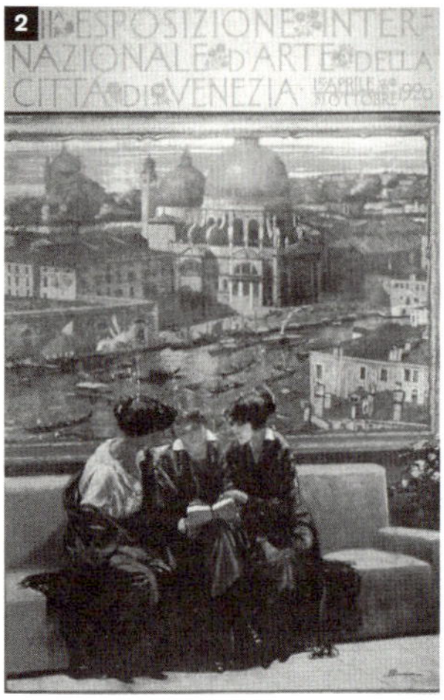

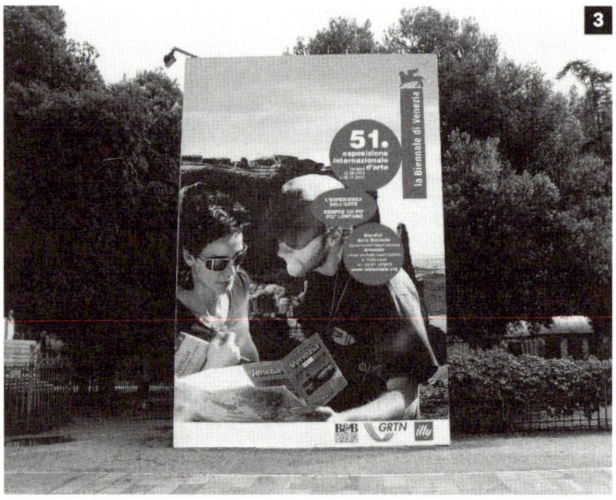

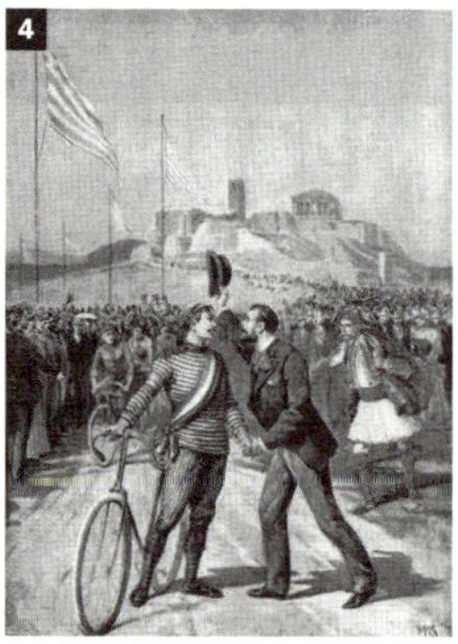

1 View of the Quai des Nations, Exposition Universelle de Paris, 1900, showing buildings for Belgium, Norway, Germany, Spain, Monaco, and Sweden.

2 Augusto Sezanne, *Manifesto della 12. Esposizione Internazionale d'Arte della Città di Venezia*, 1920, lithograph on paper, for the Venice Biennial.

3 "Tourists Looking for the Venice Biennale," 2005. Poster photographed on site outside the Venice Giardini. This is one of several posters of the same theme designed for the 51st Venice Biennial by the Milan offices of the advertising firm McCann Erickson.

theater of globalism that is the biennial. As evinced in the 2009 Istanbul Biennial, utopian questions of art's necessity could also be linked to the pragmatics of experience: "the proof of the pudding is in the eating"—judgments or "proofs" that can be provided only by the consumers of this cultural sustenance. The experience-seeking subject that these exhibitions have helped to produce is thus responsible for making judgments, but also for weighing the larger implications and longer histories of such encounters. Necessary in our present world, biennials are also necessary for questioning their own necessity. Spectacles to consume but not be consumed by, biennials and biennial culture must now include ruminating while renting rooms, critically reflecting while chatting, and—for artists, curators, and visitors alike—understanding the continuity of our desires for the world picture. ●

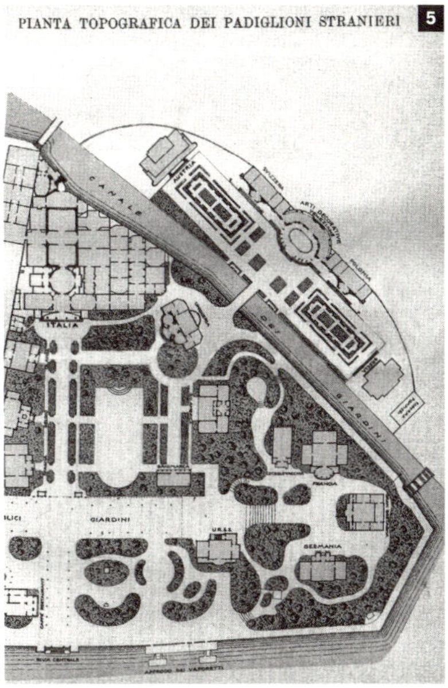

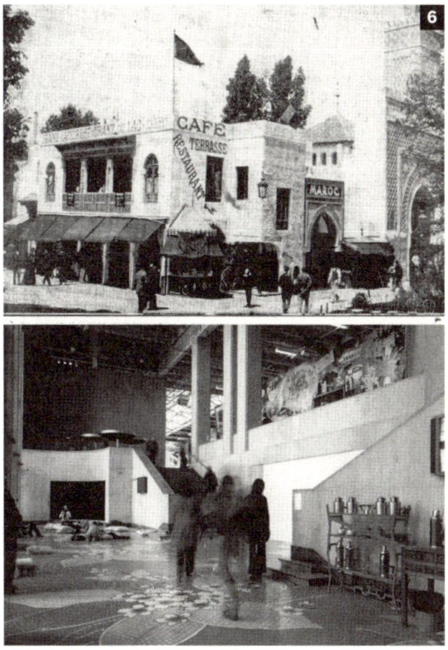

4 French competitor Paul Masson, winner of the velocipede race, being revived by Olympics founder Baron Pierre de Coubertin. Illustration by Henri Meyer, "The Olympic Games in Athens," in *Le Petit Journal*, April 26, 1896.

5 Topographic plan of foreign pavilions in 1934, Venice Giardini.

6 The Café Maroc, Exposition Universelle de Paris, 1900, and lounge culture at the Palais de Tokyo (as renovated by Anne Lacaton and Jean-Philippe Vassal, Paris), 2002.

NOTES

This essay is a revised version of a lecture given at the Bergen Biennial Conference, September 17–20, 2009.

The author is deeply grateful to the organizers of the Bergen Biennial Conference for the opportunity to rethink the arguments presented in this essay, many of which are central to the early chapters of my book-in-progress, *Desires for the World Picture: The Global Work of Art*. Research by several of the conference participants has been crucial to my thinking on the topic of biennials; in particular I would like to thank Vittoria Martini for her pioneering work on the Venice Biennial, as well as her generous help in facilitating my own research in the Biennial archives.

1 "In 1895, the municipal council of Nancy passed a resolution opposing the proposed exposition in Paris. J. Léon Goulette, editor of Nancien journal *L'Est républicain*, published a strident pamphlet, *Pas d'Exposition en 1900!*, in which he forcibly stated the feelings shared by many opponents of the Parisian fair. His most critical points were that the provinces lost revenues during the fair years, and that the exposition (and Paris) contributed to dissipation and depravity." Alfred Chandler, "Culmination: The Paris Exposition Universelle of 1900," reproduced from *World's Fair Magazine* (vol. 7, no. 3, 1987) in a revised and expanded version (January 2000) at http://charon.sfsu.edu/publications/PARISEXPOSITIONS/1900EXPO.html.

2 H. Georges Berger, *Les Expositions universelles internationales (Leur passé, leur rôle actuel, leur avenir)*, doctoral thesis, Université de Paris, Faculté de droit (Paris, 1901), p. 111. The translations are my own.

3 Ibid., pp. 112–13.

4 Ibid., p. 155. Actually, this proposal had been made much earlier by Napoleon III, after the 1855 Exposition Universelle had suffered a staggering loss of eight million French francs. According to John Allwood, Napoleon III had appointed his cousin (confusingly referred to as "Prince Napoleon") to supervise the fair and later to determine the causes of its failure: "He . . . suggested that the days of the great Universal Exhibitions were numbered and that special exhibitions, dealing with one particular subject only, should replace them." Allwood, *The Great Exhibitions* (London, 1977), p. 36.

5 Berger 1901 (see note 2), 160.

6 This number is almost impossible to verify. Robert Storr, at the conference on biennials organized in December 2005 by the Venice Biennal, put the number at 110; Rosemary O'Neill, co-organizer of the February 2006 College Art Association panel on "Installation Art in the Age of Globalization," estimated 200. Some biennials seem to appear and disappear, and others shift venues or genres; some scholars are willing to count biennials of decorative arts or design or architecture, while others restrict their enumeration to those showing contemporary art.

7 My thanks go to Rafal Niemojewski for our many conversations on the subject over the past five years. His cogent argument was recently summarized in his lecture at the Bergen Biennial Conference, Bergen, September 17–20, 2009. A revised version of this appears in this volume as "Venice or Havana: A Polemic on the Genesis of the Contemporary Biennial."

8 See Rosa Martínez: "Biennials are transgenerational and transnational[,] . . . an opportunity to break through the centers, like New York and London." Martínez interviewed by Carolee Thea, in Carolee Thea (ed.), *Foci: Interviews with 10 International Curators* (New York, 2001), p. 79.

9 Captured by the Heideggerian reference in the title of my forthcoming book: *Desires for the World Picture: The Global Work of Art.*

10 The object-containing-its-own-meaning is in fact what art history has imagined traditional artworks to be, or philosophers interpreting technologies of inscription such as those Bruno Latour once theorized as immutable mobiles. Latour, "Drawing Things Together," in Michael Lynch and Steve Woolgar (eds.), *Representation in Scientific Practice* (Cambridge [MA], 1988). Of course, Latour's own actor-network theory immediately complicates the naïve version of this position.

11 Online glossary from Bourriaud's *Relational Aesthetics* (1998; English translation 2002), http://www.gairspace.org.uk/htm/bourr.htm.

12 Venice Biennial Web site, opening statement by Daniel Birnbaum for his theme "Making Worlds / Bantin Duniyan / Hacer Mundos," http://www.labiennale.org/en/art/index.html. Note that Birnbaum, with whom I've discussed my project, importantly departs from Heidegger in insisting on multiple worlds—a nice multicultural concession.

13 For an early example of the artwork as a world, see Hieronymus Bosch, *The Creation of the World,* 1510 (Prado, Madrid); the outer panels of the triptych depict the Garden of Earthly Delights.

14 Rosa Martínez interviewed in Thea 2001 (see note 8), pp. 79–80. See also anthropologist Thomas Boutoux: "All eyes, paradoxically, are never focused on Manifesta's past editions, but on future ones." Boutoux, "A Tale of Two Cities: Manifesta in Rotterdam and Ljubljana," in Barbara Vanderlinden and Elena Filipovic (eds.), *The Manifesta Decade: Debates on Contemporary Art Exhibitions and Biennials in Post-Wall Europe* (Cambridge [MA] and Brussels, 2005), p. 213.

15 Gilles Deleuze, *Difference and Repetition* [1968], trans. Paul Patton (New York, 1994).

16 Unless explicitly cited otherwise, all references and quotes from the founding documents come from the Serie Scatole Nere, Box 1: Periodo dell'Organizzazione 1894–1895, Archivio Storico delle Arti Contemporanee (ASAC), La Biennale di Venezia.

17 In her book *Venice: Fragile City, 1797–1997* (New Haven, 2002), Margaret Plant writes that the exposition was not referred to as a biennial until after the First World War (p. 216); this must not include how it was "referred to" in the founding documents, which do mention "ad ogni biennale."

18 Plant reports that "the first opportunity to offer Venice as a showcase for art occurred when the Esposizione Artistica Nazionale for 1887 was assigned to Venice in 1883 by the Eighth Artistic Congress in Rome." Ibid., p. 215.

19 Underneath the poster's heading are printed the categories that mapped previous world's fairs experiences: Serenate, Regate, Gare Sportive, Luminarie, Freschi, Concerti, Baccanale con Redentore, Torneo Internazionale di Sherma, Gare Pirotecniche, Grandi Spettacoli Teatrali, ed Altri Eccezionali Festeggiamenti.

20 From the minutes: ". . . come omaggio aquella Monarchia che ha dato agli Italiani la Patria. (Applausi prolungati)."

NOTES

21 Minutes of the town council, April 19, 1893, cited in translation by Enzo di Martino, *History of the Venice Biennale: 1895–2005: Visual Arts, Architecture, Cinema, Dance, Music, Theatre,* trans. Barbara Trotto and Susan Candy (Venice, 2005), p. 10.

22 Headed by radical orator Fradeletto, the small Venetian advisory group had been instrumental in insisting on internationalism, which they proposed could be guaranteed by a "comitato patrocinio" (or patron's council) consisting of invited international artists. Interestingly, Fradeletto and his colleagues seasoned the comitato with Secessionists, Symbolists, and international Realist artists from the chief European countries; at the last minute someone added a few conservative academicians. Thus, artists who would have been in confrontation in their home situation (Max Liebermann, a Munich Secessionist in touch with colleagues across Europe, versus Anton von Werner, a painter of nationalist history machines and director of the Munich Academy) were brought together on the Venetian roster as members of the German "team."

23 See Elena Filipovic, "The Global White Cube," in Vanderlinden and Filipovic 2005 (see note 14), pp. 63–84. This essay has been reprinted in the present volume.

24 In 1999, Szeemann revised his own program, creating "dAPERTutto" (something like "open free-for-all"), removing the age limit on "young artist" qualifications and opening up still more of the nether regions of the Giardini—in this case, the dockyards. Here you could experience Paul McCarthy and Jason Rhoades's donut factory (reclining on a La-Z-Boy and being fed donuts coming from the machine) or other processual and/or experiential works.

25 Press release, 2005 International Istanbul Biennial, http://www.universes-in-universe.de/car/istanbul/eng/2005/press-01.htm.

26 Plant 2002 (see note 17), p. 215.

27 Venice acknowledged its entry into Napoleon's enlightenment "public sphere" by occupying the Giardini, offering art in a public garden rather than through the traditional modes of the early republic, such as private or city commissions for a doge's chapel or diplomatic hall.

28 The art activity of the United Arab Emirates, notably the Sharjah Biennial, is part of a vast set of initiatives by the UAE, including huge new research universities (King Fahd University in Dubai) and franchise museums (Abu Dhabi's branch of the Louvre). These can be viewed cynically, as being aimed primarily at buttressing a reputation abroad among the Western militarized democracies who will then invest in the enlightenment aspirations of the Emiratis so that if the latter are endangered by, say, an expansionist nuclear Iran, there will be a cultural investment in the region justifying military intervention. (Remember Kuwait?) The fact that Emiratis are not citizens, do not have a democracy, cannot vote for their government, and represent a tiny fraction of those who live in the region (most of whom are foreign workers living in sequestered quarters) has not thus far surfaced in the curatoriate or art world attending these biennials, despite common postures of political activism in these groups.

29 Pierre de Coubertin, at a meeting of the Union des Sports Athlétiques in Paris, November 25, 1892, quoted in "Olympic Games," http://www.britannica.com/bcom/eb/article/2/0,5716,115022+1+108519,00.html.

30 Berger 1901 (see note 2), 117. Quoting from *Le Figaro* (August 21, 1895), a member of the Chambre des Deputies put it this way: "On simplifia la question. Nous abandonnâmes le Luxembourg qui fut déclaré pays neutre. Et, au détriment de nos intérêts extérieurs, l'exposition fut sauvée!"

31 My French friend Marianne Cassavetta recalls her mother speaking of seeing the "giraffe women from Africa," their necks elongated with metal collars, at the 1937 Paris World's Fair.

32 The Venetian film biennial seems to be the first film festival, but scholarship on this is in its infancy. Cannes was formed explicitly in the image of Venice, intended to begin in 1939 in opposition to the Fascist control of the Venice event; war forced its postponement to 1946. The success of the Venetian strategy in the Fascist period is marked by the U. S. film musical *Top Hat,* made in 1935. Not yet at war with Italy (or critical of its Fascist government), Hollywood stars Fred Astaire and Ginger Rogers could still be flown to the Venetian Lido for a bit of glamorous fun.

33 An argument has been made that an earlier model was the series of exhibitions inaugurated in London in 1756, when the Royal Society of Arts launched its series of Fine Art Exhibitions. Open to society members and their friends, these exhibitions were not quite the public, state-funded affairs that we associate with biennial culture, but they did establish the crucial rivalry between France and England that would drive the European expositions of the nineteenth century.

34 Cited without a source in Allwood 1977 (see note 4), p. 12.

35 Robin Wilson, "Art in Process: The Palais de Tokyo," *The Architectural Review* (February 2003), http://www.findarticles.com/p/articles/mi_m3575/is_1272_213/ai_98831552.

36 This argument is worked out in more detail in my forthcoming book, *Desires for the World Picture: The Global Work of Art.*

37 Remarks on Sehgal were found on Dekabank's cultural sponsorship Web site, http://www.dekabank.de/db/en/engagement/kuw/bildendekunst.jsp, in June 2009.

VENICE OR HAVANA: A POLEMIC ON THE GENESIS OF THE CONTEMPORARY BIENNIAL

Rafal Niemojewski

IN December 2005, the Venice Biennial organized an international symposium to celebrate its 110th anniversary and to reflect upon its future. Entitled *Where Art Worlds Meet: Multiple Modernities and the Global Salon,* the event was programmed and presented by Robert Storr, artistic director of the 2007 edition of the Biennial. While there was much constructive critique presented at the symposium about the archaic structure of the Venice institution, its mission, and the demographics of its public, no attempts were made to analyze the position of the Venice Biennial among the other large-scale exhibitions taking place today in different parts of the globe. Perhaps this was because its place had already been defined and stated in the symposium program as central and hegemonic. According to Storr, the conference represented

> *La Biennale's contribution to the widening discourse surrounding the proliferation and transformation of a phenomenon it in effect created... Once La Biennale di Venezia was the only exhibition of its kind. Now there are over a hundred exhibitions deploying variants of the model on which the original Biennale was based.*[1]

Storr's comment requires closer examination, since it promulgates the assumption that the Venice Biennial, as inaugurated in 1895, is both responsible for and has given rise to the vast proliferation of biennials that has taken place almost a century later.

This assumption is not isolated; indeed, it is a commonplace so prevalent that few even question it.[2] Yet one wonders why Robert Storr, following many curators, critics, and art historians before him, would assume that all of the large-scale shows subsequent to the Venice Biennial were clearly and necessarily based on its model. It is indisputable that the Venice Biennial must be acknowledged as the first art exhibition to recur on a regular basis and as a model institution of modernity. Some of the most convincing voices highlighting the centrality of Venice's biennial in the discussions surrounding the current proliferation of biennials often leverage its presumed importance by depicting it against the background of the international industrial exhibitions and trade fairs of the nineteenth century (see, for example, Caroline A. Jones's essay in this volume). Such readings draw parallels between the nonartistic agendas structurally indebted to recurring large-scale international exhibitions of the past and present: the presumptive universality, ties to tourism, implications for urban development, openings for foreign/multinational capital investment, and ambitions for an improved visibility in the global arena. Indeed, the emergence of a new biennial is never fortuitous; rather, it is always part of a larger and often very elaborate agenda.

Biennials can and do serve as a vehicle for civic aspirations far beyond the art world, and with few exceptions they are founded on the basis of ideological and economic considerations rather than artistic ones. The introduction of a new biennial is meant to incite civic pride among the local population and provide it with a sense of belonging to the club of civilized and cultured communities, of which such ventures are traditionally indicative. What is at stake here is the recognition, or the prestige, that might be employed in the production of further wealth, or, as Pierre Bourdieu called it, symbolic capital.[3] The biennial thus functions as a generator of symbolic capital and can indirectly generate real capital via its ties, which are duly listed by Caroline A. Jones. I would argue, however, that none of these elements is specific or exclusive to the Venice Biennial or the more recent biennials. These very same agendas can be found behind the establishment of a new museum, library, theater, opera house, or any other major cultural institution, for that matter. What distinguishes a contemporary art biennial from all these ventures is that it is an art exhibition as much as it is a cultural institution or event. An analysis from the perspective of exhibition/curatorial history should thus be given an equal if not greater importance when considering the role of the Venice Biennial in relation to the other biennials currently proliferating around the world. Furthermore, it seems peculiar to give the Venice Biennial sole credit for a type of exhibition whose emergence depends equally on the developments of the large-scale exhibition format throughout the twentieth century and, perhaps more importantly, on a unique set of circumstances that gave rise to its spread.

The purpose of this essay, therefore, is to argue a different genesis of the contemporary biennial than is typically presumed and, more specifically, to reassess the relevance of the Venice Biennial as the main point of reference for the biennials proliferating around the world today. I will do so by retracing major evolutions of the recurring large-scale international exhibition format from the inception of the Venice Biennial in 1895 to the beginning of its spread in the mid-eighties with the inception of events like the Havana Biennial.

This assumes, of course, that we can comprehensively define the "contemporary biennial." It would seem that, given the multilayered, complex character of the majority of biennials of contemporary art and their number, diversity, and dynamic institutional structures, any subgrouping based on a single typology would be quite perilous. Despite this, however, by examining a wide cross-section of proliferating exhibitions and institutional frameworks and applying the rules of normal distribution, it is possible to delineate within a larger mass of biennials the prevalent curatorial and institutional models, which I designate as the contemporary biennial and the contemporary biennial organization. This selection process requires looking at biennials while taking into account their overall complexity—from the ideological and political agendas behind their creation to their physical products, such as exhibitions, catalogues, or commissioned works. It also necessitates a consideration of their contributions towards redrawing the map of the contemporary art world and rewriting contemporary art discourse, and towards the development of the new models of artistic, exhibitionary, and curatorial practices that have emerged during the period of their proliferation. The contemporary biennial can be distinguished by a strong will to negotiate its peripheral condition, to represent the ambitions of its host city, and to form infrastructures for contemporary art and the public sphere. The self-reflexivity, time- and site-specificity, rhetorical armature (increasingly interdisciplinary discourse that incorporates postcolonialism and non-Western positions), and support it provided to new forms of discursive and socially conscious art and to the new type of curator are equally distinctive features.[4]

The fact is, the number of new large-scale international shows of contemporary art introduced during the so-called period of proliferation of the biennial form has been open to debate, for the available literature provides no consensus with regard to the time frame of the phenomenon or the use and exact meaning of the imprecise term "biennial" (or its Italian equivalent *biennale*). "The term biennial is not protected by copyright and consequently is open to abuse," asserted René Block in 2000.[5] It is often used to signify any biannual art exhibition or art project, regardless of its scale, focus, content, or framework, rather than just the more specific format of the recurring large-scale international survey show of contemporary art with a particular set of goals and characteristics whose proliferation has taken place in the context of a major reshaping of the contemporary art world's topography over the past twenty-five years. The latter, more specific reading is used in most of the relevant literature, but without arriving at a precise definition of it. Block, for example, describes the proliferating format as "a new type of global exhibition established under the generic term biennial, which had a major impact upon the contemporary art scene," while Okwui Enwezor refers to it as a "mega-exhibition," and Tim Griffin as a "large-scale, transnational exhibition." Others continue to use the term biennial generically, defining its exact meaning through the range of arguments and examples they put forward.[6] In this essay, I have focused on the subject matching the more specific format described by Block, Enwezor, and Griffin and designated it as *the contemporary biennial:* the large-scale international survey show of contemporary art that recurs at regular intervals but not necessarily biannually.[7]

The model of the first Venice Biennial in 1895 was set out by a list of regulations very specific to its time and somehow similar to those governing the majority of today's commercial art fairs; any attempt to compare or apply them directly to today's biennials must keep this in mind.[8] It is also important to note that from the early days all the artworks presented at the Venice Biennial were on sale, and a percentage levied from their purchase formed a significant contribution to the biennial's budget until 1968. Nevertheless, several facts are worth highlighting to provide a context for the subsequent developments that would eventually lead to the emergence of the large-scale international exhibition as we know it today. First and foremost were its scale and international profile: the 1895 Venice exhibition featured 516 works, and nearly three-fifths of these were by non-Italians. The artworks were displayed according to the artist's country of origin and with a conspicuous attachment to the nineteenth-century notion of national schools and styles. This arrangement later developed into a system of national representation and, in terms of infrastructure, into national pavilions constructed in the Giardini at the beginning of the twentieth century. While claiming to be "international," the Venice Biennial was, in actual fact, an exhibition nearly exclusively focused on European art and thus was hardly what we might consider fully or properly international today. It wasn't until 1964, for instance, that a non-European artist, the American Robert Rauschenberg, won its main prize.

From the text published in the catalogue of the first Venice Biennial one may also learn that the exhibition's aim was to show "the most noble activities of the modern spirit" and to survey the "art of our time."[9] In practice this vanguard position was never actually assumed, beginning with the significant absence of any non-Salon art until the early twenties and continuing with a resistance toward abstract art (with the exception of Fascist-oriented Futurism) until the first postwar edition in 1948. This delay was later transformed into a particular interest in art history: the 1948 edition featured an exhibition of Impressionist paintings, and the following one, Fauvism, Cubism, and Metaphysical Paintings. At the same time visible attempts were made to make up for earlier omissions: in 1948 the main prize went to Georges Braque, and in subsequent editions it went to Henri Matisse (1950), Raoul Dufy (1952), and Max Ernst and Jean Arp (1954). Another symptom of the noticeably conservative attitudes of the Venice Biennial's selection committee was the absence of any media other than painting and sculpture until 1976, when the first photograph was exhibited. In this period the artists, whose works were selected for display by state committees, were only arriving on site for the opening and therefore didn't have any influence on how their pictures and sculptures were showcased, a fact which gradually increased the frustration of some: after the 1950 edition, for example, Giorgio di Chirico sued the Biennial for showing a group of his early Metaphysical Paintings against his wishes.

At the same time that the first edition of the Venice Biennial was presented to the public, in the U.S. the Pittsburgh industrialist Andrew Carnegie founded an art institute with the ambition of creating a museum of modern art. The exhibition series entitled the Carnegie International that was established in the following year and meant to recur annually, aimed to assemble works for that institute's collection as well as to educate audiences and attract the art world to the city.[10] Compared to the Venetian exhibition, the Carnegie International seems to have represented a model closer to today's biennials from the start in terms of its peripheral location and its form as a single large-scale international exhibition prepared by a curator after a period of extensive travel and studio visits. However, as with Venice's exhibition, relatively few avant-garde works appeared in its early editions, and it was not until Henri Matisse's work won first prize in 1927 that modern art—that period's "contemporary" art—was recognized. Similar aspirations were evoked when, more than half a century later, a wealthy industrialist of Italian descent, Francisco Matarazzo Sobrinho, established the São Paulo Biennial in 1951. Based on the original Venetian model of an exhibition comprised of national representations, the early editions of the Brazilian biennial presented a remarkably large and progressive survey of current art marked by the importation to Brazil of many works of European modernism (the retrospective show of Picasso in 1953 may serve as an example).

In many respects, these early biennials can be seen as the direct descendants of the nineteenth-century salon, now institutionalized with its own venue (the Palazzo dell'Arte in Venice, the Carnegie Institute in Pittsburgh, the complex of pavilions and exhibition halls designed by Oscar Niemeyer for the second edition of the São Paulo Biennial), expanded many times over in size, and updated with a new spirit of internationalism, yet still strongly attached to the conservative taste of the bourgeois public. In 1955, however, the first Documenta introduced a different model of a single, large-scale, perennial international exhibition.[11] This initially encompassed a broader spectrum of the *Kunst des XX. Jahrhunderts* (Art of the Twentieth Century), but after its second edition Documenta evolved toward a survey of current art production. By 1972, with the fifth edition, director Harald Szeemann aspired to turn Documenta's initial idea of representing itself as a *Museum der 100 Tage* (Museum of 100 Days) into one hundred days of events. Defined as "a process of mutually interrelated events" rather than "a static collection of objects," and as "a concentrated version of life in the form of an exhibition," it expanded the traditional limits of an art exhibition and became a lively forum for discussions, performances, experiments, and social action.[12] Joseph Beuys's *Office for Direct Democracy* and Hans Haacke's sociological survey of visitors were perhaps the most contemporary in feel. This expanded discursive format is echoed in the innumerable instances of discussions and "live" art projects that accompany many international large-scale exhibitions today. The show was also, in all respects, a reflection of recent artistic exploration, which was marked by the presence of Conceptual Art (Hans Haacke, Lawrence Weiner), Body Art (Viennese Actionists), Performance Art (Vito Acconci, Gilbert & George, Ben Vautier), Hyper-Realism, and recent experiments in urban development (Archigram, Peter Cook, Yona Friedman).

In the meantime, the Venice Biennial experienced some important developments informed by the changes in its status, which had been thoroughly revised after the thirty-fifth edition was struck by the protests of 1968. This included bringing an end to the sale of artworks and introducing a new focus on the exhibition and involvement of the artists.[13] In 1970 some of the national presentations were conceived for the first time through the close collaboration of commissioners and selected artists. The U.S. Pavilion displayed a survey of American printmaking that included an on-site working space for the artists arranged by the commissioner, Henry Hopkins. As a result, the American exhibition featured several artworks made in situ, including Ed Ruscha's *Chocolate Room,* an installation consisting of 360 sheets of paper silk-screened with chocolate that entirely covered the interior walls of one of the rooms. In the German Pavilion (then West German), Dieter Honish, the director of the New National Gallery in Berlin, together with artists Heinz Mack and Gunter Uecker (Zero Group), Karl Georg Pfahler, and Kaspar-Thomas Lenk (Op Art) established the precedent of artistically intervening in the pavilion's architecture by rearranging the appearance of the building on the inside as well as on the outside.[14] Two years later the same German commissioner entrusted the configuration of an entire pavilion to a single artist, Gerhard Richter, thereby setting the precedent for today's prevailing model of a pavilion presenting a newly commissioned work (or ensemble of works) by a single artist or group.[15] These new models of display helped bring about an important updating of the Venice Biennial. They opened doors to curatorial and artistic projects that were increasingly in sync with the latest developments in practice at that time. However, they did not solve the persistent problems that prevented the Venice Biennials of the seventies from contending with the concurrent editions of Documenta, namely, the lack of a strong, single curatorial direction that could be played out on a large scale independently from the nation-based system of funding and its political implications, and the lack of a systematic inclusion of emerging artists and practices, instead of just the already well established. The avant-garde projects at the American and German pavilions also revealed the increasing inequality between different national representations, some of which were slowly adopting more experimental methodologies while others continued to endorse the more traditional museum-like displays of modern art.

In 1980, Harald Szeemann and Achille Bonito Oliva overhauled the Venice Biennial in a radical fashion by introducing *Aperto,* a new section created as a response to the rigidity of the Biennial's structure and to the conservatism of the majority of selectors. Opening its doors to young, emerging artists without any restrictions regarding nationality, it constituted perhaps the single most important shift to have taken place in the history of the Venice Biennial since its inception in 1895. *Aperto* inaugurated changes on a structural and aesthetic level that have subsequently enabled independently curated and financed exhibitions to take place in the Arsenale during each edition of the Biennial.[16]

The four main biennials of the preglobalized twentieth century—those of Venice and São Paulo, the Carnegie International, and Documenta—should thus be regarded as the most important evolutions of the Venetian model. However, none provide a true blueprint for the contemporary biennial as experienced since the mid-eighties, which is to say, since the period of the format's proliferation. The crucial event for the history of the contemporary biennial arguably came only in 1984, when the first recurring large-scale exhibition was established in the Third World, the Havana Biennial. *La Bienal de La Habana* was groundbreaking in many ways. For the first time the focus was clearly on art coming from the Caribbean, Latin America, Asia, the Middle East, and Africa—that is, from outside the traditional centers of the contemporary art world. This unprecedented strategy of promoting peripheral art scenes as part of the global circuit—later to become one of the principal raisons d'être of the contemporary biennial—was plainly stated in the Havana Biennial's "Regulation for Participation," a trilingual brochure published and distributed during its first edition:

The Wifredo Lam Center convenes the 1st Havana Biennial in order to promote the development of plastic arts in Latin America and the Caribbean in the belief they must be recognized as a part of universal culture. In Latin America and the Caribbean, Africa and Asia, many artists involved in the quest for a genuine and contemporary form of expression do not have access to the contact and confrontation necessary to achieve international recognition of their talents. Thus, one of the main objectives of the biennial is to promote the work of participating artists on the international scene.

In consequence, the participating artists were required to be citizens of a Latin American or Caribbean country, or at least have lived in one of these two regions for a minimum of five years. The second edition was additionally opened to artists from Asia, and the third, to artists from Africa. These restrictions were relaxed a little in the fifth edition, which featured diasporic artists of Caribbean descent, such as the British artist Keith Piper.

Unlike in Venice or São Paulo, the works in the main exhibition of the first edition of the Havana Biennial, which was located in the Pabellon de Cuba, were displayed according to formal criteria rather than national origin. The Biennial stemmed from the assumption that Latin American artists were a heterogeneous group of individuals rather than mere representatives of particular countries or cultures. This perspective was also conspicuous in the layout of the catalogue, which arranged the artists alphabetically rather than by nationality. The exhibition at the Pabellon was also remarkable for its unique manner of display. Over 5,000 square meters of open-air space covered by a concrete roof was used to create a temporary multilevel maze with wooden bridges connecting the various exhibition spaces. All works were uniformly framed with raw, unfinished wooden strips, regardless of their format. Meanwhile, in the second main venue, the Museum of Fine Arts, a more traditionally hung exhibition was divided into sections according to technique, and then each of these sections was suborganized according to country. The selection of works featured in the first edition may seem a little conservative from today's perspective, for the official "Regulation for Participation" only allowed two-dimensional works—painting, drawings, photography, and prints. It is, however, important to note that from a local perspective there was nothing particularly reactionary about this focus: due to the duty-free nature of mailed printed matter as well as the affordability of its production and shipping, printed works have always been a favorite item in Latin American contemporary art exhibitions and were preponderant in several other smaller, short-lived biennials preceding Havana's, such as the biennials in Medellín and Cali (both in Colombia), with the latter being entirely devoted to the graphic arts.

With a total of 2,200 works by 835 artists, the first Havana Biennial ended up presenting one of the most important overviews of contemporary Latin American art in history.[17] Beginning with the second edition, the biennial focused predominantly on works by emerging artists by introducing a new paragraph into the regulations that allowed only works created during the five years preceding the exhibition to be displayed. This unprecedented annotation is most likely the earliest formulation of the tacit rule of contemporary biennials to privilege new work, that is, their function as surveys of the latest tendencies in art.[18] The second Havana Biennial was also the first truly global exhibition, gathering 690 artists from 57 countries and pioneering the extraordinary internationalization of art that we witness today. From early on, it was also the priority of the organizers to invite artists to Havana to install their works. In the fifth edition, 104 of the 171 participants were involved during the installation.[19] Today, many participants recall the early Havana Biennials as a unique place for dialogue among artists grappling with the restrictive costs of artistic production.[20] In having an important number of artists on site and a favorable political climate, the organizers saw the event as a space for creative encounters between artists, theoreticians, cultural workers, and the local population.[21] The biennial engaged the entire city as the exhibition venues were spread across different neighborhoods; for some of the early editions over thirty venues were used, including artists' studios and private apartments.

The Havana Biennial's innovative nature was also manifest in several other aspects. Since its inception in 1984, it has expanded the traditional model of one central exhibition into an assortment of shows, panel discussions, lectures, performances, and workshops led by artists. Although Documenta 5 (1972) already contained elements of this expanded character, this was confined to the level of artists' projects and did not concern a self-reflexive enquiry into the exhibition and the institution's own raison d'être. However, it is when looking at the themes addressed by the earliest Havana exhibitions and their parallel events that we are struck by the contemporaneity of these topics, for they continue to play a central role in the discourse of today's biennials. The first biennial (1984) focused on Caribbean cultures, while the next edition (1986) was accompanied by a conference entitled "Tradition and Contemporaneity in the Arts of the Third World." These questions were elaborated further in the fourth edition of the biennial (1991) through an exploration of the theme of "Cultural Domination and Alternatives to Colonization." The 1991 edition of the Havana Biennial marked an important turn in discussions surrounding globalization and, concurrently, in the ways the following wave of emerging biennials articulated their rhetoric. In fact, this edition was the first contemporary biennial to deal explicitly with postcolonialism before the readings of globalization through the lens of postcolonial critique began to be systematically appropriated by the discourses and frameworks of preexisting and newly established biennial exhibitions. The new variant of the Havana Biennial's rhetoric relied to a lesser extent on the "Three Worlds" model and instead shifted towards questions of the global versus the local and the center/core–periphery dialectic. In parallel, the Biennial featured from the beginning exhibitions designed to address a range of current issues, such as nomadism, displacement and marginalization, cultural hybridizations and diasporic identities, ecology, and the periphery of postmodernity—all of which now belong to the vocabulary of the current generation of biennials. The organizers privileged works expressing ethnic, religious, and cultural particularisms, thereby accentuating "difference" and a polyphony of discourse rather than seeking to communicate a universal message imposed by a single curatorial gesture.

Bringing together a selection of local and international artists, curators, critics, historians, and philosophers as well as social activists, theoreticians, and practitioners from various fields, the Havana Biennial was one of the early instances of a new type of heterogeneous discursive sphere capable of addressing current art practice while simultaneously exploring some of the most complex predicaments of our time.[22] Such generated rhetorical armature was therefore much broader than the art historical discourse accompanying the majority of museum shows at the time, which made it capable of expanding the locus of the disciplinary models that had constituted and defined artistic knowledge production up until the eighties.[23]

With the proliferation of variations of the new model established by the Havana Biennial (an international, large-scale, theme-driven survey of recent art with an extensive program of parallel events and discursive platforms that increasingly incorporated nonartistic disciplines), which was swiftly applied in places that have traditionally been marginalized (e.g., Istanbul, Johannesburg, Dakar) and later recuperated by second-tier cities in Europe (e.g., Lyon, Tirana, Seville) and the Far East (e.g., Gwangju, Fukuoka), the Cuban biennial itself began to lose its singularity around the time of its sixth edition in 1997. At that point, first regrets were expressed about the softening of the Havana Biennial's radical rhetoric, for it had begun to engage with the politics of the contemporary art world. As critic Rachel Weiss observed in 1997, the organizers of the Havana Biennial had "proved that a convincing global position can be developed from outside the usual circles of power; their task now, one fears, is to defend their achievement from its own success well enough to preserve its voice and distinctness—a problem of middle age."[24] However, the Havana Biennial remains the symbolic model for the majority of biennials created in the past twenty-five years. Paradoxically, it is thanks to the economic isolation of Cuba that Havana's biennial still represents a peripheral context in its purest form today.

The arguments listed above suggest that the Havana Biennial (as evidenced by its first five editions) represents a more accurate point of reference for the contemporary large-scale exhibition than the Venice Biennial in either its original or its current form. The arguments supporting the location of the genesis of the contemporary biennial in the Havana Biennial can be summarized and grouped into the three main areas of inquiry: its relevance from the perspective of exhibition and curatorial history, the conjuncture of historical circumstances in which it came into being, and its distinctly different reading of modernity.

While Venice had been resistant to avant-garde and non-Western art for almost a century, Havana's biennial was the first to focus strictly on recent work and prioritize art production from outside the Western core.[25] Artworks featured in the Havana Biennial were displayed according to formal criteria in a centrally curated exhibition rather than in a series of displays of works arranged according to the country of their origin, as was the case—and to some extent still is—in Venice.[26] Beginning with its second edition, the Havana Biennial was designed not only as an exhibition but as an entire constellation of events (main exhibitions, assorted group and solo shows, conferences, talks, lectures, workshops, publications, film programs, etc.) revolving around a specific thematic, artistic, and cultural focus, which thus provided it with a strong rhetorical armature and unprecedented discursive capacities.[27]

Another major difference between the two institutions in question was primarily informed less by their artistic profiles and choices than by the historical circumstances in which they came to being. The Venice Biennial was founded as a celebration of the nineteenth-century idea of the nation-state, while the Havana Biennial, in contrast, emerged with the advent of major historical transformations concurrent with the unprecedented acceleration of the processes of globalization, and thus reflected the new transnational, multicultural, and diasporic identities. To ignore these dealings and focus only on the elements of the early Venice Biennial that already contained within them a grain of the ensuing phenomenon of biennial proliferation in order to contrive a neat teleology would be a mistake.[28] Instead, one might also articulate the conditions of possibility for the appearance of what seems self-evident, conditions that are contingent in that they are products of historically unrepeatable circumstances yet are also conjecturally determined. The acceleration of processes of globalization and the passage from a polarized political situation in the world (during the Cold War) to the far more complex arrangement that Antonio Negri and Michael Hardt describe as the "Empire" provided the conditions of possibility for the proliferation of today's contemporary biennials. These historical circumstances are, in this context, far more decisive than the sway of the predecessors.[29] Therefore, the importance that I am assigning to the Havana Biennial lies in the fact that it captured and marked the period of the major transitions in the (art) world that determined the course of the proliferation.[30]

The first edition of the Havana Biennial in 1984 thus marked a turn in biennial history: the birth of a new breed of contemporary biennials born of a global context and the start of their proliferation. While many of the new biennials may, in some respects, be read as continual expressions of modernity (notably through their association with the accumulation of symbolic capital), it was the Havana Biennial that established the contemporary biennial as a platform for the critique of this same modernity. By focusing on creating horizontal connections (South–South) that provide alternatives to the art routes inherited from modernity, the Havana Biennial enabled a new type of global exhibition that debunks the myths of teleological modernity and explores the plurality of modernism. The inception of the Havana Biennial coincides precisely with (and in the process is informed by) the theorization of postmodernism, which the Havana Biennial advanced in its own way against the modernity-making machine of the Venice Biennial. It was in 1984 that American literary critic and Marxist political theorist Fredric Jameson presented his seminal essay on the cultural logic of late capitalism, a text that continues to be a resource for discussions surrounding cultural aspects of globalization today.[31] It is precisely the ways in which the Havana Biennial mirrored the new readings of globalization and modernity—in which it captured the historical, political, and geographic transitions of the eighties, and in which it introduced (and in some cases anticipated) the shifts in exhibitions-making and the discourse surrounding contemporary art—that allow us to identify the Cuban biennial as the most important point of reference for the contemporary biennial.

Situated at the juncture where global capitalism and culture intersect, where the yields of modernity can be used to critique it, the contemporary biennial is a highly fractured and fragmented entity that only acquires its full meaning once sited within a given context (whether that is Havana, Istanbul, or Singapore). The contemporary biennial can generate the public sphere necessary for discussion, articulating inherent contradictions of cultural globalization. With its ambitious and often utopian aspirations of changing the (art) world, which were first articulated by the Havana Biennial, it should be seen today as a largely unachieved project. As long as the outcome of cultural and economic globalization is still a clouded mirror, the fate of the contemporary biennial remains unpredictable with respect to both its survival (with possible transformations and adjustments) and its capacity to produce a viable and important alternative to existing institutional frameworks within the contemporary art world. ●

NOTES

This essay is a revised version of a lecture given at the Bergen Biennial Conference, September 17–20, 2009.

1 Taken from Robert Storr's text published in the program of the symposium "Where Art Worlds Meet: Multiple Modernities and the Global Salon," December 9–12, 2005, Venice, Istituto Veneto di Scienze, Lettere ed Arti.

2 This centrality of the Venice Biennial in the discussions surrounding the current proliferation of biennials is indeed commonplace among many art historians, critics, and curators (including Caroline A. Jones, Tim Griffin, Daniel Birnbaum, Charlotte Bydler, and Carlos Basualdo, to name a few). Conspicuously, those representing, or subscribing to, non-Western perspectives tend to be considerably more skeptical about its presumed relevance (for instance, Geeta Kapur, Thomas McEvilley, and Gerardo Mosquera). Other commentators who questioned Venice's position in regards to "younger" biennials include René Block and Carolyn Christov-Bakargiev. The general prominence of the Venetian exhibition is due the fact that it is one of the most popular, publicized, and discussed events punctuating the art-world calendar, and the relative lack of first-hand knowledge about biennials outside the West does not help the discussions. Even today relatively few critics and curators (and hardly any art historians) travel to see exhibitions outside the EU and the U.S. while the Venice Biennial continues to be visited and referenced by thousands.

3 The employment of Bourdieu's notion of symbolic capital (see his *Distinction: A Social Critique of the Judgement of Taste* [London, 1984]) in this context is designed to point to alternative sources of wealth other than economic (financial and industrial) capital whose value may nevertheless be redeemable and reconvertible back into economic value through a whole series of direct and indirect routes, a fact that explains the willingness of city administrators to encourage and seek investment in contemporary biennials and their sensitivity to the importance of enhancing their city's image under conditions of intensified competition.

4 Rafal Niemojewski, *The Rise of the Contemporary Biennial 1984–2009*, doctoral thesis, Royal College of Art, London, 2009.

5 Martin Glaser, "Interview with René Block," in *Das Leid von der Erde / Songs of the Earth*, ed. Barbara Heinrich, exh. cat. Kassel, Documenta and Museum Fridericianum Veranstaltungs-GmbH, 2000, p. 5.

6 Ibid., p. 5; Okwui Enwezor, "Mega-Exhibitions and the Antinomies of a Transnational Global Form," in Marieke van Hal, Viktor Misiano, and Igor Zabel (eds.), "Biennials," special issue, *MJ–Manifesta Journal* 2 (Winter 2003–Spring 2004), p. 8; Tim Griffin, "Global Tendencies: Globalism and Large-Scale Exhibition," *Artforum*, no. 42 (November 2003), pp. 153–207.

7 According to my findings, around fifty new instances of the contemporary biennial were introduced from 1984 to 2009. Less than half of these exhibitions can declare a perfect record of recurrence, while others at some point(s) encountered circumstances that led to the postponement or cancellation of one or more editions, or, in the most severe cases, to their discontinuation. Some of the most emblematic "biennials," including those of Havana and Berlin, should in fact call themselves triennials, as three-year intervals between consecutive editions have been more frequent than two-year intervals.

NOTES

Similarly, the span of time between the first and second editions of the Yokohama Triennial (2001, 2005) was four years, thereby technically making it a quadrennial. The frequency of such irregularities suggests that classifying perennial exhibitions according to the pace of recurrence can be arbitrary.

8 An official selection committee consisting of prominent artists and citizens born or resident in Venice set out these regulations in the first catalogue published in 1895. The committee had the authority to issue invitations to participating artists and to decide on the inclusion of works after an open call for submissions had been made. In his study of the early Venice Biennial, Lawrence Alloway asserted that the Venetian regulations were largely modeled on those of the nineteenth-century salons, in particular the ones that took place in Munich in 1886 and 1888. This connection, along with the committee's conspicuous inclination toward Salon art, led him to depict the early editions of the Venice Biennial as a "Super-Salon." See Lawrence Alloway, *The Venice Biennale, 1895–1968: From Salon to Goldfish Bowl* (London, 1968), pp. 33–35.

9 Riccardo Selvatico, Syndic of Venice and a member of the original Venice Biennial Commission, quoted in ibid., p. 32.

10 In 1896, the show was established as a yearly survey and presented as the Annual Exhibition. In 1950 the exhibition was renamed the Pittsburgh International and became biannual, and then in 1955 it became triannual. During the nineteen-seventies its name was changed to the International Series and it broke with the tradition of the survey show to present solo exhibitions. The show returned to its original 1896 survey-exhibition format in 1982 and was renamed the Carnegie International.

11 Until its fifth edition in 1972, Documenta recurred at four-year intervals (excepting the five-year interval between the second and third editions of 1959 and 1964), but from then on at intervals of five years. The considerably longer period of preparation (matched by a considerably bigger budget) reinforced Documenta's reputation as one of the leading surveys of contemporary art. Despite its specific pace of recurrence, many other characteristics of the post-1972 editions of Documenta (the artistic direction, selection of curators, curatorial strategies, shared lexicon, and discursive frameworks, as well as selection of works) suggest that Documenta should not be discussed separately from other recurring exhibitions.

12 Harald Szeemann quoted in Gabriele Mackert, "At Home in Contradictions: Harald Szeemann's Documenta," in Michael Glasmeier and Karin Stengel (eds.), *Archive in Motion: 50 Years of Documenta 1955–2005* (Göttingen, 2005), pp. 253–61.

13 One of the earliest commentators of contemporary biennials, Carlos Basualdo, has asserted that the way they acquired symbolic capital was paradoxically linked to their presumed independence from market logic. While Basualdo argues that the current connections of the biennial industry with the art market are often overstated, the Venice Biennial, until 1968, was a marketplace in which nearly every work bore a price tag. It is perhaps not by total coincidence that 1970 marked both the end of the sale of art at the Venice Biennial and the opening of the art fair in Basel, which was founded by the art dealers and gallerists Trudl Bruckner, Balz Hilt, and Ernst Beyeler. The rapid rise of Art Basel to the rank of one of the world's most important art events was likely due to the fact that the art fair, held in June, coincided every two years with the opening of the Venice Biennial. It could therefore cater to the community of collectors, in particular those coming from across the Atlantic looking for new marketplaces in Europe after the end of commercial activities in Venice.

14 Similar efforts took place during the Architecture Biennial in 1970 at the French Pavilion, where architects Claude Parent and Paul Virilio installed the first experimental and site-specific environment.

15 Gerhard Richter displayed his series of forty-eight grayscale paintings of identical size based on photographic portraits taken out of the encyclopedia.

16 *Aperto* continued to present works by emerging artists throughout the eighties. However, without curatorial direction strong enough to respect Szeemann's initial vision, its relevance and visibility gradually waned. The section was given a particularly important focus during the forty-fifth edition of the Biennial under the artistic direction of Achille Bonito Oliva, but then it disappeared from view once more. As the artistic director of the forty-eighth edition in 1999, Szeemann revived the concept of *Aperto* on a much larger scale with *dAPERTutto* (APERTO Everywhere), which featured works from over a hundred artists presented in the newly restored Corderie in the Arsenale. Throughout the eighties Szeemann's and Oliva's initiatives can be therefore seen as exceptions rather than as a sign of actual structural change, which only truly arrived in the nineties.

17 That is, at least in terms of quantity, even if, as several critics have noted, "it was far from an exquisite selection." Like the first edition of Documenta, the first edition of the Havana Biennial featured many historical works before shifting its focus entirely to recent art production. See Luis Camnitzer, "Report from Havana: The First Biennial of Latin American Art," *Art in America* (December 1984), p. 43.

18 As mentioned earlier, the short-lived *Aperto* section of the Venice Biennial introduced in 1980 was dedicated to emerging artists and not necessarily to new works (although these two often came hand in hand). The works displayed in that section represented only a small percentage of the total number of works presented at the Biennial, while the more systematic presentation of recent artistic production only began in Venice in the nineties (notably in 1993 and 1999).

19 This represented the highest ratio of artists involved during the installation to date. See Luis Camnitzer, "The V Havana Biennial," *Art Nexus,* no. 14 (October–December 1994), pp. 48–55.

20 See Valerie Cassel, "The Havana Biennale," *NKA Journal of Contemporary African Art,* no. 15 (Fall/Winter 2001), pp. 14–17.

21 The eighties in Cuba were a period marked by more liberal cultural policies and a considerably more open approach on the part of the Cuban government to cultural and international exchange.

22 For example, the fourth edition of the Havana Biennial (1991) featured an extensive program of parallel events including the international conference "Cultural Domination and Alternatives to Colonisation," whose list of speakers included the editors of *Third Text* Rasheed Araeen and Guy Brett, artist and critic Luis Camnitzer, historian Iván de la Nuez, cultural theorist Nelly Richard, philosopher Eduardo Subirats, and critic and scholar Jorge Glusberg among many others.

NOTES

23 The areas of thought incorporated into the general lexicon of contemporary biennials via theories of globalization and postcolonialism include sociology, architectural theory, anthropology, philosophy, feminist theory, queer theory, urban studies, cultural studies, film studies, and literary criticism. While the Havana Biennial (or any other contemporary biennial, for that matter) cannot under any circumstances be given exclusive credit for the entry of extra-artistic discourses into the realm of contemporary art, it is nonetheless significant that its early editions and the beginning of the proliferation of the new model coincided with this shift. The contribution of a new breed of globalized biennials to the hybridization of the discourse surrounding contemporary art and exhibitions should be seen as significant, particularly with regard to the progressive absorption and dissemination of postcolonial thought (or, more broadly, discourses giving prominence to the concept of alterity) and to the new voices and theories (re)articulated outside Western academia.

24 Rachel Weiss, "The Sixth Havana Biennial," *Art Nexus*, no. 26 (October–December 1997), p. 77.

25 At this writing, the contemporary art of African countries and the African diaspora still haven't found a satisfying platform of presentation in Venice.

26 As mentioned earlier, the changes announced by *Aperto* in 1980 and then subsequently applied in 1993 and 1999 can be seen as milestones in the history of the Venice Biennial. However, the archaic and questionable system of national representations continues to be this biennial's defining feature.

27 This early instance of a biennial serving as a discursive platform can be discussed in relation to broader shifts in curatorial practice and discourse and in developments in art practice, which required the establishment of new frameworks for the production, mediation, and dissemination of art. For details on this, see Paul O'Neill, "The Curatorial Turn: From Practice to Discourse," in Judith Rugg and Michele Sedgwick (eds.), *Issues in Curating Contemporary Art and Performance* (Bristol, 2008), pp. 13–28. This essay has also been reprinted in the present volume.

28 I would, however, like to acknowledge that the periodization I put forward in this paper, just like Robert Storr's genealogy, or, as a matter of fact, any other similar procedure, is to some extent a teleological construct and as such it can be criticized and disputed. In order to further assess it, I suggest comparing it to two other periodizations presented in the available literature, those of René Block and Charlotte Bydler. Block's panorama of biennials conspicuously excludes the Venice Biennial. Explaining this deliberate omission in the catalogue, Block said that he saw the Venice Biennial at that time, with its impermeable structure of individually funded and curated national representations, as the antithesis of the younger biennials he was interested in. See Block's remarks in Glaser 2000 (see note 5), p. 4; see also Charlotte Bydler, *The Global Art World, Inc.: On the Globalization of Contemporary Art* (Uppsala, 2004), p. 151. An abridged version of the latter appears in the present volume.

29 Michael Hardt and Antonio Negri, *Empire* (Cambridge [MA], 2000).

30 At this writing, the proliferation of the contemporary biennial had acquired a time-bound niche in recent exhibition history. The analysis of the dynamic of proliferation (with a significant shift occurring around 1995) allows us to pinpoint the association of the contemporary biennial and the processes of globalization to appear as truth and eventually something self-evident. The early stage of the proliferation of the contemporary biennial (1984–95) was marked by the appearance of new instances in territories largely peripheral to and disconnected from the core of the contemporary art world, which at that time was still centralized and revolved around the few Western art capitals that had been empowered throughout the modern era. The earliest contemporary biennial organizations (those of Havana and Cairo) emerged in territories then designated as being part of the Third World, which could be translated as geographically remote, and politically and economically incompatible with the centers of Western art. Others materialized in the peripheries and semi-peripheries with an analogous agenda of correcting and decentralizing the cartography of the art world inherited from modernity. One thing that these various places had in common was that they were localized on the margins of dominant culture, within the regions of the so-called social, cultural, and/or geographical periphery, or of the "Other." The vast majority of the contemporary biennials established during the second stage of biennial proliferation (roughly 1995 to the present), on the other hand, were localized in the territories that could now be best described as emerging economies or developed countries in Europe, Asia, South America, and the Middle East. With the new world order in place after the end of the Cold War, the preceding rationale based on political alliances, the theory of development, and the notion of periphery defined either geographically or symbolically could no longer be used to comprehend the second stage of biennial proliferation. Instead, it was necessary to privilege a different approach, using the nomenclature and division into strategic alliances defined by the system of the global economy and economic deregulation: the single market of the European Union including its new members from Eastern and Central Europe, the highly developed economies of the Asian Tigers, the emerging markets of BRIC and Mercosul countries, countries united by NAFTA, and the Gulf oil states. The shift in the geopolitical and economic identity of the contemporary biennial was concurrent with a change in ideological perspectives. Most of the biennials that emerged during the first phase were characterized by a strong desire to challenge the status quo of unequal power relations within the art world and the world at large. In contrast, the majority of contemporary biennials established after 1995, according to the interpretation presented by Negri and Hardt, can be read as "projects from within" that articulate their agendas according to a new world order in which ideological opposition and political blocks can no longer be easily drawn on a world map.

31 Fredric Jameson, "Postmodernism, or the Cultural Logic of Late Capitalism," *New Left Review*, no. 146 (July–August 1984), pp. 59–92. This controversial article, which would later be expanded to a full-length book in 1991, was part of a series of analyses of postmodernism from the dialectical point of view Jameson had developed in his earlier work on narrative. Other dates—associated perhaps with seminal works by Baudrillard, Foucault, Derrida, Perry Anderson, Richard Rorty, or others—could be quoted here as markers of the postmodernist critique of modernity, but Jameson's pronouncement seems as useful as any to me with regard to the contemporary biennial.

THE INVENTION OF THE DAKAR BIENNIAL (2009)

104

Yacouba Konaté

For Africa to really get away from the West implies having an exact understanding of what it costs to break away from it; it implies knowing how far the West has, insidiously perhaps, come closer to us; it implies knowing what it is, precisely in that that which enables us to think against the West remains Western; and measuring the degree to which our recourse against it may still be a trick that it puts in our way, behind which it is there waiting for us, unmoving and elsewhere.

V. Y. Mudimbe, *L'Odeur du père*

THE ADVENT OF BIENNIALS IN AFRICA

TO understand the invention of a biennial in Africa, because it is of "invention" that one must speak, one might first of all ask: Who plays the role of the People in the history of art in Africa and in the emergence of the Dakar Biennial? Who makes the history of African art? What are the infrastructures and productive forces in the field of the history of art in Africa, and what are the subjective and objective elements that make this history meaningful and valuable? These questions are approached via the framework of a theory of the history of art, conceived not as a succession of styles, but as a social and political field. The inception and institutionalization of the Dakar Biennial (Dak'Art) is the positive result of debates within Senegalese society. These historically coded discussions were and continue to be social, political, and aesthetic. They participate in the inscription of the Dakar Biennial into history. As for the event itself, it became a self-fulfilling prophecy on many levels: Pan-African, international, and contemporary.

According to the German Web site www.universes-in-universe.org, there is a total of some two hundred art biennials around the world. Among the events that have established themselves on the international cultural circuit, Africa is represented by the Cairo Biennial (Egypt), the Rencontres Africaines de la Photographie in Bamako

(Mali), and the Dakar Biennial. The Biennial of Bantu Arts, organized by the Centre for Bantu Civilisations (CICIBA) since 1985, has not been able to carve out a niche either internationally or in the region. The triennials in Luanda and Cape Town, launched one after the other in early 2007, will certainly improve the general picture with regard to major artistic events in Africa. In the meantime, Dak'Art remains the standout event for contemporary visual arts in Africa. It has forged its identity over the years, becoming a springboard for its own history and an engine of creativity. Artists make work specifically in order to take part. Dak'Art is part of the general history of biennials.

Most of the major cultural events contemporaneous with the Dakar Biennial emerged from the sociohistorical situation of the nineteen-nineties. This historical coexistence makes sense, corresponding as it does to the general renewal of social and political governance undertaken in Africa. The nineties, which worked through the consequences of the fall of the Berlin Wall, were marked by the end of the apartheid regime, which some analysts interpreted as the end of colonialism and the beginning of postcolonialism in Africa. Before the fall of apartheid, nearly everywhere in Africa the principle of the one-party state was threatened, forced to give ground and allow a political pluralism that was seen as political openness.

The age of biennials was thus, also, a time of political rupture and reorganization and, above all, a time of a general clamoring for liberties. At the forefront of this movement were the young and the working classes rebelling at the general failure of the one-party state. Biennials open up public space, that is to say, space for encounter and debate where art professionals meet and discuss cultural policies or the lack of them, or organize joint projects. In the same space, the work of the visual artists was socially and politically engaged, and in this sense they helped animate the debate on the governance of Africa and the world. Biennials in Africa were part of this general movement of social and political emancipation, a vector of its intensification. They signaled Africa's reawakening to freedom, expressing its new self-belief. In this sense, they contributed to the general logic of "enlightenment" emphasized by Okwui Enwezor with regard to the creation of Documenta in Kassel, Germany. Just as this latter event gave international expression to Germany's determination to turn a new leaf after Nazism and take part in the movement of new ideas, the creation of the African festivals also coincided with a period of rebirth in Africa. Documenta was conceived, among other reasons, as a home for forms of art that the Nazis condemned as "degenerate," particularly abstract art, and to help the moral and physical reconstruction of the city of Kassel, which had been completely destroyed by Allied bombs.

It can be agreed that the advent of biennials in Africa articulated what was at least a double movement: the reception of an unloved art and self-reconstruction. The contemporary art biennial is connected with the problematic of the reception of African art, which was seriously low in the pecking order of the international art system. It partook of the efforts to reconstruct Africa in the midst of its democratic crisis. Also, the positive PR resulting from the biennial helped put Dakar on the map, establishing a place for Senegal and Africa in the world of fine art. The African biennial of contemporary art therefore relates to the question of Africa's place in an ever more globalized world.

Theodor Adorno would have rejected blockbuster exhibitions in the style of the Dakar Biennial as a manifestation of mass art, with mass art being a form of the culture industry that turns the individual into a faceless creature, lost in the anonymous cohort of visitors, rather than stimulating people's critical potential. At the same time, are people visiting biennial exhibitions not to confront the enigma of art, helping to prove Adorno's point that "art has lost its obviousness"? Does this face-to-face between an unlikely artwork and its occasional visitor not bring with it tension and critical wakefulness? It does insofar as the viewer realizes that the contemporary artwork is not only a two-dimensional pictorial work or a kinetic and tactile work in three dimensions, but increasingly involves installations, that is to say, "spatial units that may be descriptive or imaginary, and that are capable of evoking a technological environment in order to attain the virtual." The confrontation with works is a critical moment that makes it possible to verify and evaluate the problematic character of the contemporary artwork. I recall several moments in the evolution of this problem that, in the history of Dak'Art, have proved controversial.

I have not tried to make the Dakar Biennial a theme, attempting to recite Adorno by heart. I have stirred a few moments of debate and tried to understand from the inside how the need for a major cultural event like the Dakar Biennial elaborates a kind of mass art while resisting blindness or standardization. In analyzing this question, one faces some of the problems that confront the vanquished when, as Walter Benjamin and Adorno recommended, they take it upon themselves to recount history from below—history from the loser's viewpoint. And we have gained a sense of the victor's power and resonance. When he chooses to play the viewer, he is taken on as a player. And when the match is a draw, he ends up the winner. Even more seriously, when one believes one has won, even against oneself, it would seem that the most one has succeeded in doing is producing a weak copy of his masterpieces. We refer to him, in time and in an untimely way, for better and for worse.

WHAT IS (AFRICAN) ART?

THE point of the list of misconceptions that follows is to compare differing accounts of the construction of the Dakar Biennial, starting from that initial question: Who makes history? Looking beyond the different subjects that come up in the invention of the Dakar Biennial, it is our hypothesis that the Biennial itself functions as a machine for making the history of art, of Pan-Africanism and contemporaneity. That history employs the notion of art as if it were self-evident. But this view is shared only by those who consider the notion of art as an external one that is not really compatible with African reality.

"In what sense can one speak of 'art' when one speaks of African art?" The answer to this question, which sounds deliberately provocative, is not simple. One can choose between two types of answer. The first is to state that there is no African art because there is no equivalent term in African languages. "Most African languages have no words to designate a work of art, an artist or art."[1] This conception assumes that words are the verbal confirmation of things and the events leading up to them. It thus closes the door on the unnamable or the ill-named and forgets that behind a word there is more than just a thing for which it is the more or less appropriate name. The second option is to state that African art does exist and, with generous condescension, to extend the category of art to include works produced for nonartistic purposes that can nevertheless stand up to a formal, aesthetic interpretation. The *art nègre* movement takes its place within this second approach, at a distance from those who claim that the concept of art is not African but Western, and that pseudo "African art" is at most a form of Art Brut, or naïve art—in a word, the childhood of art. It would therefore follow that what has taken its place throughout the Western and Westernized world under the label of the "fine arts"—the expression itself exudes a sense of the duty to contemplate the sublimity of these outstanding works produced by men of genius—has no equivalent in Africa. In both cases we remain caught in the vice of the postulate that, whether brutally expressed or not, boils down to this: Africa has a problem with art.

Africa has been under the Western gaze at least since the turn of the twentieth century, if not before. This recognition is part of a historical sequence that began with the modern age, if not before. It culminated with the notion of art being removed from the matrix of beauty and made to revolve around the notion of the artwork. This aesthetic shift is one of the theoretical conditions for the reception of so-called *art nègre.* It followed the depletion of the resources of classical painting whose key innovation, at least during the Renaissance, had been perspective. It also made the criteria of adroitness and technique intrinsic in the notions of *artes* and *tékhné* obsolete. When visiting museums in New York, Tokyo, Dakar, or Paris, you will often get young or older people coming up to you and asking, "Where is the art in all this? Where is the beauty? Where is the emotion?" And more than once, men and women will say—and not without justification—"Well, if that's art, then I'm an artist!" As Adorno would say, "Art has lost its obviousness."

The question of the status of art could be enriched by opening onto that of "artiality," understood as the set of objects that are, actively or potentially, art objects. "Much that was not art—cultic works, for instance—has over the course of history metamorphosed into art; and much that was once art is that no longer."[2] Jean-Hubert Martin has often formulated this question: when Michelangelo was decorating the ceiling of the Sistine Chapel at the Vatican, did he claim to be making art? In the same way, the Dan sculptor making a mask for an altar does not see the creation of beauty as his main objective, but he does render the mask concept he has been asked to as best he can, with all his talent, style, and inspiration. In the same way, photography was first seen as a technology for reproduction, and therefore for imitating nature, but later became a form of representation, like painting and sculpture. It is worth diffracting the term *art* in order to see how it is used to signify and crystallize the *artial* as the *artistic.* The extraordinary variety of versions of art goes beyond the supposed unity of art. There are different kinds of *artiality,* each one mobilizing a specific range of affects. Art is not an exclusive attribute of glorious humanity.

As for the notion of African contemporary art, it touches on the relations between Africa and the West. What Africa must do is be contemporary with the world, with or without the mediation of the West. Africans must be their own contemporaries in a world whose shockwaves they themselves feel and in which they would like to be active players. Africa is not a country but a continent. Why do people get that wrong? It all comes down to prejudice, ignorance, and misinformation—in short, to the representations that we form both of ourselves and of others. These representations concern what are common images of Africa as well as images that Africans themselves put into circulation in the inventive course of everyday life. Art is part of this everyday life. As a maker of forms and rhythms, it liberates images that may invalidate or confirm, but that fundamentally express the concerns of the man or woman engaged in abstract activities, for and by whom ordinary men abandon, more or less provisionally, their duty to create and invent: the artist. Self-expression may directly or indirectly help repair or restore one's self-image. Artistic representations remind us all that images are plastic and mobile, and that they bring internal tensions to the surface of consciousness, making painting, sculpture, or video their avatars.

THE BIENNIAL EFFECT

IN 1989, explaining the absence of African partners in the curatorial team for *Magiciens de la terre,* André Magnin pointed out that the organizers simply didn't know of any professionals likely to fit in with their projects. Of course, this justification judges itself, in that it reveals the organizers' level of information. Putting on a biennial implies having men and women who are competent or can be trained. The construction of the event is a performance that creates qualifications, that enriches the professional competence of the art workers striving to make it a success. Dak'Art can take pride in having contributed to the visibility and validation of a certain number of skills in the artistic professions. It has not only validated competence, but also actually brought it into being. The involvement of African critics and curators in defining the content of the event reestablishes the truth as to the purported lack of contemporary art professionals in Africa. Dak'Art demonstrates that a curator is someone who has been certified as a professional, but also someone who has been professionalized. Dak'Art is a platform for the professionalization of artists, critics, exhibition designers, and cultural operators.

In September 2005 torrential rain beat down on Dakar. Unusual for a Sahelian country such as Senegal, the duration and intensity of this rain caused a real natural catastrophe. The national TV channel showed men, women, and children in distress. Desperate men were explaining to the authorities that they had lost everything they had. In many neighborhoods the waves climbed up the pavement and into houses. The infiltration of water forced the inhabitants to wrap their possessions in plastic. It was like a tropical adaptation of Christo's work. This was when an important figure at the Ministry of Culture in Dakar put to me the following question: what will you say if one of these poor people asks why you devote so much money to organizing a biennial for a privileged few when the houses of Dakar's poor are flooded with rainwater? The answer that immediately came to mind was as follows: The money that we could save by cutting the Biennial would certainly not be spent on improving the poorer districts! True, poor people may not necessarily need a biennial, but they don't wait to have everything they might need before starting to love music, dance, beautiful forms, and beautiful things. The answer I actually gave was more convivial: the 300 million or so francs that Senegal agrees to pay for the Biennial are next to nothing when compared with the huge sums that we effectively need to find in order to fight flooding. Beyond these answers, the fundamental question raised by the friendly objection formulated above is that of financial viability. It is also that of the financial viability of festivals and other events. Artists and cultural professionals are on the wrong track if they respond by arguing that painting can immortalize memories of the floods of 2005 and elaborate a tropical version of Géricault's *Raft of the Medusa!* That landmark painting from 1819, which refers to the sinking of a frigate that occurred in 1816 off the Senegalese coast, speaks of the atrocious sufferings endured by its passengers for ten whole days. The work also raises the question of responsibility (who made the disaster inevitable?) and denounces the inequality of the different classes before death. The privileged passengers were saved while the less well-heeled were abandoned, left on that raft.

It is also a waste of breath answering the culture skeptics that art and culture, a fact attested by the so-called development theater, can help in the fight against malaria and AIDS and may also, let us not forget, serve to formulate more or less educational arguments on social issues such as democracy and human rights. Culture skeptics are impervious to arguments demonstrating the effects of culture on social cohesion, the construction of dignity, social development, etc. As Saint-Exupéry's Little Prince observed a long time ago, "Adults love numbers." Figures are the only language they understand, and what they expect is a mathematical demonstration of the benefits of culture in cash value. Now, most of the cash generated by culture doesn't find its way directly into its coffers, hence the joke made by Minister Abdoulaye Elimane Kane: "Yes, Dak'Art does have a structuring effect. I mean, it has a structuring effect for airlines, hotels, restaurants, shops, taxis, and gallerists."

In effect, the Biennial does often incite airplanes and hotels to work at a constant rhythm. Most of the meager budgets allocated by the public authorities and international cooperations do not go into artists' pockets but are injected into the national economy.[3] The Biennial creates the conditions for the general activation of the national economy. It follows that the real budget-eaters are not those who are singled out for attention, but the airlines, the hotels, and the communications agencies. If only a fraction of the sums spent by festivalgoers in each of these areas ended up in the Biennial's coffers, then surely it would not always need to go from financier to financier in order to make up its budget. Having been financed once, it would remain in funds for many years. And it would then no longer be seen as financially voracious.[4]

Festivals are also powerful vehicles of communication, a dimension confirmed by the many posters around the city and the coverage in the press, on the radio and television, and in various international media with an interest in African issues. Thanks to the Biennial, Senegal enjoys prime coverage in the most prominent media. Press response in and beyond Africa, plus airtime, sends images of the country's vitality all around the world. In addition to this indirect publicity for the country, there is also the aspect of diplomatic communication. The authorities of the host nations that provide limousines and cocktails for their prestigious guests use the Biennial to reaffirm their role in the subregion of West Africa, in the larger region of Africa, and in the world. This cultural diplomacy is aimed at ministers in the subregion and the higher bodies of international cooperation (European Union, World Bank, etc.), as well as at representatives of civil society such as associations and NGOs, which use the festival as an occasion for organizing initiatives and consolidating their work with urban and village communities.

ORIGINS OF DAK'ART

MAN is born of man. Such is the law of the species. But is a biennial born of a biennial? The Venice Biennial has on occasion been presented as the model purportedly "under-developed" by Dak'Art:

> *The first Dakar Biennial was organized in 1992, again with a structure close to the pavilion model of the Venice Biennial. The first edition of Dak'Art was an international exhibition of contemporary art at which artists were grouped together by nationality. In order to select and invite foreign participants, the organizers contacted embassies, foreign cultural institutions, and international organizations, using a network linked mainly to the government and supplemented by a few personal contacts. It was therefore inevitable that the first Biennial should consecrate international political relations more than contemporary art.*[5]

This presentation of events gives Venice a great deal of importance. In fact, there were no national pavilions at the 1992 Dakar Biennial of Arts and Literature. In the catalogue, the artists were presented by country for the sake of editorial convenience, as they were again in 1996, but this did not reflect the reality of the concept or the design of the exhibition. Certainly, the cultural centers of international partners facilitated the participation of artists from the countries concerned. But the Ivorians expected at this edition did not all appear and were not registered by the government. In her report, commissioned by the European Commission, Isabelle Bosman noted: "It was announced that Africa, Europe, America, and Asia would all be taking part. The reality was that several countries, especially from Africa and Asia, were represented by only one or two works by a national based in Senegal or Europe. There were few direct relations with the countries concerned."[6]

A misconception: the Dakar Biennial has sometimes been presented as a replica of the Parisian exhibition devoted to those famous *Magiciens de la terre* held at the Centre Georges Pompidou and La Villette in 1989. Not only does this way of looking at things impute goals to Dak'Art that it does not have, but it implies that if you want to refute an exhibition put on in Paris you need not only another exhibition but a whole institution. Indeed, in 1990 or 1992, how many Senegalese even knew of the existence of *Magiciens de la terre*? And furthermore, how many Senegalese and African artists and intellectuals considered that exhibition as something that urgently needed to be refuted? In the presentation texts for the Biennial of Arts and

Literature, and then of Dak'Art, *Magiciens de la terre* is nowhere to be seen. Indeed, neither the Venice Biennial nor Documenta nor *Magiciens de la terre* has claimed to have invented Dak'Art.

So, if the Dakar Biennial is neither a replica of the Venice Biennial nor an effect of *Magiciens de la Terre*, what is its origin? Of what is it the sign? How did it attain the undeniable renown that makes it one of the important events in the calendar of international biennials, and one of the biggest cultural events in contemporary Africa?

Rather than hypothesize, I propose to consider the thoughts of the social and political players who, in the field, while at the same time inventing the conditions of their everyday survival, were dealing with the shifts and orientations that have positioned the Biennial in the contemporary history of art and of Africa. The Dakar Biennial is an avatar of the Biennial of Arts and Literature. How could it be otherwise in the home of Léopold Sédar Senghor, the first president of Senegal?

Senghor voluntarily stepped down on December 31, 1980, after a twenty-year rule, retiring to France and leaving his heir apparent, Abdou Diouf, to complete his term of office. On March 29, 1984, the former president, a founding member of the Senegalese Socialist Party, was elected to the Académie Française. This was the culmination of a long campaign waged by his friend Maurice Druon, and supported by the opportune accession to power of François Mitterrand and the French Left. In 1989 Amadou Lamine Sall, the disciple that "the bard of negritude" considered the most gifted poet of his generation, and who had followed the master in his retirement in France, returned to Senegal and to the Culture Ministry. His name remains intimately linked to the implementation of the Biennial.

In his great solicitude, President Senghor, "the poet-president" who was also a critic and patron, had provided artists with a number of structures. The regime of President Abdou Diouf, when faced with the structural adjustment programs, chose not to maintain these. Consequently, important aspects of Senghor's cultural heritage were eroded. The privatization of Les Nouvelles Éditions Africaines (NEA), the transformation of the Musée Dynamique into law courts, the termination of the aid and subventions that benefited artists and poets, the closure of the Village des Arts de la Corniche in 1983— all these acts of renunciation heightened the impression of a process of "de-Senghorization," causing much nostalgia and resentment.

Artists became increasingly militant in their attitude, albeit reluctantly. For them, the opening of the National Gallery of Arts looked like no more than a feeble consolation prize. Under the directorship of Papa Ibra Tall, a comrade of Senghor's, the National Gallery hosted a Senegalo-Afro-American exhibition that featured only a handful of Senegalese artists. Those not included reacted by organizing the first National Salon of Visual Artists.

The following year, in 1986, the Salon chose an overtly political theme: "Art against Apartheid." That year, President Abdou Diouf "made the struggle against apartheid the defining theme of his tenure."[7] Since that edition, the Salon has been placed under his patronage. The decision to organize a Biennial of Arts and Literature was announced by Diouf in October 1989. Ousseynou Wade, the second secretary general of the Dakar Biennial, links this step to the realpolitik of the time. The Diouf regime was all the more ready to lend an ear to artists' concerns because it had just completed its second structural adjustment program. It was economically more comfortable and could more easily entertain the project of a Biennial of Arts and Literature, while at the same time opening a new Village of the Arts. Then, at the awards ceremony for the Grand Prizes of the Arts and Literature on August 6, 1990, when speaking about writers and artists, the head of state stated:

> *They will be offered a new expressive framework, the Dakar Biennial. As I previously announced in this same place, Dakar will be hosting the Biennial of the Arts and Literature from December 10 to 18, 1990. This regular event will enable men of culture on this continent and in other countries to meet and communicate and to share the fascinating experience of creating and recreating. Dakar will thus offer our peoples one of those moments of fraternity when a civilization creates, thinks about what it is, and prepares to go forth and conquer its future.*[8]

TOWARDS THE PAN-AFRICAN

DAK'ART began to present itself as a Pan-African arts festival in 1996. By positioning itself in this way it took as its center of gravity the intertwining of the "History of the Dark Continent" with the more or less edifying "story-ettes" of individual or collective subjects who partly or wholly identified with its destiny while at the same time moving it forward, rather as the walking man transports and projects his own shadow. It was standing up and speaking on behalf of Africa and in the name of Africa. The Pan-African option induces a theoretical position, an argument of a philosophical nature, and a style of case-making that are not unproblematic. The Pan-African role of the Dakar Biennial reduces participation by Senegalese artists in a biennial to only a limited number of places in an event for which they fought so hard—a meager share, in fact. Those who thought themselves naturally entitled to the Biennial reluctantly found themselves confirming the proverb, "There is only one hunter, but the whole village feasts."

Becoming a Pan-African arts festival meant that the Dakar Biennial exhibited fewer and fewer Senegalese works. Thus despoiled of their birthright, many have found an effective alternative in fringe events.

For Pan-Africanism the idea of African unity or union is a question not so much of essence as of meaning. It represents a determination to confront the complexity of reality while gesturing towards a historico-mythical origin. The idea is to make Africa a living pulsation, to help it live and accept itself with as much dignity and as freely as possible, and to make the idea of African unity come alive, while keeping it from a monolithic conformism. The Cairo Biennial, which is particularly open to the Middle East and to Arab countries, hosts more artists from Europe than from sub-Saharan Africa. The Dakar Biennial bases its identity on a claim to promote African artists.

In 1995 the first Johannesburg Biennial was deliberately international, in which respect it was just like all the other biennials glittering in the firmament. Africa was its space, but in terms of time it was plugged in to the simultaneity of the global village. In Pan-Africanism, Africa was engaging with its internal and external realities, with the plasticity of its fixed and shifting identities. This was an Africa that was constantly moving, open and outspread in the complexity of its children's relation to their adoptive lands, on the one hand, and to the motherland on the other. Between, so to speak, the father-earth and the mother-earth, several nodes of memories formed, and one could choose a number of them without contradicting oneself. The new information and communication technologies have changed man's relation to space and time. Africa and Africanness have consequently been potentially reconfigured. While remaining the center of gravity for men and women who feel that they are named through its history and geography, Africa is constantly shifting on its foundations, in keeping with the movements of its children and their departures and returns. The African integration effected by Dak'Art is not only internal; it is also external. Dak'Art and events like it take on board an Africa that is open to its historic divisions and dismemberings. This approach is not authoritarian: those concerned and enrolled are only artists who recognize and accept their African origin.

The opening of Africa to its diasporas sets Africanness in motion. It also reminds us that Africa is not only a geographical reality, but also an idea. In the words of Simon Njami, "an artist like Moataz Nasr discovered that he was African when he went to Dak'Art. He didn't know that such an event existed in Dakar. He went back to Cairo with a totally new physical, intellectual, and human map of Africa."

Behind the idea of Africa is a desire for Africa, a project sustained by the ambiguous energy and unconditional love and impatience of men of action. The fact of meeting up in Africa around a Pan-African project is part of this dynamic. The experience of the Biennial and of its strengths and weaknesses helps bond all those, both Africans and non-Africans, who dearly want Africa to be respected and worthy of respect. It feeds the desire for unity. For all that, however, the idea of Africa does not need to be either real or just. For it is a more or less phantasmal representation, and believers never ask for a certificate of authenticity.

This openness affects both the form and content of Dak'Art. The diaspora has accelerated the acceptance of new styles, including video and multimedia installations and performance, both at the Dakar Biennial and around Africa. It has thus exerted all its influence on the content of selections, haunted as these were by the question of so-called international criteria. From the outset, the bulk of selected artists were Africans from Europe. The selection process in place since 1996 is founded on the applications sent directly by would-be exhibitors to the Biennial's general secretariat, and it is manifest that artists from the diaspora have been better than their continental counterparts at adding the technological trappings (transparencies, slides, then CDs) to their inherent talent, and that the quality of this presentation added to the value of their works. Better informed of artistic developments because of a more richly furnished cultural environment, better equipped, and highly motivated, they quickly develop a sublimated relation to the continent. All of this stimulates the imagination and enhances art-making. Arithmetical data aside, the artists of the diaspora show that distance can be a motivation for getting more intensely involved in the questioning of origins. More than Africans living in Africa, communities that have exported the idea of Africa feel the need to keep a living connection to the continent. Culture is one way of doing so. Between history and memory, domination and resistance, it sustains the will to survive and remember in men and women living in different contexts and time frames who, despite themselves, are reinventing their identity. Leibniz's theory of the monad offers the brilliant idea of the subject's radical singularity. As a monad, each subject sees the world from a unique viewpoint, and, to speak like Aimé Césaire, from the viewpoint of a cry that only he can articulate. Depending on the amount and quality of reflexive effort put into making his particular relation to the world intelligible, the subject helps or does not help to make the world better. But the general state of efforts produced by all, validated at every moment by God, produces the best of all possible worlds. The privilege and responsibility of artists and men of culture is that they are aware that it is their role to understand and communicate their particular relation to the world.

THE BIENNIAL: A STAGE FOR THE CONTEMPORARY

ALL art bears a relation to society. It can rehearse its cultural and moral givens and change form when its social base is irremediably transformed. The notion of contemporary art adumbrates a visual space in which societies, all societies, are encouraged to be in tune with the historical and technological changes informing artistic practices. In Africa, contemporary art has been popularized by biennials and festivals. Better than museums, which are to a great extent the prisoners of the anthropological vocation of conserving heritage, and better than galleries, which are focused on the model of the artwork as something that can be transferred to a private living room, biennials have managed to find a place for this new aesthetic that validates a certain number of operations, including the substitution of the representation of the object for its presentation, the abolition of boundaries between disciplines, the subversion of style, the destructuring of forms, the transfiguration of disciplines, the integration of new media such as photography, video, installations, and all the approaches drawing on the language but not the machinery of cinema, etc. We may note in particular that contemporary art is pursuing a radical questioning of the traditional notion of approved modernism. Henceforth distanced from the models of the demiurge and the genius, the artist no longer even needs to have talent or to exhibit a particular know-how. It is enough for him to have an idea, a concept, and to ensure that he has the means to put on a powerful and even spectacular visual presentation.

The problematic of the contemporary came to the fore at the same time as major exhibitions, such as the Dakar and Johannesburg biennials. There is a factual contiguity between contemporary art and the biennial as a specific form of exhibition. The biennial as authority and institution is an element within the contemporary art system. It designates great artists in collaboration with the active community of gallery directors, museum and non-museum curators, and critics. It is worth describing the conditions in which this element emerged. Dakar has no contemporary art museum, only a national gallery, cultural centers run in cooperation with other nations, and a few private galleries. In this environment, the event that is the Biennial holds all the power that would devolve to institutions if they existed. This state of affairs endows the Biennial with immense institutional power. In fact, the Biennial assumes and exercises the power of the museum before sharing it with curators. And there is much to be shared. The time of biennials is also the time of curators. This makes the Biennial a performative instance of the contemporaneity of art in Africa.

Biennials stage the contemporary. Indeed, they have promoted this adjective, which implies certain international criteria for the selection of artists. Consequently, the Dakar Biennial has been the home of international critics and curators who, along with a few African specialists, have articulated their version of contemporary art in Africa. This construction is based not on unanimity but on debate and confrontation.

The blockbuster exhibition fits with the modern and postmodern logic of the "society of the spectacle." In the Biennial, Senegal puts Africa on stage and attempts to negotiate a place in what Heidegger defined as the time of representation. The Dakar Biennial represents Africa not only by speaking in its name, but also by its presence in places where Africa is absent: in the supermarkets of culture and the spectacle. It also represents Africa in that it gives it a new presence: a presence in the contemporary, when Africa is endlessly associated with tradition and folklore. It represents it in a different light, so to speak: it gives it a makeover. In this respect, it is a form of resistance against residual colonialism. But at least since Cain, we have known that it is not enough to destroy the other if we want to escape the power of his gaze.

AFRICA AND THE GLOBAL

THE nineteen-nineties were characterized by a play of forces on the art system that encouraged relative optimism. The fall of the Berlin Wall and the implosion of the Eastern Bloc gave wings to the discourse of globalization. One practical effect of these discourses was precisely that more and more Africans could make themselves heard in the world of contemporary art. The first African presences at the Venice Biennial (the world's oldest) are part of this context. In 1986 Venice thus saw its first participation by artists from South Africa, which was still under the apartheid regime at the time. This signal to Africa was stronger at the 1990 edition, which included five African artists: Tapfuma Gutsa, Henry Makembera, and Muyarase from Zimbabwe, El Anatsui from Ghana, and Bruce Onobrakpeya from Nigeria. Mustapha Dimé was invited to Venice in 1992, and Ousmane Sow in 1998. These timid but regular overtures whetted African artists' appetite for visibility. Could it be said that the call for an African biennial was driven by the desire to make up for the lack of visibility of African artists? To answer this question in the affirmative would be tantamount to saying that a satisfying representation of African artists at existing biennials would have removed the need for an African biennial. However, the organization of a major cultural event is not just a solution to problems of the "artistic showroom" variety; it is also an undertaking in which human resources are mobilized and remobilized on a number of levels. A lack of visibility does not mean only that Africa is not sufficiently shown. It also implies the dubious nature of those infrequent presentations in which Africa is poorly shown and inappropriately named.

In a general context where criticism is timid, galleries rare, collectors unlikely, and the public evanescent, the Biennial helps to polarize, inject dynamism, and mediate. It provides proof that an art system can exist without a formal museum. It also makes the case for contemporary African art, illustrating its existence and showing that it can be encountered somewhere in Africa, if one makes an appointment. Another challenge is to get African art away from provincialism so that, without having to go to New York or London, an artist in Bangui or Bujumbura can become known and recognized and sell his work. Unlike other major exhibitions, such as *Magiciens de la terre,* which have aroused interest and stirred debate about contemporary African art, the Dakar Biennial is held in Africa. It stands as a concrete record of the consciousness and memory of African professionals and of the general public. It does not relate to history by proxy. It is, rather, an objective given in which the main protagonists are both Africa and the situation. One important function of Dak'Art is thus to integrate it into the distribution circuits of so-called global art, which tends to mean Western art.

Recognition of Africa by the West came slowly and late. It remains incomplete and can perhaps never be complete. The fact remains that the history of this recognition shows art and artists to have been in the vanguard of a struggle that was heavily conflictual, both symbolically and in reality. This recognition has not been without violence.[9] The recognition of African art as part of universal art is the humanist aspect of a violent practice of expropriation. At first real and brutal, this has since become more diffuse, more complex.

What is at stake in a theory of African art (and therefore of a biennial of African art such as Dak'Art) is determined around a central proposition: Africa may have in some ways been "underdeveloped" (you never know), but certainly never on the level of the arts. ●

NOTES

This essay is an abridged and translated version of several chapters of: Yacouba Konaté, *La Biennale de Dakar: Pour une esthétique de la création africaine contemporaine: Tête à tête avec Adorno* (Paris, 2009).

Translation by Charles Penwarden.

1 Éliane Burnet, "L'Africain de service: Des zoos humains aux biennales d'art contemporain," *Éthiopiques*, no. 73 (2004), http://www.refer.sn/ethiopiques/article.php3?id_article=117&artsuite=4.

2 Theodor W. Adorno, *Aesthetic Theory*, trans. Christian Lenhardt (London and New York, 1974), p. 3.

3 These budgets expected but rarely obtained by FESPACO, MASA, and Dak'Art are, respectively, two million, one and a half million, and one million euros.

4 In 2008, for the 150 professionals invited by the Biennial, including the chosen artists, 300 other professionals made the trip on their own initiative. We can therefore say that in that year, for every ticket or hotel room provided by the Biennial, two others were bought by international art professionals and cultural tourists. The Biennial also has this stimulating effect where exhibitions are concerned. In 2009 there were 160 exhibitions in the unofficial part of the event and their average budget was 5,000 euros. In all, Senegalese, African, and international cultural operators invest more money in the Biennial than do its state and international partners. The sums thus injected are of benefit in the first instance to artists, for whom Dak'Art is a space for exhibiting and selling work. It is estimated that an average of three works are sold per exhibition. Of course, not all exhibitions offer works for sale. With the average price being 1,000 euros, it's easy enough to do the math.

5 Iolenda Pensa, "Les Biennales et la géographie: Les Biennales de Venise, du Caire et de Dakar," http://io.pensa.it/node/1417.

6 Isabelle Bosman, *La Biennale internationale des arts plastiques de Dakar, 14–20 décembre 1992*, audit carried out for the European Commission, p. 14.

7 Abdou Sylla, *Arts plastiques et état au Sénégal: Trente-cinq ans du mécénat au Sénégal* (Dakar, 1998), p. 138, n. 89.

8 Ibid., p. 148.

9 The violence of seizure and theft was still in evidence when the Dakar–Djibouti mission led by Marcel Griaule with, among others, Michel Leiris crossed Africa in 1929. To put it simply, while in Paris the Cubists were celebrating "negro" sculptures, scientific missions were confiscating and stealing objects from "the natives," working under the immunity provided by the colonial administration.

WHAT IS A BIENNIAL?

POTENTIALS, FUNCTIONS, AND IDEALS

THE UNSTABLE INSTITUTION (2003)

Carlos Basualdo

IN 1531, Titian bought a house with a garden on Venice's north side near the lagoon, and from here, on a clear day, he could make out the mountains that surrounded his hometown of Pieve di Cadore. Biri Grande, in the parish of San Canciano, no longer exists. The Fondamente Nuove, half a mile of docks along the island's northern edge, were built in its place just a few years after the artist's death. For unprepared pedestrians walking along the docks, the chance of seeing the Alps is but an amusing stroke of luck. And to be sure, the smog and haze seem to conspire so as to limit the landscape to the classic silhouettes of Italian cypresses in the San Michele Cemetery and some campanile or other on the island of Murano. But nevertheless, they are there. I can attest that the day we left Venice, we were deliciously surprised to see, from the vantage point of the boat that took us to the airport with all our baggage, the contours of the Alps.

Even things most categorically evident can occasionally seem invisible—not because they do not exist, but rather because, in particular moments, some act of intellectual conjuring, some configuration of action and thought, manages to conceal them from the horizon of perception. Paradoxically, I have the impression that something similar happens with large-scale international art exhibitions. It is not that they literally become invisible, since they are, precisely, a staging of enormous mechanisms of visibility, but rather that the singularity of their meaning seems to hide itself from the myriad journalists, critics, historians, and pundits, who, as one might imagine, come to be their privileged spectators.[1] Of course, I am not saying that these events do not stir up opinion. On the contrary, opinions abound, but not because there exists any set of common criteria that can be used to evaluate this genre of events. For example, a review of critical articles about the most recent editions of the Venice Biennial and Documenta in Kassel reveals enormous discrepancies, not so much in regard to the shows themselves, but rather in regard to the expectations that the realms of criticism and journalism bring to these events. Critics' insistence on setting aside the explicit intentions that, in accordance with the organizers' criteria, are used to justify the realization and subject matter of the shows would not, in itself, be so serious, especially if this were a voluntary stance. But the fact the shows are analyzed from perspectives that ultimately make these intentions invisible is, indeed, something to be taken seriously. One gets the impression, for example, that many critics respond indignantly to any suggestion of subordinating the individual works to an overly complex thematic frame—as if the primary function of these shows were to free art from intellectual overdetermination. In other cases, it is the absence of theme itself, or its frequent extra-artistic ramifications, given serious consideration—in spite of the fact that, quite often, these side-programs are structurally constitutive elements in the explicit goals of the organizers. Such a survey of the bibliography might be amusing, were it not a truly uncomfortable and even, at times, rather melancholy exercise.[2] Not only can one often reproach journalistic reviews for their numerous errors and omissions, but in many cases, a careful reading allows us to deduce that the author was not even able to visit the entire show. It should be acknowledged, however, that many of these events are simply not designed to be seen in their totality, on account of both their sheer size and the fact that they are made up of a large number of components, so that a comprehensive visit would take much more time than for other shows. Critics tend to ignore this explicit intentionality and merely react with disdain, without stopping to analyze the possible consequences of such neglect. The lack of a frame of reference to help us interpret these events becomes ever more evident, even as its development becomes more urgent. Without a frame of reference to validate it, the kind of specific operation carried out by these shows in the field of art and culture is barely, if at all, perceptible through the opinions of a host of commentators. Titian's mountains blend into the mist that conceals and disguises them. From the printed page, we discern only the repeated, interchangeable silhouettes of cypresses.

In comparison to the rivers of ink these shows unleash in both the specialized press and the mass media, the academic critical literature specifically tackling these events is relatively scarce: barely a dozen books, in two or three languages, published largely in the last decade.[3] Perhaps the two phenomena are related. Shows like Documenta or the Venice Biennial have acquired an unprecedented visibility in contemporary art—a field of culture that, until recently, was of interest, almost exclusively, to a more or less limited group of specialists. Such visibility suddenly turns these shows into desirable and even, on occasion, income-generating instruments for the political and corporate sectors. At the same time, it makes them anathema precisely for the intellectual spheres whose analytical capacity should (supposedly) elucidate their current meaning and possible potential. Of the few voices from academic circles that mention these events, the majority tends to be discrediting. Most view these shows as epiphenomena of mass culture, an indisputable symptom of the culture industry's assimilation of the project of the avant-garde—as spectacles, pure and simple, whose logic is nothing more than that of late-stage capitalism, in other words, the progressive suppression of the multiple system of values and its translation into a universal equivalent, namely, exchange value. In a way, this analytic trend implies that the oppositional nature, which characterizes the critical project in modernity, is largely foreign to the kind of exhibition that is unequivocally associated with the realms of marketing and consumption. Following this line of reasoning to the end, we may conclude that the apparent lack of criteria that journalistic criticism underscores when discussing such events is nothing more than a symptom of the expiration of its traditional function in this specific stage of the development of the culture industry.

The emergency of art criticism paralleled the formation of an international circuit in which artists, galleries, and museums each found their own places. Clearly, academic criticism, linked to universities (and, overwhelmingly, to the discipline of art history), finds its place in the same system as yet another institutional mooring. Artistic modernity is thus presented as a constellation of specific practices and institutional settings charged with discerning—and assigning—the relative values that incorporate them. The ensemble is determined by a certain way of representing the singularity of its own history and articulating the value system it produces. These institutional instances regulate the relationships between individual constituent parts, while at the same time restricting their freedom. Naturally, this assembly is not synchronic; it was not produced all at once. Instead, it is a more or less unstable product of a series of historical processes that, like sedimentary strata, eventually paired off slowly in order to produce, finally, an impression of totality. For their survival, institutions require the illusion of everlastingness, since this is what safeguards them, in the final analysis, against their contingent character. In Western countries, modern art was thought to be structured around the relative balance between a number of institutions founded on a common history or histories, that is to say, on shared values. In this order of things, the tension between production and the market finds a sort of referee in criticism and museums.[4] We could say, very schematically, that the duty of criticism has been to inscribe production into a symbolic field in a way that simultaneously makes it accessible to the effects of the mechanisms of the production of exchange value, while the duty of art history has been to recover the specific differential in the work that hinders its complete subordination to exchange value. Of the two, it was the institution of the museum—which from its origins has had a fundamentally ideological character—that sanctioned the value of the work as an exchange value, but not without first disguising it, hiding it in the folds of a particular historical narrative that the museum was supposedly responsible for preserving and intensifying.[5] Clearly, it is not difficult to imagine how any exhibition or production of works that lacks a direct association with galleries or museums—and which, even if it maintains dialogue with both the market and history, does not really meet the expectations of either—may suddenly become at least partially illegible for the system in which it is supposed to operate.

But at this point I should clarify the types of events to which I am referring. Are we dealing with large-scale shows in general? Or with the international biennial circuit? Perhaps more importantly, are we dealing with a characterization that exclusively concerns the size of the exhibition—that is, the size of its budget and the number of works included—or could this also have to do with other factors, such as the nature of the institutional framework that generates such events? Although an archeology of the large-scale international exhibition model would include many shows organized by more conventional art institutions, it seems fair to argue that biennials are the most exemplary. At first glance, biennials seem to have only their name in common. The Venice Biennial was first held at the end of the nineteenth century; it was modeled on the world expositions that had been so popular throughout that century. It would take five more decades and two world wars to found the São Paulo Biennial, which, like Venice's, continues to take place. In the brief interlude of fifteen years from 1984 (the year of the first Havana Biennial) to the end of the twentieth century, more than fifteen international biennials were established, including Istanbul (1987), Lyon (1992), Santa Fe (1995), Gwangju (1995), Johannesburg (1995), Shanghai (1996), Berlin (1996), and Montreal (1998).[6] Moreover, the specific circumstances under which these shows were established are extremely diverse; the same can be said of their resources and of the attraction they hold for both the specialist press and the general media. The Venice Biennial was the model for the São Paulo Biennial, whose initial function was to establish itself, alongside that of Venice and the Carnegie International (founded in 1896), as a world-scale event that could put its city—and country—on the map of modern culture. In 1984, the first Havana Biennial had a very explicit ideological goal: to stimulate communication between artists and intellectuals of the southern hemisphere, so as to keep the centers of economic power from monopolizing the distribution of contemporary art. Havana's success was capitalized on by a number of subsequent biennials, which had the obvious function of giving visibility to local production and promoting the cities and countries that hosted them.

Nearly all shows of this type rely on the official financial support of their respective countries or cities. A marketing component is, then, common to all of them; it is a question of publicizing the artistic and cultural potential of a city, country, or region. Few, perhaps, have been as ideologically marked in their origins as the Havana Biennial and, of course, Documenta, which has been held since 1955—initially, every four years, and now, every five—in the German city of Kassel. On the one hand, Documenta is a fortunate byproduct of the Cold War, while on the other, it was created from the need for postwar Germany to bring itself up to date with the evolution of modern and contemporary art and leave behind the painful excesses and omissions of Nazism—which, among other things, affected the practice and appreciation of modern art in that country.[7] In all these shows, however, diplomacy, politics, and commerce converge in a powerful movement, the purpose of which seems to be the appropriation and instrumentalization of the symbolic value of art. The specific motives change—Venice was originally concerned with updating a universalist ideology clearly related to European colonialism; Havana, by contrast, staged an ideological project that was diametrically opposed to this—but the type of operation is, curiously, the same. Another point of agreement consists in the fact that the majority of these shows emphasize the internationalist nature of cultural and artistic production. This is not a question of sharing a unified vision, but rather of considering internationalism as a term literally in dispute, capable of being interpreted specifically in highly diverse ways. The nature of the interests that generate the events and their common commitment to the possible horizon of internationalism seem to associate them in an intimate way with the ups and downs of modernity—and with the range of its possible interpretations. Their unstable nature—somewhat tentative, incomplete, and always subject to negotiation and readaptation—merely reinforces this tie.

In 1983, barely a year before the first edition of the Havana Biennial—the success of which contributed to the subsequent proliferation of such exhibitions—Professor Theodore Levitt of Harvard University wrote in the *Harvard Business Review:* "The globalization of markets is at hand." This was one of the first texts to use a term that would become increasingly commonplace in the years that followed. The globalization to which Levitt referred consisted in extending the logic of economies of scale to the planetary level; it was grounded in the presumed worldwide convergence of consumer tastes. In an article written for the twentieth anniversary of the publication of Levitt's text, Richard Tomkins observes: "Prof. Levitt's message was simple. As new technology extended the reach of global media and brought down the cost of communications, the world was shrinking. As a result, consumer tastes everywhere were converging, creating global markets for standardized products on a previously unimagined scale."[8] The publication of Levitt's essay coincided with a period of market openness that still continues today, although in a less pronounced way. In predicting a convergence of consumer tastes, Levitt did not seem to take into account the fact that, through the spread of new technologies and the ever more decentralized use of information, the nature of demand itself becomes more specialized. From our current perspective, we could state that the value of Levitt's thesis consists mainly in its symptomatic character. Coinciding with the information revolution that took place with the Internet (and the progressive development of communications in general), Levitt's essay foresaw a period of progressive integration on a world level, although not decentralization. In the area of contemporary art, that phenomenon is reflected precisely in the growing proliferation of this unstable institution of the large-scale international exhibition. One could venture the hypothesis that the biennials that have emerged in the last two decades have done so completely in tune with these transformations, as a result of the contrast between the tendency toward centralization, typical of the integration of markets on a global scale, and the increasing dissemination of information, which provides growing visibility for local situations and problems. Such tension, obviously, is an essential component for institutions whose aim, to a large extent, consists precisely in its representation and analysis.

It is evident that these institutions have been created with a distinct instrumental purpose: to respond to the interests that brought them about—in other words, to promote the contexts in which they take place, giving them greater international visibility, supplying them with a patina of prestige, and ratifying the supposed commitment of these different contexts to modernity and, more specifically, to the processes of economic integration associated with late capitalism. The aura of prestige that surrounds art in general—and modern and contemporary art in particular—is perfectly suited to this task. What is instrumentalized in the large-scale international exhibition is precisely the symbolic capital of modern art, tied to its own presumed autonomy and independence from market logic. Following this line of reasoning, we could reach the paradoxical conclusion that the relationship between the supposed aim of art biennials and the traditional function of museums will eventually be one of simple continuity. The symbolic value created initially by museums—as a concealed affirmation of the exchange value of objects and artistic practices—is ultimately transformed by biennials into pure utility. Perhaps this was (and, in some cases, may still be) the (ultimately naive) reasoning of many of the institutions that founded biennials. And in some cases, such reasoning may even be partially justified. Nevertheless, this equation assumes a total equivalence between what is exhibited in museums and what is exhibited at biennials. Furthermore, it assumes an agreement between the conceptual and ideological frameworks of both types of institution. Both these assumptions are erroneous.

The configuration of interests at the core of institutions like biennials clearly differs from that that gave rise to the institutional circuit traditionally linked to modernity in art (museums, art criticism, and galleries). The commercial fate of the works, for example, is neither evident nor even strictly necessary in biennials, for the simple reason that the bulk of the financing behind the event and the production of many of the projects is largely independent of art collecting (either private or state-funded). This facilitates the inclusion of practices of a nonobjectual nature, as well as works of an interdisciplinary nature and even practices pertaining to other fields of cultural production, such as cinema, design, architecture, etc.; indirectly, this ultimately stimulates the problematization of the notion of art as an autonomous activity. The inclusion of works of an interdisciplinary nature, as well as the persistent integration of discursive elements in these kinds of events, has become increasingly a constant.[9] Moreover, the sheer size of these shows—which is necessary to achieve the marketing impact expected of them—makes their insertion into highly particularized interpretative systems an absolute necessity. Without these systems, the shows would lose their ability to communicate as discrete singularities; that is, they would lack all identity. In many cases, it is even manifestly expected that the conceptual framework charged with giving these events legibility is related to local issues—at least as far as the inclusion of elements tied to the local culture is concerned. Consequently, the figure of the curator emerges as the event's conceptual organizer. In comparison with the traditional role of the museum curator, this more recent incarnation seems to be endowed with greater autonomy. It is no longer a question of the discerning critic or interpretive historian examining a specific tradition, but rather of a relatively unfamiliar figure who must negotiate the distance between, on the one hand, the value system traditionally established by critic and art historian and, on the other, the ideological pressures and practices corresponding to the institutional setting in which such events emerge. But this specific incarnation of the curator is no accident; inasmuch as these are art professionals who must respond to a variety of extra-artistic conditions and questions, their work is necessarily different from that of those who preceded them.[10] The type of knowledge they put into practice becomes less and less retrievable from the perspective of the critic or art historian, even if this is still a highly particular and specific kind of knowledge. The chain of meaning that makes sense of the group of practices assembled for such a show will necessarily be constructed around an interrogation of local histories and contexts, though always in terms of their possible relationship to the presumed internationalist horizon. The curator's work is riddled with, and overdetermined by, such problems. Perhaps we could say that the curator's ability to produce a highly differentiated form of knowledge is related to his or her degree of fidelity to the entire matrix of unique situations surrounding curatorial practice. This type of work thus implies the articulation of a reflection capable of linking forms of local culture and history with the horizon of internationalism that appears as a founding element in these events. Finally, partially freed—or better yet, forcibly liberated—from the constrictions associated with the supposed autonomous nature of artistic production, the curator finds him- or herself in the position, and with the need, to expand not only the canonical apparatus that articulates the historical narratives linked to the production of modern and contemporary art, but also the very definition of that which constitutes the artistic practice in a specific context.[11]

Paradoxically, the presumed instrumental nature of biennials may thus serve as a way to try out a series of operations whose scope is, for the most part, radical when considered within the institutional context traditionally linked to (Western) modern and contemporary art. We could classify these operations synthetically into two types: revisionist efforts, which lead to a reconsideration of the canonical mechanisms established in the historical narratives produced, almost exclusively, in Europe and the United States; and the exploration of the position of the artwork in the wider cultural context in connection with a variety of symbolic practices to which it is not usually thought to be related. An exhaustive revision of the canon and a reexamination of the autonomous nature of the work of art are actually two sides of the same coin, since an inquiry into the mechanisms that structure art history's narrative will inexorably lead us to consider historical discourse as highly ideologized and, therefore, the inevitable result of the intersection of heterogeneous and diverse practices and interests. The relationship with the local context, which is usually mandatory in these events, becomes an opportunity to exercise the historical revisionism that, in the final analysis, inescapably ends with a questioning of the ideological base that articulates the institutions of artistic modernity. With respect to the traditional institutional structure, large-scale international exhibitions can act as a kind of surreptitious short circuit. Their supposed instrumentality, signaled by a sector of academic criticism as a function of their dependence on the culture industry, could, conversely, be revealed as a juncture that facilitates the expansion of the canon and the exploration of an expanded notion of what presumes to be the artistic practice of a specific context. Needless to say, although this range of possibilities appears inscribed in the very institutional structure of such events, there is no guarantee of their realization. The figure responsible for actualizing this range of possibilities is, inevitably, the event curator. And this is because the determinations that could guarantee the effectiveness of the curatorial practice for this type of show are in no way predetermined by the institutional framework in which this practice is carried out—unlike what happens when a curator joins the traditional structure of the museum. The curator's inevitable lead role in such shows has recently given the position an exaggerated, and clearly equivocal, level of visibility in the cultural field. But this is a question of misunderstood celebrity status. Whether the curator is a mere instrument of the culture industry or a recent incarnation of the model of the independent intellectual, the possible range into which his or her decisions are introduced is at once remarkably vast and dangerously undefined.

The invisibility I spoke of the beginning of this text clearly applies to the position these shows occupy with respect to the traditional circuit of criticism, the museum, and galleries. Large-scale international exhibitions never completely belong to the system of art institutions in which they are supposedly inscribed, and the range of practical and theoretical possibilities to which they give rise often turns out to be subversive—let's not forget that museums are, first and foremost, Western institutions, and that the global expansion of large-scale exhibitions performs an insistent de-centering of both the canon and artistic modernity. Increasingly, one has the impression that the vitality of such shows seems to be a direct function of the number of visitors they attract and the dissemination they achieve in the media, and have an inverse relationship to the appreciation of specialized criticism; in terms of the politics of exclusion historically enacted by the institutions of modernity, large-scale exhibitions could perhaps be seen as occupying a role similar to that of theater in the High Renaissance, namely as "a force for the breakdown of class distinctions, even for democratization."[12] This vitality is, undoubtedly, the best guarantee of their survival. To a large extent, the conceptual horizon opened by such shows as the two most recent editions of Documenta or the first Havana Biennial remains largely unexplored. There is no doubt, however, that many aspects associated with such events have been partially absorbed and recycled by museums and galleries—a process that, while not at all recent, has visibly accelerated over the last decade. In this short span of time, for instance, a significant number of artists have, effectively, been incorporated into the canonical narrative of the postwar period. Many conventional museums have resorted to the implementation of biennial or triennial showcases as a way to increase the number of their visitors and attract the attention of the press. In some cases, the international exhibition's clear and direct influence on the traditional institutional circuit can be confirmed; in others, it is more a question of partial coincidences in the development of independent (though undoubtedly simultaneous) processes, inasmuch as that the form of internationalism we call "globalization" increasingly determines the financing and programming of a large segment of the museums in Europe and the United States. Beyond these transformations and a sense of the growing interdependence between traditional modern-art institutions and the mega-exhibition, there is still, it seems, no appropriate framework for analyzing all the implications of the large-scale exhibition. These events are constantly evaluated only in terms of the logic of institutions of modernity and not in relation to the challenges they embody. A proper historical account of the emergence of these institutions is still to be written. A clearer understanding of the implications arising from their interrogation of both the canon and the modern notion of the autonomy of art is no less essential. Although the project of the formulation of alternative versions of (Western) modernity seems to have been a driving force for many of these institutions from the start, the implications of such a radical move have not yet been theorized. The development of large-scale exhibitions can be associated with the economic and informational transformation of late capitalism—such as the expansion of tourism on a global scale and the concurrent rise in the number of museum visitors worldwide—in other words, an increasing democratization of culture, characterized by an increasing intermingling of education and entertainment. Large-scale exhibitions could well represent a possible response to these phenomena from the cultural field. Nevertheless, there is little understanding of the role they play in the culture industry and among institutions of artistic modernity. Their contribution to the cultural field has barely been taken into account. Perhaps it is precisely this sort of inquiry that would give these events the visibility they need if, among other things, we are to articulate an effective reform of the institutions of modernity.[13] ●

NOTES

Previously published in: Marieke van Hal, Viktor Misiano, and Igor Zabel "Biennials," special issue, *MJ–Manifesta Journal* 2 (Winter 2003–Fall 2004), pp. 50–61. This essay was commissioned in 2002 by the Philadelphia Exhibitions Initiative, a program of The Pew Center for Arts & Heritage, as part of: Paula Marincola (ed.), *Questions of Practice: What Makes a Great Exhibition?* (Philadelphia, 2006).

Translation by Vincent Martin.

1 It is important to note that one of the motives for writing this text stems from my participation, in various capacities, in three of the exhibitions mentioned: as a panelist in the "100 Days–100 Guests" program at Documenta 10 in 1997, and as a member of the curatorial teams of Documenta 11 (2002) and the fiftieth Venice Biennial (2003). In particular, my work on the latter two events allowed me to interact intimately with both their organizational and their conceptual aspects. This text largely stems from my embarrassment and grief before the enormous disparity and lack of analytical rigor in a good many of the reactions by the general and specialized press to these shows.

2 For a paradigmatic historical example of this kind of coverage, see Bruce Kurtz, "Documenta: A Critical Preview," *Arts Magazine* 46, no. 8 (Summer 1972), p. 30, which contains, in a nutshell, most of the usual misunderstandings of such events.

3 Although a profuse bibliography on museums certainly exists, there seems to be no single publication devoted solely to the subject of large-scale international exhibitions. Some of the more recent publications on the subject of exhibitions and curatorial practice are: Bruce Altshuler, *The Avant-Garde in Exhibition: New Art in the 20th Century* (New York, 1994); Emma Barker (ed.), *Contemporary Cultures of Display* (New Haven, 1999); Reesa Greenberg, Bruce W. Ferguson, and Sandy Nairne (eds.), *Thinking about Exhibitions* (London, 1996); Bernard Guelton, *L'Exposition: Interprétation et réinterprétation* (Paris, 1997); Anna Harding (ed.), *Curating: The Contemporary Art Museum and Beyond* (London, 1997); Susan Hiller and Sarah Martin (eds.), *The Producers: Contemporary Curators in Conversation*, 4 vols. (Gateshead, 2000–03); Katharina Hegewisch and Bern Klüser (eds.), *L'Art de l'exposition: Une documentation sur trente expositions exemplaires du XXe siècle* (Paris, 1998); Carin Kuoni (ed.), *Words of Wisdom: A Curator's Vade Mecum on Contemporary Art* (New York, 2001); Paula Marincola (ed.), *Curating Now: Imaginative Practice / Public Responsibility* (Philadelphia, 2001); Dorothee Richter and Eva Schmidt (eds.), *Curating Degree Zero: An International Curating Symposium* (Bonn, 1999).

4 A complementary account of a tension (over such issues of taste and value) between the audience and an institution devoted to public education and the promotion of art can be found in Seth Koven, "The Whitechapel Picture Exhibitions and the Politics of Seeing," in Daniel J. Sherman and Irit Rogoff (eds.), *Museum Culture: Histories, Discourses, Spectacles* (Minneapolis, 1994), pp. 22–48.

5 See Theodor Adorno, "Valéry Proust Museum," in idem, *Prisms*, trans. Samuel and Shierry Weber (Cambridge [MA], 1981), pp. 173–85.

6 See Paula Latos-Valier, "Biennales Big and Small," in *Info* (newsletter of the twenty-fifth Biennial of Graphic Art, Ljubljana) (2003).

7 For a discussion of the connection between the first Documenta and the Nazis' "Degenerate Art" exhibition, see Walter Grasskamp, "'Degenerate Art' and Documenta 1: Modernism Ostracized and Disarmed," in Sherman and Rogoff 1994 (see note 4), pp. 163–94. In Grasskamp's view, the tensions between Documenta as an art institution exemplary of postwar Germany and the questions the Nazis posed to modern art were acknowledged, ultimately, and only by implication, by the curatorial team of Documenta 5 in 1972.

8 Richard Tomkins, "Happy Birthday, Globalization," *The Financial Times*, May 6, 2003.

9 One only need mention the examples of "100 Days–100 Guests" at Documenta 10, the four "Platforms" at Documenta 11, and the events surrounding the "Archive of Contemporaneity" at the fiftieth Venice Biennial.

10 See Karsten Schubert, *The Curator's Egg: The Evolution of the Museum Concept from the French Revolution to the Present Day* (London, 2000). In the last section of this informative overview of the history of museums in the West, Schubert devotes several chapters to the changes in the role of curators in the last three decades. Although his observations are primarily concerned with museum curators, they could well be inspired by—and, indeed, seem to pertain even more to—the transformation of the curatorial role with respect to large-scale international exhibitions.

11 The consideration of art as an autonomous activity certainly leads to the inclusion of highly specialized practices in historical narratives. When this framework disappears as a prime intellectual motive, it becomes possible—and to a large extent, compulsory—to explore an expanded field of cultural production, since it would be a matter of understanding artistic practices in their possible relationships to the systems of power (economic, political, and social) that would support these kinds of shows. To a certain extent, we could say that Documenta 10 thematized precisely this process of canon revision.

12 William J. Bouwsma, *The Waning of the Renaissance: 1550–1640* (New Haven, 2000), p. 131. An interesting parallel could be drawn between the emergence of theater as a cultural practice in the High Renaissance and the position occupied by large-scale international exhibitions in today's cultural landscape. Originally distrusted because of their connections to spectacle and commerce, both phenomena experience artistic evolution partially as a function of their growing popularity, exemplifying the complex relationship between culture and spectacle that the institutions of modernity have traditionally rejected.

13 A number of institutions founded in the postwar period and dedicated to exhibiting modern and contemporary art were once not so different from the large-scale events I have been discussing, at least if we consider their original aims. One particularly remarkable example is that of the Centre Pompidou, which was established as an interdisciplinary laboratory for research on modern and contemporary cultural production. Although, while under the direction of Pontus Hulten, the Pompidou's activities seemed headed toward satisfying this goal, the center later began gradually to change into a more or less conventional modern art museum. On rare occasions, some exhibitions still display certain interdisciplinary and revisionist elements, but even so, these do not dominate the program as a whole.

THE BIENNIAL IN 1968 (1969)

Lawrence Alloway

THE BIENNIAL AND OTHER EXHIBITIONS

IN 1968, in addition to the Biennial in Venice, there were 112 other official exhibitions and fairs in Italy, some international, some local. The subjects ranged from an International Aeronautical Show in Venice to an International Container Convention in Genoa, and from automation in Milan to children's books in Bologna.[1] The contents of the Biennial are works of art, and for this reason, we tend to reserve them from participation in this orgy of contact and communication. We tend to relate them to humanism rather than to the competitive area of fairs and shows. For reasons that will emerge later, our preference has been for works of art as symbols of permanence rather than as complex structures subject to numerous interpretations. However, art is physically and conceptually mobile, which means that it can be seen in various contexts. As it is subject to the communications network of our time, physically or in terms of reproductive processes, some of art's talismanic solidity is reduced by the increase in connectivity. A work that was executed for a chapel, and stays there, can be connected with fewer artworks and environments than a work that is movable. Even here, the imaginary museum of photographs makes possible the recontextualizing of the most sacred and monumental art. The Venice Biennial is not only a demonstration of art's contextual shifts; it is, during a period of unprecedented exhibition activity, the major institution.

The 1966 Biennial showed 2,785 works by artists from 37 countries; attendance was 181,383, with 800 art critics, journalists, and free-wheelers in addition. Sales amounted to around 141,684,690 lire. These figures indicate the magnitude of the exhibition. It is large enough to bring into the foreground our ideas about the artist and his audience, the relation of the individual to the new scale and speed of international communications. Those who gravitate to an elitist view of art regard the Biennial's abundance as a dilution of art's neat essence. On the other hand, left-wing critics oppose the show too, because of the preponderance of international styles without manifest social usefulness.

What I propose here is an outline of the Biennial as an organization, one that in its history touches on unsettled problems of art in society. There are many studies of artists, schools of art, media, and iconography, but not much has been written on the distribution of art. The groups that artists formed in the past to organize their own profession have been thoroughly investigated,[2] but their more recent means of contact with an increasingly large public have been less discussed. The tendency is to study the work of art as an object, rather than as part of a communication system. As an entity in time the Biennial has been adaptive to social and politic change; it has changed basically at least three times, but it has not lost its core identity, its legibility as an institution.

In addition to the solid shows, such as the Venice Biennial, there are some that, though large, only simulate the reality of the other. It is important to clarify the comparative value of such exhibitions. Consider the Salon International de Galeries-pilotes, held at the Musée Cantonal des Beaux-Arts, Lausanne. A pilot gallery is defined as one that is devoted to the discovery of talent rather than to its merchandising, or one not identified with a constant aesthetic position. Betty Parsons in New York is an example of the former, and Denise René in Paris of the latter. At Lausanne all expenses are carried by the participating galleries, and indeed, they install their own sections. Under the circumstances rigorous control would be needed if the exhibition were to be more than simply a source of prestige for the galleries and an inexpensive show for the museum. In the first Lausanne exhibition, the Galerie Svensky-Franska, for instance, showed the work of Wols and Yves Klein. The most that could be claimed, however, is that this gallery had been the first to show them in Sweden, for the artists had already been exhibited elsewhere by that time. Thus the exhibition is a form of concealed advertising, but one likely to impress gallery clients unfamiliar with the facts.

The position of the São Paulo Biennial is more complex. The exhibition space is like an abandoned factory, and the location, out of the town, is unknown to most of the residents; the exhibition is attended only by people directly engaged in the operation. It is not, in the full sense of the word, a public exhibition at all; it is more like a convention in a remote place. Of course, the prize can be a desirable episode in an artist's ascending career, and the catalogues are circulated as evidence of the show's having taken place. As an exhibition, however, it is a kind of fiction with extensions into reality in the form of catalogues and prizes. What the catalogue can amount to is shown by the 165-page book published by the National Collection of Fine Arts on the occasion of the ninth Biennial.[3] Harold Rosenberg, who attended the opening of the sixth, has recorded its disorganization and lack of substantial art. He lumps together "the São Paulo and Venice biennials,"[4] but the comparison is absurd. It serves, in fact, to underline the accessibility of Venice, the solidity of the organization, and the high caliber of some of the exhibitions as well as of the total effect, which is, often, a profile of current trends.

THE BIENNIAL AS A STRUCTURE

THE status of the Biennial, founded in 1895 by the City of Venice, was fixed by a law of December 24, 1928, No. 3229, in which the exhibition was declared an autonomous agency ("ente autonomo"). The Agency was to provide the organization that previously had been the responsibility of the city, and the city was to hand over the exhibition buildings. The financing was to be provided by the government, the city of Venice, and the profits of the exhibition (admissions, commission on sales, catalogue receipts).[5] The law, signed by Vittorio Emanuele III and Mussolini, directed that a five-man commission be appointed to administer the Agency. It was a typical piece of Fascist reorganization aimed at greater efficiency, and it worked.

The commission's President was Giuseppe Volpi di Misurata, and he turned out to be the right man, in some respects, to preserve the stability of the organization. For one thing, he had ties of friendship with the organizers and artists of the early Biennial, such as Riccardo Selvatico, Antonio Fradeletto, and Ettore Tito, although the phase of taste that they represented was played out by the nineteen-twenties. That Volpi accepted a traditionalist view of painting and sculpture is clear from the exhibitions during his administration. Under Fascism the range of the Biennial as an international affair diminished as a tough Italian nationalism gained confidence. However, Volpi increased the scope of the Biennial by expanding into other arts. In 1930 a biennial, then annual, Music Festival began, and in 1932, a "Convegno di Poesia" (which awarded a prize to Giuseppe Ungaretti), but it did not survive a second meeting in 1934. The great success of the expansion of the Biennial was the Mostra Internazionale d'Arte Cinematografica in 1932. The cultural benefits to Italy, the conversion of so many professionals into tourists or tourist attractions and, maybe, the patriotism expressed in the Italian art in the Biennial itself, led to official recognition of the Agency's importance. A Royal Decree of 1938 allocated additional funds and sanctioned the positions of Volpi and Antonio Maraini, the Secretary General. The structure of the Biennial, whether run by the city or as a separate agency, remained constant: massive Italian coverage at the center of autonomous national exhibitions. This form, susceptible to drastic changes of content, has proved capable of absorbing cultural and political shifts without damage to the stability of the exhibition.

THE PAVILIONS

THE pavilions in the Giardini, where the exhibition is housed, are erected by each country and the styles are a vivid array of national self-images. As the pavilions are occasional architecture, they are more demonstrative than buildings put up for continuous use; they are frivolous, but sensitive to the cultures from which they originate. At a large exhibition, the total effect, the sum of the physical plant and its content of individual works, has a meaning. To look only for the pure art content within the circus of material display at large-scale shows confuses this meaning. Such an approach leads to a constant antagonism between the containing system and the exhibits contained. The exhibition itself, as we shall argue later, has a structure, and hence a message, as much as the art that it shows. Here we can approach the architecture as a model of nonverbal communication, somewhat like an exhibition. The pavilions, built and rebuilt at various times, can be divided into categories of folkloric, classicizing, and international. The Hungarian pavilion is folkloric, with a monumental Art Nouveau/Romanesque door, encrusted with four-star folk art; so is the Soviet pavilion, with dormer windows and bulging ornament, like a product of Western influence on conservative Slavic workmen. The Greek pavilion has a façade along the lines of a Byzantine basilica, with patterned brick that makes the surface look like Harris tweed. Equally folkloric is the pseudo-classicism of the Central Pavilion façade and the Italian-designed galleries across the Canal di Sant'Elena, which house Romania, the UAR (or RAU in Italy), and Yugoslavia. Flattened columns without capitals, empty niches, shallow curves: this is the streamlined classicism of official Fascist architecture, rhetorical but austere. The big portico with square columns and pinched entrance steps of the German pavilion is in the Nazi version of the style.

The classical styles are all highly indicative of their countries. Across from the Olympic Games classicism of the German pavilion is the post–Petit Trianon French pavilion, with a portico on an oval plan and delicate detailing. Between these two buildings is the British pavilion, with high steps leading up to a wide loggia, where bricks and white columns raise instant memories of Georgian style. It looks like an Italianate English country house. The American pavilion, with its tiny dome and miniature symmetrical wings, is Colonial neoclassic, halfway between Monticello and Howard Johnson. The Danish pavilion is a sharp and austere Neoclassical revival building, a reminder that Thorwaldsen has a museum dedicated to him in Copenhagen. International style shows in various forms: the Spanish pavilion, self-contained in solid walls, has a Frank Lloyd Wright look, as does the Swiss pavilion, long and low, with factory-studio windows ranged above. Later forms of international style are shown by Japan's pavilion, a dizzying bit of cantilevering entered through the *piloti*, and by Brazil's, a glass and wood box entered by a jutting concrete tunnel. Canada has built an intricate wigwam of glass and wood around a tree, presumably to symbolize a love of nature. In truth, perhaps all the pavilions are, to some extent, folkloric.

ORGANIZATION AND INFLUENCE

IN discussing an exhibition as large as the Biennial, and as important, it is necessary to confront the rumors and suspicions that are triggered every two years. The selection of the artists and the awarding of the prizes are, of course, the sensitive areas. That the choice of artists can be problematic is shown by the recent history of the United States pavilion, but the problems are administrative tangles well within the power struggles normal to institutions. The American pavilion is now sponsored by the National Collection of Fine Arts (NCFA) in the Smithsonian Institution, Washington; it decides on the museums to be invited to arrange government-backed art shows. In 1966 the invitation was issued to the Guggenheim Museum in New York and later withdrawn. According to the curator of international exhibitions in Washington, "The proposals they have finally submitted would involve expense of such magnitude that we could not undertake at this late date to raise the funds for it."[6] In 1968 an invitation was issued to the Los Angeles County Museum for Venice and then withdrawn, too. According to David Scott, director of the NCFA, "Los Angeles' was an interesting proposal but it came late, and when it did it wasn't worked out enough. On the other hand, the Geske proposal fit cleanly into our budgetary requirements."[7]

In both cases, lateness and expense are cited because they are inarguable and tolerably polite reasons. (There was a diversion in the case of Los Angeles when Edward Kienholz, a protest assemblagist included in the proposed list of artists, was rumored to be the reason for Washington's withdrawal, but he was not.) Scott said, a bit airily: "I frankly don't remember whether Kienholz was in the Los Angeles proposal.... I know they had lots of trouble over his show in Los Angeles last year, but that sort of thing never bothers us."[8] The argument about expense is doubtful, but the lateness is unquestionable. In both cases the delay originated with the directors of the respective museums, T. M. Messer at the Guggenheim, Kenneth Donahue at the County Museum. To quote *The New York Times*, "It is known that the Guggenheim delayed the final submission of its proposals to the government agency until after an initial choice by its curator, Lawrence Alloway, had been overruled by the museum's director, Mr. Messer. When the National Collection tapped the Guggenheim to do the show last December, it was generally assumed that the choice had been made specially with Mr. Alloway in mind."[9] Similarly with the Los Angeles museum, it was assumed that it received the invitation so that Maurice Tuchman, curator of modern art, would arrange the exhibition. Hopefully, the NCFA has learned enough about American museums not to try in the future to get curators when the official invitations have to go to the institution, that is, to the director. As for Messer and Donahue, they share the unusual distinction of being museum directors who have lost the Venice Biennial for their museums.

What about all the intrigue and corruption that are supposed to surround the prizes at Venice? The press is full of unsupported allegations, such as: "Leo Castelli, Mr. Lichtenstein's New York dealer and the man generally credited with 'arranging' the prize for Robert Rauschenberg two years ago . . ."[10] This was written by Hilton Kramer before the prize winners were announced in 1966, and Lichtenstein did not get one. What, precisely, the alleged "arrangement" was has never been told, and it was apparently unrepeatable two years later. The Rauschenberg success was something of a surprise, to his dealer as to others, whereas Lichtenstein's chances were somewhat optimistically viewed, by his dealer and others. To quote Kramer again, "Certainly the campaign for Mr. Lichtenstein seems well organized. The bookshops here [in Venice] are prominently displaying a bright and hastily produced illustrated multilingual paperback anthology of critical writing on Mr. Lichtenstein's work . . . Three international art journals featuring Mr. Lichtenstein on their covers . . . are very much in evidence, as is a fourth, *Art International*, published in Switzerland by an American. The last contains an article on Mr. Lichtenstein by Otto Hahn, the French critic, and has nothing about the other Americans showing here."[11]

The point that is not made by the writer is that all this activity is out in the open and cannot fairly be linked to the implied corruption of an "arrangement." The interest in Lichtenstein did not culminate in a prize (reportedly the French juror François Mathéy vetoed moves in this direction). The prize winner, for once, caused general astonishment: Julio Le Parc, an Argentine Kineticist who was definitely getting his glory ahead of schedule. The trading that goes on in international committees, as a legitimate route to a consensus, promoted him accidentally. In the following year, the Stedelijk Museum, Amsterdam, originated a retrospective of Lichtenstein, undeterred by the artist's failure to hit the jackpot at Venice. Norman Reid, director of the Tate Gallery, London, was on the jury in Venice and seems not to have voted for Lichtenstein, but he accepted the Amsterdam exhibition for his museum. Prizes cannot be viewed in isolation, as sudden bounty; they are almost always part of a series of public events. It is noticeable that Louis and Noland, and Olitski and Frankenthaler, in two successive Biennials, have interested Europeans very little, certainly less than Pop artists. The reason for this is not the inherent difficulty of the work, but is attributable, in part, to the amount of preparation by the artist's dealer. The Castelli Gallery artists, through the Ileana Sonnabend Gallery in Paris, have reached galleries, museums, and collectors in Europe. The artists of the André Emmerich Gallery, though shown in Paris at the Galerie Lawrence, had not reached a comparable point of European recognition.

The Biennial generates a mass of gossip, some garbled in the Giardini, some forgotten in Florian's. Gossip, entertaining as face-to-face communication, changes its meaning when it enters the press; here everybody's bad opinion of other people's activities is confirmed. Gossip is probably at a normal level for any comparable group, but the kind of group must be defined. Art dealing, which is a symbiote of the modern Biennial, is not a profession in the sense that law, medicine, and architecture are professions. Internal self-regulation and the suppression of doubtful claimants are at a minimum. The Art Dealers Association of America, more concerned with raising the image of the business than with regulating it, resembles the self-bestowing prestige organizations of the television and movie industries. The profits and the risks of art dealing are both great; dealers are free to improvise on a basis of personal ingenuity in ways that members of a profession cannot. There is a connection to the garment business and selling carpets which art dealing has not yet lost.

This situation does not make unfounded hints about "arrangements" any more credible: flattery, perhaps, but bribery, unlikely. The jurors, who are usually distinguished men, at least in their own countries, have too much to lose, and so have ambitious dealers. Influence is exerted in another way. It is more economical to shift the focus of the art-orientated communications network than to buy somebody. The way to reach a juror is the same way that the dealer influences the collector and the public, by taking advertisements and supplying color transparencies to journals, encouraging critics, lending to museums, cutting prices for collectors, and so on. The kind of underground activity implied by Kramer is a primitive conception; the media are the route to the juror's attention, as to yours and mine. The operation is thus in the open to an extent that people prone to conspiracy theories of events or who revere the idea of that old-time payoff find hard to believe.

THE FUTURE OF THE BIENNIAL

UMBRO Apollonio, Curator of the Historical Archives of Contemporary Art, in conversation with me, speculated on the Agency's role. He stressed that he was sharing personal thoughts, not implying policy. He pointed out that in 1968 it was becoming necessary for the Biennial to do more than be informative. The massive presentation of great numbers of works from different countries is the foundation of the show. This function of data-assembling had been the proper course after World War II, but he regarded it as basically fulfilled. The dealers, who after the war had been slow to reorient themselves to an altered art scene, were now a highly effective force in the art world. Museums all over the world, too, showed recent art in quantity, he pointed out. Possibly the prizes, which once served as a stimulus to artists, might no longer be effective in their present form. Few big international shows with a prize system had smooth prize-givings any longer. He was amused at Asger Jorn's dramatic telegram rejecting a Guggenheim International Award in 1964. I reminded him of Henry Geldzahler's attack, as Commissioner of the American pavilion, of the principle of the jury system at Venice. These were extreme examples of a general attitude, he considered. If the prize system were modified it would be possible, he hoped, to structure the exhibition around governing ideas. Today, the general knowledge of modern art, greater than it has ever been, was ready to support thematic and ideological shows. (Incidental support for this view is the shift towards informative catalogues by the National Collection of Fine Arts in their Biennial plans.) At present the Biennial is formed, as always, by the participating countries' send-ins, over which Venice has no say, and by random conglomerations on the labyrinthine walls of the Central Pavilion. What is necessary now is to discover a means to confer order on the thick samples of present activity.

THE BIENNIAL AS A PARTY

IF you visit the Biennial on the day it opens to the public, it feels as if it has just closed—there are just one or two tourists and students, some nuns (if the Patriarch has not forbidden the exhibition), and a few sailors (if the Italian Navy is using the port facilities). It is the four days of the official opening that give the Biennial a special value; here are more artists, dealers, collectors, and writers in one place at one time than can be found anywhere else in the world. Each nation gives a press party and there are other fringe benefits and entertainments. Rosalind Constable described the hectic preview period as "part vernissage, part horse race"[12] when she covered the 1962 revels. This was Hundertwasser's big year, and she describes him as "a tall, slim, unsmiling man of thirty-three, with a red fringe beard, who invariably wore a black art-velvet jacket and was accompanied by his beautiful young Japanese wife, in Japanese dress. . . . Collectors and dealers quickly beat a path to the door of the Austrian pavilion to buy him, or sign him up."[13] Recently, American collectors have given prizes with their names on them (David E. Bright was the first, followed by, for instance, Robert C. Scull). Others give parties, such as the one staged by Arnold A. Maremont, manufacturer of automobile parts and respected collector, for 130 people. They "boarded a *vaporetto* at the Hotel Cipriani" for a trip to Torcello; then back to the Cipriani for "a Lucullan feast."[14] Apart from the fact that people in the same business are usually congenial, the Biennial is an arena for making or renewing contacts, arranging shows, monographs, sales, visits, and articles. There are, too, the people who openly use the event for publicity, like Hundertwasser or Harold Stevenson, who was not in the Biennial but a beneficiary of the crowded scene. Rosalind Constable described him as "a fin-de-siècle young man from Idabel, Oklahoma . . . " "A new Michelangelo. I adore him,"[15] his dealer Iris Clert was quoted as saying. She rented a palazzo and hung banners: "Iris Clert, Piccola Biennale." The rest of this book is about the big one.

THE BIENNIAL AS A TARGET

1968 was not a great year either for parties or for developing solutions to any of the Biennial's problems; both activities were pointlessly interrupted. Venetian students, cued by student activism elsewhere in the early summer, demonstrated against the Biennial and succeeded in closing it briefly and in postponing the awarding of prizes. Biennial officials, as sensitive as the students to the high level of student dissent, closed the exhibition after the official opening. When it reopened the Giardini were crowded with police. Estimates put the number of students as low as 100 and as high as 500, but, in fact, Umbro Apollonio estimates that between two and three hundred students (eighteen or twenty-three years old) were involved.[16]

Some news media reported the affair in terms of the iconography of a global student conspiracy. According to *Newsweek,* "The Venice Biennale reeled under relentless blows of students from Italy and France *converging* (my italics) on the city of canals."[17] According to *Time,* "Revolution-minded students from Madrid, Paris, and other points began deplaning in Venice."[18] Foreign students were deplaning and more were detraining all summer long in Venice, but, in fact, they were not central in harassing the Biennial.

Most of the students were from the Accademia di Belle Arti, hardly famed as a center of student unrest and rebellion (as say, the University of Caracas is). Several months before the Biennial opened students began protesting their conservative training. By the time of the opening of the Biennial, they had already seized studios at the Accademia. Thus the Biennial was an incidental target for the students, though an inevitable one since it coincided with their action.

On June 7, less than two weeks before the Biennial's opening, a manifesto against the exhibition was published, signed by "the committee of students, workers, and revolutionary intellectuals to boycott the Biennial."[19] "The 18th of June, the day of the vernissage, the day of the cultural market, we must all be present, workmen, students, intellectuals, united in the struggle against capital, against the bosses, against bourgeois society."[20] The student manifesto, headed "Workmen, Companions," attacked the Biennial as "one of the moments in which is concretized the mechanism of repression and mystification of the culture of the bosses" (padroni). The Biennial is, that is to say, contaminated by the historical context of declining capitalism from which it emerged. The art and organization of the Biennial are both attacked for appealing to merely "a limited number of people." In fact, the Biennial and other big exhibitions function to take art out of an elite context, but this fact is not amenable to the simplistic drama of the manifesto. One of the reasons given for the boycott is that "through Venice the Biennial represents an essential moment in the articulation of a tourist activity destined for the rich. . . . And it enriches the great hotel companies together with the big industries which exploit our labor."[21] The statement is decidedly archaic, with its sociologically ignorant division of Venice into an alliance of dissenting students and Venetian workers versus rich visitors. (No doubt such resentments arise in any tourist city where most of the inhabitants exist economically at a level far below that of the tourists.)

Actual disturbances were lightweight: placards and painted slogans, small groups outside the American pavilion shouting anti-U.S. slogans, a clash with the police in the Piazza di San Marco. One poster stated: "Dopo la Pop-Art . . . Poliz Art." At one level this touches on notions of workers against strike-breaking police, but it also touches on the more generalized, and more recent, hostility to the police felt by all students, housewives, pacifists, and subgroups engaged in public protest. Referring to the police guard in the Giardini this poster also included a reference, typical for many, to the first "Esposizione Internazionale di Polizia." Another poster, with a brutal hand holding a truncheon, carried the words: "For the First Time in the World the Exhibition Is the Police! XXXIVth Biennial."[22]

A theme show, in the Giardini but arranged independently of the national pavilions, surveying the art of 1950–65, had been scheduled. This exhibition, a moderate but welcome first move towards another form of exhibition than one based on national identity, was canceled: the alarm caused by the demonstration thus weakened the first real effort to reform the exhibition system, a step that even the students had been demanding.[23] Fear of vandalism to expensive foreign works led not only to this cancellation, but to the postponement of the Biennial prizes. Prize-winning works would have been obvious, perhaps irresistible, focal points for further protest, assured in advance as they were of excellent coverage by the media.

Insurgency is the style of direct action at a time when democratic institutions have been stereotyped and poorly administered. The Biennial was reportedly attacked as "bourgeois" and "capitalist." One placard read: "The Biggest and Worst Exhibition in the Biennial is the Police," and another described the exhibition as "the Biennial of the Bosses." The continual references heard to Marx, Mao, and Che Guevara (or students shouting "Ho Chi Minh" outside the American pavilion) were probably less political than individualistic, for in Italy a communist vocabulary provides what is, fundamentally, the only common language of dissent. Whereas formerly the communists were skilled at making opportunistic use of the local forms of discontent, the position is now reversed. Communist iconography has been appropriated for use as the signal of individual revolt. Marx and Lenin are ambiguously separated from the form of society that actually embodies their ideas, the USSR. The language of dissenting students in the United States and often in Europe, though frequently derived from the theory and history of insurgent warfare, is not, with any consistency, communist.

One gesture of international support for the students came from Denmark in the form of a single-sheet leaflet, rather like the students' original statement. It was headed "Declaration Four Our Italian Artists and Comerads [*sic*]: Follow Courbet" and signed "Jens Jørgen Thorsen, Caesar, Jørgen Nash" (Asger Jorn's brother). "An iron-ring of police is now defending the exhibition-area. We thank you, Italian camerads [*sic*], for your deed! It has shown that the terror-police by all means is defending the art-police." Here is an example of shreds of communist rhetoric used to affirm a purely artistic kinship.

Various artists reacted sympathetically to the students, often on the basis of freedom and anti-institutionalism: at least fifteen Italian artists withdrew their work, as did three French artists and one each from Sweden, Denmark, and Yugoslavia. It was an opportunity for them to show kinship with the young, as well as to express some of the resentment they felt about the existing system of merchandising their wares, in which the Biennial plays a prominent role. Artists felt caught, as indeed they are, with no available alternative to dealers' galleries, museum exhibitions, and international shows.

Reports of student demonstrations and riots, mainly in New York and Paris but also in Belgrade, must surely have acted as an incentive to the Venetian students (not traditionally resolute) and undoubtedly were a source of apprehension to the Biennial officials, leading them to exaggerate the vulnerability of the Biennial to what was, in the event, very little pressure for a very short time. (The students' manifesto included the sentence "France instructs," referring, of course, to the student uprising in Paris.) The possibility of tourism's being adversely affected by a real confrontation of students and police was no doubt worrying, and close at hand was the sobering example of the Triennial in Milan, an industrial design exhibition and conference which had been prevented from opening at all by a student sit-in supported by artists.

The communications media that disseminate reports of demonstrations and riots today must be reckoned as a major contributing factor to similar events. There is an immense amount of "inside" information concerning their manipulation; this example is typical: "The crowds don't just happen. 'People have no idea how much behind-the-scenes work goes into a spontaneous demonstration,' says a Rockefeller advance man."[24] In fact, an increasing number of people have a very clear idea, with the result that middle-class students have learned the pessimism long known to the poor and underprivileged. "Passaic is decaying and all we get from the politicians are promises,"[25] says a housewife trapped in a New Jersey town. Conversely, the students, at Columbia and at Venice, know how easy it is to use the media that have contributed to their disillusionment. Thus in Venice the presence of the Biennial conferred the status of major news on what was a minor rebellion compared to those in New York and Paris, and the Biennial was not even the initial target of the demonstration.

When an artist sees his work in the Biennial he may feel trapped in the circuit of the art world, and also experience other discontents. He may feel ambivalent about the gaudier aspects of the scene he is entering. There is, too, a kind of temporal vertigo. At a big, recurrent exhibition, you have a sense of recent art behind what you are looking at now and a sense of the next art, not in form but in sequential order, on the way in. Artists concerned with the uniqueness of their own work or critics anxious to stabilize taste at a certain point are understandably oppressed by this sense of time being like a production line. Of course, being shown at Venice is a sign of recognition, but, at the same time, it is a recognition of age. Hence the belief of the Abstract Expressionist generation that retrospectives are only for the young. ●

NOTES

Previously published as a chapter of: Lawrence Alloway, *The Venice Biennale, 1895–1968: From Salon to Goldfish Bowl* (London, 1969), pp. 12–29.

1 "Official Calendar for 1968 of the International and National Fairs and Exhibitions in Italy," *The Economist,* March 16, 1968.

2 Nikolaus Pevsner, *Academies of Art, Past and Present* (Cambridge, 1940).

3 William Seitz, U.S. exhibition catalogue, 9th São Paulo Biennial, 1968. The expanded role of this catalogue by William Seitz and, to a lesser extent, of Walter Hopps's for the preceding São Paulo Biennial, typifies Washington's new requirements for catalogues, as only Alan Solomon's 1964 catalogue has done for the Venice Biennial. The intention is to produce well-documented and thoroughly argued texts in place of the eulogistic puffs in past catalogues.

4 Harold Rosenberg, *The Anxious Object* (New York, 1964).

5 "Constituzione della Biennale in Ente Autonomo," in *Storia e Statistiche della Bienniale di Venezia* (Venice, n. d. [1932]).

6 Quoted by Grace Glueck, "Guggenheim Loses U.S. Biennale Role," *The New York Times,* February 22, 1966.

7 Quoted by Grace Glueck, "Biennale, Bah," *The New York Times,* February 11, 1968.

8 Ibid.

9 Glueck 1966 (see note 6).

10 Hilton Kramer, "Art: Venice Machinations," *The New York Times,* June 16, 1966.

11 Ibid.

12 Rosalind Constable, "Part Vernissage, Part Horse Race," *Life International,* July 30, 1962.

13 Ibid.

14 Ibid.

15 Ibid.

16 Information supplied directly by Umbro Apollonio.

17 "Art, Venetian Carnival," *Newsweek,* July 1, 1968.

18 "Exhibitions: 'Violence Kills Culture,'" *Time,* June 28, 1968.

19 "Operai, Compagni," single-sheet pamphlet (Venice, 1968). The translations are by Ruth Ann Fredenthal, who helped me gather material on the student boycott.

20 Ibid.

21 Ibid.

22 Both posters were reproduced in *L'Ora* (Palermo), June 18, 1968.

23 Reform needs to take the reform of reducing national sovereignty, on the lines of the large-scale Documenta exhibitions at Kassel, financed by the city, which are controlled completely by a central committee. The second Documenta, that of 1959, was the biggest coherent survey of postwar art seen up to that time in Europe, and the fourth, held in 1968, was an imposing sample of recent work, much of it by young artists.

24 "Smoothing the Way," *Wall Street Journal,* July 3, 1968.

25 "Passaic Debating Uncertain Future," *The New York Times,* July 8, 1968.

MARKS OF DISTINCTION, VECTORS OF POSSIBILITY: QUESTIONS FOR THE BIENNIAL (2009)

150

Simon Sheikh

The collective symbolic capital which attaches to names and places like Paris, Athens, New York, Rio de Janeiro, Berlin and Rome is of great import and gives such places great economic advantages relative to, say, Baltimore, Liverpool, Essen, Lille and Glasgow. The problem for these latter places is to raise their quotient of symbolic capital and to increase their marks of distinction to better ground their claims to the uniqueness that yields monopoly rent. Given the general loss of other monopoly powers through easier transport and communications and the reduction of other barriers to trade, the struggle for collective symbolic capital becomes even more important as a basis for monopoly rents.

David Harvey, *Spaces of Capital*[1]

If the spectrally human is to enter into the hegemonic reformulation of universality, a language between languages will have to be found. This will be no metalanguage, nor will it be the condition from which all languages hail. It will be the labour of transaction and translation which belongs to no single site, but is the movement between languages, and has its final destination in this movement itself. Indeed, the task will be not to assimilate the unspeakable into the domain of speakability in order to house it there, within the existing norms of dominance, but to shatter the confidence of dominance, to show how equivocal its claims to universality are, and, from that equivocation, track the break-up of its regime, an opening towards alternative versions of universality that are wrought from the work of translation itself.

Judith Butler, "Competing Universalities"[2]

IN a dialogue on the notion of universality, American philosopher Judith Butler has suggested that we understand this concept in the plural and conflictual, and that the political task thus becomes to establish what she calls practices of translation.[3] This is not, however, a matter of translating the particular into the universal, in order to make it politically salient or effective, but rather that the universal is always a particular, competing universal. The universal is not anterior to the particular, and commonalities and overlaps can be found within such competing notions of universality, and thus also among various political movements and groups through acts of translation without transcendence. Movement here takes on a double significance, partly in the sense of concrete social movements with political aims, and partly, and more abstractly, as the movement between moments and sites of political contestation and articulation, which can be named a politics of translation.[4]

Now, the question I would like to ask is whether the contemporary forms of the biennial can be considered one such site, and what movements can be traced through and around them? In other words, what is to be translated, and through which method of translation? Obviously, the theory and history of translation in conjunction with culture is highly contested, and it is not my aim to reiterate these intellectual debates here, but only to point to one singular dichotomy in translation, that of the original and the copy, and to suggest what it could mean in a geopolitical sense. The most widespread version of translation indicates a relation between an original text in an original language and a copy that translates this text into a secondary language, leading to choices regarding fidelity, either to the original and the transfer of its meaning as accurately as possible, or to the new, secondary language and its specificity. In this theory, there is always something that is untranslatable, and that requires literary skills of equivalence on the part of the translator. It is also a theory, and practice, of translation that has colonialist implications in terms of site, privileging the originality of European culture in opposition to all the colonial copies.

THE "ORIGINALITY" OF THE BIENNIAL

IN terms of biennials, the original to be copied and exported is the biennial in Venice, held fifty-two times since 1895 and based on the concept of national pavilions, that is, with national (self-)representation, with each nation sending their best and brightest artist(s). The Venice Biennial exists as a sort of Olympic Games of the art world, complete with a first prize. However, it should be immediately noted that most of the biennials that have emerged all around the world since then have not followed this model, and indeed most of them do not make claims for a world art, but rather for a regional, cultural particularism (with universalist elements), be it in Havana or the Whitney Museum in NYC, or the ever-shifting locale of Manifesta in Europe. While this might be the predominant alteration of Venice, there is also the brief of bringing the world of art to a particular place, in effect translating the international to the local(s), be it in Berlin, Istanbul, or São Paulo, or, specifically so, the poignantly named Periferic biennial in Iasi. Finally, there are the biennials that make claims for a specific kind of art, for a certain medium as nation, one could say, such as the Liverpool Biennial and the Berlin Transmediale, among a few others.

We are thus not exclusively dealing with a culture of the copy, but with deviation and hybridity as well as repetition and simulation, with different notions of fidelity. Biennials find themselves in an unregulated and informal system, that is, paradoxically, both rhizomatic and hierarchical. Although they are directed towards several vantage points and spheres of interest, their meaning and placement can only be seen from one place at a time. They may make up one place after another for an, again, loosely defined and organized group of art professionals, but for most regular visitors, their recurrence is time-based, if not timely. In this case, they are more likely to be read in terms of the previous versions of the specific biennial and its scope, choice of artists, curators, venues, and so on, rather than an international circuit and communication of exhibitions and articulations.

While the exhibition format remains the main vehicle for the presentation of contemporary art, this does not mean that the exhibition is a singular format with a given public and circulation of discourse. Rather, the notion of an exhibition is to be understood in the plural, with different types of exhibitions speaking from different locations and positions, and with different audiences and circulations indicated and implicated, from the self-organized student show in a small provincial town to the larger (inter)national biennials that are the topic of this essay. What they share, and this is especially true of biennials, is a double sense of public and publicity: the local, physically present (if only potentially) audience and the imaginary constituency and professional field of the art world (if only potentially). There are, in the landscape of biennials, not only the original and the copy, the deviant and the hybrid, but also always a here and an elsewhere.

Biennials are placed within an ecosystem as well as an economic system of exhibitions (and exhibition venues) in geopolitical terms. They do not command the same immediate attention internationally, despite the number of (local) visitors. More people visit the biennial in Mercosul in Porto Alegre than Documenta in Kassel, for example, but historical importance in the art world, geographical placement, and media attention all play a role in the significance of a biennial's standing and influence as well. In short, a biennial builds up a brand, as well as an audience and a constituency, both locally and internationally. And with the recent growth of new biennials, especially in southeast Asia, it is becoming an increasingly competitive environment in which to vie for international attention, which affects designated centers and peripheries as well.

Take the aforementioned Documenta, although not a biennial in the proper sense of the word, which has, since its inception in 1957, taken a different route than the Venice Biennial: rather than the Olympic model of national competition, Documenta tried to make a statement about the state of art. That is, a transnational survey of the most dominant trends within contemporary art at the given moment. "Movement" was understood as artistic movement, and it was originally dedicated to twentieth-century avant-garde art in a re-education of the German people after the Second World War, and as part of an assessment of West German democratic ideals in opposition to those of its Eastern, communist Other. Its brief has naturally changed since the fall of communism in Europe, and indeed the last three versions, Documentas 10 through 12, have attempted to redefine the idea of a world exhibition of art and address the idea of a globalized world by showing art from all corners of the world as opposed to focusing on Western Europe and the U.S. However, Documenta's centrality and discursiveness have simultaneously been challenged by the many new biennials, both in its vicinity and around the world, and it remains to be seen if it can maintain its importance and place at the top of the hierarchy in the future, both in terms of discourse, attention, and economy.

BIENNIALS AND MONOPOLY RENT

MORE and more, a biennial has to create a niche market, a specific identity, reputation, and prestige that can place it on the map of the world and the art world alike. And this placement may be vastly different, and might even require speaking different languages and in two tongues. On the one hand there is the circulation of discourse of the international art world, with its system of competing universalities, as well as a competition for symbolic capital, market shares, and monopolies, and on the other the local political and economic demands for cultural significance and supremacy: the uniqueness of this culture, this country, this place. The uniqueness of a particular place and culture is not only a question of nationalism and of nation-building, though, but also a means of establishing a niche market and attracting an international audience, to generate cultural capital as well as increased revenues through (art) tourism. Biennials are, in this way, part of the experience economy, with the whole experience of the city and the exhibition being the commodity rather than the singular works of art displayed, as is, presumably, the case with art fairs.

In his book *Spaces of Capital,* social geographer David Harvey has analyzed the relationship between globalization, city marketing, and the commodification of culture through the Marxian category of "monopoly rent." Monopoly rent occurs when a producer can generate a steady increase of surplus and thus income over time through exclusivity. This is achieved either by being the only producer of a certain commodity in a regional economy, or through the uniqueness of the brand in a more global economy. The example given is the wine trade, where an exclusive vineyard can sell its wines as commodities, but also itself—the land, resources, and location. Historically, a producer of wine or beer could gain monopoly rents in its region or area by simply being the only brand available, but in a global and globalized market, the product has to have some sort of local uniqueness in order to be tradable outside its region and in order to compete for market shares with other brands being imported into its region. It has to achieve a symbolic quality besides its actual taste in order to generate revenues; therefore the wine merchants in the Bordeaux region have copyrighted the use of the name "Château" and only the producers of sparkling wine in the Champagne region can now legally call their products "champagne." Here we are dealing with a culturalization of commodities as much as the commodification of culture. However, there are also other factors involved in the wine market: specialist publications and international competitions give value judgments based merely on taste rather than origin, suddenly bringing wine from, say, South Africa, Chile, or Australia to the fore, and then there is, naturally, a competition in terms of price, which compared to the specialist judgments of taste creates a consciousness of value for money among potential consumers in a global market.

Hopefully, the parallels to the art world, and market, are obvious. Here, we also have historical centers, in a biennial context places such as Venice and Kassel, but also new, emergent players around the world, most lately and massively in Southeast Asia. Also, we have the judges of taste in the form of critics and magazines, as well as a competition on price and uniqueness in terms of locality. Venice obviously has a history, not only of its biennial, but also of its city, giving it an incredibly strong brand and attraction. Secondly, it has a centrality in terms of location, certainly within the art world, but also, from a European perspective, in terms of geography. All these factors clearly outweigh the fact that the city is very expensive for travelers. Other cities, like, say, São Paulo, are obviously cheaper to be in for the art tourist, but more expensive to travel to from most places, both in Europe and the U.S., not to mention in Asia. Indeed, the São Paulo biennial was originally based on the same principles of national pavilions as that of Venice, which also made each nation participating financially responsible, but has recently abandoned this model, presumably due to its decreasing symbolic value and credibility in the art world as such. Perhaps this format is a bit too crude within the global (art) economy?

Instead, biennials have to brand themselves differently and specifically in order not only to achieve cultural hegemony, but also to extract monopoly rent, in terms of both symbolic and real capital. They must be, on the one hand, recognizable as a certain format, a festival of art, and on the other hand be specific, *this* biennial, not *that* one. With *these* specific properties and attributions, in *this* specific place, city, region, and country. The branding of the biennial is thus twofold: partly the city as attraction and allure, giving context and value to the biennial, and partly the glamour and prestige of the biennial branding and upgrading the otherwise nondescript or even negative image of the city, region, or country. In this scenario, it is only logical that most biennials today are taking on a (at least) dual purpose, both highlighting the uniqueness of the particular place or region and its culture, as a way of cultivating the national audience and attracting an international one, *and* bringing international artists and positions to the local situation, cultivating the national citizens as international consumers and connoisseurs of culture: the lure of the local meets the glamour of the global. In other words, biennials do not only situate a place, but they also always establish a connection, and herein lies their potentiality.

INTERCONNECTEDNESS

INDEED, one of the most widespread complaints about contemporary biennials is their lack of connection to the "local" audience, but this often takes the form of a positivity of the social: that social relations and identities in a specific context are given and whole, if not holy, that the local audience is a singular group with essential qualities and shared agencies. This is a residue of the myth-making of the nation-state and its production of citizenry through cultural means, such as exhibitions and institutions, and hardly seems adequate in the postmodern and post-public condition, where identities are, at least, hybrid and multiple agencies, and even contradictory and schizoid. It is, rather, a question of how a biennial produces, or attempts to produce, its public(s) that must be analyzed and criticized. One must ask what assumptions of place and participation are at work, and what notions of subjectivity, territoriality, and citizenship are invoked. And one must ask in what way participation is valued in terms of cultural consumption and legitimation. Additionally, the "lack of local sedimentation" argument tends to overlook the potential biennials actually offer for reflection on the above-mentioned double notion of publicness: the local audience and the international one, and the art world and the world. The potential not only to address presumed existing audiences, both locally and in terms of art-world credibility and circulation, but also to create new public formations that are not bound to the nation-state or the art world. By being recurrent events, both locally placed and part of a circuit, they have the potential to create a more transnational public sphere, with both difference and repetition in the applied mode of address and the implied notion of spectatorship and public participation.

Moreover, location is to be understood in the sense of *interconnectedness:* this means not only that we connect through the public formation of the event of the biennial and the encounter with the artworks, but also that any place is always seen in relation to another place, or a series of possible places. We view other places through the prism of our own place, as subjects with history and geography. Our places of dwelling and of action are also always related to other places, whether visible or invisible, present or absent. What goes on "here" always has effects "there" and vice versa, even when we are not aware of these movements. This is, of course, the current global condition, and art today must reflect this double sense of place, public and nonpublic, presence and absence, the visible and the invisible. Any sense of locality always involves a here and an elsewhere: a constant movement between centeredness and marginality, be it in aesthetic, geographical, or economic terms, and one of the characteristics of advanced art is precisely that it allows one to see more than one viewpoint—more than one story or situation, and more than one way to look at them.

Any locality, regardless of its self-image, is connected to other places in subtle and often unexpected ways: what is produced here is consumed there, what is seen there is invisible here, and so on. This is also the situation for biennials: they find themselves in an art-world system of exhibitions and festivals (public formations), as well as in an international economy of desire. But how is this made visible to a local community, and how is it relevant to the experiences of the audience, both inside and outside the exhibition, as well as before and after the exhibition? The question is what our relationship is to different spaces, and, moreover, how continuity is established and made productive in a biennial setting. It is therefore a matter not only of what a biennial can give, or give *back,* to its community and constituency, but also of what kinds of community and constituency it can produce, put into play or suspend. The relationship between the artworks and the audience created by the exhibition is one of positionality, and as such the position of the speaker is something that must be made visible by the exhibition and its ways of display. The biennial is not only a container of artworks, but also a mass medium in itself, and must as such establish a social space, that is, a place where meanings, narratives, histories, conversations, and encounters are actively produced and set in motion. A place where connections are made and unmade, subjectified and suspended. In other words: *politics of translation.*

TRANSLATION AND LOCATION

TRANSLATION is here to be understood in multiple ways, not only as something that occurs between original and copy, and primary and secondary culture, nor only geographically, that is, as something occurring between different places, but also as being *locational,* as taking place *in situ.* However, it would also be too limited and limiting to merely understand translation as a pedagogical exercise of explaining works and their contexts to different audiences and groups. Rather, translation must be understood within the transposition of forms of language, that is, be understood in terms of exhibition display, or what I have called *modes of address,* which is the instituent practice of exhibition-making—its placing of objects and subjects within a frame and on a horizon, a world and a worldview.[5]

This has to do, then, not only with representation in the form of artworks and the (geopolitical) selection of artists, but also with public programming and exhibition design. One can, for instance, try to imagine and implement ways of showing and seeing within an exhibition design that do not follow the historical, apparently neutral museum display of the white cube—which hides its political positioning of the works and the viewers—and instead attempt spatializations that make such positions more visible and locational.

One of the ways to achieve this is *historization:* interconnectedness in time. Exhibition-making has certain historical forms of display, and a part of the biennial enterprise could be to focus on historical forms of exhibition-making, an exhibition on exhibitions. Exhibitions are, to paraphrase Walter Zanini, "microcosmoses of the possible," and as such directly connected to our political imaginary: what is possible and impossible, visible and invisible, to be done and not to be done, and so on. Biennials are not only part of the present, but also always the past, in the forms of the previous editions of the particular biennial itself, art history in general, and, naturally, the history of the place, with its contestations of space, cultural hegemonies, and forgetting and remembrance of struggles past. And by immediately inscribing itself within art history and processes of marketability and canonization of the artists included as well as of the institution of the biennial itself, it is always an investment in the future: a statement about art (and thus specific artists and practices) is an attempt to achieve hegemony, not just instantly, but even more so in the short *and* long run.

This connection with history, or with the making and unmaking of history and its relation to our view of the world, our horizon of possibilities and impossibilities, connects to an important nodal point, *the sense of place* and *the situation of exile*. These terms may seem to be strange bedfellows, especially within the context of art and culture, and its privileging of place, location, site, and specificity. Today, our sense of place has as much to do with that place's connection to other places, be they possible or impossible, permeable or incommensurable, perceivable or invisible, as with the originality of the place. Places exist through connections, within the global flows of objects and subjects, rules and (de)regulations. We can thus only sense a place through other places, albeit only from one place at a time. But we also move from place to place, geographically and politically, within larger global flows of migration. So, how exactly does one belong to a place, a culture, and a language, both as cultural producer *and* consumer? Who can speak for a place, or even *speak the place?* Is it the "local" artist and/or community, for instance, or is it, conversely, the specialist cultural producer dealing in intervention and/or site-specific strategies?

These questions have both concrete and abstract answers, but always in terms of time rather than space. Politically, citizenship is either something you are born with or something that is acquired after living legally in a given country for a certain number of years. The option of getting a new citizenship obviously varies greatly depending on the country. However, as we know from the nationalist debates that have swept Europe for the last decade, citizenship in legal terms does not equal citizenship in cultural terms. And even though cultural terms of national identity are arguably of a symbolic nature, they are perceived and discussed—culturalized—as *real*. To have Danish citizenship, for example, does not necessarily make you a "real" Dane, thus the distinction in media reports and debates between "Dane" and "Danish citizen," with the former being the real Dane. This can, of course, be even more fine-tuned when talking about a specific region or city: there may be several different people, even of the same color and creed, living in a place, but the "real" _____ (insert your place/identity of choice here) are the ones who were born here. A sense of place known as roots, indicating an organic relationship to the place. However, as mentioned before, we are, regardless of origin and current location, rarely in a position of full coherence and identity, but rather selves in the making, and on the move.

WAYS OF TRAVELING, WAYS OF SEEING

TO be on the move is, naturally, one of the characteristics of the much maligned star curators and artists of the international biennial circuit. But expertise is also implied through method, and through commitment over time: how long has a curator or artist spent in a place? How deep is their work? Even though this can be measured in terms of time, such a measure is ultimately meaningless in terms of assessment and judgment, obviously, but also in terms of critique and potentiality. Rather, we should look at what connections are made and unmade: what sense of place is analyzed through the prism of which other places? Hence, the situation of exile, both inside and outside of one's given nation or society. Exile is not just a matter of leaving a nation geographically, be it voluntarily or involuntarily, but also of leaving it conceptually and politically, that is, an exodus from the current state of affairs, from the state of the state, as it were, again both voluntarily and involuntarily. It is no coincidence, I believe, that Giorgio Agamben titled his Italian diary of 1992–94 *In This Exile,* writing as an Italian who was in Italy but somehow outside of the current hegemony, both politically and culturally.[6]

Everybody is, surely, involved in some sort of movement—even when staying still geographically, one might be moving ahead, or up or down, socially and economically. But we do not all travel in the same class and according to the same itinerary, nor even with similar destinations, or, for that matter, destinies. Some are sidelined to the margins, others exiled on Main Street, but everybody is in some sense displaced: where one comes from and where one is, or is going, is no longer the same place, neither in terms of time nor geography, and one can never go home again. Our sense of belonging and place are, in this way, becoming more and more conceptual and relational. It is therefore obvious why a major theme in contemporary art production should be an *uncertainty of place,* not only geographically, but also socially: who has access to which spaces, both generally and locally? Access should be understood not only in terms of physicality, but also symbolically and culturally. When thinking about the politics of translation implied in contemporary biennials, one must think in terms of relations of difference and contextuality, and the fragmentation of the public sphere (including a fragmentation of the art world), and what this means transnationally. One must look at connections and lines of flight between different points of departure and arrival. Such theorizing could perhaps be employed as a form of actualization; realizing, imagining, representing, and communicating that which is possible, but has not yet been implemented.

This also applies to the discussion of a decentralization and/or globalization of the art world and its biennials. Rather than viewing biennials and mega-exhibitions as essential categories with fixed representations and implications, I would suggest this contextual and relational view of them. They offer a stage, surely, but one does not have to follow the script. That is, we can look at their specific placement and relation to their surroundings, each other, and the general circulation of discourse through the art world. What is, for instance, the relationship between site-specific art projects and the notion of the local, between site-specific projects and tourism, and, finally, between tourism and migration? Often site-specific projects not only bring a cultural value to remote areas and interact with the local in a displacement of art from the centers to the margins, but also bring financial rewards to the site in terms of increased tourism. And the same can of course be stated about international biennials and other recurrent mega-exhibitions. But the notion of tourism should not be separated from another form of travel that brings about cultural exchange and interaction, that is, migration. The differentiation between these two kinds of travel indicates not only the content of these forms of travel, but also their contexts; tourism indicates legalized travel and spending, usually from richer countries to other rich and/or poor countries. Tourism equals income and enlightenment, consumption and information—just like in a biennial. Migration, on the other hand, is nowadays mostly illegal, and usually viewed as unwelcome, as it is unprofitable and culturally alien. One only has to watch the literal fence on the U.S. side of the U.S.–Mexican border, or the establishment of an internal open market in Europe while its external borders, especially those shared with North Africa and the Middle East, are increasingly guarded and closed, turning the European Union into a *European Fortress.*

Global flows are not only voluntary, as art tourism supposedly is, but also brought about by the same structures and strictures of global capitalism that produce the demand for city branding and the surge towards monopoly rent. The art world, for instance, is not so much multicultural as it is multicentered, hence the global spread of the biennial phenomenon but also the seeming interchangeability of participating artists without any shifts of signification. Perhaps, then, interconnectedness should be foregrounded over the uniqueness of place? Perhaps we should think in terms of what Sathya Rao, a network scientist from India, has called "non-colonial translation," and its nonhomogeneous and even chaotic space without residues of the colonial original and without any unifying textual-ontological plane of reference.[7] In this way art and its institutions can become public platforms that relate not only to a more or less centralized art world, but also to other fields of knowledge and modes of production in a society that seems more and more specialized and fragmented, thus creating several public, semipublic, and even counter-public spheres within the existing ones. From such formulated platforms we can relate to other spaces and spheres, indicating that biennials are not predominantly to be seen as utopias, but rather as heterotopias, capable of maintaining several contradictory representations within a single space. Obviously, biennials are part of (inter)national cultural hegemonies as well as city branding and the creation of monopoly rents, but that does not mean that they can only represent these features, nor that they can only affirm them. Indeed, they can question them by highlighting them, as well as by creating other possible connections, other ways for or concepts of stranger sociability and senses of place and placement. It is improbable that a biennial can exist without taking part in such processes of capital accumulation (both symbolic and real, of course), so the question is rather, can they do something else simultaneously? That is, can they produce something other than merely more symbolic-turned-real capital for the involved cultural producers, curators and artists alike, something else in terms of interconnected global political transaction and translation? While biennials remain spaces of capital, they are also spaces of hope. ●

NOTES

Previously published in: Jorinde Seijdel and Liesbeth Melis (eds.) "The Art Biennial as a Global Phenomenon: Strategies in Neo-Political Times," special issue, *Open* 16 (2009), pp. 68–79.

1 David Harvey, *Spaces of Capital* (New York, 2001), p. 405.

2 Judith Butler, "Competing Universalities," in idem, Ernesto Laclau, and Slavoj Žižek, *Contingency, Hegemony, Universality* (London, 2000), pp. 178–79.

3 Ibid.

4 The notion of a "politics of translation" indicates a shift from, as well as affinity with, what Michel Foucault termed "the politics of truth." But where the politics of truth has to do with a questioning of authority, and a wish for being governed in a different way, politics of translation seems to confront different regimes of truth, the ways in which truth is produced.

5 Simon Sheikh (ed.), *In the Place of the Public Sphere?* (Berlin, 2005).

6 Giorgio Agamben, "In This Exile (Italian Diary 1992–94)," in *Means without End: Notes on Politics* (Minneapolis, 2000), pp. 121–42.

7 Sathya Rao, "From a Post-Colonial to a Non-Colonial Theory of Translation," in Naoki Sakai and Jon Solomon (eds.), *Translation, Biopolitics, Colonial Difference* (Hong Kong, 2006), pp. 73–94.

BIENNIALS AS STRUCTURES FOR THE WRITING OF ART HISTORY: THE ASIAN PERSPECTIVE

John Clark

OVERALL ISSUES[1]

WHILE the history of biennial art exhibitions, beginning with the Venice Biennial (1895) and the Carnegie International (1896) in Pittsburgh, is fairly well known and the subject of research,[2] the recent role of biennial exhibitions in constituting the canonical works of contemporary art has been neither fully nor carefully examined.[3] This is a particularly important area of investigation not only because of the increase in the number of such exhibitions during the nineteen-eighties and -nineties, but also because they would appear to be functioning for contemporary art in as yet not fully understood ways as arbiters of taste, as consecrators of esteemed practice and works, and as the mediating sites or distributors of artworks, artists, and curators.[4] They are also functioning in these ways for the contemporary art produced in countries in Asia that in the main began to enjoy major international circulation only in the eighties.[5] Indeed biennials and triennials—and for brevity's sake I shall refer to all such exhibitions as "biennials," whatever their periodicity or institutional site—have increasingly been founded in various Asian countries. Biennials have functioned not merely as exhibitors of international art to local audiences, but also as exhibition sites for local art deemed worthy of attracting international attention.[6] They have served to draw contemporary art from other Asian countries into new inter-regional circuits of comparison and circulation, although only latently so in most cases. For most official organizers of biennial exhibitions in Asia, and, it would seem, for most curators and artists, biennials function by transferring the exposure of sites, works, artists, and curators from the "national" to the "international" level. They only began to function in a transnational way that transcended the national/international dichotomy in the late nineties.[7]

Most biennials, however, have the intention and actually do function to developmentally tie a city or region to an international level. These non-art and often econo-political functions of biennials are not without their art-world side effects, particularly in the flow of knowledge and sometimes of people between local communities below the national level.[8] Moreover, the increasing participation of Asian artists at international art biennials and the large number of biennials now organized in Asian countries have implications for the construction of modern and contemporary Asian art history (figs. 1, 2).

It is only recently that work has begun to appear on modernity in Asian art.[9] The notion of modernity itself permits the formation of a conception of an art that is transnationally applicable across various "Asian" contexts and allows art historians to see "Asia" as a discursively constructed space in parallel to, or as a relativizing contrast which reciprocally constructs, a modern "Western" art. It should be underlined that this position means any notion of a "modern" Asian art relativizes modern "Western" art and that the former cannot be seen as a simple stylistic transfer from the originating latter. It is highly significant that many texts on modern Western art do not acknowledge modern art outside the West, and thus deny this relativization.[10] It may well be the economic importance in the transnational relationships of Japan in the 1980s, of China in the 1990s and 2000s, and probably of India in the 2000s and 2010s that has been the motor driving the more frequent entry of Asian artists into international circuits. Or, if we sensibly bracket the reductivity implicit in economic arguments, such relationships have at the very least produced the economic context that has allowed this movement in art its own degree of autonomy.

SOME OBSERVATIONS ABOUT BIENNIAL TYPES

BIENNIALS may be simply distinguished as prescriptive international and prescriptive national exhibitions that also sometimes have a further prescriptive influence on the local dimension. "Prescriptive" here indicates that the exhibitions practice inclusion by selection, which means that an appraisal of the importance of each work or artist as a representative of current contemporary practice is made, and thus often by implication indicate a direction in which others may—or should—follow.[11]

At the Venice or São Paulo biennials, "nationally" selected artists are also shown at the "international" level. The "national" selection of a country may be intended at the same time to represent the art of a region, as with the regional Korean artists shown in a separate exhibition hall at the Gwangju Biennial in 2004. In the case of Documenta, which has basically been a quinquennial exhibition since its inception in 1955, there is a claim to a prescriptive role for the art of one nation conceived as a cultural region in the world, in this case Germany.[12] This locally prescriptive role has gradually—if not always manifestly—expanded to become the projection of a prescriptive intention for the whole international art world as conceived from that local position. While the function of prescription is thus similar if not identical across different levels, its purported scope and hegemonic intent can be of quite different orders. In the case of Documenta itself, we may consider how few Asian artists were in fact selected for exhibition there before 2007.[13] If we then consider the links between northern European and North American critical discourse and the restricted membership of the international curatorium—a select group of curators whose opinions and subsequent selections have canon-making effects, one we could call a "curatoriate" to indicate its quasi-ruling function—the hegemonic effect of Documenta becomes clear.[14] This hegemony of position exists despite Documenta's own antihegemonic claims, or even its procedures in 2002, when it appointed a U.S. resident of Nigerian origin as director, Okwui Enwezor. Documenta 11 went on to expand the intellectual positioning away from Kassel itself, and arranged various non-German sites for critical "platforms." However, the platforms were by invitation only and had the curiously hegemonic effect of privileging only some, but not all, international critical discourses presumed to have a local relevance in the places where the platforms occurred.[15]

Prescriptive exhibitions at the international level attempt to define what contemporary art is and/or how it should be articulated by their selection of sites, works, artists, and curators. One might think only the first three were involved, beginning with those funding the exhibition. The latter could be a municipal body, regional or national government, or a private corporation seeking exposure at a more prestigious international level. Those supplying the objects—that is, the artists, who often consider their own artistic position or personality as a virtual object—would clearly like to have their work circulated at an international level in order to secure greater prestige and, if possible, greater prescriptive approval or cultural "consecration."[16] The latter is not in itself an economic reward, but it may be the symbolic node of conversion for many artists, transforming them from those who contribute to cultural capital into those who derive real economic benefit from their production of objects they can then "sell" in various markets.[17]

However, the experience of viewing various biennials, together with an awareness of the restricted number of curators who actually curate these exhibitions and of the equally restricted number of artists who are selected to exhibit at them, whether by way of "national" or "thematic" selection, has led me to the conclusion that what is on show at biennials is as much the curatorial selection as any particular works or artists selected.[18]

THE CURATOR'S ROLE

EXAMINING the roles of curators leads me to note that the biennial functions as the site through which "international" and "national" curators show themselves to each other via their selections and whose "audience" is in a very real sense composed of other curators. The biennial is the site through which curators themselves are circulated and try to achieve their own further circulation.

If the "international" biennials have an external hierarchy of levels, then the institutional organization of biennials has an internal one within the structure of its curatorium, or body of single or multiple curators. These curatoria are often composed of a "master curator," "delegated" or "subcurators," and operational supplicants, or what I shall call "minion curators." For the 2003 Venice Biennial the master curator was Francesco Bonami, and the eleven "delegated" curators included Hou Hanru for *Zones of Urgency* and Molly Nesbit, Hans Ulrich Obrist, and Rirkrit Tiravanija for *Utopia Station,* among other subcurated exhibitions in the Arsenale. For the Venice Biennial of 2005 there were two master curators or "directors," María de Corral and Rosa Martínez, both acting as their own subcurators for *The Experience of Art* in the Giardini and *Always a Little Further* in the Arsenale, while the supplicant assistants or "minion curators" cited in the catalogue were Martina Bertaggia, Lorena Martínez de Corral and Paolo Cimarosti, María José Balcells, and Marimó Llaràs.

Other biennials, such as those of Fukuoka and Brisbane, have an institutional and quasi-curatorial function, for in these cases an institution nominally functions as the ultimate master curator. In Fukuoka the Asian Art Museum director seems to play a final decision-making role from time to time, just as the Gallery director does in Brisbane.[19] But in these two cases, instead of a formal single "master" curator there is a group of overlapping and hierarchically structured but delegated curatorial committees, each with its own group of minion curators, among whom I would include the various local referees who may be responsible for establishing an initial list of artists. I can't see any clear way towards claiming an equality between the organizing institution and the advisors or local curators in such cases, for the views of the latter can be, and frequently are, set aside.

Perhaps it was just such a group of master curators that was envisaged for the first Yokohama Triennial in 2002, but in effect this became a triennial composed of four separate exhibitions curated by four separate curators, each with his or her own minion curators. At least one of them, Nanjô Fumio, thought that this was inadequate and ran counter to the international experience of the organization of a biennial based on an artistic director and subdirectors.[20] The organization of the curatorium may appear to be a minor matter, but it is surely central to the impact and cultural-political dynamics of the organization of biennials, since one can imagine many kinds of subnegotiation about selection, the support of certain artists, and the discernment of themes. These all significantly vary the range of artists shown as well as the nature and potential of the exhibition as a representation of art trends at any one time, let alone as something presenting a specific conceptual position or even as a display of the period's zeitgeist.[21]

Art history has not provided much interpretation in this field, save perhaps through biographical studies of dealers and curators.[22] Many imaginary associations conjure up why this might be so. Perhaps the nakedness of the contemporary curator might be masked by the powerful fragrance worn by the artist-bearers of fabulist designs paraded before the innocent spectator, or by analogy, the flavor of your Navin as against the taste of my Rirkrit. Indeed many exhibition works are presented to the viewer as if they were preloved *objets de luxe* with a guaranteed pedigree, recognized high expense and production values, and often the hint of a genealogy of previous consecrations by other curators. Other associations include the concept of a curator functioning like a car salesman who pushes to persuade the well-heeled potential buyer that there is a substantial difference between a Mercedes and a BMW, or like a Hollywood agent trying to persuade a casting director that in *this role* in *this movie* Gwyneth Paltrow will definitely not outshine Cate Blanchett, despite the fact that any average fan would see both actresses as equally fine. Maybe we'll go with the Morimura this time, rather than the Sugimoto again . . . ?

The curator basically propagandizes a fashionable intangible, the taste on which he or she proposes all should agree. The "all" refers first, before anyone else, to other curators in the field.[23] However often curators may claim to be humble or declare the need for humility,[24] one cannot avoid the sense that their selections have actually been made not for a broader art public, in whatever manner this may be conceived, but, at least in part, with other curators in mind. The actual or key audience is this private or restricted group, notwithstanding the feigned openness or flexibility of the notional "all." Such an assessment is reinforced by the fact that minion curators,

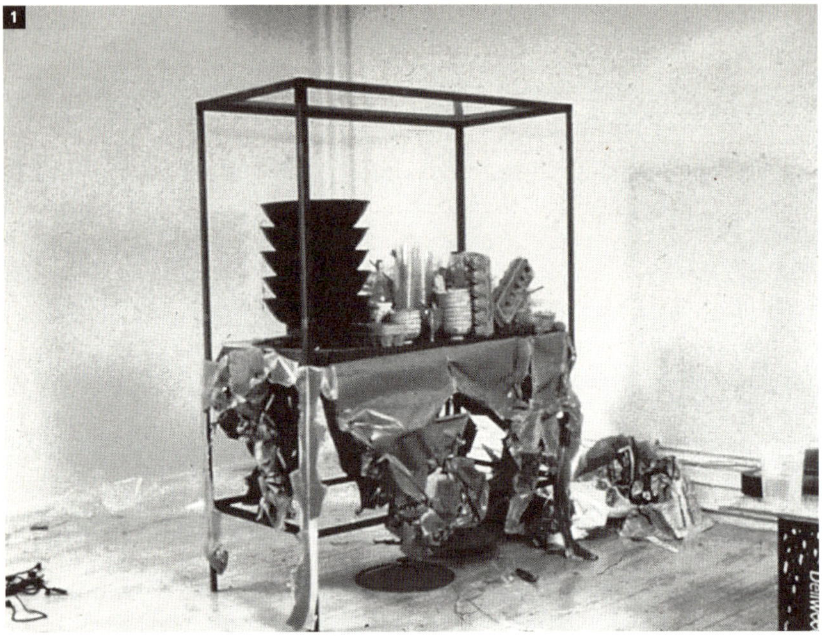

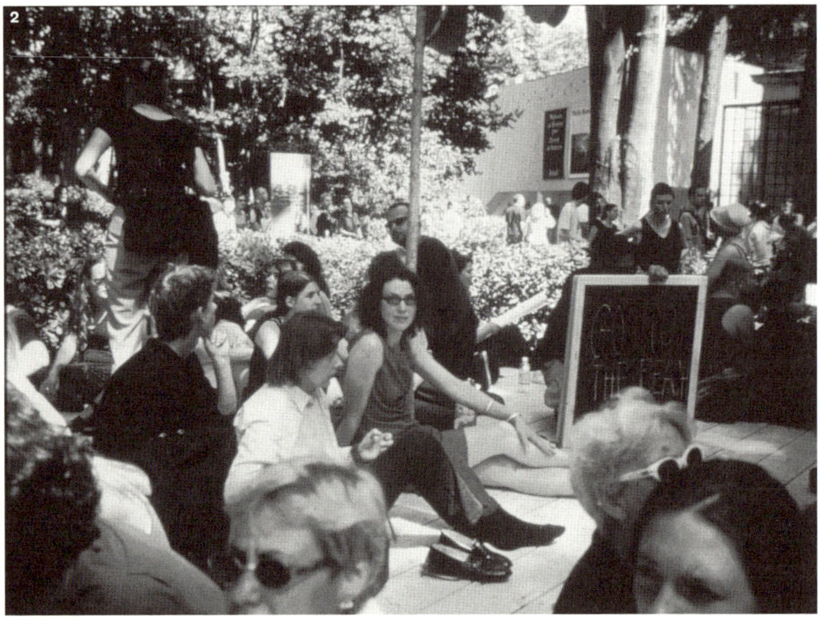

1 Rirkrit Tiravanija, *Untitled 1990 (Pad Thai),* 1990.

2 Rirkrit Tiravanija, installation view, 1999, *dAPERTutto,* Venice Biennial.

3
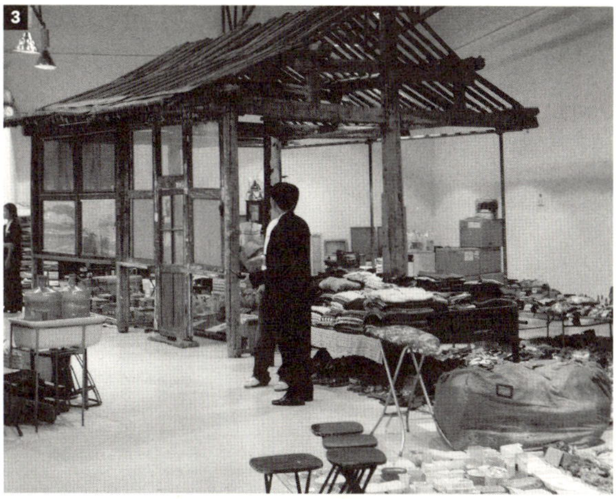

4
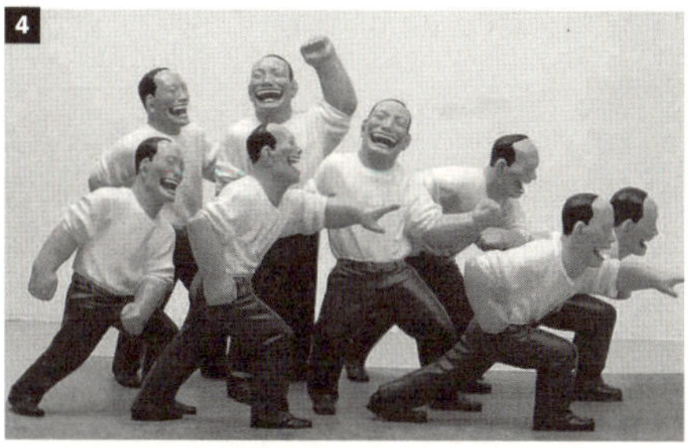

5
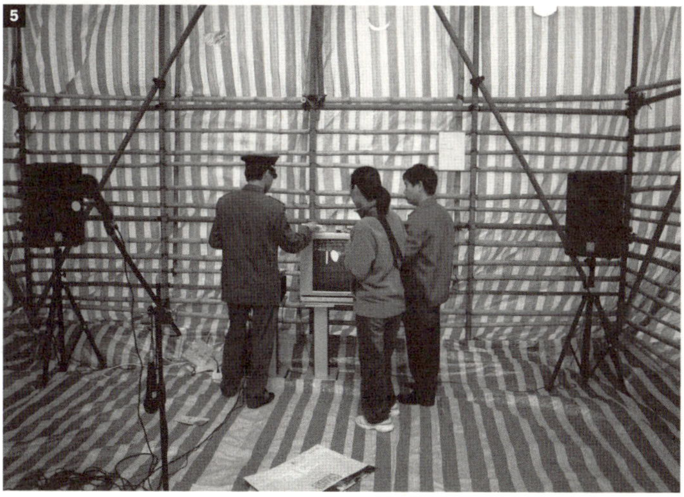

3 Song Dong, *Waste Not,* 2005, Gwangju Biennial (Gwangju Biennial catalogue, 2006). This work was later identified as a work produced with his mother on exhibition at the Tokyo Gallery.

4 Yue Minjun, *Romanticism and Realism 6,* 2003, Gwangju Biennial (Gwangju Biennial catalogue, 2004).

5 Xu Tan, *Wine for 9 September,* 2005, Guangzhou Triennial (Guangzhou Triennial catalogue, 2005). The woven cloth can be made into the woven bags widely used by Chinese people. Visitors can enter the two- or three-storey-high woven bag, in which a karaoke machine and video recorders have been installed.

who do most of the preparatory research work and make most of the primary selection assessments, place their future career advancement at risk if they question the later decisions made by higher-ranking curators.

BIENNIALS VIS-À-VIS SURVEY EXHIBITIONS

WHAT remains a subject for serious exploration, and unfortunately lies beyond the scope or interest of my research, is examining to what degree and in what way biennials have at the international level substituted for survey exhibitions of contemporary or modern art at the national level. Such surveys seem to have become a staple of institutional exhibitors of modern and contemporary art.[25]

These exhibitions may be categorized as surveys of periods, surveys of national art, surveys of the artistic production of cultural communities found within a nation or bridging national boundaries, and surveys of regional tendencies between nations.[26] Among non-national surveys are surveys of conceptual unities, surveys of the mental frames informing art or the zeitgeist,[27] surveys of art movements with a manifesto or position that may embrace different concepts, periods, or nations, and surveys of practices that are usually period-specific—being of "now," of the "last decade," or of some other close-to-the-present periodization—and defined by media or approaches to their use.

Perhaps the most interesting "chaste" comparators to biennials are the art exhibitions or competitions held to accompany the Olympic Games.[28] They appear to be "chaste" because they often claim to disinterestedly assemble art that is supposed to be representative of a host nation for a specific period. They are also deployed to officially consecrate by high cultural accompaniment the non–high culture sporting events with which they coincide—beyond *our* superlative bodies we also have *our* superlative artistic imaginations and superior collections of *our* cultural treasures.

Unfortunately Olympic art exhibitions are sometimes not well attended or given the publicity they deserve. The magnificent Papunya Tula exhibition held to accompany the Sydney Olympic Games in 2004 comes to mind in particular.[29] It was barely visited on the three occasions I went, though it included some of the country's most important paintings by indigenous artists, many of which, in a differently constituted international art world, would have already been recognized as masterpieces of our or any other age. Perhaps it is when the vagaries of particular sections of the art world are momentarily suspended on such occasions that we see what biennials might intend: the consecrated demonstration of a kind of Olympian achievement in the field of art relevant to its age and representative of the contemporary spirit. Significantly, however, they also point to the isolation of even the most achieved art in the popular discourse just as much as they display the competitive nature of national submission to biennials, whether by way of designated national pavilions or through the consecrated selection of master curators to create thematic exhibitions.

BIENNIALS AND CONTEMPORARY ASIAN ART

HOW have biennials, as specific institutions for the exhibition and thereby for the consecration of art, functioned for the contemporary art of various Asian countries? These institutions have two levels: the "international," which is hierarchically perceived as being superior or more important, and the "national," which is conceived of as being interested and "local," and therefore less important, even if it pretends to elevate local artists and their work to an "international" level. In recent years, biennials have been organized in Delhi, Dacca, Gwangju, Guangzhou, Shanghai, Beijing, and Yokohama to show local artists at an international level, but also to introduce what are in theory previously little-known international artists to the local art-viewing public. To date, there are no cross-national but explicitly regional biennials, although some are clearly intended to have that function, such as those of Dacca and Gwangju (figs. 3, 4).

These biennials appear to be caught up in, if not standing as a distanced representation of, the changing interrelations between nation-states and their cultures that are loosely called "globalism" or "globalization." The habit of taking art-world phenomena and reading into them worldviews or states of relationship between econo-political structures and cultural (or more specifically art) values has been part of modern art history since the mid nineteenth century.[30] Furthermore, in the opposite "Euramerican" methodological direction, the longing for metatheory may be a theological residue left over from the eighteenth-century European Enlightenment mediated by the developing educational and ideological structures of the modern state.[31] It would be premature to attribute all of the phenomena of new "international" biennials and their relations with "local" art worlds to "globalism," or to link these phenomena to changes in inter-state relations or to the nature of the state unit itself in order to understand international relations. There are far too many art- and art-institution-specific phenomena in play at biennials to make such a theory-down approach sensible.

Before looking at international biennials and their function as a site for the exhibition of contemporary Asian art, and at their interaction with its production, one would like to know more about biennials themselves, particularly biennials of the last fifteen or so years. It would appear that these have not been systematically researched, either because those who might have direct knowledge of biennials are tied up directly in their organization or because those involved with contemporary art criticism and theory are disinclined by their art historical training to carry out basic institutional analyses.[32] This state of affairs tends to leave no gap between the conceptual base of international curators, which is almost entirely constructed around their operational activity, and an understanding of what biennials are or how they function at a systemic level. There is, for example, a reasonably extensive series of interviews with and papers by international biennial curators thinking aloud about exhibitions, but very few if any of them want to define the system in which they are operating.[33] This means that in the current research there is no basic description of biennials and, as noted above, scarcely any analysis of their typology.[34]

Curators tend to be secretive about their budgets and artist selections. Biennials have a specific relationship to the consecration of contemporary artworks and their practices. As a specific type of exhibition site they are also related to the way certain kinds of noneconomic goods are created and made prominent through the spectacle of exhibition. The noneconomic situation of artworks, and of the artist as a kind of art performer, may metamorphose into economic benefits for the artist via the sale of works, and the work may also later be transformed via secondary sale into a kind of commodity circulation.

The questions of central concern to art history, insofar as this discipline concerns itself with contemporary art, may be grouped under four headings: circulation, mediation, units and levels of analysis, and the dynamics of art worlds.

LEVELS AND TYPES OF CIRCULATION

HOW do artworks, artists, and their curator-mediators circulate? It may seem self-evident that artworks circulate, but in fact the art object often seems like the secondary imprint of an artist-producer selected to produce a new variant of a known range of work or replicate one that is already known. However, works and their producers are not the only things that circulate; information about both does as well. Sometimes an artist achieves prominence thanks to a very small mention in an art magazine by a particular curator. I can only guess that artists often appear to achieve prominent circulation simply because their name is taken up in a variety of communications media, whether printed or electronic. This actual and virtual information-media "chatter" is taken up in a kind of mirroring process—if the signs attached to work or artist are appropriately configured—just as one might see more obviously in the repetition of a "style" or "look" in fashion magazines. Furthermore, while there are some very decent, humble curators, there are also others who make their cultural background an unspoken feature of their presence in an exhibition: curators become both quasi-artists and quasi-stars. Circulation at the international level of curators and artists, however physical their presence, does often appear to be one of symbolic simulacra. To put it in a manner that is perhaps more profound, if the phenomena of circulation are difficult to describe empirically, it is far more challenging to identify what kinds of circulation are at work and what hermeneutic models curators or art historians might deploy to understand them.

MEDIATION

THE participation of contemporary Asian art at biennials inside and outside Asia has thrown into relief the crucial role of curator-mediators who would have the public think they are somehow ethically neutral and simply operate tricky aesthetic judgments that select and position artists. In fact, such judgments are imbricated in a landscape of personal and public institutional self-interest from which curator-mediators are not only never freed, but which they may actually have to assert more concretely simply in order to function effectively. Here again we need a more precisely articulated typology of functions and units of analysis, the latter ranging from artists themselves to curators who may be nominally free of institutional attachment and others who are actually closely caught up in pursuing institutional goals as well as often formally attached to a museum of contemporary art or a nonprofit arts center. It is unclear exactly where art critics or even academics—who may be art historians or belong to other disciplines like anthropology or sociology—fit into such a typology.[35] These figures serve as another kind of mediator, for they often critically comment upon or academically analyze the judgments of curators. But the opinions of critics and academics are also part of a circulation of ideas and knowledge that itself affects mediation, and academics are increasingly moving away from mere opinion-forming mediation toward mediation through the works they select for exhibitions whose curation they themselves are involved in or lead.

UNITS AND LEVELS OF ANALYSIS

UNDER the heading of units and levels of analysis, I have begun to question whether there is actually any artwork in circulation anymore. This is partly because artworks are increasingly notional and become actual only for the limited moment of physical or conceptual reference in an exhibition, an actual or virtual site of mediation to a receiver. They are not simply concrete, physical works defined in specific media or site contexts that can be transferred between sites. And if this is true of works of art, it is even more true of the types of actors involved in art circulation. For if the role of the artist may be absorbed into, if not usurped by, that of the curator, does "art" not become simply a peculiar category of perceptual and conceptual life that itself circulates between the functions of producer, mediator, and reception? In other words, the notion that there are different kinds of actors defined by their function may have become transparent, mostly due to a change in the institutional characteristics of the siting of these actors that makes them interpenetrable.

If this is true of the units in question, levels are equally problematic. Since what we now tend loosely—but with experiential reason—to call the "global" appears to have dissolved the "national," we may now associate artistic practice in terms of the producer or mediator unit with a kind of "transnational" level at which circulation occurs between like units or their embodied functions but no longer in a manner defined by the nation-state.[36] That is, circulation has come to be defined by the distribution of like functions within nation-state entities. Of course, this does not allow for the very different cultural functions of different kinds of nation-state entities in relation to their cultural pretension or spatial aggrandizement beyond the state. Artists have often claimed to me that they just do what they do in order to make art. Curators may state they merely operate discrimination in a neutral but personal manner, but that does not change the fact that the whole context in which they do so has changed around them because of their curatorial activity.

THE DYNAMICS OF ART WORLDS

FINALLY, a range of issues involving the dynamics of art worlds has been brought out in my research. Why are artworks made and circulated? Or, put differently, what causes them to be made, or what processes of causation can we identify in their making? These may look like reformulations of long-standing issues of concern to art history, but I bring them up because we are dealing with basically new phenomena, or ones that have to be newly conceptualized. These have been identified above in terms of the fragility or interpermeability of the functions assigned to the main actors in this field as much as to the levels at and the nature of units inside or between which they operate. If these actors and units were not so unstable or redundant, we would not have to think again about the dynamics by which artworks are created, since we could simply aggregate old conceptions with the new ones: the making of works whose aesthetic features (beauty or ugliness) outstripped our social categories for handling them to give us a sense of the uncanny or of an unfathomable sublime. Artworks make us secure with the unknown, and appreciating them can in the spiritual domain take the place of religion. But now because of the interpenetration of units and what one could call "cultural worlds," the discourses in which those artworks function and the units and levels between which they flow have lost their internality, their autonomy. Just as all art is potentially now our art, so the units that structured the relations between the actors in art worlds have dissolved, even though what we see may borrow their old guises.

It may be that visual artworks are peculiarly capable of slipping across cultural boundaries and that this has always been the case. But when an artwork may be "made at" one end of the globe and "shown at" the other, then the audience that receives it and for whom it is mediated by a mediator—namely, the curator, who has been at both ends of the chain—is going to have to be differently constituted than one that was simply the local variation of some internationally sited set of tastes. Is this new, particular audience the site of a dynamic that is quite different from that of the production of an artwork for a national art salon, a dealer exhibition, or a manifesto or thematic exhibition previously confined to one art culture? What makes the work for this audience is surely the connection and the connector. I would say that the dynamic of art production has now come to privilege this connection to the extent that the artwork does not exist without it. And since the connection is supplied by the mediator-curator, it is the function of mediation and the actor who bears it that claims sovereignty in such a process: aesthetic sovereignty belongs neither to the creation of the work nor to its reception at either end of this circuit. But perhaps it does belong to those whose slippery insertions actually direct or control the circuit itself.

BIENNIALS AND THE FORMATION OF A MODERN ASIAN ART HISTORY

I HAVE deliberately couched much of the argument in the preceding four sections in general terms, without referring specifically to Asia, but my selection of illustrative figures has shown that I have had specifically Asian phenomena in mind all the time. Indeed my intention was to show that modernity might be discussed in this field, at least from a specifically Asian perspective, with a generality that can be applied to Euramerican phenomena as well. Thus is Euramerican modernity relativized.

The consequences of the rise of biennials as the sites for other-than-Asian consecration or within Asia of national consecration and later canonization are manifold. Let me name just two here: the first, evident since the removal of *nihonga* and senior artists from the Japanese artists sent to Venice from the nineteen-sixties, is the exclusion and relativization of both neotraditional and academic Western-style art as not being "of the current moment" and as retrograde if not atavist. This phenomenon, widely repeated in selections from other Asian countries for Venice by international, usually Euramerican curators, has meant that a historical link with the immediate past of many art cultures has been severed from the domain of current practice. It can be there as material or technique, but not as the constituent of art discourses as such. This has meant that an artist working within a neotraditionalist discourse such as *nihonga* is unlikely to be selected at the international level unless, like Murakami Takeshi or Nara Yoshitomo, they assimilate their conceptual position to that of their contemporaries, or to some interpretation of a zeitgeist that is clearly not that of simply repositioning art customary to a particular art culture.

The second consequence is that modern art history is continuously being recomposed by the display functions of current exhibition. Art that stays in a studio is dead, according to this interpretation, however much it is known by a circle of the artistically well-informed. These display functions are assimilated with ease into intellectual and commercial fashions, shown tellingly by the way in which the work of some video artists moves between advertising and artistic cultures, or in the way some images from popular culture can be massified into grandiose symbolic icons for art biennials. In fact, if in the twenties and thirties Art Deco fashion was a kind of parasite that fed on avant-garde art in Euramerica, then at least since the nineties advanced or thought-provoking art almost everywhere has become inalienably complicit with the flow of images and information found in the mediascape of commercial "culture" (= merchandising). The positions now are reversed: art has come to be dependent on fashion, this time *its* parasite.

The historical function of consecrating artworks as worthy of regard and then canonizing those of a near-present range of artists as valuable to collect is increasingly performed by the patronage decisions of the small group of mediators who situate themselves before cultural markets the way artists once put themselves in their mind's eye alongside other, largely passed-over masters. This stratum is increasingly in touch across national boundaries, and as its size and the frequency and scale of its activities increases, I suspect it will eventually divide itself into those oriented to the "transnational" and those oriented towards the projection of the "national" into the "international" and then "transnational" arenas. This may be accompanied sometimes with a return to a "national" domain of mediation after work at the "international" level followed by that carried out on the "transnational." Indeed, if one considers the career path of such Asian curators as Hasegawa Yûko, Nanjô Fumio, or Hou Hanru, this tendency is already plain.

It means that art history, insofar as it in part tracks selections made by such mediators, will itself start to cycle between these three levels, and the integrity of its subject will come from understanding the processes of such cycling, rather than from remaining within any single cycle. This might be where the Asian modern resides (fig. 5). ●

NOTES

This essay is an abridged version of Chapter 1 in: John Clark, *Biennales and Contemporary Asian Art: Histories of the Asian "New"* (forthcoming).

1 I am grateful to many international curators, art historian colleagues, gallerists, and collectors for materials and interviews relevant to my research on biennials, and I would particularly like to mention Furuichi Yasuko at The Japan Foundation, Ushiroshôji Masahiro at Kyûshû University, Kuroda Raiji and Rawanchaikul Toshiko at the Fukuoka Asian Art Museum, and Ulli Sigg. This essay was originally written for the Asia Society–Clark Institute of Art conference on *Asian Art History in the Twenty-First Century* held in April 2006, and an earlier version was published as "Contemporary Asian Art and Biennales: The Perpetual Modern?" in Desai Vishaka (ed.), *Asian Art History in the Twenty-First Century* (Williamstown, 2007).

2 There is a Frick Fine Arts Library bibliography, *International Exhibitions* (Library Guide Series, no. 42), available at www.library.pitt.edu/subject-guides/arthistory/. Of particular relevance here is Jean-Marc Poinsot, "Large Exhibitions: A Sketch of a Typology," in Reesa Greenberg, Bruce W. Ferguson, and Sandy Nairne (eds.), *Thinking about Exhibitions* (London, 1996). Histories of the Venice Biennial and national participation include: Lawrence Alloway, *The Venice Biennale, 1895–1968: From Salon to Goldfish Bowl* (London, 1968); Sophie Bowness and Clive Phillpot (eds.), *Britain at the Venice Biennale, 1895–1995* (London, 1995); Enzo di Martino, *The History of the Venice Biennale, 1895–2005* (Venice, 2005); and The Japan Foundation (ed.), *Venezia Biennale—Nihonsanka 40-nen / The Venice Biennale, 40 Years of Japanese Participation* (Tokyo, 1995).

3 A discussion of definitions of "contemporary art" may be found in Terry Smith, *What Is Contemporary Art? Contemporary Art, Contemporaneity and Art to Come* (Sydney, 2001). Robert Storr, curator of the 2007 Venice Biennial, led a by-invitation-only international symposium entitled "Where Art Worlds Meet: Multiple Modernities and the Global Salon" in Venice in December 2005. But I am afraid that—contrary to Stephanie Britton's "Biennials of the World: Myths, Facts, and Questions" (*Artlink* 25, no. 3 [September 2005], p. 34), where she refers to "mountains of ideas, analysis and critiques"—after some reading I do not find the literature on current biennials to be particularly rich, save for what are mostly practitioner discussions. Among these are the following: Alex Farquharson, "I Curate, You Curate, We Curate," *Art Monthly (UK)*, no. 269 (September 2003); William Furlong et al., *La Biennale di Venezia 1999* (Wimbledon, 1999); William Furlong et al., *Venice Biennale 2001* (Wimbledon, 2001); William Furlong et al., *Venice Agendas 2003: A Series of Three Breakfast Meetings* (Wimbledon, 2003) (I am grateful to William Furlong and Wimbledon School of Art for copies of these publications); Tim Griffin et al., "Global Tendencies: Globalism and the Large-Scale Exhibition," *Artforum* 42, no. 3 (November 2003); Walter Grasskamp, "For Example, *Documenta*, or, How Is Art History Produced," in Greenberg, Ferguson, and Nairne 1996 (see note 2); Mari Carmen Ramírez, "Brokering Identities: Art Curators and the Politics of Cultural Representation," in Greenberg, Ferguson, and Nairne 1996 (see note 2); Ralph Rugoff and Larry Rinder, "In Conversation," www.stretcher.org/archives; Ralph Rugoff, "Rules of the Game," *Frieze* 44 (January/February 1999); Terry Smith, "Biennales in the Conditions of Contemporaneity," *Art and Australia* 42, no. 4 (Autumn 2005).

4 This often takes place in a quasi-cultural market, before artworks actually become objects in art markets for purchase. In place of the two-level notion of a primary gallery and secondary investment art market, beloved out of self-interest in the trade talk of gallerists and auction houses, a four-level conception of art markets may be of more interpretive use:

1. artist to artist or artist to client for cultural esteem
2. artist to curator for cultural consecration
3. artist to gallery to client for economic sale
4. gallery to gallery, collector-investor to other collector-investor for monetary sale, or to institution for esteem and sometimes tax benefits.

5 "Circulation" may be identified as a key concern of current art history insofar as it addresses the link between museum and gallery practices and the definitions of contemporary art. For a review of some issues see the "Circulation" workshop papers available at http://www.arts.usyd.edu.au/art_history_film/research/workshops.shtml.

6 This term is not unproblematic and hinges on the nature and level of units between which "internationality" is supposed to take place. For a discussion of the problem of units see John Clark, "An Australian Creative Space: Where Is Australian-Asian Art Now?" in Dianne Waite (ed.), *2006 / Contemporary Commonwealth* (Melbourne, 2006), pp. 26–33.

7 Indeed, not-for-profit and artist-run spaces are increasingly trying to get around national mediators and international curators by organizing direct exchanges between themselves that bracket both the "national" and the "international" levels. See Duksung Women's University, Alternative Space Loop, and Yellow Sea Publications, *The 2nd "In-Between" International Alternative Space Conference: Globalism and Alternative Spaces* (Seoul, 2004). There are many examples of artist-to-artist exchanges that exemplify noninstitutional exchanges, such as the *Womanifesto* exhibitions in Thailand since 1995; see Brian Mertens, "Womanifesto 2001," *Art Asia Pacific*, no. 36 (2002).

8 The Fukuoka Asian Art Triennial has made particular efforts with residential artist programs which link up with broad sectors of the Fukuoka population. See Matsuura Jin, "Notes on the Artist-in-Residence Programme," in *Artisto in rejidensu seikaten* (Fukuoka, 2002).

9 For an introductory outline of the problem of modernity in Asian art see the entry "Modern and Contemporary Asian Art" at *Grove Art Online / The Dictionary of Art*, http://www.oxfordartonline.com/public/. For a more academic overall view see my "Modernities in Art: How Are They 'Other'?" in Wilfried van Damme and Kitty Zijlmans (eds.), *World Art Studies: Exploring Concepts and Approaches* (Amsterdam, 2006). The first book in this area, to my knowledge, was *Modern Art of Asia* (ed. Japan Cultural Forum, Tokyo, 1961). A conference that systematically brought various parts of modern and contemporary art into comparison was "Modernism and Postmodernism in Asian Art" held at the Australian National University, Canberra, in 1991, and most of the papers were published in John Clark (ed.), *Modernity in Asian Art* (Sydney, 1993). My own overall study is *Modern Asian Art* (Sydney and Honolulu, 1998). The general bibliography in this field—the 2007 edition of the *Bibliography of Modern and Contemporary Asian Art*—that serves as a guide for students can be downloaded at http://www.arts.usyd.edu.au/departs/arthistory/staff/jclark.shtml.

NOTES

10 Clearly the life histories, intellectual placement, and personal investment of the Western scholars studying modern Western art may account for this refusal. See my review of Hal Foster, Rosalind Krauss, Yves-Alain Bois, and Benjamin Buchloh, *art since 1900: modernism, antimodernism, postmodernism* (London, 2004): "A Short Review of a Very, Very Long Book," *Yishu: Journal of Contemporary Chinese Art* (December 2005). Unfortunately the printed version of my review left out my original list of Asian artists mentioned in this book who, except for Gutai, were all largely active in New York; for this, see note 16 below. The published review also used the term "Euro-American," not that of "Euramerican" that since 1998 I have argued we should use; see Clark 1998 (see note 9), pp. 11–12. Significantly, North American writers find the term "Euramerican" more problematic than, for example, Chinese or Japanese writers. This does not remove the need of those in Asia outside Euramerica first of all to understand their own modernities, and then to grasp how these may or may not fit into a wider perspective on modernity in art other than the available and Euramerica-centered one.

11 In his *L'Art contemporain international: Entre les institutions et le marché (le rapport disparu)* (Nîmes, 2002), Alain Quemin discusses "prescriptive countries" in contemporary art from an assemblage of factors including size of population and GDP per capita, the role of leading institutions and collectors, and the numbers of artists ranked in international comparative indices such as *Kunstcompass.* See Rohr-Bongrad Linde et al., *Kunst=Kapital, Der* Capital *Kunstkompass von 1970 bis heute* (Cologne, 2001).

12 In fact, when it was founded in 1955, Documenta was meant to be held every four years and has only become in subsequent decades a once-every-five-years event. The shifts between the tenor of the early Documenta curated by Arnold Bode and the later exhibitions have not gone unnoticed: "Today, the levity and transience of contemporary art would have driven a man like Bode to despair." René Block, "Never Play Sorcerer's Apprentice," in Carin Kuoni (ed.), *Words of Wisdom: A Curator's Vade Mecum on Contemporary Art* (New York, 2001), p. 28.

13 As far as I am aware, Matthew Ngui from Singapore was the first in Documenta 10 in 1997.

14 For other signs of this hegemony, see the Asian artists thought worthy of inclusion in Foster, Krauss, Bois, and Buchloh's *art since 1900* (see note 10), which mentions only the following: Ay-O, Gutai Group, Hsieh Tehching (Xie Dejing), Kusama Yayoi, Motonaga Sadamasa, Murakami Saburo, Ono Yoko, Paik Nam-jun, Shiomi Mieko, Shiraga Kazuo, Sumi Yasuo, Tanaka Atsuko, Rirkrit Tiravanija, Yoshida Toshio, Yoshihara Jiro, and Yoshihara Michio.

15 Indeed, if there are different kinds and levels of prescription in operation at various biennials, these themselves have a quite clear hierarchy between "international" biennials, such as Documenta and those of Venice or São Paulo, "national" biennials, such as those of Guangzhou, Shanghai, Beijing, Gwangju, or Yokohama, and "local" biennials, such as that of Chengdu or the Triennial of Chinese Art, whose second edition in 2005 took place in Nanjing. Alongside these levels of biennial are found what might be loosely but effectively understood as "quasi-biennials," that is, exhibitions of "nationally" selected art shown overseas as a representative selection from current practice. See Pauline Yao, "The Second Triennial of Chinese Art: History in the Making," *Yishu: Journal of Contemporary Chinese Art* 4, no. 5 (September 2005).

16 Pierre Bourdieu writes that "*consecration* cycles perform the fundamental operation of social alchemy, the transformation of arbitrary relations into legitimate relations, de facto differences into officially recognized distinctions." He later goes on to say that "the endless reconversion of economic capital into symbolic capital, at the cost of a wastage of social energy which is the condition for the permanence of domination, cannot succeed without the complicity of the whole group"; Bourdieu, *Outline of a Theory of Practice,* trans. Richard Nice (Cambridge [UK], 1977), p. 195. Also see Bourdieu's *La Distinction: Critique sociale du jugement* (Paris, 1979), pp. 463–65. How this is articulated on a global scale may be seen in Quemin 2002 (see note 11), pp. 136–72.

17 From my limited and personal observation of gallery purchasing interactions, there would seem to be a profound asymmetry between the volume/level of "sales" of contemporary art and patrons' wish to "purchase." Above a certain price for the artist, even a very low price relative to the work, skills, and materials involved in production, "selling" characterizes the nature of an exchange, usually from artist to gallery to client, but "buying" hardly characterizes the client's situation. Whether giving money for a work for pleasure or social esteem or investment (and usually all three), the buyer is not choosing between comparable or *equivalent* goods. The choice is between *different* goods whose price he or she will pay according to a desirability market usually both by private taste and public fashion, and not directly some utilitarian evaluation of satisfaction, quality, or need-fulfillment. There is no equivalent calculus between the artist's need to sell and the client's wish to buy, and both are usually articulated in quite different domains, the one economic, the other mostly as a store-symbol of cultural capital that will only be converted to economic capital at a deferred date.

18 A research database has been compiled for this project from names of Asian artists and the curators, including those of Asian origin, at selected biennials and other art exhibitions from 1989 to 2004. The exhibitions where the artist or curator appeared were awarded points that were ranked according to the importance of the exhibition, both for China and for all Asian countries. All the implications of this data have yet to be fully analyzed. In the case of China, the total sample was of 157 curators (as of November 2005, this number will slightly increase), and there were 19 curators with 4 points or more. With the actual points given in brackets, the top five curators were Hou Hanru (23), Chang Tsong-zung (13), Huang Du (09), Nanjô Fumio (09), and Harald Szeemann (08). In the case of Asia overall, a total of 103 curators and 15 curators had 4 points or more. The top six curators were Harald Szeemann (10), Nanjô Fumio (10), Kim Hong-hee (07), Apinan Poshyananda (05), Hasegawa Yûko (05), and Tatehata Akira (05). In the artists' database, for China there were 858 artists overall, with 55 artists with 10 points or more. The top eight artists were Cai Guoqiang (36), Xu Bing (30), Fang Lijun (26), Zhang Peili (25), Geng Jianyi (22), Huang Yongping (22), Yang Fudong (21), and Zhang Xiaogang (21). For Asia overall, there were 632 artists and the top ten artists had 10 points and above. Those artists were Heri Dono (17), Anish Kapoor (14), Kim Soo-ja (14), Miyajima Tatsuo (14), Navin Rawanchaikul (11), Ono Yoko (11), Hatsushiba-Nguyen Jun (11), Yanagi Yukinri (11), Montien Boonma (10), and Funakoshi Katsura (10).

NOTES

19 If one may unsatisfactorily judge by informal, unattributable reports. The Queensland Art Gallery director, Mr. Doug Hall, refused a request for an interview for this research. In the circumstances I felt unable to continue with a plan to interview curators since—whatever may be right or wrong about subsequent interpretations—one topic of this research was to model such decision chains where information was available and reliable. For relative transparency in this field, see Toshiko Rawanchaikul, "How Were the Artists Selected?" in Igarashi Rina (ed.), *The 3rd Fukuoka Asian Art Triennale 2005* (Fukuoka, 2005), pp. 030–033.

20 See Nanjô Fumio, "Yokohama Toriennaare 2001 kôki – sono tenmatsu no kojinteki memorandamu," *Aica Japan Newsletter*, no. 2 (November 2001).

21 For example, the Venice Biennial of 2003 included just such a zeitgeist survey, *Painting in the Twentieth Century* at the Museo Correr.

22 See, inter alia, Meryle Secrest, *Duveen: A Life in Art* (Chicago, 2004); Sybil Gordon Kantor, *Alfred H. Barr Jr. and the Intellectual Origins of the Museum of Modern Art* (Cambridge [MA], 2002); and Alice Goldfarb, *Alfred H. Barr, Jr.: Missionary for the Modern* (Chicago, 1989).

23 There are an increasing number of "chat" texts on curating practice, including Carolee Thea, *Foci: Interviews with Ten International Curators* (New York, 2001), and Kuoni 2001 (see note 12). A very useful collection with a comprehensive analysis of the functions of art in such events is Lewis Biggs, "'Art, Money, Parties' and Liverpool Biennial," in Jonathan Harris (ed.), *Art, Money, Parties: New Institutions in the Political Economy of Contemporary Art* (Liverpool, 2004). The broader problems of the "celebritization" of artists and curators are touched on in John Walker, *Art and Celebrity* (London, 2003).

24 As, for example, the exhortation to "Live Humble" in Marcia Tucker, "Become a Great Curator in Six Simple Steps!" in Kuoni 2001 (see note 12), p. 170.

25 In the contemporary Asian area there is a discussion by Kamiya Yuki, "A Potential Role of Asian Art in the International Art Scene: A Study of Asian Art Exhibitions in the United States and Japan," in Duksung Women's University et al. 2004 (see note 7).

26 As in exhibitions like *The Birth of Modern Art in Southeast Asia: Artists and Movements,* curated by Ushiroshôji Masahiro and held at the Fukuoka Art Museum in 1997, or Tatehata Akira et al., *Cubism in Asia: Unbounded Dialogues* (Tokyo, 2005).

27 The title of Harald Szeemann's *When Attitudes Become Form* (Bern, Kunsthalle, 1969) was clearly invoked in Philippe Vergne's publication *How Latitudes Become Forms: Art in a Global Age* (Minneapolis, 2003).

28 These would make an elegant study in their own right. There were art exhibitions at the Tokyo, Seoul, and Sydney Olympics. There is a study by Richard Stanton, *The Forgotten Olympic Art Competitions: The Story of Olympic Art Competitions of the 20th Century* (Victoria [BC], 2000). Significantly, the Venice Biennial is located on the site of a previous national exhibition of Italian art and the current building being used for the British Pavilion was once the café for the Italian national exhibition. One is thus led to the question, Are biennials actually a kind of "national" exhibition projected onto the "international" level where the "nation" no longer exists as the legitimating site but only as a source of materials for producers and mediators?

29 The Sydney exhibition was *Papunya Tula: Genesis and Genius,* Art Gallery of New South Wales in association with Papunya Tula Artists, 2000 (catalogue by Hetti Perkins and Hannah Fink).

30 The *locus classicus* is Jacob Burckhardt, *The Civilization of the Renaissance in Italy* [1860], trans. S. G. C. Middlemore (London, 1951).

31 Art history since the mid-nineteenth century has been the result of an uncomfortable series of positions established between a changing *weltanschauung* and an unstable conception of art. On this, see Hans Belting, *The End of the History of Art,* trans. Christopher Wood (Chicago, 1987), p. 15.

32 Apart from the work of Quemin (see note 11) and Charlotte Bydler (*The Global Art World, Inc.: On the Globalization of Contemporary Art* [Uppsala, 2004]); an abridged version of the latter appears in the present volume. The place of the Fukuoka Asian Art Triennial in Japanese international cultural flows is analyzed in detail in Kishi Sayaka, "Bijutsukan 'Ajia' to deau toki – Fukuoka Ajia Bijutsukan no setsuritsu to tenkai," in Hirano Kenichirô, kanshû, *Sengô nihon no kokusai bunka kôryû* (Tokyo, 2005).

33 See Kuoni 2001 (see note 12).

34 The exception is Charlotte Bydler's work; see Bydler 2004 (see note 32) and the abridged version of her book included in the present volume.

35 This is because art criticism in news media is largely lifestyle-oriented mediation designed for a niche market in order to increase the attractiveness of the newspaper for advertisers, and is often in any case linked to those commercial galleries able to secure such exposure for their artists.

36 See Clark 2006 (see note 6).

THE CURIOUS CASE OF BIENNIAL ART

Jan Verwoert

NEW INTERNATIONALISM AS IDEAL AND GENRE

WHAT does art do in a biennial? Let's say that it seeks to voice what matters to people in particular places in a manner that allows others to understand. If the spirit of contemporary art biennials is characterized by the hope of building a new global consciousness, the art on show proposes ways to embody it. In this sense, then, art in biennials reflects a desire and a need: the *desire* to share specific experiences in a situation of international exchange, and the *need* to find a mode of artistic expression that could accommodate the conflicting demands of experiential specificity and cross-cultural comprehensibility.

This conflict echoes the challenge that modernist avant-gardes set themselves: to find an artistic idiom that would convey originary intuitions in a globally understandable language. The crucial difference, however, is that the context within which we perceive the need for such a means of communication now is no longer defined by the dream of a unitary language, a revolutionary ism, an art that would accomplish the impossible and faithfully articulate mythic origins through universal forms. The exposure of the megalomaniacal nature of such isms has left us—and here "us" is meant to refer to anyone who is experiencing the current historical moment in the light of this disenchantment—in a difficult position in which we may still share the desire for art to produce genuine insights through cross-cultural communication, but know that (potentially insurmountable) cultural differences must be acknowledged if imperialist chauvinism is to be shunned. Expressive of this hope and reserve, the tone in which art speaks in biennials is thus marked both by a residual belief in the possibility of a free exchange *and* a heightened awareness of its limits.

Arguably, the rekindling of the hope for a free international artistic culture is a consequence of the events of 1989. After the impediments to exchange imposed by the rival superpowers of the Cold War had (largely) been lifted, it became strikingly apparent that the experiments in artistic form commenced during modernism were in fact continued, visibly or underground, in and out of sync with each other, in all kinds of places around the world; therefore, to grasp this legacy and develop its potential in a truly global framework would in fact be the task of the generation that witnessed this historical moment of transformation.

With the demise of the bipolar world order, however, the intricate geopolitical conditions of the history of the present became equally clear: On the one hand, today we face a world shaped by the brutally overriding logic of industrial *modernization* that transformed countries everywhere according to its dictates and linked all of them through a global infrastructure of pipelines, flight routes, satellite connections, and invisible cash flows. On the other hand, this logic of compulsive modernization turned out to have been interpreted in ever so many slightly but distinctively different ways in each and every country, region, or place affected by it. So while industrial modernization constitutes a failsafe *tertium comperationis* between any two places in the world, we have come to understand that, culturally, there were many modernities instead of just one, each of them a singular result of how the forces of modernization were locally applied, mediated, and opposed in historically unique ways.

The ramifications of this situation manifest themselves in the changed conditions under which art is produced and exhibited globally. The new awareness of the specific histories of local modernities has created a curiosity for the many yet-unheard stories that are there to be told, while the global infrastructure provides the armory of modern communications media to tell them and a system of cheap air travel that allows storytellers to be flown in and find new listeners. However, there are also no limits to the likelihood of failed encounters created by the confusion of technical possibilities with actual chances (and reasons) to share an experience. Just because a film, for instance, is now easily shot in digital video and delivered by courier (or data dump) to urban exhibition spaces anywhere in the world doesn't necessarily mean that this cultural transfer generates the potential of a meaningful encounter. But what cross-cultural modes of sharing experience are we looking for, then? After nearly twenty years of biennials proliferating worldwide, this question still begs for an answer, especially now that a (notoriously precarious, yet still somewhat feasible) infrastructure has been created, while the initial idealism of the biennial spirit may be on the verge of becoming exhausted by its routine invocation. It's not just that the concept of presenting global culture locally has been strained as a mantra of cultural marketing. Certain modes in which artworks tend to communicate in biennials—selling cultural difference as a thrill, enigma, or piece of information—seem to have by now become so recognizable that (in conversations among art professionals) these works can casually be referred to in terms of a *genre:* "biennial art."

That an idealistically promoted form of art should now be identifiable as a genre—and therefore as inherently *generic*—makes "biennial art" as prone to mockery as Abstract Expressionism was when, by the sixties, the disparity between the high-minded rhetorics used to advertise it (as a world language) and the formulaic nature of many of its proponents' works became all too obvious. To perform the rites of mockery as a means to throw questionable routines into relief is tempting, but in the end it's potentially productive here only as a ceremony to openly summon and exorcise the spirit of cynicism to which overly idealist ventures in art are bound to give rise. So, if in the following sections of this essay the implications of the use of the term "biennial art" as a genre are unfolded in a somewhat more caustic manner, this is done in order to foreground which forms of biennial discourse may have exhausted themselves, but also, ultimately, to raise this question: given that we have established the means to create a culture of international artistic exchange on biennials, what are the artistic, social, and political ends, criteria, motifs, and modes of communication we really want to embrace?

A CURSE THAT STICKS: THE USE OF THE TERM "BIENNIAL ART"

AS vague as it essentially remains, the term "biennial art" has the effect of a curse. This is because as a term describing a genre it designates a particular type of art. And it is in this act of primary typification that the curse takes hold. For if a *type* is easily identified, works that fulfill it are by definition marked out as *tokens* to a type—and hence instantly disqualified as merely *tokenistic* (i.e., derivative, calculating, flat, etc.). In this sense, the criticism notoriously leveled at art exhibitions dedicated to international exchange is already built into the term "biennial art": the contention that biennial exhibitions wallow in *tokenistic representations of cultural diversity* and display works by artists who make a career out of allowing themselves to be exploited in this manner. Like most figures of speech used to craft tendentious arguments, the term "biennial art" defies further specification in terms of its content precisely because its meaning lies in its use. It does what it says. It lays a curse on the exhibitions, artworks, and artists that are associated with the business of rendering the representation of cultural identity easily consumable for larger audiences by narrowing its horizons to fit expectations.

Apart from their impact on the subject addressed, a side effect of figures of speech that do what they say tends to be that they position the speaker. Once uttered, the curse of "biennial art" applies equally to the one who pronounced it. This is because in order to be in the position to know the discontents of a global exhibition industry, one must have traveled the world and thus experienced it firsthand. To use the term knowingly therefore means to implicate oneself in the discourse on the malaise of professional art-viewing as an initiate, and hence to identify oneself as a (world-weary) art professional. If we were to picture this gesture of self-implication literally as an act of cursing oneself, we could imagine a convention of sorcerers and sirens at which each participant, as a sign of modesty, appeared in the guise, in terms of transfiguring victims, of their animal of choice. (I'd go as a goat. How about you?)

To pick particular artworks as examples of the principles of biennial art and its discontents may seem tempting. Yet, it is part and parcel of the power of rhetorical typification that its logic remains unchallenged when individual tokens are presented as literal (counter)evidence. Sweeping assumptions made in his name, for example, are not invalidated when someone tracks down—and determines the preferences of—an actual plumber called Joe. If the attempt has any value it is comic value, due to the lack of humor it betrays. In their analysis of biased discourse, Etienne Balibar and Immanuel Wallerstein even go so far as to suggest that debating whether this or that token individual fits the (stereo)type or not is in itself, in fact, the dubious joy that prejudices generate. This is why we entertain them: opinionated discourse allows us to have opinions (e.g., "All Xs are Ys; only Z from next door is a little different") and feel important about it.[1] But let's not go there (yet).

Instead, let's risk a conjecture about what may be at stake—and for whom—in a debate in which the term biennial art is prominently used. If we were to focus on art production rather than institutions in this regard, one question to raise would be: is a new *modus operandi* for building an artistic practice enabled by the particular conditions that biennials provide? If one is, beyond this, prepared to acknowledge that international biennial art exhibitions do not just offer a set of career options (alternatives to the art market) but actually constitute a different public consciousness for art, then the next question would be: has art created for biennials in fact generated a new *set of criteria* for understanding what art can do when it goes global? The first question would seem to invite a social/political commentary on how the conditions offered by biennials has created a new set of options and strategies for performing the role of the artist. As it requires faith in the capacity of international biennials to open up a different horizon of art experience, the second perspective of inquiry, in turn, calls rather for a more hopeful philosophy of art's potential to communicate across cultural boundaries on the basis of a different set of terms. In the following sections I will try to pursue first the one and then the other line of speculation.

THREE MODES OF DELIVERING "BIENNIAL ART": PLAYING THE JOKER, THE THIEF, OR THE BOY/GIRL SCOUT

THE crux of a social/political commentary on the prevalent modes of performing the role of the artist is that it tends to presuppose that artists are operating *strategically* when they do what they do in order to become recognized in the field of art. While in many cases this arguably won't be too far off the mark, the contention that, quite generally, the trajectory of any artistic practice could be described in terms of a consistent strategy makes social/political discourse analysis prone to a particular brand of cynicism. Since ulterior ends that transcend the calculus of strategic means are generally assumed to be mere delusions (that social agents just entertain to sustain faith in their practice), the sociological study of operations in the field of art notoriously arrives at the conclusion that art-making is motivated by predictable interests in the benefits of social distinction. The fatal attraction of systemic sociology lies in the undeniable fact that its reductive form of description yields graphic results:[2] art-world sociology tends to read like a colorful caricature. This is unsurprising, since artists, next to dictators and drunks, have always been popular subjects of persiflage. It is where there is ego, status, or grace to be deflated by foregrounding the prosaic material aspects of someone's existence that the reductive gaze finds its most thankful objects. Perhaps it helps to foreground rather than deny this aspect of analysis. So, rather than donning the cloak of objectivity, as art sociology habitually does, I will openly continue these speculations in the *key of caricature* at the risk of being crude, but in the hope that the graphic characterizations yielded by the reductivist approach will be offset by the blatancy of (over)simplification.

If there is a *modus operandi* that biennials foster because they depend on it, it's that of the artist as communicator. This is because, unlike the head of a museum or *Kunsthalle* who will be granted some time to educate and charm a local audience gradually, biennial organizers face the demand of having to offer—within the temporal parameters set by the duration of the exhibition—an art to their audiences that can communicate quickly and, on the spot, deliver its content. The performance models that biennial culture has nurtured are hence first and foremost *modes of delivery.* The three most prominent types of delivery performers developed within biennial culture are: (1) the joker, (2) the thief, and (3) the Boy/Girl Scout.

Jokers are easy to grasp. They simply deliver *thrills* that are magical enough to make an audience feel charmed but not so demanding that they feel excluded. Thieves are more complex. They understand the economy of desires just as well as jokers do, but choose a different strategy by which to operate within it. Instead of spectacular over-gratification, thieves opt for clandestine ways of rarification. Thieves steal and deal in *secrets* (i.e., smoking mirrors), their most precious secret being the mirage of a cultural identity centered around an undecipherable trauma that glints like a ruby in the dust when one tentatively points a spotlight in its direction. Biennials offer optimal conditions for the trade of jokers and thieves. If they were forced to operate in a local context, they would eventually run out of jokes or get busted. The international biennial circuit, in contrast, allows jokers and thieves to keep moving and to perform the selfsame trick over and over for unprepared audiences. In their understanding of themselves, Boy/Girl Scouts do not succumb to the immoral politics upon which jokers and thieves build their careers. Boy/Girl Scouts are on a mission. What they deliver are *help* and *information.* They do collaborative projects, site- specific interventions, and documentary videos or informative displays. Whether the help offered is ever needed, however, usually remains as debatable as the question of whether the information presented had not already been long available to anyone bothered to read the papers regularly. But innocence is bliss.

In theory, all three types of performers—can and do—also operate outside the biennial circuit. Yet in practice, biennials are the school that hones their most crucial skill for efficient delivery: the tight *sense of timing* required to move into a given place, bedazzle, deceive or come to the rescue, and then move out again in no time. So even if the jokers, thieves, and Boy/Girl Scouts continue their careers elsewhere, their work remains marked by the legacy of biennials as the site where they became initiated into the artistry of their trade.

For writers these role models are unfortunately not as readily available. To play the joker is the prerogative of the critic working for local or daily newspapers whose position in the local political battles and hierarchies affords him or her the power to be populist and to flaunt this or that opinion depending on the mood of the day. Critics who live an itinerant life comparable to that of biennial artists will never have the backing of local power structures or the nationwide readership that are necessary for the cultivation of a persona baroque enough to permit playing the joker in this manner. The thief, in turn, is more or less impossible to embody for a writer. The writer must speak, whereas the thief must remain silent. Critical writing is a bad medium for the stealing and keeping of secrets. And poetry pays even less than criticism. To opt for the Boy/Girl Scout model would thus seem to present the only means of joining in on the play. It works well for writers, not least of all because the practice of regurgitating available information has proven to be compatible with a university career as an institutional backup plan. There is, however, a fourth model that is less easy to adopt for visual artists and more suited to those who know how to use language as an elegant means of distancing oneself from the problematic situations in which one finds oneself entangled: the model of the critic as the cosmopolitan cynic who portrays the world from the panoramic viewpoint of an imaginary watchtower. This is a delusion, too. But enough of this mean chat.

To go beyond the caricature of successful models we would have to presuppose that there is more at stake in the culture of biennials than the strategical need to survive in the closed economy of desires created by the alignment of international art circuits with local power structures and audiences. To assume that there is more implies a leap of faith. This leap would take us back to the initial promise of international artistic exchange, the modernist idea that to communicate across cultural boundaries is a genuine expression of artistic *freedom*. And this freedom in a critical modernist tradition means freedom from commodification. The main force of commodification at play in the biennials' economy of desire today is the pressure to perform an identity and deliver consumable chunks of communication. In the light of this *pressure to perform and deliver,* biennial art must indeed seem like a caricature of tokenistic cultural engagement. Whether this pressure is imposed from the outside by sponsors and audiences or was always already internalized as the new moral imperative of the cultural industries is difficult to determine. Still, it's fair to say that it governs the current politics of cultural production globally. So, to counteract this pressure would be a prime objective of critical art, thinking, and curating.

Now, if the spirit out of which this discontent with the pressure to deliver simulacra of cultural communication is born is a modernist yearning for a free form of international exchange, then the task for critical art, thinking, and curating would be to work through the implications of this notion of *free communication* anew in the light of the changed conditions with which the current postmodern, postcolonial geopolitical situation confronts us.

What is there to communicate in the first place? Jokers will proclaim that it's a witty idea that resonates with the spirit of the local. Thieves will close their eyes suggestively to insinuate that it's a traumatic narrative of identity. Boy/Girl Scouts will come for a site visit to search for something interesting to discuss. All of them will deliver something. But none will activate the potential to address and renegotiate the conditions of communication that art could have in a situation of cross-cultural exchange. The crux of the matter may be that we intuitively still understand communication primarily as a means by which to *convey content.* Due to its functionalist bias, however, this understanding already paves the way for the commodification of communication. If we picture there to be a distinct entity—or "content"—transferred from artists to audiences, this image in fact models the conditions of communication on those of a closed economy in which a clearly defined currency circulates. As a currency, content can be thrills, secrets, or information. It makes no difference, really. It's all interchangeable material that feeds the machine. Those who are called upon to supply it are thus reduced to the status of "content-providers." If we refuse to accept this concept of a closed economy of communication and the limiting terms of exchange it imposes any longer, the question to address would be: how could biennials be more than a global marketplace for content-providers?

THIEVES OR CREATURES LIKE US: TOWARDS A SENSUALIST ETHICS OF BIENNIAL ART AESTHETICS

ARTISTICALLY and philosophically (and socially and emotionally, if you will) the challenge then lies in thinking communication differently by rejecting the false premise that it is a form of content management. But what is there to communicate if not content? The answer is limits. When people meet and intuitively work out how to relate to each other, the implicit subject of their communicative interaction is, first and foremost, the limits of communication. Each party will communicate its limits and propose a mode of getting around them. Performatively speaking, communication is an encounter on a threshold defined by the mutual limits of understanding. The renegotiation of this boundary is what the performance underlying communicative acts is initially concerned with. This is a rough paraphrase of how Jean-Luc Nancy develops his phenomenological account of communication as a performance *on*, or rather *of*, a threshold.[3] Taking this account of an initial encounter as a model for literary (or in the widest sense, artistic) communication, Nancy then develops a set of criteria to describe the ethical quality of a certain mode of performing the threshold.

The ethics that he identifies as inherent to the acts of writing and reading is a mutual dedication to struggling with the limits of understanding that both writer and reader avow when the one seeks to make him- or herself understood through writing and the other seeks to understand through the act of reading. As the writing, beyond being print on paper, is only brought to life in the process of this struggle, the experience of reading writing is the sensation of a threshold coming into being. The work in fact *is* that threshold; it constitutes it. The experience of encountering a potent work is the realization that the encounter itself is made possible through the emergence of a threshold (an opening as much as a boundary) on which the experience (of the work as a threshold) occurs. To attune oneself to the intricate dynamics that allow for a threshold to emerge and be negotiated is the ethical stance that Nancy espouses. The mutual avowal of the emergence of a threshold in the exchange between reader and writer is what he terms the ethics of a “literary communism.” The spirit out of which this kind of communism is born is not that of an identity invoked, but of a limit avowed. Speculatively, then, the question to be addressed to biennial culture could be: how can we go beyond an understanding of international biennials as a platform for the delivery of content towards an actualization of their potential to become sites where the collective avowal of the limits that form the threshold to a different kind of communication could be enacted?

This question applies to how the entire exhibition communicates the threshold on which it seeks to communicate. But it also very much relates to the mode in which the works in the exhibition bring into being the limits at which the experience of/in the exhibition then becomes possible. To formulate in prescriptive terms how this should ideally happen, however, would be absurd. If we recognize the *freedom* to negotiate at or over a threshold as the key quality at stake in this ethics of communication, then to impose moral protocols on the dynamics of the encounter would obviously defeat the idea and destroy its spirit. In search of criteria that delineate what mode of communicating limits would seem desirable (and what mode would not), however, it seems almost inevitable that we must distinguish between different manners in which the threshold can be avowed or dissimulated.

An easy target to hone in on would be work that does not even acknowledge the significance of negotiating boundaries and unthinkingly passes over the threshold to impose itself on the viewers, be it through overwhelming aesthetic thrills or by bludgeoning them on the head with hard facts and newsworthy information. But this would take us no further than the stock-in-trade criticism of biennial art usually goes. Rather, the limit at which things get critical is set by works that do precisely what an ethics of performing the threshold in principle would ask for: the staging of the threshold as such, and no more than that. Picture an empty shoebox, a few oranges left behind on workbenches, a puddle of water in an empty factory hall, sloping ribbons suspended in midair, an illuminated curtain, a melancholy long shot on 16mm film of nothing much happening . . . and you see contemporary examples of an aesthetics of sheer potentiality that give you all you desire, and nothing more. It is true that work that deliberately remains on the threshold to evoke a sense of the possible (the desirable, the lost, the hidden, the disappeared, the miraculous) defies the pressure to deliver positive content. It also acknowledges that our negotiations of boundaries in art are deeply steeped in the politics of desire. It does this by putting desires into play. Before you know it, that precious experience of something that is next to nothing is all you want. It's the dance of the veil or the game of *fort-da*, the psychoanalytic formula for negotiating the terms of desire, enacted in nuce. So where does playing peek-a-boo on the threshold take us? It would lead us to admit that all "thieves like us" do is steal from one another what none of us has: that precious little something that would make us feel we had gotten the best we'll ever get.

Bringing content back in is no help. Just because someone talks to you about something doesn't mean that they aren't out to seduce you (or bore you to death). The dynamics of desire (hope and belief) will, in some form or another, always play a crucial role in how attention is attracted and held when the contract that will determine our relationship to a person or an artwork is tacitly negotiated on the threshold of communication. As thieves, it would seem, we therefore always meet. The question is only if, besides that, we could also meet in another guise—for instance, as *fellow creatures*. To speak of creatures here is in no way meant to invoke a humanist sense of a basic condition of similarity. On the contrary, as creatures we all smell, taste, look, and sound (a little but decisive bit) differently (when we get happy, sad, hungry, angry, lazy, excited, or bored). And it is this difference that, on a sensual level, also constitutes—and plays across—the initial threshold of communication.

This is a given, and therefore is no guideline. The simple avowal of that creaturely remainder of difference would literally, however, already make all the difference. A bond between creatures, no matter how tentative, would at least seem to be a more promising point of departure for future communication than a deal between thieves. There is something about sharing an aspect of one's creaturely condition, at the risk of complete embarrassment, that just might put communication on a different footing. This is not to suggest that sharing a creaturely moment through art (or writing) on the basis of a particular taste, look, sound, or scent would in any way ensure a better form of communication. On the contrary, taste, looks, sound, and scent may in fact remain elements of the incommunicable, or remainders of that which does not compute or translate but nonetheless affects the other and in doing so creates the threshold of the encounter. Accents, too, are exemplary in this regard. In an international context, art (or writing) inevitably speaks with an accent, and an accent neither computes nor translates. Still, phenomenologically speaking, it is the first sensual experience you struggle with when you encounter a person or work on the threshold to another linguistic realm. This is not written in praise of authenticity, for accents can easily be faked (and doing so is endless fun). It is only to say that beyond the elegant manipulation of potentialities that make a threshold appear there might be certain remainders of opacity—stuff that tastes, looks, smells, or sounds peculiar—which, when acknowledged and brought into play at the risk of embarrassment, give a different tone or touch to a work.

Admittedly, taking a sensualist ethical position in regard to art that seeks to effect a form of cross-cultural communication remains tricky. The global culture of biennials has frequently been criticized for encouraging a form of art tourism that revives the most dubious kinds of bourgeois, if not colonial, customs of going round the world to consume cultural difference as if it were a culinary treat. To renounce any allegiance to this tradition (and the idiocy and arrogance it implies) is imperative. But to pretend we were packaged and posted off as brains in a vat when we go to see or show work and talk to people in the context of an international biennial exhibition would be ridiculous.

The point, rather, is to appreciate and develop sensuality—or *sentience*, in an expanded sense—as a form of intelligence that determines the conditions of communication precisely by creating thresholds that are barriers as much as ports of entry. This is not least because discussing biennial art in terms of *representation* seems bound to get stuck in (apologies against) the allegation that these representations were tokenistic, just as analysis of the modes of artistic *performance* on the biennial circuit leads to the predictable conclusion that these performances are strategic. To resituate the debate about what, at a biennial, art could be and do in a scenario that grants some freedom to speculate about perspectives, we may want to revisit the question of an inherent ethics of aesthetic experience. To do so would mean to abandon the exhausted vocabulary of postwar humanist internationalism and to experiment with a different artistic and philosophical language in order to articulate what may be at stake when we have a sensual encounter with someone or something at the limits of our understanding and on the threshold of a different form of communication.

In the context of an international biennial exhibition, to experiment with a different form of artistic communication—one that defies the pressure to deliver content just as much as a politics of smoke and mirrors—is to work on the conditions for the production of a different kind of consciousness, one that would reflect the global topology of fragmented yet interconnected modernities precisely by throwing into relief how those modernities differ and touch on their limits. For modernity is the limit that all modernities share, as life in different countries, in very particular ways, has been—and continues to be—*pushed to its limit* (of productivity and exhaustion) by the global forces of modernization. It is in this liminal zone that we meet, as we get pushed into it from different directions. Each life or modernity has its own particular limits—on one side, touching, and on the other that one global limit, that fault line constituted by the push of modernization.[4] How can a form of consciousness that would touch on the(se) limit(s) in art—and thus articulate the experience of meeting in the zone that opens up around the limit(s)—be produced? Perhaps to touch on a limit and make it tangible is not to transgress it, but rather, as Irit Rogoff has suggested, to dwell upon, linger on, and inhabit it.[5] The temporality of learning how to inhabit a limit is indeed fundamentally different from the sense of timing that the mode of instantaneous delivery requires. It's a long-term exercise of the mind and body, a discourse that continues over many years—the time it takes for a language to acquire strange new inflections due to exposure to the accents of others. Beyond the pressure to perform and deliver representations, the continued conviviality of creatures inhabiting the zones of sentience on the thresholds between local modernities may, in the end, even entail being freed from the demand to enact and represent only the identity assigned by one's passport. Through contagion and transference, the demon of one modernity may instead pass from the body that hosted it before to a body formed by another modernity and speak through the mouth of that other body with a different voice, though retaining a peculiar accent that betrays that it came from without. It's messy. In fact, the point is that it's not yet messy enough. So if there is a good reason for artistic, curatorial critical experiments with the conditions of cross-cultural communication on biennials to continue, it's that two decades are not nearly enough time in which to attempt to inhabit the zones of sentience on the thresholds between our modernities. More time is still needed for art and thought to get entangled in a manner that would be as painfully and joyfully messy as a global art consciousness deserves to be. ●

NOTES

This essay was specially commissioned for *The Biennial Reader*.

1 See Etienne Balibar and Immanuel Wallerstein, *Race, nation, classe: Les identités ambiguës* (Paris, 1988), Chapter 1.

2 I am here paraphrasing an argument that Eve Kosofsky Sedgwick develops in depth in her fabulous essay "Paranoid Reading and Reparative Reading, or, You're So Paranoid You Probably Think This Essay Is about You" (in idem, *Touching Feeling* [Durham (NC) and London, 2003], pp. 123–52). She argues that systemic theoretical approaches, particularly of sociological and psychological provenance, are "strong affect theories" because they leave one with a world explained and no surprises to fear and, in this sense, provide the joys of the paranoid mind to know always in advance what was and is going to happen.

3 Jean-Luc Nancy, "Literary Communism," in idem, *The Inoperative Community* (Minneapolis, 1991), pp. 71–81.

4 To describe the spatial logic of such a liminal zone, Deleuze and Guattari draw on the mathematical model of Riemann's space, inside of which, if I understand it correctly, the positions of points and planes are not defined through fixed metric coordinates but rather through the *tactic connections* that occur around the *borders* of the fields, which together form a patchwork of territories. See Gilles Deleuze and Felix Guattari, "A Thousand Plateaus," in *The Mathematical Model (Multiplicities)* (London and New York, 2004), pp. 532–33.

5 To think about approaching the threshold between conflicting modernities not in terms of a single act or intervention, but in terms of a *long-term* effort of inhabiting this conflict, of staying in there, is a proposition Irit Rogoff made in her contribution to a panel in the context of the Art Sheffield biennial of 2008.

THE HAVANA BIENNIAL: A CONCRETE UTOPIA

198

Gerardo Mosquera

THERE is a certain amount of idealism in every biennial, just as there is in any exhibition. Donna de Salvo has even said that curators "trade in ideals."[1] This idealism comes from narratives of enlightenment and humanism that have been deeply built into art. In his report on the 1997 conference in Bellagio that was a pioneering antecedent of the 2009 Bergen Biennial Conference, Michael Brenson underlined the opposition between the realistic approach to curatorial issues of the curators who participated and the heroic, in some cases messianic ambitions of the biennials they were curating.[2] Although we are now living in more cynical times, it is true that around every biennial hovers a feeling that the event will contribute something positive to the human spirit, or even make this world better. On the other hand, the practical goals of biennials are frequently the result of optimism about the functional possibilities of culture, which sometimes prove to be a failed myth—in the short run at least. Is the fact that some 200 periodic contemporary art exhibitions take place all over the world the consequence of the need for art or just the *use* of art?

I am going to discuss here what we could consider the ultimate utopian biennial: the Havana Biennial in its first editions.[3] The Havana Biennial was born in the utopian context of the Cuban Revolution out of the desire to transform international power relations connected to the circulation and legitimation of art. No less idealistic were its more down-to-earth political and ideological ends.

It is amazing how misrecognized the historic relevance of the Havana Biennial has remained. An "itinerary of silence," as Gayatri Chakravorty Spivak would call it, has obfuscated the groundbreaking role the Biennial has played in changing mainstream hierarchies and giving the international circulation of art the scope it enjoys today, thereby breaking these away from the very restrictive situation that prevailed in the mid eighties. Since I am going to analyze an event that is not well known and has not yet been legitimized, I have to provide a factual account. It is, in fact, an uneasy task for me to discuss the Biennial, for I was one of its founders. Fortunately, however, I resigned immediately after its third edition was held in 1989.

The Biennial was part of Cuba's strategy of organizing every kind of international event in all fields as a way of publicizing its political messianism and crafting a positive image of itself. For the Cuban regime, representation has always been a priority that has surpassed the country's scale and economic means. The first Biennial took place in 1984 and therefore became the fourth biennial (after those of Venice, São

Paulo, and Sydney) and the sixth international periodic art event to be established, following in the footsteps of the aforementioned biennials, the Carnegie International, and Documenta. The Biennial was supported by the Cuban government, which, in turn, was subsidized by the USSR at the time. (fig. 1)

The reason for the Cuban regime's intense spending on cultural activity has always been ideological and involved strong international activity. We can consider this to be either utopianism or political expediency, or both. However, we would be restricting our view on this policy if we were merely to think that its only purposes were to promote socialist ideas, to fight against the isolation imposed on Cuba by the U.S., to showcase a positive image of the country, and to co-opt Cuban and Third World intellectuals (fig. 2). It's true that since 1959 the country has been an outpost for revolutionary and ideological struggles by virtue of its combination of geographic location and political messianism. The Cuban revolution has always had an expansionist agenda and has been involved in revolutionary warfare and subversion throughout the world. Apart from some obvious differences, Cuba's approach to the arts has been similarly aggressive.

If Cuba had managed to maintain considerable political autonomy during certain periods of its history, by the eighties it was completely inserted within the Soviet bloc. However, Cuba was a strange member of the bloc, given that it is a Caribbean country with a very distinct culture located only ninety miles from the U.S. with clocks that show the same time as New York and a long and consistent modernist tradition that began in the early twentieth century... The Cuban revolution was one of the toughest and most radical in history, but, since it happened in a Caribbean country famous for its music and nightlife, it was also, as Che Guevara once put it, a "revolución con pachanga," or "revolution with a party." Cuba had a genuinely Latin American and Third World cultural and political agenda that was sometimes at odds with the Soviet Union's communist orthodoxy. And as part of the role of beachhead for communism and Soviet policy that Cuba had always played, its peculiar character was used in those days to try to make Cuba into a Third World leader. In aspiring to this status it was competing with China, which opposed the Soviet bloc and was also trying to claim a leadership role. This confrontation was the reason why neither Chinese artists nor artists of Chinese descent were invited to the first Havana biennials. Therefore, for historical, political, and cultural reasons Cuba had an inclination towards Caribbean, Latin American, and Third World cultures on the one hand,

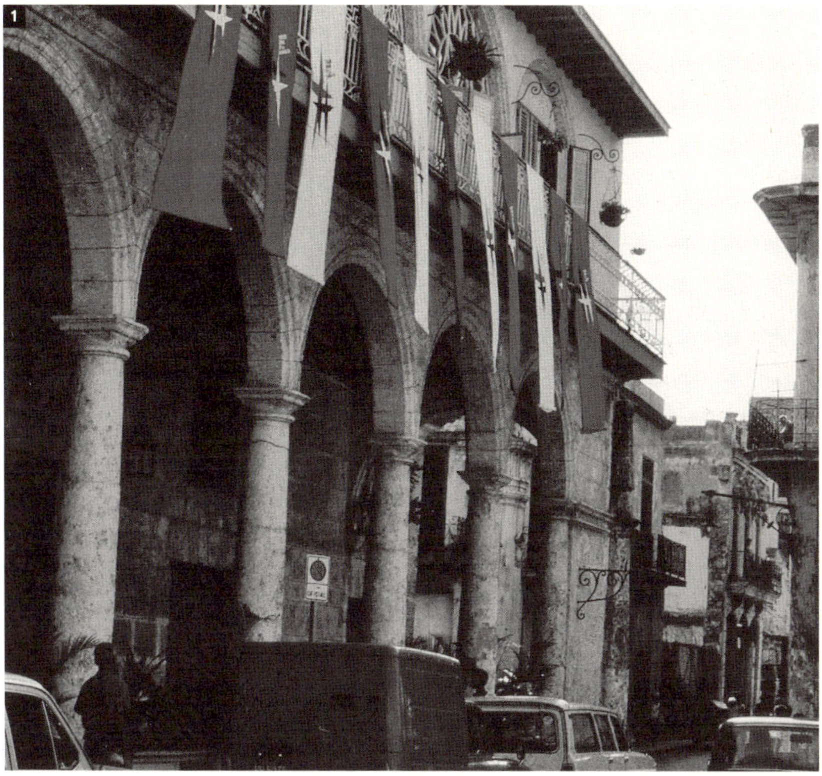

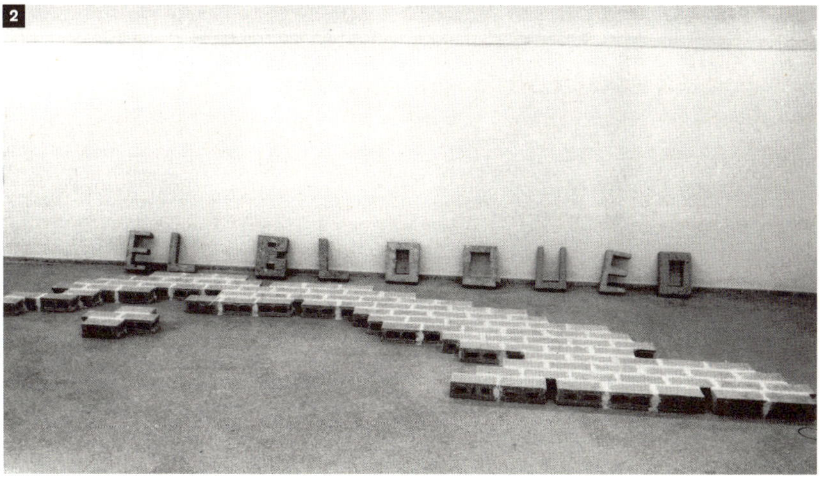

1 Banners printed with the logo of the Havana Biennial were hung throughout the city in 1986.

2 Tonel, *El bloqueo*, 1989, Havana Biennial.

but on the other, this inclination was exploited and supported by the Soviet bloc as a means of gaining political influence over other Third World countries.

The institutional backdrop I have just roughly outlined also possessed some positive aspects that made the historic role played by the Havana Biennial possible. The Cuban regime launched the event in the pursuit of political goals, and while it may have remained unaware of the Biennial's artistic and cultural scope and importance, it was smart enough to leave its creation to a team of specialists from the visual arts field. The government gave the curators considerable latitude, interfering only in decisions that would have a direct political impact, such as the exclusion of the Chinese or the inclusion of North Korean artists. Such policy has been typical of the Cuban regime, which has generally allowed the arts and culture a considerable degree of freedom, although these areas have experienced numerous repressive episodes. It was also clear that in organizing an event dealing with such a vast range of countries and artists it would not be possible to maintain a restrictive Marxist ideological frame. So, the Biennial was conceived as an open space in which contemporary artists, critics, curators, and scholars from Africa, Asia, the Caribbean, Latin America, and the Middle East, as well as from the diasporic communities of these places in Europe and North America, could meet and become acquainted with each other's work and ideas beyond questions of ideology or pure politics. This was the Biennial's most important and utopian aspect, but the event was also pragmatic in the sense that it responded to the practical need to create a platform for research and promotion at a time when artists from the "peripheries" (most of the world) were unknown beyond their local contexts. Of course, in so doing the regime was successfully contributing to the fulfillment of its practical goal of becoming a Third World leader. At the same time, however, the Biennial was satisfying a critical need for the presentation of contemporary art outside the mainstream and making room for its curators' sincere commitment to doing work that was inspired by a vision they considered to be of global importance. The Biennial thus embodied a convergence of governmental politics and a plausible commitment to transform the circulation, knowledge, and legitimation of contemporary art on a global scale with a vision for the future.

It is crucial to consider that the Biennial was born in the context of a radical cultural renovation being carried out in Cuba by a new generation of visual artists and critics that had emerged at the end of the seventies. The so-called New Cuban Art[4] transformed forever the conservative, ideology-oriented official culture that had prevailed during that decade, pushing the Ministry of Culture, to which the Biennial reported, to cultivate a more liberal policy. The young artists involved in this developed a critical, postmodern, internationally open approach to art, a fact that helped create the more liberal climate that was essential to shaping the Biennial's nature and providing it with an environment in which a healthy artistic and cultural spirit could bloom. At the same time, the event functioned as a platform for launching Cuba's new artists.

Held in 1984, the first Havana Biennial was huge, though restricted to Latin America for logistical and organizational reasons, and was launched as a sort of test or training experience. The second edition held in 1986 achieved a scope that extended throughout the Third World. It was the first global contemporary art show ever: a mammoth, uneven, chaotic bunch of more than 50 exhibitions and events presenting 2,400 works by 690 artists from 57 countries.[5] The Biennial's variegated structure made it a true urban festival, a *pachanga* that involved the whole city.[6] More importantly, never before had artists, curators, critics, and scholars from Buenos Aires to Kingston, and from Brazzaville to Beirut and Jakarta met "horizontally." What made this Biennial historic was not its curating but its curatorial perspective. If its curating suffered from the vastness and swiftness of the task and from a lack of knowledge, preparation, and organization, the event's curatorial standpoint was nevertheless the result of a clear vision that anticipated the internationalization of contemporary art that we enjoy today. Thus the Biennial's idealistic agenda hit its mark, triggering the foundation of other biennials in the "peripheries." The importance of this breakthrough at the time is more evident when we notice that even today a lack of South–South interaction persists.

By the mid eighties, segregation was very critical in the visual arts. The preexisting periodic international art events, such as the Venice Biennial and Documenta, were far from being global ones: only five percent of the artists who participated in them were not from Western Europe or North America. Thus the Havana Biennial created a new, truly international "other" space while acting at the same time as a gigantic "Salon des Refusées" that involved most of the world. The Biennial was born out of utopianism, but also out of a spirit of action: we thought, if we are marginalized, then let us create our *own* space, our own networks, values, and epistemes, and project them into the world; it is a goal that we have only very partially achieved. If the Biennial in those days only included artists from the Third World, this was done in order to confront their exclusion and a lack of intercommunication and networking, never because the event organizers considered that some sort of "Third World art" existed as an ontological category distinct from that of "Western art." As Luis Camnitzer has said, the Biennial was not about "otherness" but about "itness."[7] The Biennial recognized and emphasized artistic and cultural differences, but within a shared, postcolonial practice of contemporary art, thereby providing little room for traditional or religious aesthetic-symbolic production; this was one of its main differences from *Les Magiciens de la Terre.* In this sense it was foreseeing the current way in which art is created and consumed internationally, a process that involves the increasing role of a plurality of new artistic and cultural subjects and art scenes around the globe. Paradoxically, as a result of its focus on contemporary art, the Biennial was accused of being Westernized.

The first Havana Biennials were conceived as organisms consisting of shows, events, meetings, publications, and outreach programs rather than as exhibitions. Along with the main program there was also a constellation of exhibitions and diverse events organized by various spaces and institutions distributed throughout the city. This model intended, ideally, to employ a more diverse approach at the general level while cultivating a specific thematic, artistic, and cultural focus for each particular event. It pioneered an awareness of the need to change the traditional model of the biennial. However, the Biennial never got rid of the contradiction of keeping the large, customary blockbuster exhibition, which tended to be regarded by many as "the biennial" while the rest of the events were considered fringe ventures.

The Biennial was idealistic in both international and local terms. The diversified, open, gridlike structure of the first editions was largely determined by their wish to achieve a broader social and educational impact and a deeper involvement with the city. Entrance was free, and the Biennial was discussed both in the media and in schools; the Biennial was everywhere. Artists and critics worked at cultural institutions in the city's neighborhoods, they talked and danced with people at grassroots parties, they were mugged, had love affairs, were joined by students who volunteered to put the shows and workshops together . . . Even if they were not exhibiting at the Biennial, most local artists became involved with the event in one way or another.

A meaningful element of the Biennial's program in the early days was its "utopian" bar. We were always concerned with providing an accessible space where participants coming from different continents, many of whom felt isolated, would be able to meet one another informally and exchange ideas. This was not so easy in the Cuba of the mid eighties, before the country was opened up to tourism and when the few bars, cafés, and restaurants were usually terrible and overcrowded. As a result, the two bars that the Biennial created at its main exhibition venues were even included in the second Biennial catalogue's list of exhibitions and events, where they were called "meeting places." The bars were emblematic of one of the Biennial's main ideals and achievements: the establishment of a space for encounter and for the sharing of knowledge as part of the goal of creating a "horizontal" South–South platform very much based on personal contact between people from different art worlds.

By 1989, however, the new Cuban artists were trespassing the boundaries that the Cuban regime was prepared to tolerate. Their criticism of Cuban society and their deconstruction of the nation's official rhetoric had become too radical, and was consequently suppressed. Many artists went into exile, and the intense, dynamic liberal climate that had prevailed in the eighties changed. Then, during the third Biennial's opening days, the Berlin Wall fell. After that, Cuba proved unable to reinvent itself in the new post–Cold War landscape and thus became a fossil. Instead of responding to the new and challenging times, it introduced minor changes to keep everything the same. Although we could say that the Biennial's vision was already forging new times, the event was not independent enough to escape the changes that the country itself was suffering. Thanks to the Biennial organizers' efforts, the editions of the early nineties managed to maintain the event's original character. Eventually, however, the Biennial did evolve into just another standard international art exhibition, instead of activating its innovative orientation and experimentation with new methods and strategies, and this was partially a consequence of losing its acting utopia. In Camnitzer's words, the Biennial mutated from "an alternative independent forum" into "a provider of the international market."[8] The Biennial has also become a paradoxical global event in that it is always curated by essentially the same official team. As a result, a lack of curatorial focus and of a rigorous, uncompromised selection of artists has always afflicted the Havana Biennial, and its centralism has predisposed it to a certain authoritarian, bureaucratic, and even repressive stance, as was made evident by the instances of indirect or blatant censorship that have occurred in the last editions.

The idea of utopia has been a driving force behind the creation of biennials, mainly in nonmainstream places, and behind the positive transformation of these events in the attempt to respond to the new realities of our time. Perhaps the best reason to create a biennial is that you want to experience an exhibition that does not yet exist, so you decide to make it yourself so that you can enjoy it. Utopia can function as an impulse for agency, as a machine for positive transformation. However, it can also be a way of ignoring the intricate realities of art and its production, circulation, and consumption. I have lived this utopia and have seen firsthand the worst thing about it: its idealistic dreams produce the most cynical, traumatic, and Orwellian attempts to force dreams to transform a reluctant reality—utopia creates its opposite.

Perhaps Ernst Bloch's notion of a "concrete utopia"[9] could be useful in defining the Havana Biennial. Unlike what he called an "abstract utopia," the result of wishful thinking, voluntarism, and imposition that is incapable of interaction with the real world, Bloch argued that a "concrete utopia" can anticipate and help build the future, for it is the result of hope and desire as forces for change. He proclaimed that our imagined vision of the future plays a role in the creation of our actual future. But this can only work if a concrete, practical utopia functions as an agent in activating potential that actually exists in the real world, rather than imposing a uniteral messianism. Even more, this concrete utopia needs to be a partial utopia; it has to move away from the "changer la vie" obsession that pushes utopia towards totalitarian unrealism. Finally, this concrete utopia should also be a utopia on the move—a dynamic force that changes in response to new times and situations. Utopia is always a dangerous tightrope. Its ambivalence is rooted, as a warning, in the impossible paradox that the term itself embodies: etymologically, utopia means both "good place" and "no place." ●

NOTES

This essay is a revised version of a lecture given at the Bergen Biennial Conference, September 17–20, 2009.

1 Donna de Salvo, "Notes on Curating," in Carin Kuoni (ed.), *Words of Wisdom: A Curator's Vade Mecum on Contemporary Art* (New York, 2002), p. 48.

2 Michael Brenson, "The Curator's Moment," in Zoya Kocur and Simon Leung (eds.), *Theory in Contemporary Art since 1985* (Malden [MA], 2005), pp. 61–65. This essay has also been reprinted in the present volume.

3 See a broader discussion of the subject in Gerardo Mosquera, "The 3rd Havana Biennial 1989 in Its Global and Local Contexts," paper for the international conference *Exhibitions and the World at Large,* Tate Britain, London, April 3, 2009, from which I have borrowed here.

4 See Luis Camnitzer, *New Art of Cuba* (Austin, 1994), and Gerardo Mosquera, "The 'New Cuban Art,'" in Ales Erjavec (ed.), *Postmodernism and the Postsocialist Condition: Politicized Art under Late Socialism* (Berkeley, 2003), pp. 208–46.

5 *Segunda Bienal de La Habana '86: Catálogo general,* exh. cat. 2nd Havana Biennial (Havana, 1986).

6 For its paradigmatic involvement with the public I remember in particular Julio Le Parc's workshop with young artists that consisted of playful, interactive interventions at a park in the El Vedado neighborhood. There was also the impressive transformation of the space of the Petit Trianon–looking building of the Museum of Decorative Arts by young Cuban artists who participated in Marta Palau's workshop. An amazing, open, public fashion show took place with models performing at night on a catwalk that was built in a colonial plaza at Habana Vieja, wearing dresses made out of fabric designed by Cuban artists (the project was called *Telarte*), while a crowd composed of people from the neighborhood, visitors, and the local art world enjoyed it.

7 Luis Camnitzer, "The Biennial of Utopias," in idem, *On Art, Artists, Latin America, and Other Utopias,* ed. Rachel Weiss (Austin, 2009).

8 Ibid.

9 Ernst Bloch, *The Principle of Hope* (Cambridge [MA], 1986).

THE CURATORIAL

EXHIBITION OF AN EXHIBITION (1972)

210

Daniel Buren

MORE and more, the subject of an exhibition tends not be the display of artworks, but the exhibition of the exhibition as a work of art. Here, the Documenta team, headed by Harald Szeemann, exhibits (artworks) and exposes itself (to critiques).

The works presented are carefully chosen touches of color in the tableau* that composes each section (room) as a whole.

There is even an order to these colors, these being defined and arranged according to the drawn design** of the section (selection) in which they are spread out/presented.

These sections (castrations), themselves carefully chosen "touches of color" in the tableau that makes up the exhibition as a whole and in its very principle, only appear by placing themselves under the wing of the organizer, who reunifies art by rendering it equivalent everywhere in the case/screen that he prepares for it.

The organizer assumes the contradictions; it is he who safeguards them.

It is true, then, that the exhibition establishes itself as its own subject, and its own subject as a work of art. The exhibition is the "valorizing receptacle" in which art is played out and founders, because even if the artwork was formerly revealed thanks to the museum, it now serves as nothing more than a decorative gimmick for the survival of the museum as tableau, a tableau whose author is none other than the exhibition organizer.

And the artist throws her- or himself and her or his work into this trap, because the artist and her or his work, which are powerless from the force of habit of art, have no choice but to allow another to be exhibited: the organizer.

Hence, the exhibition as a tableau of art, as the limit of the exhibition of art.
Thus, the limits art has created for itself, as shelter, turn against it by imitating it, and the refuge that the limits of art had constituted are revealed as its justification, reality, and tomb.

D. B., February 1972

* Translator's note: The French word *tableau* has multiple meanings; it can refer to a painting, a scene, a chart, a table, a board, a picture. Since there is no adequate English translation for Buren's literal and metaphorical use of the word here, it is preferable to retain the original.

** Translator's note: Buren uses the word *dess(e)in*, a combination of *dessin*, drawing, and *dessein*, plan or design.

WHERE ARE THE ARTISTS? (2004)

212

Daniel Buren

WHY do I precede this brief reflection with a text that is more than thirty years old?

Simply because it seems that the question/proposition "Should the next Documenta be curated by an artist?" and what I wrote in 1972 about another Documenta are absolutely linked.

Thirty-two years ago, Harald Szeemann—who as the general organizer of the exhibition was the first to be concerned by this text—found it intelligent, naturally, but excessive, and hundreds of leagues away from his personal attitude, which he claimed was exclusively that of a person who, after having analyzed the production of the largest number of living artists, was choosing those who seemed to him to produce the most interesting works and, from there, was putting them together in the most suitable manner by arranging their works in the best possible fashion and even, often, by following the desires of those who know best how to express them.

What could be more natural than this response? It is a bit like a good deed. The perfect organizer's good deed. There is no reference to the personality of the organizer in this declaration, nor any pretension to "create" the event. This implies that if there is an event, the invited artists will have created it, not the organizer!

Nevertheless, and despite his comments or his denials, my text indicated and could not have invented that other things were already at play.

These are things which H. S., more than any other organizer of the period, had already brought to light, since he was by far the most gifted and easily the best of his time (and of those who, afterward, tried to imitate him) in the realm of group exhibitions. Hence, it seems to me, the accuracy of the text "Exhibition of an Exhibition," which analyzed the possible perverse effects of large group exhibitions that were emerging at the start of the most promising exhibition organizer's career.

Judging from a tendency that could already be felt in 1972, today we can assert that the proclivity of most exhibition organizers is to conform as exactly as possible to what this text was already anticipating. So much so that it has become a sort of stylistic epidemic, an artistic genre in itself, a rampant competition in which the organizer proclaims as loudly as possible that he or she is the artist of the exhibition, and to such an extent that Harald Szeemann, who found my 1972 text attributing to him the role of principal artist of the exhibition inappropriate, today claims to be an "author of exhibitions," undoubtedly out of fear of being outdone and of appearing simply like a nice organizer from the past. However, one must be careful to not misunderstand; the big change in this late-coming proclamation is not that Harald Szeemann has transformed the way in which he has conceived of his exhibitions, nor that he has over-personalized everything he has undertaken. It is simply that, at the end of the sixties and at the beginning of the seventies, no exhibition organizer concerned with his or her career would have dared claim out loud that they were the authors of whatever exhibition they were in charge of, and they would have been even less inclined to claim they were the artists! Even if it had been the case, to say so would have denigrated the invited artists, who would not have hesitated to let them know in no uncertain terms, and who would have undoubtedly rebelled. But times have changed (fig. 1)!

We have come full circle and the generalized passivity of artists in the face of this situation is even more serious than it was thirty years ago. Since if in 1972 they could still turn a deaf ear and a blind eye to the ways in which they were being used, the straightforwardness of our epoch (which others might call cynicism) makes it entirely improbable that artists today do not know what is being plotted and what is being declared and the kinds of discourses surrounding them!

Just as it is hard to know if the chicken or the egg came first, it is also difficult to make out if this situation stems from the suicidal passivity of artists, automatically engendering organizers capable of bypassing or even replacing them at a moment's notice, or if the artists, having other fish to fry when confronted with the impertinence of certain organizers/manipulators, would have literally pushed themselves to the side by disparagingly watching the spectacular emphasis of the exhibition organizer to his own detriment, and above all to the detriment of his work as the exclusive center of the exhibition, which it naturally should be, for better or for worse.

Today, it is possible to imagine that we are not far-off from having a large-scale international exhibition directed by a great organizer-author who proposes the first exhibition without any artists at all!

Enough of these nightmares, and without wanting to specify all of the reasons for such a slippage here, it is certain, however, that the affirmation of one (the organizer as author or artist) and the passivity/acceptance of the other (the work of art as a

1
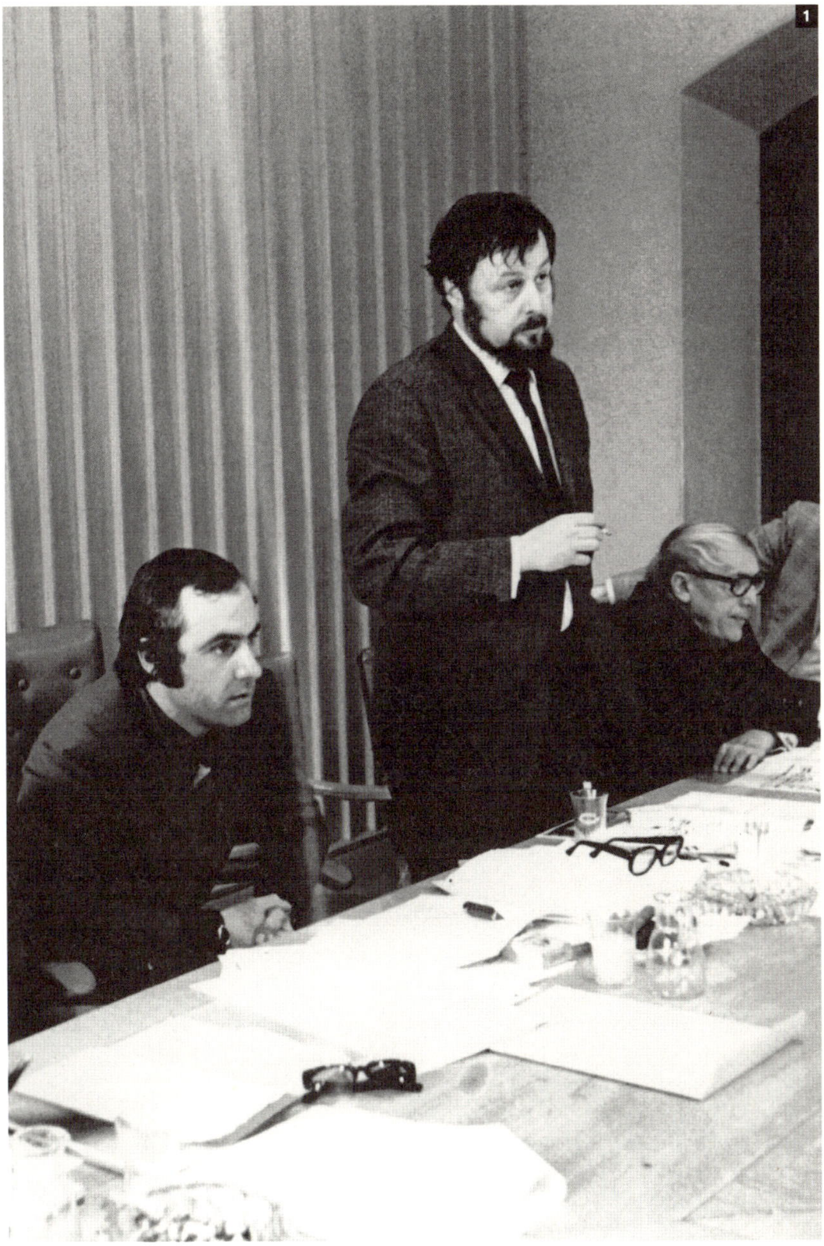

1 Harald Szeemann at Documenta 5, 1972.

colored stroke in a large fresco that escapes him or her) are two sides of the same problem: the present crisis of living art and how it is shown.

It is also, in most cases, proof that the couple "organizer versus invited artists" is no longer homogenous, but one that looks even more like a forced marriage just asking to be broken up. All the more so since, as everyone today knows, this infernal couple is made up of one who dominates and one who is dominated. The same people always play these roles, without any possibility for reversal. The former are always more dominating, while the latter are always more dominated.

However, if most invited artists were to refuse the role assumed by certain exhibition organizers, it is worth betting that they would no longer work in the atrocious way that some of them have been working, and we would never again see Robert Ryman's works on pink walls under the pretext of innovation!

I also have to assert here, so as not to be misunderstood, that I cannot imagine for one second an ambitious group exhibition without an organizer. The role of the organizer is very important in the selection and the mise-en-scène, when it is necessary, and it seems impossible to me to do without it. The organizer exists and must continue to exist. I am not calling into question their existence, just their manner of existing.

However, the problem underscored above—that is, the meaningless, because excessive, domination exercised by the author or artist-organizer—is even more crucial with regard to large-scale international exhibitions today; from Kassel to Venice, from Lyon to Istanbul, this has been evident for years. All of the large-scale international exhibitions are currently in a state of crisis, and I would not be surprised if one of the major causes is the problem we are concerned with here: the reversal of roles ratifying the organizer as author and the artist as interpreter.

Is it possible today to do without the organizer-artist or the organizer-author and return to the organizer-interpreter? In the absolute, the response is yes, of course, but it seems to me that the current situation is not moving in this direction; on the contrary.

We want to personalize everything, spectacularize everything, and individualize everything to the extreme. We no longer accept that the organizer remain in the shadow of the invited artists.

In the face of such a trend we can understand better why, with the help of laziness, organizers/authors have attained such importance in relation to the selected artists. Instead of studying the dozens and dozens of works presented, we can simply transfer all interest, criticism included, onto the shoulders of a single person, the organizer-author! What a relief! We put all of the works in the same basket and we throw praise or criticism at whomever has put them in it and carries it; that is, the author of the compilation. And just as we go from compilation to compilation, we go from exhibition to exhibition, taking off or adding one or two pieces just as we take off or add a singer or two from a compact disc. And there you have it! We are made to believe that we have an entirely new exhibition every time!

So, the question remains: How do we get out of this cul-de-sac, this vicious circle?

From this perspective, your question has the advantage of redistributing the cards. Could a large-scale exhibition like Documenta be entrusted to an artist? If the tendency remarked upon here continues to hold, my response would undoubtedly be "yes." For the artist-organizer would erase the faults inherent in the organizer-artist. For example, it would be worth betting that the announcement of an artist-organizer, whoever he or she might be, would cause an immense outcry of lamentations from the choir of the majority of all the other panic-stricken and destabilized artists.

This will be a varied and serious song. Its reasons for being will be intelligent, stupid, and revealing at the same time. They will be founded on jealousy on the one hand, and fear of the artist-organizer's positions on the other. Artists, exacerbated individualists if ever they existed, would show that their corporatist spirit is not as remote as it may seem. One would notice, then, that the critiques suddenly raised by the announcement of the name of an artist-organizer had never been raised by the announcement of any organizer-artist. This a priori predictable reaction already bears within itself the fruits of extremely positive debates, for they reveal a state of fact that has been occulted for over thirty years.

Undoubtedly other kinds of faults inherent to the choice of the artist in question would crop up, but given that an experiment of this sort has yet to be attempted (apart from much more modest experiments undertaken here and there by artists as different as Duchamp or even Kosuth or myself), it seems a bit too early to mention it. What other reasons—besides opening up a real debate—are there for welcoming an artist-organizer, even though such a possibility would certainly not be revolutionary? First and foremost, an initiative of this sort could bring the dulled, even anesthetized, artistic tribe out of the torpor it has been in for years now. Second, it seems to me that the artist in question would continue working as usual but in another way, and this parameter alone would immediately allow for a clear perspective on the exhibition itself, both for the artists who would accept or refuse such an invitation and for those (amateurs and professionals) who would critique the exhibition once it opened.

Now, this putting into perspective with regard to artistic work over the long term, verifiable in the works, does not exist when an exhibition organizer, whatever his or her talent, suddenly becomes an organizer-artist or author of an exhibition. His or her talent is linked to nothing else than the exhibition in question and the theme he or she has decided to develop, which in most cases is a bit too insubstantial to be a "work"! However, the theme chosen by the usual organizer-author, which will enable commentators to exercise their eloquence, is never remarked upon by the invited artists, whether it interests them or not. They will just as soon agree to participate in the exhibition of another (or the same) author-organizer that develops a diametrically opposed theme, which their (same) works will aim to illustrate as well (that is, as poorly) as the preceding exhibition, period, and so on.

If exhibition organizers today defend the status of author it means that they consider that the work resides in the exhibition produced (which becomes their work) and that, as I wrote in 1972, the exhibited works, the fragments that make up the corpus of this exhibition, are not really artworks but have become, at best, accents, particular details in the service of the work in question, the exhibition of our organizer-author. At the same time—and this is where the problem has become pointed enough to create the crisis in which we find ourselves—the "fragments" and other "details" exhibited are, by definition and in most cases, completely and entirely foreign to the principal work in which they are participating, that is, the exhibition in question. On the other hand, if the organizer of the exhibition is a full-time artist, it is worth betting that he or she will take enormous risks and that his or her vision will be more explicit, less neutral, more engaged; in a word, it will make more sense than that of an organizer by profession, whether or not he or she proclaims him- or herself an author. The latter will only be able to work by using the work of others or, if you like, by using work that is docile enough to fit into their own discourse, which strongly risks corresponding to current, fashion, or tastes.

For at least thirty years now there have been abundant examples of organizers rigging up group exhibitions in their own way in order to make "works"; and their own way is not always up to the works employed, to say the least. All the more so because, in most cases, their "works" are nothing but even more large-scale imitations of certain artistic movements or research that they pillage for their own benefit, vulgarize, and attach to all of the invited artists, who, generally lacking in mistrust, find themselves cursed with a costume that does not fit them, when it isn't a big red nose that the organizer-author/clown has placed smack in the middle of their face. At least with an organizer chosen from among artists (those capable of assuming and willing to take on such a delicate and dangerous role would certainly not be very numerous!) we would know a little bit more precisely the spirit in which they position themselves in relationship to the world. We could read the exhibition with much more perspective and more seriously than we seem to be able to do under the reign of the organizer-authors. At least, I think so.

Yet, why does such a possibility (that an artist organize the next Documenta) seem so original and so surprising, even improbable, once it is considered in the space of the plastic arts, whereas, a priori, it would not pose any problems in other cultural realms? Without pretending to respond to this strange situation, it could be useful to look around and to try to understand why what may be evident elsewhere is hardly conceivable here.

Who is most often nominated to be the head of an opera house? A highly skilled musician (interpreter, composer, or director of an orchestra, or all of those things at once). Is an artist, a painter or sculptor, nominated to run an important museum? Never. Actors, directors, authors, or someone who engages in all three activities are frequently hired to run theaters. Are living artists nominated to run art centers? Never. Publishing houses often entrust complete collections—from the choice of authors to the writing of texts—to a writer, a philosopher, a novelist, or an essayist. Are artists named directors or editors-in-chief of art magazines? Never!

It is not rare to find writers, playwrights, musicians, and directors in charge of rubrics treating literature, theater, music, and cinema in journals, magazines, or other reviews. Is it possible to find an art criticism column written by an artist? Never!

The only exception to this quasi-generalized and systematic exclusion of artists from positions in which decisions are made is in the very area in which they work: art schools. Why? It's a mystery!

The aim of these reflections is not to study the reasons for the absence of artists on the front lines of all of the domains cited above, where certain of them, if it were possible and if they so desired, could undoubtedly have their place. Yet, if we wager that we could decipher the reasons, would we be any closer to knowing what an artist is today? What is their role in society? What do we offer them and why? What do we never offer them and why? What role do we assign to them, really? And why does their place seem to become even more restricted as time goes by?

Given the far from brilliant state that contemporary art finds itself in today, it seems entirely appropriate that certain artists could assert their presence exactly where it is never solicited. The organizers/authors/artists of large-scale exhibitions provide results we already know: Documenta transformed into a circus (Jan Hoet) or even as a platform for the promotion of curators who profit from the occasion in order to publish their thesis in the form of a catalogue (Catherine David) or as a tribune in favor of the developing politically correct world (Okwui Enwezor) or other exhibitions by organizer-authors trying to provide new merchandise to the ever voracious Western market for art consumption, which, like all markets, must ceaselessly and rapidly renew itself in order not to succumb, hence, in order to bring about: *Magicians of the Earth* by J. H. Martin, the Chinese and the breathless "youth-ism" of H. S.

Others, undoubtedly too influenced by the history of art of yesterday and today, forget that even if they do admire the gesture of a creator like Duchamp for having put a mustache on a fake Mona Lisa, or the research of artists like Sylvie Fleury or John Armleder, this does not give them the right to hang a Bernard Buffet on a Sol Le Witt wall drawing, or to place a doghouse sold by Gucci in front of a Claude Levêque.[2] In doing so, at least they should not add to the taste for such banality the pretension of calling themselves an "author" by generalizing the attitudes of artists who have already proved themselves elsewhere on the scale of an entire exhibition.

To be an organizer-author is surely not to make fun of art at its own expense, especially since there are already a good number of artists who do so quite well and thus one is only shamelessly imitating them.

There are swarms of examples of doubtful worth and I think, at such a level of "non-thinking," that occasionally putting an artist (or several artists) in charge of a large-scale exhibition like Documenta would help to redistribute the cards, as I indicated above, and perhaps help us to see the questions that living artists today are posing, whatever their age, a bit more clearly.

If it is indispensable that every organizer play a creative role when exercising his or her profession (whether they are artists themselves or curators), then it is less obvious that the result of this creativity, the exhibition produced, is a work in itself. And if this is the case, what about the "works" that make it up?

Therefore, the question that remains, and the one worth asking, is whether an exhibition that brings together a large number of different artworks can become a "work" itself.

Whether the response is yes or no, from the moment that a group exhibition is signed and defended by a veritable author who would also be, for the space of this exhibition, its organizer, strong evidence would be given on this subject that only an artist, it seems to me, can provide today. ●

NOTES

Previously published as: "Exhibition of an Exhibition," *Documenta 5: Befragung der Realität – Bildwelten heute*, ed. Harald Szeemann, exh. cat. Kassel, Museum Fridericianum, 1972, Section 17, p. 29; and "Where Are the Artists?" in Jens Hoffmann (ed.), *The Next Documenta Should Be Curated by an Artist* (New York and Frankfurt, 2004), pp. 26–31.

1 Generally speaking, the art magazines created and financed by artists themselves are those whose editors-in-chief or associates do everything for the magazine, and those that are published irregularly and that never fail to collapse (which does diminish their quality).

2 This is in reference to an exhibition in Avignon during the summer of 2003 signed by Eric Troncy, organizer-author of the exhibition.

THE CURATOR'S MOMENT: TRENDS IN THE FIELD OF INTERNATIONAL CONTEMPORARY ART EXHIBITIONS (1998)

Michael Brenson

In August 1997, fifteen curators from Africa, Asia, Australia, Latin America, Europe, and the United States met at the Rockefeller Foundation's Conference and Study Center in Bellagio, Italy, to consider the rapidly developing field of international contemporary art exhibitions. Conceived by Noreen Tomassi, director of Arts International, and Tomás Ybarra-Frausto, associate director of arts and humanities at the Rockefeller Foundation, the conference was designed to enable curators struggling with the extraordinary and in some ways unprecedented challenges posed by international contemporary art exhibitions to share their ideas and concerns. The moderator was Kinshasha Holman Conwill, director of the Studio Museum in Harlem, who helped shape the program. Each curator made a presentation, as did Betye Saar, representing the artists' perspective, and Saskia Sassen, professor of urban planning at the University of Chicago and an expert on globalism. Tomassi asked if I would be interested in attending the conference and then writing a report that would be made available that fall to the participants, as well as to other curators and funders.

Tomassi knew of my interest in international exhibitions when I worked for the New York Times (1982–91). *In Barcelona in 1993 I had attended "Crossing Cultures," one of several international conferences Arts International has organized to consider pressing issues in art and culture. I had written on the issue of art and community and had worked as a consultant for the Rockefeller Foundation, which financed the Bellagio conference, an event that was remarkable in its thoughtfulness, intensity, and candor.*

After listening to heads of international biennials and triennials speak with one another for three days about their hopes and concerns, it was clear to me that the era of the curator has begun. The organizers of these exhibitions, as well as other curators around the world who work across cultures and are able to think imaginatively about the points of compatibility and conflict among them, must be at once aestheticians, diplomats, economists, critics, historians, politicians, audience developers, and promoters. They must be able to communicate not only with artists but also with community leaders, business executives, and heads of state. They must be comfortable with people who have devoted their lives to art and culture, with people who neither like nor trust art, and with people who may be willing, if they are convinced that art serves their interests or is sufficiently connected to their lives, to be won over by an artist or an exhibition. As much as any artist, critic, or museum director, the new curator understands, and is able to articulate, the ability of art to touch and mobilize people and encourage debates about spirituality, creativity, identity, and the nation. The texture and tone of the curator's voice, the voices it welcomes or excludes, and the shape of the conversation it sets in motion are essential to the texture and perception of contemporary art. The focus on Catherine David, curator at the Jeu de Paume in Paris, throughout the one hundred days of her 1997 Documenta 10 was not an aberration.[1] For the foreseeable future, the ambitions, methodologies, and personal styles of the curators responsible for major international contemporary art exhibitions will be as essential to their content as any artist's work.

In the midst of the recent chapter in the history of museums that was largely defined by the ethnicity- and identity-based exhibition, Mari Carmen Ramírez, curator of Latin American art at the Jack S. Blanton Museum of Art in Austin, Texas, and another participant in the Bellagio meetings, recognized the importance of curators' working across and between cultures. In her 1994 essay "Brokering Identities: Art Curators and the Politics of Cultural Representation," an analysis of the history of Latin American and Latino exhibitions in the United States, she noted the "transformation of the curator of contemporary art from behind-the-scenes aesthetic arbiter into central player in the broader stage of global cultural politics." If this transformation was evident to her in 1994, how much more complete it must have been in 1997, the year of five international biennials—in Cairo, Havana, Venice, Istanbul, and Johannesburg—as well as Documenta. Look at the issues embedded in these exhibitions: nationalism versus internationalism or transnationalism; indigenous cultures versus global media; handmade traditions versus technological networks; respect for the intimate experience of art versus a belief in curatorial interventions that can make the artistic message, and sometimes even that intimacy itself, broadly accessible; and belief in the intrinsic value of art versus an obligation to put art in the service of extraordinary social and political needs. The urgency of these issues underlines the challenges facing the curatorial profession to think deeply about multiple audiences and to allow individual curatorial perspectives to be invigorated by radically, even shockingly, different experiences of space and time, memory and history. These unframable high-stakes biennial projects do not reward curatorial business as usual. Like those curators who work outside galleries and museums to develop projects that propose reimagining the site of, the audience for, and perhaps even the nature of the art experience, the biennial curator cannot succeed without a hands-on involvement in every aspect of the program. For the new curator, the clear-cut division of responsibilities between the curatorial, administrative, education, marketing, and public information departments that has been a reality in large museums in the United States for well over a decade—a division that has tended to detach many curators from their audiences and blind them to the nonaesthetic interests their museums are serving—is inconceivable. If this division exists, meeting their responsibilities is impossible.

While large international contemporary art exhibitions are helping to expand the roles and responsibilities of the curator, many artists find themselves having to develop in aesthetic and political climates of increasing suspicion and constraint. Throughout the United States, the political right is ridiculing artists, and even the idea of the artist; within the contemporary art community, there is now widespread contempt for any tendency to romanticize the individuality, personality, hand, and heroism of the artist. Monograph and biography are now the most disparaged forms of art history. Not surprisingly, much of the most respected new art in Europe and the United States is defined by a noticeable degree of self-effacement. It is intended to draw attention to ideas, processes, and situations—not to itself as an object (if that is what it is) or to its makers. In October 1997 I heard Kristaps Gelzis, a young sculptor in Riga, Latvia, say that he liked Documenta 10 because "it was not concerned with the artist but with process," and Andy Goldsworthy, an English landscape sculptor, remark, while constructing one of his delicate, undulating walls of unattached stones at the Storm King Art Center in upstate New York, that he wanted to make work that "would take credit for itself." In other words, as the curator becomes a more and more visible player in the world of contemporary art, more artists are concealing their egos to prove to the art community, to the general public, and to themselves that they are worthy of respect.

At the same time, the presentation of art is more dependent on the curator than ever. There seems to be a consensus that when art from one culture is shown in another, it cannot speak for itself. Because of the inevitably loaded nature of the responses of a museumgoer in New York, let's say, or Washington, D. C., to contemporary art from Zaire, Colombia, or Cambodia, the idea of a museum's presenting an object from one culture in such a way that it would offer an intensely private object-to-visitor encounter to someone from another culture, in which no one or nothing else is welcome and viewers are free to respond as they please, is increasingly unacceptable in the United States. Sufficient clues must be given to enable viewers to orient themselves to the work and to provide viewers unfamiliar with the conditions in which it was created at least some sense of what it means to appreciate it on its own terms. Hand in hand with an awareness of the challenges of presenting art from one culture in a very different cultural context is a growing awareness within museums that art exhibited in any museum is seen by many people who feel they have little or no access to it and that they need to be encouraged to feel that the aesthetic experience belongs to them as much as to anyone else. The perplexing combination of curiosity and distrust, respect and exploitation, that defines many institutional approaches to audience cannot be explored here. What needs to be stated is that the increasing institutional awareness of the importance of the audience has made curators more visible as mediators between art and its publics.

The increasing centrality of the curator has also been reinforced by the emergence of installation as the standard form in which contemporary artists around the world are working. Installations involve selecting and arranging in a space often shared by visitors. They may also involve writing and educating. Installations were designed, in part, to contextualize and therefore empower themselves by inscribing within them an awareness and even the look of a gallery or museum. By so doing, however, they implicitly acknowledge the curator's inescapable authority. Blurring the line between artist and curator builds into the experience of art a heightened awareness of the curator's reality.

Yet I have so many questions. How did we reach the point where we expect art to respond to the needs and aspirations of peoples and nations? Are there limits to what art can be asked to do? Why have the expectations for art increased at a time when the individual artist is feared, not only in the United States but in many other countries as well, and the artist's voice is being systematically deconstructed? What are the political implications of approaching art as a means to an end, rather than an end in itself, or both a means and an end? Is it the responsibility of the curator to ensure respect for the integrity of a work of art, which can survive, miraculously, even if the art points everywhere but toward itself and all the walls between it and the world around it seem dissolved? At what point does approaching a work of art in terms of what it can do, rather than in terms of what makes it unlike any other work, or indeed anything else, bring to mind nightmares of instrumental thinking?

TRANSPARENCY

THE discussions in Bellagio underlined the importance of several related constellations of words. The constellation that includes "impurity," "partiality," and "incompleteness" suggests the rejection of any assumption of absolute authority, conclusive knowledge, or human or cultural essence.

Another constellation includes words like "hybridity," "reciprocity," "negotiation," and "reconciliation," suggesting the pressing need many people feel to listen to one another and to acknowledge and communicate with realities different from their own. These constellations are familiar and, among many cultural communities in the United States, widely accepted. Their usefulness in helping people to consider themselves and their relationships to others in an increasingly decentralized yet interconnected world is, to me, incontestable. These constellations of words clarify not only the attitudes of curators but also the complexity and the general goals of many of the big international contemporary art exhibitions. It was apparent from the meetings that all the biennials are hybrids, shaped by different interests, some of them competing. Many are conceived within a nationalistic framework intended to develop national confidence and pride, yet the art they present may argue against nationalism and even against the idea of a nation. It was also apparent that if it were possible to produce a cross section of the structure of any of these exhibitions, it would show layer upon layer of negotiation and reconciliation. And many of the curators want the actual exhibitions to inspire both local dialogues and dialogues with other biennials and nations.

What concerns me here is a third constellation. It includes words like "self-consciousness," "openness," and "transparency," and phrases such as "declaring yourself." Several of the curators emphasized the importance of self-consciousness, which implies a sophisticated awareness of the histories and implications of the ideas they are working with and of the economic and political systems they are working within, as well as an ability to build this awareness into their curatorial presentations. Vishakha N. Desai, director of the galleries at the Asia Society in New York, asserted that curators must "own up to taste," define their positions, and explain where they are coming from and what they cannot yet understand. She spoke about "recognizing our own fallibility" and sharing that recognition with audiences. "We are as much products as creators," she said. For Okwui Enwezor, the artistic director of the 1997 Johannesburg Biennial, part of the responsibility of the curators is to say, "This is what I am doing, and it is not the final word." In a private conversation, Enwezor spoke about "creating a space of vulnerability." This wonderful phrase reflects the wish of many of these curators to conceive an exhibition experience in which intimacy, accessibility, and self-disclosure are welcomed and audiences are encouraged to express their ideas and feelings by participating in the collective production of meaning. The importance of participation and interactivity in Documenta 10 helped convince some of the curators in Bellagio that, in the words of Virginia Pérez-Ratton, the director of the

Museo de Arte y Diseño Contemporáneo in San Jose, Costa Rica, "Documenta was coming into another century with this show." This constellation of words indicates how much the generation of curators now coming into power believes in responsibility and generosity. It also reveals how essential hospitality and trust have become to the success of most ambitious cross-cultural curatorial endeavors.

The issue for me is not the spirit of these words or their importance to this artistic moment. The issue is ensuring that the difficulty of being self-conscious, of making oneself transparent, of declaring oneself, is understood. When I recently heard U.S. politicians at an economic conference talk about the need to be more "open and transparent," it was clear to me how easily these words can become conventions. One of the problems is that words or phrases calling for greater openness and transparency tend to be understood politically, economically, sociologically, or aesthetically. Rarely are they understood to be meaningful within all of these frameworks. Even more important, rarely are they understood psychologically. The confidence with which the words are now being used in the field suggests less an unending process, in which any sense of control is ultimately illusory, than finality, as if it were possible to declare oneself once and for all in that moment, or as if it were enough to be able to declare oneself in such a way so as to get what one desires from a specific situation. As a result, these words tend to promise the relinquishing of authority without delivering it. If the difficulty of the words is not acknowledged, then their use can become pat and manipulative. When this is the case, they do not become a way of sharing power—or, in the words of the Brazilian artist Mauricio Dias, of "exchanging territories"—but rather simply of reinforcing power at the curatorial, institutional, or political end.

The currency of words like openness and transparency leads me to ask, How much can we reveal and how much must we hide, and how does the line between revealing and concealing structure the tone and conversation curators are trying to create? How much does being open and transparent challenge power and how much does it reinforce it? What is the relation between transparency and mastery? What kind of sharing of power is really desirable, or possible, within an exhibition that must communicate authority to be credible? Which artists, curators, and peoples are likely to support these words, and which are not? Is a curator trying to put a biennial on the map in a part of the world largely removed from the immediate possibility of economic and political power more or less likely to argue for these words than a curator in a country where such power is taken for granted?

What does it mean to "declare yourself"? Does it mean being up front about the goals of a show? And is that possible when the goals of these exhibitions may be manifold, from supporting art and artists in one place, to providing an overview of the contemporary art situation, to putting an entire culture, country, or even part of the world on the international art map? Does "declaring yourself" mean defining taste when an exhibition driven by both transnational awareness and national needs will always go beyond individual taste? Does it mean sharing with audiences the ideological premises and aims of an exhibition likely to overflow any ideological framework in which anyone tries to put it? Arguing for a particular kind of art and for thinking about it? Situating the exhibition within the history of exhibition approaches and curatorial methodologies? Historicizing the exhibition and its place within the tradition of that biennial and of the city itself, as Paulo Herkenhoff did in Bellagio in his cogent overview of the 1998 São Paulo Biennial, of which he is chief curator? Discussing funding sources and defining the problems and compromises that are inevitable in biennials, and how these compromises end up shaping the show?

What about the personal implications of openness and transparency? Do these words mean defining oneself in race, class, and gender terms—terms that are evolving all the time? Do they mean defining oneself in terms of geography, of family history, of the psychological and social formation of one's style? What about individual ambition? How is that talked about? And what about the obsessiveness and narcissism that, as Herkenhoff indicated, are inextricable and indeed necessary components of most meaningful curatorial ventures?

In short, while words and phrases like "declaring yourself" and "making yourself transparent" can help establish a climate of exchange and engagement, they do not, in themselves, lead to what I think most of the curators want to encourage but are also somewhat wary of encouraging: risk. In addition, they do not, by themselves, acknowledge that the candor and honesty many of the curators were calling for depend not only on introspection and goodwill but also on performance and style. In the best memoirs, which have become one of the dominant literary forms of this time, candor is always both exposure and creation. Openness and transparency must have a form to inspire people to believe in them, and when they have that form, they are already both an unmasking and a transformation. Just as important as the will to be open, then, is the form in which a curator is able to be open. This form, in turn, will affect the tone and texture of the exhibition. The ability to be open and transparent in ways that inspire trust and risk is one of the talents that can link curatorial and artistic creation. The ultimate test of the form may be whether, and in what ways, it allows itself to be open to question.

As Desai recognized, these words lead directly into the identity issue. "Making transparent and self-conscious brings identity to the fore," she said. At the same time, the words expose the immense complexity of the concept of identity. Anyone using this constellation of words is, in effect, acknowledging this complexity. He or she is also suggesting that words like "negotiation," "reconciliation," and "hybridity" apply not just to people's relations to others and to the world around them but to the processes of everyone's inner life. These words and phrases—openness, transparency, self-consciousness, declaring yourself—therefore have the potential to restore the radicality that has been largely lost from the other two constellations of words. When the difficulties of these words emerge, the meanings of hybridity, negotiation, reciprocity, and partialness become dramatic. "Self-consciousness," "openness," and "transparency" call attention to an instability and danger that seem so much of the moment and yet so basic to the human condition that it is both topical and primal. At the same time, these words pose a question many artists and curators are struggling with: How can awareness and acceptance of instability and uncertainty become a source of community, knowledge, wonder, and revelation?

HEROIC / NONHEROIC

ALTHOUGH the constellations of words that shaped the discussions of curatorial identity in Bellagio are insistently, even adamantly, nonheroic, the exhibitions discussed are, with the exception of the Venice Biennial and the Carnegie International, both of which have been around since the nineteenth century, heroic at their cores. In the biennials that have emerged since the Havana Biennial was inaugurated in 1984, art is a means that enables curators to work toward breaking the isolation of their peoples and regions and redefining national and international relationships. In most of these exhibitions, art is also seen as a means of improving society and making the world better. Enwezor expressed his hope that the second Johannesburg Biennial would be "a celebration of South African independence" that worked toward the "reconnection of South Africa to the world." Remi Sagna, the secretary general of the 1998 Dakar Biennial, defined one aim of his show as making Dakar a Pan-African center. Herkenhoff said the goals of his 1998 São Paulo Biennial included "the formation of the gaze of young Brazilians" and reforming São Paulo's institutions. "It's not for art's sake," he said. "It's for the sake of the education of society." Caroline Turner, the director of the first Asia-Pacific Triennial of Contemporary Art in 1993 in Brisbane, spoke of the importance of educating Australians about the changing identity of Australia, "which is no longer a Western outpost," and, by so doing, changing "the way Australians see the region through the art." For Lillian Llanes Godoy, the director of the Centro Wifredo Lam in Havana and the organizer of all five Havana Biennials, "Art is very important for the survival of humanity." She is convinced her biennial and other exhibitions of this genre can contribute to "the construction of a more balanced world."

For the curators in Bellagio, as a group, a more balanced world is not possible without more equal representation in the corridors of cultural power. Margaret Archuleta, curator of fine arts at the Heard Museum in Phoenix, made clear that her responsibility at the meetings, "and it's a heavy responsibility," was to speak for Native Americans, who are almost always excluded from the most prominent international artistic events. "How do they get to participate in this arena?" she asked. This was a question, she said, that she had to answer for her people. Ramírez, too, like several others, raised the issue of representation. Part of her job as a curator and scholar, she said, is to understand why artists from Brazil, let's say, are often included in these shows while artists from Bolivia are left out. For her, it is imperative to render visible the dynamics of those international circuits that give artists in some countries, and from certain ethnic backgrounds, a greater chance of being recognized internationally than others.

Curators did communicate their passion for art and the importance of standards. Llanes: "Our aim is to show the best art in our country." Pérez-Ratton: "I have been traveling for years, and I am sick of all the bad Central American art I saw.... We have to try and get the quality people into these shows." Enwezor: "We have to deal with issues of art." His responsibilities in Johannesburg, Enwezor said, included making distinctions in quality and clarifying the different ways in which "artist" is defined.

Being an artist is not the same in Africa as it is in the United States, he said, and not the same in Nigeria, where he was born, as it is in South Africa, which he described as "a divided country, horribly wounded," where the "situation of the artist is a life-and-death matter." Enwezor indicated his discomfort with any curatorial or critical language that does not allow for the possibility of using passionate words, like "love" or "beauty," to describe the encounter with art.

One of the reasons that the Havana Biennial is so widely respected among biennial curators is that the aesthetic and the political were inseparable and equal in it from its inception. Llanes believed in Cuban and other Latin American artists. She wanted to provide a space for artists "who do not have space in the world." She wanted to enable countries and regions that were strangers to understand one another better. In biennials that emerged in the nineties, however, the relationship between aesthetic and political needs has been less seamless. The need to empower and connect regions and peoples can seem so great, in fact, that the first message sent out by recent biennials as a group is not: see what the art in them and in their countries or regions has achieved and has to say to the world, but rather: consider what the art in them is intended to do. The issue here is tricky. The same political needs and circumstances that define the urgency of these exhibitions—if they were just surveys of good art, few people in other countries, and perhaps even in the countries where the exhibitions were held, would feel a desire to visit them—can also make them seem contrived and manipulative. The same needs that convince some people to take these exhibitions seriously make others uneasy with them.

The conflict between a commitment to art and a commitment to using art to serve other agendas is not just a biennial issue. In the fiercely contested yet unforgettable *Magiciens de la terre* in Paris in 1989, its curator, Jean-Hubert Martin, in his effort to reveal to the West the continuing vitality of artistic traditions in non-Western cultures, installed almost all the non-Western works in an exhibition context that had little or nothing to do with the intentions of the artists who created these works and the traditions they served. In many of the multicultural, identity-based exhibitions of the early nineties there were layers of disjunctiveness: between the art (non-Western in origin) and the site (often designed for modernism), between the art and many of its audiences, and between the personal nature of some of the art and the representational or liberation causes the curators were asking the exhibition to serve.

While the new biennials grow out of the climate that produced exhibitions like these, they also reflect the conflict between the commitment to and the use of art in museums whose narrowness helped make multicultural exhibitions necessary. In New York, hardly anyone informed about art institutions is under the illusion that any of the city's big museums cares first and foremost for art, no matter how brilliant and sustaining their exhibitions may be or how exemplary they may be in caring for the art entrusted to them. Curatorial programs serve institutional and board interests and agendas that are economic, social, and political as much as they are aesthetic. These interests, more than the needs of artists or of contemporary art, are at the forefront of exhibition programming in powerhouse museums in the United States. Using art in the service of causes that may not be its own is a complicitly accepted part of American museum life. The news media not only refuse to question the ideological structures of big museums but hold up some of them as models of aesthetic responsibility. The more blatant conflict that can exist in biennials between commitment to art and commitment to using art should be considered with this recent exhibition history and with museums in mind.

The first biennial issue is legitimation. "The entire debate about legitimation is at the center of what international biennials are trying to do," Enwezor said. What is being legitimated? Art? Artists? Curators? Institutions? Traditions? Cultures? Communities? Cities? Regions? Nations? What is the process of legitimation? It certainly involves giving exhibition space to local and national artists and showing the people who live in those locations what the artists can do. It involves showing people from different parts of a continent and from other continents what the artists, cultures, and inhabitants of a region are capable of. By becoming a recognized event, covered by newspapers and art magazines and attended by people from the region and perhaps from all over the world, the local is validated in a way in which few local cultures anywhere—not even in urban centers like New York, Los Angeles, Berlin, or Tokyo—can now validate themselves. While perceiving the local's desire and claim for international recognition, international and transnational communities are not only pressured into focusing attention on the local but are also given evidence of their own authority by recognizing the power of their legitimizing machinery in the local's eyes. In this astonishingly complex and frequently collusive game that demands as much self-consciousness as possible, the local, the regional, and the international can legitimate one another.

What legitimates most? Is it that art from a region appears in an international exhibition? Is it that a region that may have been previously unidentified in technologically advanced nations with contemporary art, and, as a result, with modernity, mounts such an exhibition and therefore takes its place in its own eyes, and in the eyes of the world, as a nation with a rightful claim to the present? Is it critical acceptance and appreciation? By whom? Is it market interest that enables local and regional artists unknown before a biennial to enter major collections and participate in other international exhibitions? Is it the effect of the exhibition two, five, and ten years later on the artistic life of the region? If the Dakar Biennial, as Sagna defined it, has multiple goals—including making known the art in Africa without ghettoizing Africans, providing a place where African artists can meet and debate with one another, and generating interest in African art outside Africa—what most determines success or failure? If the Havana Biennial is, in Pérez-Ratton's words, a "legitimator of Latin American art"—an exhibition many artists from Africa and Latin America attend to understand what other artists from these regions are doing—with minimal attention from the mainstream Western news and art media, is the biennial nevertheless enough of a legitimating force that it should require, in its own eyes and in the eyes of all those who depend on it, no other form of legitimation? What does the value still placed on the machinery of recognition in Western Europe and the United States mean in postcolonial exhibitions born from liberation struggles?

"What is it we are making?" asked Madeleine Grynsztejn, curator of twentieth-century art at the Carnegie Museum of Art and the director of the 1999 Carnegie International, a triennial exhibition. "Why? For whom?"

While the burden of legitimation is enough by itself to suggest the heroic nature of the new biennials, just putting these shows together is heroic as well. The legwork, tenacity, tact, forbearance, flexibility, assertiveness, and cunning demanded of a biennial curator are startling. Many must negotiate with unreliable funders and fight for their artists and ideas within chronically unstable political conditions. "Every day the government changes," N. Fulya Erdemci, director of the International Istanbul Biennial, said. In every city that is the site of a developing biennial, the art infrastructure is limited at best. Erdmeci spoke about asking for help from everyone, including her brother and other family members. Her photographer was her best friend. She herself helped to pack the art "like babies." Llanes spoke about the absence of a budget from the Cuban ministry of culture in the last two Havana Biennials and "solving problems day by day." She got help from the mayor, institutions, the army. After listening to her talk about the physical and mental exhaustion she has felt after her biennials ended, describing her effort as heroic seems like an understatement.

While trying to understand the nature of biennials, it is important to consider the contrast between the heroic nature of most of these exhibitions and the language of modesty and humility curators use to define an appropriate curatorial style. It is also important to consider the contrast between a profound suspicion of religious responses to art in some of the curatorial presentations—and of the kind of theological language that was commonplace not too long ago to describe the encounter with a painting or sculpture—and the widespread faith in the transformative, even healing power of biennials. Herkenhoff, who was incredulous when he cited an example of the eucharistic language with which the encounter with modernist art has sometimes been described, nevertheless asserted that the São Paulo Biennial has the ability to give its city a "soul." Many of the curators would be extremely wary of any messianic view within an artist's work, yet many biennials have a messianic dimension. While the art many of the curators in Bellagio support is conscious of itself as art and limited in its spiritual claims, the causes the art is intended to serve may be as idealistic and grand as those served by early- and mid-twentieth-century paintings and sculptures inspired by spiritual or utopian beliefs.

Is the conflict between faith and knowledge still appropriate in an age in which the nearly irresistible appeal of the new technology seems to be its combination of information and magic? Any large overview of contemporary art is likely to swing between faith and consciousness, balancing either toward skepticism or belief but never entirely eliminating the other side. Certainly no biennial can afford to dismiss the spiritual and hope to appeal to multiple audiences. Soon after the Bellagio conference, I visited a sculpture park near Vilnius called the Sculpture Museum of the Centre of Europe, built after Lithuania's independence in 1991. On a Saturday afternoon, two couples came to the park directly after their weddings. They wanted to touch the sculptures and be photographed around them. Clearly they believed the sculpture and the park blessed them. I asked its founding director, thirty-year-old Gintaras Karosas, how often this occurred. He answered, "All the time." Whether it is in the art shown or in the belief in what art can accomplish, the biennial curator, however strong his or her insistence on self-consciousness and context, takes the human faith in artistic magic seriously.

The contrasts, or tensions, within the languages of the curators, or between their words and their exhibitions, lead me to what I see as one of the major unresolved issues in the new biennials: modernism. In the three days of meetings at Bellagio, modernism was a purely negative presence. It was acknowledged as the driving cultural force when the Venice Biennial, the Carnegie International, the São Paulo Biennial, and Documenta were founded. Once this acknowledgment was made, declaring the need for a new biennial model inevitably followed. The kind of faith that characterized the responses to a great deal of modernist art by the many people devoted to it was assumed to be antithetical to the kind of engaged, questioning response many of the biennial curators are after. Modernist exhibitions like *Qu'est-ce que la sculpture moderne?* in Paris in 1986 were cited as examples of the kinds of narrow and exclusionary museum surveys unacceptable now. For these curators as a group, modernism, with its essentialism and its totalizing, unifying impulses, was so objectionable in today's postmodern world that it had to be either ostracized or singled out as an enemy to be overcome.

But I can't imagine these shows without modernism. Only in modernism do I find a comparable concentration of belief in progress, education, healing, and transformation. Only in modernism do I consistently find that acute awareness of vulnerability and limits combined with heroic ambition and will that is shaping the identities of a number of the biennial curators. This combination has been a decisive feature in some of the best European and American art from Paul Cézanne and Jackson Pollock to Bruce Nauman and Felix Gonzalez-Torres.

By raising the issue of modernism, I mean to be neither provocative nor accusatory. My aim here is to try to make it easier for curators at the end of the century to use whatever art and ideas are available to help them develop and clarify their positions. I don't think it is possible to understand the level of hope and faith in these shows—to understand how curators reached the point where they believe art can meet such overwhelming needs—without being open to the many sides of modernism. The curators of these extraordinarily hybrid shows cross many worlds. Any attitude or position that prevents them from using any of the art in this century to clarify their aims and develop their ideas, and to make sure this hybridity can be rendered visible and approached as a source of knowledge and strength, particularly in countries where modernism has never been seen in depth, is not helpful.

THE FUTURE

DESPITE all the crucial questions they raise, and also *because* of these crucial questions, biennials born from deep cultural and political needs will make a difference. They will be festivals for art in which all those who attend will find something that pleases or moves them. They will create new audiences and new bases of information. They will introduce different regions to unfamiliar approaches to art and people in art-world centers to unfamiliar regions. They will foster debate about the meanings of national and international and about what it means to be an artist at the end and at the beginning of a millennium. They will encourage other cities and countries to consider building artistic and cultural infrastructures. They will make clear that many cities and countries are capable of being seats of cultural power.

These exhibitions will also help build respect for art and culture throughout the world. Perhaps the most important message of the biennials as a phenomenon is that the curators who organize them and the organizations that sponsor them believe in the future. The newer biennials argue implicitly that the places and countries that house them have a future, that the future is there to be built collectively by people of goodwill everywhere who want to join in, and that in the process of conceptualizing the future, art matters.

If this message is so moving to me, it is partly because my country does not seem to believe either in art or in the future. In the United States, only a relatively small number of people believe that art can have an impact on the world. The assault against the National Endowment for the Arts, the government agency that has given a limited but decisive amount of funding to the arts since 1965, has been relentless for nine years. The United States Information Agency, which for years sent American artists abroad and enabled them to establish connections with other artists and bring back home the lessons they learned from their contacts, now provides almost no money for cultural programming and largely defines American culture in terms of Hollywood and the entertainment industry. The assault on art and artists in the American media, and the exploitation of the anxieties about artists by conservative political interests, has made it impossible for the United States, as a nation, to view art with confidence. It will be a long time before the United States is remotely comfortable with artists, contemporary art, and the artistic imagination.

In short, at the moment when many other countries with little or no immediate possibility of economic and political power have set out to realize dreams of gaining power through art, the government and the mass media of the United States have been trying to evict art and artists from the American dream. One of the telling ironies of this discomfort with art and artists is that it is helping to level the playing field internationally. By inhibiting the ability of American art to function as an aesthetic, economic, and political force, the government and media have ended up serving postcolonial cultural aspirations outside the United States. As a citizen of this country who believes in the artists here, who has spent years fighting for them, and who will always fight for them, I find this situation painful on many levels. But it must be acknowledged. And curators in other countries must know that while there is an extraordinary breadth of knowledge and experience among art professionals in the United States, and while art and artists here will continue to be essential players on the world's artistic and cultural stages, the art system in the United States can no longer dominate as it once did. The eruption of biennials is evidence of a historic change.

Three interrelated issues must continue to be debated if the new biennials are going to be clear about what they are and what they want to achieve. The first issue is legitimation. To what degree are the sources of legitimation for the biennials that have emerged since 1984 determined by geopolitical conditions? By practical necessity? By emotional and psychological needs? If exhibitions do not depend at all on Western goodwill and support, like the Asia-Pacific Triennial, which looks toward Asia, do they become more or less necessary and desirable in other parts of the world? Where? To whom? Can biennials with shared histories and goals help legitimate one another? What legitimates most? What needs most to be legitimated?

The second issue is audience. It came up constantly in Bellagio without ever being engaged. It inspired some fertile remarks. Llanes's statement—"a lot of artists I detest, but I respect the audience"—made sense on many levels. It reminded me of all the artists I now value whose work I did not like or respond to for years, but whom I kept in the back of my mind because of my respect for their supporters. It reminded me that art cannot gain a real foothold anywhere unless it is engaged by the communities who live with and around it, regardless of whether the curators are sympathetic to the tastes and aesthetic assumptions of community members. Is it possible for curators to have candid, even contentious discussions with colleagues about the many audiences they are trying to reach, which ones they feel most and least responsible to and why, how to build lasting relationships with them, and how these relationships shape the understanding and possibilities of art within an exhibition or museum?

The final issue is the one that will not go away: quality. The language in which art from non-Western cultures is being defended is still often one of representation. The focus of attention is not on what a work has to offer—poetically, thematically, psychologically, philosophically, and politically—but the cause the artist serves and the political struggle with which he or she is identified. Biennials offer an opportunity to transform the chasm between the language of representation and the language of quality into a space in which many of the people demoralized by this split can make a place for themselves. We have to begin to talk about art in ways in which everyone has something to lose. People have to write and lecture about art in ways that leave them exposed. If a critic were asked to argue for an artist in a public event in an unfamiliar country, it would all but oblige him or her to think in terms of issues and words that could cross cultures. Both the positive and the negative responses to the presentation and to the artist would be revealing. If cross-cultural debates about art and artists continue to be part of the programs of biennials, and if these debates are published, perhaps in some collective biennial publication, they could help locate the words and the approaches to language that now carry maximum feeling and thought. The biennials can help develop a poetics for contemporary art that has not been recognized or that does not yet exist. ●

NOTES

Previously published in: *Art Journal* 57, no. 4 (Winter 1998), pp. 16–27.

1 Documenta is a huge and enormously influential exhibition of contemporary art that takes place every five years in Kassel, Germany. Each Documenta has a different curatorial team and therefore offers a distinct perspective on art at that moment. Catherine David's Documenta was multidisciplinary, with an unprecedented attention to film. It was unusually innovative and interdisciplinary in its programming, offering daily platforms for thinkers of all kinds, including scientists, philosophers, and political activists as well as artists. It emphasized ideas and issues, which led influential American journalists to criticize the exhibition for providing insufficient pleasure. David approached art and art exhibitions as forms of engagement in which everyone who participated had an opportunity to better understand and take on the intellectual, cultural, and political challenges of the world.

Participants in the Bellagio conference:

Margaret Archuleta, Curator of Twentieth-Century Art, The Heard Museum, Phoenix; René Block, Director, Museum Fridericianum, Kassel; Michael Brenson, New York; Germano Celant, Curator of Contemporary Art, Solomon R. Guggenheim Museum, New York; Kinshasha Holman Conwill, Director, Studio Museum in Harlem, New York; Vishakha N. Desai, Director of the Galleries, Asia Society, New York; Okwui Enwezor, Artistic Director, Second Johannesburg Biennial; N. Fulya Erdemci, Director, International Istanbul Biennial; Lillian Llanes Godoy, Director, Centro Wifredo Lam; Madeleine Grynsztejn, Curator of Twentieth-Century Art, Carnegie Museum of Art, Pittsburgh; Paulo Herkenhoff, Chief Curator, Fundação Bienal de São Paulo; Virginia Pérez-Ratton, Director, Museo de Arte y Diseño Contemporáneo, San Jose, Costa Rica; Apinan Poshyananda, Associate Director, Centers of Academic Resources, Chulalongkorn University, Bangkok; Mari Carmen Ramirez, Curator of Latin American Art, Jack S. Blanton Museum of Art, Austin; Remi Sagna, Secrétaire Général, Dakar Biennial; Caroline Turner, Deputy Director, Queensland Art Gallery, Brisbane.

THE CURATORIAL TURN: FROM PRACTICE TO DISCOURSE (2007)

240

Paul O'Neill

INTRODUCTORY CONTEXT

IT was in the late nineteen-sixties that Seth Siegelaub used the term "demystification" in order to establish the shift in exhibition production conditions, whereby curators were beginning to make visible the mediating component within the formation, production, and dissemination of an exhibition.

> *I think in our generation we thought that we could demystify the role of the museum, the role of the collector, and the production of the artwork; for example, how the size of a gallery affects the production of art, etc. In that sense we tried to demystify the hidden structures of the art world.*[1]

During the sixties the primary discourse around art-in-exhibition began to turn away from forms of critique of the artwork as autonomous object of study/critique towards a form of curatorial criticism in which the space of exhibition was given critical precedence over that of the objects of art. Curatorial criticism differed from that of traditional Western art criticism (i.e., linked to modernity) in that its discourse and subject matter went beyond discussion about artists and the object of art to include the subject of curating and the role played by the curator of exhibitions. The ascendancy of the curatorial gesture in the nineties also began to establish curating as a potential nexus for discussion, critique, and debate, where the evacuated role of the critic in parallel cultural discourse was usurped by the neocritical space of curating. During this period, curators and artists have reacted to and engaged with this "neocriticality" by extending the parameters of the exhibition form to incorporate more discursive, conversational, and geopolitical discussion, centered within the ambit of the exhibition. The ascendancy of this "curatorial gesture" in the nineties (as well as the professionalization of contemporary curating) began to establish curatorial practice as a potential space for critique. Now the neocritical curator has usurped the evacuated place of the critic. As Liam Gillick pointed out:

> *My involvement in the critical space is a legacy of what happened when a semi-autonomous critical voice started to become weak, and one of the reasons that happened was that curating became a dynamic process. So people you might have met before who in the past were critics were now curators. The brightest, smartest people get involved in this multiple activity of being mediator, producer, interface and neo-critic. It is arguable that the most important essays*

about art over the last ten years have not been in art magazines but they have been in catalogues and other material produced around galleries, art centers and exhibitions.[2]

Accompanying this "turn towards curating" was the emergence of curatorial anthologies. Beginning in the nineties, most of these tended to come out of international meetings between curators, as part of curatorial summits, symposia, seminars, and conferences, although some of them may have taken local curatorial practice as their starting point. Without exception, they placed an emphasis on individual practice, the first-person narrative, and curator self-positioning—articulated through primary interviews, statements, and exhibition representations—as they attempted to define and map out a relatively bare field of discourse.

Alongside this predominantly curator-led discourse, curatorial criticism responded with an assertion of the separateness of the artistic and curatorial gesture—when such divisions are no longer apparent in contemporary exhibition practice. I would argue that such a divisive attempt to detach the activity of curating from that of artistic production results in resistance to recognition of the interdependence of both practices within the field of cultural production. Moreover, the mediation of hybrid cultural agents through the means of the public exhibition is overlooked.

THE CURATORIAL TURN

Exhibitions have become the *medium through which most art becomes known.*[3]

EXHIBITIONS (in whatever form they take) are always ideological; as hierarchical structures they produce particular and general forms of communication. Since the late eighties, the group exhibition has become the primary site for curatorial experimentation and, as such, has generated a new discursive space around artistic practice. The group exhibition runs counter to the canonical model of the monographic presentation. By bringing a greater mix of people into an exhibition, it also created a space for defining multifarious ways of engaging with disparate interests, often within a more transcultural context. Group exhibitions are ideological texts which make private intentions public. In particular it is the temporary art exhibition that has become the principal medium in the distribution and reception of art, thus being the principal agent in debate and criticism about any aspect of the visual arts.

Exhibitions (particularly group exhibitions, art fairs, temporary perennial shows, and large-scale international art exhibitions) are the main means through which contemporary art is now mediated, experienced, and historicized. Just as the number of large-scale, international exhibitions has increased since the nineties, so has the respectability of the phenomenon of curating been enhanced. Similarly, writing about exhibitions has further reinforced the merit of curatorial practice as a subject worthy of study. As a tactic, "This may either be a compensatory device, a politicized attempt to consider works of art as interrelated rather than as individual entities, or a textual response to changes in the art world itself."[4]

The critical debate surrounding curatorial practice has not only intensified, but as Alex Farquharson has pointed out, even the recent appearance of the verb "to curate," where once there was just a noun, indicates the growth and vitality of this discussion. He writes: "New words, after all, especially ones as grammatically bastardized as the verb 'to curate' (worse still the adjective 'curatorial'), emerge from a linguistic community's persistent need to identify a point of discussion."[5]

Indicative of a shift in the primary role of curator is the changing perception of the curator as carer to a curator who has a more creative and active part to play within the production of art itself. This new verb "to curate . . . may also suggest a shift in the conception of what curators do, from a person who works at some remove from the processes of artistic production, to one actively 'in the thick of it.'"[6] Ten years previously, when writing about cultural production, Pierre Bourdieu noted that the curator (inter alia) added cultural meaning and value to the making of art and artists:

> *The subject of the production of the artwork—of its value but also of its meaning—is not the producer who actually creates the object in its materiality, but rather the entire set of agents engaged in the field. Among these are the producers of works, classified as artists, . . . critics of all persuasions, . . . collectors, middlemen, curators, etc.; in short, all those who have ties with art, who live for art and, to varying degrees, from it, and who confront each other in struggles where the imposition of not only a world view but also a vision of the art world*

> *is at stake, and who, through these struggles, participate in the production of the value of the artist and of art.*[7]

As cultural agents, curators and artists participate in the production of cultural value, and exhibitions are intrinsic and vital parts of what Theodor Adorno and Max Horkheimer termed the "cultural industries" associated with: entertainment; mass culture; the communications enterprise of mass reception; and the consciousness industry.[8] Exhibitions are, therefore, contemporary forms of rhetoric, complex expressions of persuasion whose strategies aim to produce a prescribed set of values and social relations for their audiences. As such exhibitions are subjective political tools, as well as being modern ritual settings, that uphold identities (artistic, national, sub-cultural, "international," gender- or race-specific, avant-garde, regional, global, etc.); they are to be understood as institutional "utterances" within a larger culture industry.[9]

BIENNIAL CULTURE AND THE CULTURE OF CURATION

ONE of the most evident developments in contemporary curatorial practice since the late eighties has been occurring on an increasingly international, transnational, and multinational scale, where the "local" and the "global" are in constant dialogue. In *Contemporary* magazine's special issue on curating, published in 2005, Isabel Stevens produced a substantiative list of eighty official biennials/triennials throughout the globe to be held between 2006 and 2008. Terms such as "biennial," "biennale," or "mega-exhibition" no longer refer to those few exhibitions that occur perennially, every two years or so: they are now all-encompassing idioms for large-scale international group exhibitions, which, for each local cultural context, are organized locally with connection to other national cultural networks.[10] Biennials are temporary spaces of mediation, usually allocated to invited curators with support from a local sociocultural network. They are interfaces between art and larger publics—publics that are at once local and global, resident and nomadic, nonspecialist and art-worldly.

In what Barbara Vanderlinden and Elena Filipovic call the "biennial phenomenon," such "large-scale international exhibitions" reflect the cultural diversity of global artistic practices and call into question the inertia of public art institutions that are unwilling or too slow to respond to such praxis.[11] Biennials have become a form of institution in themselves; their frequency has resulted in an index of comparability. In a rather prophetic essay written in the early nineties, Bruce Ferguson, Reesa Greenberg, and Sandy Nairne had already begun to question the fundamental idea of international survey exhibitions. Their collective essay ended with this paragraph:

> *However progressive the political or economic intentions behind them, international exhibitions still invite a presumption that the curators have access to an illusionary world view, and that spectators may follow in their wake. But a more specific and sustained engagement with communities and audiences, creating meanings beyond the spectacular and mere festivalizing of such occasions, may produce a new genre of exhibition. It seems that in order to accommodate both artist's needs and audience demands, the new exhibition must have reciprocity and dialogue built into its structure. How successfully this is accomplished will determine international exhibition maps of the future.*[12]

As was predicted, these event-exhibitions have shaped new social, cultural, and political relations in a more globalized world, where the traditional biennial model is maintained through discourse on cultural policy, national representation, and internationalism, thereby enabling cultural travel, urban renovation, and local tourism. Alternately, it is arguable that they have become polarizing spaces that legitimize certain forms of artistic and curatorial praxis within the global culture industry.

Very few biennials are of the scale of Documenta, Johannesburg, Venice, or even Istanbul. Many tend to be improvisatory, localized, and modest in their aims. Here I am interested in the general-specific homogeneity produced by the institution of the biennial, not the heterogeneity of the myriad of localized cultural statements. The populist perception of the activity of curating has changed in large part due to the spread of biennials in the nineties, whereby new degrees of visibility and responsibility were placed upon the curator. Apart from the particular issues of scale, temporality, and location, the activity of curation made manifest through such exhibitions is articulated as being identity-driven; therefore an overtly politicized, discursively global, and fundamentally auteured praxis prevails, in spite of the many variable forms they have taken on. The biennial form as a global exhibition model has driven much of the art world's global extension since 1989, when *Magiciens de la Terre* began the process. Biennials have become the vehicle through which much art is validated and acquires value on the international art circuit. Now such "global exhibitions" often have as their main theme "globalization," while questioning the ideological underpinning of the exhibition itself as a product of that process.

Despite any curatorial self-reflexivity in recent large-scale exhibitions that may exist towards the global effects of "biennialization," the periphery still has to follow the discourse of the center. In the case of biennials, the periphery comes to the center in search of legitimization and, by default, accepts the conditions of this legitimacy. Charles Esche suggests that the globalization of art within large-scale exhibitions has, through a process of standardization, absorbed the difference between center and periphery. According to Esche, the "center first" model of global art, largely begun in 1989, still holds sway over much of the museum and biennial culture. It requires "the key institutions of contemporary culture officially to sanction the 'periphery' in order to subsume it into the canon of innovative visual art."[13] Even though many of the artists in each exhibition may have developed their practice on the fringes of the recognized art world, "their energy is validated and consumed by the center and therefore the relationship between rim and hub remains in place. This is, of course, how globalization generally operates—sometimes to the economic benefit of the patronized but rarely in the interests of maintaining their autonomy and sustainability."[14]

The exhibition's ritual of maintaining a given set of power relations between art, display, and reception is particularly true of what John Miller called the "blockbuster exhibition," which tends to incorporate anachronistic elements while recuperating any dissent from viewers as part of the totality of the overall event. In consequence, a "cycle of raised expectations and quick disillusionment" is both predictable and overdetermined. Miller argues that the "mega-exhibition" is an ideological institution that reifies social relations between artworks and spectator. As the explicit purpose of these shows is to offer a comprehensive survey of artworks on a demographic basis, the terms of discourse are treated as predetermined, rather than being "transformed in the course of art production and therefore subject to contradiction and conflict."[15]

According to Miller, to critique these exhibitions on the basis of curatorial choices made within the established framework would be to ignore the ideologies underpinning the institutions that are responsible for them. He suggests that such institutions often treat and address audiences as a concrete social constituency, whereby artworks are relegated to being mere "raw material" within the "total artwork" of the exhibition (gesamtkunstwerk), thus privileging the curator's subjectivity, so that the outcome of the exhibition-form is naturalized as an organic inevitability within the organization's institutional framework, producing an illusion of curatorial inspiration and genius.[16]

I would argue that during a period of transformation since 1989 the notion of exhibitions as authored subjectivities produced dominant discourses around "mega-exhibitions." Although more recent biennials have moved away from the single-author position towards more collective models, a globally configured exhibition market has persisted with a curator-centered discourse. Discussions, lecture programs, conferences, publications, and discursive events are also now a recurrent and integral part of such exhibitions, and in the case of some exhibitions, such as Documenta 10 and especially Documenta 11, discursive events formed the very foundation of the project. As Elena Filipovic suggested:

> *This striking expansion goes in tandem with curatorial discourses that increasingly distinguish the biennial or mega-exhibition as larger than the mere presentation of artworks; they are understood as vehicles for the production of knowledge and intellectual debate.*[17]

In many ways the expanding network of biennials has effectively embraced art and artists from the peripheries beyond a dominantly Western European and American internationalism, but as Jessica Bradley has argued, they function as a more responsive and spectacular means of distribution:

> *One that can efficiently meet the accelerated rate of exchange and consumption parallel to the global flow of capital and information today . . . while curatorial aspirations are frequently concerned with addressing cultures in flux and eschew cultural nationalism, the motives for establishing these events may nevertheless reside in a desire to promote and validate local, culturally specific production within a global network.*[18]

It is the inter-relational attributes of both culture and location that are the most obviously marketable aspects of the global tourism upon which they depend. Locality embodied within tourist spots, local specialities, sites, culture, and their consumer produce are some of the most reliable economic revenues for local communities. During these times of "culture as spectacle," artistic production is a catalyst for culture to be globalized, attracting financial investments as well as audiences. Biennials (and art fairs) are happening in more and more cities, which have adopted cultural tourism as a means of securing a place in the international arena of economy and culture, wherein artists, curators, critics, art dealers, patrons, and sponsors nurture a clearly defined production system through labor division, which produces hierarchical roles for the participants.[19]

As an important agent within the global cultural industry, a new kind of international curator was identified by Ralph Rugoff as a "jet-set *flâneur*" who appears to know no geographical boundaries and for whom a type of global-internationalism is the central issue.[20] In particular, the role of the nomadic curator within large-scale exhibitions is to select and display "international" art through a visible framing device: a subjective (curatorial) system of mediation that has the notion of inclusivity as one of its central thematics. The rise of the global curator has less to do with the old embedded power structures within the art world than with a change in the form of inherited cultural significance. Capital is now circulated through new reputational economies. Here, practice, which has long been prioritized over discourse within the culture industry as a whole, is now dependent on being translated back into discourse in order to facilitate more equivalent practice, thus enabling the maintenance of the existing superstructure. As Benjamin Buchloh identified in 1989, there is an urgent need for articulating the curatorial position as part of art discourse, where practice as "doing" or "curating" necessitated a discourse as "speaking" or "writing," in order for the curator's function to be acknowledged as part of the institutional superstructure at the level of discourse:

> *The curator observes his/her operation within the institutional apparatus of art: most prominently the procedure of abstraction and centralization that seems to be an inescapable consequence of the work's entry into the superstructure apparatus, its transformation from practice to discourse. That almost seems to have become the curator's primary role: to function as an agent who offers exposure and potential prominence—in exchange for obtaining a moment of actual practice that is about to be transformed into myth/superstructure.*[21]

This interest in discourse, as a supplement or substitute for practice, was highlighted in Dave Beech and Gavin Wade's speculative introduction to *Curating in the 21st Century*, in which they stated that "even talking is doing something, especially if you are saying something worthwhile. Doing and saying, then, are forms of acting on the world."[22] So, it seems fair to characterize the discursive as an ambivalent way of saying something vis-à-vis doing. This may seem a somewhat optimistic speculation, as Mick Wilson argues in his assessment of the productive powers of language, which have been part of the stock assumptions of a wide range of experimental art practices and attendant commentary.[23] This tendency has been given further impetus by what he calls "the Foucauldian moment in art of the last two decades, and the ubiquitous appeal of the term 'discourse' as a word to conjure and perform power," to the point where "even talking is doing something," with the value of the discursive as something located in its proxy for actual doing within discourses on curatorial practice.[24]

The "rise of the curator as creator," as Bruce Altshuler labeled it,[25] has also gathered momentum. The ever-increasing number of global biennials has provided what Julia Bryan-Wilson claims to be prestigious "launching pads for the curatorial star system" in "the age of curatorial studies," in which the "institutional basis of art is taken as a given, and the marketing and packaging of contemporary art has become a specialized focus of inquiry for thousands of students."[26] If the nineties were all about a new professionalization during a period of globalization, they now seem to represent acceleration in the global art exhibition-making market followed by a settling-down period. Only now can we begin to evaluate the processes of translation that accompanied these productions and recognize that curating as distinct moments of practice is significantly divergent from curatorial discourse.

Beatrice von Bismarck provided an example of this bifurcation between curatorial practice and discourse, so that professionalization and differentiation within the art world have turned curating into a hierarchically arranged job description, whereby "internationally networked service providers" offer their skills to a diverse exhibition market, when curating as practice is understood in discourse as something that is distinct from its understanding as a job title:

> *Of the tasks originally associated with the fixed institutional post, curating takes only that of presentation. With the aim of creating an audience for artistic and cultural materials and techniques, of making them visible, the exhibition*

becomes the key presentation medium. In contrast to the curator's other duties, curating itself frees the curator from the invisibility of the job, giving him/her an otherwise uncommon degree of freedom . . . and a prestige not unlike that enjoyed by artists.[27]

Within curatorial discourse, the figure of the curator operates at a level previously understood as being the domain of artistic practice, where in Foucauldian terms such discourse is "the general domain of all statements, sometimes as an individualizable group of statements, and sometimes as a regulated practice that accounts for a certain number of statements."[28] Thus, curating-specific discourse engenders a requisite level of prestige necessitated by the dynamics of contemporary curating. Practice alone does not produce and support such esteem; rather, distinct moments of practice translate into a hierarchical "common discourse" of curating as it is understood through its discursive formations. While internationalism is now at the core of practice with the biennial industry, its accompanying curatorial discourse functions to maintain the superstructure of the art world on a much wider scale than ever before. Where the biennial curator is a well-traveled subject, the curators of exhibitions are already engaging in a complex network of global knowledge circuits that traverse and overlap with the other: each "biennial" is "in conversation" with the next, providing yet another momentary place of exchange of curatorial discourse across exhibitions; each exhibition is in dialogue with the next, as well as with the world it claims to reflect.

CURATOR AS META-ARTIST, ARTIST AS META-CURATOR

SINCE the late eighties, the shift away from curating as an administrative, caring, mediating activity towards curating as a creative activity more akin to a form of artistic practice was indicated by Jonathan Watkins's polemic on curating written for *Art Monthly* in 1987. Using Oscar Wilde's idea that objects were transformed into art by the critic through writing, Watkins provocatively argued that curating was a form of artistic practice and that curated exhibitions were to be likened to Marcel Duchamp's "Readymade Aided" artworks, where the display or exhibition is aided by the curator's "manipulation of the environment, the lighting, the labels, [and] the placement of other works of art."[29]

Watkins's loose description of what role curators/artists/critics take on within an exhibition context may no longer be completely in synchrony with the development (over the last eighteen years) of curatorial practice beyond the parameters of gallery or museum exhibition displays. Yet Watkins's belief that curating is a "necessary, if insufficient, medium through which the communication between art and its audience takes place"[30] seems in tune with the way in which the cross-fading of individual positions within our cultural economy has aided the transformation of artistic practice. Its slight shift away from an author-centered cultural hierarchy towards a post-productive discourse, in which the function of curating has become another recognized part of the expanded field of art production.

Almost twenty years after Watkins's polemic, the "curator as artist" question remains one of the key debates within curatorial discourse: it is still being discussed within many contemporary art magazines such as *Frieze* and *Art Monthly.* In 2005, writing for his monthly column in *Frieze,* curator Robert Storr expressed his fears about the notion of the curator as an artist by refusing to call curating a medium since it "automatically conceded the point to those who will elevate curators to the status critics have achieved through the 'auteurization' process." Storr also situates the origins of the idea of the curator as artist in Oscar Wilde's 1890 essay "The Critic as Artist" (where it is the eye of the beholder that produces the work of art) rather than in Barthes' poststructuralist analysis of authorship. Storr's conclusive response—"No, I do not think that curators are artists. And if they insist, then they will ultimately be judged bad curators as well as bad artists"—ends up reiterating "the artist/curator divide and inadvertently returns the power of judgment to the critic."[31]

Storr's rejection of the notion of curating as a form of artistic practice and his refusal to call curating a medium represents one of the ongoing tensions within critical debate surrounding curatorial discourse since the late eighties. Yet, as John Miller has argued, the specter of the curator as meta-artist began to haunt large-scale international exhibitions after Jan Hoet's Documenta 9 in 1991, when Hoet put himself forward as a curatorial artist who used a diverse range of artworks as his raw material. For Miller, the momentum of the artist-curator, or the artist as meta-curator, had already been building up from the work of artists linked to institutional critique who had taken curatorial prerogatives and the works of other artists into their own practice, such as Group Material, Julie Ault, Louise Lawler, Fred Wilson, Judith Barry, and others working in the U.S. in the eighties. Miller argues, however, that Hoet's technique of "confrontational hanging" was less about the exposure of "non-reflexive assumptions about what makes up an exhibition and what that might mean"[32] for the work of artists within heavily imposed curatorial structures, and more about "the willfully arbitrary juxtaposition of works, equat[ing the curator's] artistry with free exercise of subjectivity."[33]

The idea of the curator as some type of meta-artist became prominent in the nineties, and according to Sigrid Schade, "curators [now] sell their curatorial concepts as the artistic product and sell themselves as the artists, so the curators 'swallow up' the works of the artists, as it were. In such cases, the curators claim for themselves the status of genius traditional in art history."[34] Dorothee Richter echoed this view when she stated:

> *Since the eighties, we can see another shift in the roles ascribed to artists and curators: It seems perhaps as if a shift in power in favor of the curator has taken place, especially since the role of the curator increasingly allows for more opportunity for creative activity. Thus, the curator seems to employ the artistic exhibits in part as the sign of one text, namely, his or her text.*[35]

Richter suggests that the presentation of an exhibition is a now a form of curatorial self-presentation, a courting of a gaze whereby an exhibition's meaning is derived from the relationship among artistic positions. This, she argues, is represented by the codependent idea that the curator and artist now closely imitate each other's position.[36]

In 1972, the artist Daniel Buren wrote "Exhibition of an Exhibition," where he claimed: "More and more, the subject of an exhibition tends not to be the display of artworks, but the exhibition of the exhibition as a work of art."[37] At the time, Buren was referring both specifically to the work of curator Harald Szeemann and his curation of Documenta 5, and to the emergence of the idea of exhibition organizer as author. Buren was suggesting that works were mere fragments that make up one composite exhibition, and although having not changed his position, he later updated his initial thoughts in 2004:

> *[Artworks are] particular details in the service of the work in question, the exhibition of our organizer-author. At the same time—and this is where the problem has become pointed enough to create the crisis in which we find ourselves—the "fragments" and other "details" exhibited are, by definition and in most cases, completely and entirely foreign to the principal work in which they are participating, that is, the exhibition in question.*[38]

Buren's disdain for the tendency of large-scale exhibitions to acquire the status of quasi-artwork where the work of the curator transforms the work of the artist into a useful "fragment" in his or her own work of exhibition as art still prevails. Buren claimed that this can and has taken on many guises in the more recent past:

> *The organizers/authors/artists of large-scale exhibitions provide results we already know: Documenta transformed into a circus (Jan Hoet) or even as a platform for the promotion of curators who profit from the occasion in order to publish their own thesis in the form of a catalogue essay (Catherine David) or as a tribune in favor of the developing politically correct world (Okwui Enwezor) or other exhibitions by organizer-authors trying to provide new merchandise to the ever voracious Western market for art consumption, which, like all markets, must ceaselessly and rapidly renew itself in order not to succumb.*[39]

But the great irony of Buren's statement is that it is a published response to the question as to whether *The Next Documenta Should be Curated by an Artist* (2003) proposed by curator Jens Hoffmann as a part of his own curatorial project/exhibition/publication. By enabling Buren's text and other artists, Hoffman's intention was to pass to artists the critical and curatorial voice and to include them in the discussion around the effectiveness of an artist-led curatorial model, but Mark Peterson states, it "ultimately uses a similar curatorial strategy as the one he is criticizing, namely to invite artists to illustrate his thesis."[40] Peterson goes on to argue that Hoffmann's position only appears to be one of self-reflexivity, as the curator attempts to involve artists in questioning not only his own practice but the various mechanisms and dynamics of his medium and his profession and how exhibitions gain form, yet ends up deflecting attention away from his own curatorial trap. This may in part be true, but Peterson's position, not unfamiliar as a general viewpoint, again places the curator and artist in opposition to one another.

According to Zygmunt Bauman, it is precisely because of an absence of a single, universally accepted authority within contemporary culture that curators are becoming "scapegoats . . . because the curator is on the front line of a big battle for meaning under conditions of uncertainty." Bauman adds the term "scapegoat" to a long list of ingredients for a curator's role, which he lists as animator, pusher, inspirer, brother, community maker, and someone who makes people work and things happen and someone who inspires artists with ideas, programs, and projects. He also adds that "there would be an element of interpreting, of making sense of people, of making them understand, giving them some sort of alphabet for reading what they see, but cannot quite decide about."[41]

According to Bauman, art has become recentered around what he calls "the event of the exhibition," where the dominant experience of art is generated by short-lived temporal curatorial events and only secondly, if at all, by the extemporaneous value of the work of art itself. It is mostly the work of art exhibited in a widely publicized art-world event that can meet the standards set for its global consumption, and the only way it might stand a chance of being seen is by maximizing its shock value, its scale, and its visibility so as to avoid the risk of boredom or submission, which would strip it of its "entertainment value."

As well as their temporal and transient nature, large-scale international group exhibitions have tended to lend themselves to thematic shows. It has been argued that such projects prevent artists from realizing their "true potential" and even that this emphasis on the curatorial project has quite serious implications for the status and roles of art and artists. For example, Alex Farquharson questions exhibitions that foreground their own sign-structure, for they pose the risk of using art and artists as constituent fibers or pieces of syntax subsumed by the identity of the whole curatorial endeavor. He argued that we are more likely to remember who curated *Utopia Station*, ongoing since 2003, than which artists took part, forgetting that Rirkrit Tiravanija (an artist) was one of the curators. For Farquharson, projects such as Hans Ulrich Obrist's *Do It* (1993 onwards, www.e-flux.com) and *Take Me (I'm Yours)* (Serpentine Gallery, London, 1995), or *A Little Bit of History Repeated* (Kunst-Werke Berlin, 2001), curated by Jens Hoffmann, result in the relegation of artists to the role of deliverers of the curators' conceptual premise, while curatorial conceit acquires the status of quasi artwork.[42] This more than common opinion seems to yearn after an upholding of the cultural value of the artist over the curator within contemporary art exhibitions and generates serious problems for the overall question of advocacy within the art world. As Gertrud Sandqvist has warned, the curated exhibition is not intended merely to reinforce the identity of the artist, or of the curator. Instead of seeing curating as one of the rare, more intellectual positions in the processes of art circulation, there is a danger that curators may become mere agents for the artists as part of their own tactics for reputational gain. But if the public exhibition holds any potential as a producer of meaning, then its purpose must differ from that of the art market, and that of the individual artist.[43] Finally, as Maria Lind has pointed out, reverence towards the work of art has its own problematic: it is suspiciously close to resting upon ideas about art as detached from the rest of our existence; and it often conceals the concept of a curator as "pure provider" who simply supports an artist without affecting the exhibition and its reception.[44]

THE SAME OLD STORY OF REPRESSED HISTORIES: BY WAY OF CONCLUSION, THE BEGINNING

PRIOR to the nineties, few historical assessments or curatorial paradigms existed, let alone a discourse specific to contemporary curatorial practice. As an historical discourse, curating still has yet to be fully established as an academic field of enquiry. In *The Power of Display: A History of Installation at MoMA* (1998), Mary Anne Staniszewski proposed that Western art history had forgotten to take into account the functions performed by curating, exhibition design, and spatially arranged exhibition-forms. For Staniszewski, our relationship to this past is not only a question of how art is now seen to have been part of this history, but what kind of documentation and evidence of its display has survived. She writes: "What is omitted from the past reveals as much about a culture as what is recorded as history and circulates as collective memory."[45]

Visual effect, display, and narrative are central to any curated exhibition. The exhibition remains the most privileged form for the presentation of art; thus display may be understood as the core of exhibiting. Staniszewski suggests that the history of the exhibition is one of our most culturally "repressed" narratives. The contextualization of space and its rhetoric have been overshadowed by the context of art in terms of epochs and artists' oeuvre, despite the fact that exhibition installations have had such a crucial significance for how meaning is created in art. One of the key factors in the production of artistic posterity is the dominance of the modernist "white cube," which eliminated the context of architecture and space as well as that of institutional conditions. According to Thomas McEvilley, the endurance of the power structures inherent to the white cube centers on that

> *of undying beauty, of the masterpiece. But in fact it is a specific sensibility, with special limitations and conditions that is so glorified. By suggesting eternal ratification of a certain sensibility, the white cube suggests the eternal ratification of the claims of the caste or group sharing their sensibility.*[46]

Hans Ulrich Obrist is one of numerous curators to have mirrored Staniszewski's assessment by stating: "Seeing the importance of exhibition design provides an approach to art history that does acknowledge the vitality, historicity and the time and site bound character of all aspects of culture."[47] He has claimed that this amnesia "not only obscures our understanding of experimental exhibition history, [but] it also affects innovative curatorial practice."[48] In many of the interviews I have conducted over the last few years, contemporary curators often refer to the amnesiac effect of missing literature, and what Brian O'Doherty called "radical forgetfulness" towards innovative pre-white-cube exhibition forms. So the institutionalization of "the white cube" since the fifties meant that "presence before a work of art means that we absent ourselves in favor of the Eye and the Spectator."[49] According to O'Doherty such a disembodied faculty meant that art was essentially seen as autonomous and experienced primarily by formal visual means.

Aside from the series of essays that made up *Inside the White Cube,* first published in *Artforum* in 1976, there had been very little subsequent examinations of display practices of the early twentieth century, less still the notion that contemporary art curation was affected by any lack of contextualizing history. The nineties could be said to have begun the process of remembering during a moment of emergency when curatorial programs had little material to refer to by way of discourse specific to the curatorial field.

It was within this epistemic gap that contemporary curatorial discourse began to take shape in the nineties and a generation of curators emerged during what Michael Brenson called "the curator's moment."[50] I would argue that the prioritization of all things contemporary within recent curatorial projects, alongside the concentration on an individualization of the curatorial gesture, has created a particular strand of discourse that is hermetic at times. At the same time it is self-referential, curator-centered, and, most evidently, in a constant state of flux: curatorial knowledge is now becoming a mode of discourse with unstable historical foundations.

From surveying the key debates within publications dedicated to contemporary curatorial practice, it is apparent that curatorial discourse is in the midst of its own production. Curating is "becoming discourse" in which curators are willing themselves to be the key subject and producer of this discourse. So far, for those unwilling to accept the provision made for the figure of the curator within the reconfigured cultural field of production, critical response has been maintained at the level of an oversimplified antagonism, where the practice(s) of artist and curator are divided, separated out, and set in opposition to one another. If this policing of boundaries continues, the gap between curatorial criticism and curator-led discourse will only widen further. ●

NOTES

Previously published in: Judith Rugg and Michele Sedgwick (eds.), *Issues in Curating Contemporary Art and Performance* (Bristol and Chicago, 2007), pp. 13–28.

1 Paul O'Neill, "Action Man: Paul O'Neill Interviews Seth Siegelaub," *The Internationaler,* no. 1 (August 2006), pp. 5–8.

2 Gillick, quoted in Saskia Bos, "Towards a Scenario: Debate with Liam Gillick," in *De Appel Reader No. 1: Modernity Today: Contributions to a Topical Artistic Discourse* (Amsterdam, 2005), p. 74.

3 Reesa Greenberg, Bruce W. Ferguson, and Sandy Nairne, "Mapping International Exhibitions," in Reesa Greenberg, Bruce W. Ferguson, and Sandy Nairne (eds.) *Thinking about Exhibitions* (London and New York, 1996), p. 2.

4 Ibid.

5 Alex Farquharson, "I Curate, You Curate, We Curate," *Art Monthly* 269 (2003), pp. 7–10.

6 Ibid.

7 Pierre Bourdieu, The Field of Cultural Production (New York, 1993), p. 261.

8 See Theodor W. Adorno and Max Horkheimer, "The Culture Industry: Enlightenment as Mass Deception," in idem, *Dialectics of Enlightenment* (1944), trans. John Cummings (London and New York, 1997), pp. 120–67.

9 See Bruce W. Ferguson, "Exhibition Rhetorics," in Greenberg, Ferguson, and Nairne 1996 (see note 3), pp. 178–79.

10 See Isabel Stevens, "IT'S SO TWO YEARS AGO," *Contemporary* 21, no. 77 (2005), pp. 22–32.

11 See Barbara Vanderlinden and Elena Filipovic (eds.), *The Manifesta Decade: Debates on Contemporary Art Exhibitions and Biennials in Post-Wall Europe* (Cambridge [MA], 2005).

12 Greenberg, Ferguson, and Nairne 1996 (see note 3), p. 3.

13 Charles Esche, "Debate: Biennials," *Frieze* 92 (2005), p. 105.

14 Ibid.

15 John Miller, "The Show You Love to Hate: A Psychology of the Mega-Exhibition," in Greenberg, Ferguson, and Nairne 1996 (see note 3), p. 270.

16 Ibid., p. 272.

17 Elena Filipovic, "The Global White Cube," in Vanderlinden and Filipovic 2005 (see note 11), p. 66. This essay has been reprinted in the present volume.

18 Jessica Bradley, "International Exhibitions: A Distribution System for a New Art World Order," in Melanie Townsend (ed.), *Beyond the Box: Diverging Curatorial Practices* (Banff, 2003), p. 89.

19 Ivo Mesquita, "Biennials, Biennials, Biennials . . . ," in Townsend 2003 (see note 18), pp. 63–68.

20 See Ralph Rugoff, "Rules of the Game," *Frieze* 44 (1999), pp. 47–49.

21 See Benjamin Buchloh, "Since Realism There Was . . . ," in *L'Exposition Imaginaire: The Art of Exhibiting in the Eighties* ('s-Gravenhage, 1989), pp. 96–121.

22 Dave Beech and Gavin Wade, *Curating in the 21st Century* (Walsall, 2000), pp. 9–10.

23 See Mick Wilson, "Curatorial Moments and Discursive Turns," in Paul O'Neill (ed.), *Curating Subjects* (Amsterdam and London, 2007).

24 Ibid., p. 202.

25 See Bruce Altshuler, *The Avant-Garde in Exhibition: New Art in the 20th Century* (New York, 1994).

26 Julia Bryan-Wilson, "A Curriculum for Institutional Critique, or the Professionalisation of Conceptual Art," in Jonas Ekeberg (ed.), *New Institutionalism, Verksted No. 1* (Oslo, 2003), pp. 102–3.

27 Beatrice von Bismarck, "Curating," in Christoph Tannert and Ute Tischler (eds.), *MIB–Men in Black: Handbook of Curatorial Practice,* (Berlin and Frankfurt am Main, 2004), p. 99.

28 Michel Foucault, *The Archeology of Knowledge* (London and New York, 2003), p. 30.

29 Jonathan Watkins, "The Curator as Artist," *Art Monthly* 111 (1987), p. 27.

30 Ibid.

31 Robert Storr, "Reading Circle," *Frieze* 93 (2005), p. 27.

32 John Miller, "Arbeit Macht Spass?" in Jens Hoffmann (ed.), *The Next Documenta Should Be Curated by an Artist* (Frankfurt am Main, 2004), p. 59.

33 Ibid.

34 Sigrid Schade, "Preface," in Barnaby Drabble and Dorothee Richter (eds.), *Curating Degree Zero: An International Curating Symposium* (Nuremburg, 1999), p. 11.

35 Dorothee Richter, "Curating Degree Zero," in Drabble and Richter 1999 (see note 34), p. 16.

36 Ibid.

37 See Daniel Buren, "Where Are the Artists?" in Hoffmann 2004 (see note 32), p. 26. This essay has also been reprinted in the present volume.

38 Ibid.

39 Ibid.

40 Mark Peterson, "Open Forum," in Hoffmann 2004 (see note 32), p. 80.

41 Zygmunt Bauman, "On Art, Death and Postmodernity—And What They Do to Each Other," in Mika Hannula (ed.), *Stopping the Process: Contemporary Views on Art and Exhibitions* (Helsinki, 1998), p. 31.

42 See Farquharson 2003 (see note 5).

43 Gertrud Sandqvist, "Context, Construction, Criticism," in Drabble and Richter 1999 (see note 34), pp. 43–44.

44 Maria Lind, "Stopping My Process: A Statement," in Hannula 1998 (see note 41).

45 Mary Anne Staniszewski, *The Power of Display: A History of Exhibition Installations at the Museum of Modern Art* (Cambridge [MA], 1998), p. xxi.

46 Thomas McEvilley, foreword in Brian O'Doherty, *Inside the White Cube: The Ideology of the Gallery Space,* 4th ed. (Berkeley and Los Angeles, 1999), p. 9.

NOTES

47 See Hans Ulrich Obrist and Gilane Tawadros, "In Conversation," in Susan Hiller and Sarah Martin (eds.), *The Producers: Contemporary Curators in Conversation* (3) (Newcastle, 2001).

48 See Hans Ulrich Obrist et al., "Panel Statement and Discussion," in Paula Marincola (ed.), *Curating Now: Imaginative Practice? Public Responsibility* (Philadelphia, 2001).

49 O'Doherty 1999 (see note 46).

50 See Michael Brenson, "The Curator's Moment: Trends in the Field of International Contemporary Art Exhibitions," *Art Journal* 57, no. 4 (Winter 1998), pp. 16–27. This essay has also been reprinted in the present volume.

QUESTIONS OF AUTHORSHIP IN BIENNIAL CURATING

Federica Martini and Vittoria Martini

CURATORS AS AUTEURS?

AROUND 1968, when Roland Barthes and Michel Foucault wrote two seminal texts that would deeply influence reflection about authorship and postmodern literature and theory, student protests advocated new forms of collectivism.[1]

In his essay "Death of the Author," Barthes pointed out that, traditionally, "book and author stand automatically on a single line divided into a 'before' and an 'after,'" while "in complete contrast, the modern 'scriptor' is born simultaneously with the text... There is no other time than that of the enunciation and every text is eternally written 'here' and 'now.'"[2] Responding to Barthes' claim, Michel Foucault outlined the notion of the "author's function" in an essay entitled "What Is an Author?" and argued that it

> *results from a complex operation whose purpose is to construct the rational entity we call an author... Nevertheless, these aspects of an individual, which we designate as an author (or which comprise an individual as an author), are projections, in terms always more or less psychological, of our way of handling texts... In addition, all these operations vary according to the period and the form of discourse concerned.*[3]

Seen from the perspective of the art world, it was precisely in this period that the authorial role of the curator was being discussed. The question, however, was not so much whether the curator-as-author was or should be "dead," but whether one can speak of a curator as author at all in relation to the making of an exhibition.

Following Barthes and Foucault and their definition of the author as "a cultural process specific to a period in time," it can be argued that the "cultural process" called "curating" with its specific agent, the "curator," begins taking shape at the same time. Before World War II, the organization of exhibitions was the task of what was called the "museum curator," with the title's implications of attachment to a stable institution and attention to building up and caring for a permanent collection. That role, as the etymological roots of *curare* or "taking care" imply, was mainly related to the interpretation of art and the preservation of artworks.[4] In the decades after World War II, there was a shift from this type of "museum curator" toward what would eventually be called an "exhibition *auteur*," which is to say, the role of the "curator" as we understand it today.[5]

This shift and the debate about what a "curator" is and does only really began in the nineteen-sixties. Acting no longer as "an Apollinairean prophet" but as a "scholar educated through the acquaintance with artists, museums, and universities," a new figure emerged who was not necessarily an art historian, but was passionate about contemporary art practices and traveled to meet artists and visit exhibitions, an intellectual who made value judgments based on his or her own experience and taste.[6] When this new figure was called upon to organize an exhibition, he or she would invite artists coherently following his or her specific critical view as informed by a theme or issue. The exhibitions organized by Seth Siegelaub, Lucy Lippard, and Harald Szeemann, among others, contributed to the general overhaul of the way exhibitions were made.[7] And as a result of such efforts, new definitions of this professional figure that operated particularly in the contemporary art field were proposed.[8] Among them, one of the most influential was Szeemann's "exhibition maker," a formula with which he started defining himself in 1969, when he quit his job at the Kunsthalle Bern and began making exhibitions on a freelance basis.[9] The definition of this new role of curator and the resulting discourse of curatorial authorship arguably ran parallel to the establishment of new forms of collaboration between artists and exhibition makers. Indeed it was in the late nineteen-sixties that the rise of what art historian Bruce Altshuler calls "the curator as creator" enabled the inscription of "subverting the exhibition format" as a task on the agenda of exhibition organizers.[10] It was at that time that critical reflection upon the relationship between the artwork and the exhibition space, something that since the early avant-garde movements had been mainly taken up by artists, became part of curatorial work.[11] As a result, in the first half of the seventies, a new epistemological model of thematic exhibitions emerged that proposed a nonlinear organization of the exhibition discourse. It offered itself as a counterpoint to chronological and anthological organization by movements and monographic exhibitions, and, as we will see, would eventually largely replace it with regard to the organization of large-scale perennial exhibitions like biennials, which would become increasingly important platforms for curating. The attention to the contemporary art scene and the philosophy of "curating the new" promoted through such biennials fostered a change in attitude regarding the organization of exhibitions and eventually contributed to the growing importance of the curator's position. Over time, curators' work thus proved to be less about "caring for" in the sense of preserving art than about "discovering" lesser-known artists, movements, and scenes, a veritable profession shaped by master courses, thematic symposia, and conferences.[12] Their role in the construction of the exhibition as an authored object also became more and more defined over time, so much so that by 1998 an exhibition installation conceived by curator Henri Langlois at the Musée du Cinéma in Paris was defined as an "oeuvre d'esprit" in a court of law and thus deemed akin to the work of an "author" in other domains, earning it the protection of French copyright law.[13] If the curator in our present day has become, unquestionably, an "author," it makes sense to look back at the history and development that led up to this.

CURATORIAL AUTHORSHIP

IN the sixties, the reorganization of curatorial work may also explain the growing disquiet against the "Venice Biennial" attitude towards exhibition-making in the same decade and, with it, the critical examination of its multisite structure. In 1966 critic Bruno Alfieri commented that the Venice Biennial had failed to appoint someone who was clearly "in charge of the cultural outset" of the exhibition.[14] In contemporary terms, his question would sound like this: who is curating the Venice Biennial? The fact is that even up until the mid-sixties the Venice Biennial—widely considered to be the oldest of the perennial exhibitions—was not organized by a "curator," but instead by committees of officers and art history professors, or what was collectively called a "biennial council."[15] Accordingly, the Venice Biennial, like the other major large-scale perennial exhibition of that time, Documenta, was occupied with a focus on "re-writing history."[16] Since 1948, the Venice Biennial had tackled the task of filling in the historic gaps caused by twenty years of Fascist dictatorship.[17] Documenta, on the other hand, was founded in 1955 with the aim of "producing history" in the particular context of postwar Germany, which was burdened with the legacy of Nazism.[18] It was precisely in this period and in this context that Alfieri asked who was "in charge of the cultural outset" of biennials, especially the Venetian one. And, as his query implied, don't such large-scale international exhibitions need a "cultural signature," or, in other words, an author?[19]

This issue may sound outdated today, when nearly a dozen curatorial study programs and over 200 biennials are well established around the world and when biennials in particular have positioned themselves as a third institution competing with universities and museums in the writing of contemporary art history and are even proving to be a crucial debating ground with regard to curatorial strategies.[20] Therefore, when retracing the curatorial history of large-scale exhibitions, we also have to question the authorial position that curators have taken in the writing of both art history and the curatorial history of biennials, and wonder about when, through what debates, and how those authors became visible.

In regard to this, the Venice Biennial occupies a peculiar position, being the only perennial show characterized by a "multicell" structure due to the dissemination of the exhibition in multiple national pavilions.[21] As early as 1968, the national representation system adopted in Venice was already considered unproductive and questionable. Much debate thus developed around the idea of abolishing national pavilions and every "preconstituted space" in favor of "contingent structures, built upon the artist's request[,] ... spaces devoted to aesthetic events, a 'ring' where free action is possible, beyond any spatial and temporal bond."[22] Nonetheless, during the seventies the problem of the multicell structure was partially overcome thanks to a thematic approach that was framed by several international conferences attended by the representatives of the various national pavilions.

As a consequence of the debates about the pavilion structure of the Venice Biennial, the first thematic biennial took place in 1976, bringing together both the Palazzo delle Esposizioni and all national pavilions around the theme of *Ambiente, partecipazione, strutture culturali* (Environment, Participation, Cultural Structures). Under the coordination of artistic director Vittorio Gregotti, several exhibitions were organized by individual curators. Following on this path, the space of the 1978 Venice Biennial was again unified by a common thematic denominator, *Dalla natura all'arte, dall'arte alla natura* (From Nature to Art, from Art to Nature), though it was organized by two curatorial teams. Presented as a "research field proposed by a collective of international critics," the open theme offered a means of creating a space for free and critical analysis, and was perceived as a way to contrast with the art market system.[23] Somehow the fragmented spatial structure that the thematic approach was trying to solve was translated into a multiplication of curatorial views. Ever since, a unifying theme has been a leitmotif in contemporary art biennials, which are scattered throughout the urban space. And while biennials are thus, as a result, guided by an apparently universal or collective question/subject to which they are meant to respond, for which they are to provide a background, or about which they are meant to create debate, curatorial teamwork (that is, collective curating) within biennials, though it does occur occasionally, is far from the norm.

THE BIENNIAL AS A CURATORIAL LABORATORY

IT was at the Venice Biennial and at rival perennial exhibitions like Documenta that the first theme-based group shows were organized by the new figure of the curator, who was now explicitly in charge of the cultural outset of the exhibition, thereby effectively becoming the "author" of the show.[24] As early as 1968, on the occasion of Documenta 4, Arnold Bode was listed in the catalogue as being responsible for "Exhibition direction" (*Ausstellungsleitung*) rather than general direction (*Leitung*). The Documenta council's reorientation around the exhibition concept, which was eventually emphasized by the "exhibition maker" attitude that Szeemann cultivated in the creation of the show's fifth edition in 1972, made Documenta the first large-scale exhibition that, historically, may be recorded as the work of a single curator.[25]

In this context, Szeemann's "exhibition maker" approach met the large-scale perennial exhibition's quest for an author in the sixties, so the practice of a "council" deciding on the artistic fate of the exhibition came to an end. Arguably, then, the question of the authorship of biennials is rooted in the crisis of the historic-informational model[26] of the perennial exhibition itself.

Following internal organizational problems during the 1968 edition of Documenta, Szeemann was appointed "Secretary General" and charged with sole responsibility for the exhibition.[27] As art historian Hans-Joachim Müller has pointed out, besides the "coordinating" connotation of his appointment, the term used made explicit reference to the political role of the UN's Secretary General. Szeemann didn't aim to "democratize" the making of the Documenta, however; he made this clear when describing himself as "a Secretary General with the widest range of authority and a team of 5–7 executors in a d5 working group, so no huge commissions, no votes, no playing games with the names of the artists, but seven people who are responsible and reach the final decisions, together with the secretary general."[28]

Nevertheless, within this "authoritarian" structure we can see the beginning of new forms of collaborative curating that would come of age more fully at the end of the eighties. The collaborative structure outlined by Szeemann for Documenta 5 seems to have anticipated the trend of having a central curator and a network of collaborators.

Along with outlining the curator's vision of the art world, biennials and their large-scale exhibition counterparts have thus taken on the role of a laboratory for curatorial practice, thereby providing a context for investigating issues of authorship in contemporary art production. It is perhaps no coincidence that throughout the eighties the curator's role gained increasing visibility[29] while the dissemination of postmodern theories made the debate around the "death of the author" a common topic of discussion in university circles.[30] In relation to precisely this, the French philosopher Jean-François Lyotard wrote in 1979 about the end of "metanarratives" and, as a consequence, the end of their "great heroes."[31] In the invitation letter that curator Rudi Fuchs sent out to artists asked to participate in Documenta 7 in 1982 we find a similar wording, although the subtext animating Fuchs's intention is somehow opposite to Lyotard's hypothesis about the loss of "narrative functors." Subtitled "A Story," Documenta 7 seems, in fact, to merge a subjective curatorial proposal with other voices. However, as we read in the letter, the overall project was based on an individual authorial position, for it was Fuchs's identification and definition of his choice of contemporary issue that unequivocally determined the theme and approach of that edition of Documenta:

> *I see this exhibition as a story, and have even thought about using this word in the title... For me, however, that suggests something very precise: first a journey, then an account of it... The art of our contemporaries has not yet a defined history. It started at some time and somewhere: the depart [sic] from the classical tradition, the path toward the new! This departure meant leaving behind the magnificent, shared language of the classical period. Everyone now speaks the dialect of their own tradition—they speak of their home, their history.*[32]

Later on in the same letter, Fuchs aligns the collaboration with Documenta 7's "Artistic Board"[33] with the collapse of classical unity and grand narratives that led, in Lyotard's terms, to a "cloud of narratives." Behind the comprehensive backdrop of his claim ("Everyone now speaks the dialect of their tradition ... their history"), it is not at all clear who is speaking for whom: Are the curators speaking for the artists? Or are the works speaking for the artists or for the curators? This ambiguity is emphasized by Fuchs's opening statement, in which he remarks that an exhibition's concept (or story) can really be "formulated" only in the real space, "when the works are actually there." Still, this idea of cowriting the exhibition in collaboration with the Artistic Board and the artists is in fact contradicted by his use of the first person in the letter ("I see this exhibition as a story") and by his decision to build walls in the previously wall-less Museum Fridericianum, which led to a directed path for the viewing of a kind of authored narrative. Thus, though partly suggesting a collective authorial position in his text, Fuchs's inscriptions in the exhibition space bore a strong individual-author orientation: "We practice this wonderful craft, we construct an exhibition after having made rooms for this exhibition. In the meantime, artists attempt to do their best, as it should be."[34]

In Jan Hoet's 1992 Documenta, this subjective attitude was pushed even further. The curatorial team working with Hoet,[35] which he described as an ensemble of "fellow voyagers of discovery and antennae," was not "conceived as a democratic forum."[36] In a letter in which he explains his curatorial position with regard to Documenta 9, Hoet claimed not to have a specific exhibition concept ("I only built a structure that suggests a concept"):

> *The ninth Documenta is a Documenta of places; its topography is the supporting, load-bearing framework. But it is also a Documenta of the artists, because they are the ones that create the spaces within this framework ... My Documenta sets out solely from the artists, from their work.*[37]

Again, the apparent multiauthor structure of the exhibition is denied by the facts. The framework within which Hoet selected the artists and the exhibition spaces may have been inspired by the artists and the curatorial team, but the final, subjective choice was made by Hoet himself. Thus throughout the history of exhibition-making, one can identify two opposite trends: on the one hand, there have been perennial exhibitions that foregrounded the creation of curatorial one-man shows, like Hoet's Documenta, in which an individual curator positions him- or herself as a prominent figure; on the other hand, biennials and other large-scale exhibitions have also actively contributed to the dissemination of collaborative curating.

MULTIPLE VIEWS AND AUTHORSHIPS

THE proliferation of contemporary art biennials in the nineties has contributed to a large degree to the addressing of questions concerning recent changes about authorship in curatorial practice. A quite new form of cooperation that came of age with biennials is that of the correspondent, that is, the curator/art expert based in a city/node of the international art scene that offers advice on the selection of artists and guides the biennial curator in his or her visit/discovery of local artists and institutions. First made visible in the exhibition structure of Jean-Hubert Martin's *Magiciens de la terre* (1989), this type of correspondent acts as an informant in the work of "translation," interfacing his or her view of the "local scene's language" with that of the curator. The fact is that from the seventies through the eighties the thematic orientation of contemporary art biennials had often taken on the features of a monolithic narrative distributed in several spaces, a kind of gesamtkunstwerk that relied on artists' works as a means of expressing the curator's vision.[38] In 1997 this tendency, as well as the notion of the curator as author, was brought into question by Okwui Enwezor, who was artistic director of the second Johannesburg Biennial that year:

> *There is a tendency among curators and artistic directors to take the old model of seeing themselves as authors, so to speak. In order to move beyond this habit, in which we do not allow ideas and processes to be complicated, we have chosen to make Johannesburg into a different kind of forum. I decided to invite curators from different parts of the world, and my only restriction for them was that it would not be nationally based. I want them to go beyond their own territorial proclivity.*[39] *Still, the possibility of a truly collective curatorial process is not merely a matter of involving more than one person, as several biennials projects showed in the nineties, but of actually allowing for what could be called multiple authorship among curators to emerge.*[40]

In this regard, although it was the mandate of a singular curator, Catherine David's Documenta 10 arguably resulted in a far more plural exercise than other projects that were supposedly more collaborative. Putting forward her critical analysis of Documenta, and positioning her project within the questioning of large-scale exhibitions and contemporary culture, David clearly stated her temporal (Retroperspective) and spatial (Parcours, Limits, Borders) vision. Within this visible frame, artists were invited to debate and interact with a Documenta that was defined as "a type of laboratory," a place for "experiment, for conflict, for controversy."[41]

Similarly, for Documenta 11 Enwezor showed a deep concern for the process that produces the working framework that leads to the realization of an exhibition. He worked with a curatorial team to shape an exhibition that was intended to be a "constellation of ideas," in order to connect "the formality of the exhibition" with "the idea of communities of discourse."[42] In Enwezor's view, contemporary art curators belong to a transnational community of discourse and share a common research field that aims at "[making] room for new forms of knowledge."

Enwezor's approach to the group show's structure stressed discursive production, as he explained in the exhibition statement:

> *The basic concept of Documenta 11 is based on the formulation of a series of five platforms—public discussions, conferences, workshops, books, film and video programs—that try to describe the present location of culture and its interfaces with other global systems of knowledge.*[43]

The multiplicity of the contemporary cultural scene was not resolved here via a multiplication of views, but via a *change of paradigm*. The concept underlying the exhibition was not a mere theme, but a research tool that helped to build a plural discourse.

In a different fashion, Achille Bonito Oliva curated the 1993 Venice Biennial entitled *I Punti cardinali dell'arte* (The Cardinal Points of Art) in a similar attempt to undermine the way the big picture of contemporary art is produced within biennials. Bonito Oliva invited several curators to work on fifteen exhibitions and suspended the system of national representation. This allowed the German Pavilion, for example, to present the work of both a German artist and a Korean-born one. According to the "rules of the game" established by the Biennial's artistic director, the unifying theme became a device for producing multiplicity. Ventriloquist and polyphonic, Bonito Oliva's Biennial interpreted the perennial show as a tool for orienting—and disorienting—the audience through contemporary cultural production.

Ten years later, Francesco Bonami's 2003 Venice Biennial also intervened in this trend by making the plurality of the curatorial team the main concept of his exhibition project.[44] Entitled *Dreams and Conflicts: The Dictatorship of the Viewer,* the fiftieth Venice Biennial was articulated as an ensemble of group shows, each conceived by a different curator and installed, one show after another, in the Arsenale. As Daniel Birnbaum, who was one of the participating curators and later went on to become director of the biennial, pointed out, "[Bonami's Biennial] was a heterogeneous event, and in a way the biennale to put an end to the biennale as an experimental form. It tried to exhaust all the possibilities at once, and pushed the plurality as far as possible."[45] Bonami's multiplication of the individual curatorial view enabled the institutionalization of multiple authorship within the Venice Biennial. In selecting eleven curators, Bonami criticized the mechanism of the Venice Biennial that, after the experiences of *Aperto*'s curatorial teams in the nineteen-eighties, had returned to an individual curatorial structure during the nineties. In his biennial, the historical crisis of the great exhibition model and of the Venetian institution after four consecutive years of Szeemann's direction (he curated the 1999 and 2001 editions) came together with claims about the crisis of the curator as auteur. Therefore, taking the fragmentation of contemporary times as a starting point, Bonami emphasized the obsolescence of individual curatorial vision to the advantage of a multiple spatial organization, whereby the Biennial was presented as "an exhibition of several curators' exhibitions" and not as a collective exhibition project.

In a conversation with Bonami, Igor Zabel questioned the "curator's power position" and highlighted his or her role in making choices and establishing the criteria of selection.[46] These choices and selection criteria, as seen before, are actually the very places in which the authorial position of the curator is constructed, as Stéphanie Moisdon and Hans Ulrich Obrist also showed in the 2007 Lyon Biennial. A "game attitude" resonated in their biennial, where the biennial invitation system was turned into a visible exhibition concept. In biennials, curators invite artists to exhibit; in Moisdon and Obrist's biennial, curators invite other curators to show their curatorial vision, thereby delegating the choice of a large part of the artworks in the exhibition to others. Entitled *The History of a Decade That Has Not Yet Been Named,* it involved forty-seven curators and art critics, all of them participants in a historical and geographical game aiming at defining a list of the artists who best represented the first decade of the twenty-first century. As Moisdon and Obrist wrote in the catalogue, "The structure [of the Lyon Biennial's] game provides both a thinking space to think over the notion of the collective at the turn of this new century, as well as a medium to produce crossings and potential histories."[47] The selection system typical of biennials is here openly linked with the task of writing art history, and the process leading to this history is exhibited at the same level as the artworks.

One of the aims of the 2009 International Istanbul Biennial, organized by the curatorial collective What, How and for Whom (WHW), was to criticize this traditional biennial format that had been exposed by the 2007 Lyon Biennial.[48] WHW aimed at "giving the public some form of 'agency,' [and] making choices that would boost their capacity for action" in opposition to the system of spectacle that makes perennial shows "high-end branding tools for promoting tourism in metropolitan cities."[49] To do this, WHW made a single exhibition that put its finger on some of the expectations and implications of collective curating.[50] In a footnote to their text, they summed up their role as a collective of individuals curating together:

> *Curating the Istanbul Biennial is gravely complicated by the fact that it has no secure budget to fall back on, making it a deviant hybrid. The situation is further complicated by the fact that WHW is a collective of four curators, but it does not produce for four: instead of four biennials, it produces only one. Still, WHW eats and generally consumes for four persons, and even more . . . This fact presents an additional financial burden to be taken into account.*[51]

In the backdrop of WHW's analysis, we can see that though always developed on a collaborative basis—involving selection committees, consultants, and dialogues with other actors in the art world along with the artists and the audience—biennial curating is often forced to be perceived, at least in name, as *individual work*.

HERE AND NOW

IN a chapter devoted to "quickness" in his *Six Memos for the Next Millennium*, Italo Calvino compared the difference between the nineteenth-century novel's speed and that of the twentieth-century avant-garde novel with the difference between horsepower and the technologically advanced velocity of the car. As Calvino implies, and as the international avant-garde proved earlier in the twentieth century, each epoch needs to find new formats and writing devices in order to account for its revolutions, traumas, and changing realities. The task of curating today should be no different. But what type of curating and what kind of curator are needed? As Gianni Vattimo puts it, our epoch may be one of "weak thought"—a moment with a plurality of relative truths rather than a single absolute truth. Curating in such a time might, then, have to respond and give form to such a reality by inventing a way of thinking that undermines the notion of sure and indisputable statements, offering instead a multiplicity of truths that enable the acceptance of different viewpoints and imposing none of them as absolute.

In order to establish the possibility for actual coauthorship, however, there is no point in hiding the subjective nature of curatorial processes behind objective claims. One interesting trend developed by a few twenty-first-century biennials is the reflection on how these individual views become intersubjective. As Barthes reminds us, "there is no other time than that of the enunciation and every text is eternally written 'here' and 'now.'" And it is precisely in its ability to show a narrow, critical image of a specific time that the biennial's interest lies. This global picture of contemporary art and culture will be more productive the more it clearly assumes and brings into question the relativity of individual curatorial visions. The notion of the singular, unequivocal curator as "author" seems to be in tension with that possibility, so as our epoch unfolds before us, new possibilities and definitions for the author and the exhibition he or she produces may have to be found. ●

NOTES

This essay was submitted in response to the 2009 Bergen Biennial Conference's "Call for Biennial Knowledge."

1 Roland Barthes' "Death of the Author" was published in 1968 and translated into English in 1977, while Michel Foucault's "What Is an Author?" was published in 1969 and translated into English in 1979.

2 Roland Barthes, "Death of the Author," in idem, *Image, Music, Text,* trans. and ed. Stephen Heath (London, 1977), p. 145.

3 Michel Foucault, "What Is an Author?" in idem, *Language, Counter-Memory, Practice,* ed. Donald F. Bouchard, trans. Donald F. Bouchard and Sherry Simon (Ithaca [NY], 1979), p. 127.

4 See David Levi Strauss, "The Bias of the World: Curating after Szeemann & Hopps," in Steven Rand and Heather Kouris (eds.), *Cautionary Tales: Critical Curating* (Rotterdam, 2007).

5 An early critique of the curator as author is included in Douglas Crimp's "The Art of Exhibition" (in his *On the Museum's Ruins* [Cambridge (MA), 1993]), which focuses on Rudi Fuchs's Documenta 7 (1982).

6 The need to "make contemporary art exhibitions in a critical way," writes Giorgio De Marchis, results from the assumption that critique is the most productive way to represent contemporary artistic research. Under these circumstances, contemporary reality starts to provide themes that become modes of operation for exhibitions; see De Marchis, "Mostre e attività critica," *Metro: An International Review of Contemporary Art* 13 (1968).

7 Between 1969 and 1973, Lucy Lippard organized several "numbered" shows, the first being *Number 7* at the Paula Cooper Gallery in New York (1969). On this occasion, she positioned herself not as the exhibition's curator, but as "a compiler." The subsequent shows were *557,087* (Seattle, 1969) and *955,000* (Vancouver, 1970). Just like contemporary artists' practice in those years, all of these shows were "scattered" and "fragmented." Like conceptual artists of the day, she also worked with instructions and produced several books. See Lucy Lippard, "Curating by Numbers," in "Landmark Exhibitions," special issue, *Tate Papers,* no. 12 (Fall 2009), and the exhibition-as-book projects of 1969. From 1964 to 1966, Seth Siegelaub ran his own gallery in New York, Seth Siegelaub Contemporary Art. Collaborating with Conceptual artists such as Robert Barry, Douglas Huebler, Joseph Kosuth, and Lawrence Weiner, he curated several groundbreaking exhibitions and experimented with different formats, including interventions in the public space and books. He curated *Xeroxbook* (1968) and *January 5–31, 1969* (1969), "publication/exhibitions" editorial projects for which Siegelaub intermixed several artists' interventions, "but [which] were effectively his artists' books." See Charles Green, *The Third Hand: Collaboration in Art from Conceptualism to Postmodernism* (Minneapolis, 2000), p. 9. Since his death, Harald Szeemann's curatorial work has been discussed in several publications, including Tobia Bezzola and Harald Szeemann, *Harald Szeemann: with by through because towards despite: Catalogue of All Exhibitions, 1957–2005* (Zurich, 2007), and Florence Dérieux, *Harald Szeemann: Individual Methodology* (Zurich, 2007).

8 Bruce Altshuler, *The Avant-Garde in Exhibition: New Art in the 20th Century* (New York, 1994).

9 See Hans-Ulrich Obrist, "Mind over Matter," in idem, *A Brief History of Curating* (Zurich, 2009), pp. 80–100.

10 See Altshuler 1994 (see note 8).

11 In curator Paul O'Neill's words, a "curatorial turn" took place in the sixties, when "the primary discourse about art-in-exhibition began to turn away from forms of critique of the artwork as an autonomous object of study/critique towards a form of curatorial criticism, in which the space of exhibition was given critical precedence over that of the object of art." O'Neill, "The Curatorial Turn: From Practice to Discourse," in Judith Rugg and Michele Sedgwick (eds.), *Issues in Curating Contemporary Art and Performance* (Bristol and Chicago, 2007), pp. 13–14. This has also been reprinted in the present volume.

12 The first one in Europe opened in 1987, at the Magasin d'Art Contemporain, Grenoble. It was preceded by the Whitney Independent Studio Program, which officially opened in New York between 1967 and 1968.

13 Nathalie Heinich and Michael Pollak, "From Museum Curator to Exhibition Auteur: Inventing a Single Position," in Reesa Greenberg, Bruce W. Ferguson, and Sandy Nairne (eds.), *Thinking about Exhibitions* (London, 1996), p. 60.

14 Bruno Alfieri, "Editorial," *Metro: An International Review of Contemporary Art* 12 (1966), p. 5.

15 Ibid.

16 This is demonstrated by the number of exhibitions about major art historical movements and artists of the last forty years that were organized between the end of the nineteen-forties and the mid nineteen-fifties in Venice and Kassel. Between 1948 and 1956, the Venice Biennial dedicated group and solo shows to such historical artistic movements as Impressionism, Pittura Metafisica, Fauvism, Cubism, Der Blaue Reiter, Die Brücke, and De Stijl. Many of these historical trends were also presented in the first Documenta in 1955.

17 With its foundation in 1895, the Venice Biennial helped to form a national vision of contemporary art in a freshly unified Italy, while also aiming to position Venetian artists in a broader national and international context. From the beginning, as historian Marla Stone has highlighted, international artists outnumbered the Italian participants. This trend was gradually reversed from 1927 to 1934, when Fascism first infiltrated the administrative structure of the Venice Biennial, eventually reducing the international presence on the selection committee and reshaping the Biennial into a "national culture center." See Marla Stone, *The Patron State: Culture & Politics in Fascist Italy* (Princeton [NJ], 1998), pp. 32–43, 200–202. Sections devoted to literature, cinema, and theater were gradually added to the fine arts exhibition, with the latter being increasingly influenced by national contests aimed at building Fascist iconography. In 1934, Hitler's visit to the German pavilion was emblematic of the political backdrop affecting the Venice Biennial under Fascism and World War II. The Golden Lion awarded to Robert Rauschenberg in 1964 symbolically ended the period of historic recovery begun in 1948, and marked a shift towards the new thematic group show format discussed in this essay.

18 Walter Grasskamp, "For Example, Documenta, or, How Is Art History Produced?" in Greenberg, Ferguson, and Nairne 1996 (see note 13), pp. 48–56. The first edition of Documenta occurred in 1955 and was intended to reconnect and reconcile German public life with international modernity after the end of Nazi dictatorship.

19 Alfieri 1966 (see note 14), p. 5.

NOTES

20 See Charles W. Haxthausen (ed.), *The Two Art Histories: The Museum and the University* (New Haven, 2002). Jean-Marc Poinsot has highlighted the "writing history" vocation of contemporary art museum group shows during the nineteen-eighties; see Poinsot, "Large-Scale Exhibitions," in Greenberg, Ferguson, and Nairne 1996 (see note 13), pp. 41–47.

21 Lawrence Alloway, *The Venice Biennale 1895–1968: From Salon to Goldfish Bowl* (Greenwich, 1968), p. 136. In 1907, the Biennial's General Secretary, Antonio Fradeletto, proposed hosting foreign artists indedicated national pavilions to be constructed within the enclosure of the Giardini.

22 See "Proposte per la Biennale, una tavola rotonda, un progetto," *Metro: An International Review of Contemporary Art* 15 (1968), p. 23.

23 See "Viaggio nella natura dell'arte," in B78 (Venice, 1978), p. 1. In 1963, René Berger, director of Musée cantonal des Beaux-Arts, Lausanne, and a member of international Juries of the Venice Biennial, inaugurated the first Salon international des galeries-pilotes, which was also inspired by the will to overcome the limits of the national representation system in Venice. See Yves Aupetitalot and Catherine Lepdor (eds.), *Inside the Sixties: gp 1.2.3. Le Salon international des galeries-pilotes à Lausanne 1963, 1966, 1970* (Lausanne, 2002).

24 The trend can be also seen in the few perennial exhibitions of the time, like the São Paulo and Paris biennials, but is most visible by examining the example of Venice. On the wave of the 1968 protests, the exhibition aimed at being "more problematic, [and] far less museological" (see the general catalogue of the 1970 Venice Biennial). The first example of this trend in Venice was *Ricerca e progettazione: Proposte per un'esposizione sperimentale* (1970). More committed to the present and aiming to have the audience actively interact with the themes it explored, Ricerca e progettazione was the first exhibition in the history of the Venice Biennial that explored the visitors' role in the exhibition project. Organized according to different thematic guidelines, the exhibition also attempted to overcome disciplinary separations within the Venice Biennial.

25 See Michael Glasmeier and Karin Stengel (eds.), *Archive in Motion: 50 Years of Documenta 1955–2005* (Göttingen, 2005).

26 As early as 1957, in a symposium on the Venice Biennial, art historian Sergio Bettini argued that the Venice Biennial's audience was not looking merely for information when visiting perennial exhibitions, but also for "cultural orientation"; see Bettini, *Atti del convegno di studio sulla Biennale Venezia, Ca' Loredan, 13 ottobre 1957* (Venice, 1957), p. 31. In this context, perennial exhibitions are no longer meant to present exhaustive surveys of past trends or the contemporary scene, as according to the traditional historic-informational model. Instead, biennials are now expected to make critical statements that open up new debates and overall readings of contemporary cultural production.

27 Hans-Joachim Müller, *Harald Szeemann: Exhibition Maker* (Ostfildern, 2006), pp. 38–39.

28 Ibid., p. 157.

29 See Yves Michaud, *L'Artiste et les commissaires: Quatre essais non pas sur l'art contemporain mais sur ceux qui s'en occupent* (Nîmes, 1989).

30 See Andreas Huyssen, "Mapping the Postmodern," in Joseph P. Natoli and Linda Hutcheon (eds.), *A Postmodern Reader* (Albany, 1993), p. 141, and Sherrie Irvin, "Appropriation and Authorship in Contemporary Art," *British Journal of Aesthetics* 45, no. 2 (April 2005), p. 124.

31 In this fashion, the French philosopher Jean-François Lyotard wrote in 1979 about the end of "metanarratives" and resolved that the narrative function was losing its functors, its great hero, its great dangers, its great voyages, its great goal. It was being dispersed in clouds of narrative language elements—narrative, but also denotative, prescriptive, descriptive, and so on.

32 Rudi Fuchs, letter to invited artists (1981), quoted in Glasmeier and Stengel 2005 (see note 25).

33 The artistic board included Coosje van Bruggen, Germano Celant, Johannes Gachnang, and Gerhard Storck.

34 From the Documenta 7 catalogue, quoted in Crimp 1993 (see note 5), pp. 240–41.

35 The team consisted of Bart de Baere, Pier Luigi Tazzi, and Denys Zacharopoulos.

36 Quoted in Glasmeier and Stengel 2005 (see note 25), p. 335.

37 Jan Hoet, introduction to the Documenta 9 catalogue, quoted in ibid., p. 334.

38 The phenomenon can be read in the light of Bertolt Brecht's analysis of culture consumption, in which he suggests that in modern times the artwork can be "sold" without its author; the fame of the author without the work that determined his or her success, and a partial or modified version of the artwork can operate as a substitute for the whole work. Conversely, the curator's vision can also be "sold," in a way, without the artworks, and an exhibition's discursive frame can substitute for the actual narratives and qualities of the individual artworks it includes. See Brecht, "Il processo dell'opera da tre soldi," in idem, *Scritti sulla letteratura e sull'arte,* ed. Cesare Cases, trans. Bianca Zagari (Turin, 1973).

39 Carol Becker, "A Conversation with Okwui Enwezor," *Art Journal* 58 (Summer 2002). The curatorial team included Hou Hanru, Kelly Jones, Yu Yeon Kim, Gerardo Mosquera, Collin Richards, and Octavio Zaya.

40 An altogether different idea of "multiple authorship" takes shape around the "textualization of space and the spatialization of discourse" called for by Miwon Kwon, which raises this question: if the artist is the author of the spatial discourse and the narrative determining the "apparition" of the artwork, when an artist and a curator collaborate, are they coauthoring the exhibition? Philosopher and art theoretician Boris Groys has noted that the "identification of selection and creation" in art, which dates back to Marcel Duchamp, became crucial again in nineteen-sixties' installation practice. In installations, artists show "their personal practices of selection" and contribute to reducing the gap between curatorial and artistic work. What Groys thus implies is that both making installations and making exhibitions demand choices—of sites, objects, artworks, sources—a view that allows him to theorize a coauthorship condition for curators and artists. See Miwon Kwon, *One Place After Another* (Cambridge [MA], 2002), p. 29, and Boris Groys, "Multiple Authorship," in Barbara Vanderlinden and Elena Filipovic (eds.), *The Manifesta Decade: Debates on Contemporary Art Exhibitions and Biennials in Post-Wall Europe* (Cambridge [MA], 2005), pp. 93–95.

41 Catherine David, Documenta 10 press conference, 1997, quoted in Glasmeier and Stengel 2005 (see note 25), p. 352.

NOTES

42 Carol Becker, "A Conversation with Okwui Enwezor," *Art Journal* 58 (Summer 2002). The Documenta 11 curatorial team included Carlos Basualdo, Ute Meta Bauer, Susanne Ghez, Sarat Maharaj, Mark Nash, and Octavio Zaya.

43 Okwui Enwezor, foreword and introduction of the *Documenta11: Short Guide,* quoted in Glasmeier and Stengel 2005 (see note 25), p. 374.

44 For the 2003 Venice Biennial, Bonami invited curators Carlos Basualdo, Daniel Birnbaum, Catherine David, Hou Hanru, Massimiliano Gioni, Molly Nesbit, Hans-Ulrich Obrist, Gabriel Orozco, Gilane Tawadros, Rirkrit Tiravanija, and Igor Zabel.

45 "The Archeology of Things to Come: Daniel Birnbaum," in Obrist 2009 (see note 9), p. 237.

46 Igor Zabel, "The Power of Proposing Things, of Taking Risks: A Conversation with Francesco Bonami," in Marieke van Hal, Viktor Misiano, and Igor Zabel (eds.), "Biennials," special issue, *MJ–Manifesta Journal* 2 (Winter 2003 - Spring 2004), p. 181.

47 Stéphanie Moisdon and Hans-Ulrich Obrist, *The History of a Decade That Has Not Yet Been Named (*Zurich, 2007), p. 10.

48 Based on Bertolt Brecht's question "What keeps mankind alive?" The question is taken from the title of a renowned song from Brecht's *The Threepenny Opera* (1928).

49 WHW (eds.), *What Keeps Mankind Alive?—The Texts* (2009), p. 95.

50 In the first pages of the catalogue, WHW also exposes the "coauthorial" role taken on by public institutions when they interfere in the choice of the exhibition sites and narrow the budget for producing the artists' projects, two elements that deeply influence the shaping of any Biennial; see ibid.

51 Ibid., p. 96.

ON CURATORIAL RESPONSIBILITY

276

Raqs Media Collective

ZIMMEDARI / RESPONSIBILITY

IS it possible to speak of curatorial responsibility in the making of biennials?

In Hindustani-Urdu, one of the languages we find ourselves thinking and speaking in, the word for "responsibility" glosses as *zimmedari*. Zimmedari, coming from the Arabic root *zimma*, meaning "guarantee," by way of Persian into Hindustani-Urdu, suggests the notion of being a guarantee of something or someone. A *zimmedar* person, therefore, is someone who is willing to act as guarantor, to compensate for the consequences of an action. Often he is also an *izzatdar* person, a person of honor. It is evident that this sense of the word touches upon our understanding of custodianship, of what it means to care enough for something or someone so as to stand as its guarantor to the wider world—to be, in a sense, its *curator*.

Now, this meaning of standing as guarantor, which also requires a caring if not "careful" aloofness from the object in question, seems to preclude too intense an involvement with that for which one stands as guarantor.

The taking on of the role of curator by an artist involves the risk of compromising the attempts to keep at bay the imagined conflicts of interest between the engaged, passionate, subjective production of meaning and affect (art practice), and the careful, apparently disinterested, ostensibly objective imperative of display, arrangement, and discourse (curation).

We confess here that we are deliberately setting these two terms up as a crude binary pair, as hypotheticals, if only for heuristic purposes.

What is the tacit nature of the compromise inherent in the morphing of the artist into curator, or of the curator into artist?

We could speak of it as the risk of a state of suspension of the convention of a phenomenological distinction between production and display, or between artistic entanglement and curatorial distance, such that the prospect of retrospective, studied contemplation is contaminated by the imperative to make meaning and affect happen kinetically, in the "here and now" of the making of an exhibition.

What, we might then ask, is the recompense that might be demanded from an artist-curator for hazarding the contamination of contemplation by production? A sketch for an answer could be sustained productive contemplation—not just the curation of experiments and experience, but also the curation of reflection—a practice that dares to be theory, and that must be held accountable if it fails to be theory, that is, if it fails to both make and show and sense and be and think at the same time.

Theory for its own sake might be more elegant, and practice, in and of itself, may be more robust, but practice that is also theory, while it may be both inelegant and frail, is at least a "better failure" than what we would consider to be the "disabling," intimidating success of either theory or practice on its own terms.

If the practice of the artist-curator fails to embrace (in a fulsome way) the odd contradiction that might entail the simultaneity of making—showing and thinking all at the same time—then he might as well retreat into being either artist or curator, and give up the ambition of being both at the same time.

In other words, *if artist-curators fail to fail better* ("failing better" is the leap of faith in favor of which Sarat Maharaj argued at the 2009 Bergen Biennial Conference[1]), for fail they well might, especially as they might end up privileging at least one of either "making," "showing," or "thinking" even as they attempt to juggle all three heroically, then they can truly be held accountable for not offering adequate recompense for their folly—for not living up to their obligation to stand as a guarantor to their publics for their temerity in straying from the tried and tested conventions of curating done by curators and of art produced by artists without an adequately theoretical practice or a practically grounded theory.

As long as the division of labor between producer and interpreter, and between artist, curator, and critic, is maintained, so can the conceit of the distinction between practice and theory, but the moment that this distinction is erased, practice must embody theory and theory must inform practice. The tendency towards an increasing conceptualization and dematerialization of artistic practice suggests that the artist-curator might be a figure who has already emerged; it's just that some curators might be reluctant at times to recognize this when they look at an artist's body of work—they might have the uncanny, out-of-body experience of having their own practice reflected back at them in the artist's immaterial labor.

If this is the case, if the line between artists and curators is steadily blurring, then curatorial responsibility entails that the practice of curation, and the making and *look and feel* of an exhibition must be possessed by a commensurately sophisticated argument or narrative or allegory that can withstand ruthless interrogation, at least at the hands of the artworks that constitute the exhibition. The idea that argument, narrative, or allegory must simultaneously be able to walk upright as finely tuned, well honed, fully formed practice. A responsible exhibition is one that can look good and think acutely, not one that thinks cleverly yet acts shabbily, or one that looks handsome but thinks dull, predictable thoughts.

What this rules out is the use—or, should we say, abuse—of contemporary art exhibitions to provide makeovers and cosmetic surgery for ageing and depleted rhetorical expressions borrowed from the social sciences, journalism, or even art history and aesthetics. And here we mean the reciprocal trade in the course of which words such as "globalization," "First and Third Worlds," "nations and national identities," "center and periphery," and even the holy grails of "truth," "beauty," and the "migration of forms" acquire the rejuvenating glamour of an immersion in the art world even as they bestow on the same art world the mellow patina of academic respectability, usually expressed in a badly written, jargon-laden, grammatically and semantically uneven, high-brow (non-)English.

While we might have spiraled onwards from the morphing of attitudes into forms towards the transformation of latitudes into forms, we have, at least, the urgent responsibility to ensure that our platitudes do not become our norms. Instead, we could ensure that our exhibitions become sites where concepts learn to walk in the world, taking a tumble if need be and acquiring the flesh and muscle tone of feelings, and that they become laboratories of knowledge that are not necessarily only about art, and not necessarily endless, internally referenced engines about art and artists, but in and of the world, and of ourselves, through art.

This is a first step in our answer to the question about what might constitute curatorial responsibility for we "artist-curators." Now let's take the second step.

RESPONSIBILITY THEORY

IT is time to take a longer and more considered look at responsibility. Almost nothing in the literature of aesthetics, curation, or biennals seriously considers the question of responsibility. It is our hunch, and we are open to being corrected, that the insurance industry, through its daily operationalization of complex notions of moral hazard, has a more serious understanding of responsibility than the contemporary art world does.

Boris Groys, when speaking of aesthetic responsibility, said: "Today, everyone is subjected to an aesthetic evaluation—everyone is required to take aesthetic responsibility for his or her appearance in the world, for his or her self-design."[3] His take on aesthetic responsibility rests ultimately on his understanding of the subsumption of the role of the artist into the status of the artwork, such that the artwork formerly known as the artist is asked to take responsibility for his or her appearance in the world, exactly, and as exactingly, as it is demanded of politicians, celebrities, and terrorists. While Groys' discussion is useful and engaging, especially when it is counterintuitive, it still does not provide us with an answer to the question of what it means to assume the burden of the representation of our ideas and concepts in and through the bodies and bodies of work of people other than ourselves, which is what curating is all about in the first place.

Curatorial responsibilities in a more technical sense may denote, in a museum context, the obligation to care for and protect fragile or precious objects in perpetuity, or at least for a long time. Here, we might see the need to think about Hans Jonas.[2] (Jonas is a philosopher deeply concerned with responsibility, especially within an ecological framework.) Needless to say, a biennial curator who damages the objects or processes in his custody is acting irresponsibly, but this is an obvious and banal point to make.

We may extend this notion of responsibility to the care and concern for the well-being of artists—the obligation to ensure that artists are not ripped off or treated unfairly, that they encounter a context of conviviality, and that their work is presented as well as it can be. Speaking of conviviality, we may remind ourselves of the ways in which the "arrangements" of Documenta 11 in the days leading up to the opening, for instance, included a canteen where all artists and everyone on the curatorial team, all assistants and technicians, could have a simple buffet meal at lunchtime, a circumstance that not only provided wholesome, simple nourishment at a low cost to the organization, but also led to many chance encounters in the soup queue that turned into lasting friendships. This was an invisible consequence of an invisible, modest decision in a grand exhibition, but it has had a profound effect on the lives of many artists and curators, some of whom were assistants and interns at the time.

It may also extend further, to a sensitivity to the needs of communities that constitute the publics of the exhibition. Large exhibitions are funded by the taxpayers' money, so curators have a responsibility to spend it wisely, or at least with a degree of democratic accountability to the public that pays twice—first to fund the exhibition (and the sometimes not insubstantial curatorial fees), and then again in buying tickets. Does this require curators to attend to whether or not the occasionally intractable opacity of contemporary art needs to be made more hospitable to the experiences of Joe Public? Perhaps it can, if enough attention is given to mediation and education. On the other hand, are artists and their expressive autonomy shortchanged in this desire for accommodation? Do the desires of the artist and the demands of the public stand in opposition, say, in the case of a work that either "gives offence" or may be perceived to give offence? Situations in which such conflicts arise require mediation, the undertaking of which can also be a part of the question of curatorial responsibility.

An international exhibition stages encounters between local and global realities, and the terms of this encounter can be heavily burdened by the dynamics of power. A rich regional government that foots the bill of a biennial may instrumentalize the participation of outsiders to earn itself the cultural capital of cosmopolitan credibility at a discount. On the other hand, foreign art-world elites may patronize, misunderstand, misrepresent, exoticize, and alienate local realities. The global carbon footprint of a biennial may undermine any claims to local sustainability. Entrenched local interests might use the opportunity of a biennial to reassert their hegemony, foreclosing the limited available options for the opening up of narrow cultural spaces in the region. A biennial may be an urban renewal exercise involving eviction and forced resettlement; it may also be the occasion when issues of eviction and dislocation are revealed, analyzed, and dramatized in highly public ways. Curators can find themselves becoming unknowing brokers for real estate companies or knowing impresarios for political satraps. They might find themselves caught in the cross fire of several simultaneous ethical and cultural-political dilemmas that involve difficult political and economic choices. They may overreach themselves, underplay their hand, or risk everything by wagering nothing.

Whatever the case may be, in each instance the guilty curators (and here we are assuming we are all at least charged guilty) would probably throw their hands up and say that they were battling circumstances beyond their control. These circumstances can be budgets, the tantrums of star artists, the naïveté and inexperience of emerging artists, technical and architectural constraints, the gallery system and the art market, academism, history (either of the biennial form in general, or of the particular biennial concerned, or of the region), political repression, corruption, or whatever else may be the power most likely to appeal to each given curator's particular eccentricity of victimhood.

THE PRINCIPLE OF ALTERNATE POSSIBILITIES

BUT does this appeal to force majeure, to threat, to powers greater than the prestige of curatorial office absolve curators of moral responsibility? Do we not have an obligation to account for our failures just as much as the right to enjoy the fruits of our successes? To answer this question we have to make a short detour into the narrow but interesting field of "responsibility theory" in ethics.

Now, there are two kinds of responsibility theorists: (a) those that accept the excuses of those who say they could not have done otherwise, and (b) those who don't.

This division is easy to understand; it is as simple as the division between blind free will and absolute determinism, and is expressed succinctly in what is known as the Principle of Alternate Possibilities in ethical theory. The Principle of Alternate Possibilities forms part of an influential argument for the incompatibility of responsibility and causal determinism, and goes something like this:

(1) An agent is responsible for an action only if said agent is free.
(2) An agent is free only if causal determinism is false.
(3) Therefore, an agent is responsible for an action only if causal determinism is false.

However elegant it may be, the Principle of Alternate Possibilities is not very useful, because real-world examples rarely, if ever, correspond to the absolute polarities of free will and total determinism. Rarely, if ever, could a person really have absolutely freely done other than what he did in any given circumstance because of the constellation of social, historical, political, juridical, economic, biographical, psychological, interpersonal, and cultural determinants of the action in question. The reality of an action usually, if not unvaryingly, involves an admixture of determination, chance (which is also a kind of determination), coercion, will, and liberty. Does this absolve us all of moral responsibility? No, it doesn't.

How, then, can we assign moral responsibility? When do we accept or reject a curator's plea that he should not be made to bear moral responsibility for not having been able to fully realize his curatorial dream because of a host of external and "objective" conditions?

Among those who try to reconcile the need for locating moral responsibility, a degree of free will, and a dose of determinism are the people who say that free will is not incompatible with determinism because an agent is free to do otherwise when he would have done otherwise had he wanted to do otherwise. Agents may possess free will, according to this tradition of conditional analysis, even if determinism is true.

FRANKFURT'S OBJECTIONS

AN alternative view, rigorously argued by the ethicist and philosopher Harry Frankfurt,[4] who is otherwise known for his incisive and fertile book entitled *On Bullshit*[5] (which we highly recommend), holds out a series of fascinating possibilities that draw a stricter line insofar as the location of moral responsibility is concerned. We must confess that we are more partial to this view, especially because we constantly hear curators, artists, and intellectuals lament the "force of history."

For Frankfurt, a person is *not* morally responsible for what he has done if he did it *only because he could not have done otherwise.*

We draw your attention to the subtle but very significant difference this view possesses with respect to the earlier position. The earlier position stated: A person *is* morally responsible when he is *free to do otherwise*. He is free to do otherwise when he *would have done otherwise had he wanted to do otherwise*. In other words, he is free to do otherwise only when the factors inhibiting his desires are absent. Since this is rarely the case, he is not morally responsible for most of his actions.

Now let's return to Frankfurt's formulation: A person is *not* morally responsible for what he has done if he did it *only* because *he could not have done otherwise*, that is, if even *nonaction*, rather than *action*, was *not* available to him as a viable option.

We can identify such situations as those in which there is a total arrest or withdrawal of agency, not because of either inertia, lethargy, or compliance, but because of the active, preventive, and nonpunitive intervention of a more powerful actor.

We want to stress here the difference between actual preventive force and punitive action, and it is this difference that we now wish to explore, following from Frankfurt, by trying to think about instances in which the question of moral responsibility cannot be avoided, regardless of the presence of determining or coercive factors.

A person is morally responsible for doing what he is expected to do if he did it while being indifferent to either the potential rewards for or the threat of having to face the consequences of his action, that is, if his desire for carrying out the action outweighs his calculation of the loss or gain that might accrue to him as a result of doing it.

A person is morally responsible for doing what he did even if he did it knowing that there was a threat to him as a consequence of his not doing what he was being expected to do. In such cases we could argue for diminished responsibility rather than absent responsibility, either because (a) he does not risk testing the limit of whether or not the threat to him can be actualized, or resisted, by his insistence on doing what the wielder of the threat asks him not to do, or (b) he does not take the route of withdrawal, or that of refusal, evasion, or reticence, all of which could also be alternatives to doing what he is expected to do, or (c) he refuses to outwit the wielder of the threat such that his refusal to do what he is expected to do is *performed* in a manner that makes it impossible for the threat holder not to misread it as compliance.

In this case we could speak of "false" or "ironic" compliance or subversion *disguised as compliance*. This is a kind of "dissimulatory" compliance that actually undermines the intent of the person wielding the threat, or power, perhaps by revealing an inner contradiction that the wielder of the threat or power would rather have kept concealed.

Each of these instances is mappable across curatorial arguments for action and inaction, and different modes and methods of staging shows. For instance, the trope of "national representation" that is much discussed in relation to biennials, through exaggeration, irony, or even deadpan, low-key performativity, can be, hypothetically, used to send up and subvert national representation if a situation exists in which a curator feels he cannot but work with the trope of national representation due to "pressure" from the authorities that control a biennial and/or its purse strings. A failure to adopt a critical strategy—either simply, confrontationally, and openly, or through disguise and dissimulation—in the face of an oppressive official mandate cannot absolve a curator of having compromised his responsibility for critical vigilance in the face of the hegemonic power of an intellectually and morally vacuous category.

COMMITMENTS

AND now, we can return to the question: Is it possible to speak of curatorial responsibility in the making of biennials?

Responsibility, after all, is all about being "answerable." To be "responsible" means, first and foremost, to answer, to respond, to be responsive. We could say that *curatorial responsibility* consists in taking the position of being a custodian of the ethical, authorial, pragmatic, and programmatic energies that act in concert to transform the occasion of a biennial into a process whereby (for the duration of the event) a space of creativity, display, and discourse is rendered public in a manner that articulates criticality, intelligence, pleasure, and an informed response to the matrix of social and political relationships that tie local contexts to global realities.

The thoughts and notes that we are presenting here arise at the intersection, or commons, of our collective's intersubjective practice and involve some strands of thought that are recent as well as others that go back many years and reflect our hybrid, equivocal, hermaphrodite position as artists who also happen to have occasionally curated.

What brings the three of us in Raqs to work everyday (and has kept us together for the past seventeen years) are a desire to ask questions and a dissatisfaction with the answers, even if they are of our own devising. We seek refuge from certainty in all we do. This means that our work often expresses our deep and enduring skepticism regarding narratives built out of unexamined ideas about identity, property, progress, memory, and security, or barely examined yet overextended (sometimes to the point of exhaustion) terms like globalization, identity politics, nations, nationality, nationalism, postcolonialism, centers, and peripheries.

Our response to the assault of these barely examined, overextended terms is to cultivate a daily and diligent garden of doubt (about every aspect of their operation) from which we harvest many different kinds of fruits and flowers, most of which have been artworks, texts, and situations, and some of which have been exhibitions.

This is the "critical public space" that exists, firstly, between the three of us. A public space comes into existence the moment you have more than two people, because at least one person at any given time is a witness (a public) to the dialogue of the other two. And a triangulation such as ours is thus, by definition, a miniscule but highly critical public space populated by synergies as well as disagreements that have lasted for more than seventeen years. And everything we do, whether as artists or curators, is simply an exercise in extending the boundaries of this critical public space to include ever-larger constellations, whether of people, of practices, or of institutional spaces, invitations, and imperatives.

We see ourselves more as citizens of a federated republic of practices than as the subjects of nations and the mere objects of history. This means our commitments and fealty generally lean more towards the things that we make, see, read, listen to, and participate in—images, words, sounds, and situations—rather than to abstract and static concepts that are determined by factors and forces beyond our control. These forces out of our control include the regime of passports, visas, citizenship, and static constructs of identity, but also the more mundane issues of funding and the very different degrees of support for artistic practice in different parts of the world that attempt to describe and define all our work, the agendas of all of which we ourselves usually have no role in determining. We did not determine our sexes, our ethnicities, our mother tongues, our nationalities, or the extent of the funding to which we have access. These were determined for us by biological, historical, and cultural factors that predate us all. What we can determine, and take responsibility for, is our attitude towards these factors and how we allow or enable or trick ourselves, individually and collectively, to respond to them. Are we coerced by them, complicit in them, indifferent to them? Are they indifferent to us? Are we able to construct zones of autonomy with, within, without, against, or despite them? Are our responses to them conducive to the conditions of their continued life, and to the continued life of our practice?

The question of how biennials could be responsibly curated in the future requires us to think a little bit about time, because any questions about the future are really enquiries about how we want something to continue, or about how prepared we are to ensure its continued existence.

We might anticipate the writing of (future) histories of art simply by ensuring that the definitions and criteria of practice that we put into place in the present are open enough to accommodate expansions and transformations that challenge our present state of understanding about what constitutes art. In this way, the art history of the future will find it possible to recognize our current work as making room for what today's art might evolve into tomorrow.

We think that the times we live in are sharp and interesting, dangerous and rich in possibilities. Negotiating history, like a pedestrian calculating how best to cross a street busy with speeding cars, can be a risky business. Predicting the future of this negotiation is less useful than cultivating the skills necessary to remain sharp, street-smart pedestrians. We keep our eyes on the road and our feet on the ground, especially since we know that the hands upon the wheels on the road may belong to agents who have command over greater amounts of horsepower than we can muster by ourselves.

We find that time doesn't run in only one direction, people don't just belong to one place, feelings don't just have one color, and every conversation has an infinity of possible endings. Our work, as artists and as curators, is in the end only a means for enjoying the sense we have of this plenitude. Our responsibility as curators, or, for that matter, as artists, is, then, to paraphrase Hans Jonas, *a correlate of power* (for power, read "enjoyment of plenitude") *and must be commensurate with the latter's scope and the scope of its exercise.*

Jonas is unique in actually giving us a temporal, durational sense of the understanding of responsibility. He talks about adding a "time horizon to the moral calculus"—a dimension that is missing, in his estimation, in Kant's understanding of the moral imperative. Jonas can thus speak of the requirement that human beings, in order to qualify as moral agents, act in such a way that they *"do not compromise the conditions for an indefinite continuation of humanity on earth."*

Again, a modest rephrasing of this imperative, when applied to curatorship, in our opinion, would mean: to act in such a way that *we do not compromise the conditions for the continuation of the life of the questions with which we deal.*

Let us, at the very least, not kill the issues we deal with by presenting them in such a manner that they no longer remain open questions. Are our wares local, global, here, now, laden with familiarity, or bearers of their own estrangement? Let's let these issues—at least for the time being, if not for forever—remain open questions. Let's not close the file on them by the manner in which we "curate" them. Let's make sure our custodianship of these questions does not become the condition either of their imprisonment or of our being taken hostage by them.

Let us at least allow ourselves, from time to time, to maintain our confidence and assurance about what it means to be something in abeyance in order that we may yet be surprised by who or what we might still become. ●

NOTES

This essay is a revised version of a lecture given at the Bergen Biennial Conference, September 17–20, 2009.

1 Sarat Maharaj in discussion with Carlos Basualdo, "Are the Traditional Paradigms Still Relevant Today," Bergen Biennial Conference, Bergen, September 17–20, 2009.

2 See Hans Jonas, *The Imperative of Responsibility: In Search of an Ethics for the Technological Age* (Chicago, 1985).

3 See Boris Groys, "Self-Design and Aesthetic Responsibility," *e-flux Journal,* no. 7 (June 2009), http://www.e-flux.com/journal/view/68.

4 See Harry Frankfurt, "Alternate Possibilities and Moral Responsibility," *Journal of Philosophy* 66, no. 23 (1969), pp. 829–39.

5 Harry Frankfurt, *On Bullshit* (Princeton [NJ], 2005).

RETHINKING BIENNIALS: MODELS AND FORMATS

HOW TO BIENNIAL?

THE BIENNIAL IN RELATION TO THE ART INSTITUTION

292

Maria Hlavajova

TO biennial or not to biennial: *that is the question.* Having been asked to ponder this, I wonder whether the state of things is really so wretched that a complete dismissal of the biennial phenomenon needs to be meditated upon? But no; as we learned from Shakespeare's protagonist Hamlet, questions of this nature are uttered as a means of pausing before undertaking action. The exercise thus provides a welcome opportunity in the realm of art, where the endless carousel of events, fueled by the spectacle and populist choices, rarely provides an occasion to take the time to imagine itself otherwise. To pose this question is thus an occasion to try to grasp the seemingly unrestrained development of the *biennialization* of the art world that has so overwhelmingly redefined our field, particularly since the beginning of the nineties, and to think about not only its alarming features (as there are many) but also, and more importantly, the *possibilities* it itself embodies, as well as what must be done for these possibilities to come to life.

I am not entirely convinced that the way we have discussed biennials so far has been constructive, especially given the undertone of undirected cynicism and unchallenged opportunism that is often so readily—and unnecessarily!—employed. I have come to believe that this sort of "cynicism" was employed by many to disguise a feeling of guilt—perhaps for having said "yes" to the opportunity to work on a biennial, or perhaps for having taken an active part in a culture that always already embraces criticality as a harmless outlet for oppositional voices according to today's neoliberal logic. By this logic, the refusal to participate is not the kind of grand heroic gesture it perhaps once was, but this does not justify the uncritical ride of those who have readily submitted their curatorial voice to the political and economic status quo with only one aim on their minds: not to engage in changing the system, but to make it work for themselves. Having observed these developments, and occasionally having taken an active part in them, I am convinced that we have to engage in thinking about biennials responsibly and build actively on the legacy of those undertakings that (at least) tried to transform the mere opportunity of organizing an art festival into a possibility for the agonistic repoliticization of cultural labor.

These conditions affect how we might respond to the hyperbolic instruction of the question of whether "to biennial or not." One does not need too many theoretical insights to understand the simple truth that "we *will* biennial," and also that—and here we need to say it for once—perhaps "we *should* biennial." To deal with this responsibly, we first need to change the focus from "*whether* we should biennial" to "*how* should we biennial" (if not even to "*what* should we biennial"), a process that involves discussing the ways and circumstances in which things are done, and indeed what these *things* that are to be done actually might be. Then, with the experience and knowledge we have at our disposal, we need to see if and how one can find an emancipatory dimension in a phenomenon that so closely mirrors the flows of neoliberal capital.

One area of knowledge that we must inevitably tackle in order to move on to these crucial questions of *how* and *what* to biennial (questions that this essay admittedly cannot resolve) is to try to create some understanding of where biennials stand *as* and *among* art institutions. Such a discussion needs to happen in at least two fields of tension: the one that exists between "exhibition" and "institution," and the ones that exist in the landscape of art institutions as such, searching for the pockets of ambiguity between and among these that hopefully allow us to think through new possibilities. Necessarily, in the absence of a concise critical and theoretical body of work on this issue, some concrete examples of projects need to be invoked, so I do this here by making reference to projects with which I have been involved, letting the tone and the language of my discussion oscillate between the theoretical and the experiential. But first let's remind ourselves that speaking about "*the* biennial" is an impossible task, as no single form representing this entire hybrid field of cultural endeavor exists. However, as much as it may be impossible, it is also inevitable if we want to further our discussion about this critical phenomenon of our contemporaneity. Yet the thoughts that follow here should be seen only as a set of provisional schematic suggestions in need of further examination.

It is rather customary that in the context of discussing the contemporary "biennial phenomenon" we tend to reflect on it in one of two ways: we see biennials either as *exhibitions* or as *institutions*. These views are sometimes set in opposition to each other, but often they are used in a vaguely interchangeable way, and so the distinction between these two tropes is too often overlooked and even more rarely conceptualized. While it may be that biennials are *both* exhibitions and institutions simultaneously, dealing with the distinction in a conscious way might help to further our discussion.

Reducing biennials to exhibitions appears relatively limiting, although there is an overwhelming tendency among advocates of biennial culture to try to place the history of biennials within the history of exhibitions, a discourse that has grown rather fashionable in the last couple of years. Only rarely, however, do biennials make it onto the list of exhibitions we customarily come up with when thinking of, as we often call it, "one of the most vital" narratives of our cultural history. Such an (impromptu) list usually includes, to name just a few of the usual suspects, Edy de Wilde's 1969 *Op losse schroeven* and Harald Szeemann's *When Attitudes Become Form* of the same year, Kaspar Koenig's *Westkunst* of 1981, Jean-Hubert Martin's *Magiciens de la terre* of 1989, Valerie Smith's *Sonsbeek* of 1993, and Okwui Enwezor's *Short Century* of 2001, which are then interwoven with Szeemann's, Catherine David's, and Enwezor and his team's respective Documentas and perhaps Charles Esche and Vasif Kortun's Istanbul Biennial of 2005. You can take this selection for what it is: an improvised, provocative attempt to suggest that the history of exhibitions as it stands in the theoretical discourse today is, in fact, relatively separate from that of biennials (or even "biennial exhibitions"), with only occasional points of intersection. Also problematic is that what this offhand list includes displays the Western, if not a specifically Eurocentric, perspective on (and of) exhibition-making, despite the genuine attempt at de-Occidentalization at which some of the shows aimed. Newer biennials lacking a Western provenance do provide an important, even crucial counterthrust in our attempt to move beyond such center-first models of exhibitions and institutions, although in many cases they attest to no more than what we already know: that art and economic globalization are fellow travelers. On many other occasions, however, these biennials represent a serious possibility and provide concrete examples of how to engage with local conditions in a politicized way and how to extend the scope of our understanding of what the meaning of exhibitions can be in different political geographies, thus simultaneously recontextualizing and subverting the dominant views of Western hegemony to which the West itself continues to cling.

This (erroneous) interchangeability of the notions of the biennial as an institution or as an exhibition has to do, I believe, with a lack of what one could call "historicity." In order for the next biennial exhibition to succeed, it would seem, it needs to concentrate its efforts on overwriting what came before in order to recharge the biennial form's reputation for innovation and newness. The history of exhibitions mounted by any one biennial institution (think of Manifesta or the Berlin Biennial, for example) must therefore necessarily be the history of separate, independent, unrelated, eccentric, disparate curatorial projects that are in fact often brought to life through a principle of opposition to previous editions or even through a strategic denial of what has been done before. Thus it is relatively common that if the past (in other words, previous editions of a given biennial) is in any way present in new biennial iterations, it is brought about through the trope of negation. Add to this the establishment of short-term, temporary, and, to the greatest extent possible, exclusive alliances with the figure of the curator, from whom the biennial borrows his or her fame, knowledge, networks, etc., only provisionally, and the identity of the biennial must necessarily be unstable, always in flux, and difficult to articulate in terms of continuity or as something more than just the sum of its editions over time. What we have, then, is a series of "one-offs" with no obvious or readable conceptual link. Yet let's not confuse this with the specific properties that the biennial institution does provide: a "given" outside that does not originate from the exhibition or its concept (though it can be thematized by the project), such as, for example, the uniqueness of the city (as in the cases of Berlin or Iasi, and most of the locations of Manifesta), the nation (as in the cases of the biennials in Venice or São Paulo), or the region (as, at times, with Manifesta, but also in the case of the only edition of the Brussels Biennial). These are properties that make the biennial prone to act relatively seamlessly within the game of capitalist distribution, consumption, and promotion, thereby making the biennial a catalyst of financial investments, popular interest, and global networking.

We now know that it is undeniable that the exhibition format *is* the primary vehicle on which biennials rest, but let's acknowledge for the time being that the radically diverse projects that take place under this label, hand in hand with the expanded field of contemporary curating, involve not only production and display but also, and progressively even more importantly, the production of discourse and the distribution of knowledge. And who says that biennials need to be exhibitions at all? Rather than "perfect exhibitions" (which in his opinion must be organized by museums), I recall curator René Block saying that the biennial should become "a workshop" for contemporary art, something that would provide an opportunity for "encounters between local and international artists" that would encourage work and exchange. In various corners of the world, some biennials have begun maturing away from exhibition/event culture and have embarked on moving beyond a spectacular, large-scale, international exhibition-festival, making themselves the producers, educators, and hosts of long-term artist residencies and discursive programs that transpire in between the perennial exhibitions. This is a development that is critical, especially in the particular conditions of locales where such possibilities are not offered through the work of any other (public) cultural institutions, or at least not in an interesting or innovative way. Yet in the cases when the crude machine of the biennial imposes itself from the outside and threatens the cultural work of the existing (progressive) institutions in a particular locality—art centers, museums, or academies—only because it is better equipped to operate in close proximity to the economic dogma of the day, this might create a new urgency for us to debate the place of the biennial in relation to other art institutions. In other words, it is vitally important that the function of the biennial and its meaning for the public sphere be measured against the background of the social, political, and cultural functions of the art center and the museum (in fact, all existent infrastructural, locational, and relational coordinates) within the concrete circumstances under question. This perspective is indispensable to the attempt to articulate the space in which the biennial could bring something to the table that *isn't already there* and *would not exist otherwise.*

Before moving on to outline the second "field of tension"—that is, the position of the biennial in relation to other art institutions—I want to provide a brief clarification about what I mean when I refer to "art institutions." I use the notion of the art institution not as a vast, all-encompassing system of values, norms, and customs as sociology customarily identifies the Institution with a capital "I," but merely as a way to address one of the players within the larger field of art, an art institution with a lowercase "i": as sociologists would put it, a concrete organization of people, buildings, things, and meanings, such as museums, *Kunsthallen*, art centers, and—of course—art biennials. Let's remind ourselves that in this sense there is no contradiction between the art institution and the biennial, the latter being but one of the many possible "species" to which this term can be applied. To keep it simple, I will speak of the biennial as a biennial in order to distinguish it from the (other) art institution I have in mind.

At the risk of oversimplifying things, I would like to suggest the following: if it is largely believed that the contemporary version of the biennial as we know it, the kind that has mushroomed across the planet in the last two decades, is to some extent an outcome of dissatisfaction with rigid (static, inflexible, immobile, hegemonic, slow, etc.) art institutions (and here I am thinking mainly of the large-scale museum in the so-called West, maintained to protect the bourgeois public sphere through either the nationally-oriented model or its neoliberal equivalent, which is driven by populism and entrepreneurial principles), I would like to suggest that some of today's smaller and medium-scale organizations (such as some art centers or *Kunsthallen*) are in fact a reaction to and an outcome of disillusionment with both old-fashioned museum-type structures *and* what the contemporary biennial has come to represent. The (overwhelming) exodus of independent curators to small- and medium-scale contemporary art centers mainly across northwestern Europe (and partially to academia, or some combination of the two) that occurred at the end of the nineties launched a new trust and belief in the potential of the art institution. This move radicalized the possibilities of what art institutions might be by bringing in experience from outside their own tradition, experience that also included inside knowledge of international contemporary art biennials (let's not forget that many of the independent curators who took on such directorial roles had curated biennials in the previous decade). Unlike classic institutional organizations, these "new institutions" ("experimental institutions," "post-institutions," or institutions expounding the curriculum of "institutional creativity," as some protagonists of this new institutional ethos have labeled them) are capable of responding to the post-Fordist requirements of flexibility, horizontal organizational structures, and even mobility. And unlike biennials, they are capable of investing in notions of continuity, locality, and concentration. They operate in the space between historicity and innovation, translate efficiently between the local and the global, and readily engage in a negotiation between political agendas and economic competition.

What do I have in mind? It might be useful now to look at a concrete example of such medium-scale art institutions, and in this case the one I am familiar enough with to discuss is BAK, basis voor actuele kunst, an institution envisioned as a space dedicated to thinking from, about, and through art that I was lucky enough to think through conceptually from the very beginning nearly eight years ago and now run as its artistic director. In many respects BAK was envisioned as a concrete yet experimental conceptual response to my experience with the successes and failures of Manifesta 3, the Ljubljana edition of the nomadic European contemporary biennial that I co-curated in 2000. This curatorial project involved rethinking the processes of translation between the international and the local, reorienting the consuming body of the nomadic tourist art audience into a complex and multilayered policy of "zero visitors," shifting the position from which we were speaking from knowing to not-knowing, reworking the spectacular into the reflexive and research-based, investing in collaborative and participation-driven work, and transforming the temporal into the long-term, and promotion into commitment. All in all, this meant thinking of BAK as an art organization that completely invested itself in a sustainable model of engagement with subjects of global urgency, but at the same time engaged with its local constituency in order for art to exercise its public voice. If my experience with biennials was shaped by the imperatives of the spectacle, speed, immediacy, and erasure—and all this in a locale with which a sense of close familiarity and understanding simply cannot be established in less than two years—then BAK became a possibility for engaging in reflexivity, historicity, continuity, discursivity, participation, production, fluidity, intimacy, and criticality.

So what happens if, for the sake of experiment, we "superimpose" an art institution like BAK on the institution of the biennial, as occurred in the case of the Brussels Biennial?

The Brussels Biennial took place only once, towards the end of 2008. Having ended up as it did in a nightmarish organizational and financial bind as a result of hugely problematic maneuvers and irresponsible governance on the part of the Biennial at the expense of the participating artists and art institutions (the organization was dissolved with a declaration of bankruptcy in mid 2009), the Brussels Biennial should serve as a discouraging example in our discussion on the meaning of the biennial today. It also evinces a painful realization of the scale of the lack of responsibility that the art world sometimes displays when bringing to life (yet) another art institution in the form of a biennial, an act that ought to be imperatively and urgently subjected to serious reconsideration and reflection. Yet, the Brussels Biennial still might help us pursue our line of thought about the relation of the biennial to the art institution, because it was comprised of a number of exhibitions pieced together by various art institutions under the Biennial's name.

When the Brussels Biennial's organizers extended an invitation to organize individual exhibitions that together would constitute the new biennial project to a number of public, state-funded art institutions rather than to individual artists or curators, it was assumed that this was a constructive and certainly noteworthy attempt to reorient the tired model of biennial exhibitions.[1] Charles Esche and I—respectively the institutional curators of the Van Abbemuseum in Eindhoven and BAK—took it as a challenge to transpose the ethos of working in a public art institution to the framework of a biennial. This new construction obliged us to think about our institutional contributions in a rather new way in comparison to the "routine" (if one can use this word) curatorial work of selecting, commissioning, installing, etc. We jointly contributed a project to the Brussels Biennial under the title *Once is Nothing*, and saw it as an opportunity to rethink the biennial, knowing that to date biennials had been developing in overwhelming synchronicity with the art market and the commercial gallery circuit rather than with public institutions. At the same time, the context of the Brussels Biennial made us think about what the art institution can learn from biennials, which have managed to become cultural devices that mobilize unprecedented interest in contemporary art, reaching far beyond the art world's "in crowd," for better or for worse.

Although BAK and the Van Abbemuseum work in their own distinct ways and with different mandates—respectively those of a contemporary art center and those of a contemporary art museum—both institutions share an interest in continuity in the exploration of art's agency in our time and place. BAK and the Van Abbemuseum are also both concerned with the question of memory and the preservation of what has existed, whether we are referring to the objects in an art collection, a collection's archives, a discourse, or the forms of knowledge that we each seek to produce. Without the survival of such projects and products, our institutions' activities make little more sense than everything else in today's transient spectacular event culture, in which each new production tries to outdo or undo the accomplishments of its predecessor. The questions that we as directors of these institutions constantly ask ourselves have to do with the value of exhibition-making in general—its rapidity, continuity, and frequent pseudo-originality. The way in which we allow projects of significance to be inscribed in our memory and the ways in which discourse has developed around exhibitions we believe are of key consequence are among the things we need to consider.

So how can one perform these considerations on a biennial's stage? Adding our concerns to the additional conceptual parameters of the first Brussels Biennial (which largely concerned the legacy of the project of Brussels's modernization connected to the 1958 Brussels Expo, as well as the region spreading across the Netherlands, Belgium, and parts of Germany that Rem Koolhaas has called the "Eurocore"), we put together an exhibition based on another biennial exhibition, dealing with the notion of modernity in a very precise way. The exhibition was entitled *Individual Systems* and was curated by the late curator and writer Igor Zabel. The show was articulated from the perspective of the beginning of the twenty-first century and took into consideration the major shifts in the world's global political (and thus cultural) geography that had been brought about by the events of 1989. The show was also part of a larger biennial project, the 2003 Venice Biennial, which (not unlike the one in Brussels) had been conceived as a patchwork of relatively unrelated exhibitions put together by the multiple voices and visions of a number of curators. In this context, Zabel's unpretentious exhibition was somewhat lost in the cacophony of the spectacular projects that surrounded it; those who visited Venice that year will likely remember the overwhelming, if not anaesthetizing, volume of artworks more than the individual works of art (or exhibitions) themselves (fig. 1). In contrast to this disquieting reminder that curatorial practice of late readily sides with neoliberal demands for spectacle and entertainment, *Individual Systems* insisted on the conventions of exhibition-making that, in the name of the works of art it encompassed, require time, space, and concentration. *Once is Nothing* attempted to reconstruct, however partially, the *Individual Systems* exhibition, or perhaps, rather, the very qualities of time, space, concentration, and even wit that the original exhibition evoked (fig. 2). Based on the show's embodiment in 2003, the version of *Individual Systems* that appeared in Brussels took the form of an interpretation of the exhibition's architecture, letting the void in its midst speak for the works of art that were physically absent (fig. 3). A reference catalogue of "the show that wasn't" and a new project by Belgian artist Patrick Corillon helped us mark a space for ourselves and for the audience, one in which a visitor could pause to consider questions about exhibition-making and biennials, institutional responsibility, continuity, and memory, and to engage with the key element of empowerment that art has to offer: imagination. In other words, we created a space of inaction in which to pause—a space for thinking things differently, for posing questions like the one at the core of the present discussion: to biennial or not to biennial . . . ?

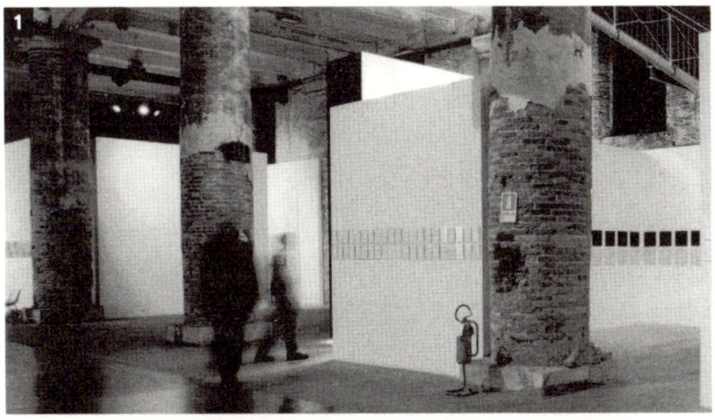

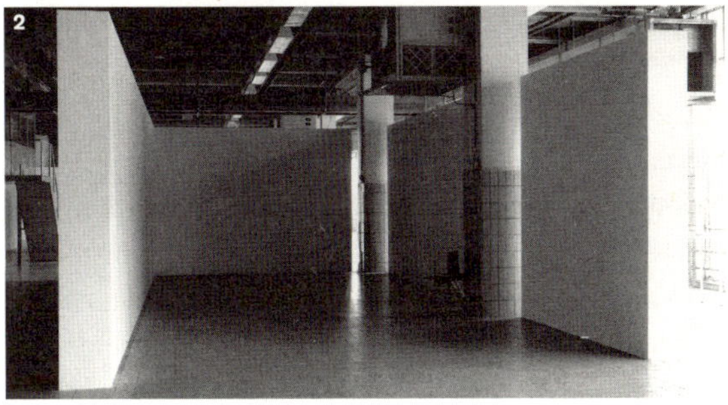

1 Installation view of *Individual Systems*, curated by Igor Zabel, 50th Venice Biennial, 2003.

2 Installation view of *Once is Nothing*, presented jointly by BAK, basis voor actuele kunst (Utrecht) and the Van Abbemuseum (Eindhoven), Brussels Biennial, 2008.

At this point, please allow me a brief detour. The conceptual twist of inaugurating the Brussels Biennial with contributions from public art institutions has its precedents and followers, although these are as varied as the number of cases in play. Think, for example, of Charles Esche and Hou Hanru's provocative curatorial gesture in 2002's Gwangju Biennial, its Part 1 entitled *Pause*, which was dedicated to and determined by artists' initiatives and independent art spaces from all around the globe (which Hanru famously called the embodiment of his "fuck the museum" strategy), or of the recently opened Istanbul Biennial curated by the curatorial collective What, How and for Whom (WHW), a group that could be viewed as an art institution in itself, or even of the recent appointment of a number of "curatorial groups, artistic and interdisciplinary collectives and/or existing institutions" to curate Manifesta 8 in Murcia next year, an appointment that is an expression of "Manifesta's aim to experiment with innovative curatorial models and methodologies" in search of "a new working model for Manifesta 8."[2] Whether this is a true search for a new working model or just a way to guarantee that someone will pay the bills in the end is, at this point, debatable. But whatever the case may be, we are witnessing a development in which the boundaries between and the initial juxtaposition of the art institution and the institution of the contemporary biennial are put under pressure and in which the antagonisms of the past are being rephrased in the agonisms of the now.

At this point, let's try to look at the notion of *repetition* one more time, as it might help us to create some understanding of where the potential of biennials lies both in the here and now, and in the future. In the concrete case of the Brussels Biennial exhibition *Once is Nothing,* my co-curator and I determined it was important to try to reconstruct—or to *repeat,* as it were—an exhibition with inspirational power from the past that we believed was otherwise running the risk of being forgotten in these times of immense acceleration and overproduction in the art world. We based this attempt in the adage "einmal ist keinmal" that the great novelist Milan Kundera thematized in his 1984 book *The Unbearable Lightness of Being,* which reminds us that once is, in fact, nothing; in other words, if an exhibition happens only one time, then it might as well be as if it had never happened. In the concrete case of *Once is Nothing,* what we therefore meant to do was, as art historian Walter Grasskamp has put it, "to change perspectives, to present an alternative to the usual art-historical point of view," which tends to forget (or actively erase) artworks or other artistic or intellectual endeavors that seek meaning beyond the loud and the spectacular. Indeed, we have to keep this in mind if we seriously and responsibly mean what we say: it is one of our goals to charge the narrative of the exhibition's history with the history of biennial exhibitions, and chances are high that this will be a successful project, as biennials have the potential to represent to a great extent what Grasskamp taught us such history-writing needs: "art-historical extracts."

In the end, the *Once is Nothing* exhibition was a repetition in a "Deleuzian" sense, performing or bringing to life, as it were, certain ideas of the philosopher Gilles Deleuze regarding the concept that time forms neither a cycle nor a straight line. As a consequence, this means that the ambition of bringing back an identical or faithful copy of what already was or is cannot be fulfilled, and any attempt to do so would be foolish and utterly wasteful. In fact, in Deleuze's view repetition is intimately bound to difference, and thus it is only when something is "repeated as something other" that its distinct qualities can be revealed.

In this vein of thinking, the biennial model must be confronted with an opportunity to move beyond the "survive and reproduce" strategy through which it has, in the overwhelming majority of cases to date, faithfully mirrored a world that is today bereft of any horizon, of any possibility to conceive of itself that is different than what we already know: a world in which the artistic, the cultural, the political, and even the philosophical have been, to a large extent, subsumed by the regime of economics.

Yet as mentioned earlier, if a number of biennials have managed to mature away from this self-satisfactory exposure of contemporary-art-as-lifestyle and have embarked on reactivating if not radicalizing the potentials of art in terms of political emancipation, it is precisely this that I believe should be carried on through the notion of Deleuzian repetition. This means nothing more than doing the same—repeating that it is in the possibility of art to imagine the world otherwise and that there is an unknown horizon that has yet to be named. It means doing the same in order to change, to produce something different in the collective imagination, to resuscitate the possibility of change or the transformation of the status quo—to repeat the message of the possibility until it becomes a popular belief, so to speak. And this is a task perhaps more likely to succeed today than it was even a year ago, after the global economic crisis put the notion of the stability of the world system into question. This is one of the reasons we should talk about biennials now.

As much as it is important to repeat the message of emancipation, and to insist on it time and time again, it is also essential to consider how and to whom biennials speak, for in at least one respect biennials are far better than an art institution at attracting a visiting public. At biennials, art world professionals are not the exclusive beneficiaries: other people from local communities who are perhaps less learned about current discourse on art but more curious about art's possible place in their lives and the world form the majority of most biennial audiences. However, it is not only the sheer scale of the biennial audience in comparison to that of an art institution, but also precisely this overlap, this combination of cosmopolitan, nomadic, *and* local communities and constituencies, that forms a social space with potentially unprecedented power: the art world and the world at large, so to speak, a new social space in which new imaginaries can be brought to life.

Despite these lofty words and ideals, however, we must acknowledge that the biennial is not a metaphysical hydra-headed creature, but just a blunt instrument in the hands of professionals from the various fields that intersect in the world of art. "How to biennial" is not a given; instead, it needs to be carefully reconsidered anew each time. Perhaps we can find a productive sign pointing in this direction. When the Istanbul Biennial opened in 2009, its curators wrote that their project sought "to rethink the biennial as a meta-device with the potential to facilitate the renewal of critical thinking by extracting thought from the immediate artistic and political context where it takes place." One might like or dislike the exhibition that the Biennial's curators put together, but one thing is clear: it had a beating heart, a yearning to imagine the world differently. Well, the opportunity—as well as the responsibility—to do this is entirely ours. ●

NOTES

This essay is a revised version of a lecture given at the Bergen Biennial Conference, September 17–20, 2009.

1 The first Brussels Biennial was comprised of individual exhibitions curated by a number of contemporary art organizations invited by artistic director Barbara Vanderlinden: B.P.S.22, espace de création contemporaine de la Province de Hainaut, Charleroi; BAK, basis voor actuele kunst, Utrecht; Drik, Images, Communication & Information Technology, Dhaka; Extra City, Centrum voor Hedendaagse Kunst, Antwerp; L'appartement 22, Lieu Indépendant pour la Création Contemporaine, Rabat; MuHKA, Museum van Hedendaagse Kunst Antwerpen, Antwerp; Van Abbemuseum, Eindhoven; and the Witte de With Center for Contemporary Art, Rotterdam.

2 E-flux announcement, September 4, 2009.

3

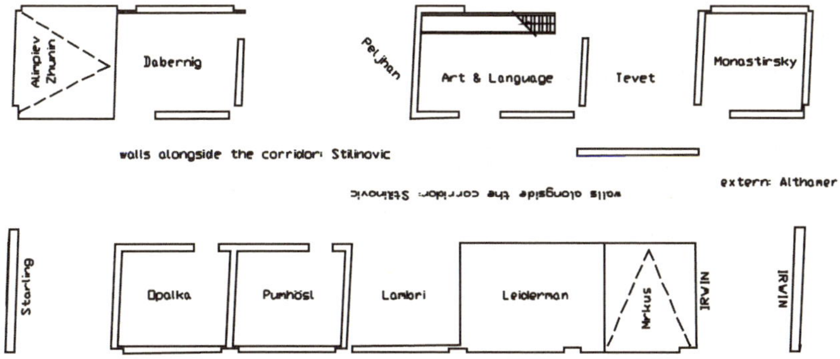

Individual Systems, Venice Biennial (2003).

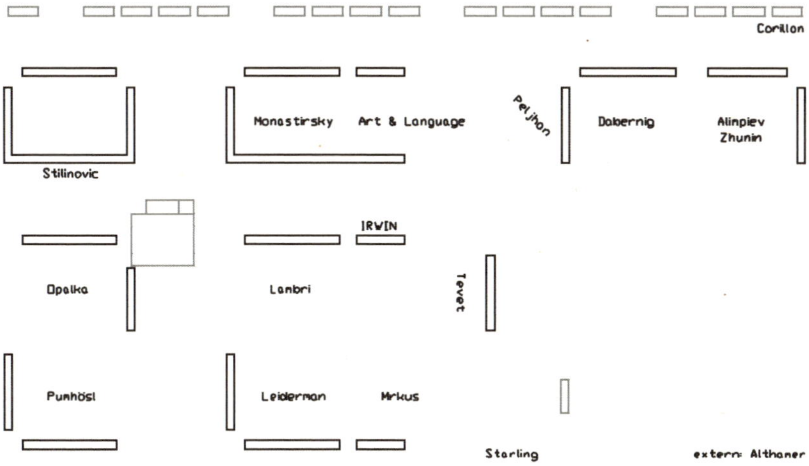

Once is Nothing, Brussels Biennial (2008).

3 Floor plans of *Individual Systems*, curated by Igor Zabel, 50th Venice Biennial, 2003, and *Once is Nothing*, presented jointly by BAK, basis voor actuele kunst (Utrecht) and the Van Abbemuseum (Eindhoven), Brussels Biennial, 2008.

BIENNIALS OF RESISTANCE: REFLECTIONS ON THE SEVENTH GWANGJU BIENNIAL

306

Ranjit Hoskote

GENEALOGIES

MUCH biennial discourse is set between the twin poles of euphoria and melancholia, or written under the sign of crisis. In this essay, I propose a modest view of the redemptive, if seemingly utopian dimension of biennial practice. My account is developed from the experience of co-curating the seventh Gwangju Biennial (Korea, 2008) with Okwui Enwezor and Hyunjin Kim. I also have in mind more spectral moments, such as the Delhi Biennial that has been vigorously discussed but may never come to be, and the India Triennial, a Third Worldist cultural initiative inaugurated with great optimism in the late nineteen-sixties, now long defunct, that some are seeking to revive.

In order to best understand biennials today, one might begin with the multiple genealogies of the biennial—some of the foundation myths of the form, if you will.

Discussing the formative roles played by the journal of record and opinion, the *magasin* or department store, and the museum in the evolution of bourgeois culture in nineteenth-century France, Chantal Georgel shows how these three elements were closely related and mutually mirroring institutions. As organs of a culture premised on the dressing-up of raw ambition and acquisition in the costume of taste, the journal, the department store, and the museum shared a structural disposition and mode of display, as well as the same theoretical vocabulary and aura of prestige. As Georgel observes:

> *The press, the museum, and the department store, all born during the century of industry, were each in their own way and in complementary fashion "machines" of capitalism. While the department store offered its clients the pleasure of consuming the products of private accumulation, the press sold its readers the pleasure of accumulated information—an image of mastery that justified the title of "museum" and, indeed, represented the ideal museum. For its part, the museum allowed its visitors to possess objects that were inaccessible—objects that could neither be bought, since they were inalienable, nor fully understood, except by an elite of amateurs or art appreciators—and as such invested with high cultural prestige.*[1]

The biennial, born in the late nineteenth century and classically embodied by the Venice Biennial (founded 1895) with its axial logic of presenting the world's most vital and magisterial artistic production through a system of national pavilions, emerges from the same ethos but is a hybrid. It marks the intersection of several mutually opposed forms of display. While it inherits some of the aura and magisterial nature of the museum, constructed as an elite experience shared graciously with the general public, the biennial also has much in common with other late nineteenth-century manifestations of the imperialist appetite for consuming the world's resources: the expo, the zoo, and the pageant. From another perspective, and opposed to this indulgence in the spectacular, the biennial could be seen within a conceptualist lineage of exhibition-making: the show as a testing ground for artistic innovations, a laboratory in which to experiment with new ways of activating the relationship between viewers and artworks, between artworks and their site, and between artworks and their architecture of display. For the biennial is neither exclusively nor even primarily a space of spectacular display, but rather a discursive environment: a theater that allows for the staging of arguments, speculations, and investigations concerning the nature of our shared, diversely veined, and demanding contemporary condition.

The sense of community, of shared purpose and shared travail, among transnational curators today has its origins in the traveling exhibition practices of the epoch of high imperialism. Discussing the colonial-period expositions of the arts, crafts, sciences, and ethnography that were conceived, mounted, and circulated by European commissioners in the colonies of India and Australia during the late nineteenth century, Peter H. Hoffenberg writes:

> *Commissioners travelling in India after the popular Calcutta International Exhibition were recognised in local bazaars as "The Exhibition Wallahs."... The exhibitions not only circulated objects and information, but also created and sustained communities of experts, many of whom were both imperial and national.... Contact at the shows and the constant exchanges of displays between the exhibitions provided the shared experiences necessary for this sense of communal identity and continuity, generated at the nexus of political, social, and cultural boundaries.... Exhibitions quickly evolved into a floating institutional foundation for imperial and national art and science experts.*[2]

Substitute "imperial" with "global" and "exhibitions" with "biennials" in this passage, and we bring it almost seamlessly up to date.

Travel can lead to the insight of direct encounter—to the dismantling of canonical criteria and long-established conventions of viewing and representation. It can help the cause of de-exoticizing the "Other" as a subject of inquiry or an object of desire and display. It can help restore suppressed or excluded content. It can make for a confluence of energies and perspectives. At the same time, as is well known, it can produce a dichotomy in the reception of contemporary cultural practice: a schism between mobile publics, which travel constantly from one transnational venue to another, and anchored publics, which embrace a notion of the local that can be defensive at its best and parochial at its worst. As one of the key zones in this schism, the contemporary biennial could address itself to unraveling the tight weave of the local while texturing the blandly global with greater intricacy and specificity. It could also, by inserting itself into the public consciousness of its site, reduce the tension in a host city that might sometimes see itself as a hostage city.

Thus another semantic and operational landscape that the biennial inhabits may be indicated by reference to Barbara Kirshenblatt-Gimblett's positioning of the museum between the knowledge establishment and the tourism industry. In her *Destination Culture: Tourism, Museums, and Heritage* (1998), she writes:

> *Museums have long epitomised a product-driven ethos, reserving for themselves the prerogative (in the public interest) to determine what they want to say and show. This prerogative is a legacy of the bifurcation of entertainment and edification during the last half of the nineteenth century, when the public museum and art gallery as we know them came into their own. . . . Until recently, a long history of public service, scientific research, education, social amelioration, cultural elevation, and local enthusiasms has insulated museums from the customer focus of the modern tourism industry.*[3]

The biennial, it would then seem, occupies a middle ground between entertainment and edification; it can maintain a museum-like authority while accommodating itself to the fact that it is part of its host city's plans for urban renewal, expansion, or international visibility. And while it is important to situate forms in relation to their anterior histories, the occupational hazards of looking back are manifest: you might be turned into a pillar of salt, for instance, or be returned without hope of reprieve to the condition from which you were about to be redeemed.

There is yet another starting point, a new horizon located, well, at the horizon: I'm referring to the *biennial of resistance,* or biennials located in transitional societies that mark the stake of these societies in the global scenario. I would argue that a biennial of resistance marks its host site's claim to the world-historical importance of its own dramas of consciousness and of its own regional modernity, which emerges from the local and yet is imbricated with global circumstances. It often testifies to the belief, held by the progressive elite of a transitional society, that cultural expression can articulate a political drive towards emancipation, dignity, and an optimistic appraisal of historical predicaments. This is, in its own special way and often against the odds, a heroic stance. Among such biennials, I would include the São Paulo Biennial (established 1951), the India Triennial (inaugurated in 1968 and pursued somewhat erratically since), the Havana Biennial (founded in 1984), the Asia-Pacific Triennial (launched in 1993), the Gwangju Biennial (founded in 1995), the Johannesburg Biennial (founded in 1995 but dissolved after its second edition due to financial difficulties), and the Delhi Biennial (discussed in successive annual conferences organized by a group of critics, curators, artists, and academics between 2005 and 2007 but never realized). As often happens with such courageous enterprises in what are frequently adverse conditions, not all have survived or flourished. I would particularly underscore the Johannesburg Biennial, the India Triennial, and the Delhi Biennial as embodying three of the possible negative fates that can befall a biennial. The Johannesburg Biennial incarnates the collapse of a biennial owing to the fall of the municipal financial structure meant to sustain it. The India Triennial is an instance of a biennial lapsing into neglect and oblivion as a result of the loss of its original propulsive ideological fervor and the political commitment of its organizers, followed by a bureaucratization of culture, which causes the fossilization of an inspiring idea into a set of routine commissioning procedures traced over diplomatic treaties of cultural exchange between the host nation-state and other nation-states (figs. 1, 2). As for the Delhi Biennial, raised as a hope and dream through spirited discursive exchanges, it failed to translate itself from the domain of intent, reflection, and discursivity into the rough theater of practice; the reason for this was the reluctance or inability of its convenors to form crucial pragmatic and material alliances with civic institutions, governmental bodies, and patronal agencies.

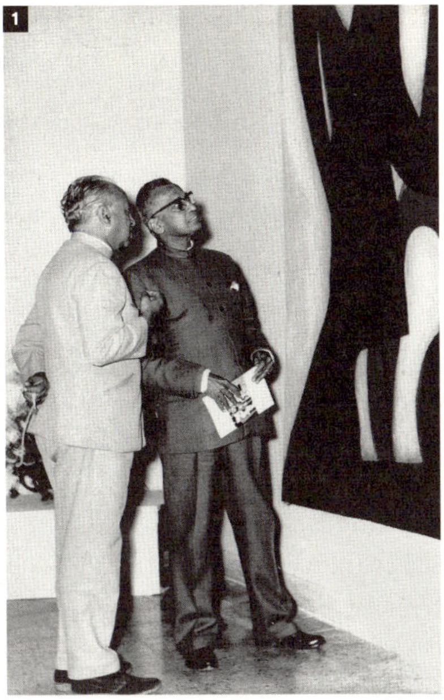

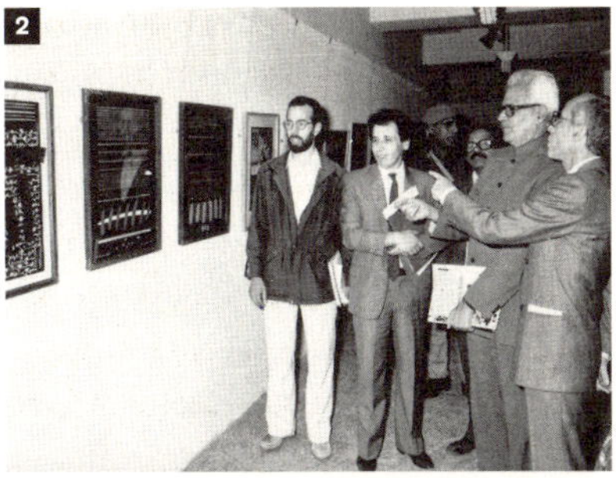

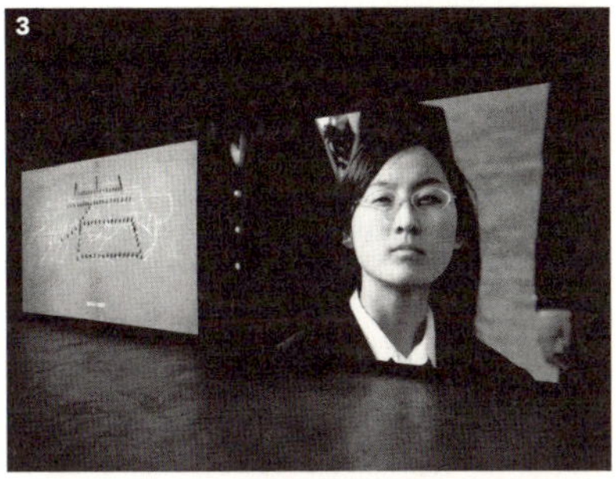

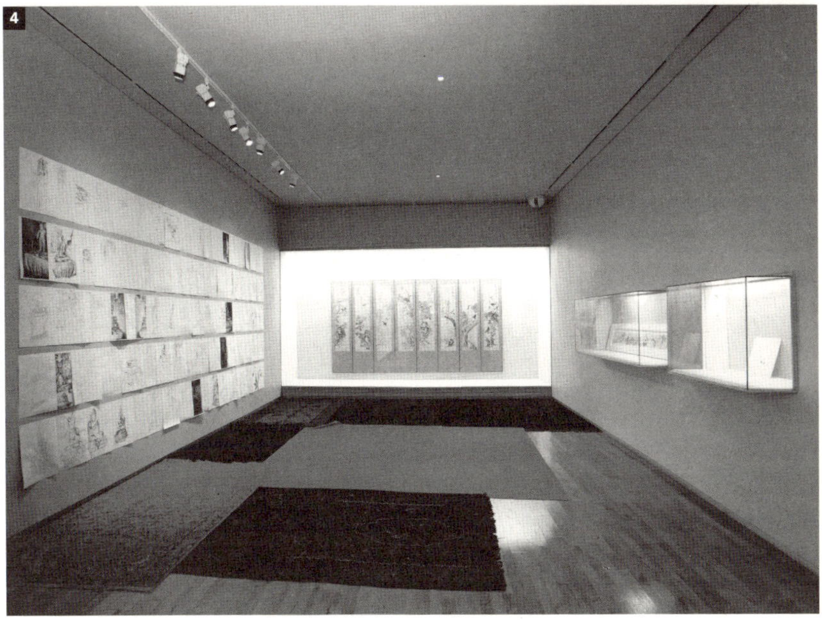

1 Photograph from the archives of the India Triennial showing the novelist, art critic, editor, and curator Mulk Raj Anand, the Triennial's founding director, in New Delhi in 1968.

2 Photograph from the archives of the India Triennial showing the inauguration of the fourth edition of the India Triennial in 1978.

3 Nina Fischer and Maroan el Sani, *Spelling Dystopia*, 7th Gwangju Biennial.

4 Works by Stefano Arienti and the Venerable Uijae, 7th Gwangju Biennial.

All of the manifestations of the biennial of resistance that I have enumerated here articulate what we may term the emergence of a global South, a network of sites of cultural production sharing common questions, themes, and, indeed, a common precariousness. Observe that these platforms take their stand on the ground of newly evolving regionalities—whether mobilized under the sign of Latin American and Caribbean solidarity, of Afro-Asian unity, of a post–Cold War position of Asia-Pacific solidarity, or of an emancipatory politics that has transcended long-standing antagonisms, as in post-apartheid South Africa.

All these experiments, as well as the biennials of resistance that continue to extend themselves despite prevailing constraints, mark a cumulative counterpoint to the Venice Biennial as the universal template for the biennial as form and medium. Their existence demonstrates that there is a substantial non- and perhaps even counter-Venetian history of the biennial form that has yet to be narrated. Such a future program of history-writing would have to take into account both the "will to globality" (to use Okwui Enwezor's phrase) expressed through the biennials of resistance, as well as their potential for the generation of a "critical transregionality" (to cite a term that my colleague, cultural theorist Nancy Adajania, and I have been using). Both these proposals will be unpacked in the sections that follow.

WILL TO GLOBALITY?

IN 1997, when the consequences of globalization had only just begun to unfold, Okwui Enwezor wrote:

Here identity no longer signals what we are or how we define, refine, reify, and contest who we are and where we come from. It has become an ideological problem we struggle to solve. And despite its difficulties, it remains a fascinating object of the transcultural, transterritorial, and transnational narrative of the human enterprise.[4]

As the politics of identity has now passed into the hands of demagogues who orchestrate caste mobilizations and ethnic discord, I find myself thinking more often about selfhood as a transitive performance rather than a conscriptive clause, one that we craft using cultural materials that we have chosen and woven together with an ideology of resistance. This selfhood is not compromised by an oppressive politics; it is not based on pseudo-primordial identities constructed in a war of positions. Indeed, it is a refusal to be named and shaped by the interpellation of such entities as nation-state, religion, and region. As we open conversations in different cities and find empathetic interlocutors far from home, while traversing the Silk Roads of today, we realize the extent to which we depend on floating contexts beyond such entities: contexts kept alive by e-mail, Facebook, and Skype, colloquium exchanges and co-curated exhibitions, and the enduring collaborations that are born through these encounters. We also think about the accounts of the disenfranchised, who, as Enwezor has put it, likewise manifest a "will to globality" yet do not or cannot subscribe to the prevailing dogma of globalization: the vast, invisible, inaudible narratives of refugees, forced migrants, ecological outcasts, and illegal immigrants, which bring us to an appreciation of diaspora and exodus.

A dynamized definition of intercultural being emerges from such intense communication and collaboration across distances, one based on the values of participation and mutuality: it grants us the *locus standi*, the right to be heard, to enter into a variety of debates across the planet responsively and at oblique angles. To be a cultural practitioner today is to perform intercultural selfhood. To map our lives and affiliations correctly, we shall have to redraft the inherited atlas of belonging.

While discussing (at a forum in Berlin in 2008) the manner in which the cultural energies of Islamic societies have historically exceeded the bounds variously legislated for them by Orientalist scholarship, home-grown theocracy, and Cold War geopolitics, I put in play a concept that Nancy Adajania and I have been calling "critical transregionality," which is "the strategic and imaginative freedom that cultural practitioners may exercise, in order to link regions on the basis of elective affinities arising from common cultural predicaments, jointly faced crises, and shared choices of practice—as against the determinism of territorial contiguities dictated by military and economic cartography."[5] Critical transregionality is not conceived as a mode of escape from the pressures and urgencies of the globalized local; it is not a romantic embrace of difference, an exercise in cultural adventurism, or a politically approved dialogue with the exotic. Rather, it is the appropriate performative mode for an intercultural selfhood: its practitioners reject insularity and provincialism and ground themselves in a productive engagement with urgency and crisis in varied locations. Through a lattice of exchanges, they translate a belief in global responsibility into a stance of global responsiveness.

Perhaps it is time for us to address our global present in this spirit of critical trans-regionality, to configure new continents of affinity that correspond more genuinely to our desires and aspirations than the geographer's superseded, merely physical fictions. Perhaps, also, we may reflect on how a large exhibition of international art might propose such new continents of affinity.

ANNUAL REPORT

THE seventh edition of the Gwangju Biennial engaged with the dilemmas evoked thoughout this essay by staging itself as an invitation to a series of conversations: among works, among curatorial practices, among forms of image-making, and among types of exhibition-making. What resulted was *Annual Report: A Year in Exhibitions*, the seventh Gwangju Biennial, which emerged from eighteen months of research trips, studio visits, and exchanges, and was structured around three intersecting axes: "On the Road," with its resonances of Kerouac, a wild journey of self-discovery but also a workmanlike survey of developments, an atlas and a calendar; "Position Papers," with its air of taking stock of the exhibition, of how it can be deconstructed and rephrased in order to mark different temporalities within the global contemporary; and "Insertions," with its sense of announcements, notices, and events unpacking their freight of significance, a sort of almanac. In the process of realizing this project, we saw the biennial as a parliament of narratives, an investigation into the diverse and sometimes unsuspected starting points of a global contemporary that is collegial, collaborative, and coproduced by actors remote from one another in location, working not only in New York, Berlin, Tokyo, Singapore, Delhi, and Vilnius, but also in Asmara, Jogyajakarta, Alexandria, and Isfahan.

What became clear to us was that this biennial, indeed any biennial as such, also marks a complicity, an intimacy, among curators, artists, and institutions with regard to their interests and desires. And this may be the occasion to make explicit the poetics of biennial-making as a form. I would allude here to the contested legitimacy of curatorial desire, which shuttles between pretext and context without being able to name itself, and to the way in which the curator, while not perhaps being an artist or inheritor of the modernist artist's mantle alongside the contemporary artist in Groys' sense, is still one who makes worlds from the materials of trust, passion, urgency, vulnerability, and attentiveness.

Annual Report was conceived and designed to function as an interplay among various scales of elaboration. The contexts of display that it represented were drawn from across the spectrum of exhibition venues: the public museum, the commercial gallery, the alternative space, the college gallery, and the small museum with a special focus. *Annual Report* thus led its viewers through a fluid constellation of artistic positions and display spaces, some referring by metonymy to the original contexts of reception, and others presented as edited extracts: viewers could pass from intimate exhibitions to grand monographic surveys, from individual galleries to ensemble presentations (figs. 3, 4). The range of curatorial expressions varied from a procession choreographed as a major public event to a documentation of the understated but eventually momentous transformation of four Southeast Asian avant-garde artists into curators whose work has had a seminal impact in their region. This edition of the Gwangju Biennial cut against the grain of the biennial as a venue of consumption by bringing viewers constantly up against important questions: Why do we mount exhibitions at all? What is our model, the ransacked emporium of themes or the production set of ideas? And can the biennial function as a liminal space—part nomadic archive, part temporary museum, part spectral repository? It is an occasion that opens itself up to multiple readings and addresses different publics. It is also a traveling text that allows itself to be annotated by diverse interpreters of the scene: not only the native informants and parachute ethnographers of the old and still residually present international exhibition system, but also many other participants acting at various levels of engagement, competence, and intensity.

When we show, tell, and read across cultures, we traverse not only cultural differences; just as crucially, we also traverse different relationships between poetics and politics, and between expressiveness and criticality, as phrased by individual artists. Our universalism is bruised, our tongues learn idiolect, and we begin to decipher as readily as we breathe. The process is not an easy one. While looking at Thomas Demand's enigmatic settings without protagonists or Atul Dodiya's isolated personae, we try to translate the strange, soul-possessing melancholia of another into our own. While experiencing Ken Lum's labyrinth of darkness or Zarina's never-to-be-completed maps, we struggle to accept that our own homelessness, fear of the unknown, and yearning for euphoria can be encrypted in the retrieval system of another. Perhaps this is what a biennial can do at its best: it can act as a platform of interpretations, a clearing house for readings, a hermeneutic space between archive and adventure.

THE STUDIO OF STUDIOS

AMONG the questions our research for the seventh edition of the Gwangju Biennial provoked were some concerning the feedback loop between the biennial and the studio.

Does the biennial provoke a shift in studio practice? What, today, is the studio? And where, today, is the studio? Given that the way in which art is now conceived and produced is so greatly distributed across personnel, processes, and sites, the studio is a multifocal and multilocal sequence of decisions whose activities are elaborated, improvised, and aggregated in time rather than generated in a single space reserved for the purpose. Or else images produced in one framework—whether as reportage, footage, or preparatory work—migrate to another framework and discover an afterlife.

Shilpa Gupta produces her video works, nuanced with compassion as well as irony, under threat of surveillance and interrogation in the heavily militarized countryside of Kashmir. MY-DA-DA trace their path through the ethos of sport in order to evoke the macho athletics of neoimperialism. Bani Abidi (re)searches for her images in the securitized public spaces of Pakistan's metropolitan centers, developing a typology of cordons and barriers that is really an oblique portrait of an embattled society. Kohei Yoshiyuki's unsettling photographic accounts of the nocturnal sexual adventures of couples and groups in a Tokyo park through the nineteen-seventies leave us in a dilemmatic space between pity and terror, and, more self-estrangingly, between revulsion and prurient interest: the series of photographs offers a portrait of the tragic, vulnerable underside of an aggressively confident capitalist society, but also problematizes our position as viewers, turning us into half-embarrassed interlopers or privileged voyeurs.

In a profound sense, the biennial becomes the studio of studios: where the constant attendance of viewers repeatedly unknots the work of art, and the interplay of ensuing interpretations repeatedly completes it only to release it again and leave it open for other perspectives.

CONVOCATIONS

ANNUAL REPORT addressed and reconciled various energies that distinguish the public sphere of Gwangju, and relayed these into the larger circuit of international cultural practice. We retained the Biennial Hall as a symbolic center that was important to many in Gwangju—demonstrating our responsiveness to the inherent, ascribed symbolism of a local site—and also extended ourselves into the breathing fabric of the city, distributing the biennial, interweaving it into the civic domain. This was achieved by various improvisations and platforms: first, by inviting the city's people into the galleries of the Biennial Hall and the Gwangju Museum of Art; but also, and equally importantly, by entering into a dialogue with Gwangju's history of democratic resistance through the processional media of "Spring"; by referencing Gwangju's lineage of spiritual questors and nationalist literati through the use of the hermitage-like spaces of the Uijae Museum of Korean Art; by staging part of the biennial at Cinema Gwangju, the city's Art Deco cinema hall, and thereby forming a connection with its strong film constituency; by reanimating the Daein Traditional Market as a space of artist-led social renewal and by hosting some of the sessions of the Global Institute, its platform for "experiments in transnational education," there.

Annual Report attempted to make a cogent case for the development of new forms of assembly, new convocations, as we take forward the process of activating conversations between mobile publics and anchored publics around contemporary international cultural practice. This would help participants across the globe to shuttle between regional histories and global histories, reorienting themselves from one narrative to the next. What might we discuss at these convocations? The power of infinitives, perhaps: to disclose the complicities between an official contemporary and its unacknowledged cousins; to celebrate the carnivalesque; to document the half-forgotten; to allude to elusive historical realities; to annotate our encounters. We work between the incessancy of theoretical articulation and the riddlelike silence of history, and between the volatile rhetoric of political elites and the absolute secrecy of the strategic operations through which they exploit the planet. Our convocations could help generate modes of comprehending, critiquing, and resisting these opposite hazards. They could rescue us from being conscripted by the cause of a single past or being mortgaged to a single future.

The demands of such a practice are strenuous, and often revolve around the trope of translation: interpretation, the making and re-making of meaning. Are we here to gain epiphanic pleasure, to perform contextual labor, or to gain discursive leverage? Whatever our choice or mandate, the biennial serves to generate the possibility of new forms of attentiveness, new forms of pedagogy and intellectual exchange.

WHAT DO WE CALL NORMALITY HERE?

ON one hand are ranged the large, even colossal and (as some would suggest) hypertrophied biennials and other festivals of success, whether achieved or hoped for. On the other hand spread the panoply of microlevel initiatives that build loci of belonging, sites of assembly, and communities. It is only through the use of scales of elaboration that we can bring the baroque and the infinitesimal, the overwrought spectacular and the down-to-earth do-it-yourself modes of production, together in a constructive dialogue. Without such scales of elaboration, we would not only lose perspective, but also render ourselves unable to account for the multiplicity of contemporary cultural practice as it proceeds from various sources in widely divergent and disparate initiatives.

This leads us to an awareness of the political activations that a biennial can trigger. By inserting itself periodically into a given locale, a biennial can perform an interrogative and transgressive rather than merely ornamental function. It could ask, each time in a different and destabilizing register, What is normality? What do we call normality here? Let us expose the norms that undergird and define this normality. The biennial can thus function as a laboratory for disruptive insight.

To my mind, one of the deep and subliminally defining horizons for *Annual Report*—which lay outside the biennial landscape—was the memorable, controversial, and historically responsive exhibition titled *Information*, organized by the Museum of Modern Art, New York, in 1970. The show was conceived by MoMA's curator, Kynaston McShine, as an "international report" on the directions taken by an emerging generation of artists.[6] Departing from its practice, MoMA decided not to have a curator choose the works for *Information;* instead, it invited 150 artists to submit proposals that were then reviewed by McShine and developed into site-specific works. As Mary Anne Staniszewski has put it, the exhibition became a landmark because it opened itself up as "an arena for Conceptualism's challenges to the institutions of art." It also marked the emergence of a new art situation, one distinguished by a confrontation between artwork and exhibition context. *Information* demonstrated the advent of a versatile, multitasking, intellectually sophisticated, and tactically adroit "breed of 'artist-worker'[:] . . . 'cultural producers' [who] were consciously creating work that engaged the institutions within which art is displayed, distributed, and received" and who were given the opportunity to deploy "new Conceptualist strategies to question the frameworks within which aesthetic meaning and value are generated and maintained."[7]

This richly confrontational new art situation was perhaps best dramatized by the work that Hans Haacke (who was also represented in *Annual Report*) contributed to the show. Called *MoMA Poll,* Haacke's work turned a politically loaded question into an artwork, orchestrating an elegantly simple yet explosive politicization of the viewing experience. Haacke used the quotidian device of the opinion poll to underline for viewers the links between MoMA's governing body, as symbolized by Governor Nelson Rockefeller, and President Richard Nixon's brutal militarism in the fraught context of the Vietnam War. Haacke thus disrupted the classical modernist aesthetic experience of the isolated art object and, as Staniszewski writes, "expanded the aesthetic framework of the work of art to include the institutional domain of the museum."[8]

By keeping the relationship between the artwork and the institutional circuits within which it gains significance productively unstable, the biennial could look beyond the connoisseurial or enthusiastic audience of the present and anticipate a viewership that has not yet come into being. It could play with conditions of impossibility and force connections among ostensibly unrelated regimes of meaning. Here, for instance, Taryn Simon mobilized for us the visual experience of things concealed or remote that can never normally be seen; Iman Issa de-familiarized a generic metropolitan environment with the faintest trace of an aura, the edge of menace; and Praneet Soi rendered the horrors of Abu Ghraib with the delicacy of a miniaturist, losing none of its potential to shock and presenting it as an homage to Goya as well. Hassan Khan's work disoriented us deliberately, navigating us toward recognition of how the gesamtkunstwerk can be rescued from its own totalitarian overtones and rendered capable of proposing a library of surprises. Huma Bhabha's meticulously articulated postapocalyptic scenarios, industrial translations of the antiquarian, propelled us towards a palimpsestic reading of the historical cycles of violence and renewal.

And so a biennial could develop into far more than a concourse of dazzling names and commodifiable objects. It could become a crucible for transformative experiences.

RECALIBRATING THE BIENNIAL

I would like to conclude by reminding us of the constant and productive tension between institutionality and resistance, and between self-perpetuation and self-disruption, within the biennial form. The biennial is a structure of recurrence, but it does not mark a simple repetition. Rather, I would argue that it embodies the more complex trope of recursion, or *ricorso:* a revisiting and a reorientation in which not only the way, but also your own traveling self is refashioned.

How do we recalibrate the biennial? How do we deal with the totalizing possibilities immanent in the encyclopedic form of the biennial? How do we undo the teleologies of Euro-American modernity? How do we disentangle the diverse temporalities within the global, or testify to the complicities and coproductions of the contemporary?

For this, the biennial must cease to be an atlas and begin to function as an almanac (from the Arabic *al-manaqqa,* a navigational guide), not as an ordered and annotated archive, but as a richly surprising genizah.

I would be inspired by the biennials of resistance in this project. They offer us insights into how the biennial can shift from search-engine mode to being a tool of investigation and how we may construct new fields of research premised on the "not yet." We must reflect on ways of redistributing the biennial in time rather than space, addressing questions of scale and duration, so as to reconfigure it as a field of proposals and relationships and conversations.

What is crucial is that the biennial serve as a means of activating audiences and seeking interlocutors, a means of transforming local consciousness (the vexed "local" that is no longer native). Can it be an inclusive, nonalienating spectacle?

What is the "apertural responsibility" of a biennial in this regard? I would like to pursue this question, especially by reference to what might be called the demotics of viewing—how do people view art, or cultural production more generally, in various locales? Can the biennial adjust its protocols to such local practices of viewing and experiencing?

Eventually, we move towards the possibility of a mutual transformation of consciousness, as the "international art world" meets the "local" and as the hope of a mutual renewal, a reciprocality, a mutuality emerges. Finally, a biennial should be a wager on an ecumene, a world that can really be home (from the Greek *oikos*). ●

NOTES

This essay is a revised version of a lecture given at the Bergen Biennial Conference, September 17–20, 2009.

1 Chantal Georgel, "The Museum as Metaphor in 19th-Century France," in Daniel J. Sherman and Irit Rogoff (eds.), *Museum Culture: Histories, Discourses, Spectacles* (London, 1994), p. 119.

2 Peter H. Hoffenberg, *An Empire on Display: English, Indian, and Australian Exhibitions from the Crystal Palace to the Great War* (Berkeley, Los Angeles, and London, 2001), pp. 31–32.

3 Barbara Kirshenblatt-Gimblett, *Destination Culture: Tourism, Museums, and Heritage* (Berkeley, Los Angeles, and London, 1998), p. 137.

4 Okwui Enwezor, "Travel Notes: Living, Working, and Travelling in a Restless World," in *Introduction to Trade Routes: History and Geography*, exh. cat. 2nd Johannesburg Biennial (Johannesburg, 1997), p. 12.

5 Ranjit Hoskote, "Retrieving the Far West: Towards a Curatorial Representation of the House of Islam," in Shaheen Merali (ed.), *Re-Imagining Asia: A Thousand Years of Separation* (London and Berlin, 2008), p. 121.

6 Kynaston L. McShine (ed.), *Information*, exh. cat. New York, Museum of Modern Art (New York, 1970), p. 1.

7 Mary Anne Staniszewski, *The Power of Display: A History of Exhibition Installations at the Museum of Modern Art* (Cambridge [MA] and London, 1998), p. 269.

8 Ibid., p. 271.

THE GLOBAL WHITE CUBE (2005)

322

Elena Filipovic

The history still to be made will take into consideration the place (the architecture) in which a work comes to rest (develops) as an integral part of the work in question and all the consequences such a link implies. It is not a question of ornamenting (disfiguring or embellishing) the place (the architecture) in which the work is installed, but of indicating as precisely as possible the way the work belongs in the place and vice versa, as soon as the latter is shown.

Daniel Buren, "Function of Architecture"

FIRST, THE MUSEUM

NEW YORK, 1929. A sparse, singular row of artworks lined the palest of walls in the Museum of Modern Art (MoMA) in New York, a display strategy that Alfred Barr Jr. imagined after a visit to the Folkwang Museum in Essen two years earlier.[1] The walls became somewhat lighter upon arriving on American shores and even whiter over the years, moving from beige-colored monk's cloth to stark white paint by the time the MoMA moved into its new permanent home on West 53rd Street.[2] But the essence of the museum's aesthetic project was there from the start. With it, other details followed: Windows were banished so that the semblance of an outside world—daily life, the passage of time, in short, *context*—disappeared; overhead lights were recessed and emitted a uniform, any-given-moment-in-the-middle-of-the-day glow; noise and clutter were suppressed; a general sobriety reigned. A bit like its cinematic black-box pendant, the museum's galleries unequivocally aimed to extract the viewer from "the world." For this and other reasons, the minimal frame of white was thought to be "neutral" and "pure," an ideal support for the presentation of an art unencumbered by architectural, decorative, or other distractions. The underlying fiction of this whitewashed space is not only that ideology is held at bay, but also that the autonomous works of art inside convey their meaning in uniquely aesthetic terms.[3] The form for this fiction quickly became a standard, a universal signifier of modernity, and eventually was designated the "white cube."[4]

No tabula rasa, the white cube is an indelibly inscribed container. Far more than a physical, tectonic space (monochromatic walls delimiting a certain geometrical shape), the art world's white cube circumscribes an attitude toward art, a mode of presentation, and an aura that confers a halo of inevitability, of fate, on whatever is displayed inside it. The legibility of the artwork *as work* is contingent upon the structuring of that legibility by its surroundings—Marcel Duchamp taught us that. From the MoMA's whitewashing forward, the white cube became a cipher for institutional officiousness, fortifying the ultimate tautology: an artwork belongs there because it is there. (The fact that the artwork is bracketed off from the world also undermines the impression that it might be related to, or the same as, the stuff of everyday life.) In that space of encounter, the ideal viewer (white, middle-class) is also constructed—well behaved, solemn, disembodied, and able to focus on the singularity of the work of art with an uninterrupted gaze.[5] Particular to the white cube is that it operates under the pretense that its seeming invisibility allows the artwork to speak best; it seems blank, innocent, unspecific, insignificant. Ultimately, what makes a white cube a white cube is that, in our experience of it, ideology and form meet, and all without our noticing it.[6]

Years after Barr invoked the white cube as the hallmark of the MoMA's exhibition spaces, Hitler approved of its use for the interior of the Haus der Kunst in Munich in 1937, the Nazis' first architectural project after coming to power. That monumental new building with its interior of vast well-lit gallery spaces, all white and windowless, opened with the *Grosse deutsche Kunstausstellung* (Great German Art Exhibition). The white container and sober display served to make the painted idyllic landscapes and bronze Aryan bodies on view seem natural and innocuous, despite the belligerent motives that underlay their selection and presentation. Driving home the point, the demonstration was doubly staged; the *Grosse deutsche Kunstausstellung* was the "acceptable," positive pendant to the somber, densely cluttered, and apparently disorganized show *Entartete Kunst* (Degenerate Art) that opened in a nearby archeological institute the following day.[7] Thanks to such a contrast, the artworks in the former seemed all the more righteous and those in the latter all the more abhorrent. There is no denying the coincidence: when the aestheticization of politics reached terrifying proportions, the white cube was called in.

New York and Munich, 1929 and 1937. The larger architectural frames for these white cubes are not comparable, and their respective regimes, it goes without saying, were worlds apart. Conflating them is not my purpose. Rather, I wish to highlight the usefulness, efficacy, and versatility of an exhibition format that has become a standard. If the white cube managed to be both the ideal display format for the MoMA's *and* the Third Reich's respective visions of modern art, despite their extremely different ideological and aesthetic positions, it is because the display conceit embodied qualities that were meaningful to both, including neutrality, order, rationalism, progress, extraction from a larger context, and, not least of all, universality and (Western) modernity.[8] Their examples are relevant today not only because they laid the foundations for how the white cube came to signify over time, but also because the subtle and not so subtle political ambitions of their exhibitions remind us of the degree to which pristine architectonics, immaculate backdrops, general sparseness, and the strict organization of artworks on the walls *matter*. The subjugation of artistic production to a frame at once "universal," neutral, ordered, rational, and ultimately problematic for what that so-called universality implies and hides, points to a predicament with which artists and curators have grappled ever since: exhibitions, by their forms, entangle the viewer in a space at once physical and intellectual, but also ideological.

NOW, BIENNIALS AND OTHER LARGE-SCALE PERENNIAL EXHIBITIONS

FAST-FORWARD, virtually everywhere, sometime here and now. Like modernity, the white cube is a tremendously successful Western export. Its putative neutrality makes it a ubiquitous architectural surround (an "architectural inevitability," Rem Koolhaas would say) for artworks in museums, but also for galleries and art fairs that transform commercial environs into what look more and more like mini museal spaces. Given that galleries and art fairs have a financial interest in making goods for sale appear as if they have already been legitimized by museum-like spaces, not to mention their frequent desire to keep the poetry or violence of everyday life out of the realm of becalmed shopping, this is hardly surprising. It makes less sense, however, within the context of the recurrent, large-scale international exhibitions that have proliferated around the world.

Sometimes referred to in shorthand as "mega-exhibitions" or "biennials" (even those that do not, strictly speaking, occur biannually), the various large-scale international exhibitions about which I speak distinguish themselves from typical group shows staged in museums, art centers, or *Kunsthallen* in large part through their connection to the Venice Biennial, the first perennial international salon of contemporary art inaugurated in 1895. This parentage implies a temporality and spectacularity that is their own: these punctual manifestations recurring every two or three or even every five years, as is the case with Documenta, lack real visibility beyond the duration of their exhibitions; they have an explicit ambition both to represent their region, host city, or nation and to display a decidedly international panorama of contemporary production, an ambition that influences the scale and general circumstance attached to the event; and they often are dispersed over multiple public spaces and institutional sites. If these relatively basic features unite large-scale international exhibitions and biennials, an ocean of differences can separate their ideals and histories. A number of them find their origins in contexts of profound political and cultural transition, for example, Documenta and German postwar reconstruction, the Gwangju Biennial and the democratization of South Korea, the short-lived Johannesburg Biennial and the end of apartheid, or Manifesta, European Biennial of Contemporary Art and the fall of the Berlin Wall. These and others have used the particularity of their historic, cultural, and geographic situation to define an institutional focus, a striking example being the Havana Biennial's ongoing engagement to offer a platform for artists from the "Third World." Whatever their individual histories, however, the ambition to be a counter-model to the museum and its traditional exhibitions is a significant defining feature of such events.

Most biennials and large-scale international exhibitions in fact were founded in reaction to nonexistent or weak local art institutions unwilling or unable to support the most experimental contemporary cultural production. These perennial exhibitions, therefore, perceive themselves as temporally punctual infrastructures that remain forever contemporary and unburdened by collecting and preserving what the vagaries of time render simply modern. The aim to be the paradigmatic alternative to the museum cuts both ways, however, with positive and negative distinctions. The proliferation of biennials in the nineteen-nineties rendered them new privileged sites for cultural tourism and introduced a category of art, the bombastic proportions and hollow premises of which earned it the name "biennial art," a situation that knotted the increasingly spectacular events to market interests. That mega-exhibitions can be compromised is a frequent lament, but in their best moments, they offer a counterproposal to the regular programming of the museum as well as occasions for artists to trespass institutional walls and defy the neat perimeter to which the traditional institution often strictly adheres when it organizes exhibitions (although museums, it must be said, are increasingly challenging their own once-staid protocols). Moreover, mega-exhibitions have also been platforms for challenging and heterogeneous artistic forms from around the world, often addressing some of the most politically charged issues of the period. Just as importantly, they have been known to elicit some of the most intense questioning of artistic practices through the expanded idea of where such an event's borders lie. Interdisciplinary discussions, conferences, and lectures that take place on or near the premises of exhibitions or, as was the case with Documenta 11, in several locations around the world are increasingly integral to these events. This striking expansion goes in tandem with curatorial discourses that increasingly distinguish the biennial or mega-exhibition as larger than the mere presentation of artworks; they are understood as vehicles for the production of knowledge and intellectual debate.

As Carlos Basualdo suggests, "the configuration of interests at the core of institutions like biennials clearly differs from that which gave rise to the institutional circuit traditionally linked to modernity (museums, art criticism, and galleries)."[9] In many ways, he is correct. If, however, "muscums are, first and foremost, Western institutions," then biennials, as Basualdo reasons, avoid being so almost by definition because "the global expansion of large-scale exhibitions performs an insistent de-centering of both the canon and artistic modernity," rendering the two qualitatively different.[10] While such an optimistic position champions the positive effects of the increasing number of biennials worldwide, it tends to overlook some of the ways they perpetuate the museum's most questionable paradigms.[11] Despite the numerous reasons to extol mega-exhibitions, it is necessary to examine the curious discrepancy between their accompanying discourses as well as the extraordinary promises they seem to offer and the conventions through which they frame the artworks on view.

GLOBALLY REPLICATED

Is it conceivable that the exercise of hegemony might leave space untouched?

Henri Lefebvre, *The Production of Space*

NO one seems to want to speak about it, but no matter how fervently biennials and large-scale exhibitions insist on their radical distinction from the idea of the museum, they overwhelmingly show artworks in specially constructed settings that replicate the rigid geometries, white partitions, and windowless spaces of its classical exhibitions, that is, when biennials are not simply bringing artworks into existing museums without altering their white cubes. Timeless, hermetic, and always the same despite its location or context, this globally replicated white cube has become almost categorically fixed, a private "non-place" for the world of contemporary art biennials, one of those uncannily familiar sites, like the department stores, airports, and freeways of our period of supermodernity described by anthropologist Marc Augé.[12] One of the crucial particularities of biennials and large-scale exhibitions, however, is that they are meant to represent *some place*. Their specificity is precisely their potential to be specific—site-specific, if you will, and time-specific as well. The fact that the main exhibition format used in a recent biennial in Dakar looked like that used in Taipei a short time ago or like that used in Venice twenty years ago seems to contradict such an idea. Forays beyond the box and into the city or its environs are part of what visitors expect from biennials, but such "special projects" held outside museal spaces often make up a relatively small percentage of the whole event and, in some cases, don't figure at all. Instead, the requisite mixing of "local" and "global" artists, recurrent themes generalizing the contemporary condition (their titles say it all: *Everyday, Looking for a Place, Art Together with Life*), and a singular, age-old display strategy diminish the distinctions between geographically distant events. The paradox, of course, is that the neoliberal model of globalization against which many of these biennials position themselves thrives on and itself produces just such homogenization.

There are exceptions to this rule. Biennials such as those in Havana, Istanbul, Johannesburg (while it lasted), and Tirana, all of which happen to represent the so-called margins of the art world, historically have often reflected the particular economic, political, and geographic conditions of their localities through their inventive and often hesitant exhibition forms. Rare editions of other biennials, like Paulo Herkenhoff's edition of São Paulo in 1998 or Francesco Bonami's edition of Venice in 2003, stand out for the ways in which they revised typical biennial norms and forms. Still, the list of cities that have hosted large-scale exhibitions in the last decade using and reusing white cubes to display large portions of the artworks selected for inclusion is seemingly endless: Berlin, Dakar, Pittsburgh, Luxembourg City, New Delhi, Taipei, São Paulo, Sharjah, Frankfurt, New York City, Kassel, Sydney, Prague, Seville, etc. Their reliance on traditional museum exhibition formats is questionable for numerous reasons, including, as Catherine David suggests, the fact that many contemporary aesthetic practices no longer correspond to the conditions for which the white cube was built.[13] Just as troubling is the presumption that the profound diversity of histories and cultures that these biennials aim to represent should be equally legible in such a space. Determined to present themselves as an alternative to the museum, these large-scale exhibitions attempt to give voice to cultures, histories, and politics underrepresented within that institution. The fact that the most seemingly progressive biennials and their curators, vaunting the most heterogeneous of art forms, so often adopt a unique and now ossified exhibition format suggests that some of the most pernicious tenants of the museum and the history of modernism it embodies remain fundamental to their functioning.

As Brian O'Doherty, one of the white cube's most perceptive theorists, notes, "the history of modernism is intimately framed by that space; or rather the history of modern art can be correlated with changes in that space and how we see it." More than "any single picture," he further states, "that white ideal space . . . may be the archetypal image of twentieth century art; it clarifies itself through a process of historical inevitability usually attached to the art it contains."[14] The white cube often supports the modern museum's other historiographic devices, including a linear, evolutionary history of art (think Alfred Barr's famous "torpedo" of modern art) with its decidedly Western perspective, limited temporal schemas, and unidirectional notions of influence. Given this, one wonders why this most dutiful spatial accomplice has continued to proliferate almost without question when we have become more conscious in recent decades that "modernity" is a construct that has suppressed, obscured, or transformed whole cultural histories and their producers. If globalization, as is so often maintained, problematizes the binary opposition of the national and the international, defying national borders and unhinging dominant cultural paradigms to allow the entry of histories, temporalities, and conditions of production from beyond the West, then why do so many conventional structures remain at exactly those sites that seek to undermine the epistemological and institutional bases of these structures? The white cube is, to cite O'Doherty again, "one of modernism's triumphs," a Western conceit constructed to uphold some of its most cherished values, including what Igor Zabel called the common presumption that "Western modern art is . . . modern art, that modernization [in the visual arts as well as in other areas of cultural and social life] is Westernization."[15] While it may not be surprising that the museum has been slow to dismantle these paradigms, why have biennials not done so? To question Basualdo's notion of decentering: can a true decentering of traditional notions of modernity be fully accomplished so long as the Western museum's frame is exported as the unquestioned context by which to legitimize an apparently expanding canon?

To Lefebvre's queries about whether space can be innocent and whether hegemonies might leave space untouched, the answer—as he knew well—is "no."[16] And so it is for the space of the exhibition. There are diverse ways an exhibition can resist, asserting its social and political relevance in our contemporaneity. To focus on select aspects, therefore, is admittedly to hold in suspense a reading of the others. Still, the "ideology of an exhibition," as theorist Miško Šuvaković persuasively contends, is not "an aggregate of [the] oriented and entirely rationalized intentions of its organizers," nor is it the "messages that the authors of an exhibition are projecting and proclaiming in their introductory or accompanying texts."[17] Instead, he concludes, it lies "between the intended and the unintended." Or, to put it slightly differently, the ideology of an exhibition lies between the discursive statements of purpose and the aesthetic-spatial result that manage more or less effectively to translate the intentions of the artists and curators involved. An examination of several editions of Manifesta, Documenta, and the Gwangju Biennial thus will focus on the discursive and structural armatures supporting these exemplary recent projects and, inevitably, on the ways in which the white cube has haunted or still continues to haunt them.

MANIFESTA

MANIFESTA, European Biennial of Contemporary Art was inaugurated in 1996 as a platform for cultural exchange within newly unified, post-Wall Europe. The paucity of dialogue between artists, institutions, and curators across Europe (despite the dramatic historic changes), the phenomenal multiplication of biennials, and their increasing concretization and inflexibility are all factors that profoundly influenced the project. As a result, the new biennial was imagined not only as an alternative to the museum, but as an alternative to the typical biennial as well. Thus Manifesta's most unique feature was conceived—each edition was to be held in a different peripheral European city. Rejecting some of the inherent nationalism of geographically fixed events and eschewing art-world capitals in favor of locations with less established or visible infrastructures for art, Manifesta seemed to want to use its shifting locations and explicit focus on emerging European artists to rethink the form and specificity of large-scale international exhibitions.

For each edition, the selected curatorial team mounted its exhibition across a number of local institutional sites. The main venue was typically a contemporary art museum or *Kunsthalle*—the Museum Boijmans Van Beuningen for Manifesta 1, the Casino Luxembourg for Manifesta 2, the Moderna galerija Ljubljana for Manifesta 3, and the Frankfurter Kunstverein for Manifesta 4. (Manifesta 5 was an exception to this rule, with only a small portion of the show displayed in a local contemporary art space, the Koldo Mixtelena.) Exhibiting in such established venues was no doubt a pragmatic gesture: given Manifesta's itinerant existence, it would be difficult to start from scratch each time. Moreover, the designation of local museums, contemporary art centers, and other cultural sites as exhibition spaces was a vital element, it was reasoned, in the collaboration between Manifesta and its host cities. However, in this process, the white cube seemingly had been accepted as a kind of "international-style" exhibition frame, an internationally recognized container that was deemed appropriate almost no matter where the project moved or the nature of the artwork being displayed.[18] Whereas the incredible promise of such a project lay in the possibility of producing fundamental shifts in successive editions as they traversed Europe, Manifesta's exhibitions have remained relatively true to known biennial formats and standard museal display aesthetics.

Although no edition of Manifesta to date has abandoned the white cube, a remarkable fragility, informality, and tentativeness did characterize several editions, distinguishing them in the face of the otherwise visual sophistication and high-gloss spectacle of most perennial events. However, the modesty and ad hoc character of the display in Manifesta's first edition in 1996 had already begun to fade somewhat with the second edition two years later and seemed to have been lost altogether by the fourth edition of 2002. The reasons for this are hardly simple and the attachment to traditional museum spaces and their formats is perhaps the symptom of the resistance that biennials like Manifesta encounter when they consider departing from established expectations for such events. An anecdote about the city of Stockholm's decision not to host the second edition of Manifesta after having seen the first in Rotterdam is telling: the dozen venues across which were dispersed predominantly subtle and small-scale or otherwise unspectacular artworks and performances hardly seemed to cater to the ambitions of a city looking to place itself on the cultural (tourist) map. For city officials shopping for a biennial, there was little that seemed likely to draw the same crowds or press as more established mega-exhibitions. This story suggests that there was pressure on Manifesta to conform to the idea of what a biennial should look like—which meant not only grand artworks displayed in visible concentration, but the appropriately conventional "museum hang" and white partitioned spaces to properly enframe them.

Another theoretical problem with abandoning the white cube remained, one perhaps even more fundamentally troubling to such exhibitions: how to display works of art by as yet unknown artists, often with an aesthetic sensibility that is as yet unrecognized by most viewers, or artworks that are not easily recognizable *as art* in spaces that do not announce themselves as bastions for art? Might not the artwork be mistaken for mere "stuff"? And wasn't it desirable that artists new to the international art world avoid this confusion at the moment of their *entrée* into that world? (Not to mention that the emerging curators relatively new to the international art world might have felt they were expected to demonstrate that they could organize a biennial that looked the part.) To imagine that the art that Manifesta showed or that the survival of a new institution like Manifesta indeed *depended* on the white cube, however, would be to accept the dominance of Western modernity's structures as the ground against which everything else must be read in order to be considered legitimate at all, a highly problematic assumption and one contingent on precisely the kind of normalization that Manifesta claimed to want to question.

Efforts to highlight the specificity of a Manifesta exhibition in a particular place as well as its specificity as a biennial could instead be seen in the themes that both the displaced exhibitions and the artworks on view addressed, including homelessness, hospitality, diasporas, borders, and immigration. Perhaps more than any other biennial, Manifesta's various editions can be said to have consistently probed topics crucial to intellectual, cultural, and political debates of the nineties. The third edition in Ljubljana in 2000 underlined these debates in a programmatic way. Its large number of politically engaged works, rejection of slick display strategies, active discussion program initiated by local thinkers, and collaboration with the RTV Slovenia to use local television broadcasts as a fifth venue were uniquely appropriate given the region's war-torn history. Relatively little was done, however, to engage in more than a thematic way the show's concerns with what it called Europe's "borderline syndrome." Thus, in the end, the significant distinctions between the exhibition formats of the editions themselves arguably were hard to discern.

Manifesta 5, held in Donostia–San Sebastián in the politically troubled Basque region of northern Spain, might be seen as an exception since it took urbanism as a theme at the same time as it incorporated actual urban rehabilitation into the exhibition as a constitutive element. In collaboration with the Rotterdam-based Berlage Institute, the curators instigated theoretical reflection on the revitalization of one of the region's poorest districts, the Pasaia Bay area, and had two of the area's disaffected factories, Casa Ciriza and Ondartxo, restored with the intention that they would serve the community after the run of the show. The largest portion of the exhibition, shown in the Casa Ciriza and thus framed by the defunct fish warehouse's postindustrial ruin and larger impoverished context, avoided the physical accouterments of the white cube, as did the portion held in the sixteenth-century former monastery Museo San Telmo; yet, what was staged in these venues and those others that did resort to white cubes amounted to a rather conventional show. While the urban renewal project was an important step towards asserting that biennials could be the motors for lasting local change, in the eyes of a number of critics, the exhibition missed an opportunity to render the historical, political, and cultural specificity of the location more integral to its form or to the artworks selected. As one reviewer concluded, it "could have been mounted almost anywhere."[19]

Ultimately, Manifesta's past exhibitions as well as its symposia, discussion forums, and parallel events have attempted to encourage curators and institutions to think about the limits, transformations, and particularities of Europe as an idea as much as a physical place but never productively incited the connection between this thinking and the reinvention of the project's structural form. After all, given Manifesta's concerns, why demand that it take the form or occupy the space of a conventional museum exhibition? Why not imagine truly experimental exhibition forms that emerge from both the specific sites in which Manifesta finds itself and the issues that make holding a biennial there and then relevant or even urgent? And why not imagine that even those cities less able to replicate Western European museum standards and lacking the same level of financial commitment might actually host a Manifesta edition, inventing new idiosyncratic forms for the event? As experimental platforms that define new models for exhibiting, the peripatetic editions could thus better reflect Manifesta's stated ambitions.

If questions such as these have beset the project from the start, the sixth edition seems to have used them as a point of departure. The curators of Manifesta 6, still in the planning stages, have announced that this upcoming edition in Nicosia, a geographically isolated, culturally and politically divided site with only minimal resources for the production and presentation of art, not to mention a historically fraught relationship to Europe, will exchange Manifesta's punctual, traditional exhibition in favor of the extended duration and pedagogical process of an art school. It appears that the biennial's newly envisaged form and temporality emanate from an attempt to respond to some of Cyprus's multiple historic overdeterminations, including its locus between Europe and the Middle East (a first foray outside of Europe for Manifesta) and its role as paradigm of the conditions and consequences of globalization today. For what sense could another mega-exhibition have in such a location today? If goods can traverse its international borders with relative ease, people still cannot, caught as they are in the political instrumentalization of ethnic and national identities. In place of a biennial as showcase for contemporary cultural goods, the sixth edition purports to use the increased facility of movement across borders made possible by student visas to construct a bi-communal, international forum for process, experimentation, and exchange built from the artists' extended presence at the site in order to respond to the realities of its ethnically divided host city. What the visiting spectator will be able to experience, how such things as process and cultural translation can be rendered visible in an art exhibition-as-school, and whether some of the complexity of what has for so long been the "Cypriot problem" will be adequately addressed in the result remain to be seen, but this shift for

Manifesta suggests that the specificities of its site have come to serve as the foundation for imagining a new formal model for this biennial.

DOCUMENTA

DOCUMENTA began in 1955 in the hope of rehabilitating the image of postwar Germany, transforming the bombed-out town of Kassel and its most iconic extant structure, the Neoclassical Museum Fridericianum, into the center of the art world every five years. The one-hundred-day quinquennial quickly came to be considered the most serious and among the most prestigious mega-exhibitions of its kind.

One can hardly say that for the tenth edition of Documenta in 1997 artistic director Catherine David devised radical, new display strategies to recast the physical appearance of the white cube. While the artworks on display were largely political in content, their presentation in the Museum Fridericianum bore little evidence that the traditional museum format or the Western avant-garde canon was under attack. The highly problematic role of the white cube was, however, an essential tension underlying Documenta 10. A reflection on what David called its "spatial and temporal but also ideological limits" was central to the conception of her project.[20] The seeming inability of the museum's "universalist model" to accommodate some of the most experimental and exemplary contemporary cultural production determined her objective to conceive an exhibition that included the program "100 Days–100 Guests," a mammoth series of daily public lectures, theater performances, film screenings, poetry readings, discussions, and other events in Kassel.

Conceptually, "100 Days–100 Guests" began with the premise that presenting a panorama of recent visual art was not a priori the best means of representing contemporaneity. As David suggested in the short guide to the exhibition, "the object for which the white cube was constructed is now in many cases no more than one of the aspects or moments of the work, or better yet, merely the support and the vector of highly diverse artistic activities."[21] Nor was the *exhibitable object* the most representative of every culture. She further explained:

> *For reasons which have partially to do with interrupted or violently destroyed traditions, as well as the diversity of the cultural formations that have sprung*

from colonization and decolonization and the indirect and unequal access these formation have been given to the forms of Western modernity, it seems that in many cases the pertinence, excellence, and radicality of contemporary non-Western expressions [find their] privileged avenues in music, oral and written language (literature, theater), and cinema forms which have traditionally contributed to strategies of emancipation.[22]

All cultures, she thus contended, are not equally served by the white cube. David's resulting project, with predominantly Western figures featured in the show's historical "retroperspectives," more recent but still largely American and European artwork on view in the exhibition spaces, and the work of non-Westerners overwhelmingly relegated to the lecture and events program, admittedly offered a Eurocentric perspective of *visual* art. But, instead of imagining yet another "Museum of 100 Days," as Documenta had been nicknamed at its founding, she aimed to present more heterogeneous works—and through more heterogeneous means—during "100 Days–100 Guests." Both conceptually and physically central to the exhibition (its stage stood in the middle of the Documenta-Halle), the events program could also be experienced live on the radio and via the Internet, or consulted as recordings in the exhibition, constituting a growing archive both in and, potentially, beyond Kassel.[23] David thus effectively transformed Documenta from a spectacular visual arts exhibition into a hybrid site for the representation of diverse cultural production. The result opened Documenta to the kind of political engagement and diversity of mediums and cultures that no other such exhibition in the West had seen—what many critics in turn lamented as an overly political, theory-driven, and aesthetically impoverished show. In fact, David's move to counter the mega-exhibition's usual spectacle was consistent with the audacious assertion that it is impossible to continue to innocently perpetuate the museal exhibition format as the legitimate frame for all works of art from all places. The exhibition and events program thus staged the very limitations of the white cube. And in critically reflecting on the way hegemonic forms operate, Documenta 10 used the conceptual and discursive structure of the last edition of the millennium to encourage others to do so as well, a role that was, as David suggested, no less political than aesthetic.

For the eleventh edition of Documenta in 2002, artistic director Okwui Enwezor and his co-curators aimed to transform the geographic, conceptual, and temporal constitution of the event, conceiving a series of five "platforms," the first four of which were themed conferences (in one case including a workshop and film screenings) held in Lagos, Saint Lucia, New Delhi, Vienna, and Berlin over the course of eighteen months.[24] The discussions deliberated such issues as the recent impact of globalization on the world or the violent legacy of colonialism. Although far from a literal rehearsal of the exhibition, they also mapped out the concerns at the heart of the fifth exhibition platform. Reiterating the terms of the larger project's postcolonial critique, the stridently political artworks and accompanying curatorial statements rendered explicit the need to question Western imperialism, including its perpetuation through such notions as modernity, the avant-garde, universality, and democracy.[25]

The first four platforms were, by most accounts, thought-provoking if academic affairs, at once dislocating the singular site of Documenta and situating critical research and theoretical reflection at its heart. Despite the fact that relatively few visitors and participants actually attended the conferences, these proceedings were integral to the form of Documenta 11, which expanded the boundaries of this art event traditionally held in a provincial European town and transformed it into a transnational, interdisciplinary, multilayered manifestation. While these events overturned the strictures of Documenta's hallmark one-hundred-day exhibition in Kassel, the fifth platform appeared to be a decided *return to order.* Impeccable arrangements of white cubes and black boxes recurred throughout almost all of the show's multiple sites. Even though the exhibition largely occupied the stately Museum Fridericianum, keeping with Documenta's typical practice, here as well as in the massive, newly inaugurated Binding Brauerei and the Kulturbahnhof one encountered a display even more museal, conservative, and rarefied than in previous editions.[26] Exceptionally, a few of the exhibition projects extended outside the museum, seeming all the more to confine that platform to neatly delineated display spaces.[27] It was as if, in creating four other platforms out there in the world, the curators had decided that the fifth in Kassel would replicate even more closely a museum space cut off from that world. The exhibition brought, as one critic noted, "issues of genocide, poverty, political incarceration, industrial pollution, earthquake wreckage, strip-mine devastation, and news of fresh disasters *into the inviolable white cube.*"[28]

This is not to suggest that the means by which display strategies structure perception and art history were entirely overlooked. As one of the curators attests in his catalogue essay:

> *Art exhibitions also frequently adopt linear models to represent historical flux and the relationship between past art and recent production. To be sure, there is a correspondence between the linearity of these narratives and their tacit—or implicit—totalizing will. . . . The ideological effects of these types of exhibition strategies are well known: the consolidation of an artistic canon, and therefore the staging of a series of mechanisms of inclusion and exclusion that assures its permanency.*[29]

He and the other curators of Documenta 11, therefore, tried to imagine a "structure that would allow the works to coexist in a heterogeneous and nonlinear temporality."[30] Indeed, as such an effort suggests, an exhibition's politics are inevitably a politics of (identity) representation, articulated in the selection of works and in the ways their strategic display rethink certain established ideals. Once the works were selected, however, Documenta 11, being largely composed of recent art, did not seem to fully question the ideological legerdemain of traditional museum shows, except insofar as it dispersed historical works from the nineteen-seventies throughout the exhibition. If Documenta 11's notable breadth of representation (with significantly more visual artists from non-Western nations than any previous edition) and the displacement of the four platforms sought to challenge occidental paradigms and champion instead "those circuits of knowledge produced outside the predetermined institutional domain of Westernism," then corseting the exhibition portion in exactly that predetermined institutional paradigm most intimately connected with the development and historicization of occidental modernism effectively undermined many of the supposed objectives of the project.[31]

Examining the fifth platform in this way inevitably simplifies the breadth and theoretical complexity of a much larger project, but it also underlines the silence which allows the white cube to function, even in those projects most consciously and explicitly positioned against the hegemony of modern Western forms. Why, one might ask, expand Documenta into different parts of the world through the four discussion platforms only to encase most of the over four hundred works from five continents in Kassel within the West's least questioned framing devices? A hasty response might be that bringing together works of art from vastly different cultures requires using a uniformly prestigious or valid frame through which they can be experienced—the necessary fiction sustaining this being that the white cube is a neutral, legitimate frame. The issue was rehearsed, one might say, in one of the essential queries of "Democracy Unrealized," the first platform of Documenta 11: can democracy, a fundamentally Western concept and hegemonic political form, serve as a legitimate benchmark for the constitution of society in the postwar period, even in nations with vastly distinct histories and cultures? One could also ask the same of the white cube in relation to large-scale exhibitions. Of course, the underlying stakes of these two questions might seem, on the surface, wildly different, but both suggest that there is an imperative need to problematize (Western) models that quietly perpetuate themselves as unquestioned universals.

THE GWANGJU BIENNIAL

THE Gwangju Biennial, East Asia's first large-scale contemporary art event, was founded in 1995 at a high point in the biennial boom. With memories of nearly two decades of political oppression still present, including the 1980 massacres that accompanied a citizen uprising for democracy, the new biennial was imagined as a bandage for old wounds and a means by which to provide the city with a positive, forward-looking profile. Critics decried the overly Western focus of the first two editions as well as their seeming inability to draw attention to the specificity of the emerging Asian art scene or, for that matter, those of other cultures less well-represented in Asia. As a result, the biennial's third edition in 2000 was revamped, initiating a strong Asian focus accompanied by a declaration of commitment to becoming a forum for artistic practices outside the West. Broadcasting that the biennial would "pursue globalization rather than westernization, diversity instead of uniformity," officials marked their seriousness and new focus by building a multistory, convention center–like exhibition complex, which was inaugurated with the 2000 edition.[32] Ironically, at precisely the moment that Gwangju and its biennial hoped to demonstrate their entry into a globalized art world, this new permanent exhibition structure incorporated generic Western display tropes in the form of a series of flexible but neatly arranged white cubes. For biennial officials, to be globally relevant meant replicating the "universal" exhibition backdrop.

The fourth edition in 2002 opposed this strategy. Entitled *P.A.U.S.E.* and directed by Wan-kyung Sung, the biennial was composed of four curated exhibitions or "projects" that in different ways engaged the vestiges of Gwangju's uneasy past and contemporary condition, including a series of site-specific installations in a former military prison, a project to reconstruct the area around the city's abandoned railroad tracks, and an exhibition concentrating on the Korean diaspora. *Project 1: Pause,* curated by Hou Hanru and Charles Esche and held in the biennial hall, was the largest part of the biennial, and the curators conceived it as a "context specific event" rather than a panorama of recent art. Asia's transformed urban reality provided the context for questioning art's "global–local negotiation" and imagining possible alternatives to the homogenization and acceleration of late capitalism.[33] The conditions of art production in contemporary Asia and beyond the Western world more generally, where structures to support experimental artistic practice are rare or nonexistent, determined the curators' decision to show dynamic recent cultural production by artists who had self-organized outside the occidental art world's capitals.[34] As a result, they conceived an exhibition that included some twenty-five independent collectives and artist-run organizations from around the globe, mostly from Asia and Europe but also from the Americas and India. These groups were invited essentially to self-curate their participation in the biennial, retaining incredible autonomy and shifting the role of the biennial curator. The result was less a presentation of discrete artworks than a biennial as a workshop for artistic experimentation, since bringing together artist collectives from around the world was meant to empower and mobilize, acting as "a first step towards a global network of independent, self-organizational, and resistant structures for creation."[35] By highlighting the possibilities of collective self-organization in the face of institutional inertia, the biennial engaged in a real dialogue with its local context, offering artists multiple models of self-sustainable cultural production.

"Hou and Esche seemed to want to subvert both Eurocentrism—with its fellow traveler, a certain patronizing exoticism—and 'the museum' as an institution," one critic noted, adding that "in much of Asia, these two issues are deeply intertwined."[36] *Project 1: Pause* translated its conceptual ambitions into an equally remarkable form: in collaboration with architects, the artist groups were asked to conceive display pavilions or reconstruct the actual spaces in which they typically worked and exhibited. A sprawling frame of steel and plywood delimited these pavilions, the ensemble redressing the biennial hall's exhibition spaces with evocations of a frenzied global metropolis. The resulting makeshift structures connecting the different parts of the exhibition rendered tangible the physical qualities of various international art spaces and conceptualized something about the practices seen within them. The pavilions and reconstructed independent art spaces varied wildly, from a Bedouin tent printed with images of Western cities overlaid with Muslim iconography (AES Group from Moscow) and a carpet-lined photocopying facility for Xeroxing reduced-priced copies of the catalogue during the exhibition (Kurimanzutto from Mexico City) to reconstructions of an apartment interior (IT Park from Taipei) or a meeting room (Project 304 from Bangkok). They also implied, as did the urban evocations of the larger exhibition frame, that the particularities of artistic practices were connected to and imbricated in the actual structures that allowed their experimentation. Suggesting that colonialism insinuates itself through the appropriation of the Other's monuments, demonstrating how capitalism's means could be used against itself, or illustrating that the most apparently quotidian gathering spot could be the site of intense cultural exchange, these structures within the larger exhibition refused the white-cube form but also demonstrated that the aesthetics of a display space are not separable from the ethics of an art practice.

THE END(S) OF THE WHITE CUBE

TO have begun to question the use of the white cube in recent large-scale perennial exhibitions by addressing the foundation of the modern museum and the historical and political implications of certain exhibition spaces, extreme as those examples may be, was not merely for rhetorical effect. By so doing, I intended to underscore that the framing of art, no less than the selection of artworks, is fundamental to the ideological dramaturgy that we call an exhibition. A curious silence regarding this phenomenon remains in discussions of biennials and related large-scale exhibitions. Yet, one could say that the "crisis of biennials" that so many critics have decried lies not so much in the proliferation of these events as in the proliferation of a *form*, which, more often than not, remains the same over time and across space despite the vast differences in the issues such exhibitions are meant to illustrate, their relationships to their individual local contexts, the works they present, the institutions that sponsor them, and the institutional and other histories they interrogate along the way.

At a moment when art remains one of the few modes of critically resisting hegemonic global transformations and when the engagement and experimentation of many artists remain a source of promise for the future, exhibition forms need all the more urgently to be intelligent, sensitive, and appropriate means for rendering that work public. To insist here on the way in which some of the politics of an exhibition inheres in its form is not, however, to advocate the promotion of a cult of the curator or the conflation of his or her role with that of the artist. Nor does it mean to suggest that curators, institutions, or their exhibition spaces generate the meanings of contemporary artistic production. Artworks, however much an element in the construction of the meaning of an exhibition and, dialectically, also subjected to its staging, nevertheless also articulate aesthetic and intellectual positions and define modes of experience that resist their thematic or structural frames.[37] Yet, as any number of exhibitions can amply testify, an exhibition is no mere sequence of artworks, good or bad, thematically unified or formally disparate. Nor is an exhibition's worth and meaning the sum (if one could measure them in this way) of the combined worth and meaning of the various works of art on display. Instead, the manner by which a selection of artworks, a tectonic context, and thematic or other discursive accompaniments coalesce into a particular form is at the heart of *how an exhibition exhibits.* This, after all, is what distinguishes an exhibition from, say, an illustrated essay: the articulation of a particular physical space through which relations between viewers and objects, between one object and others, and between objects, viewers, and their specific exhibition context are staged.

What then is the role of biennials and large-scale exhibitions today? How might they be more self-reflective about how meaning is expressed in the very structures they provide visitors with for thinking, acting, and viewing a show? How can the postcolonial project of cultural translation prevent itself from being betrayed by the frame through which art is shown in order to allow these large-scale exhibitions to live up to their potential as sites from which to question the consequences of global modernity? How too might they register some of the hesitancy and instability that their discourse would have us believe is integral to their projects?

There are perhaps no easy answers, nor is the issue without its own contradictions. But a change lies above all in the recognition that the aesthetic and discursive premises on which an exhibition is based—the issues its curators and artists wish to defend, the intellectual positions they seek to express—need to be more fully articulated in the forms exhibitions take. Of course, it is not evident what forms might be appropriate to the vast cultural and formal heterogeneity of contemporary artistic production—supple enough to accommodate diverse practices, respectful enough to reveal the inherent, individual logic of artworks, and quiet enough to allow an intimate relationship between artwork and viewer. The answer is surely not singular. The now global white cube certainly should not be supplanted by another model that will become *the* biennial standard. Merely inserting works in crumbling industrial buildings or any number of other "exotic" locales is not the solution either. Instead, the future of biennials is to be found in a sensitivity to how the coincidence of works of art and other conditions (temporal, geographic, historic, discursive, and institutional) *locate* a project and how that "location" can be used to articulate an aesthetic project that is respectful of its artworks and speaks to its viewers. This requires the willingness of curators and institutions to think through more complex relationships to sites, artworks, and the intellectual propositions of an exhibition—a prospect that may require more time for exhibition research and preparation as well as greater collaboration between artists, curators, and institutions, but also the courage to risk a result perhaps more vulnerable and hesitant as it departs from an authoritative format. In the end, none of this will guarantee consistently memorable shows, but thinking through an exhibition's form will facilitate the development of more engaged and dialectical relationships between artworks and their presentation frames as well as projects and viewers that are more aware of the ideological entanglements of the structures and strategies they experience every day.[38] Only then will biennials and mega-exhibitions emerge that assert themselves fully as the "models of resistance" that they promise to be, which does not necessarily mean the end of the white cube in all cases and for all places so much as initiating a critical relationship to its ends.[39] ●

NOTES

Previously published in: Barbara Vanderlinden and Elena Filipovic (eds.), *The Manifesta Decade: Debates on Contemporary Art Exhibitions and Biennials in Post-Wall Europe* (Brussels and Cambridge [MA], 2005), pp. 63–84.

1 For a discussion of Barr's strategic adaptation of the white cube based on European exhibition models, see Christoph Grunberg, "The Politics of Presentation: The Museum of Modern Art, New York," in Marcia Pointin (ed.), *Art Apart: Art Institutions and Ideology Across England and North America* (Manchester, 1994), pp. 192–210.

2 See also Mary Anne Staniszewski, *The Power of Display: A History of Exhibition Installations at the Museum of Modern Art* (Cambridge [MA], 1998).

3 As Grunberg (1994 [see note 1], p. 206) argues of Barr's whitewashing of the MoMA: "The white, neutral and ideology-free gallery space constitutes the physical materialization of MoMA's selective amnesia. More than anything else, the 'white cube' epitomized the attempt to escape from the realities of the external world, belying modernism's original claim for the integration of art and life. . . . The physical confinement and limitations imposed by the installation reveal MoMA's selective appropriation of modernism."

4 Artist and critic Brian O'Doherty, the white cube's earliest commentator, probably first coined the term in the mid-seventies. His series of three articles entitled "Inside the White Cube," originally published in *Artforum* in 1976, remain the most thorough and engaging study of the phenomenon. They have been collected and reprinted with later articles on the subject in his *Inside the White Cube: The Ideology of the Gallery Space* (Berkeley, 1999).

5 Over the last decade, various studies have begun to make evident the manner in which the museum, from its origins, has been an ideologically laden and disciplining site crucial to the formation of subjectivity. The white

NOTES

cube is in many ways the culmination of its Enlightenment project. See, in particular, Douglas Crimp, *On the Museum's Ruins* (Cambridge [MA], 1993); Tony Bennett, *The Birth of the Museum: History, Theory, Politics* (London, 1995); and Donald Preziosi, *The Brain of the Earth's Body: Art, Museums, and the Phantasms of Modernity* (Minneapolis, 2003).

6 Indeed, the white cube is no more a tabula rasa than the white surface is in architecture more generally. The seminal work on this subject is Mark Wigley's *White Walls, Designer Dresses: The Fashioning of Modern Architecture* (Cambridge [MA], 1996). Whitewashed spaces, Wigley argues, were far from accidental, blank, or silent, and although his study concentrates on the beginnings of the use of white in modernist architecture of the nineteen-twenties and -thirties, the whiteness of museums, galleries, and biennial exhibitions in the decades since similarly speak volumes.

7 Numerous studies have thoroughly discussed these two exhibitions, including Stephanie Barron (ed.), *"Degenerate Art": The Fate of the Avant-Garde in Nazi Germany* (Los Angeles, 1991); Neil Levi, "'Judge for Yourselves!'—The Degenerate Art Exhibition as Political Spectacle," *October* 85 (1998), pp. 41–64; and Berthold Hinz, "'Degenerate' and 'Authentic': Aspects of Art and Power in the Third Reich," in Dawn Ades et al. (eds.), *Art and Power: Europe Under the Dictators, 1930–1940* (London, 1995), pp. 330–34.

8 A discussion of the Third Reich's paradoxical conceptions of modernity and diverse exhibition strategies is not possible here. While the above cited studies have brilliantly treated many of these issues, what interests me is the ways in which the white cube was indoctrinated early in the twentieth century as a vehicle for the projection of diverse, even contradictory, ideals. There are, as I have pointed out, some shared significations of the display conceit, including legitimacy, neutrality, and—albeit differently for Barr and Hitler—a modernity that is resolutely Western. This last point may sound contradictory, since what counted as "Western" was also very different for both men and their respective institutions. Moreover, one could argue that the art shown in the *Grosse deutsche Kunstausstellung* was like Albert Speer's monumental Neoclassical structure, hopelessly caught between past and present, more backward-looking than "modern," in the way we have come to think of the term. However, for Hitler, the presentation of newly made works of art at the Haus der Kunst (the only ones that could legitimately represent their time) contrasted with those of the avant-garde and everything gathered in the *Entartete Kunst* show, which were dismissible as degenerate *and* essentially non-Western or at times degenerate *because* non-Western (the discourse that accompanied the show was explicit, while the primitive "African" lettering of the posters for the *Entartete Kunst* show attempted to underscore the point).

9 Carlos Basualdo, "The Unstable Institution," *MJ–Manifesta Journal* 2 (Winter 2003–Spring 2004), p. 57. This essay has also been reprinted in the present volume.

10 Ibid., p. 60. For a discussion of the degree to which museums have historically been Western institutions founded on colonial imperialist principles, see Preziosi 2003 (see note 5), pp. 116–36.

11 Across various texts, from his curatorial statement for his exhibition *The Structure of Survival* at the fiftieth Venice Biennial in 2003 to his essay for the Documenta 11 catalogue, Basualdo has interestingly engaged the discursive and display strategies in large-scale international exhibitions. If I point here to what has been overlooked in his most explicit treatment of the question in "The Unstable Institution," I do so in part because that essay is a rare example of serious consideration of the biennial phenomenon, and it is remarkable that it does not acknowledge how the endless replication of the white cube in biennials relates to the Western-museum model he discusses.

12 Marc Augé, *Non-lieux: Introduction à une anthropologie de la surmodernité* (Paris, 1992).

13 That argument is a central premise of Documenta 10 and is discussed at length in David's introduction in *Documenta X: Short Guide* (Ostfildern, 1997) as well as in Robert Storr, "Kassel Rock: Interview with Curator Catherine David," *Artforum* 35, no. 9 (May 1997), p. 77.

14 O'Doherty 1999 (see note 4), p. 14. Igor Zabel astutely discusses the ambivalent possible meanings of the recent use of the white cube in exhibitions ("The Return of the White Cube," *MJ–Manifesta Journal* 1 [Spring–Summer 2003], p. 57), and I agree that the meanings of the display conceit are hardly univocal over time. Nevertheless, we should not allow this fact to keep us from recognizing the form's historical overdeterminations nor let its proliferation as an ideal standard in biennials and other mega-exhibitions go on without questioning.

15 Ibid., p. 79; and Igor Zabel, "We and the Others," *Moscow Art Magazine* 22 (1998), p. 29.

16 Henri Lefebvre, *The Production of Space,* trans. Donald Nicholson-Smith (Oxford, 1991), p. 11.

17 Miško Šuvaković, "The Ideology of Exhibition: On the Ideologies of Manifesta," *PlatformaSCCA*, no. 3 (January 2002), p. 11, available online at http://www.ljudmila.org/scca/platforma3/suvakovicengp.htm.

18 Robert Fleck, one of the show's curators, employed this term in the catalogue for Manifesta 2 ("Art after Communism?" *Manifesta 2, European Biennial of Contemporary Art* [Luxembourg City, 1998], p. 195). He provocatively argued that after the Wall fell and equal access to such things as video games and Coca-Cola was established, essential differences between artistic production in the former East and West disappeared to be replaced by what he called an "international style."

19 Jordan Kantor, "Manifesta 5," *Artforum* 43, no. 1 (September 2004), p. 259. See also Susan Snodgrass, "Manifesta 5: Turning Outward," *Art in America* 92, no. 12 (December 2004), pp. 68–73. The show almost completely, and perhaps understandably, avoided directly addressing the deep political tensions in the region, the site's most striking particularity. Instead, the curators opted to construct unspoken analogies to the local situation by displaying a number of artworks that pointed to such things as identity construction, geopolitical strife, and territorial borders elsewhere in the world. However, the inability of the exhibition to more actively or inventively engage with the complex specificity of its location, especially given that this "nomadic" biennial had chosen a Basque city for ostensibly those reasons, left many viewers feeling that the analogies were too few, too distant, or too abstract to resonate with the local reality.

20 David 1997 (see note 13), p. 11.

21 Ibid.

NOTES

22 Ibid., pp. 11–12.

23 The massive publication that accompanied Documenta 10, *Documenta X: The Book* (Ostfildern, 1997), a collaborative project between David and Jean-François Chevrier, conceptually carried through this premise, but it in no way attempted to reproduce on the page the exhibition or events or otherwise represent the diverse artworks. Instead, it served as a parallel intellectual, political, historical, and cultural anthology of Europe across several key historical moments.

24 The four conference platforms—"Democracy Unrealized" (held in Vienna and Berlin), "Experiments with Truth: Transitional Justice and the Processes of Truth and Reconciliation" (held in New Delhi), "Créolité and Creolization" (organized as a workshop that was closed to the public and held in Saint Lucia), and "Under Siege: Four African Cities: Freetown, Johannesburg, Kinshasa, Lagos" (held in Lagos)—found their most public expression in the publication of the proceedings in four eponymous volumes published by Hatje Cantz in 2002 and 2003.

25 See Okwui Enwezor, "The Black Box," in *Documenta 11, Platform 5: Exhibition* (Ostfildern, 2002), pp. 42–55. For a thorough and cogent discussion of the various platforms, see Stewart Martin, "A New World Art? Documenting Documenta 11," *Radical Philosophy: A Journal of Socialist and Feminist Philosophy* 122 (November-December 2003), pp. 7–19.

26 Critics repeatedly noted that the spaces were exceptionally "elegantly proportioned" and "restrained," what Peter Schjeldahl ("The Global Salon: European Extravaganzas," *The New Yorker* 78, no. 17 [July 1, 2002], p. 94) described as a "global salon." Another critic (Jens Hoffmann, "Reentering Art, Reentering Politics," *Flash Art* 34, no. 231 [July–September 2002], p. 106) praised it as "almost perfect, at least in terms of what a traditional art exhibition can be." In one of the few reviews that addressed the contradictions inherent in the aesthetic of the display strategies of Documenta 11 in relation to the content of the artworks, Massimiliano Gioni ("Finding the Center," *Flash Art* 34, no. 231 [July–September 2002], pp. 106–7) proclaimed: "Everything is presented in an almost clinical manner, verging on seamless slickness. Disorder is at the core of the exhibition, but the show itself speaks in a very clear, at times didactic tone. . . The trouble with this edition of Documenta also lies in this attitude, for it renovates themes, artists, and languages, but it does not readdress the format of the exhibition or truly question our role as spectators."

27 Thomas Hirschhorn's dense and sprawling *Bataille Monument* created for Documenta 11 was one such project and a perfect example of the way in which subversive content and architectonic/display form meet (this, one could say, is central to Hirschhorn's entire oeuvre). Its insistent engagement with its displaced location on the outskirts of Kassel (through its use of vernacular materials, a local Turkish workforce to install and maintain the monument, and explicit dedication to the local immigrant community) enacted its own commentary on the relationship of margin to center and political injustice activated by the exhibition.

28 Kim Levin "The CNN Documenta: Art in an International State of Emergency," *Village Voice,* July 3–9, 2002, p. 57, emphasis added. Also available online at http://www.villagevoice.com/art/0227,levin,36174,13.html.

29 Carlos Basualdo, "The Encyclopedia of Babel," in *Documenta 11, Platform 5: Exhibition* (Ostfildern, 2002), p. 60. See also Derek Conrad Murray, "Okwui Enwezor in Conversation with Derek Conrad Murray," *NKA: Journal of Contemporary African Art,* no. 18 (Spring–Summer 2003), pp. 40–47.

30 Ibid.

31 Enwezor 2002 (see note 25), p. 54.

32 Cited in Charlotte Bydler, *The Global Art World, Inc.: On the Globalization of Contemporary Art* (Uppsala, 2004), p. 131. In her exceptional recent study, Bydler situates the Gwangju Biennial's history within the broader context of contemporary art and globalization. An abridged version of this book appears in the present volume.

33 Hou Hanru, "Event City and Pandora's Box: Curatorial Notes on the 2002 Gwangju Biennale," *Yishu* 1, no. 2 (July 2002), p. 91.

34 See Hou Hanru, "Initiatives, Alternatives: Notes in a Temporary and Raw State," in Philippe Vergne, Vasif Kortun, and Hou Hanru (eds.), *How Latitudes Become Forms: Art in a Global Age* (Minneapolis, 2003), pp. 36–39. The fourth Gwangju Biennial seemed to respond in advance to what Charles Esche ("Debate: Biennials," *Frieze,* no. 92 [June/July/August 2005], p. 105) has argued is the most pressing issue for such events since, as he insists, "the biennial needs above all to ask what kind of global culture it underwrites and how that support is made manifest."

35 Hanru 2002 (see note 33), pp. 91–93.

36 Jonathan Napack, "Alternative Visions," *Art in America* 90, no. 11 (November 2002), p. 94.

37 I actually believe in the agency of the artist as author, and a singular author at that. This does not preclude the exhibition from providing a context for *reading* the work (otherwise, I have written in vain) but that context does not, to my mind, fundamentally *change* the artwork nor does it annihilate the dialectic relationship between both—exhibition and artwork—and the potential sense of each constructed by the encounter.

38 Such a turn would be a positive shift for the museum as well, which has arguably also been rethinking its own exhibitions' forms, in many cases in response to and under pressure from its biennial counterpart. The museum haunts this essay even as its particularities—but also its important social contributions—remain insufficiently discussed. Museums unquestionably serve a vital role and one that will always be distinct from that of mega-exhibitions. Still, neither institution is monolithic despite the need to refer here to the values of each in schematic terms; space limitations have kept me from being able to treat the issue in a more nuanced way, but one should not go away with the impression that museums/*Kunsthallen* (and their directors and curators) have not historically struggled with the ideological signification of the white cube, nor that these institutions have not at times been the sites for truly engaged and innovative projects. The relationship between the large-scale international exhibition and the museum—one of exchange and articulation of difference that has been important for both sides—is a subject awaiting thorough study.

39 The term is Okwui Enwezor's and is mentioned in his "Mega-Exhibitions and the Antimonies of a Transnational Global Form," *MJ–Manifesta Journal* 2 (Winter 2003–Spring 2004), p. 31. This essay has also been reprinted in the present volume.

CHANGES IN THE STRATEGIES OF (RE)PRESENTATION AT THE SÃO PAULO BIENNIAL

Vinicius Spricigo

INTRODUCTION: INSTITUTIONAL CRITIQUE OR CRISIS?

THE twenty-eighth São Paulo Biennial curatorial project presented itself as a critique of the Biennial. At his first press conference after his appointment as curator, Ivo Mesquita declared that the São Paulo Biennial had fulfilled its original mission of consolidating a local artistic system and promoting the international projection of Brazilian art.[2] Thus, curators Mesquita and Ana Paula Cohen's concept was that it would be the moment to convert the exhibition into a platform for reflection and debate on the biennial system across the international art circuit,[3] taking the history of the São Paulo Biennial itself as a point of reference, through a political strategy of reactivating its memory and archive.[4] The concrete result was the creation of a "Reading Floor," a "flexible archive"[5] set on the third floor of the Biennial pavilion,[6] including an exhibition space, a library with catalogues of different biennials and periodic exhibitions from around the world, and a conference hall. The second floor of the Ciccillo Matarazzo building was left empty, while the first would, in principle, be made into a public square (as in Oscar Niemeyer's original design), thereby establishing "a new relationship between the Biennial and its surroundings—the park, the city—which open up like the Greek agora, a space for encounters, confrontations, frictions."[7] It was a sort of conversion of Niemeyer's project into an architectural metaphor for the curatorial proposal, rendering the public dimension of the building explicit while harboring inside it a process of critical reflection on the institution (figs. 1, 2).

It may have been appropriate, after all, that some of the press labeled the twenty-eighth edition "the void Biennial," in spite of the curators' protests and the last-minute choice of architecture as the symbol of modernity's utopias and impasses. The proposal to transform the pavilion's ground floor into a public square was changed not only because of the (budget-motivated) abandonment of the idea of removing the casements in the pavilion's downstairs windows, but also because of the heavy security apparatus set up after a group of spray painters tagged the empty space on the second floor. The curators declared the incident a criminal act of vandalism

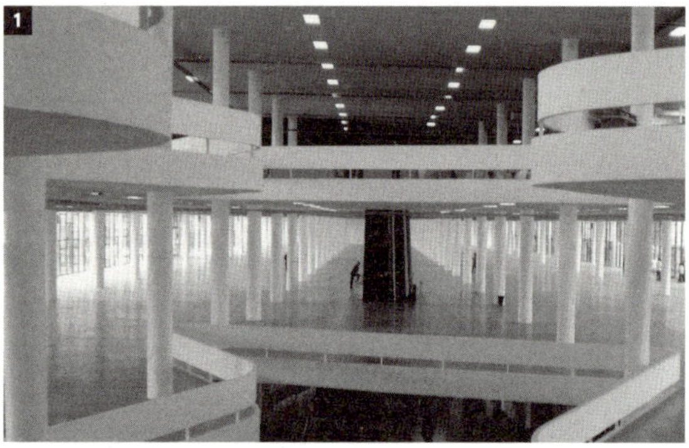

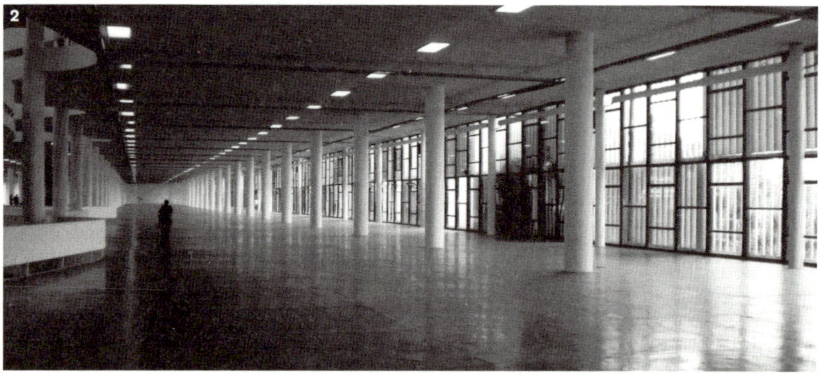

against the city's cultural heritage and installed a system of checks similar to the ones that have been found in international airports since 9/11. This was the central point in Fábio Cypriano's critique,[8] which questioned the legitimacy of the choice of Ivo Mesquita's curatorial project, the undeclared interest in the use of public funds, the reasons for the demotion of curator Thomas Mulclaire, the lack of public attendance at the debates, etc. The episode was also referred to by architect Ligia Nobre, cofounder of the social organization EXO experimental org (www.exo.org.br), a platform for field research in art and urbanism in São Paulo active between 2002 and 2007. Emphasizing the contradictions between the discourse and the practice of the curators, she remarked: "The Biennial called the taggers criminals, and Cohen disqualified them as 'those people from the periphery' during the press conference. This is not quite the kind of 'living contact' that she and Mesquita promised. If the twenty-eighth Biennial claims to be a public space of social inclusion, should it not be open precisely to 'those people from the periphery'?"[9]

1, 2 The empty Oscar Niemeyer pavilion during the 28th São Paulo Biennial, 2008.

Ironically, the incident at the exhibition's opening was symptomatic of a crisis in the public sphere that had already been addressed by the Biennial's previous edition. In a debate at the time, Renato Janine Ribeiro commented on the present condition of Sé Square in the center of São Paulo. Once an important meeting place for public manifestations in the nineteen-eighties, such as those of the movement for direct presidential election after twenty years of military dictatorship, it lost its social dynamic after its remodeling by the local administration, becoming a space where the most visible form of "participation" is the work of taggers and graffiti artists.[10] Another example of the impasses created by the process of modernization in São Paulo is Luis Carlos Berrini Avenue. Seen from the perspective of the favela on the opposite side of the Pinheiros River, it reflects the country's extreme social and educational inequality, as well as the urban paradigm of protection and control discussed by Spanish artist Antoni Muntadas in relation to the end of the public sphere and the sensation of fear that leads to the installation of fences, gates, and surveillance systems.[11] We are witnessing what Brian Holmes called "the urbanization of blindness" in reference to the way in which the Paris protests of 2005 did not manage to disrupt the flow of tourists or the city's cultural life.[12] During the preparation of the twenty-seventh São Paulo Biennial in 2006, a crime syndicate known as the PCC (Primeiro Comando da Capital, or First Commando of the Capital), whose leaders controlled drug traffic by mobile phone from behind bars, attacked police stations and public transportation, thereby succeeding in bringing a metropolis of eighteen million inhabitants to an almost complete standstill.

The taggers' radical response, and the heavy-handed repression of their activity on the part of the Fundação Bienal de São Paulo, evidenced the displacement of the conceptual axis of the Biennial's last two editions. Speculation on the concept of art in terms of formal experimentation and evolution, or even the overcoming of the Western canon, that was characteristic of the nineteen-nineties has given way to a discussion on the politics of art and other aspects of "life in common" and the crisis of representation.

It is the relation between the end of the politico-cultural project of modernization in the late sixties on the one hand and the "void" used as aesthetic or institutional-critical strategy on the other that allows me to question the premise from which the curators of the twenty-eighth São Paulo Biennial set out in 2007. The curators' argument was that the Biennial had already achieved its initial goals (or its historical mission) to the extent that it had made São Paulo into one of the great centers of world art. However, I believe that such a perspective belies the teleological appeal of the notion of progress implicit in "grand narratives" that has been criticized by postmodern and postcolonial theorists in their analysis of the historical construction of European modernism and the tensions inherent in core–periphery relations. Besides, Mesquita and Cohen's idea dates back to the developmentalist discourse of the nineteen-fifties and the belief in the emancipatory promises of modernity, making no reference to the various fates of the modernist project or the partial accomplishment of its aims.

The (counter)argument here is that the initial project of the modernization and internationalization of the Brazilian art system proposed by the São Paulo Biennial reached its conclusion a long time ago, when the boycott led by Mário Pedrosa against the tenth Biennial in 1969 as a strategy to protest the military dictatorship started a phase that went down in Brazilian cultural history as "the cultural void."[13] By adopting a different historical reading, this article critically reflects on the role of the São Paulo Biennial today. My goal is to examine the artistic and cultural debate that has taken place around the São Paulo Biennial over the last fifty-seven years and to identify its central questions in order to facilitate a critical reflection on its history and its role as a political and cultural project. Firstly, we will look at the project of the São Paulo Biennial, initiated in 1951, in view of the significance the exhibition has had in the reformulation of notions of identity in Brazilian art in terms of their connection to the modernization and cultural transnationalization that characterized Brazil in the nineteen-fifties.

In many ways, the Biennial's history belongs to the period of the consolidation of the developmentalist project and of the flourishing of nationalistic, identitarian discourses in the first half of the twentieth century. The specific project of the São Paulo Biennial resulted from the progressive ideas of Brazilian entrepreneur Francisco "Ciccillo" Matarazzo Sobrinho, founder of the São Paulo Modern Art Museum,[14] and from the city's situation in the postwar period as the center of the country's aspirations for modernization and industrialization. Today, it is one of the largest metropolitan regions in the world and personifies the contradictions of a country "condemned to be modern," to borrow Mário Pedrosa's words.

For a country that had become independent from Portugal (1822), abolished slavery (1888), and established a republican regime (1889) all within a single century, modernity[15]—as a project with its sights set on a certain degree of historical development—represented the opportunity for breaking with the colonial past and submission to European domination. The main goal of Latin American modernization was to dissolve the colonial relationship in which the periphery produces primary commodities and consumes manufactured products. At the cultural level, this situation of colonial dependency expresses itself when "the colony is ethnographic material that lives off foreign-produced cultural imports."[16]

Colombian thinker Jesús Martín-Barbero, a key figure in cultural studies in Latin America, understands modernization as a political action promoted by the Brazilian state with the support of self-appointed progressive elites and with the goal of effecting societal transformation. Carried out by a centralizing state, as Martín-Barbero writes, this action is focused on industrialization and the reorganization of the economy:

> *From the nineteen-twenties on, the majority of Latin American countries engaged in a reorganization of their economies and a readjustment of their political structures. In the promotion of an internal market and the employment of a growing labor force, industrialization was undertaken with import substitution at its center, thereby making state intervention, through investment in transport and communication infrastructure, decisive. Therefore, even when the start of the industrializing process responded to the international market's functioning conditions, there were differences in the scope and rhythm that corresponded to the degree of the development of the "national project"—differences that would forge each country's bourgeoisie from the second half of the twentieth century.*[17]

Martín-Barbero stresses the ambivalence in Latin American modernization and modernism: the process of creating a distinctive cultural identity and becoming a nation, in the modern sense, led traditional societies to follow the steps Western Europe had taken towards modernity, and thus to adopt hegemonic countries as a point of reference against which to measure their achievements.[18] Brazilian modernization, however, would be out of step with its European model, with the result that "being out of step" would define our cultural difference.

> *If it is true that different processes of national formation follow different rhythms and paths, it can also be said that a fundamental rearrangement of the ensemble of these diverse trajectories would take place in the 1930s . . . Firstly,*

in the belief that the originality of Latin America as a whole and of individual Latin American countries was constituted by factors that escape the logic of capitalist development. Secondly, in the perception of modernization as the recovery of wasted time, which therefore identifies development with a definitive ceasing to be what one used to be in order to finally become modern. The discontinuity that we try to see here is situated in another key, one that allows us to break with both an ahistorical, culturalist model and a cumulative-rationality paradigm, with its pretension of unifying and subsuming within a single time all the different sociohistorical temporalities. This enables us to think at once what backwardness meant in historical terms, not as in a time that would have stopped, but in its historical production; and what, in spite of backwardness, exists in terms of difference, cultural heterogeneity, the multiplicity of temporalities of indigenous, black and white, and the time produced by their mixture.[19]

This passage is worth quoting at length, for it provides evidence of the sophistication of the idea of temporal discontinuity as a tool with which to comment on modern development in the periphery of capitalism, avoiding simplism and trying to conceive of a modernity that cannot be reduced to imitation, or of a difference that cannot be exhausted in backwardness. Avoiding the mistake of positing an "ideal" modernism in core countries and of adopting an evolutionist view of history according to which the fate of Brazilian civilization would be to arrive at some predetermined state, Martín-Barbero emphasizes the contradictions that allow us to rethink the appearance of Brazilian modernism. Finally, as an attempt to overcome the colonial tradition of cultural dependence, Brazilian modern art sought its own local specificity, adopting the supposedly "universal" model of the internationalist current that became hegemonic in the postwar period, which had abstractionism and painting as its main vehicles.

European modernism would appear, then, as a model to be imported and adapted to the local context. It is a spatial displacement, an "idea out of place," to borrow one of the most important hypotheses for the interpretation of the relationship between our economic dependency as a peripheric country, which has resulted from colonialism, and the recourse to models imported from core countries also in the symbolic field, as developed by literary critic Roberto Schwarz.[20]

Anthropologist Renato Ortiz[21] points out the ties in Brazil between modernism and the construction of a national project. The self-awareness of cultural dependency led to an effort to overcome the established hierarchical relationship between core and periphery and the dynamic of emulating foreign models as a task carried out through the creation of a Brazilian modern art and a distinctive, unified cultural identity for the entire nation. Therefore, "modernism, modernity, and modernization are interchangeable terms for us"; modernism in Brazil would thus be "an idea out of place" that is being progressively adapted to a developing society.[22]

Inaugurated by the São Paulo Modern Art Week of 1922, Brazilian modernism was the starting point for a project of national culture and a search for the "Brazilianness" of our art. While modernism contested local specificities and proclaimed a universal myth, the Brazilian modernist movement posed the question of what Brazilian art was. "Paradoxically, internationalist modern art set Brazilian culture on the path of self-examination."[23]

There is, however, a fundamental difference between this first modernist moment and the internationalization of Brazilian art that occurred after the war. Notions of a culturally dependent situation inherited from the colonial period and of imported artistic canons give way to a questioning of cultural imperialism and U.S. hegemony during the Cold War.[24] In line with public policies for the affirmation of modern art and North American postwar cultural diplomacy, the political and cultural project of the São Paulo Biennial was, for better or for worse, a decisive step in the modernization of the Brazilian art system and the country's insertion in the international scene.[25] In the words of Lourival Gomes Machado, the first artistic director of the São Paulo Museum of Modern Art Biennial, "by its own definition, the Biennial should accomplish two main tasks: to place Brazilian modern art not merely in confrontation, but in living contact with world art; and at the same time to seek to establish São Paulo as an art center on a global scale."[26] It is no surprise that these words were made into the slogan of the Biennial's 2008 edition. In this regard, the São Paulo Biennial saw, on the cultural plane, an opportunity to break with a situation of dependency by defining the specificities of Brazil's local art production and promoting its inclusion on the international scene.

The Biennial's first impact on the local artistic sphere, as is well known, served to promote the rise of the movement of Constructive Art in Brazil. It was, in fact, an artist coming from this context—Hélio Oiticica—who went on to theorize the Brazilian avant-garde and the conditions of aesthetic experimentation in peripheral contexts,[27] thereby shaping what remains today a frame of reference for the analysis of the process of internationalization of Brazilian art and the different consequences of the appearance of popular culture in Brazil.

Now, in order to understand the "living contact" that the São Paulo Biennial produced until the early seventies, we cannot forget art critic Sônia Salzstein's remark that, despite the pressures of internationalization, Brazil developed a singular experience that resisted any homogenizing tendency. She writes: "It was an experience that could not be simply explained as a foreseeable effect of the expansion of Euro-American modernity nor as an epigone version of it, showing no more than regional interest or relevance."[28] Examples of such relevance include, to mention but a few, the formal experimentations of Neoconcretism, the theoretical and poetic formulations of Ferreira Gullar and Oiticica, and the "tropicalist" cultural effervescence that preceded the diaspora of Brazilian artists in the "years of lead" of the dictatorship.[29]

From the nineteen-eighties on, during the process of democratic reorganization of Brazilian society, the projects designed by Vilém Flusser and Walter Zanini[30] around the appearance of new languages and developments in Conceptual Art, as well as the reconstitution of the local art circuit, shrouded in doubt the policies of (re)presentation and the modernist discourses through which the identity of Brazilian art was defined.[31] Besides, as a consequence of the processes of cultural globalization, the expansion of Western modernism beyond the established standards of artistic internationalism sparked a "crisis of representation" in the Biennial in which the conventional dichotomies (local/global, core/periphery, modern/traditional, etc.) seemed to become obsolete.[32]

IN THE GUISE OF A CONCLUSION

HERE, therefore, without ignoring the transformation that took place or the institutional and geopolitical contexts that have existed since the nineteen-seventies, we will discuss the insertion of the São Paulo Biennial in the dynamic of global art. In this new global order of the art system, a certain number of responses to present problems, or the "postmodern condition," were articulated by curators Nelson Aguilar (1994–96), Paulo Herkenhoff (1998), Lisette Lagnado (2006), and Ivo Mesquita (2008).

The recent changes in the São Paulo Biennial may show that the institution is moving away from a perspective oriented by the discourses of contemporary art's hegemonic centers. Turning inwards to explore its own history, it has examined its modernist foundations, seeking to question its relation to Euro-America in the terms put forward by Oswald de Andrade in his 1928 "Anthropophagic Manifesto."[33] At least this was the device employed by curator Paulo Herkenhoff in 1998 in order to maximize the Biennial's affirmation of Brazilian art, a process that had begun in 1989 with Stella Teixeira de Barros being appointed as the curator of the Brazilian representatives' work. In his words, "Anthropophagy is one of the first concepts of Brazilian culture to enter the international grammar of art,"[34] offering an alternative and counterpoint to the so-called Western interpretation of the history of art, which neglects the multiplicity of existing modernisms and sets of parameters of exclusion (fig. 3).[35] A few years earlier, for the twenty-second Biennial, curator Nelson Aguilar had already organized special rooms for Oiticica, Lygia Clark, and Mira Schendel in order to affirm the belief that the work of local artists was on the same level as that of the more renowned representatives of other nations (figs. 4, 5).[36] This strategy would be discontinued due to the Biennial's institutional crisis around the turn of the century and only taken up again in 2005, when Oiticica's work was chosen to provide the conceptual paradigm for the twenty-seventh São Paulo Biennial. His texts became the theoretical frame of reference for the elaboration of the curatorial project presented by Lagnado. In a text on Oiticica of 1966, the critic Mário Pedrosa first used the term postmodernism when proposing the passage of art to a "state of culture."[37] This reversal of perspective, which identifies a Brazilian artist as the precursor of such a significant shift, makes room for new interpretations of the international development of contemporary art.[38] It also allows one to speak about contemporary art exhibitions from the point of view of the Brazilian experience, thus revealing the São Paulo Biennial's local contribution to the global phenomenon of the spread of biennials around the world.

Inspired by Roland Barthes' 1976–77 Collège de France lectures, the twenty-seventh São Paulo Biennial started many months before the opening of the exhibition with a program of international seminars inspired by Documenta 11's platforms and Documenta 10's "100 Days–100 Guests" program in which the team of curators directed

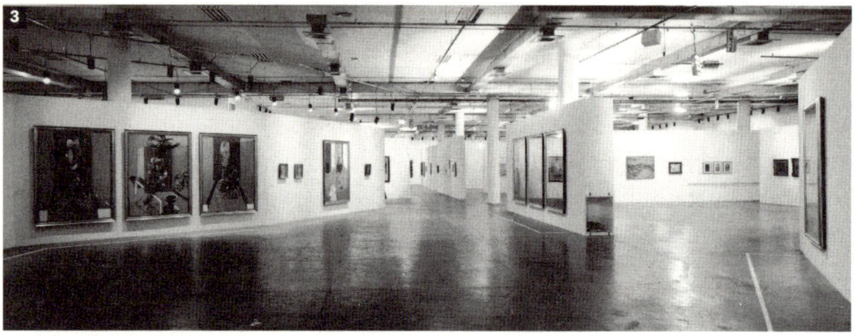
3

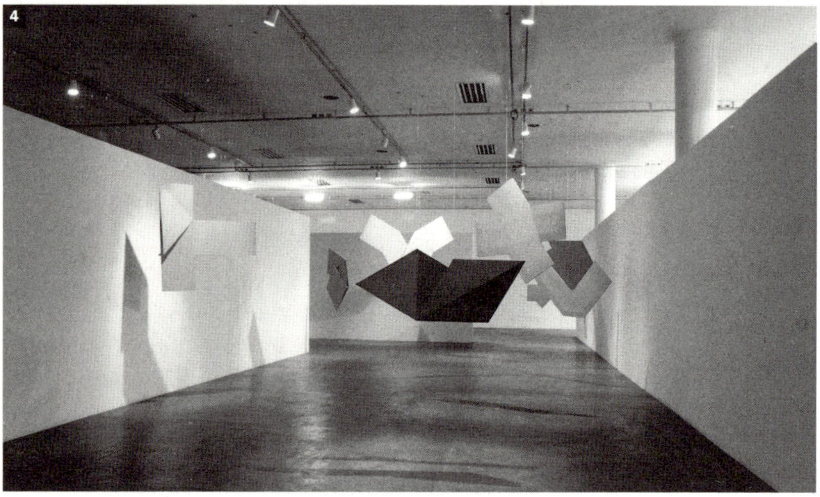
4

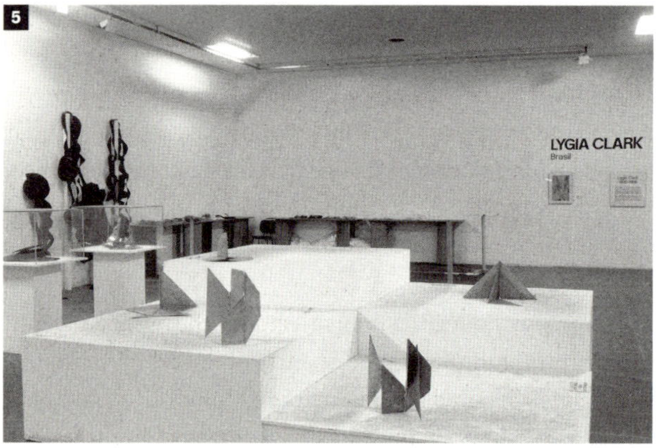

5

by Lagnado (Cristina Freire, Jochen Volz, José Roca, Rosa Martínez, and Adriano Pedrosa) offered the general public access to the ideas that informed the whole exhibition.[39] The intention was to replace the Venetian model of national pavilions with a platform of debates on "the political" (that is, "life in common") in which the blurring of boundaries between the public spheres of art and politics would set in motion a program of self-critique and the deconstruction of the limits of these institutions. The twenty-seventh Biennial's response to the so-called crisis of representation was thus to abolish national representation altogether, "a system that undermined the possibility of establishing a project independently from the authority of constituted powers," and give "a political dimension to an exhibition of such importance to the city, to Brazil, and to the world."[40]

Looking back at the twenty-seventh São Paulo Biennial's curatorial project three years later, it seems to me that there were two distinct visions at play: one that reached back to institutional critique and the work of Conceptual artists like Daniel Buren, Hans Haacke, Dan Graham, and Marcel Broodthaers (who was the featured artist at the first of the international seminars), and one that turned towards contemporary production, placing emphasis on a political art that was sociological in nature and visibly seeking contact with so-called marginalized communities. In a certain way, the background for this discussion was the idea of a "reconstruction" of a public sphere that traversed a reflection on architecture and urbanism (another theme of the seminars) and political projects that incorporated the recognition of the other. In the realm of the visual arts, this recognition was linked, for example, to the inclusion of "modernisms" produced outside the legitimizing centers of Western modern art. ●

3 *Salas especiais,* Francis Bacon room, 24th São Paulo Biennial, 1998.
4 Hélio Oiticica, *Relevos Espaciais* (Spatial Reliefs), 24th São Paulo Biennial, 1998.
5 Lygia Clark room, 22nd São Paulo Biennial, 1994.

NOTES

This essay was submitted in response to the 2009 Bergen Biennial Conference's "Call for Biennial Knowledge." It is a slightly revised version of the text that appeared in: *Global Art and the Museum* (2010), online journal of the ZKM | Zentrum für Kunst und Medientechnologie, Karlsruhe, http://globalartmuseum.de/site/guest_author/254.

Translation by Rodrigo Nunes.

1 This text presents some reflections arising from my doctoral thesis, which was developed at the University of São Paulo's School of Communication and Arts and financed by the São Paulo State Foundation for the Support of Research (FAPESP). The São Paulo Biennial became the focus of my research around the time of my collaboration with the coverage of the twenty-seventh edition's seminars, which I coauthored (with Liliane Benetti, from the Center for Research on Modern and Contemporary Brazilian Art, University of São Paulo's School of Communication and Arts) for the Web site of the Art Museum Permanent Forum project (www.forumpermanente.org). I thank Liliane for helping me revise the seminars and elaborate some ideas about the relationship between the aesthetic and the political that have remained with me to this day.

2 See http://bienalsaopaulo.globo.com/.

3 Fundação Bienal de São Paulo (ed.), *Em vivo contato,* exh. cat. 28th São Paulo Biennial (São Paulo, 2008).

4 The Wanda Svevo Historical Archive, originally the Contemporary Art Historical Archive, was created in 1954 by Wanda Svevo, secretary of the Modern Art Museum of the São Paulo Biennial. It presently occupies a 400-square-meter area on the second floor of the Fundação Bienal de São Paulo.

5 The system was conceived by Ana Paula Cohen for the Istmo project; see http://www.forumpermanente.org/.rede/proj-istmo/.

6 The Ciccillo Matarazzo Pavilion, former Palace of the Industries, was designed by Oscar Niemeyer and has hosted the São Paulo Biennial since its first edition in 1957. It is part of a set of buildings in Ibirapuera Park that was opened in 1953 for the city of São Paulo's four-hundredth anniversary.

7 São Paulo 2008 (see note 3).

8 Fábio Cypriano, "Um acordo de cavalheiros em vivo contato," *Fórum Permanente de Museus de Arte* (December 17, 2008), http://www.forumpermanente.org/.imprensa/a-recepcao-da-28a-bienal-de-sao-paulo/um-acordo-de-cavalheiros-em-vivo-contato/.

9 Ligia Nobre, "Taggers Get into 'Living Contact' with Vacant São Paulo Bienal," *Art Review,* November 4, 2008.

10 Seminário Reconstrução, 27th São Paulo Biennial, June 9–10, 2006.

11 "The Social in Art: Between Ethics and Aesthetics," round-table discussion with Claire Bishop, Antoní Muntadas, Sônia Salzstein, and Paula Trope, School of Communication and Arts, University of São Paulo, November 9, 2006.

12 Brian Holmes, "Beyond the Global 1000," conference paper given at CIMAM, Pinacoteca do Estado de São Paulo, November 2005.

13 The term (coined by the journalist Zuenir Ventura) expressed the disappointment arising from the rupture between the modernizing process and the ideals of emancipation—an association, which led to the political support of many leftwing intellectuals to the modernizing impulse, according to whose logic political democracy would be a natural consequence of economic growth.

14 The first biennials were promoted by the São Paulo Modern Art Museum, founded by Ciccillo Matarazzo in 1948. In 1962, with the creation of the São Paulo Bienal Foundation, the MAM ceased to exist and its collection was donated to the University of São Paulo. Intellectuals and artists who opposed the MAM's extinction refounded it in the following years. Today it occupies a space in Ibirapuera Park.

15 In the sense in which I use it here, "modernity" signifies a stage in the development of European and North American societies which served as the ideal model for agents of modernization in Latin America.

16 Roland Corbisier, cited in Renato Ortiz, *Mundialização e cultura* (São Paulo, 2000), p. 93.

17 Jesús Martín-Barbero, *Dos meios às mediações: Comunicação, cultura e hegemonia,* 2nd ed. (Rio de Janeiro, 2001), p. 227.

18 Ibid., pp. 226–30.

19 Ibid., pp. 225–26.

20 Roberto Schwarz, "As idéias fora do lugar," in *Cultural e Política* (São Paulo, 2001).

21 Renato Ortiz, *A moderna tradição brasileira: cultura brasileira e indústria cultural,* 5th ed. (São Paulo, 1994).

22 Ibid., p. 209.

23 Carlos Zilio, "Da Antropofagia à Tropicália," in Adauto Novaes (ed.), *O nacional e o popular na cultural brasileira: Artes plásticas e literatura* (São Paulo, 1983), p. 14.

24 Hans Belting, *O fim da história da arte: uma revisão dez anos depois* (São Paulo, 2006), pp. 51–58.

25 Mário Pedrosa, "A bienal de cá pra lá," in Aracy Amaral (ed.), *Mundo, Homem, Arte em Crise,* 2nd ed. (São Paulo, 1986), pp. 254–56.

26 Lourival Gomes Machado, "Apresentação," in *Catálogo da I Bienal do Museu de Arte Moderna de São Paulo* (São Paulo, 1951), p. 14.

27 Hélio Oiticica, "Esquema geral da Nova objetividade brasileira," in *Projeto Hélio Oiticica,* exh. cat. Rio de Janeiro, Centro de Artes Hélio Oiticica, 1992.

28 Sônia Salzstein, "Pop as a Crisis in the Public Sphere," in Kobena Mercer (ed.), *Annotating Art's Histories* (London, 2005), p. 102.

29 Despite that many artists stayed in the country, the nineteen-seventies have become marked by the idea of the "cultural void" advanced by journalist Zuenir Ventura in order to place the period in opposition to the preceding decade's hegemony of left-wing culture. See Zuenir Ventura, *A crise da cultura brasileira* (Visão, 1971).

30 Zanini was the first to occupy the post of São Paulo Biennial curator; until the seventies, the function was performed by a general director.

31 See Aracy Amaral's texts on the internationalization of the Brazilian art system and on the history of modern art in Latin America, such as *Textos do Trópico de Capricórnio: Artigos e en-*

NOTES

saios (1980–2005), Vol. 2: Circuitos de arte na América Latina e no Brasil (São Paulo, 2006).

32 Nestor Canclini, *Culturas híbridas: Estratégias para entrar e sair da modernidade,* 2nd ed. (São Paulo, 2003).

33 The Manifesto was inspired by a Tupi ritual consisting of devouring the bravest captives from the enemy army in order to absorb their vital force. Displaced onto the field of culture, the concept of anthropophagy has become a metaphor for Brazilian culture's relationship with its European "matrix". Through its association with the exotic or primitive character of cannibalism, it signals a specific position of the development of an artistic avant-garde in the context of the rediscovery of the Brazilian modern tradition by nineteen-sixties Tropicalism. According to Hélio Oiticica, the experimentalism that characterizes our modernism can be understood as a process of the creation of a new, Brazilian artistic language through the incorporation of other, international languages—for instance, Pop Art and the "Nouveaux Réalistes" of French critic Pierre Restany.

34 Paulo Herkenhoff, "Bienal 1998: Princípios e processos," *Trópico,* April 24, 2008, http://pphp.uol.com.br/tropico/html/textos/2973,1.shl.

35 Fundação Bienal de São Paulo (ed.), *Núcleo histórico: Antropofagia e histórias de canibalismos,* exh. cat. 24th São Paulo Biennial (São Paulo, 1998), p. 22.

36 Nelson Aguilar adopted the concept of "rupture with the medium" to question the traditional categories of "beaux arts" and the notion of artwork itself, confronting the Western modernist canon and the universalist conception of art. Hélio Oiticica, Lygia Clark, and Mira Schendel were thus chosen by the curator as "beacons" of national production for the twenty-second São Paulo Biennial. Clark and Schendel represented Brazil at the 1968 Venice Biennial, but did not achieve the recognition of the international art circuit. After a retrospective held in Rotterdam, Paris, Barcelona, Lisbon, and Minneapolis ten years after his death in 1980, Oiticica finally achieved a certain visibility outside the country, with his work displayed at Documenta 10 (1997) and at the Tate Modern (2007). There are doubts, however, as to the effect of inserting the names of a few Brazilian artists in the international circuit in terms of the recognition and systematic presence of Brazilian art outside the country, and about the benefits of building up a profile abroad to the consolidation of the local art system. See Ana Letícia Fialho, "Mercado de artes: Global e desigual," *Trópico,* 2005, http://pphp.uol.com.br/tropico/html/textos/2551,1.shl.

37 Mário Pedrosa, "Arte ambiental, arte pós-moderna, Hélio Oiticica," *Correio da Manhã,* June 26, 1966.

38 Lisette Lagando, "O 'além da arte' de Hélio Oiticica," *Trópico,* July 8, 2007, http://pphp.uol.com.br/tropico/html/textos/2882,1.shl.

39 Adriano Pedrosa, "Como curar junto," in Lisette Lagnado and Adriano Pedrosa (eds.), *27ª Bienal de São Paulo: Como viver junto* (São Paulo, 2006), p. 84.

40 Lisette Lagnado, "No amor e na adversidade," in Lagnado and Pedrosa 2006 (see note 39), p. 53.

TALKING AND THINKING ABOUT BIENNIALS: THE POTENTIAL OF DISCURSIVITY

Bruce W. Ferguson and Milena M. Hoegsberg

RECENTLY, there has been a development in the biennial genre toward so-called discursive exhibitions.[1] These include exhibitions that question the format of the curatorial project from within, or foreground symposia, platforms for discussion, research, and educational programming, which is to say, they attend to pedagogy, aesthetics, and knowledge production. One might in this case also speak of the emergence of curatorial projects that could be called "durational": long-term, process-oriented works-in-progress that unfold over the course of several months, or even years.[2] If the "discursive turn" in exhibition practice more generally has shifted the focus from the exclusive presentation of concrete and autonomous objects (display) in art institutions of various kinds (museums, art centers, *Kunsthallen*) towards the engagement of the audience in listening, reading, studying, or participating rather than merely looking, it has in the last decade become more and more the case that biennials and other such perennial exhibitions have become privileged platforms for exhibiting discursivity. From the "100 Guests–100 Days" program of Catherine David's Documenta 10 to the attempt to make an exhibition-as-school for Manifesta 6 to the 2008 São Paulo Biennial's self-investigation and focus on a discussion about biennials, perennial exhibitions are arguably more and more the site for the discursive.

MULTIPLICATION WITHOUT MULTIPLICITY

ONE question might be why these "discursive biennials" are starting to appear now, just when the biennial is actually doing better than it ever has in terms of both numbers and cultural status. It seems that this new kind of biennial emerges at a point of discontent among art professionals relating to the enormous proliferation of biennials worldwide and, more importantly, what these do and do not accomplish. In the art world, there is a growing sense of a collapse of the biennial's curatorial relevancy and thus of its consequence. Surveys of a cross section of recent biennial catalogues reveal a consistent awareness that the promise of the contemporary art biennial, especially as a platform for true global exchange and as a departure from the museum, has not been fully realized.[3] Critique of the biennial might be summarized as follows: despite its promise, the biennial has given rise to a new set of problems, including predictable and stagnant curatorial intellectual patterns; a limited pantheon of artists whose forms of production and networks of distribution (including their commercial gallery affiliations) are traditionally hierarchical; the misuse of site-specificity as a practice, which has been transferred from the specifics of contextual intensity to an assimilatory aesthetics of style and faux social commitment; and the architectural mimicry of museums in the form of the modernist "white cube."

The dramatic increase of contemporary art biennials, beginning in the nineties, and the issues to which they have given rise can be contextualized on many fronts. The biennial multiplication occurs as a part of an extraordinary increase in contemporary art activities. The biennial pandemic must be seen in the context of a wholesale eruption of more and larger undergraduate art programs and graduate art schools, the plethora of new commercial art galleries, a vast number of new museums, new consultants, new and substantial art prizes, new investors, and new collectors, as well as new publications and immensely enlarged art audiences worldwide. The emergence of curatorial schools and the need for greater employment opportunities developed simultaneously.

The art world of the nineties very closely shadowed and mimicked the same period's inflated stock market. Nation-states, municipalities, regions, cities, civic organizations, and private corporations alike embraced this emerging cultural and economic tendency, mythologizing contemporary art's potential in order to market cities or regions and place them indelibly on the global map through promises of economic prosperity and social prestige. "Biennial" quickly became a generic brand name, with the inherent promise of international relevance. The growing demand for contemporary art reflects the wide recognition of art's potential to serve social, political, and economic ends, in both the public and private sectors. The increase in biennials signals, in other words, a continuation of a far-reaching instrumentalization of contemporary art, in particular as a tool for dealing with issues such as education, cultural diversity and integration, cultural tourism, urban and social regeneration, and identity politics.

The world-weariness of art-world members who bemoan the excess of biennials seems often to pertain to the widespread sentiment that too many biennials look and feel the same—what some critics have called the biennial's homogenizing effect, or the "biennial syndrome."[4] In large part this seems due to the repeated showcasing of well-known artists who are invited by established recurring curators and who often represent received academic wisdom and dominant museum, or even market, values. Continuously giving the curatorial floor to the usual suspects at the most visible biennials sets a narrow standard for a biennial's success. More consequentially, biennial curators often hold one or more other full-time positions, and their time for deep research or extensive studio visits is thus often severely limited. Hou Hanru, the frequent-flyer curator par excellence, remarked in a public interview, no less, that he had conceived both the title and the concept for the tenth Lyon Biennial in a matter of "a few days" after returning from a visit to Lyon.[5] Needless to say, an exhibition conceived under such a self-imposed deadline means that Hanru, like many curators before—and likely after—him, will make standard and predictable choices. One corollary result has also been the emergence of what have come to be called "biennial artists," artists with a ubiquitous presence in many major international sites whose particular installation work has become closely identified with the vision of their curatorial advocates. Although biennials have made visible many great artists who might otherwise have been overlooked, they have also resulted in predictable inclusions and a lack of experimentation with either form or content. In other words, the perennial elitism that is associated closely with the power of economic and social status in the collecting world of museums, private collectors, and markets has become the imperious standard for biennials as well. As a result, social and career networking opportunities remain one of the important motivations for attending biennials professionally, rather than an interest in the art's potential for meaning.

Daniel Birnbaum, for instance, director of the fifty-third Venice Biennial, has suggested that there are only twenty-five biennials with "serious curatorial ambitions," although he estimates that there are at least a hundred of them in total.[6] His comment reflects a powerful segment of the art world's immovable criteria for a successful spectacle that continues to rest distinctly on the participation of established players in the circuit. However, this attitude overlooks the privilege of its own position. Keeping in mind that no one has either the time or the money to visit all existing biennials, biennial fatigue must be contextualized in other terms as well.

The proliferation of biennials in the nineties accompanied the highly mythologized "globalization" of the world. Globalization is often understood as being similar to historical imperialism, whereby a dominant culture exports its infrastructures and values to a subordinate culture. But globalization in the late twentieth century seems less like these historically imposed systems, because it is often invited into the foreign culture, as in China's particular "socialist" embrace of capitalism. Globalization is perhaps more usefully explained as "the spread of modernity," in John Tomlinson's words, and thus can be seen more powerfully as "cultural loss" than as imperialism per se.[7] Just as the birth of sixty-six independent countries between 1945 and 1968 produced a postcolonial discourse, in the nineties the new biennials arose within an unprecedented worldwide population explosion and contiguous migration to urban centers.[8] These developments were combined again with the wholesale creation of new nations from the fragmentation of older ones in Eastern Europe and Africa. Indeed, despite "exhaustion" at the centers, many voices have yet to be heard. The Venice Biennial, for instance, has expanded to include seventy-seven nations officially, but the United Nations recognizes one hundred and ninety-two registered countries. Even all these countries do not necessarily represent the multiple diasporas of the world. Nation-states are often out of step with the networks of communication and economic, as well as artistic, discourses. As Okwui Enwezor has argued, one positive effect of biennials has been the explosion of the myth of a lack in artistic practice in parts of the world outside the West.[9] Speaking from a postcolonial perspective, Homi Bhaba too has said, "the globe shrinks for those who own it; for the displaced or the dispossessed, the migrant or refugee, no distance is more awesome than the few feet across borders and frontiers."[10] In other words, biennial exhaustion can only be afforded by those privileged enough to already have homogenizing power or by those who lack intellectual curiosity about new forms and new voices.

The recent emphasis on what can be called "discursivity," for lack of a better term, seems to emerge as a response to all of these intertwined concerns: the power brokering of the West; peripatetic international curators and artists intervening insensitively in a local situation; the lack of impact on communities and the lack of structures for cultural sustainability after a biennial's occurrence. Concurrently, it should be underscored that despite the credit curators are given for this "turn" by other curators, of course, it is equally if not more true that this new exhibition form reformulates something of the aesthetic conceptual practices of the late sixties and early seventies as a kind of dematerialization of the exhibition form, or as a deconstruction of it, at the very least, in the face of redundant curatorial practices and the museumification of the biennial. For instance, Joseph Kosuth, one of the great thinkers of the Conceptualist practices of four decades ago, has created a method of working that oscillates productively between curatorial practices and installation practices, and problematizes both. Another example is the artist Peter Greenaway, whose curatorial practice in museums overlapped with his filmic interests to the extent that his most recent work has been a form of interpretative art history using film as an investigatory tool. There is no question that the practices of many artists from the Conceptualists forward has led to this curatorial "turn" toward discursivity and its subsequent theorizing. Even prior to Documenta 10, which is often considered a watershed moment for a certain intellectual or discursive exhibition practice within academic and curatorial circles, it is possible to think of Joseph Beuys, Group Material, Dan Graham, Andrea Fraser, Joseph Grigley, the Center for Land Use Interpretation, Max Dean, and countless other artists, cultural collectives, and organizations who developed "action research" in the arts.[11] Certainly, much of this work has its roots in Beuys's notion of art as "social sculpture," regardless of the interpretation of that term. This is an area for more intense research, one distinct from the all-too-easily-drunk Kool-Aid of "relational aesthetics."[12] The point here is not to take away credit from the curators, who folded the implications of some artistic practices into their own, but to give credit to the work of artists for the shifts occurring not only in biennials, but also in the exhibition practices and programs of a number of art centers internationally.

However, as a result of both the early and continuing work of artists and now-new curatorial thinkers, this small group of biennials can be viewed as a potential space for critique of both the form of the biennial itself and the underlying conditions of the exhaustion generated by it. Like the relatively loose genre called "the novel," which can accommodate many different structures and forms, including the "anti-novel," the biennial template does not dictate its content. The attempt to reuse a potentially successful formula—the biennial—does not have to be predictable or comforting, nor based in either market values or a surplus of theory. It can be reimagined.

The manifestations we are interested in here undermine the power relations outlined above through a deliberately wide social engagement. The "discursive" biennial, in theory, could circumvent the self-fulfilling ambitions of mutual power-brokering and circular leverage—the mutual back scratching that can be heard worldwide. Daniel Birnbaum's candid defense of established boundaries of art protocol, and the narrow understanding of "relevance" it reinforces, could be avoided by the "discursive" exhibition per se.[13] The new emphasis in these biennials also represents a shift in focus towards a deep and committed interest in local contexts. Not coincidentally, the biennials we have in mind—few of which we can discuss here—are not always included in the limited roster of the "grand tour" and often take place in locations in which the biennial fills a gap in the artistic community by becoming a genuine alternative, a platform for the dissemination of existing local practices and ideas that may not be discussed elsewhere.

So far, no single biennial has seemed capable of resolving all of the key issues raised by curators, artists, and art critics. Several biennials have elements that point to the possibilities for the future of the genre. This leads us to think about "knowledge production" rather than the style or nomenclature of "discursive biennials," "durational exhibitions," or parameter "turns." The biennial, however defined, has, in many ways, replaced the museum as a trope of interdisciplinary investigation, acting in much the way the museum did when the notion of postmodernism was introduced. Because museums act to reinforce culture, not to change it, postmodernism revealed that the museum was actually another institution of sameness, not difference. But, at that same moment, academics from many disciplines migrated to the museum as the site of multiple kinds of intellectual investigations, represented by the idea of a "field" as opposed to a discipline. We consider the biennial to be just this kind of heterotrophic field, and this is where our interest lies.

The discursive biennial signals a migration of the prerogative of knowledge production through art from the museum and the academy to the biennial. It is a process that has now started but may never conclude, and of course the museum and the academy will undoubtedly continue to wield their own forms of knowledge.[14] It is a process that involves theory, practice, and the inevitable gap between them. Therefore, it seems possible that this is an historical moment that, like the interrogation of the museum well over two decades ago, is not a result of exhaustion or of a fashionable claim for "turns" over other forms of curatorial or artistic engagement. Instead, it represents a real need to start to differentiate and designate how knowledge is now produced and reproduced in this expanding form in ways that are significantly distinct from the traditional institutional modes. Ivo Mesquita and Ana Paula Cohen's 2008 São Paulo Biennial in Brazil, an exhibition devoted to the thinking of exhibitions as such, is one example. Intended as a theoretical pause and a reconsideration of the biennial's original mission, this exhibition spoke to the very real historical need to understand what a biennial system is all about as a powerful alternative to the museum system that has been in place for over a hundred years.[15]

The shift towards education thus makes sense on a number of levels. If biennials are capable of creating "alternative experience," and therefore potential platforms for the advancement of contemporary art, they are thus powerful vehicles for the production of new knowledge. Again, we must return to the question of the audience for whom biennials are intended/organized. In places outside the established art centers, biennials are major points of access and exposure to international art for citizens or artists who do not have the economic means to travel or who do not enjoy the convenient exposure of the so-called centers. Thus, what might seem an almost intolerable repetition of "over-exposed" art to an informed audience, hungry for the new and novel, may be just what makes the exhibition productive and effective for a local audience elsewhere. Judging from the mixed response among local audiences to the 2008 São Paulo Biennial, the choice to reduce the quantity of art radically in order to leave room for reflection was probably only really appreciated by the already devoted art audience. There was a professional recognition of the difficult circumstances, including budget restraints and conventional politics, of this specific biennial, but local audience responses nonetheless reflected disappointment in not seeing art. Like many other biennials, this particular biennial suggests that the relation between knowledge for the public and knowledge for the cognoscenti is as tense as the frisson between local and global representations, or between local relevance and international visibility.

The provisional historical remedy to some critiques of the biennial has been "site-specificity," a two-fold solution to the issues of regional relevance on the one hand, and the "neutrality" of the white cube on the other. As Elena Filipovic has poignantly argued, the perpetuation of biennials of predictable "form"—the articulation of a particular kind of space and the ideology that underpins it—undermines "the vast differences in the issues such exhibitions are meant to illustrate, their relationships to their individual local contexts, [and] the works they present."[16] Seeming to respond to the criticism of the homogenizing white cube, biennials (for instance, in Liverpool and Istanbul, or in New Orleans) have commissioned new projects for nondesignated art spaces, using sites particular to the host city's or region's history, or tweaking and re-siting existing work to speak to the specific locale. Now, however, placing work outside the white cube in resonant spaces such as abandoned factories or community centers has the potential to become a superficial and undemanding solution to the "local issue." Miwon Kwon points out in her pioneering study on art and locational identity that the success of site-specific projects relies on a complex set of relations between "the distant poles of spatial experience described by Homi Bhaba." She clarifies that "only those cultural practices that have this relational sensibility can turn local encounters into long-term commitments."[17] By relational, we can infer the back and forth of authentic dialogue—of responsible commitment to site and context in artistic and curatorial practices.[18] In retrospect, the site-specificity movement, then, might be seen as a transitional stage to the "discursive," a pivot in the movement from art to audience.

CASE BY CASE

INSITE in San Diego/Tijuana is an example of a sustained practice that has deliberately tried to reconcile the simultaneous desire for internationalism and local engagement.[19] Since its inception, it has concentrated on artists and artworks that focus on border issues between the United States of America and Mexico. The biennial has ambitiously attempted to continuously investigate its own process, making adjustments in response to issues raised by previous editions. What made inSite_05 so singular is that its budget was spread out over two years to sustain a research process that culminated in new "interventions" in the public domain across two cities in two countries. The long-term agreements with the invited artists served to ensure that the projects had local relevance and encouraged a more genuine, even "ethical," engagement from outside artists with the political and social issues present at a local level. For this edition, artists were required to come for six-week residencies in four intervals—an introductory area visit, primary research, a proposal, and the execution of the resulting project/public presentation—culminating in a public phase of three months. Local artists were paid the same as visiting artists, and all were expected to partake in residency-related activities. In all aspects of the project, the emphasis was on *process* and *sustained dialogue*. Audiences were invited to survey the research, proposals, and processes of the biennial in a public presentation *before* the actual implementation of projects.[20]

InSite sets itself apart in its efforts to inhabit and negotiate the global and the local "without disempowering the local or diminishing the art," to use Lewis Bigg's cautionary words.[21] Its interest in sustained engagement is, however, also somewhat evident in other biennials. Documenta 10, curated by Catherine David, instigated worldwide discussion groups, films, and other events, a methodology to some extent followed in the next Documenta by Okwui Enwezor. Both followed on the example of Joseph Beuys's daily interventions in the name of the Free University and his durational projects, including tree planting at an earlier Documenta. If the number of biennials exploring the format as a platform for dialogue, discussion, and exchange—at least in principle—is a significant modification, there are clearly evolving movements in knowledge production, including a shift of focus to issues regarding the sustainability of local arts environments, dialogues among artists and practitioners from inside and out (for example through residencies), and exchanges of experiences through intense engagement with multiple tiers of audience members.

Another recurring thread is the effort to shift the focus away from the opening events, which are usually very exclusive, to an understanding of the exhibition as an evolving, more inclusive event—a program. The notion of the exhibition as an ongoing *process and prolonged engagement*, sometimes preceding and sometimes extending past the run of the exhibition, is also evident in biennials that place greater emphasis on relationships with artists, the process of artistic production, and the production of new audiences. The sixth Mercusol Biennial in Porto Alegre, Brazil, remains unique in its transformation of the exhibition into a "pedagogical experiment" about education and audience, for it produced a new model entirely.[22] The Mercusol Biennial is uncompromising in its emphasis on vast statewide educational initiatives, which are critically fundamental to its structure, content, and program.[23] The exhibition's teaching and learning programs both preceded the exhibition and continued after it ended, proactively producing engaged audiences of significant proportions. Another example of this kind of turn was the *Encuentro Internacional de Medellín* 07 (2007 International Encounter of Medellín) in Medellín, Colombia, organized and programmed by a team of curators from the region.[24] It too stressed local educational initiatives and explored the exhibition as an ongoing process with much less focus on the "grand" opening. According to curator Ana Paula Cohen, the biennial's weekly programming had a high local attendance rate, bringing in substantive numbers of people (up to 200) on weeknights.[25] Yet the exhibition received very little attention in the international press, partly, perhaps, because the word "biennial" was missing from its title. The Medellín exhibition further exemplifies how the current biennial knowledge depends on the circulation of ideas and information, and as a result draws primarily on biennials that have the infrastructure to print and distribute international publications and garner attention from international curators, critics, and media.

Biennials that take their cues from less spectacular exhibitions, and curators who are willing to risk shifting away from the spectacular event-based biennial toward more humble projects and less prestigious artists, will undoubtedly be part of this new shift. The concern for cultural sustainability shifts the attention from display to dialogue, and thus defiantly counters the "spectacle" condition that motivates impatient browsing and quick judgments, rather than reflective viewing and contextual understanding. The "durational" exhibition may also be one way to encourage return visits, which facilitate a more intense engagement with the exhibition and the individual works in it.

Already, several biennials have made publications or wide information distribution an integral part of the exhibition or created distinct discursive spaces or hubs for educational programming. *In Living Contact* (São Paulo), for example, produced several publications with text, images, and contributions by writers and artists that were distributed freely in São Paulo. In addition, the curators designated the ground floor of the main building as a public plaza for ongoing performance, programming, and contemplation. The fifth Berlin Biennial in 2008 invested considerable effort in creating a program with events every night for the run of the biennial, which benefited Berliners as well as visitors.[26] The program featured sixty-three nightly events—performances, lectures, film screenings, and workshops—throughout the city in cooperation with different institutions. The first (and only) edition of the U-TURN Quadrennial for Contemporary Art held in 2008 in Copenhagen also aimed for ambitious pre-programming. Entitled *Meta-Exhibition*, it began in the year leading up to the biennial, thereby creating local awareness about the upcoming biennial and benefiting from the presence of visiting artists and critics in advance.[27]

The United Arab Emirates' contribution to the 2009 Venice Biennial is also exemplary of a context-sensitive exhibition practice. Entitled *IT'S NOT YOU, IT'S ME* and curated by Tirdad Zolghadr, it concentrated on (in wall-text panels, the audio guide, and the catalogue) the full deconstruction of the exhibition itself by its participants by relating it to the term "pavilion," its origins in world's fairs, and some of the possible interpretations in advance of and after the experience. Just like at the 2009 Istanbul Biennial, where the WHW (What, How and for Whom)[28] collective of four curators showed their budget on public posters and unapologetically analyzed their choices in terms of the representation of countries, gender, age, and other data, the exhibitions we are advocating can be said to be striving for a high level of transparency, the kind you get with professional sports, where every bit of information—good or bad—is widely circulated and in the hands and minds of everyone from professional journalists to amateur enthusiasts.

Interestingly, the discursive exhibition also has exemplary models outside the biennial form in durational projects initiated by both curators and artists. Manifesta 6, itself nomadic, had the mandate to create an art school as an exhibition in Nicosia in Cyprus. Anton Vidokle's project entitled *Night School*—a year-long symposium focused on research and production—successfully emerged from that unsuccessful biennial and migrated, ironically, into the New Museum in New York in 2008. The project stands as an interesting case study of an experiment in self-organized collectivity within an institution that may prove useful as a model for components of future discursive biennials.[29]

Knowledge production, of course, happens on the levels of both discourse and practice. Closing the gap between text and object, and between theory and practice, seems pertinent to the process of rethinking the biennial. Reading a selection of twenty introductory essays from international biennial catalogues over the past nine years reveals that there has been a keen awareness of the issues inherent to biennials and an avowed interest in reconsidering their premises, or promises. However, attendance at the same biennials reveals a distinct disconnect between the rhetoric, or "art speak," used to express curatorial agendas and the actual visual and visceral experience of them. To name a few of the many possible examples, Prospect 1 2008 in New Orleans, U-TURN in Copenhagen, and Daniel Birnbaum's Venice Biennial are all examples of well-intended rhetoric—the conceptual framework and goals outlined in the press materials and catalogue—that was not fully reflected in the exhibition itself. The gap between rhetoric and what is actually on view is often due to the fact that written materials such as catalogues are generally planned, written, and published well ahead of the installation of the actual exhibition. In the worst-case scenario, they become little more than visual memory aids for visitors, or stand-ins for the experience of the real thing for those who could not attend. Even if a catalogue has substantial essays by insightful writers, there is a strong likelihood that their texts will not, or truly cannot, address the actual experience of the exhibition, and thus amount to little more than an incomplete archival record, or, quite often, an academic conceit. *The Manifesta Decade* and *[Situational] Public*, the latter documenting inSite_05 and published a year after the event ended, are among the very few examples of ambitious publications that push the conventional exhibition catalogue well beyond its usual function as an anticipatory promotional tool to become a form of critical pedagogy. The use of the publication as a serious platform for the reflection on the format may prove a small but important strategy in the shift under discussion here.

The gap between intention and outcome may be the issue most productively addressed by newer exhibition practices, particularly in relation to the global/local tension. Although almost all non-Western biennials conceptually position themselves as an alternative to the international circuit through some focus on the local, each one attempts to legitimate itself, to some degree, within contemporary art's global "system of validation and hierarchic differentiation," in Matei Bejenaru's words.[30] A calculated combination of local flair—a selling point of *particularity* for many biennials—and international scope seems to remain a prerequisite for having useful visibility in the international art world. This double-edged sword of differing conditions between local and global production, is, not coincidentally, the most pervasive biennial discontent, taken up by artists and curators alike. The focus on a repetitive roster of artists and curators cuts even deeper when juxtaposed with each biennial's local host city or region. Centrality and regionality as competing and antagonistic pressures seem to have been omnipresent in the postwar biennial structure. At the center of the debate is the question of whether "art," however it is defined, can be an instrument of universal exchange and values in opposition to the degree to which it is always local in some way. The desire to be both global and local is inherent to a large degree in the promise and promotion of each biennial. The question raised by the recent trend towards discursivity in exhibition practices, including in biennials, is whether it indicates a symptomatic crisis in the field, an exhaustion or "saturation" of the biennial genre, or a new maturity and renewed interest in the role of exhibitions in/towards the production of knowledge. Will "discursivity," however imprecisely defined, be able to produce genuine alternatives—economic, cultural, or philosophical—within the equally imprecisely defined genre known as the "biennial"?[31] Can the potential of discursivity become more than a form of professional validation and the "curatorialization of education"?[32] For it seems that discursive exhibitions might be seen as productive endeavors that embrace the responsibility to produce exhibitions as meaningful engagements within a specific context and location, to impact social and cultural infrastructure and diverse communities in positive ways.[33] Such curatorial projects, both real and hypothetical, would deliberately oppose the short-lived spectacular nature of most current biennials ("exhibitions as display") and intentionally counter the repetitive and superficial peripatetic involvement of the "tourist" curator, commissioner, and/or artist. Moreover, the potential of discursivity in exhibition-making might then become a form of critical inquiry into the operating conditions and processes of the art world and its value systems as a producer of new knowledge and meaning for contemporary art, and as a model of performative reform in the biennial genre.

Discursive exhibitions have genuine differences from other kinds of curatorial projects, but they should not be fetishized as radicalism or extreme difference for its own sake. If we see the "discursive biennial" as indicative of a new set of strategies for producing knowledge in the field, indeed as a pedagogical and intellectual opportunity, it is clear that there are hints, histories, programs, and engagements at work already. It is also clear that they are partial, or that, as in the case of the "white cube dilemma," there has not yet been enough critical analysis to determine the extent of new and useful models. The work to be done should include genuine attention to curatorial practices that fall outside the most-visited biennials, and seriously entertaining the idea of epistemic blind spots and the need for crucial distinctions pertaining to locality.[34] However, the conscious and responsible actions we have outlined here will hopefully alter the way we see biennials in the future and, most importantly, the way in which the art of today and tomorrow can continue to flourish productively under the incomplete signs of democracy and social justice, as well as those of aesthetics and pleasure. ●

NOTES

This essay is a revised version of a lecture given at the Bergen Biennial Conference, September 17–20, 2009.

1 The introduction of discursive exhibitions into the biennial field is paralleled by an increasing number of symposia and publications alongside, or even in the place of, the biennial itself, of which the Bergen Biennial Conference, where a version of this paper was delivered, is one. As it happens, the Bergen Biennial Conference occurred precisely the same weekend that "d Documenta," a conference subtitled "toward DOCUMENTA (13)," was held in Turin, Italy.

2 The term "durational" is borrowed from Paul O'Neill's lecture at the Bergen Biennial Conference, Bergen, September 17–20, 2009. O'Neill has elsewhere extensively discussed the notion of an epistemological turn in curatorial and artistic practices towards the discursive. See his essay in the present volume.

3 In principle and in structure, the biennial has been and continues to be seen as more flexible and thus more capable of responding to contemporary art than the majority of museums, which are comparatively slow-moving, impeded by bureaucratic structures, expensive infrastructures, and specific historical politics.

4 The term is used by Carolyn Christov-Bakargiev in an interview with Tracey Clement in *Artlink* (vol. 28, no. 1, http://www.artlink.com.au). Per Kvist analyzes the term as both a sign of disease and as a reference to the Stendhal Syndrome in his essay "Art and the Biennials," in idem, *Lokalisert / Localised* (Bergen, 2009), p. 149.

5 Valentina Sansone, "Hou Hanru: 2009 Lyon Biennial," *Flash Art* (July–September 2009), p. 36.

6 "Venice Biennial 2009 Guide," *The Art Newspaper,* no. 203 (June 2009), p. 3.

7 John Tomlinson, *Cultural Imperialism* (Baltimore and London, 1991), p. 175. In summary, Tomlinson writes: "Globalization may be distinguished from imperialism in that it is a far less coherent or culturally directed process. For all that it is ambiguous between economic and political senses, the idea of imperialism contains, at least, the notion of a purposeful project: the intended spread of a social system from one center of power across the globe. The idea of 'globalization' suggests interconnection and interdependency of all global areas which happens in a less purposeful way . . . More importantly, the effects of globalization are to weaken the cultural coherence of all individual nation-states, including the economically powerful ones—the 'imperialist powers' of a previous era."

8 Clifford Geertz, *The Interpretation of Culture* (New York, 1973).

9 Okwui Enwezor interviewed by Paul O'Neill, "Curating beyond the Canon," in Paul O'Neill (ed.), *Curating Subjects* (Amsterdam and London, 2007), p. 116.

10 Miwon Kwon, *One Place after Another: Site-Specific Art and Locational Identity* (Cambridge [MA], 2004), p. 166.

11 More recently, exhibitions such as *The Art of Participation: 1950 to Now* at the San Francisco Museum of Modern Art, California, in 2008 and *theanyspacewhatever* exhibition held at the Guggenheim Museum in New York, also in 2008, attest to attempts to capture the discursive "turn" in art practices and to historicize them.

12 Nicolas Bourriaud, *Relational Aesthetics* (Paris, 2002).

13 "Venice Biennial 2009 Guide," *The Art Newspaper,* no. 203 (June 2009), p. 3.

14 For example, the growing number of curators taking on jobs in MFA and curatorial programs will undoubtedly generate a parallel discourse.

15 The twenty-eighth São Paulo Biennial, *In Living Contact,* created "a range of exhibition and dissemination apparatuses to mediate contact between the audience and the production of knowledge in a collective event of such scope," which included turning the ground floor of the Biennial Pavilion into a public forum, leaving the second floor open and the architecture exposed, and presenting a library of the history of the biennial alongside the exhibition of works of art.

16 Elena Filipovic, "The Global White Cube," in Barbara Vanderlinden and Elena Filipovic (eds.), *The Manifesta Decade: Debates on Contemporary Art Exhibitions and Biennials in Post-Wall Europe* (Cambridge [MA], 2005), p. 79. This essay has also been reprinted in the present volume.

17 Kwon 2004 (see note 10), p. 166.

18 Site-specific sensitivity is also characteristic of the seminal curatorial work of Mary Jane Jacob in the nineties and, for instance, projects by France Morin.

19 InSite was initiated by Michael Krichman and Carmen Cuenca in 1992. The project is dedicated to the realization of bi-national collaborative arts partnerships between nonprofit and public institutions in the San Diego–Tijuana region. Operating through a unique collaborative structure that is based on the active participation of cultural and educational institutions in the U.S. and Mexico, inSite is focused on promoting artistic investigation and the activation of urban space.

20 Osvaldo Sanchez and Donna Conwell (eds.), *[Situational] Public: inSite_05 / Art Practices in the Public Domain San Diego-Tijuana* (Installation Gallery, 2006).

21 Lewis Biggs, "Foreword," in Paul Domela (ed.) *International 2004: 18 September–28 November, 2004* (Liverpool, 2004).

22 Sofía Hernández Chong Cuy, "Class Action," *Modern Painters* (March 2008).

23 Created in 1996, the Mercosul Visual Arts Biennial Foundation, based in Porto Alegre, the capital of Rio Grande do Sul, is a private, not-for-profit foundation dedicated to organizing the exhibition and events that comprise the Mercosul biennials. For the sixth edition in 2007, chief curator Gabriel Pérez-Barreiro intended to renew the event and consolidate the success of the five previous editions not only by changing the curatorship model but also by intensifying the process of internationalizing the show and activating an extensive education program.

24 *Encuentro Internacional Medellín 2007* was curated by Jaime Cerón, Ana Paula Cohen, José Ignacio Roca, and María Inés Rodríguez. The biennial's thematic focus was "hospitality in a physical, discursive, and political sense," and its program engaged multiple platforms or "Activation Zones," including exhibitions, television, and radio.

25 Authors' conversation with Ana Paula Cohen, October 2009.

NOTES

26 The fifth edition of the Berlin Biennial, which was founded in 1996 at the KW-Institute for Contemporary Art, was curated by Adam Szymczyk and Elena Filipovic.

27 U-TURN was the first international festival of contemporary art held in Denmark. It was curated by Charlotte Bagger Brandt, Solvej Helweg Ovesen, and Judith Schwarzbart, who won a competition initiated by the Danish Arts Council for the establishment of a festival for contemporary art in Denmark in 2006; see http://www.uturn-copenhagen.dk/UK/27061/Exhibition.

28 The Zagreb-based curatorial collective WHW consists of Ivet Curlin, Ana Devic, Natasa Ilic, and Sabina Sabolovic. The 2009 Istanbul Biennial was entitled *What Keeps Mankind Alive?* While we cannot account for the project in its totality here, the biennial's concept and programming clearly took on the problematic structure of the biennial itself. A "Red Thread" program (in Berlin and Istanbul) included a number of artists, cultural theorists, curators, architects, and urbanists who were gathered, to quote the curators, "in an effort to initiate discussions and a critical examination of the social, temporal, and spatial limitations of representative 'event' culture such as the contemporary art biennial. The loose structure of different formats stretched over time tried not to obsess about the blunt opportunism of urban promoters using art to put themselves on the world map. Instead, the programme joined with the already widespread discontent with a sort of art that is over-determined by a regime of public visibility and discussed the transformation of the productive status of artists in the context of a 'biennalization' of the art sphere." See http://www.iksv.org/bienal11/icsayfa_en.asp?cid=9&k1=footnotes&k2=re.

29 Taraneh Fazeli, "On Site: Class Consciousness: Taraneh Fazeli on Night School," *Artforum* (Summer 2009), pp. 129–32.

30 Matei Bejenaru (curator of Periferic 5), "The 'Periferic' Project: A New Beginning," http://www.periferic.org/periferic5_en.html.

31 We say "imprecisely defined" because this is a wildly fluctuating database dependent upon a lack of definition. In the 2009 issue of *Open,* a Dutch publication dedicated to the analysis of biennials, Thierry du Duve estimates the number of biennials to oscillate "between 80 and 140," while Irit Rogoff definitively states that "there are now 146 (known) biennale exhibitions around the world," although the texts of the publication are punctuated by maps of only 91 biennial locations. We take biennial to mean "recurring temporary international exhibitions," so as to include exhibitions such as inSite and the once-every-five-years Documenta.

32 Paul O'Neill "Introduction," and Mick Wilson, "Curatorial Moments and Discursive Turns," in O'Neill 2007 (see note 9). *Curating Subjects* is a very articulate synopsis of the field of discussion within the debate further explicated in the anthology that follows.

33 This is a reference to the idea of artistic engagement with place, following Claire Doherty's discussion of the new geographers, as "a notion of place as an intersection of social, economic, and political relations, rather than a bounded geographic location"; see O'Neill 2007 (see note 9), p. 103.

34 Sarat Maharaj used the term "epistemic blindness" in his contribution at the Bergen Biennial Conference, Bergen, September 17–20, 2009.

THE POLITICS OF A GLOBAL ART WORLD

THE GLOBAL ART WORLD, INC.: ON THE GLOBALIZATION OF CONTEMPORARY ART (2004)

Charlotte Bydler

INTRODUCTION[1]

ART has had a long-standing romance with cosmopolitanism and internationalism. The ideal cosmopolitan (from *cosmos,* the ordered totality of the universe, and *polites,* citizen) is distinguished by a universal cultural competence and love of art. The Fine Arts are a sort of monument to the cosmopolitan community, their cultural heritage. Cosmopolitan art culture expects global acclaim. At some point, *international contemporary art biennials* became spectacular arenas where internationalism and nationalism intersected. But is it justified to speak about contemporary art as a global phenomenon? Cultural and national borders both seemed to proliferate and fade away during the nineteen-nineties. Indeed, borders in themselves became a metaphor of contemporary cosmopolitan life in these circles.

> *Today as never before, all countries are experiencing the reality of life on the edge of a frontier—one result of the process of globalization. From one end of the Americas to the other, there are freely moving flows of trade and investment capital, social networks, mutual commitments that present risks and opportunities. Borders, the saying goes, both separate and unite. Yet the saying needs to be amended, since borders are gradually being erased, even as the concept of border broadens in meaning in the face of a new cultural reality.*[2]

International recognition could not be won at the price of lost sovereignty. The authenticity of and concern for national art culture were pitted against contemporary internationalism. In Gwangju, for example, matters were complicated by the association of modernity with military invasions and the rise of the U.S. in world politics and culture. Hence, modernization became equal to Westernization, and global postmodernism carried the Westernization of contemporary art that cultural modernism began one step further.[3] This called for an underlining of the national character within the international genre of the art biennial. According to Lee Yongwoo, curator of the first Gwangju Biennial:

> *The [G]wangju International Biennale has quite a different purpose compared to other biennales of the West. While the Venice Biennale was about tourism promotion and cultural nostalgia, drawing upon European sentiment and the grand tour of one hundred years ago, [G]wangju International Biennale is about probing Korea's modern history and treating its wounds.*[4]

A great number of biennial and other exhibition catalogues have called for attention in the name of *the globalization of contemporary art.* Art critics and international exhibition commissioners predicted how *globalization effects* would homogenize and (or) broaden participation in an integrated *global art world.*[5] In this context the *global* signifies not a world-culture inventory, but "a problem-based monocultural aesthetic agenda that elicits transnational engagement."[6] In contrast, postmodernist relativism and the internationally spectacular biennials promised to end the hegemony of the U.S. and western Europe in the contemporary arts.[7] Rival peer groups and art centers emerged in places like Havana, Istanbul, Johannesburg, Gwangju, and São Paulo. Wider knowledge about art traditions was suddenly in demand, with an expanded international art world judged by institutional art theory.[8]

1

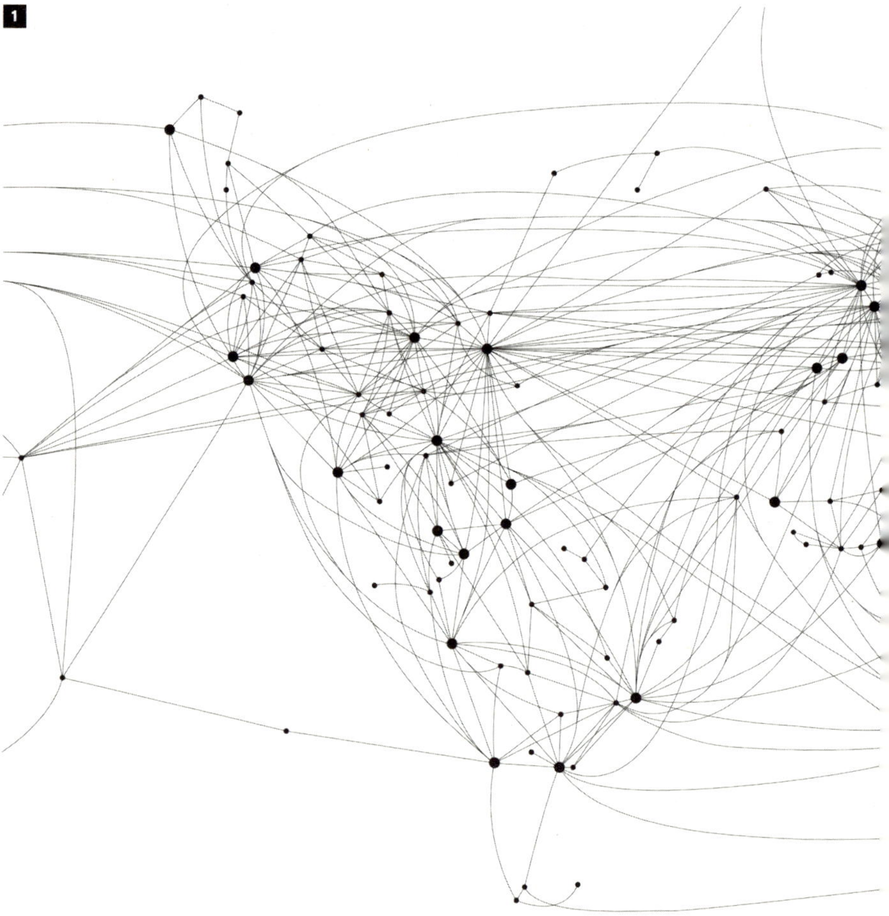

1 Langlands & Bell, *Air Routes of the World (Day)*, digital drawing and silk-screen ink on paper, 2001.

New chapters and areas in the history of art unfolded, as seminar organizers and art critics looked for names to interpret the new course of events. And a new generation of readers turned to the Canadian media theorist Marshall McLuhan's description of how telecommunications remodeled the world in the image of a "global village" with a new sense of community, a new mind-frame. Artists supported themselves for years in various residency programs and circulated among biennial shows as urban *nomad artists*. The question of location seemed hopelessly obsolete and even meaningless to artists who lived in one country, worked in a second, and exhibited in yet another, or who released their work instantly to electronic sites (fig. 1).[9]

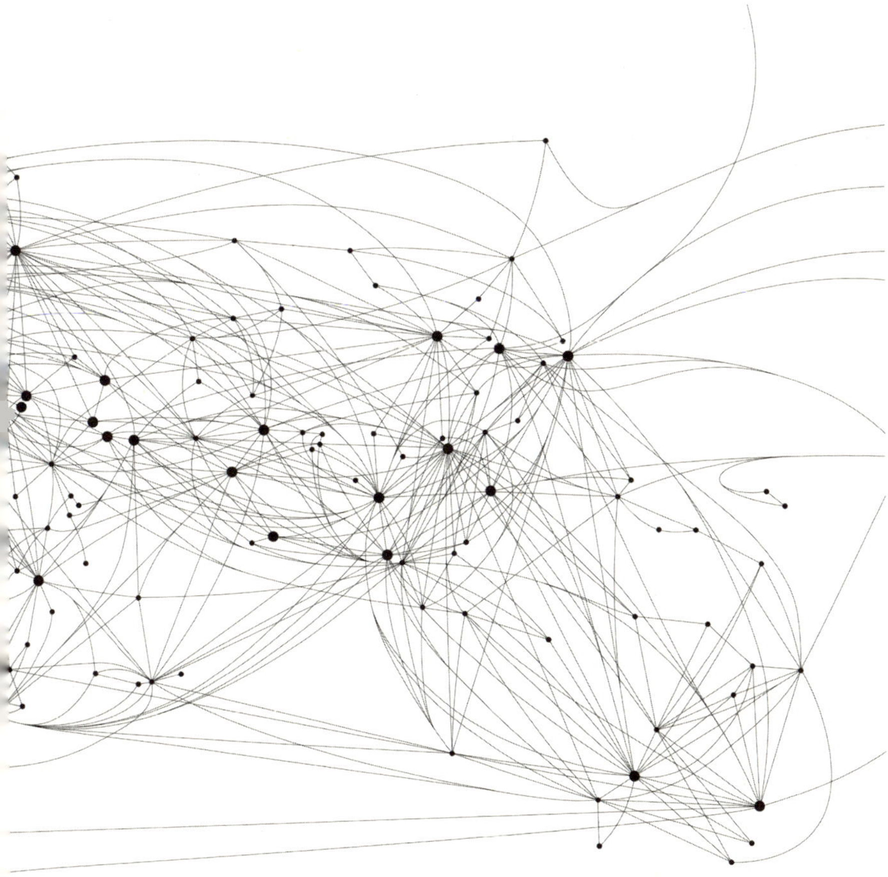

Some critics praised the multicultural competence of these cosmopolitans. But seen from another perspective, the globalization of contemporary art followed an old economic and technological pattern, whereby the circulation of art practices was tied to a global division of labor. Digital technology opened up new ways and places for the accumulation of wealth while it closed others. By the eighties, new financial centers and global cities emerged in some Southeast Asian countries. This, in turn, affected international cultural tourism and art markets. Strategic adaptation and coordination of time and space for the establishment of safe, reliable, and affordable infrastructure—both physical and for telecommunication—enabled geographically far-flung relations to be entertained with a minimum of time and effort. The available communications technologies shaped knowledge and references as much in art worlds as in any other professional community during the decade. This provided professionals with real-time updates on art trends around the world, but it also underpinned the separation of internationally connected cultural production from its local counterparts. From the networked horizon, the art world seemed like a McLuhan-style smooth and integrated global machine, where local events resounded globally and where all art was equally relevant and judged by similar standards. Had this been true, had there been such a world, artists would have worked anywhere on the planet.

To talk about the *globalization of contemporary art* suggests speaking about an inclusion, diffusion, or expansion of practices referred to as *art*. To index the main positions and their contradictions in this discussion, I must first state the obvious: the use of communications technologies surely brought *some* people and art worlds closer, but *globally* did not tie together all of the world from Qaanaaq, Greenland, to Banjul, Gambia, to Hobart, Tasmania. Nevertheless, intensified international relations in the "global village" brought intimations of a homogenized and hegemonic art history, the *expansion* of one community into other areas:

> *Indian, Chinese, and southeast Asian scholars write Western-style essays and books, adopt Western armatures for their arguments, hold exhibitions and colloquia, create departments and curricula, all in the Western manner. The discipline itself has been exported and has found new homes, and countries such as China and India are producing art histories compatible with Western ones.*[10]

Elsewhere, homogenization seemed to be the effect of a *contraction* of the contemporary art world (geographically or demographically to varying degrees). As observed in the national vindications of biennial rhetoric, still other tendencies pointed towards a *pluralization* of contemporary art and art history. The familiar heterogeneity in artistic practices provided a case in point, and professional specialization within the academic field clearly reveals the impossibility of mastering the globality of art practices. Indeed, it seemed like globalization had decentralized the art world and ended general (Western) art history's hegemony.

If the pluralization of artistic standards dissolved art historical hierarchies, are we still speaking about the same thing—one artistic practice? Short of a formula that captured art's universal, transhistorical essence, an art world-system with an anchoring in economically strong art institutions assumed responsibility for the arbitration of art status. Yet if globalization united local nodes in an art world-system, the ghost of artistic quality haunted the core art world. If anything qualified as art in the classificatory sense, there had to be a reason for why the records of art history were more discriminating.

This quick attempt to map positions within the global–local nexus is restricted to a corner of the contemporary art scene. Hopefully, something of the difficulty in making sense of the contradictory changes referred to as the globalization of contemporary art transpires. It is not only an issue of finding the best way to describe the globalization of the art world in terms of expansion, contraction, or diversification. If there is no reasonably consistent artistic practice and matching art concept, the art world cannot be a field or object of globalization. Thus, the definition of art becomes a problem of some dignity. What if there was always already art (special versions, subcultures, artistic archives, or whatever we call it) all over the world? Would the perceived globalization then be confined to a particular subculture with a particular sense of quality? In that case, judging by the examples in circulation, the globalization of contemporary art barely made it beyond contemporary art museums. Only slightly caricatured, the positions on the globalization of contemporary art are either that the art of the world is subjected to the quality arbitration of a few ("Western") institutions in Europe and the U.S., *or* that contemporary art is literally a free-for-all.

POINTS OF DEPARTURE

GLOBALIZATION must be studied diachronically, because it manifests itself as changes in practices and events, and even changes their totalization. By the nineteen-eighties, the visibility of globalization processes was greatly enhanced by electronic communications and economic deregulation. Globalization became a buzzword that could be applied in all areas of life. Economic Management, Social Sciences, Media and Communication Studies, Cultural Studies, Area Studies, and not least the avant-garde art world rapidly developed an expertise within their various fields.[11] Each area championed its own specialty, be it the global flow of the digital economy, personal identity games, network geographies, or activist counter-movements. In a basic and trivial sense, the term globalization describes a process whereby relations of mutual influence or dependence join particular events and phenomena around the world. The concept is part of the core vocabulary in many fields, not least of all in academia, even if authorization by dictionaries lags behind.[12]

Globalization describes a process of totalization or universalization in which totality is understood as meaning a worldwide or exhaustive enumeration and classification. However, any sense of a planetary inventory or exhaustive classification conflicts with the use of *globalization.* This is not to say that it is a mistake to talk about contemporary art as a globalized phenomenon. But *in what sense can we say that contemporary art has been globalized?*

To enable a discussion of what I am calling "the global art world," it is important to go into the concept of art as it is seen in academic discourse, to highlight its function in historicism. Definitions of "art status" conform to the archives (collections of art, libraries, academic capital) that are at hand in core communities. As the label suggests, institutional art theories (including historicist versions) represent a narrow and selective view of the totality of relevant artistic practices. Calling the art scene *global* or even *expanding* is begging the question "which art?" I have restricted my study to this *avant-garde art world-system,* a professional field that is centered on the international capitalist market. This means that I take *art* to be that which could be traded in this community's mainstream, and omit incompatible practices. All existing alternative art worlds (ethnic, indigenous, local, folk, outsider, graffiti, traditional, amateur, etc.) fall outside the scope of this investigation. For the same reason, the authorities and literature invoked here privilege a general history of art and what usually goes by the name of institutional art theory.

A timeline of the concept of art is problematic as a basis for investigations of globalization processes. In search of a totalizing entity, according to which a line could be drawn between the "before" and "after" of the globalization of (contemporary) art, I returned to the explosion of interest in the international in the avant-garde art world around the mid-eighties. The novelties included theoretical impulses from areas such as postcolonial studies or media and communication studies with a broader conceptualization of the international, and a geographically or demographically reformed canon of artists and authors. It looked like these important shifts concerned one particular totality—the *art world-system as a labor market.*

The art world-system as a labor market is not entirely coterminal with the capitalist economy. There is a gray zone of unpaid work that is remunerated with social capital within the professional field of contemporary art. The art field is not necessarily where the agents make their living—hence the avant-garde art world retains a certain autonomy. With a labor-market focus, investigations pay attention to cultural, political, and economic parameters.

To study globalization in the professional art world-system, I have looked at aspects of the contemporary avant-garde art world in biennial exhibitions and made connections with institutionalized art history. This labor market hinges on a consensus regarding taste and artistic value. It is hardly controversial to say that art practices are social phenomena; like other cultural phenomena, they form a focus for particular communities. This means that each community will embrace the more or less totalizing and distinct set of values and habits that characterize a culture in an anthropological sense. A community can be expected to have its own canon of artists and theoretical authorities, and its own views of artistic quality. Socialization in such an art world is equivalent to embracing (or at least understanding) its values.

To say that the art world that underpins the concept of art is constituted by language games is but half the truth—or a euphemism with its roots in a reluctance to speak about the art world-system in economic terms, as a marketplace inscribed in an international division of labor. One anchor in this intricate system is constituted by the prestigious museum collections that adhere closely to the norms of general art history. These collections slow down imagination, not to mention reform. A museum's identity is constituted by its collections; they define its area of expertise, and which curators and directors it can attract and recruit. Surely museums do more than display their collections, but even in temporary exhibitions and programming, even if in critical terms, interests and expertise are informed by the collections. Thus the collections are constantly actualized and valorized, precisely because they are considered worthy of critical reevaluation. It should be obvious why museum boards have not pursued their supposed desire to redesign their collections. It is not that they are conservative or part of a conservative art world. Imagine that a museum board actually decided to follow the recommendations of its critics and simply sold parts of its collections, replacing them with more neglected works. This would probably be the end of the private donation of art collections, which usually come with the expectation that the donation will be kept forever, if not also displayed. Museums cannot make overall shifts in collection policy without committing institutional suicide: knowledge of the particular art history that has been invested in collections, curators and directors (and their connections), supporters ("friends of the museum" associations and the like), and sponsors is very difficult to abolish using only the insights of the New Art History and Cultural Studies or their more recent offspring, Visual Culture Studies.

This institutional anchoring ties in with general art history, but also with the international freelance labor market. But at this point I think it is necessary to ponder a *negation* of my totalization—the globalization of the art world-system as conceived in this way. It could only be expected that, for example, international migration and projects like the European Union would further the internationalization of the cultural labor market, but by no means in all directions, and certainly not for everybody. Is it reasonable to talk about worldwide engagement? Labor-market globalization works in a virtual and conditioned manner—it creates a standing army of potential workers. In theory, could *place X* or *person X* be engaged for the benefit of the larger totality, the *labor market Y* (with multiple centers and subcategories that nevertheless refer to a common bank of practices, references, and financial resources)? It should be possible to answer this question with qualifications: either yes, under specific circumstances, or no.

The degree of global adaptability among freelance cultural workers as much as among scholars of art history or museum employees depends on the issue of an individual's habitus or disposition in favor of either reform or conservation. Ideally, everyone is eligible for any position in the field of the liberal art world-system. In practice, however, the field is discriminating. The parameters for attaching subject positions to individuals are described by interpellation. Judith Butler has outlined how material artifacts are employed in the interpellation of subjects through language.[13] Butler talks of an ongoing discursive interpellation into subjecthood that works by invoking a context that includes earlier instances of interpellations (rather than adopting Louis Althusser's view, whereby ideological interpellation is constituted in repeated rituals that make the subject meaningful). Interpellation empowers as well as limits the individual by making him or her dependent on interaction with external parties and a set record. The pretext of interpretation provides such an occasion, when someone is prompted to realize some of an artwork's virtual meanings. The artwork becomes a cue for the interpreter to be interpellated by discourse—to accept or reject positioning in the value-habit nexus of an art world-system.

THE BIENNIAL INDUSTRY

THE number of international art biennials surged rapidly in the eighties and nineties, as perceived by the art professionals within the Euro-American avant-garde. In fact, it would be more correct to say that the core of the art world-system became *acutely aware of a number of* biennials. This interest was highly selective, directed towards certain avant-garde art biennials. Given its focus, the core art world cannot be expected to know about all biennial projects that failed to be realized, ceased to exist (like the Paris Biennial, discontinued in 1985), or only took place once (like the Hamburg Peace Biennial of 1985).[14] Yet the partial core perspective of the art world-system is universalized.

The globalization of contemporary art has been said to end U.S. domination, and to mark a decentralization or pluralization of the post–World War II art world-system. With reference to the biennial examples above, I think this is a liberal utopia. The recent globalization processes in the avant-garde art world are of concern only in terms of the labor market, with its characteristic international labor division. The artists, curators, and critics have the inalienable right and freedom to submit their works in equal competition with the most prominent members of this marketplace.

René Block has suggested a biennial typology based on organization: (1) the Venice model, a grand world exhibition with national representation; (2) the Sydney model, representing smaller scale biennials organized around a curatorial theme, where invited artists depend on external financial support; (3) the Gwangju model, referring to biennials that select artists independent from represented countries; and finally (4) Manifesta, which represented a model for a shifting location as well as curatorial team.[15] I find it prudent to link layout and funding in the categorization. However, the characters of the biennials cited above have shifted over time, and have generally moved away from the national (or regional) representation found in World Expos. The Venice Biennial of today, for instance, is not that different from the Manifesta or Gwangju biennials. Nations pay for their citizens' participation, and curatorial responsibility is taken on by international freelancers. Importantly, Block's model biennials are selected from the part of the avant-garde art world that received the most European attention at the time. International biennials could equally well have been categorized according to the art world—for example, avant-garde biennials, biennials for new media art, or for paintings, prints, or sculpture.

I suggest another type of categorization. This alternative broader cultural categorization yields different type-models, dates, and locations. The biennials fall into three broad groups: (1) the capitalist-philanthropic enterprises initiated at the end of the nineteenth century up to the mid-twentieth century, several of which were initiated by strong-headed patrons (the Venice Biennial, the Carnegie International, and also the more recent São Paulo and Sydney biennials); (2) the events that originated in the post–World War II period, marked by bloc politic or (underdevelopmentalist) reaction against such alignment (Documenta, the postwar Venice Biennial, the Havana Biennial, Dak'Art, and the international biennials of graphic arts in Krakow, Ljubljana, and Buenos Aires); and (3) the flexible production- and event-oriented variety of the 1990s and 2000s (the Istanbul Biennial, Gwangju Biennial, Manifesta, and the Sharjah Biennial).

I hesitate, however, to ascribe an underlying meaning to each of the biennials, because they are rife with potential meanings. Therefore, each biennial cultivates its (protean) image through press material, catalogues, guided tours, posters, and pamphlets. The nineteenth-century philanthropists at the Great Exhibition of 1851, or the Carnegie International (since 1896), were partially driven by the noble wish to better the souls of workers, employees, and the general public. They arranged for the masses to see the exhibitions through subscription excursions, reduced entrance fees, published guides, and so on, to enhance their education. In a similar fashion, Documenta was charged with the rehabilitation of avant-garde art in post–World War II Germany. Visitors to the first Documenta were met by a wall of photographs of what was labeled "Primitive Art" from all over the world. The National Socialist

Party's aggressive dislike of stylized, nonfigurative modern art was countered by an installation that presumably demonstrated that this kind of art had *always already* existed. This strategy of the legitimation of modern art continued up through the third edition. The fourth through sixth editions chose another strategy for legitimacy: Bazon Bock's *Besucherschule* (Visitors' School).[16]

Through the biennial context itself, artistic practices are disembedded and then reembedded. With each new edition comes a fresh audience, for which the biennial organizers need to reinvent or repeat the history of the particular biennial. No memory of the preceding edition is stored with the audience, judging by the catalogue texts. The global-art-world audience cannot be expected to be capable of interpreting artistic production from all over the world. Spectacular art events obviously need to cultivate their audiences and teach them to read artworks. Hence, periodical exhibitions like Documenta and the Venice, Johannesburg, Manifesta, Taipei, Sydney, and Gwangju biennials provide guided tours and have extensive outreach programs.

The original Documenta strategy of juxtaposing *world art* and *avant-garde art* was echoed in *"Primitivism" in 20th Century Art* (New York, 1984), *Magiciens de la terre* (Paris, 1989), and *Plateau of Humankind* at the 2001 Venice Biennial. The latter have been seen as ham-fisted attempts to legitimize "world art" in avant-garde art institutions. But is it not the other way around? Wasn't it the curators who had to respond to a public that often finds the avant-garde hermetic and arrogant? There are large and loud pressure groups, and exhibition commissioners partly depend on public financial means. This audience could surely recognize *world art* as paradigmatic *museum items* that gave some credibility to the avant-garde as *art*.

NATIONAL REPRESENTATION AND GLOBAL ART IN GENERAL

THE art world's globalization has brought back questions of how representative the stars of the avant-garde art world are. Harald Szeemann's totalizing curatorial reform of the Documenta (1972), and later his and Achille Bonito Oliva's introduction of *Aperto* at the Venice Biennial (1980) were decisive steps towards an author-position in the avant-garde art world. In *Aperto*, a zeitgeist could be felt. The invitation procedure was professionalized—it was about global artistic value that had been purged of national interest. National pavilions suffered a parallel reduction in status, as part of an official nation-state promotion apparatus.

Even the slight knowledge of non-European art histories brought along by the numerous traveling artists, curators, and critics effectively questioned the legitimacy of the Occidental version of the art world—let alone the knowledge required by foreigners who entered the cultural labor market in Korea, Japan, or Brazil. Thus, it was not surprising that reviews of Documenta 10 and Documenta 11 thought that the choice of curators was meant to compensate for the disproportionate number of white males among curators and artists. In any case, the fiftieth Venice Biennial (2003) introduced a change: instead of acting as the sole curator of *Aperto,* Francesco Bonami enlisted eleven co-curators and made each responsible for one subsection. The explicit intention was to dispose of the outdated model of an omnipotent curator. The distributed curatorship resulted in visually coherent *Aperto* shows and a new size record. Yet the split between the national pavilion section and the subsections of *Aperto,* which wholly conformed to the art world mainstream, remained in place.

The constant assurance that the representation of nation-states (in or outside national pavilions) is a thing of the past should be enough to cause suspicion. The outraged complaints confuse the nation-state as the basis for national identity with an administrative element of the inter-state system. Globalization processes surely have exploded the idea that national borders delimit a single community. The nation-state system leaves little place for anything other than states as partners in international collaboration. The capacity to do something about the national representation per se, not only as symbolized by national pavilions in Venice, is thus less convincing. In fact, since support to artists follows national channels, curators have done what they could to ignore nation-state categories. In 1997, the Nordic pavilion included work by Mariko Mori and Mark Dion; in 2003, artists for the Dutch pavilion were also chosen on the basis of their importance to the Dutch art scene, irrespective of their passport nationality or place of birth, to mention just two cases.

National representation is not a thing of the past. On the contrary, access to the cultural economy of a core or at least semiperipheral country is crucial for an artist to be represented. Within the system of national representation, the invitation of an individual artist with a deviant passport may signify that national identity (or even the concept of the nation-state) no longer matters except in a metaphorical and (actually) utopian register. A poorer country without substantial institutions (galleries, museums, magazines, policy, and money) stands no chance of competing with heavyweights like Britain, the U.S., Germany, France, Japan, or South Korea. Without a significant presence on the art market, such countries are "simply not partners in the game."[17] National representation in pavilions is criticized for being outdated, but the art world looks favorably on entirely new biennials. National representation is accepted as a valid project when it moves up in scale. On this level, the performance of the host nation of a biennial can be rigorously analyzed even from a geopolitical standpoint, something that is avoided in connection with the analysis of artworks. The repeated denial of the significance of nation-state representation in the art world as something that only temporarily lingers, as a remnant of the past, is either wishful thinking or a smoke screen that permits business as usual. This is all too apparent to artists from the periphery.

THE SUBJECTS OF PERIPHERIES

BIENNIALS not only attract attention and a large audience, but also create contact interfaces that do not involve any permanent prestige institutions. Ideally, this constitutes a win-win situation, but as we have noted, biennials obliterate the connections between semiperipheries and peripheries. They promote a centralized structure, with communication extending outward like the spokes of a wheel. Career opportunities have made artists and critics desert their home countries. Even if they were unofficial ambassadors of their countries abroad, such migration means a cultural brain drain on the nation-state level within the periphery.

As the historian, curator, and critic Ahu Antmen has observed, the agenda and actual location of a biennial are closely linked in the semiperiphery. Many critics and reviewers complain about the political motives behind "the biennials that have been multiplying around the developing world for a generation."[18] This is not the problem, however. All biennials are situated geographically and politically, but not all biennials are situated for an external gaze. It seems to have been forgotten that both Manifesta and the Venice Biennial thematized the fall of the Berlin Wall and the subsequent dissolution of European nation-state borders. In Johannesburg, the

Truth Commission and issues of race, history, identity, and power were a substantial foil for the biennial, and in Gwangju a similar interpretative landscape involved the students' democratization movement, its suppression, and the subsequent political catharsis.[19] In addition to the situation in current politics, all of these biennials were organized for the core art-world audience. Hence, the curators needed to address the core–periphery situation, which the third Gwangju Biennial did through its promotion of Asianness in opposition to Occidentalism and the sixth Istanbul Biennial did by promoting fundamental heterogeneity and individualism that contrasted with art-world norms. This self-presentation for the eyes of a core art-world subject confirmed the hierarchy. And this peripheral perspective politicized the biennials.

However, even if contemporary art was being produced all around the world, there was still a clear line between artworks for the globalized art world and "folk art" or artworks produced by artists aimed at municipal, national, or regional levels. In 1989, Jean-Hubert Martin, then director of the Musée national d'art moderne, curated the exhibition *Magiciens de la terre.* The exhibition, shown in Paris at both the Centre Georges Pompidou and La Grande Halle, was heralded as "the first truly international exhibition of worldwide contemporary art"[20] and has a complex intertextual history. The idea emerged in discussions between Martin and the French artist Robert Filliou as a way of addressing the issue of a truly international art exchange, one that did not stop at the ping-pong game between artists from Western Europe and those from the U.S., one without hierarchies regarding "Western" and "non-Western" art. Martin, who was appointed director of the Paris Biennial in 1985, first planned to replace the biennial's traditional format (whereby participating nations' representatives selected the artists).[21] Instead, the result was a major international exhibition. In the case of *Magiciens de la terre,* and to some degree in that of the Venice Biennial's *Aperto,* curators researched local art worlds and transferred the artists they found to the global avant-garde. A curator would spotlight new talent in order to challenge the canon and brand the show.[22] The categories "local," "regional," and "global" are highly unstable, overlap, and have primarily served art historians and interpreters as a means of excusing (or explaining) the separation of art that circulated at very local or regional levels from the artworks and artists considered (at a certain point in time by certain institutions) to be part of the canon, that is, the universally—or globally—required knowledge.

REGIONAL ART WORLDS

SOME art-world communities expanded during the nineteen-nineties, but *international contemporary art* and *local contemporary art* remained separate art practices for different fora and audiences. Art worlds outside the urban network remained marginal in terms of globalization. The unity of the global art village was maintained at the price of the subordination of quirky, heterogeneous local art worlds, which were considered as being less enlightened and prestigious than their international counterparts. This did not deprive the local production of its "art" status, but its artistic quality was slighted as being less interesting, or even irrelevant.

Several cases could be cited to show that people at certain institutions in Europe and the U.S. have had a decisive influence on artistic practices and merit.[23] However, a glance at a few biennials demonstrates that there is no distinct Euro-American-influenced sender sphere, or its counterpart, an African-Asian-Latin American receiving sphere within the art world-system. It makes more sense to talk about core areas, semiperipheries, and peripheries (plus external parts) that do not necessarily follow nation-state boundaries. We can also read patterns of contact hierarchies in the art world-system from the cross-references to several biennial appearances in artists' *curriculum vitae.*

As a human practice, we can assume that art is global. In terms of relationships of knowledge or contact, art has been more or less widely distributed, even if exchange was confined to the elite subcultures of traders, griots, and aristocracies, and even if global qualities were restricted to the dissemination of artifacts and practices, with users having little chance to partake in the management of meaning. What stands out as the more interesting issue is the regional character of art. Regions are here defined by networks of cultural impact, which means that they overlap geographically.

The quest for a position on the roster of global art leads to a question of cultural authority. New York is the center of an avant-garde art region that covers the world, whereas Venice and Kassel are respectively centers of Europe and North America, Johannesburg is an African and Latin American center, Sydney is a center of a region that includes South and East Asia as well as New Zealand, São Paulo is a center of a region that includes North America as well as Latin America, and Havana is a center of an area that includes Africa, the Caribbean, Latin America, and Asia. In fact, although geographical proximity is important, it is not the only vital force in the formation of a region.

Biennials are important for international exposure, for tourism, and for both local and guest artists, and not least of all where there is weak state support for artists and institutions—a situation that surely creates a need for cultural festivals. Where the state budget does not allow for a national art museum, a biennial may be the next best thing.

GLOBALIZED INTERPRETATIONS

Art should be international in form and national in content.

Kim Levin, International Biennale and Cultural Regionalism Conference, Gwangju, 1994

ON the occasion of a pre-biennial conference in Gwangju in 1994, the U.S. art critic Kim Levin (a regular contributor to the *Village Voice* in New York) passed on a post-Soviet joke then making the rounds in the international avant-garde art world. Of course, the joke referred to the aesthetic dogma of Socialist Realism: national in form and socialist in content. The aesthetic ideal in Levin's travesty was just as uncompromising as Stalin's Doctrine of fifty years before—but even more internationalized and with a liberal leaning. It said that everything goes, as long as it can be consumed on the international market as having an exotic national character.

The globalization of art has often been ascribed to the advent of postmodernity, and more precisely the postmodern relativism that sustained democratization through the pluralization of the art scene. Avant-garde critics had treated the aesthetic ideal of modernist art (whatever that was) as an international or universal language. The same category of critics-turned-postmodernists looked upon modernist visual arts as being by definition ethnocentric. The U.S. critic Clement Greenberg, the preferred modernist enemy of the influential postmodernists connected with the U.S. journal *October*, allegedly approached a work of art with closed eyes. It was only when he was right in front of the artwork that he finally opened them for an entirely fresh and unbiased impression. This illustrated the ideal of the contextless aesthetic experience: if approached without inhibitions, good art would be recognized by anyone. Greenberg called the art he liked "avant-garde art" and the art that he disliked "kitsch," which meant that he drew a distinction for judging the two things by different standards (and dismissed one by the other's standard).[24] In opposition, postmodernist critics have foregrounded the coded and culture-specific nature of artistic practices and aesthetic experiences.

Seen from the far end of cultural relativism, all artworks need contextualization and interpretation—if not transcultural translation—in relation to each particular audience. Advocating a postmodern exhibition practice based on local criteria, Thomas McEvilley wrote in his catalogue essay for *Magiciens de la terre* (1989) that the worst thing is when (former) colonial powers exhibit ethnographic artifacts from the Third World recontextualized as art in accordance with modernist practice. This is paramount to forcing a foreign design and intentionality upon the objects and their creators, which represents a perpetual violation of the foreign culture ("une violation perpetuelle de l'integrité de la culture étrangère"). By implication, the creators were not aware of their own intentions; thus, the discriminating eyes of Western so-called connoisseurs were needed to see what the objects were really destined for.[25]

Which is the more global and relativist of the two positions? For one thing, the postmodernist protagonists of cultural relativism have accused Greenberg the Modernist of acting like the universalized yardstick of artistic value. However, the postmodernists then universalized the importance of a local critic like Greenberg by treating him as an icon of global modernism. Secondly, Greenberg's much criticized distinction between kitsch and avant-garde art implied a culturalization of artistic value. It enabled him to treat kitsch and avant-garde art as separate entities, separate value systems, and to dismiss that which he disliked as irrelevant to the category of art. But in fact, a postmodernist like McEvilley used a similar strategy to draw a line between global art and local art, or artifacts. Whereas the first is culturalized as a Western art concept, the latter is culturalized as a territorialized, contextualized, non-Western artistic practice. Both sets of culturalizations see the two art cultures as noncommunicating vessels, and both are against exhibiting artworks of different orders together. If this should in any case happen, the tendency is for reviewers and critics to assume that the standards of a Western art concept operate by default.[26] A postmodernist would probably not speak in terms of artistic quality, or say that local art is bad. Nevertheless, the result is the same as that of Greenberg's culturalization of value in kitsch: what I do not understand is irrelevant—I do not exhibit it, pay for it, or even look at it; I dismiss it.

Analogously, many biennials have culturalized the art concept and unpacked the globalization of art in different ways. Exhibition practices, texts, and even casual talk on the globalization of contemporary art have universalized particular art definitions, artistic practices, audiences, and art history. This shows that each biennial is situated within a region. Practices among artists, critics, and curators circulate in a decidedly regional fashion. Granted the limits of this exchange, the event horizon at institutions in the European and U.S. core avant-gardes nevertheless expanded. Around the nineteen-eighties, their outlook was internationalized to a degree that could be compared with the period prior to World War II and the Cold War.

Given this regional culturalization (that is, glocalization), avant-garde art concepts should not be allowed to carry too much weight, for they are constantly redefined. It may be, for example, that Asian countries had no avant-garde art concept to match gallery practices prior to the post–World War II era (and contact with Europe and the U.S.); indeed, neither did several European countries. The point is, however, that this is irrelevant since the avant-garde art market, not its art concept, determined positions in the art world-system for artists in peripheral areas in both Asia and Europe. Globalization does not diffuse a Western art concept; how could it, when the avant-garde market encourages a use of visual practices that break with art concepts globally?

A prerequisite for participation in this avant-garde is the infrastructure of artists' residencies, the freelancers, educational exchange programs, and the occasional recruitment of noncitizen curators or directors at prestigious art institutions. All of the above serve to constitute a globalized professional network. For this cultural labor market, I use *globalized* in the sense of globe-girdling. It is the arena of a large number of freelancing or project-employed curators, artists, assistants, cultural theorists, reviewers, and essay writers whose work makes up the art world-system. Tapping into the capitalist economy and the interstate system for everything from academic exchange to safe air transportation, for project employments, temporary exhibitions, and residencies of limited duration, the art world-system reaches every reasonably peaceful spot on the globe in some way. Cultural workers of all nationalities are welcome, provided that there is a budget. The host cannot make too much of a long-time economic commitment. This is a limitation on permanent positions at art institutions, if they are available to noncitizens on the cultural labor market.

APPROVAL AND DISAPPROVAL

Often, in the rash to go global, exhibition organizers seem to have overleaped the stage of tending directly to their own nation's artistic identity. Their global ambitions require an exhibition of artistic excellence that will instantly grab the art world's attention. In pur-

suit of this goal, biennial curators have tended to pick from the same list of critically favored international artists, creating uncomfortably similar shows, as with Johannesburg in 1995 . . . and São Paulo in 1994 . . . , from which their own society's history and needs had mostly been erased. (In the case of the Johannesburg Biennale, which suspended operations in 1998 when government support dried up, this strategy seems to have backfired.)[27]

Immediately after South Africa's first democratic elections in 1994, a biennial was set up in the important commercial center of Johannesburg. It was loosely modeled after the Venice Biennial, but added South African artists and assistant curators in the various national sections for convenient apprenticeship and networking. The second edition (1997), which was led by Okwui Enwezor, earned Johannesburg the name of one of the hottest spots on the globe within the avant-garde art world. Local critique, however, was devastating. Assessing local discontent with what was perceived as the star status of guest artists and curators, Clive Kellner claims that the "emphasis ultimately fell on representation and exposure," which were not equally distributed.[28]

The Johannesburg Biennial was discontinued after 1997, despite the international appeals that circulated on the Internet and other efforts to resurrect it. The São Paulo Biennial, in Brazil's busiest industrial city, was the object of a similar art-world rescue expedition. The twenty-fourth edition in 1998, which was curated by Paulo Herkenhoff, involved a team of over eighty curators and a gigantic outreach program, which made it into one of the largest contemporary art events ever. Unfortunately, this tour de force threw the biennial foundation into serious economical difficulties, and this in turn motivated a controversial reorganization.[29] The avant-garde art world started a new Internet appeal to save it. And in the spring of 2003 a similar appeal was made in support of Momentum, the Nordic biennial in Moss, Norway.

What does this ambivalence signify? The resentment among amateurs versus the enthusiasm of professionals on the local level, and the international professionals' criticism of international biennials versus their immediate support of a threatened biennial? Like a fraternizing wind, the biennial format spread through the art world-system in various idioms, from new media to globalization and postcolonial and Third World criticism. Somehow, avant-garde art turned into a popular spectacle, an event. Critics cautioned that biennials streamlined contemporary art into a globally homogeneous commodity, and reviewers who had the opportunity to see several international biennials complained that the same artists appeared everywhere.

The biennials brought the globalization of artistic practices to a broader audience of otherwise sporadic museum- or gallery-goers. This was surely a win-win situation both for the avant-garde and the administrators of public spaces and fiscal means. Similar to the Great Exhibition in London 1851, the biennials are a sort of *democratic* alibi for contemporary art. There is something for everybody. They attract attention, appeal to a large and mixed audience, and create contacts in nations that have no modern or contemporary art museums. They are a permanent success in many places. The fifty-third Venice Biennial opened in June 2009, the eleventh Havana Biennial followed later the same year, and Manifesta 7 was held in Italy in 2008. Biennials and other periodical exhibitions help to place a city, a region, or a nation "on the map." Guest artists, audiences, critics, and curators ensure international press exposure, fully booked flights, and crowded hotels and restaurants for the host city, region, or even country. The visiting international art world vitalizes the local economy as well as the local art life. This may be one reason for the support that the biennial format enjoys across the field, a support that spans the distance between local political representatives and the avant-garde art world.

However, the globalization of material practices does not imply that their meaning or related interpretations are also globalized. That is an unfounded tenet of historicism. A limited set of similarities between different cultures cannot be generalized in reference to the *entire* culture—just like people who use stone tools do not really provide insight into what life was during the Stone Age. In themselves, artifacts cannot reveal individual beliefs in much detail.[30] By analogy, similarities in artistic practices with far-flung geographical distribution do not reveal the causes behind their dissemination, or even say much about particular interpretations. Several (sub) cultures have a common touchstone—for instance, Jerusalem—yet remain distinguished by their ability to imbue focal icons with different meanings.

Theoretically, the dissemination of the biennial format around the world could follow from the material infrastructure of global capitalism *without* entailing cultural globalization. For the end result of a conceptual globalization, international biennials need the ubiquitous framework of international symposia, catalogue essay authors, and tour guides. Similar to what was seen within nineteenth-century world exhibitions, visitors encounter a "distinction between the exhibits themselves and the plan of the exhibition."[31] Catalogues, plans, talks, and signs are there to fill the gap. The historical archives (the actual artworks on display, the physical location of the exhibition, local pretexts, and political history) are pushed in certain directions by these words, these *con*-texts. They are counter-weights—more or less efficient, more or less controlled by the organizers—in anticipation of reviews and the general public's reaction. Without this framework of ongoing interrogations, the material would not be silent; it would be highly ambiguous.

It is clear that any method for interpreting biennials as well as artworks on display is a learned method. Even when formal education is offered, interpretations are in large part produced and circulated at a subcultural or regional level. Shared artistic values and interpretations presuppose a certain participation or group membership of people who share enough of a habitus to make up a community. Following Bourdieu, a habitus is, strictly speaking, a personal set of naturalized and half-unconscious predispositions, practices, and habits that are passed on through family life and other social events. It conditions the individual for participation in a field. The interpretative community that I am after here is closer to a discursive field, but it does not conform to the outline of a shared labor market. Hence, it is hard to imagine that an interpretation can have global distribution. Instead, I am looking for a *global distribution of value.*

INDIVIDUAL INVESTMENTS

IN the end, it seems like the avant-garde art world depended on core states that could manage infrastructure and funding demands. Even so, the fact that artists from peripheral and external areas could enter this art world has often been seen as "proof" of its autonomy regarding official nation-state policies. Even if this particular art world happened to sit firmly within the national-institutional infrastructure, individuals have shifted their positions by changing their country of residence or even their citizenship. The negotiation of an individual position at the intersection of the semiautonomous professional art world and a national cultural budget is paralleled by Immanuel Wallerstein's image of a malleable and expansive capitalist world-economy that is supported and regulated by the more static nation-states.[32] Both art worlds and the capitalist economy happily incorporate and digest contributions that seem useful from the outside or the peripheries.

In search of the globalization of globalization, thus, I turn to individual investments in the avant-garde art field. Positions in the art world-system involve the subject interpellation of artists, interpreters, and audiences. Parts of the historical archives (that is, all the documented examples, the artworks, exhibition venues, or historical pretexts that happen to be at hand) are there to be picked up and interrogated in any conceivable way. Hence, once information and communications technologies have provided salient local examples of globalization processes, they also acquire symbolical value. Colonialism and postcolonial trade routes may have brought forth a less fortunate telecommunications infrastructure, but a peripheral position is still a way to connect with the core, as I think was demonstrated by the seventh Havana Biennial (2000). Individuals can use a semiperipheral or even peripheral position, just as well as a core position, to relate to a core archive of historical monuments.

Either way, in the core there are opportunities for willing candidates to be involved in the processes of subject interpellation. Individuals in the (semi)periphery can transfer to a subject position at the core of a field through strategic interpellation and the use of historical archives. Paradigmatic artistic *oeuvres*, like that of Marcel Duchamp, are selected from museal collections, and theoretical (but just as material) knowledge is invoked from libraries and the faculty that constitute the capital of academia. Either way, the value system is confirmed. It is transferred, taught, and learned in a new context. Conceptions of globalization processes are themselves globalized through a series of subject interpellations.

THE END: RELATING THE INTERNATIONAL / INTERNATIONAL RELATIONS

AN interest in art historiography, in the guise of a critical mission, has provided a context for the investigation of the contemporary art scene. Current changes in the avant-garde art scene have called for critical shifts and revisions in art history, and academia has incorporated the international experience of students, faculty, and contemporary artists. The ongoing questioning of fundamental categories of art history, such as the concepts of *art* and *history*, and the material archives—and, of course, the possible intersections of these—reveals a long-lived discontent with traditional hierarchies of subjects and media. Yet, hitherto art history has to a large extent been unable to change the way introductory textbooks, canonical artworks, authors, and representative museum collections are composed. I locate the reason for this in the collections themselves, which form part of the cultural heritage, so to speak, of the national art culture with its infrastructure of institutions and funding. The international dissemination of this heritage, which is brought about by the institutional infrastructure that connects particular parts of the world, often along postcolonial lines, is another part of the resistance to change.

The globalization of contemporary art has been conceptualized in contradictory ways as a global art world in the process of either homogenization or diversification, either expansion or contraction. As geographical distances seemingly vanished with faster and intensified interaction within certain segments of the art world-system, the globalization of contemporary art was seen as turning the community of the art world into a "global village."

The experience of mutual understanding and shared artistic values has underpinned an image of expansion and homogenization of the art world-system on the model of a particular art world. This model was identified as a "Western art concept," more or less adapted from institutional art theory. However, proponents of institutional art theory have for some time also experienced changing expectations among audiences, critics, and artists. The widening cultural labor market supplies new historical examples and references to authoritative literature and artworks that were unfamiliar to the "Western art concept."

Clearly, the globalization of the avant-garde art world has not radically democratized it or made it more geographically inclusive. Whatever happened at the turn of the millennium after the opening of prestige biennials in Cuba, Korea, or Turkey, local centers did not replace the major art-world center, New York. An intricate legitimization process could be observed between aspirant and affiliated nodes within the globalizing art world. An area that was external to the art world-system would take a first step towards incorporation in establishing an upscale biennial (an exhibition, a museum, a studio program, or a department of art history). The aspirant, of course, needed to ascertain its social and political stability, as well as demonstrate its reliable infrastructure of services, electricity, and communications for the safety of goods and payment. In return, the core would turn an interested eye to the local scene, where it attracted local artists. If it was interesting to the career of artists, curators, and critics in the core, the newcomer was subjected to a larger, international division of labor. The authority of the core is confirmed by the subsequent peripheralization of local prestige institutions.

Biennials offer career opportunities where the international division of labor manifests itself as the art world's separation into "curated and curating nations," as the founder of the Havana Biennial, Gerardo Mosquera, has remarked. We have seen artists and curators circulate between biennials, which strengthens the claim that what we have is indeed one integrated market for their labor, one art world-system. Curators tend to start in the newcomer category of biennials and continue on to more established ones, or make the reverse course when they themselves carry enough institutional weight to give leverage to a semiperipheral biennial. In Wallerstein's terms, we could see the development of a core in the art world-system, surrounded by semiperipheries that aspire to a more prominent position. There is potential mobility: peripheries could be promoted to semiperipheries, and external areas could turn into art-world peripheries. When established critics and a sufficiently large audience found a biennial presentation convincing, it could be greeted as a peer/competitor.

I think of the parable of the blind men who were asked to describe an elephant from their respective positions at its trunk, tail, and stomach as a characterization of how the globalization of contemporary art is conceptualized. Each conceptualization image is a totalization based on a rather narrow selection of material. Each field, each technology, conceives of globalization in a slightly different manner than that mentioned before. The event scene that is described by the early new-media theorists and present-day utopianists was basically produced in this fashion. Unable to see beyond the connected nodes, what was most striking about the digital networks seems to have been the number of nodes and exotic languages. The blind spot of connectivity is located precisely where it did not reach. To a certain extent, biennials demonstrate similar differences in their perception of the whole and disagree over which totalizations are relevant in terms of globalization, postcolonial relations, and the "Three Worlds" model.

Globalization and historicism are thus intertwined subjects. The narrative efforts to describe relations in history become reality in the process of the description of the whole art world-system. The available narrative structures for the international also form the arenas for its realization. Those present at the exhibitions and colloquia are also represented as discourse. This situation in discourse theory often presents the category of the political in vague and oblique ways.

As much as we would like to think that we are free to speak to the academic world-system or art world-system, structural limits impede this freedom. Authors are distinguished by an ongoing interpellation into subject positions as authorities. They are called on to perform as they currently do, as catalogue essayists and academic authors, without any great possibility of recontextualization or intervention in each particular context. Each pretext in asking a particular keynote speaker to give a paper at a conference initiates an interpellation of the speakers. The contractors would, naturally, have some idea of what they can expect. This does not preclude the achievement of individual long-term goals within the context of a slightly deviant theme. The point is that achievements that arrive later, or in other arenas, may require authoritative and legitimizing merits from biennial catalogues and conferences as a stepping-stone. Nevertheless, as later events they are *invisible, absent* from the horizon of the cultural politics at hand.

The interpellation builds up a power field around the keynote speakers that is difficult to evaluate because its effects are delayed and displaced, and hence invisible. Indeed, it is rarely possible to point to a concrete individual achievement in the institutional sphere in general. Because of the rather structured academic legitimation process, a good performance demands a high degree of conformity. Once an institutional position is secured, however, the individual has more options to negotiate.

Most art historians would acknowledge that Art History was written based on Eurocentric premises. The problem is that it still is. Gerardo Mosquera was perplexed when a Texas exhibition of work by Luis Camnitzer, Alfredo Jaar, and Cildo Meireles that he described (in Spanish) as "bringing together three of the most important conceptual artists today" was translated to say that the show included "three of the most important artists *from Latin America,*" thereby disqualifying them from universal importance. As Mosquera has put it,

> *It is still considered normal to write about contemporary art [and about art of historical periods as well – author's comment] in explicit or implicit terms of universality, without taking into account not only non-Occidental art, but also that which remains outside the big circuits. Criticism too often takes as its basis the history of art as a teleological argument constructed from the Occident with global pretensions.*[33]

Similarly, as a mode of relating the international within international relations, *globalization* has a referential ambivalence between being world-embracing (planetary) and exhaustive. The artistic practices that are tied to international biennials are patently not about globalization in the planetary sense. They are examples of the regional distribution of cultural practices, in this case within the historical infrastructure of capitalism, and show how effectively a particularism—an exhaustive self-portrait—can become a universalized claim. Still, the use of "global" tends to vacillate between these two senses of the word. The generalized particular can be the innocent result of proper scholarly practice, selection processes, and a continuous editing of useless or insignificant fragments that are subsequently removed from the frame. These same pieces could otherwise have formed evidence of the inconclusive and nonplanetary nature of objects under study.

In this ambivalent fashion, globalization is globalized, and enters into the realm of subject formation. This works to the degree that people are interpellated into subject positions, which they also are whenever they exercise their critical capacity. The (post) colonial *enabling violation*, as Gayatri Chakravorty Spivak calls it, that is paramount to what I called historicism's little lie in the context of art history is couched in the knowledge that within the parameters of the mainstream there is space for a certain radical politics and interrogation. The parameters of the mainstream, however, include a disavowal of the consciousness of false prophets and less authoritative authorities, the ignorance couched in conventional knowledge, and the myopic focus on topics under current debate. The historiographical consequences are the canonization of a general art history *and its critique* by authors who are careful not to lose their focus on particular museum collections, or on investments in this representative knowledge. ●

NOTES

This essay is an abridged and revised version of the book: Charlotte Bydler, *The Global Art World, Inc.: On the Globalization of Contemporary Art* (Uppsala, 2004).

1 I am very grateful for all the work that this volume's editors, Elena Filipovic, Marieke van Hal, and Solveig Øvstebø, as well as Helene Lazaridis have done in composing this text out of excerpts from my doctoral thesis, *The Global Art World, Inc.: On the Globalization of Contemporary Art* (Uppsala, 2004). All merit is theirs, and I assume the responsibility for any mistakes that may appear.

2 Gerardo Estrada and Eloisa Haudenschild, "Forewords," *inSITE97: Private Time in Public Space*, exh. cat. San Diego/Tijuana, inSite, 1997.

3 Yongwoo Lee, "Remapping the Borders," in *Beyond the Borders: 1995 Kwangju Biennale, Volume 1: International Exhibition of Contemporary Art*, exh. cat. Gwangju Biennial, 1995, p. 23.

4 Ibid., p. 14.

5 Dorthe Abildgaard, "Global Expansion of the Art Scene," *Danish Contemporary Art Foundation Newsletter*, 2000–2001.

6 Emily Apter, "On Translation in a Global Market," *Public Culture* 13, no. 1 (2001), pp. 1–12.

7 Benjamin H. D. Buchloh, "The Whole Earth Show: An Interview with Jean-Hubert Martin by Benjamin H. D. Buchloh," *Art in America* (May 1989), p. 158.

8 "El final del siglo xx se caracterizó por la proliferación de espacios de circulación para el arte contemporáneo, el 'boom' de los museos, las biennales, las ferias, espacios alternativos, sitios virtuales son la muestra de una mediatización de la que no está exenta la curaduría de la exposicion es." See "Intercambio des experiences en el arte contemporáneo: Crónicas, controversias y puentes: Desplazamientos, proyectos, paseos," in the program of the Simposio Internacional sobre Teoría de Arte Contemporáneo, Patronato de arte contemporáneo, Mexico City, January 24–26, 2002, p. 7.

9 Renée Green, "No Easy Places: At This Moment in Vienna . . . ," *Public Culture* 13, no. 1 (2001), pp. 139–54.

10 James Elkins, *Stories of Art* (London and New York, 2002), p. 150.

11 Tim Griffin, "Global Tendencies: Globalism and the Large-Scale Exhibition," *Artforum* (November 2003), p. 153.

12 The term "globalisering" was introduced in the 1992 edition of the Swedish *Nationalencyklopedien*, but it is only used to refer to the field of human ecology; see *Nationalencyklopedien* (Malmö, 1992), p. 522.

13 Judith Butler, *Excitable Speech: A Politics of the Performative* (London and New York, 1997).

14 The 1985 Paris Biennial was a failure that attracted only 35,000 visitors and caused a deficit of several million francs. Thierry Raspail, "The Lyon Biennial," in Barbara Heinrich (ed.), *Das Lied von der Erde / The Song of the Earth*, exh. cat. Kassel, Museum Fridericianum, 2000, p. 33.

15 René Block, opening speech, Biennials in Dialogue Conference, Kassel, Documenta Halle, August 3–6, 2000, linked to the biennial exhibition *Das Lied von der Erde / The Song of the Earth* at Kassel's Museum Fridericianum. Among earlier biennial conferences, Block mentioned a more exclusive meeting staged in 1997 by the Rockefeller Foundation and Arts America in Bellagio, Italy. On that occasion, Okwui Enwezor talked about the upcoming second Johannesburg Biennial (1997), Paulo Herkenhoff described his plans for the 1998 São Paulo Biennial, and Madeleine Grynsztejn talked about the 1999 Pittsburgh Carnegie International. Also at the Kassel conference, Igor Zabel explained that Manifesta was planned to be independent of participant countries' individual capacity for fundraising and instead was to pool all resources, but in the year 2000 did not have sufficient funding and depended on various national resources; Zabel, panel statement, "What Our Village Needs Now . . . Biennial Localisation Factors," Biennials in Dialogue Conference, Kassel, Documenta Halle, August 3–6, 2000.

16 See Walter Grasskamp, "'Degenerate Art' and Documenta I: Modernism Ostracized and Disarmed," in Irit Rogoff (ed.), *Museum Culture: Histories, Discourses, Spectacles* (Minneapolis, 1994), pp. 163–94; and idem, "For Example, Documenta, or, How Is Art History Produced?" in Reesa Greenberg, Bruce W. Ferguson, and Sandy Nairne (eds.), *Thinking about Exhibitions* (London and New York, 1996), pp. 170–72.

17 Zsolt Petrányi, "Interview with Pawel Sosnowski," in *Monitor: Arsenale vs. Giardini: Little Warsaw in Venice*, exh. cat. Venice Biennial, Hungarian Pavilion, 2003. Sosnowski was the curator of the Polish Pavilion at the 2003 Venice Biennial.

18 Ahu Antmen, "Tree to a Bare Forest: A Story of the Istanbul Biennials," in exh. cat. Kassel 2000 (see note 14), pp. 15–23.

19 Ibid., p. 16.

20 Jean-Hubert Martin, quoted in Buchloh 1989 (see note 7), p. 211.

21 Ibid., p. 150.

22 Gerardo Mosquera remarked that the Havana Biennial had become sort of "a shop window for critics and curators from the centres" where they could engage in "a kind of 'scouting for third world' talent"; ibid., p. 15.

23 It was René Block's reputation as a curator that gave the Istanbul and Sydney biennials their breakthrough. To give another example, David Elliott, co-curator and jury member at the fifth Dak'Art Biennial (2000), reported that he suggested adjustments to the biennial director Rémy Sagna; Elliott, interview with the author, September 13, 2001.

24 Clement Greenberg, "The Avant-Garde and Kitsch" [1939], in Gillo Dorfles (ed.), *Kitsch: The World of Bad Taste* (New York, 1970), pp. 116–26.

25 "Les intégrer dans l'intentionalité d'un dessein étranger et faisant de même avec leur goût, représente.une violation perpetuelle de l'intégrité de la culture étrangère. Cela suppose que les créateurs ne comprenait pas les intentions contenues dans leurs propres objets, et qu'il fallait l'oeil soi-disant supérieur du connoisseur occidental pour leur expliquer à quoi leurs objets étaient réellement destines." Thomas McEvilley, "Ouverture du piège: L'exposition postmoderne et 'Magiciens de la terre,'" in Jean-Hubert Martin (ed.), *Magiciens de la terre*, exh. cat. Paris, Centre Georges Pompidou, 1989, p. 21.

26 See, for example, Mårten Arndtzén, "Kultursäkter: Aletheia – det fördoldas verklighet, Göteborgs konstmuseum; Sites of recurrence, Borås konstmuseum," *Expressen*, October 21, 2003.

27 Thomas McEvilley, "Report from Dakar: Towards a Creative Reversal (2000 Dakar Biennale of Contemporary African Art)," *Art in America* (January 2001).

28 Clive Kellner, "Notes on the Johannesburg Biennale," in exh. cat Kassel 2000 (see note 14), pp. 24–27.

29 The reform-minded international curatorial committee for the twenty-fifth São Paulo Biennial that was to occur in 2001 (Ivo Mesquita, Adriano Pedrosa, Barbara Vanderlinden, Cuauhtemoc Medina, Louise Neri, and Lilian Tone) intended to dispose of the working model of multiple national pavilion representation plus one Brazilian section. Instead they planned to divide the biennial into two sections: one exhibition of contemporary art and one historical exhibition. The contemporary section would have focussed on issues around art institutions, artistic practice, and social reality. However, the committee resigned and the biennial was postponed. See Abildgaard 2000–2001 (see note 5).

30 For a critique of ethnocentric historicism, see Claude Lévi-Strauss, *Race et histoire* [1952] (Paris, 1987).

31 Timothy Mitchell, "Orientalism and the Exhibitionary Order" [1989], in Donald Preziosi (ed.), *The Art of Art History: A Critical Anthology* (Oxford and New York, 1998), p. 462.

32 Immanuel Wallerstein, *The Modern World-System I: Capitalist Agriculture and the Origins of the European World-Economy in the Sixteenth Century* (New York and London, 1974); idem, *The Modern World-System II: Mercantilism and the Consolidation of the European World-Economy, 1600–1750* (New York and London, 1980); idem, *The Modern World-System III: The Second Era of Great Expansion of the Capitalist World-Economy, 1730–1840* (New York et al., 1989).

33 Mosquera, "Cocinando la identidad," in *Cocido y crudo*, exh. cat. Madrid, Museo Nacional Centro de Arte Reina, 1994.

ARRIVEDERCI, VENICE: THE THIRD WORLD BIENNIALS (1993)

Thomas McEvilley

THE Venice Biennial, founded in 1895, is the oldest and, along with Germany's Documenta series, the most influential of Europe's major recurring international exhibitions. Both those shows occur in formerly imperial nations and reflect a Eurocentric history, for they concentrate not just on Western art but on the art shown in the West's prominent commercial galleries. Now, however, as the colonial era fades, the biennial tradition has spread beyond the Western world. With the postmodern shift of emphasis from the previous centers to the previous margins, the idea that one's own city, wherever it may be, can act as an international hub has become widely available.

Recently a number of recurring, usually biennial, international survey exhibitions have appeared in non-Western, often previously colonized capitals. The spectrum of difference exhibited at these shows suggests varying relationships with the West: some artists identify with or at least acknowledge the Western tradition, some condemn it. At one extreme are non-Western biennials that are directly involved in the Western moment. The Sydney Biennials, for example, closely resemble the survey shows of Europe and the U.S.; though they do examine Australian artists, including aboriginal artists, they are primarily Euro-ethnic. (But then, Australia is basically a First World nation.) The São Paulo Biennial similarly explores the Western "cutting edge" while shifting emphasis somewhat toward Latin America. The work in these shows is often based in postmodernism, but the curators' residual sense of center emanates a continuing modernist aura.

Other shows are not merely non-Western geographically but take place within more distinctly non-Western cultures. Several have begun quite recently—1984 was a pivotal year. These exhibitions' inaccessibility to the vast majority of Western critics, and the truly daunting difficulty of getting information about them in the West (some of the biennials I discuss here I was unable to see, and I write on them from their catalogues, themselves hard to find), are part of their story, and part of their paradox. The institution of the international juried show may be a Western phenomenon, but the Third World biennials are sprouting with or without Western attention; clearly they have audiences and cultural functions of their own, quite independently of their resemblance to Western art practice. On the other hand, these exhibitions are often committed to the project of becoming "modern," or modernist in a classical sense. The New Delhi Triennials, the Cairo Biennials, and the Bantu Biennials (usually held in Libreville, Gabon), for example, largely eschew historical regional styles; there is little that looks "Egyptian" or "Islamic" in the Cairo shows, and little that looks "Indian" in New Delhi. There is an implication, rather, of a community of taste adjusted to Western tendencies of a couple of generations ago, when the West's idea of internationalism was still founded on an assumption of modernist universals. But if works in the indigenous traditions are not apt to be seen, neither are the Western modernist works that lie in the background: many of the works seem to be Third World embodiments of classical modernism, with admixtures of regional points of view. They resemble, for example, the so-called Shona African sculpture that traveled the U.S. last year, a smooth amalgam of modernist motifs from the heyday of Brancusi with a nod to the African styles that influenced him.

Again like classical modernism, much of the work—especially the sculpture—emphasizes craft in a way that postmodern Westerners tend to regard, somewhat arrogantly, as archaic. The Western viewer may have trouble with this art, for much of it looks like what we might see as kitsch modernism: "mushy abstract paintings with pyramids in them," as one American summarized the Cairo Biennial. Yet a great deal of this sort of work is now being produced around the world, and the ambitions of at least some of it could intrigue a postmodernist: a picture exhibited by Zairean artist Kamba Luesa at the second Bantu Biennial in 1987—a loosely allover field of mazelike abstraction coalescing here and there into hints of faces—is titled *Cultural Identity*. Perhaps the Western art world needs to find a way to understand this art's meanings and gradations. It's not as if European influence on non-Western traditions was ever a one-way transaction, and given postmodern practices of quotation and appropriation, the aesthetic processes at work in these exchanges, which are going on more all the time, should already be part of our vocabulary.

The oldest of the non-Western biennial-type shows are the New Delhi Triennials, begun in 1968. Their historical priority, among other traits, reflects the fact that many Indian artists and intellectuals have come to accept the legitimacy of a multicultural heritage, acknowledging their selfhood as simultaneously Hindu and Moslem, Asian and European, and are interested in forging a cooperation between East and West in which each incorporates elements of the other without losing its selfhood. There have been problems: instead of impaneling its jury locally, for example, the second Triennial, in 1971, reached out to an international jury including the European curator Pontus Hulten and the Mexican writer Octavio Paz, but the catalogue revealed in a small-print footnote that neither of these luminaries could attend the jury meeting "due to indisposition." Still, the Triennials have remained far more global in reach than their Western equivalents. The 1982 Triennial set delegations from Czechoslovakia, Iraq, Nepal, Bangladesh, Vietnam, Nigeria, Egypt, and Sri Lanka alongside those from France, Germany, and Britain. The United States sent just one artist, Vernon Fischer, whose postmodern takeoffs on the "Nancy" comic looked strangely out of place among the other works of Third World modernism.

A show that has striven to go beyond the influence of classical modernism is the Istanbul Biennial, begun in 1987 and curated in 1992 by Vasif Kortun under the influence of the *Magiciens de la terre* exhibition held at the Centre Pompidou, Paris, in 1989. Most of the art in Kortun's show was postmodern in type, and what modernist-style art there was looked decidedly out of place. The emphasis was on varieties of neo-Conceptual installation, a mode that seems to be becoming a global style for the time being. It may be that the genre's emphasis on iconographic coding gives it a linguistic function at the same time that it ends linguistic boundaries.

Outstanding pieces in Istanbul by artists who would be (and in some cases have been) at home in Venice or Kassel included Belgian artist Jan Fabre's installation of bathtubs and owl sculptures (*The Scheldt*, 1989), British artist Damien Hirst's claustrophobic office, and Polish artist Mariusz Kruk's furniture crucified by hardware. The Turkish artists represented were no less proficient: Gülsün Karamustafa's installation of wastebaskets stuffed with quilts and Hale Tenger's ranks of priapic midgets entitled *I Know People Like This*, both of 1992, were among the most striking and likable works.

In the catalogue, Kortun describes Istanbul not as a center but as a place "in the middle," "situated between North and South and [severing] Asia from Europe as a 'non-space.'" Yet the Biennial was generally oriented northward, with only Israel lying to the south. The special resource the show offered because of its location was the surprisingly strong presence of Central European nations. This might have been the first major international exhibition of which one could straight-facedly say "The Bulgarians stole the show." And indeed Nedko Solakov's two-room installation—which showed the Earth age of the universe winding down in a hilarious yet profound toilet-bowl intrusion from another world and time—seemed to be widely appreciated, as did the wooden machines of Lyuben Kostov, which constituted a comic drama of a man both applauded and eradicated. The primarily Westernizing nature of the Istanbul show may have reflected Turkey's desire to enter the European community. The setting, a former fez factory renovated by the well-known Italian architect Gae Aulenti, was telling: Turkey had outlawed the fez in 1925 as part of the Westernizing program of Kemal Atatürk. Here its place of manufacture was turned to a Westernizing use.

The United States Information Agency, which generally handles U.S. participation in biennial-type shows, asked Patricio Chavez of San Diego's Centro Cultural de la Raza to curate the American contribution. The result denounced the intervention in the Western hemisphere begun by Christopher Columbus—a popular theme in the quincentennial year of 1992—and featured installations by Amalia Mesa Bains, David Avalos, and others. These works might have seemed intelligent and visually dynamic in America, but I spoke to a number of non-Americans who saw them as parochial and self-absorbed—as failing to represent the cultural diversity of the U.S., let alone of the contemporary world. Yet here more than anywhere else in the exhibition, or in most others like it, was a straight-out rejection of Western values. Indeed a minor contretemps ensued when the USIA got cold feet and canceled the show, which was sent anyway through independently obtained funding.

The exhibition that has rejected Western values most thoroughly is the Havana Biennial. Once known explicitly as the "Third World Biennial," this show rarely showed First World artists: in its nine years of life, which covered a crucial period in postmodern art, it shifted from an emphasis on Latin America (along with some representation of Spain and Portugal) in 1984 toward a broader sense of Third World solidarity in 1991, when the third Havana Biennial included artists from Korea, the Philippines, India, Thailand, Egypt, and Sudan.

These exhibitions were based on, among other things, the premise that the world art system is "a system of apartheid."[1] Curator Gerardo Mosquera saw the centering of the Third World in its own culture as a part of a new global era: "If most of the world," he wrote, "aspires to new international orders in the economic and information realms, seemingly it would also be necessary to defend a new international order of art and culture."[2] This new international order was not supposed to reject Western culture entirely, yet was to transform it beyond recognition. "We, the Africans, the Asians, the Latin Americans," Mosquera wrote, "have to shape Western culture, as the 'barbarians' shaped Christianity. I am certain that the result will not resemble today's Western culture."[3] The Havana Biennials tended to emphasize Latin America's relationship with Africa more than with Europe or the U.S.; Mosquera, for example, has written on the elements of Bantu visual tradition in contemporary Cuban art.

Still, despite the Havana Biennial's premise of providing an alternative to Western modernism, much of the work displayed there echoed modernist abstraction and near abstraction. The Biennial's emphasis on photography may have reflected the Marxist ambience, with its technological and documentary emphasis.

The Bantu Biennial, or more properly the Biennale de l'Art Bantu Contemporain, is regional in tone, focusing on artists from southwestern Africa. Much of the work invokes modernist universals, but the Brancusi-like pieces of Angolan sculptor Afonso Massongui and others don't simply imitate modernism; on the contrary, they reflect an awareness that Brancusi drew his work in part from African models. Thus they promote an Afrocentric shift in emphasis: the true universals are to be found in African art, from which modernism stole. Works like those of Central African Republic painter Jean Tubind Mokouna are more explicitly political but no less hybrid, combining the theme of opposition to apartheid with the heritage of French Impressionism.

The Cairo Biennials are more Europe-oriented and use the English language in their catalogues. In 1984, their first year, all the prizes went to artists from the Arab world (from Egypt, Kuwait, Sudan, and Iraq), but by the third event, in 1988, the awards included Europeans as well. The fourth Biennial, in November 1992, showed art from 41 countries including various European nations, the U.S., and a few Far Eastern and Latin American nations, along with a heavy representation from the Arab world and Africa. By and large, however, countries like France and Germany did not send the same artists they generally send to Western shows such as Venice's, nor, for that matter, did India.

The Third World offerings were mostly modernist-style painting and sculpture: a Western viewer would quickly link Mohamed Hagra's white-marble *Labourers* (1992), say, to the tradition of Henry Moore and Barbara Hepworth. It's not in condescension but in recognition that the Western viewer connects such work with European models, yet it is altogether possible that the modernist influence has by now become local tradition, with Arab-world artists of a generation ago serving as the models for these contemporaries. Part of the point of this modernist-type work would seem to be a desire to present a façadelike impression of the visual mode of a "developed" culture. As in the New Delhi Triennials, one often has the sense here that the rest of the world is still trying to embrace the aesthetic values of Western modernism. The idea that modernist art grew partly from African sources doesn't seem to have found favor in Cairo.

As in Istanbul, the U.S. exhibit in Cairo, curated by Kathleen Goncharov, was the most confrontational in this Biennial: an installation by Fred Wilson called *Re: Claiming Egypt,* combining this artist's familiar museum interventionism with an Afrocentrism based on Cheik Anta Diop's and Martin Bernal's idea of ancient Egypt as a generator of Western culture, and with a more generalized critique of colonialist attitudes and their aftermath. Using some objects bought in the Cairo markets and others signifying contemporary African-American culture, Wilson constructed the scenario of a room in a colonial administrator's home. Western, Egyptian-influenced furniture stood amid vitrines filled with purchases from the bazaar, some of them souvenir copies of objects in Cairo's archaeological museum. On the floor large pots lay as if spilled, with tape recorders in them from which spoke a variety of French and English voices, saying things like "I want what you have, I want to figure it out, I want to get inside of it, I want to overpower it; it's not really yours, it belongs to the world." Meanwhile, from an Egyptian-style pot, a voice replied in Arabic, "It's mine, it's always been mine, I may not talk about it, I may not even think about it, but it's mine." Nearby, another voice said in African-American cadences, "They think we have no history, but though we have never met, we are you and you are us," asserting the unity of diasporic Africans and present-day Egyptians. A text in Arabic, on a traditional Egyptian gown lying on the floor, asked, "Is the West more interested in the past than in the present? Is it more threatened by the contemporary culture than by the ancient?" Other elements included T-shirts printed with Afrocentric slogans and the music videos of Queen Latifah and of Michael Jackson (as King Tut), and so on. Perhaps understandably, Wilson's work had Egyptian critics inquiring what school or movement he belonged to.

The Dakar Biennials, emerging in the city of both Diop and the great postcolonial filmmaker Ousmane Sembene, are more solidly black African. And if the main essay in the catalogue for the 1992 show is titled *Dak' Art 92: Les Promesses d'un rendez-vous international* (The promises of an international rendezvous), the organization that mounted the exhibition is called *The Dakar Festival for the Revival of the African Arts.* Still, the exhibition included work from Canada, Japan, Portugal, Sweden, Italy, Mexico, and elsewhere besides Africa and the African diaspora. The work was generally somewhat more current in terms of Western styles than that in the Bantu Biennials. Some of the modernist-style art, such as the beautiful paintings by Fode Camara and Iba N'Diaye, has been shown in New York. Bangladeshi Ahmed Shahabuddin's expertly executed canvases seemed derived in part from Francis Bacon.

Other works were primitivizing sculptures, like the Belgian artist Jephan de Viliers' mixed-media fetish, or the Cameroonian Pascal Kenfack's *Ancestral Presence*, a wood sculpture alluding to traditional African styles. A bridge between Africa and the West was provided here and there, as in the mediating works of Ouattara, Diagne Chanel, and others whose works refer both ways.

As in Istanbul, the USIA chose a minority curator for the American show—Corinne Jennings of New York's Kenkeleba Gallery. But the result addressed colonial issues very differently than the Istanbul or Cairo delegations. Jennings focused on the African-American tradition of abstract easel painting from the Harlem Renaissance, a tradition for the most part excluded from the art-historical record of white society. Yet the Harlem Renaissance was inspirational not only for other diaspora communities but for African culture too. Jennings's show of five artists ranged from Joe Overstreet, a Color Field and post-Color Field painter inspired as much by French Impressionism as by the Harlem Renaissance, to Leonardo Drew, a younger artist who has lately come to the attention of the white American art audience. In addition, the handsome and eloquent works of abstract painters Frank Bowling, Mildred Thompson, and Mary O'Neal took the ambiguous trip back to the island slave fortress of Gorée, on the Senegalese coast at Dakar.

This has had to be a selective survey. Other shows, both actual and planned, could be mentioned, such as the first Asia-Pacific Triennial of South Brisbane. Writing from New York, without having personally visited all the exhibitions under discussion, I'm sure my information in this article is in some cases out of date and my catalogue-based reporting in need of fleshing out. Geographically and chronologically widespread, the Third World biennials are simply impossible for most critics to watch closely enough fully to understand their differences and commonalties of purpose.

Still, as multiplying sites of intercultural communication, and as instances of changing global relations, are these biennials signs of the developing postcolonial world family? The idea of such a family has been found in both East and West since ancient times. The Cynics taught that all human societies formed a vast culture, the world community or *cosmopolis*.[4] Zeno the Stoic, in his *Republic*, called for a world government based on brotherly love. "The world is the mother of us all," wrote Seneca in the first century AD. In south India a Tamil poet of the first or second century AD echoed the sentiment: "Every country is my country and every person is my kinsman."[5] (The downside of this idea, of course, is the fact that the family can be an inwardly torn and hostile community.)

Like the family drama, the postcolonial situation is a play of deep and obscure shiftings of identity. The process of postcolonial readjustment is going on; no doubt it includes covert power strategies and identity appropriations, but previously colonized peoples and cultures are constructing their own places to stand and their own networks of relationships. And art, which both embodies tradition and allows direct intervention in it, is a fit medium for the search. As different cultures present their images to one another in these more or less open exchanges, the forces that shape the world are laid out in diagrammatic clarity only to shift as they both incorporate and resist one another. Out of the tumult of images, perhaps a new vision will be born. ●

NOTES

Previously published in: *Artforum* (November 1993), pp. 114–16.

1 Gerardo Mosquera, "Speakeasy," *New Art Examiner* 17, no. 1 (November 1989), p. 13.

2 Ibid.

3 Ibid.

4 See, for example, Diogenes Laertius VI.22.

5 Quoted in X. S. Thani-Nayagam, "Indian Thought and Roman Stoicism," *Tamil Culture* 10, no. 3 (1963), p. 17.

THE MARCO POLO SYNDROME: SOME PROBLEMS AROUND ART AND EUROCENTRISM (1992)

Gerardo Mosquera

THE second Havana Biennial, held in 1986, included an installation by the Cuban artist Flavio Garciandía entitled *El síndrome de Marco Polo* (fig. 1). Various ambiguous images depicted the adventures of a popular character from the comics—a captain in the wars of independence in the nineteenth century and a symbol of Cubanness—during and after a trip to China. The work, drawing on forms of Orientalist kitsch, humorously questioned the problems of intercultural communication. The character, like Marco Polo, was a pioneer in the experience of understanding the Other, but his chances of bridging two cultures were lost through the suspicion provoked by both sides, especially from his.

We had to wait until the end of the millennium to discover that we were suffering from the Marco Polo Syndrome. What is monstrous about this syndrome is that it perceives whatever is different as the carrier of life-threatening viruses rather than nutritional elements. And although it does not scare us as much as another prevalent syndrome, it has brought a lot of death to culture. Only now has an understanding of cultural pluralism and the usefulness of dialogue begun to spread to such an extent that the intercultural problematic has become a major issue.

The possibility of a more diversified consciousness has been opened up, while the question of ethnicity and nationality fills the new maps with many colors. Dominant Eurocentrism—the main symptom of the disease—is undergoing a critical treatment increasingly more effective in its power of persuasion. All these mutations have targeted art, presenting it with urgent and very complicated problems. Only some of them will be touched upon here.

The notion of Eurocentrism is very recent. In anthropology we find an acknowledgment of ethnocentrism in the eighteenth century,[1] and a consolidation of the idea of cultural relativism by Boas before the end of the nineteenth century. But, until recently, this idea had not significantly infiltrated the studies and interpretations of art and literature, centered as they were in criteria of values linked to the myth of the "universal." The discourses called postmodern, with their interest in alterity, have gradually introduced a more relativist attitude to the scene. A new consciousness of ethnicity is taking shape as a result of several contemporary processes, among them decolonization, the greater space gained by the Third World in the international arena, the influence of ethnic groups from the margins in the great northern cities, and the increase of information and improved facilities in travel and communication.

Postmodernism itself, as Geeta Kapur suggests, could be regarded as a consequence and not as a description of a "realigned universe" through the praxis of societies previously completely marginalized.[2]

Eurocentrism is different from ethnocentrism. It refers not only to the ethnocentrism exercised by a specific culture but also to the often forgotten fact that the worldwide hegemony of that culture has imposed its ethnocentrism as a universal value, and has persuaded us of it for a long time.[3]

Here we leave the rather aseptic field of cultural relativism to come up against social problems and issues of power. The fact is that, from the Industrial Revolution, the global expansion of capitalism began to involve the whole world in an economic process which had Europe as its center, and which, from then on, determined the course of the planet. Western metaculture established itself through colonization, domination, and even the need to articulate this in order to confront the new situation within itself. Even so, Amílcar Cabral went so far as to say that imperialist domination "was not only a negative reality," and that "it gave new worlds to the world."[4] Modernity, full of good intentions, contributed not a little to this planetary cultural revolution, although Adorno, Horkheimer, and Huyssen have connected its negative aspect with imperialism.

Ethnocentrism always suggests the naive vanity of a villager who, as José Martí said, assumes that "the whole world is his village," believing everything originated there even if it had been imposed on him through conquest. Eurocentrism is the only ethnocentrism universalized through actual worldwide domination by a metaculture, and based on a traumatic transformation of the world through economic, social, and political processes centered in one small part of it. As a result, many elements of this metaculture cease to be "ethnic" and become internationalized as intrinsic components of a world shaped by Western development. But if these components are irrefutable, so should be the need to end the lack of focus, limitation, boredom, and injustice of planning the world like a one-way street.

The very fact of the rise of the idea of Eurocentrism demonstrates an awareness of the monocultural trap in which we have all found ourselves prisoners. I say "all" because Eurocentrism affects not only non-Western cultures but the West itself, given the widespread impoverishment of perspective inherent to any monism. The tragedy is that the notion of Eurocentrism is also *made in the West,* even though, as

Desiderio Navarro has pointed out, it is starting to take shape, especially in Eastern Europe, at those peripheries exposed to closer contact with non-Western countries.[5] Colonialism brought about a split whereby non-Western countries took on board the problems of their own cultures in the sphere of traditions isolated from the contemporary scene at the same time as they adopted those of the West, without making a connection capable of transforming both of them to the benefit of their own interests and values in the existing global situation. This has started to change. Roughly, three moments can be summarized: first, the cultures that we currently call traditional were "arrested" by Western expansion, which carried forward, according to its point of view, the great centrifugal development of art and science from the eighteenth century, generalizing it as "universal"; second, the realization by one faction of thought in the Western world of the absurdity of this situation ("Not a single Ibn in the index to *Literary Theory!*" René Etiemble eloquently exclaimed, thereby disqualifying the classical work of Wellek and Waren); and third, anti-Eurocentrism from non-Western positions has begun to be systematized.

This does not mean a return to a past prior to Western globalization, but the construction of a contemporary culture—one capable of acting in today's reality—from a plurality of perspectives. This development is a matter of some urgency, since we are running the risk that the West, apart from anything else, may also give the Third World a philosophy of intercultural exchange and a critique of Eurocentrism. Such a self-critique, despite its good intentions and its indisputable value, would perpetuate the distortion produced by its single perspective and existing circuits of power.

Postmodern interest in the Other has opened some space in the "high art" circuits for vernacular and non-Western cultures. But it has introduced a new thirst for exoticism, the carrier of either a passive or a second-class Eurocentrism which, instead of universalizing its paradigms, conditions certain cultural productions from the periphery according to paradigms that are expected of it for consumption by the centers. Many artists, critics, and Latin American curators seem to be quite willing to become "othered" for the West.

The problematic of Eurocentrism and the relations among different cultures is particularly complex in the contemporary visual arts, where the Marco Polo Syndrome embodies a double-edged sword. Art, in today's conception of a self-sufficient activity based on aesthetics, is also a product of Western culture exported to others. Its full definition is also very recent, no older than the end of the eighteenth century. The aesthetic tradition of other cultures, like that of the West in other periods, was a different kind of production, determined by religious, representational, and commemorative functions, and so on. Today's art in these cultures is not the result of an evolution of traditional aesthetics: its very concept was received from the West through colonialism.

This generates contradictions and brings the evils of dependency on and mimicry of the centers. But it forms part of the postcolonial challenge, because our cultures should not lock themselves in isolating traditions if they want to take part in today's dynamic and offer solutions to their own problems. Instead, what should be done is to make traditions work within the new epoch. The problem is not preserving them but vigorously adapting them. The question is how we may also *make* contemporary art from our own values, sensitivities, and interests. The de-Eurocentralization in art is not about returning to purity, but about adopting postcolonial "impurity" through which we might free ourselves and express our own thought.

A paradigmatic case of these complexities can be seen in the Cuban artist José Bedia (fig. 2). White and blue-eyed, this artist of popular origin practices the *palo monte,* an Afro-Cuban religious and cultural complex of Kongo origin. A graduate and ex-professor of the Instituto Superior de Arte de La Habana, Bedia is a sophisticated, well-informed Western artist with a wide range of resources at his command. But his conceptually oriented work, in its content rather than in its language, is mostly based on the cosmology of the Kongo still alive in Cuba, a result of his interest in a contemporary reflection on the problems of the human being derived from the Kongo's interpretation of the world. His work intelligently takes advantage of openings, resources, and sensitivities from current art of the centers, to confront us with a different vision. This syncretism also occurs in his technique, effortlessly integrating technological, natural, and cultural elements, drawing and photography, and ritual and mass-cultural objects, all within the sobriety of an analytic discourse. He also appropriates "primitive" techniques, but not in order to reproduce their programs: he creates elements with them that articulate his personal discourse and iconography. Bedia is making Western culture from non-Western sources, and therefore shifting it towards a de-Europeanization of contemporary culture. But, simultaneously, we could say that he is making postmodern Kongo culture. Besides which, he opens himself up to so-called primitive cultures in what he has called a voluntary transculturalization in reverse: from his "high art" education to a "primitive" one.[6]

Although this is an intellectual process, it is also interiorized in the artist, given the mestizo character of his own cultural background.

The Marco Polo Syndrome is a complex disease that often disguises its symptoms. The struggle against Eurocentrism should not burden art with a myth of authenticity that, paradoxically, may add to the discrimination that Third World visual art suffers on the international circuits. This myth precludes its appreciation as a living response to contradictions and postcolonial hybridities, and demands instead an "originality" defined according to tradition and old cultures corresponding to a situation long since passed. More plausible is to analyze how current art in a given country or region satisfies the aesthetic, cultural, social, and communicative demands of the community from and for which it is made. Its response is mostly mixed, relational, appropriative—anyway, "inauthentic," and therefore more adequate to face today's reality.

One of the great Eurocentric prejudices in the critique and history of art is the complete undervaluing of this production as "derivative" of the West. Third World artists are constantly asked to display their identity, to be *fantastic*, to look like no one else or to look like Frida... The relatively high prices achieved by Latin American art at the great auctions have been assigned to painters who satisfy the expectations of a more or less stereotyped Latin-Americanicity, able to fulfill the new demand for exoticism at the centers. As a consequence, Rivera is valued well above Orozco, Remedios Varo more than Torres García, and Botero considerably more than Reverón.[7] In other cases, all contemporary practice is discredited as spurious. Witness the opinion of an eminent Africanist: "Authentic African art is that produced by a traditional artist for traditional purposes and according to traditional forms."[8]

In this view, Africa is tradition, not the present. An anti-Eurocentrism like this freezes all African cultures, relegating them to a museum, without understanding that they are living organisms that need to respond actively to the reality of their time. If we have to fight relentlessly against colonialism, which castrates much contemporary art from the Third World, we should not do it through nostalgia for the mask and the pyramid.

Extreme relativism constitutes another danger. It is said that a village may be ignorant of what happens in the neighboring village, but knows what happens in New York. Anyone who has ever traveled through Africa knows that it is often easier to go from one country to the next via Europe. One of the worst problems of the southern hemisphere is its lack of internal integration and horizontal communication, in contrast with its vertical—and subaltern—connection with the North. The cultures of the South, so diverse, confront common problems derived from the postcolonial situation, and this has determined structural similarities in the mosaic. "Speaking about the Third World and wrapping up in the same package Colombia, India, and Turkey"[9] is as rhetorical as ignoring what unites, or might unite, them in their confrontation with hegemonic power, even if it is just poverty.[10] These cultures urgently need to know and think of each other, to exchange experiences, to embark on common projects. A radical conception of relativism should not exacerbate their isolation, separating them from our efforts to approach the Other and learn from him or her (even about things we don't like, as Venturi would say). If postmodernity places otherness in the foreground, it does so through a process of infinite differentiation which eliminates even the necessity of choice.[11] The strategy of the dominated moves towards integration through what unites them, and activates their difference "in the face of international postmodern dominance."[12] South–South "Robinsonism" benefits only the centers by entrenching North–South verticalism. If the translation of one culture into another in all its nuances is impossible, this should not preclude their capacity for mutual closeness, enrichment, and solidarity. Jorge Luis Borges said that Quixote is still winning battles against his translators.[13]

The myth of universal value in art, and the establishment of a hierarchy of works based in their "universality," is one of the heritages of Eurocentrism that continue to survive, despite our becoming less naive with respect to the "universal," which has so frequently been a disguise for the "Western." But this should not disable our reception of artwork beyond the culture that made it; even if that response is "incorrect,"[14] it may still generate new meanings. Art is very linked to cultural specificity but possesses a polysemic ambiguity open to very diverse readings. We live in a "great time of hybrids," as a Mexican rock star once sang,[15] that offers an unconventional challenge by reinterpreting instead of rejecting dependency on the great circuits. In contemporary experience, contextualization, recycling, appropriation, and re-semanticization gain more and more power as a consequence of increased interaction among cultures.

The critique of Eurocentrism forms part of a new awareness of the ethnic, the consolidation of which would sense, for the first time, the possibility of a global dialogue among cultures capable of facilitating a cure for the syndrome. However, in the visual arts, little progress has been made in this direction. Contemporary, nontraditional

1

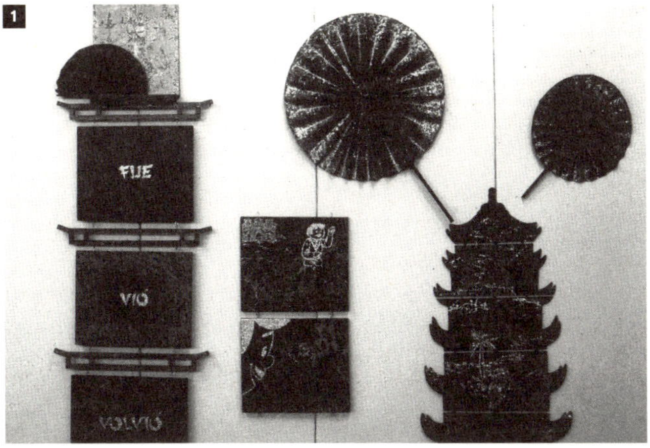

2

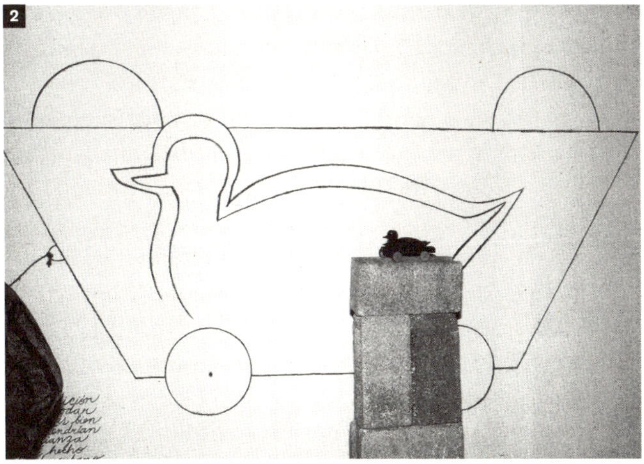

production from the South finds few outlets. Excluded from the great centers and supposedly international circuits, its presence in exhibitions like *Primitivism in Twentieth-Century Art* or *Magiciens de la terre* is insignificant, despite the fact that it could have contributed a lot more, especially by deepening and problematizing their perspectives.[16] The "contemporary artistic scene" is a very centralized system of *apartheid*.[17] More than being Eurocentric, it is Manhattan-centric. But, I insist, the barrier is not only South–North due to center–periphery relations of power, but also South–South, as a consequence of a postcolonial deformation.

1 Flavio Garcilandía (Cuba), *El síndrome de Marco Polo* (installation detail), 1986, Havana Biennial.

2 José Bedia (Cuba), *Toy for an African Child* (installation view), 1989, Havana Biennial.

Despite its deformed structure, the dictates from the center and the imposition of their arrogant judgments of art, the diversification of artistic circuits clashes with the difficulties of intercultural evaluation already pointed out. Critics, curators, and historians have a great responsibility in this sense. To paraphrase Harold Rosenberg, we should realize that the way towards an intercultural evaluation of the work of art is not just a question of seeing, but also of listening. Careful account should be taken of how an artwork functions in its context, what values are recognized there, what sensibility it satisfies, what perspectives it opens, what it contributes... Only after such thorough understanding would we recognize the messages of interest that art can communicate to the viewers addressed by the exhibitions, and how it can contribute to a general enrichment. Given that it has been demonstrated that the role of the viewer is fundamental in art and literature, this does not mean that one only sees from one's self and one's own circumstance, but also that reception is active and therefore capable of expanding.

The fundamental problem for exhibitions and texts with an intercultural meaning is communication: on the one hand, to inform and contextualize, and on the other, to orientate towards what interests new receivers. As mediators they must accept compromise, but need to make an effort to avoid centrisms and clichéd expectations. It is easy to say it, but in practice we are far from possessing exemplary solutions.

Apart from polyfocal, multiethnic decentralization, one last problem is that the dismantling of Eurocentrism demands an equally pluralistic revision of Western culture. When Robert Farris Thompson assigned Fu-Kiau Bunseki, a traditional Kongo expert, to comment on the "Africanist" painting of Picasso,[18] he was not simply making a gesture of deconstructing in reverse the appropriation of African sculpture by modernism, and making eloquent the ingenuity of his concerns with universality. He was also opening up a pluralistic methodological perspective. Not only in the sense of an erudite explanation of traditional Africa through others inspired by it. Bunseki's analyses deepen our appreciation of those works, and even of a Western point of view. Cubism revolutionized the visual culture of the West by appropriating formal resources from Africa. But these forms were not free-floating; they were designed to support specific meanings that can also function, on a more general level, within the coded system of Picasso's paintings. Those forms belong to a cosmic vision whose perceptual foundations continue to be present in the new vision by which the Cubists transformed Western painting, even without their acknowledging the functions and meanings of their African models.

Intercultural involvement consists not only of accepting the Other in an attempt to understand him or her and to enrich myself with his or her diversity. It also implies that the Other does the same with me, problematizing my self-awareness. The cure for the Marco Polo Syndrome entails overcoming centrisms with enlightenment from a myriad of different sources. ●

NOTES

Previously published in: *Third Text* 6, no. 21 (Winter 1992), pp. 35–41.

1 For instance, see John Hunter, "Inaugural Disputation on the Varieties of Man" [1775], in *The Anthropological Treatises of Johann Friedrich Blumenbach,* ed. and trans. T. Bendyshe (London, 1865), pp. 357–94.

2 Geeta Kapur, "Tradición y contemporaneidad en las bellas artes del Tercer Mundo," in *Debate abierto: Tradición y contemporaneidad en la plástica del Tercer Mundo,* exh. booklet, 3rd Havana Biennial (1989), p. 12.

3 Gerardo Mosquera, *El diseño se definió en Octubre* (Havana, 1989), pp. 31–33.

4 Amílcar Cabral, "O papel de cultura na luta pela independencia," in *Obras escolhidas de Amílcar Cabral,* vol. I (Lisbon, 1978), pp. 234–35.

5 About the double condition of European borders as Western bastion and contact zone, see Leopoldo Zea, *América en la historia* (Mexico City and Buenos Aires, 1957), pp. 118–54.

6 See his testimony in *Made in Havana: Contemporary Art from Cuba,* exh. cat. Sydney, Art Gallery of New South Wales; Brisbane, Museum of Contemporary Art; and Melbourne, Australian Centre for Contemporary Art (Sydney, 1988), p. 20.

7 A critical interpretation of Botero from this perspective can be read in Luis Camnitzer, "Boteros: Falsos y auténticos," *Brecha,* August 16, 1991, p. 20.

8 Joseph Cornet, "African Art and Authenticity," *African Arts* 9, no. 1 (1975), p. 55.

9 Néstor García Canclini, "Modernismo sin modernización?" *Revista Mexicana de Sociología* 51, no. 3 (July–September 1989), p. 170.

10 Mirko Lauer, "Notas sobre plástica, identidad y pobreza en el Tercer Mundo," in *Debate abierto* (see note 2), pp. 19–27.

11 Kapur 1989 (see note 2), p. 11.

12 Nelly Richard, "Latinoamérica y la postmodernidad," *Revista de crítica cultural* 2, no. 3 (April 1991), p. 15.

13 Jorge Luis Borges, "La supersticiosa ética del lector," in idem, *Páginas escogidas* (Havana, 1988), p. 105.

14 Boris Bernstein, "Algunas consideraciones en relación con el problema 'arte y etnos,'" *Criterios,* nos. 5–13 (January 1983–December 1984), pp. 266–67.

15 Rodrigo González changed his old Castilian aristocratic name into Rockdrig, and became one of those who transformed rock into a vehicle of expression of marginal youth and lower classes in Mexico City by using international rhythms for local ends.

16 Rasheed Araeen, "Our Bauhaus Others' Mudhouse," *Third Text,* no. 6 (Spring 1989), pp. 3–4; James Clifford, "Histories of the Tribal and the Modern," *Art in America* 73, no. 4 (April 1985), pp. 164–77, reprinted in *The Predicament of Culture* (Cambridge and London, 1988); Gerardo Mosquera, "'Primitivismo' y 'contemporaneidad' en jóvenes artistas cubanos," *La revista del sur* 2, nos. 3–4 (1985), pp. 52–55, reprinted in *Universidad de La Habana,* no. 227 (January–June 1986), pp. 133–39.

17 Gerardo Mosquera, "Speakeasy," *New Art Examiner* 17, no. 3 (November 1989), pp. 13–14.

18 Robert Farris Thompson, "Breakshadow Art (Pasula Klini): Towards an African Reading of 'Modernist Primitivism,'" in *Rediscovered Masterpieces of African Art* (Paris, 1988), pp. 65–73.

MEGA-EXHIBITIONS AND THE ANTINOMIES OF A TRANSNATIONAL GLOBAL FORM (2004)

Okwui Enwezor

World exhibitions glorify the exchange value of the commodity. They create a framework in which its use value recedes into the background. They open a phantasmagoria which a person enters in order to be distracted. The entertainment industry makes this easier by elevating the person to the level of the commodity.

Walter Benjamin, *The Arcades Project*

INTRODUCTION

IN the last few years, a new figure of discourse that seeks to analyze the impact of global capitalism and media technology on contemporary culture has asserted that the conditions of globalization produce new maps, orientations, cultural economies, institutional networks, identities, and social formations. Their scale not only delimits the distance between here and there, West and non-West, developed and underdeveloped, but also, by the depth of its penetration, embodies a new vision of global totality and a concept of modernity that dissolves the old paradigm of the nation-state, replacing it instead with the numbing logic of spectacular capitalism. In this sense Guy Debord was quite correct to think of capitalist logic and its effects on modern social relations as the "immense accumulation of *spectacles*."[1] However, there are ways in which one can deviate from Debord's classic analysis of capitalistic spectacle by looking penetratingly at other discourses of spectacle that are the exact obverse of this conclusion; this essay will address these discourses later on.

The putative discourse around globalization—particularly in relation to modern and contemporary art as they are embedded in museums, models of large-scale international exhibitions, the culture industry, etc.[2]—are carried through and through by the same systems of rationalization to be found in the neoliberal market logic of spectacular capitalism. Such systems of rationalization not only have an economic dimension, but they are also expressed within a political and cultural discourse of homogenization and integration of the dominant culture industry. It is here that models of large-scale exhibitions and modern and contemporary museums have come to see their programs and projects of the global integration of recalcitrant modernity challenged. Such challenges have come to articulate the notion that the conditions under which cultural and artistic productions today are made, and the complexity of institutional discourses that mediate their circulation and insertion into broader global networks, face the risk of homogenization when placed *in toto* within the ideology of global capitalism. On the other hand, there is the view that sees in the globalization of contemporary art a great and necessary development of late modernity into a sphere of greater inclusion of artistic practices that extend the discourse of modernism. Such extension is also seen to mediate the historical relationship between the classical aesthetic language of European high modernism and those other modernisms that offer a differential interpretation of what is modern in modern art.

Yet what this discourse has so far not made clear is: to what end? Or does the discourse around the globalization of art, museums, exhibitions, academies, universities, and their various industries return us to the cynical absorption and integration of a range of counter-hegemonic contemporary practices and cultures that seek to highlight the crucial factors of difference, experimental cultures, and recalcitrant notions of art into an already well-honed system of differentiation and homogenization? If we are to have any meaningful debate about the nature of this venture around globalization and art, we would do well to remind ourselves that the historical transformation currently underway must not simply be seen as merely a fanciful notion that impedes serious thinking about the very nature of art, but a transformation whose potential dehistoricizing, delegitimizing import is yet to be taken full measure of.

If globalization has opened up new axes of contestation in which a number of antinomies have become apparent, antiglobalization discourses, unlike the old debates of postmodernist critique of grand narratives, have supplemented a discourse that was always about the negotiation of knowledge and power with a radical rethinking of the deleterious effects of global capitalism's lack of recognition of such negotiations, especially within the field of art. According to Pierre Bourdieu,

> *The literary or artistic field is a* field of forces, *but it is also a* field of struggles *tending to transform or conserve this field of forces. The network of objective relations between positions subtends and orients the strategies which the occupants of the different positions implement in their struggles to defend or improve their positions (i.e., their position-takings), strategies which depend for their force and form on the position each agent occupies in the power relations [rapports de force].*[3]

Within the field of modern and contemporary art, we are locked in this tension of *rapports de force.*

Today antiglobalization has been derisively—often through ideological intentions—constructed as antimodern, nationalist, anti-Western, and archaic subaltern impulses. Conversely, any embrace of the potentialities of globalization as a means of broadening the space of international participation across a range of cultural, social, and political spheres has been decried as a neoliberal, capitalist attempt to assimilate into the West non-Western spaces and subjectivities. Even where the spaces of inclusion are mutually and dialectically embraced across the borders of ethnic, racial, cultural, gender, and sexual difference, the pull of and pressure to hold on to the coordinates and demands of certain identifications remain strong. For certain there are no easy answers to these oppositions. Still, it is possible to look at the issues, as I shall try to do in the rest of this essay, from the perspective of a number of structural and philosophical differentiations within which we can understand the current discourse of modernity, contemporary art, and globalization.

There are two models of thinking about the present situation. On the one hand, there is a vigorous expansion of museum and exhibition programs as well as academic curricula in order to rethink standard art historical views of modernism and contemporary art, as well as to integrate cultures hitherto thought marginal to the intellectual economy of Western modernism. On the other, there remains a staunch resistance to such a critical rapprochement between classical Western modernity and its counterpart in developing material economies of the non-West. Recently, there have been several retreats into academic highhandedness, through specious historical denunciations on the matter of differential modes of modernity and contemporary artistic practices that strongly resist inclusion in the center of Occidentalist discourse. Such denunciations have made their claims through recourse to what amounts to a theology of modernism propagated from the peculiar view of the Western avant-garde, but without situating that avant-garde within the larger, complex political determinations of colonialism and imperialism that made it possible. Increasingly, a number of influential historians and journals, through recourse to notions such as medium specificity, post-mediumness, artistic autonomy, institutional critique, artistic particularity, and so on, have encouraged this Occidentalist reiteration of modernity and art with very little said about the historical conditions under which art is produced and practiced throughout the entire modern period.

Yet it would be futile in this debate (without necessarily making any easy concession as to the value of the global) not to recognize that much of what has been constituted as the fact of globalization, as the historical rupture par excellence, has done little to help us understand those historical conditions under which the labor of art and culture is manifested. However, the presumption that globalization and its alliance with market liberalism and politics brings us further along the road in the long arduous march towards modernity is today kept in check by a number of oppositional activities and critical negotiations that have recently arisen to force new debates about its disciplinary and institutional efficacy. I shall mention only briefly two areas around which these debates are being waged. One is in the domain of the cultural and social production of identity. The other is in the political and economic area of democratic rights, national sovereignty, and economic self-determination.

For metropolitan audiences the most visible of the struggles around globalization is often seen in the mediated activities of a loose network of social movements, labor and environmental organizations, and NGOs (what I shall call the Porto Allegre contingent), and through antiglobalization marches such as those recently witnessed in Genoa, Seattle, Prague, and Montreal.[4] But there are yet other views of such struggles, "Third Worldist" in their perspective, only nominally antiglobal,[5] and much more sophisticated insofar as they are embedded in historically determined analysis of global regimes and are above all concerned with questions of justice and socio-political-economic agency. This second phalanx of struggle attacks globalization from the point of view of its attempt at hegemonic control over vast areas and systems of production and knowledge (whereby those "everyday users," as Michel de Certeau calls them, are systemically disadvantaged and deprived of the means to assert their agency[6]). If we add another point of view from the "Third Worldist" position, we see the rigorous critique of globalization as antidemocratic, especially in its ideological support of forces of liberal market capitalism that continually seek to harness globalization's surplus value, forever increasing profit motive while failing the simplest test of citizenship, transparency, and ecological responsibility. One example is Ken Saro-Wiwa's MOSOP movement (Movement for the Survival of the Ogoni People), directed against the shameful conduct of Shell Petroleum in the oil fields of Nigeria and its complicity in the murder and intimidation, as well as the suppression, of the democratic rights of their opponents. The other example is the Union Carbide tragedy in Bhopal, India. There are, in fact, countless examples that clearly show the horrific conduct of global corporatist exploitation of developing economies, from Nike's sweatshops to pharmaceutical companies' expropriation of indigenous knowledge without paying copyrights.

In these debates, it requires only a cursory probe to see that within the defining features of globalization, with its apotropaic promises, are inscribed a range of antinomies. Some of these antinomies are historical, based on a disequilibrium of power and material resources, while others are built around careful cultural reflexes that manifest themselves in the form of resistance to the hegemonic force of supranational global forums controlled by the forces of industrial and technological capitalism. It needs to be noted, as well, the degree to which resistance from within the institutions of the West to other forms of knowledge inscribes another level of antinomy. Likewise, the imagined community[7] of global culture, seen from the point of view of new transnational artistic communities, forms of global exhibition enterprises, and museums, and telegraphed through the networks of global exchange and reception systems such as the media, is no less fraught with these antinomies, saturated as they are with forms of institutional governmentality that constantly obviate the possibility of interpretive regimes that can allow new insights of the cultural complexity of the global present to emerge within the spaces of art and culture.

But must contemporary culture and art and the discursive as well as the market-orientated sites in which they are produced, reproduced, marketed, or exhibited be subjected to and put into the service of enunciating the radical shift in paradigm increasingly apparent in the complex, systemic delocalizations of capital, labor flows, markets, and technologies of communication and mediation ("between the Net and the Self"[8]) that globalization is said to have engendered? How do institutions of art integrate the slower, more critical cultural shifts that arrive in the wake of these transnational, denationalized, global transformations? Where does the final arbitration about the status of the work of art occur today, especially in view of the bourgeoning and ever more diversified range of options that exist in quite prolix forms of curatorial procedures in museums and exhibition spaces, media, catalogue historiography, commercial galleries and auction houses, private collections, and informal economies of art? These questions serve to articulate the critical rift we are witnessing today within the proliferating systems of contemporary art. Equally, they reveal a space of instability as the contemporary art arena expands, tracing, as they mutate, the complex mechanisms of translation and interpretation that exist in the domain of various institutional forms of modern art (the museum and the academy being two long-standing examples). In the end, if the fact of globalization, as is often pronounced, is the unhinging of the proscriptions of institutional modernism by mobilizing new artistic thoughts, practices, and conditions of production, we see levered into relief the central problematics that shadow and foreshadow the anxieties of the present artistic context within which a range of actors—curators, exhibitions, museums, collectors, media, market—perform.

It is my intention to explore some of the underlying problems that arise at the juncture where global capitalism and the cultural intersect. I am primarily concerned here with analyzing the nature of the museum and mega-exhibitions today. To do so, I will first focus on three broad areas—the market, institutions, and the media—in order to examine the impact of the three on a range of subsystems within the contemporary artistic framework such as exhibition models, curating, artistic practice, and epistemes of contemporary art. This analysis will then fold back to articulate how each of these systems and subsystems exist in the present social, cultural, and political climate within which contemporary art functions. Finally, the remaining part of this essay will be situated within a theoretical reflection on modernity.

MEGA-EXHIBITIONS AND MUSEUMS AS TRANSNATIONAL GLOBAL FORMS

I SHALL begin with a general look at large international exhibitions of contemporary art and the recent discourses that analyze their present proliferation. In the summer of 1997, I was a participant in a three-day conference organized by the Rockefeller Foundation and Arts International (both institutions are headquartered in New York) on the subject of large-scale international exhibitions, including biennials. The conference was convened with the tacit hope of understanding the critical shifts being initiated within the context of the mega-exhibition's structures and global dimension. Held in a beautiful villa situated on top of a small cliff that overlooks the small northern Italian town of Bellagio on Lake Como, with the Italian Alps hovering on the horizon, it was an edifying place to be secluded to think and work through the travails of contemporary art and the alarmingly mutating map (some would protest) of the international art economy. The very notation of mutation strikes me, though, as highly suggestive of the kind of disorder that systems of knowledge that have been the bedrock of Western imperialism have been plunged into when confronted with the critical values of other forms of knowledge. However, I would prefer not to speak of either mutation or disorder but of the transnationalization, translocalization, and denationalization of the international contemporary art economy. This was most clearly delineated by the diversity of the speakers at the conference, who came from São Paulo, Venice, Istanbul, Dakar, Perth, Pittsburgh, Costa Rica, Havana, Austin, Sydney, Bangkok, Johannesburg, and many other places.

This chief focus of the conference was to raise questions and articulate the new demands on cultural and artistic production as they became more and more unhinged from the stable ground of local sites (the nation-state) and turned into increasingly transnational endeavors. And here I should like to say that such endeavors were not only artistic, but political, social, and economic as well. The formation of an itinerant phalanx of artistic strategies and curatorial concepts that respond directly to this shift in global capitalist and media logic required forms of critical analysis that could properly understand their significance and hopefully recode the complex dialectics between globalization and the long process of modernization towards market-based economies on the course of which much of the developing world has been set since the early days of decolonization. Furthermore, what such an analysis would seek to comprehend is the impact on institutional practices, in both the West and non-West, as contemporary art expanded into the domain of the neoliberal global market.

One important point that dominated the deliberations was the relationship between multiculturalism, multiethnic metropolitan identities, local cultures that have few cosmopolitan attachments except in terms of relations of power and production, and the circulatory logic of capital, as well as, finally, the spatial and temporal disjunctures that lie at the heart of modernity, especially as expressed through different filters of colonial and postcolonial discourses. It was a rare opportunity to debate many of the crucial issues around which contemporary art, exhibitions, museums, and art academies were being defined and to see them fully caught in a transitional and transnational nexus. Suffice it to say that there was no conclusion reached at the conference, except the promise we all made to each other about how important it was to meet again. And, indeed, we have met again and again as the wild spiral of new biennials or forms of biennials have entered the global framework. I shall not give a count of how many such exhibitions presently exist. But I'm sure they run into the hundreds.

In its expansionist mode, as well as in its insatiable propensity to absorb even the most arcane of artistic grammars and scales of production, biennials have come to exemplify not only important scenes of cultural translation and transnational encounters between artists, art markets, institutions, and various professionals, but also a negative impression of its form as an agora of spectacle has come to define its relationship to art. While this tendency towards spectacularization and dispersion into what Adorno and Horkheimer defined as the culture industry may be true, it nonetheless requires further explication to make obvious the fact that not all biennials function according to a logic of spectacle. Even if they wish to, limitations in economic and institutional circumstances militate against their move into being purveyors of spectacle. In truth, most biennials, particularly those working in and addressing specific artistic contexts, oftentimes work as low-budget, modest projects. Within that kind of framework, the scale of the works is usually more modest, portable, and intimate, while the appearance of site-specific works and that of the exhibitions seem rather improvisational and often compensatory. Making these distinctions still does not give us a full picture of the motivations behind the exponential increase in large-scale international exhibitions, whose chief attribute is the heterogeneity of strategies and objects they assemble.

I would like to examine some of the reasons why a new global culture of biennials has emerged at this historical juncture. I shall be brief. To do so, I will largely bypass discussions that have made of biennials the descendants of a genus known as the world exhibition. I will also not evoke what is believed to be its prehistory in the accumulations of so-called *Wunderkammern*. My interest is in the present historical context. Why biennials?

HISTORY AND TRAUMA

IF we exclude the Venice Biennial and Carnegie International in Pittsburgh, most if not all large-scale, cyclical exhibitions that currently exist within the international framework are largely post–World War II activities. Of these, I have been interested in the degree to which the desire to establish such an exhibition forum has been informed by responses to events connected to traumatic historical ruptures. Documenta, and more recently the Gwangju Biennial in South Korea and the Johannesburg Biennial in South Africa, exemplify such institutions. The founding of these three institutions closely mirrors the political and social transitions of each of the countries where they are situated. In the case of Documenta, the critical signpost is Germany's post–World War II attempt to rebuild the basis of its destroyed civil society as well as the artistic and intellectual communities depopulated by the Nazi pogroms that led to the exile and death of many important thinkers and leaders of the avant-garde. The Gwangju and Johannesburg biennials were both founded during critical moments in the political and social transitions of South Korea and South Africa respectively. For South Korea, it was the turn to democracy after years of repressive military dictatorships, and for South Africa, it was the end of apartheid. These events signified to the rest of the world that the ground for the work of the imagination, as a fundamental part of society in transition towards democracy and the development of new concepts of the citizen, is an important part of the transition.

MODERNITY AND MODERNIZATION

RECENTLY, while waiting my turn at a barbershop in Brooklyn, New York, I happened to cast a glance at a publicity bill pinned up on a wall with the heading "Black Inventors." On the chart was listed every conceivable invention one can think of, from the toothpick and the ironing board to stabilizing instruments for the space shuttle, airplane engines, computer hardware, etc. But the entries that caught my attention were the first four on the list. They read as follows: culture = African, alphabet = African (Egypt), writing = African (Egypt), paper = African. Having lived in the United States for twenty years, I was fairly familiar with the ways through which many African-Americans assert their sense of cultural worth in response to Western cultural marginalization. From the days of slavery through the height of the Civil Rights Movement to the Black Power Movement, part of the construction of African-American cultural value and worth is a battle waged on the grounds of the fanciful ideology of origin. Given the basic historical schism between the United States and its black citizens, I was not surprised, though I was still struck by the deft deployment of the entries of the poster, which sought to underline the precondition of social visibility for any knowledge-based society. And if Africa is the primal scene of civilization, having invented culture—the alphabet, writing, and paper—then it must also be the basis for the ontological construction of modernity as such through a range of inventions which culture, the alphabet, writing, and paper made possible. As crude and bombastic as this list may seem, its presumptions are almost identical to the ways in which Western epistemological thought constitutes the dimensions of knowledge-based society as essentially springing from the European imagination. Here, we can say, is an obvious example of one antinomy of global culture, the struggle over cultural legitimation.

It is striking then to see through this ideological struggle to establish the prehistory and history of the modern world, how the text of historical legitimation has been written out of the bitter imposition of indenture, marginalization, and opposition to these through counter-hegemonic strategies. I would, therefore, like to offer the view that one consequence of Western imperialism and colonialism is the degree to which culture and societies seen to be marginal to Western culture have written, out of the antagonism of European imperial conquest and hegemony, a complex narrative of the human lifeworld. Having started from the Brooklyn barbershop, let us stay in the contemporary and cosmopolitan Western realm and explore what this antagonism looks like today from the perspective of someone like Jürgen Habermas. In the second volume of *The Theory of Communicative Action*, Habermas offers a most perspicacious view of the question of an institutionally determined sense of culture:

> *In the past decade or two, conflicts have developed in advanced Western societies that deviate in various ways from the welfare-state pattern of institutionalized conflict over distribution. They no longer flare up in domains of material reproduction; they are no longer channelled through parties and associations; and they can no longer be allayed by compensations. Rather, these new conflicts arise in domains of cultural reproduction, social integration, and socialization; they are carried out in subinstitutional—or at least extraparliamentary—forms of protest; and the underlying deficits reflect a reification of communicatively structured domains of action that will not respond to the media of money and power. The issue is not primarily one of compensations that the welfare state can provide, but of defending and restoring endangered ways of life. In short, the new conflicts are not ignited by distribution problems but by questions having to do with the grammar of forms of life.*[9]

Through Habermas we may then approach the second antinomy as being predicated on cultural plurality, difference, and *questions concerning the grammar of forms of life.* We can then say that within the broader discourse of regimes of representation, decolonization complicates the classical texts of international and global curatorial work, the art historical work bound to the institutional domains of the museum and the academy, and the conception of the ideal public. Decolonization reorients and transforms the priority placed on the productive and representational values, as well as the multifarious objects, texts, and images of Western artistic modernity. With decolonization and the emergence of postcolonial states as well as the dispersion of many postcolonial subjects to far-flung places, a new figure of the modern subject in the global metropolitan circuit became much more visible, challenging, by its mere presence, such Enlightenment concepts as *liberté, egalité,* and *fraternité.*

For the postcolonial state the pressure to modernize and develop not only the superstructure of the state, but also the substructure of culture became the contemporary manual for exiting peripheralization. Modernity as such, and the desire to modernize, that is, to leave behind backwardness, became a tacit agreement to re-Westernize, to be reintegrated into a neocolonial scheme in the name of progress, institutional development, and access to technology. It is in light of these two movements—between modernity and modernization—that certain forms of mega-exhibition and museum can be understood. The São Paulo Biennial founded in 1952 certainly offers one key example. Founded by a member of an immigrant Italian family and modeled after the Venice Biennial, the São Paulo Biennial was designed to mediate for a modernizing Brazil the iconography and innovations of the Western artistic avant-garde and to bring to Brazil historical works of European art so as to present the view of Brazil's cultural continuity and contiguity with European culture. This conceit of cultural continuity and contiguity is an interesting one insofar as the founder of the Biennial wished to present Brazil in the company of advanced visual culture and therefore separate it from other Latin-American countries.

One way of understanding the function of the mega-exhibition and museum complex is to think about how they operationalize the discourse of modernity and modernization in relation to use and exchange value. Even mega-exhibitions in the West do not exclude themselves from instrumentalizing this discourse of modernity and modernization. Two recent examples of micromanaging the emergence of global culture in peripheral locations in Europe as supra-state policy are provided by the formation of Manifesta and the idea of the "European Culture Capital," a title which cities bid for like the Olympic Games in order to play host to the avatars of advanced artistic and curatorial initiatives. The clear impetus for many large-scale international exhibitions as such is not necessarily to bring about a more complex understanding of artistic movements to local publics through the symbolic use and exchange of forms and ideas of international advanced art but to propagate a certain will to globality. By so doing such exhibitions seek to embed the peripheral spaces of cultural production and institutional articulation in the trajectory of international artistic discourse. Modernity and modernization mean, then, not only to develop a greater proximity to the institutional patronage of international artistic spheres but also to acquire and master its language, to harvest its surplus resources, and ultimately to position and promote the periphery as a genuine destination of artistic modernity. I shall not speak here of some of the links to economies, tourism, regional revitalization, nationalism, etc., as it is obvious that they all figure as part of the complex mechanism at play in the formation of large international exhibitions or the building of new museums.

ENACTING THE DIASPORIC PUBLIC SPHERE: MOBILITY, MEDIATION, AND PROXIMITY TO THE WEST

EVEN if the desire for modernity and modernization propel some institutions of international contemporary art, it would be misleading to think of them, especially those that exist outside the context of the large industrial centers of the West, as merely mimicked copies and pale imitations (pardon the pun) of the authentic thing as it is constituted in the West. The very notion of proximity to the West as a strategy enunciated within the dialectical framework of the relations of power inherent in the development of the discourse of artistic modernity is a double-edged sword. Such a sword cuts a swath between the revolutionary and emancipatory portents of the postcolonial critique of master narratives and the nationalist rhetoric of tradition and authenticity. From the foregoing then, we can say quite clearly that the periphery does not simplistically absorb and internalize what it does not need. Nor does it vitiate its own critical power by becoming subservient to the rules of the center. In the wake of the globalization of culture and art, the postcolonial response to it has produced a new kind of space, a discourse of open contestations which does not spring merely from resistance, but rather is built on an ethics of dissent. Therefore, in its discursive proximity to Western modes of thought, postcolonial theory transforms this dissent into an enabling agent of historical transformation and thus is able to expose some Western epistemological limits and contradictions.

Let me be more demonstrative. In his book *Modernity at Large: Cultural Dimensions of Globalization*, Arjun Appadurai put the issue of what I have called open contestations in a much more elegant way when he tells the story of the circuitous map of global cultural networks in the twin instances of mass mobility and mass mediation as paradigms of globality and locality. He writes:

> *As with mediation, so with motion. The story of mass migrations (voluntary and forced) is hardly a new feature of human history. But when it is juxtaposed with the rapid flow of mass-mediated images, scripts, and sensations, we have a new order of instability in the production of modern subjectivities. As Turkish guest workers in Germany watch Turkish films in their German flats, as Koreans in Philadelphia watch the 1988 Olympics in Seoul through satellite feeds from Korea, and as Pakistani cab drivers in Chicago listen to cassettes of sermons recorded in mosques in Pakistan or Iran, we see moving images meet deterritorialized viewers. These create diasporic public spheres, phenomena that confound theories that depend on the continued salience of the nation-state as the key arbiter of important social changes.... In this scene, both persons and images often meet unpredictably, outside the certainties of home and the cordon sanitaire of local and national media effects. This mobile and unforeseeable relationship between mass-mediated events and migratory audiences defines the core of the link between globalization and the modern.*[10]

What exactly does Appadurai mean when he writes about diasporic public spheres? Who and what is the public that is referred to here? Does not the very concept of diaspora as a historical condition through which global cultural processes are mediated confront us with another antinomy in the dialectic between the tribal and the modern, particularly in circumstances where diasporic cultures indigenize themselves on the soil of other entrenched values? Here, I return once more to the Brooklyn barbershop scene, but now seen from the purview of its proliferation, not on the occasion of the journey out into slavery and indenture, but on the basis of its inscription into and passage through the global scene of cultural translation. Today, the Brooklyn barbershop represents the site of another diasporic public sphere, a new transnational locality embedded in the networks of knowledge, labor (intellectual and manual), trade, tourism, immigration, technology, and finance. Writ large, the diasporic public sphere articulates the distinctive travelogue of twentieth-century modernity while writing new concepts of translocalization and transnationalization of culture within twenty-first-century globalizing processes. The diasporic public sphere offers the clearest example of what Néstor García Canclini, in his book *Hybrid Cultures,* calls strategies for entering and leaving modernity. This to and fro movement predisposes Michel de Certeau's "everyday user" towards the instrumentalization of his/her own agency. The diasporic then delineates late modernity's transnational, transcultural, postcolonial, and global attitudes towards such concepts as identity, culture, nationality, and citizenship. It postulates an open-ended relationship, with a variety of institutional productions and private experiences, between professional and personal identity models. The diasporic, through its twists and turns, from indeterminacy and contingency to indigeneity, shows us, in a paradoxical sense, both the limits of identity discourse and the fate of all *leitkulturen*[11] in the wake of the mass mobility not only of people traveling beyond home, nation, race, ethnicity, and continent but also of all forms of migratory knowledge, cultural iconography, artistic objects, contemporary subjectivities, and the networks of their distribution, mediation, and interpretation.

If I have dwelled on the notion of the diasporic public sphere, it was to show how intertwined it is with the conditions of the global, even when it objectifies the ceaseless contradictions and antagonism between the two, especially in the ways in which questions of center and periphery, local and global, national and regional, enlightened and backward, mobility and stasis, citizen and subjects, and cosmopolitan and provincial sit within them. One visible space where one often encounters these contradictions and antagonisms is in the social, political, and cultural sphere of the global city. As it emerges from the spatial and temporal disorientation of the global city, the diasporic public sphere becomes the space where the problems of translation for culture arises. Avid for the critical incarnation of new forms of experimental production, cultural translation in the global present confronts us with a way to begin again, whereby the past is neither a foreign country nor simply the authentic name of origin. From the foregoing we can then say that the recent phenomenon of biennials in the periphery should not be bemoaned as a readymade example of the biennial syndrome. Instead, there is a need to see in the biennial phenomenon the possibility of a paradigm shift in which we as spectators are able to encounter many experimental cultures without wholly possessing them.

SPECTACLE, SPECTATORSHIP, AND MEGA-EXHIBITIONS

BUT what of the critique that biennials and other large-scale exhibitions foster an environment of speculative artistic enterprises and of spectacle, and in so doing undercut the critical autonomy of artistic practices from being appropriated by forces of the market, ideology, and media? I will address this critique in two ways: one, through the idea of what I shall call "strategic globality," and the other, through the idea of spectatorship. I will formulate my argument through a reading of Guy Debord's *Society of Spectacle* and Michel de Certeau's idea of the everyday user as not a passive consumer and receiver of culture but an active participant and agent whose critical engagement with culture makes the complexity of its meaning more focused. Pierre Bourdieu, in his study *The Field of Cultural Production,* imagines the field of culture as a habitus where position-takings among users and producers create a strong dialectical framework through which culture makes its institutional, ideological, conceptual, and other practices visible. From these assumptions I would like to address the question of multiculturalism as one moment when the contradictory aspirations of users, agents, producers, institutions, and communities converge.

Before we look at the multicultural bogeyman, let us first examine the question of exhibitions of art as spectacle. It has been often argued that the chief value of all institutional forms of mega-exhibitions (biennials, triennials, Documenta, cultural capitals, festivals of culture, blockbuster exhibitions of modern and classical European art, ethnographic exhibitions, world's fairs, etc.) is grounded in the domain of spectacle and the spectacularization of art and culture through the process of diffusion and reproduction of excess. While this is certainly the case, I would argue that such exhibitions address themselves not to the ideal viewer whose senses have already been co-opted and homogenized into the institutional logic of display and transformation, but a general viewer who represents an unknown demographic in the fragmented network of global cultural exchange. This general spectator I see lined before us in the field of spectatorship that articulates itself, not inside Debord's critique of spectacle but as a new instance of spectatorial experience through diffusion and differentiation.

Thus, the general field of spectatorship as an active field of everyday users, agents, producers, and position-takings, in the context of recent postcolonial, postimperial discourse, inserts a new spectator whose gaze upon the mottled screen of modernity is counter-hegemonic/counter-normative, and not simply counter-cultural. It is in the sense that postcolonial subjective claims (multiculturalism, liberation theology, resistance art, feminist and queer theory, questions of third cinema, antiapartheid, environmental and ecological movements, rights of indigenous peoples, minority demands, etc.) deviate from the hegemonic concept of spectatorial totality and render it fragmentary. It brings up all sorts of counter-hegemonic conceptions of looking and of how ideas of art and culture may be rearticulated and reimagined in the wake of the globalization of social temporalities that have emerged at the end of the long cycle of the world system of capitalism.[12]

Though there have been many celebrations of the death of multiculturalism in the service of a higher, more exemplary *leitkultur* motif, we must continue to remind ourselves that what the multicultural paradigm opened up was a space (to return to the term again) of open contestations and deliberations around what James Clifford has noted as the "radically asymmetrical relations of power" that was the rule in most institutional practices. And despite some of the shortcomings of multicultural discourse, its ethical project of citizenship, recognition of difference, tolerance, and respect for other cultures and forms of living remains today quite salient. No more so than in the post–September 11 return to the old asymmetrical discourse of the clash of civilizations. Multiculturalism at its best is inclusive and makes clear the complex cultural and social maps of all globalizing societies. It unbinds the discourse of art and culture from the false natal bonds of ethnocentrism, while showing powerfully and critically that relations of exchange between cultures are also necessarily adumbrated by strong relations of power. And it is in the realm of power that multicultural discourse showed that when placed at the service of nationalistic identification, power could easily turn into tools of exclusion and marginalization.

As we rethink the values of the emergent forms of spectatorship that give a new critical insight into the historical condition of globalization, I would like to conclude by invoking, through the political critique of imperialism by Michael Hardt and Antonio Negri in their book *Empire,* what a new horizon of spectatorship—the space of open contestations and deliberations—means for non-nationalist art and culture. In *Empire,* Hardt and Negri claim that former domains of relations of social production became untied from the nation-state apparatus and its imperial program. And with this unbundling, a new type of sovereignty, within a regime which they have given the name "Empire," has emerged. It is a movement that mobilizes the force of critical counter-hegemonic movements whose sovereignty supersedes the nation-state's imperial claims to such things as territorial autonomy, self-determination, a view of economic totality, and an ability to regulate all economic and cultural life. Since "Empire" has no boundaries, no limits, and since it encompasses what they call a spatial totality (that is, it is everywhere), the counterpoint to its pernicious global apparatus is to be found in the resistance logic forged outside its sphere of influence.

If, as this stellar work argues, "the sovereignty of nation-state was the cornerstone of the imperialism of European powers constructed throughout the modern era," how can we properly situate today the phenomenon of mega-exhibitions that still function under the imprimatur of the nation-state's view of culture? While there can be no singular answer to this question, Hardt and Negri begin such a discussion by insisting that mega-exhibitions have adopted the idea of the global from the perspective of the imperial and colonial mode of differentiation and homogenization, absorption and diffusion. They have not been attentive enough to that differentiated position of general spectatorship that announced simultaneously the twilight of the nation-state and the dawn of empire. As such, I will claim that Debord's notion of the "society of spectacle" was only partially attentive to the new sovereign power that is to come in the wake of "Empire." In Debord's scheme, such a sovereign power was flattened out by the spectacle-producing effects of capitalism. Everything, all social life, was seen to be caught in the optical haze of mediation, perpetually ringed by the fearful machines of media absorption. The logic of the spectacle was on the one hand a colonial one as Debord rightfully showed. On the other hand, this reading of the symptomatic logic of imperial discourse did not completely displace it. The society of spectacle, then, was one concerned chiefly with the negative dialectic where the relations of production, circulation, dissemination, reception, and acculturation proper to the European domain of culture find their expression. It did not, however, probe deeply into the discrepant categories of spectacle whose energies and modes of articulating their strategic globality within domains of cosmopolitan networks and relations of social production are strictly anti-imperialist and counter-hegemonic. Such strategies of globality introduce into the contemporary artistic and cultural circuits new relations of spectatorship whose program of social differentiation, political expression, and cultural specificity reworks the notion of spectacle and constructs it as the site of new relations of power and cultural translation. It is here that I believe that certain cases of mega-exhibitions function, especially when viewed through Mikhail Bakhtin's notion of the carnivalesque. The gap between the spectacle and the carnivalesque is the space, I believe, where certain exhibition practices, as models of resistance against the deep de-personalization and acculturation of global capitalism, recapture a new logic for the dissemination and reception of contemporary visual culture today. ●

NOTES

Previously published in: *Documents* 23 (Spring 2004), pp. 2–19. An earlier version of this essay was delivered as one of "The Thyssen Lectures on the Iconology of the Present" at Humboldt University, Berlin. The author wishes to thank Professors Horst Bredekamp and Sarat Maharaj for their invitation there. Another version was later delivered at Columbia University on February 14, 2002, as part of the Sawyer Seminar on cultural effects of globalization, organized by Professor Andreas Huyssen.

1 Guy Debord, *The Society of Spectacle,* trans. Donald Nicholson-Smith (New York, 1995), 12.

2 For a more theoretical discussion of the concept of the "culture identity," see Theodor Adorno, *The Culture Industry: Selected Essays on Mass Culture* (London and New York, 1991), pp. 98–106. See also Adorno and Max Horkheimer, *The Dialectic of Enlightenment,* where the idea of the "culture industry" is used to denote the mass phenomenon that seems currently to have overtaken the museological presentation of art. Following in the wake of the institutional success of art as part of the industry of mass culture and media is the rise of curatorial programs in universities and specialized art academies. To be noted here, of course, are the almost two decades of expansion that has led to the proliferation of international and local biennials as models of the commodity culture of global capitalism and its great appeal to the diffusion of artistic practice, with little heuristic function and content, but rather as pure visuality in relation to mass culture.

3 Pierre Bourdieu, *The Field of Cultural Production: Essays on Art and Literature* (New York, 1993), p. 30. Emphasis in the original.

4 Surely, Antonio Negri and Michael Hardt, through their book *Empire* (London and Cambridge, 2000), have come to represent the fashionable theorists of this conjunction.

5 Here I wish to distinguish between the kind of resistance to globalization that is in the relation to its current form, whereby the highly technological economies dictate the terms of global trade through forums they control, such as the International Monetary Fund, World Bank, World Trade Organization, etc., while developing economies wield little policy leverage in determining the course of their economies. It is to be noted that much of the developing economies' resistance of globalization is not antimarket in its position but against the policies of supernational global institutions' imposition of stringent structural adjustment programs through such devices as Bretton Woods.

6 See Michel de Certeau, *The Practice of Everyday Life,* trans. Steven Rendall (Berkeley, 1984).

7 See Benedict Anderson's superb study of nationalism and the idea of community from their archaic, premodern sense to their modern incarnations through the formation of the nation-state and the concept of citizenship, which mixes both the archaic and premodern aspects of community to the modern juridical conception of citizenship as political commitment and allegiance to a higher sovereignty. Anderson, *Imagined Communities: Reflections on the Origin and Spread of Nationalism* (London, 1991).

8 See Manuel Castells, *The Rise of the Network Society* (Oxford, 1996), p. 3.

9 Jürgen Habermas, *The Theory of Communicative Action* (Boston, 1984), p. 392.

10 Arjun Appadurai, *Modernity at Large: Cultural Dimensions of Globalization* (Minneapolis, 1996), p. 4. Appadurai's deployment of migratory audiences through the figure of the mobile spectator, whose encounter with the objective world is mediated through forums of global technologies, closely resembles Manuel Castells's observations regarding subjectivity and modernity. Within conventional narratives of globalization, Castells locates "a fundamental split between abstract, universal instrumentalism, and historically rooted, particularistic identities." From such a split the coordinates of identity and subjectivity become enmeshed in the polarities between mobility and mediation, a position Castells sees as "a bipolar opposition between the Net and the Self." Castells 1996 (see note 8), p. 3.

11 This refers to a controversy in Germany, whereby a German parliamentarian advocated that for immigrants to become full citizens and therefore to assimilate and integrate themselves into the German cultural context, they should, as it were, adopt German culture as the lead culture. In a manner of speaking, this means that whatever cultural context any immigrant may have originated from, and which hitherto represents a value that structures the deepest commitment of that immigrant's identity, should be suppressed or made secondary and subjugated within the proliferate presence of a German *leitkultur.*

12 See Fernand Braudel's very important account of this long cycle, what he has called "temporalities of long duration," in his *Civilization and Capitalism: The Fifteenth Century to the Eighteenth Century,* vol. 3, trans. Sian Reynolds (New York, 1984).

THE GLOBALIZATION OF THE FALSE: A RESPONSE TO OKWUI ENWEZOR (2004)

George Baker

This society eliminates geographical distance only to reap distance internally in the form of spectacular separation.[1]

Whenever individuals lose the capacity to see things for themselves, the expert is there to offer an absolute reassurance.[2]

Guy Debord

I would like to begin rather inauspiciously by admitting how massively unqualified I am to respond to such a lecture. At the same time, I will also immediately claim that perhaps my lack of qualification is a virtue here, as the situation of globalization has much to do with the promoting or demoting of a certain set of skills and institutional positions. I will admit right up front that I am a "biennial Luddite." I have been a practicing art critic for about six years now, and yet I do not go to mega-exhibitions. I resent their insistence that it is to them that all artistic attention must be paid. I resist their claim that it is now only through them that artistic importance is to be measured. I get lazy in the face of their attempt to make all intellectuals involved in the field of art into itinerants in an updated version of the Grand Tour or a parody of forced migration. I shiver at the thought that resisting biennial culture, or "festivalism" as it has also been called, is now to be equated with resisting challenges to Western imperialism and cultural hegemony. I avoid mega-exhibitions during the few times when I have the opportunity actually to be near one of these beasts. On the other hand, I rarely have the opportunity to be near one of these beasts. And this dynamic of exclusion—as opposed to all that has just been said about "inclusion"—is one important phenomenon that I want to address in my response.

I do not think we will get very far in our understanding of mega-exhibitions if we do not attempt more rigorously to define globalization itself. It seems to me important to view it as a *process*, differentiating the term "globalization" from "the global" somewhat like we do "modernization" from "the modern." And then the question becomes, what exactly is entailed in this process? Is it not, as Gayatri Chakravorty Spivak has claimed, the "financialization of the globe"? Is it not, indeed, the *Ameri-*

canization of the globe? In this lecture about exhibitions and globalization, we did not unfortunately hear much—if anything—about art and artists, and so let me cite now the words of an artist attempting to define globalization: "First and foremost, globalization is the penetration of the multinational corporate economy into every nook and cranny of human life. It is the latest incarnation of an imperative that has long been accepted as a vital necessity . . . The first law of proto-capitalism: Markets must multiply through foreign trade or they will stagnate and die. . . . What is largely missing from the current picture is any sense of material resistance to the expansion of the market imperative."[3] These are the words of the photographer Allan Sekula.

Even with this small range of definitions in hand, a number of questions arise. Why do you insist on referring to globalization in terms of rupture, as—in your words—the "historical rupture par excellence"? This language of rupture sounds to me a lot like the language that once surrounded the discourse of postmodernism within the art world. The "rupture" of postmodernism is now replaced by the "rupture" of globalization, and an aesthetic or even anti-aesthetic term gets replaced now—significantly—by an economic one. And yet perhaps neither term should be properly viewed as a rupture, but as an intensification of a much longer historical process. Rupture connotes amnesia to me. And globalization seems much more a strategy of what Theodor Adorno would have called "false totalization" rather than the fragmenting force claimed for it here.

My second major question would be: who and where is the audience for mega-exhibitions? I ask this question faced with the crucial importance spectatorship and audience issues occupied by the end of the lecture, while any trace of an audience seemed strangely absent to me in the earlier half of the talk. I would venture the following reasons for this absence: mega-exhibitions entail a violent assault on the traditional notion of an audience for art, even an assault on the idea that art needs an audience or a public at all. If "mega" here means big, we are faced with exhibitions that are *too big,* that suffer from a gigantism that echoes and serves the contemporary gargantuan scope of a newly global economy. Mega-exhibitions cannot be taken in, digested, understood, or read in any complete manner, and this sublime scale serves the function of obfuscation. They are constructed by curatorial authors as labyrinthine narratives whose plot evades any attempt at being followed, never mind critiqued. The baroque curves of contemporary architecture seem simple compared to the layout of current exhibition design, and the parallel weighty tomes of contemporary architects—S, M, L, XL—are rivaled by mega-exhibition catalogues that mock the now quaint scope of even biblical narrative by calling themselves simply *The Book*—I refer of course to the catalogue for Documenta 10, a book, by the way, too large for many to be able to afford to purchase it (in fact, with a book this size, you don't own it, you only glance at it in libraries, in other institutions, which seems a telling destination to me). This phenomenological violence that mega-exhibitions pose to their spectators is only augmented by the social violence entailed by art's increasing mediation through this form. One often hears that biennials create access to artistic culture for local audiences. And this they certainly do. But it seems necessary to contemplate as well how this mediation of art actually bars access to culture to local audiences, providing full access only to an increasingly narrow cadre of experts and professionals and creating a class conflict between those tied to the space of particularity and those whose job it is to circulate endlessly through the spaces where art only ever partially reveals itself. Mega-exhibition culture seems to be bound up with the question of exclusion: as contemporary museums become much more inclusive than their traditional mandate allowed, biennials succeed to the place of arbiter of the canon, to the judgment seat of artistic importance and status. But who else is excluded in this process of the professionalization and specialization of art that biennial culture entails? Your choice of words in the lecture gives some clues. You speak of "biennials" as offering "transnational encounters between artists, art markets, institutions, and various professionals." I find it telling that this transnational encounter excludes the public as traditionally conceived; it seems to have no place in this new space. Later you also speak of hoping to locate the nature of mega-exhibitions within a quite specific nexus: that of the "market, institutions, and media." You speak of the various "actors" working through this globalized space: "curators, exhibitions, museums, collectors, media, [the] market . . ." Some very important actors have fallen out of these last equations—artists, for one. Critics as well, and perhaps especially. They are not needed or wanted anymore. For in the moment of globalization and the rise of the mega-exhibition, what we actually witness for perhaps the first time is the *total institutionalization of the practice of art,* the onset of art's *total administration* or *total bureaucratization.* Curators replace artists in such an economy in the same way as experts replace critics.

Reproduction becomes more crucial than production, the container more important than the contained. These critical goals of postmodernism from twenty years ago, what it called the shift from "work to frame," have now been transformed into the opposite of criticality: they have become the iron-clad law of administrative recuperation. In such an economy, I have to admit that it becomes quite distressing to hear a curator denounce "institutional critique"—as well as notions of "medium-specificity," "artistic autonomy," "artistic particularity"—as a reiteration of "Occidentalist" modernity and as amounting to a "theology of modernism" propagated from the view of the Western avant-garde. (Obviously I hear as the target of such remarks the journal *October*, of which I am now an editor, and the work of Rosalind Krauss). All of these artistic strategies *are* strategic and contingent, poised today against the homogenization of capitalist globalization as they were deployed yesterday against the nation-state and the fascist rigidity of capitalist industrialization. In this denunciation of institutional critique as Occidentalist, in this frustration with the recalcitrance and historical memory associated with artistic specificity, I hear the new rapaciousness proper to the ascendancy of the global curator; if I am wrong in this regard, we should discuss our differences on this matter.

Two models for the structure of mega-exhibitions seem to run through the latter half of your talk. I will summarize your positions as the Trauma Model and the Nation Model. These models raise at least two questions for me: First, while I agree with your important observation that postwar biennials seem to emerge in locations of historical trauma, I wonder if your optimistic portrayal of this emergence can stand. Are biennials the place where the "work of the imagination" takes hold in the wake of historical trauma, a model of transition, or are they rather manifestations of official culture that are bound up with historical trauma in a much more insidious way—as tools to cover over ruptures, to spread amnesia, to deny the magnitude of historical loss through a false euphoria of plenitude? In this more pessimistic perspective, the mega-exhibition and the biennial would be the form of cultural mediation proper to the gap of historical trauma—not its "working through." It thus makes sense that an exhibition like Documenta was for decades an exportation of New York to German soil, an Americanization of the European world exhibition following the logic of the long Americanization of the world that is now known as globalization.

My second question undercuts the first: are not most biennials and mega-exhibitions actually built upon the Nation Model that you trace to the Venice Biennial and its immediate offspring, the Saõ Paulo Biennial? To ask this question is to position biennial culture in opposition to the positive globalization you otherwise espouse, to see biennial culture as a kind of Olympics that *preserves and serves* the Western imperialist model of the nation-state rather than challenging it. This is a point that you indeed stress. And yet the second implication of this question is to wonder whether we are then stuck with a biennial culture that is either archaically nationalistic and explicitly Occidentalist (the Nation Model)—and that thus *reveals globalization as a process of Westernization, not its critique*—or a mega-exhibition structure that conversely instantiates the global mediation of art in the form of historical trauma and amnesia. I am provisionally associating the biennial with the Nation Model, and the mega-exhibition with the Trauma Model, but this does not seem to me to be a very productive dilemma or position to be in, and perhaps biennials should, in such a situation, not be embraced as a solution but as the problem.

If these are two models for the production of mega-exhibitions, two models similarly bifurcate your approach to their reception: the Frankfurt School model of the "public sphere" and Guy Debord's society of the spectacle. These models, however, are notoriously incompatible. The question we are left with is: are mega-exhibitions part of the bourgeois public sphere that was formerly embodied in the museum, or are they signs of the utter dissolution of that public sphere into the rigid passivity compelled by spectacle? I'm not sure that one has to choose one or the other—we might be engaged in a battle where these two sides of the equation are still at war, where we can choose in fact to preserve the public sphere function that all exhibitions conceivably serve. And yet you devise counterstrategies for both sides of this equation, offering up the crucial notion of a diasporic public sphere on the one hand, and a counter-hegemonic spectatorship on the other. Both of these strategies depend upon fragmentation, and your lecture ultimately arrives at the opposition of Diaspora to the condition of the Global, an opposition that I find incredibly useful and important, as a process of fragmentation is opposed to one that depends upon totalization. In fact, throughout your entire talk, I wish you had spoken about diaspora as opposed to globalization, for I think your earlier theorizations of globalization as rupture are actually more about the challenges to Occidentalism posed by diaspora and not by the more thoroughly economic process of globalization. And yet, just as there are "false totalizations," such as the captation of the public sphere in the model of the nation-state or the rigidification of community into the "agora of spectacle," I would also suggest that there are "false fragmentations" as well. I would like to know why the notion of the diasporic public sphere needs to be expressed in biennials, why it is only through such mediation that we are meant to see, in your words, "the possibility of a paradigm shift in which we as spectators are able to encounter many experimental cultures, without wholly possessing them." I would like to know more about how a counter-hegemonic spectatorship can be sustained, and why again biennials and mega-exhibitions are the place of its devising (and here I guess I am asking you to speak about some of your own curatorial strategies in your work within the mega-exhibition format). For the fragmentation of the institutions of art and culture enacted by biennials today is, as I have implied, another mode of these institutions' consolidation; the perceptual sublime of the mega-exhibition seems dedicated to a fragmentation that blinds, rather than empowers, its spectators.

I don't think we can just wish away the spectacularization inherent in this mode of fusing institution and media that all mega-exhibitions entail. For Debord, media was a euphemism for spectacle. And by the term media, he would explain, we try "to describe a mere instrument, a kind of public service which with impartial 'professionalism' would facilitate the new wealth of mass communication which has at last attained a unilateral purity." However, here "decisions already taken are presented for passive admiration. For what is communicated are *orders;* and with perfect harmony, those who give them are also those who tell us what they think of them."[4] Total institutionalization, total administration, integrated spectacle: this is the historical juncture from which mega-exhibitions arise. And while ultimately I accept and support your privileging of the diasporic, the counter-hegemonic, and the fragmentation of all false totalities, I wonder why it is assumed that this force is to be found in the culture of biennials, in the mediation of the mega-exhibition. We might have to devise new strategies and new diasporic, as opposed to global, forms. So for one last time: I would like to stand against the mega-exhibition, to reaffirm the right to laziness of the biennial Luddite, but hopefully not to end up buttressing the occidental, or worse, to appear like the raving lunatic from that brilliant film *Network,* stepping into the media pulpit only to urge spectators to act out their impotence, run to their windows, throw up their arms, and yell, "I'm mad as hell and I'm not going to take this anymore!" It is instead to urge us to doubt that global biennials prove that the society of the spectacle was a European, imperial phenomenon. An anti-imperialist spectacle might now be envisioned, but I would see this neither as a mode of freedom or criticality nor as the mode in which the projects of the diasporic subject might prosper. Rather, we must be aware and resist a situation that Debord actually knew and wrote about and warned against as, in his words, a "globalization of the false" that could only lead to "a falsification of the globe."[5] ●

NOTES

Previously published in: *Documents* 23 (Spring 2004), pp. 20–25.

1 Guy Debord, *The Society of the Spectacle*, trans. Donald Nicholson-Smith (New York, 1994), p. 120.

2 Guy Debord, *Comments on the Society of the Spectaclc*, trans. Malcolm Imrie (London, 1990), p. 17.

3 Noël Burch and Allan Sekula, "Notes for a Film," *October* 100 (Spring 2002), p. 83.

4 Debord 1990 (see note 2), p. 6.

5 Ibid., p. 10.

THE IMPACT OF THE TWO JOHANNESBURG BIENNIALS ON THE FORMATION OF A "NEW SOUTH AFRICAN ART" (1999)

Sabine Marschall

THE recent national elections, five years after South Africa's first General Elections formally ended apartheid, mark a time for retrospective contemplation.[1] It is also an apt time to look at the transformation of the visual arts scene and the formation and development of a "new South African art." The two largest, most prestigious, and probably most significant events in the recent history of South African art were without doubt the Johannesburg Biennials: *Africus* (1995)[2] and *Trade Routes* (1997).[3] Both biennials were major international exhibitions, where a "new South African art" was shown not only to an international audience but also—unlike previous overseas exhibitions—to South Africans themselves. Perhaps more importantly, both biennials exhibited local art alongside works from a wide array of countries in Africa and other parts of the world, thus placing South African art in a global context and reflecting the relationship of South African art to the international art scene.

Nevertheless, there are significant differences between the two Johannesburg Biennials in terms of organization, curatorship, selection, modes of display, public reception, and in terms of the works of art themselves. These differences provide valuable insights into the development of South African art and the ongoing process of the formation of a new canon and a new identity in post-apartheid South Africa. This paper will neither discuss individual works of art, nor address any specific points of criticism that have been levied at the biennials. Rather it will focus on the impact of the two biennials on South African art production and the emergence and development of a "new South African art."

One such influence was the unprecedented amount of discussion and debate that the two exhibitions drew. In a country where the art world has always occupied a marginal position and art criticism is still in its infancy, it is significant that art matters occupied the limelight, although not necessarily favorably, thus contributing to the initiation of a public debate on art.

The first Johannesburg Biennial, *Africus,* scheduled to coincide with the first anniversary of the 1994 General Elections, was designed to introduce local artists to the world and give South African art status and international recognition, following decades of cultural boycott and international isolation. Organized by Christopher Till and Lorna Ferguson, the event attracted artists from sixty-three different countries and an estimated attendance of 50,000 people.[4]

Reflecting the recent changes of the political landscape and the prevailing spirit of reconciliation and enthusiasm for transformation among virtually all sectors of society, *Africus* was concerned with inclusivity, democratic structures, education,[5] and outreach programs. Proposals for the exhibition of South African works were solicited not solely through established institutional channels but through newspaper adverts aimed at anybody interested in art matters. Ten exhibitions of South African works intended to showcase the diversity of local art production were eventually chosen, each exploring a different theme and most centering on a particular medium.[6] The primary curatorial premise for the exhibition of South African art was the presentation of a revisionist art history focused on closing gaps and redressing imbalances that had resulted from a long tradition of racially biased art historiography.[7] To that effect, *Africus* aimed at presenting a highly diverse selection of visual art forms that reflected the demographic profile of the South African population: Many participating artists were black, self-taught or informally trained, and from disadvantaged socioeconomic backgrounds. Works with a craftlike character, such as Lazarus Seoka's *No Limits, No Frontiers* or Bonnie Ntshalintshali's *Untitled,* would not, until fairly recently, have been considered for inclusion in a canon of South African art, but rather displayed in a separate craft category. Furthermore, *Africus* included art from community art centers (such as the *Caspir* from Katlehong Artists Collective), murals (e.g., Community Mural Projects, outside the Electric Workshop), traditional pottery (exhibition: *Africa Earthed*), various photographic pieces, graphic art from workshop initiatives, and contributions from the San or Bushmen community project at Schmidtsdrift (Qwaa, *Self-Portrait*). These works were presented alongside paintings, sculptures and installations by established, academically trained white artists such as Clive van den Berg (*The Mine Dumps Project*), Willem Boshoff (*Alphabet for the Blind*), and Jane Alexander (*Untitled*). The biennial catalogue, too, contained contributions by less established but promising young scholars. The type of essays, epitomized by the title of Thomas McEvilley's article "Here Comes Everybody,"[8] reflects the concern for inclusivity and a radical redefinition of the canon of South African art.

The ideological ground for the first Johannesburg Biennial's postmodern diversity concept had been prepared by a few revisionist publications of the late eighties and two important exhibitions, namely, Ricky Burnett's *Tributaries*[9] in 1985 and Steven Sack's 1988 exhibition *The Neglected Tradition: Towards a New History of South African Art.*[10] However, while almost all works featured in *The Neglected Tradition* would quite comfortably fit into the Western idiom of "fine art," *Africus* included traditional

African art and craft and presented these works on equal terms with contemporary modern art, following the concept of the controversial but influential 1989 *Magiciens de la terre* exhibition in Paris.

The postmodern multicultural South African group show presented in *Africus* perfectly matched the current political ideology of the newly elected Government of National Unity and the "new South Africa's" image that was officially being promoted nationally and internationally: the democratic, multicultural "rainbow nation," concerned with reconciliation and redress, and the celebration of African heritage and culture as part of a gradual process of re-locating South Africa in Africa.

Numerous multicultural diversity shows of South African works followed *Africus* nationally and abroad. A local example is the 1996 *Jabulisa* exhibition; international examples of the same year are *Common and Uncommon Ground: South African Art to Atlanta* and an exhibition at the Adelson Gallery in New York with the telling title *Simunye / We Are One*[11]—a well-known slogan introduced by the newly transformed South African Public Broadcaster. However, it is significant to note that the latter show, directed at an international, primarily American audience at a commercial gallery, contained a much less inclusive selection of artists. Works that a Western audience would consider craft or "folk art" were largely left out and the selection of black artists focused on well-known names, such as Willie Bester or Kagiso Patrick Mautloa.

Opinions differ regarding to what extent *Africus* functioned as a precedent for these exhibitions as well as for the rearrangement of permanent collections in public art museums.[12] Nevertheless, while its influence may not have been direct, *Africus* endorsed and gave credibility and international status to new paradigms and the widely perceived need for more democratic structures and more representative selection procedures prevailing within the South African art world at the time. This is reflected in changing museum acquisition policies, a certain degree of restaffing with affirmative action objectives in various art institutions, the restructuring of academic art history programs, the reordering of permanent collections, and the development of new themes and paradigms around which contemporary and older works could be regrouped.[13] In short, while *Africus* was certainly not alone in inventing the all-inclusive new South African "rainbow nation" art, it certainly endorsed it and publicized it to a much greater degree than any exhibition or publication on South African art had done before.

The biennial's high-flying empowerment and redressing objectives and its democratizing stance had raised high expectations, and its shortfalls provided ample grounds for criticism. The inclusion of community art was perceived by some as tokenism and as an act of political correctness. The catalogue was criticized for its obscurity and inaccessibility.[14] A disappointed David Koloane, perhaps the only black critic of the biennial, points out in his highly critical review the many lost opportunities of *Africus* in terms of its empowerment objective.[15] Furthermore, the distribution of funds, personnel, and other resources was revealed to be in blatant discord with the recommendations of the government-appointed Arts and Culture Task Group (ACTAG).[16] Says Powell: "It is not enough, as the Biennale's organizers have done, to throw everything into a melting pot; the question is, whose hand holds the spoon?"[17] While this is not the place to investigate the validity of these criticisms, they certainly highlight the significance of the biennial in exposing issues of financial control, curatorial strategies, and the constructedness of any representation of South African art to a broader public.

Despite its many shortfalls, one of the successes and achievements of the first Johannesburg Biennial was the curatorial training program, which had an important impact on the local art scene.[18] The second was the unprecedented amount of international exposure for South African artists and subsequent opportunities for international travel, funding, exhibitions, and other forms of international exchange. This new international interface, as well as the local presence of international artists' works, provided new stimuli for many South African artists, broadening their vision and introducing them to new materials, techniques, and modes of expression. A marked increase in installation art, including new electronic media, was noticeable at the second Johannesburg Biennial, both among South African artists and in general. Examples among the South African works include Bernadette Searle's *Com/fort,* Penny Siopis's video installation *My Lovely Day,* and Stephen Hobbs's CD-ROM *Dusk Till Dusk.* This shift in media, as well as the prominence of more intellectualized, conceptual, and abstract work, could be interpreted to reflect South African artists' increasing alignment with international trends, as some art critics seem to imply.[19] But it appears far more plausible that the emphasis on conceptual work and installation as a medium represents highly selective curatorial choices rather than a reflection of the status of contemporary art in South Africa.[20]

It is significant to note that the organizers of the second Johannesburg Biennial, as opposed to the first, never claimed their selection of South African art to be truly representative. The aims and objectives of *Trade Routes: History and Geography* differed considerably from those of *Africus*, prompting the adoption of a completely different curatorial concept and organizational structure. The experience of the first biennial had highlighted the need to entrench and expand the newly forged network of international linkages and develop an exhibition that was more focused and more professional. The position of artistic director was subsequently advertised internationally, leading to the appointment of Nigerian-born, New York-based Okwui Enwezor, who worked with a multinational team of six curators.[21]

The biennial organizers felt that the intention of *Africus*—to introduce the diverse art traditions of South Africa's "rainbow nation" to the world—had been achieved, thus removing the need to present another highly inclusive, nationally representative selection of works from South Africa.[22] In fact, *Trade Routes* questioned the very validity of national boundaries and the concept of "nationalism."[23] Although one of the exhibitions, *Graft* (curated by Colin Richards), contained only South African works, the conventional organization of artworks in national pavilions was abandoned throughout the show. All works were arranged around the theme of global trade routes, exploring issues of identity and territory in the cosmopolitan world of the "global village," a topic aptly reflecting South Africa's own negotiation between opening and closure, the desire for internationalism and increasing xenophobia. The strong emphasis on contemporary African art, for which the biennial received much praise, further contributed to the re-location of South Africa in Africa.

Trade Routes was clearly about the integration of South African art into a global international context.[24] The selected number of South African works was considerably smaller than in 1995 and demonstrated a significant departure from the previous biennial's obsession with inclusiveness and regionalism. None of the six exhibition venues[25] was located in the townships, there were no fringe exhibitions, and no community art or craft works were included. The concern for equal representation had been replaced by an unspoken concern for "high-standard" and international competitiveness. There was no apprehension among the organizers about the fact that many of the South African works emanated from privileged spaces, and the enormous gap between works by black versus white artists that had characterized the first Johannesburg Biennial appeared largely closed at the second. The race issue was played down in the spirit of postcolonial theory, which had by now become increasingly influential in academia and intellectual circles in South Africa. In fact, the exhibition was praised by critics for its lack of patronizing inclusiveness and fair representation of other "Third World" contributions.[26] It has recently been pointed out that while the curator's persona is waxing in international art exhibitions, the artist's persona is waning, receding behind the often impersonal façade of the installation, which has become the standard medium of international art production.[27] This new "focus on the work itself," which allows the race issue to become less visible and prominent, may have important implications for art in South Africa.

The spirit of *Trade Routes* reflects a significant shift that had taken place in the two years between the first and the second Johannesburg Biennials. The reasons for this shift are manifold, ranging from the conceptual expansions and opportunities opened up by the first Johannesburg Biennial to new government policy on the arts. Clive Kellner suggests that the foundation of the National Arts Council (NAC) with its strong redress agenda, which, simply put, amounts to support for rural crafts at the expense of what are perceived to be "elitist" forms of art-making, may have pushed some artists to connect more strongly with the art world overseas to obtain funding and opportunities for exhibitions.[28] The obsession with inclusivity championed by *Africus* was an extremely important trajectory in the process of redefining the canon of South African art, but the exhibition's criticism also exposed the problematic nature, if not the impossibility, of true representation and multiculturalism, as well as the danger of patronization and, ironically, the exclusivist possibilities inherent in a pluralist approach.[29]

By the time the famous *Art against Apartheid* exhibition, which had occupied the walls of Parliament in Cape Town since the change of government, was replaced by "rainbow art" in 1988,[30] the political correctness of the selection approach had already acquired a taste of staleness and conservatism within some parts of the art world. There are strong indications in South Africa today that resistance to political correctness in the arts is mounting, and the arts, it may be added, only reflect a broader societal phenomenon. There are only a few, however, who voice their dissatisfaction and criticism publicly, among them Robert Greig, who recently published a poignant newspaper article entitled "Wailing worthies have hijacked culture for use as a weapon against originality in the arts." States Greig: "Increasingly, we are asked to appreciate and support works and artists because of hard-luck baggage or because of their noble intentions. The notion that one appreciates a work primarily because of what it is, in [*sic*] its own terms . . . is becoming foreign."[31]

As Sue Williamson critically remarked, the urgent sense of democratization, the obsession with inclusivity, and the pressure to reflect the demographic composition of the population had a profound and often questionable effect on selection processes for exhibitions, museum acquisitions, the art market, and art publications.[32] While public art galleries, most of which currently have no acquisition budget or very limited resources, are still busy catching up and filling gaps left by past collecting practices, there is a growing concern that acquisition policies may tend towards political overcorrection.[33] A recent newspaper report even suggested that white conceptual artists may become the new "neglected tradition" in South Africa.[34] A profound interest in art matters had prompted Albie Sachs, a highly respected anti-apartheid activist of the old South Africa and Constitutional Judge in the new, to write a thought-provoking and trend-setting paper arguing against political correctness in the arts and what he called "solidarity criticism" as early as 1990.[35] In a recent eulogy on his late artist friend Lionel Abrams, Sachs not only warns against parochial regionalist agendas—"an African-centred universe must not cut itself off from the world"[36]—but also takes the daring step of explicitly defending the Eurocentricity of Abrams's work and praising him for not adapting his style to "new concepts of South Africanism."[37] In short, as the second Johannesburg Biennial suggests, it appears that the pendulum is swinging back.

The first indication of this trend is perhaps Sue Williamson and Ashraf Jamal's book *Art in South Africa: The Future Present,* published at the end of 1996. Like *Africus* this publication appears to provide a more or less representative overview of contemporary art from South Africa, but the selection of artists and presentation of works differed considerably. There is no grouping around themes or media; instead, forty artists are presented one after another in random order, each with some illustrations of works, a photo of the artist, and some text. Most artists featured in this volume are white, academically trained, and clearly conversant with international trends and art practices, such as Sue Williamson herself, Jane Alexander, Robert Hodgins, William Kentridge, Malcolm Payne, Penny Siopis, and Kendell Geers. The relatively few black artists included are without exception more established artists like David Koloane, Johannes Segogela, and Kagiso Patrick Mautloa, or examples of extraordinary success stories like Moshekwa Langa or Sandile Zulu, who rose from humble artistic origins to international fame within a short period of time (Zulu, for example, won first prize at the 1998 Seychelles Biennial).

Back to the second Johannesburg Biennial: reviews by international critics attest to the perceived success and tremendous importance of *Trade Routes* within international art circles. Dan Cameron, for example, in his review for *Artforum,* predicting that the second Johannesburg Biennial may turn out to be the most important exhibition of the nineties anywhere in the world, wrote: "*Trade Routes: History and Geography* is the first global exhibition to transform the promise of postcolonial theory into a tangible reality, thereby almost completely exorcising the ghost of 1989's *Magiciens de la terre* from the curatorial lexicon."[38] But among the South African population, *Trade Routes* met largely with apathy. Although most local commentators indicted the show for its elitism, inaccessibility, and irrelevance, factors that were made responsible for the low attendance figures, it must be noted that South Africa has a long tradition of indifference to art, which can be traced to the deficiencies of the country's education system.[39]

A few local critics honed in on the international praise, most notably Kendell Geers, artist, curator, art collector, and art critic for the Johannesburg *Star Tonight,* who wrote prolifically in defense of *Trade Routes* and Okwui Enwezor's curatorial approach.[40] Although the editor of *The Star Tonight* claims that Geers always writes without advantaging or disadvantaging himself,[41] it is significant to note that Geers himself is a predominantly conceptual artist.

Local art critic Hazel Friedman astutely observed that biennials—"more as institutions than as events—constitute a microcosm of power relations in the real world."[42] The case of Kendell Geers epitomizes a problematic characteristic of the art world in South Africa in general that invariably affects the construction of a new canon. The problem is the persisting elitism and diminutive size of the South African art world. A very small number of role players, some of whom, as in Geers's case, even occupy multiple roles, are in a position to wield enormous influence. Geers, for example, has also edited the book *Contemporary South African Art: The Gencor Collection* (1997). It contains an essay by Nigerian artist and writer Olu Oguibe with the telling title "A Place in the Centre: South African Art at the End of the Century." His account of South African art follows precisely the globalist agenda and international competitiveness of *Trade Routes.* Singling out a few South African artists whose work has "sufficient rigour to place them favourably alongside their contemporaries around the world,"[43] Oguibe mentions Kendell Geers first, then Willem Boshoff and the installation work of Kay Hassan, followed by a much briefer mention of Moshekwa

Langa, Willie Bester, Jane Alexander, Penny Siopis, and others. All these artists had already featured in Williamson and Jamal's *Art in South Africa: The Future Present.* It is a list that consists of academically trained white artists and previously disadvantaged black artists who have gained international recognition, firstly because—it could be argued—their visual language largely conforms to international expectations of "standard" artistic production, and secondly because their work allows itself to be interpreted along the lines of current theoretical discourses—even though the artists themselves may never have intended such interpretation and some of them may not even be familiar with the relevant theoretical underpinnings. Their success implies that neither race nor disadvantage prevents a truly talented artist from producing "high-quality" work and succeeding internationally.

The polarization of opinion about the biennial's success, which, as Jen Budney points out, has been presented by some biennial supporters as a matter of bourgeois philistinism versus the progressive cultural politics of the art establishment, highlights the essential dilemma that afflicts the production and exhibition of art in South Africa as well as the construction of a new canon.[44] The art world in South Africa on the whole remains deeply divided, just as the country itself remains divided. With no art education in most black schools, a general lack of art patronage, financial constraints, and the general low-priority status that art has on the national agenda, it will not be easy for any future biennial or large art exhibition to shed its elitist, exclusive image.

What seems clear is that the divide runs no longer primarily along racial lines as in the past, but along the lines of visual language and/or the ability to engage with current theoretical discourses. The newly forged international alliances and close orientation of some artists, black and white, towards the international art scene, will persist, even after South Africa has ceased being the "flavor of the month" in terms of current world interest. Others will never be able to benefit from these opportunities. As South Africa has become much more closely connected to the world, the expectations and "standards" of an international art scene will invariably influence the production of art and the formation of a new canon. ●

NOTES

Previously published in: *Social Dynamics* 25, no. 2 (1999), pp. 119–37.

1 This article is based on a paper presented at the Association of Art Historians (AAH) annual conference in Southampton, April 1999. The author's participation was made possible in part through the financial assistance of the Centre for Science Development (CSD).

2 February 28–April 30, 1995.

3 October 12, 1997–January 12, 1998; it reopened January 8–18, 1998.

4 Ivor Powell, "*Africus:* Another Planet," *Mail & Guardian,* May 5–11, 1995, p. 28.

5 A unique feature in this regard was the curator trainee program.

6 1. International Print Exchange; 2. Objects of Defiance / Spaces of Contemplation; 3. Inside Out; 4. Africa Earthed; 5. Cavewall to Canvas; 6. Volatile Colonies; 7. My Area; 8. Taking Liberties: The Body Politic; 9. Space / Displace; 10. Artists in Residence.

7 Decades of racially segregated and biased education, and of a lack of art training and other opportunities for blacks had created a deeply divided art world in South Africa and an almost insurmountable disparity between the work of black and white artists. These discrepancies and the shortfall of black artists' works in terms of informed artistic standards had previously justified the exclusion of black artists' works from the "canon" of South African art.

8 Thomas McEvilley, "Here Comes Everybody," in Johannesburg Transitional Metropolitan Council (ed.), *Africus: Johannesburg Biennale* (Johannesburg, 1995), pp. 53–57.

9 *Tributaries: A View of Contemporary South African Art,* curated by Ricky Burnett and held at the BMW warehouse in Johannesburg in 1985.

10 *The Neglected Tradition* (Johannesburg Art Gallery, November 23, 1988–January 8, 1989) was the very first exhibition that traced the development and influence of black South African artists. It marked the first time that a major South African art gallery had devoted serious attention to black artists. The well-researched catalogue was the first significant book on the subject, laying the foundation for a more serious investigation of black artists in South Africa. To many people of the general public the very existence of black art was a revelation.

11 *Simunye / We Are One* contained work by artists like Johannes Segogela, William Kentridge, Walter Oilman, Norman Catherine, Willie Bester, Zwelethu Mthethwa, Kendell Geers, Penny Siopis, and Kagiso Mautloa; see J. Pfeffer-Engels's exhibition review, "Insight: Four Artists from South Africa and *Simunye / We Are One,*" *African Arts* (Winter 1997), pp. 75–77.

12 Williamson (idem and Ashraf Jamal, *Art in South Africa: The Future Present* [Cape Town and Johannesburg, 1996]), for instance, sees *Africus* as the prototype of the South African multicultural diversity show, while Carol Brown, director of the Durban Art Gallery (DAG), maintains that by 1995 the postmodern diversity approach was already a generally accepted, common notion. She ascertains that the postmodern rearrangement of the Durban Art Gallery's so-called Pink Room, where local art is displayed, towards the end of 1995 was not influenced by *Africus* (Brown in conversation with the author, Durban, March 1999). Clive Kellner, who was involved in the organization of both biennials, emphasizes that *Africus* did not necessarily so much function as a model for other exhibitions, but did have a profound effect on individuals in the art world, thus introducing new paradigms indirectly (Kellner in conversation with the author, Johannesburg, March 1999).

13 The South African National Gallery mounted a retrospective exhibition spanning the decade from 1985 to 1995, which has been characterized by one reviewer as "a voluntary exposure in the spirit of national reconciliation" (Jacqueline Nolte, "Review of Contemporary South African Art 1985–1995," *Third Text* 39 [Summer 1997], pp. 95–103). While revealing embarrassing gaps and imbalances, the exhibition also demonstrates that there are subtle ways of influencing the reading of the existing works by placing them in new contexts and grouping them around themes informed by current discourses.

14 "Every significant art publication assumes the existence of common knowledge and jargon, but in *Africus* we frequently have the paradox of democratic sentiments couched in a manner guaranteed to baffle all but a thin slice of the educated elite. . . . In short there is a lack of concern for the basic needs of the intelligent nonspecialist and for later readers who would not be approaching the material in the same pressure-cooker political and cultural atmosphere that characterized the change from an apartheid government to a democratically elected one. This is jarringly at odds with the democratizing goals of the show, and it is almost certainly not the impression that the organizers and catalogue editors wished to leave us with." Garth Claassen, "*Africus* Johannesburg Biennale, 1995," catalogue review, *African Arts* (Spring 1997), p. 87.

15 Koloane suggests, for example, that the international academics attending the biennial conference could have been invited to run workshops with local artists, teaching them how to write successful funding applications, etc. ("*Africus:* The Johannesburg Biennale—A Perspective," *African Arts* [Winter 1996], pp. 50–56).

16 As Ivor Powell (1995 [see note 4], p. 28) maintains, less than five percent of the biennial's funding resources were allocated to community projects and development, and only two of the twenty-odd exhibition venues were located in black townships.

17 Ibid., p. 30.

18 Williamson and Jamal 1996 (see note 12).

19 See, for example, Kendell Geers, "Let's Get ahead as an Art Capital," *Tonight (The Star),* January 12, 1999.

20 Admittedly, any curated exhibition involves selection processes. Furthermore, the organizers of the second Johannesburg Biennial never claimed to display a truly representative selection of South African art. Nevertheless, what is significant to note within the context of this paper is that curators, while claiming to reflect global trends, often actually set them. In the case of the second Johannesburg Biennial, for example, the emphasis on installation and highly intellectual conceptual work was justified through contemporary international art practices. By predominantly selecting local works that conform to such practices, competitive South African artists may subconsciously be geared in this direction.

21 The core exhibition *Alternating Currents,* with over sixty-five artists from every part of the world, was organized by Enwezor himself and New York–based Octavio Zaya. Satellite exhibitions including another seventy artists in Johannesburg and Cape Town were organized by Chinese curator Hou Hanru (Paris-based); Kelli Jones from the Walker Art Center; Yu Yeon Kim, founder of PLEXUS (based in New York and Seoul); Gerardo Mosquera from Cuba; and Colin Richards, the sole South African on the team; see Dan Cameron, "October 15, Johannesburg," *Artforum* (December 1997), p. 22.

22 Kellner 1999 (see note 12).

23 Brenda Atkinson, "Routes to Global Culture," *Mail & Guardian*, October 10–19, 1997.

24 As art critic Hazel Friedman ("The Curator as God," *Mail & Guardian*, October 10–16, 1997) enthusiastically put it: "And South African artists are no longer the coy-but-keen debutants at the international art ball. They're part of the global club of cultural nomads, curated overseas shows and international dealerships."

25 *Trade Routes* exhibited the work of more than 160 artists from sixty-three countries in six different venues, four of them in Johannesburg (The Electric Workshop, Museum Africa, the Johannesburg Art Gallery, and the Rembrandt van Rijn Gallery) and two in Cape Town (The Castle and the South African National Gallery); see "Johannesburg Biennale Reopens," *The Star*, January 7, 1998.

26 "The most exciting aspect of the 2nd Johannesburg biennale was its across-the-board selection of artists from places like Cuba, Japan, Mali and Slovakia not as 'other' artists—beneficiaries of a kind of charity or praiseworthy open-mindedness, which is the norm in most curating—but as mere artists with something interesting to say" (Jen Budney, "Who's It For? The 2nd Johannesburg Biennale," *Third Text* 42 [Spring 1998], pp. 92–93). See also Kendell Geers "Building Bridges across Continents," *Tonight [The Star]*, October 30, 1997; idem, "Okwui Enwezor Vindicated," *Tonight [The Star]*, October 29, 1998.

27 Michael Brenson, "The Curator's Moment: Trends in the Field of International Contemporary Art Exhibitions," *Art Journal* 57, no. 4 (Winter 1998), pp. 16–27. This essay has also been reprinted in the present volume.

28 Kellner 1999 (see note 12).

29 Karin Preller ("The 1995 and 1997 Johannesburg Biennales as a 'Reflection' of Contemporary South African Art," *DeArte* 57 [1998], p. 28), in her recent article on the two Johannesburg Biennials, suggests that "the post-apartheid, post-modern, pluralist situation," which characterized the two biennials, may be "as puritanical and exclusionary as the previous scenario (informed by Eurocentric, modernist conditions)" by foregrounding certain "politically correct" issues in selection processes and eliminating all work that does not conform to certain expectations.

30 Henry Ludski, "'Rainbow' Art to Greet MPs," *Sunday Times*, November 15, 1998.

31 Robert Greig, "Wailing worthies have hijacked culture for use as a weapon against originality in the arts," *Sunday Independent*, May 4, 1997.

32 "Of course, the mix of artists has to suitably reflect the demographic composition of the population, and the delicately phrased question 'Is the artist, er . . . black, or white?' has sometimes preceded a sale—or, when the wrong answer [was] given, prevented its coming about" (Williamson and Jamal 1996 [see note 12], p. 9).

33 See Warren Siebrits's remarks in "The 'Neglected Tradition' Is Back Home," *Mail & Guardian*, September 5, 1997; Jill Addleson in conversation with the author, Durban, 1998; Kellner 1999 (see note 12).

34 "The 'Neglected Tradition'" (see note 33).

35 See Albie Sachs, "From Solidarity to Artistic Freedom," *Weekly Mail*, February 2–8, 1990.

36 See idem, "Visions of Proust in the Shower," *Sunday Independent*, August 9, 1998.

37 Ibid.

38 Dan Cameron, "October 15, Johannesburg," *Artforum* (December 1997), p. 22.

39 Marion Arnold already pointed out this broadly based apathy towards art in an article on visual arts and art museums published in 1990 ("South Africa in the Nineties: The Visual Arts and the Art Museum," *DeArte* 41 [April 1990], p. 23), attributing it to the "defective South African education system" under Nationalist rule. Unfortunately, in the new South Africa, little has been done to improve the situation of visual art education for the majority of the population.

40 In an article entitled "Building Bridges across Continents" of 1997 (see note 26), for example, Kendell Geers wrote: "[Okwui Enwezor] has produced the most important exhibition anywhere in the world this year. Hardened art travelers who follow the important exhibitions were brought to their knees in Johannesburg. *Trade Routes* will be remembered for the first exhibition ever to successfully present works by contemporary African artists alongside the very best of their European and American counterparts, without compromising either. Our artists can finally take their places in a highly competitive international market." He attributes the negative local response to parochialism, the education system, lack of support from political and business leaders (see Geers, "Being Topical Doesn't Mean that It's Art," *The Star*, November 13, 1997), as well as general "ignorance, xenophobia and fear" resulting from the country's long years of isolation.

41 Peta Krost, "The Fine Art of Causing a Stir," *Saturday Star*, January 24, 1998.

42 Friedman 1997 (see note 24).

43 Olu Oguibe, "A Place in the Centre: South African Art at the End of the Century," in Kendell Geers (ed.), *Contemporary South African Art: The Gencor Collection* (Johannesburg, 1997), p. 127.

44 Budney 1998 (see note 26).

HEGEMONIC SHIFTS AND THE POLITICS OF BIENNIALIZATION: THE CASE OF DOCUMENTA (2008)

Oliver Marchart

LET'S state it clearly: a biennial is something thoroughly political, and not just in a metaphorical sense.[1] Along with the activities and policies of other artistic institutions, such as the exhibition-making and collecting practices of museums and foundations, the contemporary policy of biennialization—the global spread of the perennial, large-scale exhibition format—plays directly into political policies. That refers, of course, first and foremost to local politics, since biennials and similar events, such as the selection of European Capitals of Culture, contribute to more efficient marketing of cities and regions.[2] Beyond the added economic value for the region, however, the policies of nation-states also play a role. Thus biennialization contributes in no small measure to the construction of local, national, and continental identity. The format of biennials is directly connected to that of world exhibitions, which supported the domestic nation-building of colonial and industrial nations during the nineteenth century. Is it possible to conceive of a politics of biennialization that could change something in the world for the better—and not just in the "art world," which thinks it is the world? Or more precisely, is there a possibility that large, thematically focused exhibitions could have an effect on society—say, by introducing into the public debate political themes that would not otherwise get much attention? Such a political function of public spheres for art would be at cross purposes with current forms of ideological nation-building used by museums and biennials, just as it would be at cross purposes with the economic function of the art world as a marketplace in which goods and services are negotiated.

That possibility is by no means precluded. It must be remembered that so-called peripheral biennials in particular form their own networks and open up channels of communication and translation that can prove valuable locally. Biennials offer "important scenes of cultural translation and transnational encounters."[3] It may be objected that this is true only for the elite of functionaries of the art field and a few biennial hoppers, but, in fact, biennials and other similar large-scale cultural events always represent points of attraction for political movements, organized under the protection and in the shadows of the spectacle, knowing how to use its opportunities for self-promotion. Walter Benjamin pointed out that world exhibitions were "places of pilgrimage to the commodity fetish," where the exchange value of commodities was idealized and people were offered phantasmagorias of diversion;[4] in certain respects, they were politicized by others or could, at least, be exploited politically: "For the Paris world exhibition of 1867, Victor Hugo issues a manifesto: 'To the Peoples of Europe.' Earlier, and more unequivocally, their interests had been championed by delegations of French workers, of which the first had been sent to the London world exhibition of 1851 and the second, numbering 750 delegates, to that of 1862. The latter delegation was of indirect importance for Marx's founding of the International Workingmen's Association."[5]

Intentionally or unintentionally, large exhibitions—if only because of the sudden amassing of infrastructure and the availability of the media for self-promotion—can become facilitators of political statements—that is, those external to the art field. Even today, Documenta in Kassel—solely as a result of the media attention it generates—attracts political groups, whether or not they are invited. For example, an activist network by the name of kein mensch ist illegal (no person is illegal) was founded, like a distant echo of the meeting of workers' delegations in the nineteenth century, in the "hybrid workspace" of Documenta 10 in 1997, and it still exists today.

THE IRONY OF THE POLITICAL

THUS a certain irony clings to the politics of biennialization: not irony in the humorous sense, but irony in the materialist sense—an objective irony. On the one hand, Western large-scale exhibitions whose purpose is nation-building (and hence, implicitly, subject-building) bring enormous symbolic, prestigious infrastructural resources into play. In a sense, that makes them giant ideology machines or, more precisely, hegemony machines of the dominant (read: bourgeois, nation-state, Occidental, European) culture. Their political significance is therefore enormous. On the other hand, however—and this is the irony—such exhibitions will never succeed in completely controlling the effects they produce. Wherever resources are available, they will be tapped by the unauthorized. The dominant discourse reproduced and kept in circulation by such hegemony machines can be read differently than it was intended to be. And it could get worse: the apparatus itself can fall into enemy hands. Subsequent factions announce their ambitions and demand changes (in the case of the generation of the sixties, for example) or even convert the apparatus to make it available for other purposes. By hijacking institutions, the dominant culture's apparatus for cultural reproduction can be at least partially appropriated, taken apart, and rebuilt in a different way. In the art field in recent years, for example, there has been talk of a "New Institutionalism"[6] that, in contrast to earlier waves of institutional critique in art, was not about isolated interventions into the apparatus of exhibition but rather about the organizational and curatorial takeover of this apparatus itself. The goal of this takeover was to open up the art institution in question, to create a space of criticism, to make experimental formats possible, and to call into question institutional hierarchies, work relationships, and the circumstances of institutional production in general. At best, the apparatus is taken apart and put back together, but it is never destroyed as such. That means one does not simply retreat into critique of the institution and, in the process, keep one's hands clean, but rather first overcomes all fear of getting involved with the institution, however arduous this might be.

The apparatus can thus be made useful for a progressive canon shift in the field. This makes it possible to state and depict some things that could not be expressed before; other things, however, can no longer be expressed, or have to be reformulated hegemonically in order for this to happen. This does not necessarily occur suddenly; the loss of hegemony of the dominant culture can happen gradually. One analytical approach is particularly well suited to describing such tortuous processes: the hegemony theory originally developed by Antonio Gramsci and then expanded by Ernesto Laclau and Chantal Mouffe through discourse analysis.[7] It could be said that the Marxist Gramsci developed historical materialism into an *ironic materialism*. The structure of hegemony is always objectively ironic. "Hegemony" describes an unstable balance between social forces struggling for dominance. This unstable equilibrium of forces, in which there are always dominant and subordinate forces, is established by the network of institutions of civil society within the meaning of one side. "Hegemony" does not describe the flowerpot that the dominant side has already won in the shooting match as much as it does the *power relationship* between the rival forces. No one "possesses" a hegemony; they have to struggle constantly for its dominance. In fact, hegemony can never be achieved completely, since there are always other forces that want to get involved. Gramsci proposed the metaphor of a "war of position"—referring to the trench warfare of the First World War—for this constitutively tangled situation. A war of position—think of Verdun—is based on a system of narrow and winding trenches, so that it is often not at all clear where the front is located. The objective irony of hegemony lies in the fact that the one's own fortifications can end up in enemy hands as soon as the front—that is, the equilibrium of forces—shifts. Then they can help the enemy establish its hegemony. To put it another way, institutions are not "neutral" as apparatuses, and they definitely possess a certain life of their own, but nothing about the formats of large-scale perennial exhibitions determines that they will always spread nationalist and racist ideologies in the way that world exhibitions once did.

1
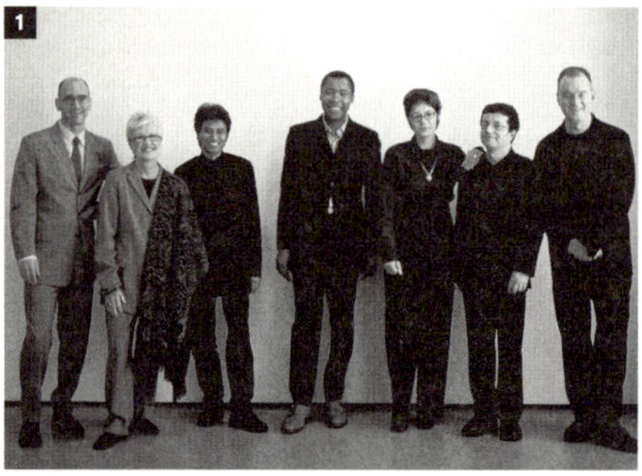

2
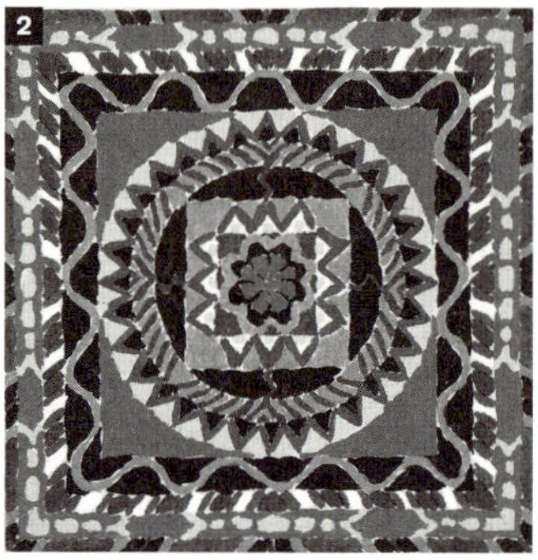

3
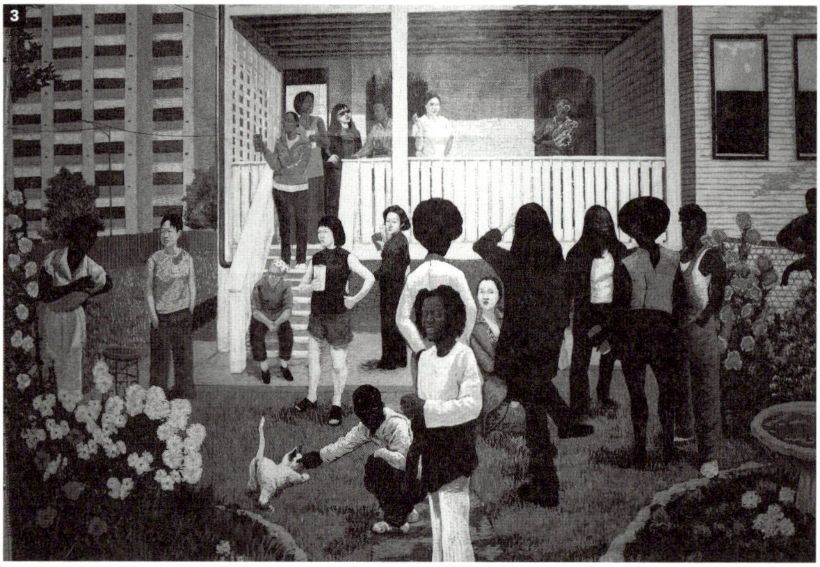

4
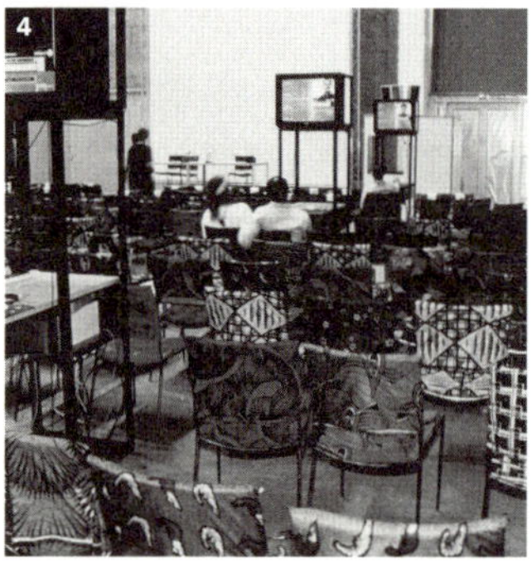

5
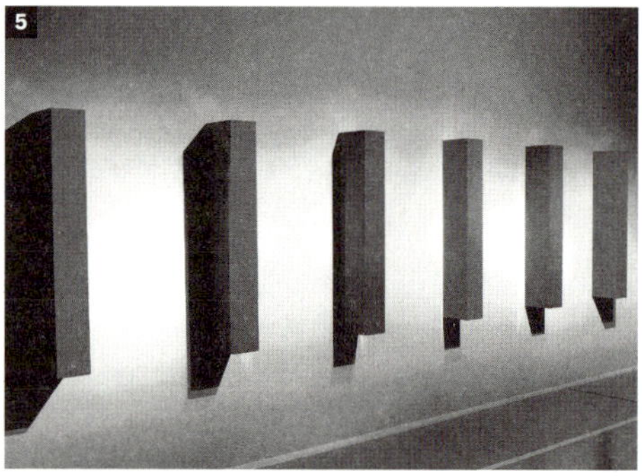

1 Documenta 11 curatorial team (L to R): Carlos Basualdo, Susanne Ghez, Sarat Maharaj, Okwui Enwezor, Ute Meta Bauer, Octavio Zaya, and Mark Nash.

2 John McCracken, *Tantric,* 1971.

3 Kerry James Marshall, *Garden Party,* 2003–2007.

4 Franz West, *Dokustuhl,* 1997.

5 John McCracken, *Fire,* 2007.

TECTONIC SHIFTS IN THE ART FIELD

ON the contrary, today we are witnessing an antihegemonic shift that has seized even the institutions of the dominant bourgeois culture itself—or at least some of those institutions. Using the examples of the tenth, eleventh, and twelfth editions of Documenta, we will study more precisely how anti-canonization and hegemonic shifts can be advanced (or, conversely, reverted) *using the appropriated institutional means of the apparatus.* If Documenta 10 and Documenta 11 took a canon shift already latently present and condensed it symbolically into a break with the art field's past that had progressive effects, then Documenta 12 could be said to have done the opposite. These shifts can be traced along several fault lines. In what follows, I will limit myself to the axes of politics, postcolonialism,[8] and theory.

The shift in canon initiated by artistic director Catherine David's Documenta 10 and then radicalized by Okwui Enwezor's Documenta 11 (which he co-curated with a team of collaborators) took place along several axes and culminated in a break with the past against which later biennials and exhibitions in the field must be measured (fig. 1). Roger Buergel's Documenta 12 (co-curated with Ruth Noack) was therefore confronted with a problem in relation to the two exhibitions that preceded it. With its depoliticized aestheticism, it demonstrated that no politicizing will remain unchallenged forever. It could be formulated polemically: as can be demonstrated along the axes outlined, Documenta 12 wanted to help the educated petty bourgeoisie regain its right to enjoy art. Documenta 12 intended to bring back—that is, neutralize—the breaks and shifts produced by the two Documentas before it into the bourgeois dominant culture, specifically by means of strategies such as formalizing, ornamentalizing, decontextualizing, detheorizing, and Occidentalizing the works presented. In comparison to Documentas 10 and 11, their successor's strategies combined to create an overall strategy that Gramsci would have called *transformism.* Once again, the irony of the political is revealed here: the institutional means appropriated for the canon shift is now employed by the dominant culture to defuse everything rebellious or unpopular about it. Antihegemonic breaks are smoothed over and integrated into the hegemonic formation.

We learn from Gramsci that the front lines between social forces never run clearly, and all institutions and actors intersect multiple times. What is more, the "fortresses and casemates," in Gramsci's words, of the exhibition complex cannot be adopted from one day to the next, nor can shifts in the canon be undone from one day to the next. Every hegemonic shift leaves behind an altered terrain from which every opponent has to proceed.

This can be demonstrated for the biennial complex using the example of the history of the past three Documenta exhibitions. For example, Documenta 10 succeeded in legitimizing a certain politicizing of the practices of art and exhibition at the "center" of the art field (even if it was merely an imaginary center) that had already been underway for some time in the more marginal areas of the art field. Much the same could be said of Documenta 11 and the way it made the problems of postcolonialism visible. Both exhibitions introduced (or reinforced) an—accumulating—canon shift that changed the terrain for future Documenta curators in a way that could not simply be ignored. The decision in favor of a rollback could not make everyone forget what had happened previously, as if Documenta 10 and Documenta 11 had never taken place. Both the integration of political works and the integration of non-Western artists had become imperatives in the biennial complex or, at least, for Documenta. A Documenta like Documenta 12 simply could not ignore this imperative. Instead, it had to develop strategies for integrating political works on the one hand, and depoliticizing them on the other—strategies for making their content and intentions invisible behind an aestheticizing, formalizing, and mystifying veil. It had to develop strategies to recenter the center of the Western art world that Kassel had marked every five years until Documenta 11 decentered it; it had to reprovincialize Kassel, re-Germanize it, and ultimately re-Kasselize it.

And yet—and this is the good news for those attached to the idea of a politically, theoretically, and aesthetically progressive exhibition of any sort—no rupture can be mended completely; nothing can be fully absorbed. Once an antihegemonic canon shift has occurred, it inscribes itself into the hegemonic formation of the art field (and also, therefore, into the hegemonic formation as a whole), for once the coordinates of the field have shifted, this shift cannot be undone but can only be taken up by another shift and thus transformed. As everywhere else in the order of the political, no ground gained, however minimal, is for naught, since it makes the dominant society work for its hegemony by defending it against attack.

The thesis is that the canon shifts that were inaugurated in Documenta 10 and so concentrated in Documenta 11 in particular could not be absorbed unproblematically. This was not primarily because they took place in the imaginary center of the art field, and *at the same moment* this center was decentered by Documenta 11, it was used by it *as a center.* This reveals once again one of the aspects of objective irony that apparently lie in the nature of struggles over the canon: it is not usually advantageous for marginalized discourses to remain at the margins. That is a luxury that can only be enjoyed by those who have already found their regular place in the center and are just making a brief excursion into the marginal zones. Even *anti*canonization seeks representation in the center. The decentering of the center should not, therefore, be confused with the elimination of it. On the contrary, the central apparatuses of the art field—and here, in turn, the more central apparatuses *within* the field to which most biennials and Documenta belong—are of inestimable value for the reproduction of hegemonic formations and can, ironically, be placed in the service of *anti*hegemonic projects for the same reason.

What such a central apparatus of the biennial complex can achieve above all is to lend symbolic legitimacy to marginalized discourses. The brilliance of the center was used while at the same time the hegemonic West was—at least in part—dislodged from the center. Any other strategy would, predictably, have failed. For example, in what might be called a more anarchistic spirit, the institution's power to lend legitimacy could have been destroyed, and Documenta allowed to fail, but that would only have robbed those responsible of an apparatus with the power to recanonize. Or this center of the exhibition complex could have been ignored from the outset, but then it would have been left to the hegemonic dominant culture. Both options would have been neither hegemonic nor antihegemonic strategies, but merely an expression of political capitulation. The theory of hegemony teaches us that one cannot be afraid of occupying the center, even if one allows oneself the luxury of lining up against all centers at the end of the day.

POLITICIZING AND DEPOLITICIZING (THE FIRST SHIFT)

SO let us turn to the hegemonic shifts symptomatically manifested in the center of this field: first at Documenta 10, curated by Catherine David, and then at Documenta 11, curated by Okwui Enwezor. These are considered to be the "most political" of all the Documenta exhibitions until that time. David parted ways with the imago-centric approach of her predecessor, Jan Hoet, who was responsible for Documenta 9 in 1992, and presented her project in urban space, especially transitional areas, to say nothing of spaces of communication like the Internet, for the first time, and in a "hybrid workspace" in the Orangerie. The integration of works with political concerns seemed scandalous to some critics, who even perceived it as a kind of oppression, if not censorship, of apolitical artists.

Despite its reference to politics and public urban space, Documenta 10 did not simply revive Harald Szeemann's first concept for Documenta 5—that is, the concept of an "event"—but rather attempted to produce the *conditions for the possibility* of publicness without being able to anticipate whether publicness would in fact *emerge*. Publicness is not something that is already lying around "in the street." Publicness only emerges at the moment of conflict—for example, when the space of street traffic becomes the political space of the public sphere. This criterion of conflict is what distinguishes the public sphere as political space from the marketlike placebo public sphere of the bazaar or the lobbyist's space of the front or back room. This onset of the political, of antagonism, cannot be prejudiced institutionally. So Documenta 10 and Documenta 11 were probably not so much political in the strict sense of the political, of antagonism, as they were *analytical* in relation to politics and social/cultural conflicts. In essence, these exhibitions saw themselves as instruments of cognition, or as cognitive weapons, rather than as directly political. This explains the documentary and conceptual nature of many of the works. Hence it was primarily on globalization or the postcolonial constellation that the two exhibitions, each in its own way, shed political light.

Documenta 11 in particular radicalized in several ways the strategies of exhibiting in the form of increased *politicizing*, a *decentering of the West*, and an uncompromised *theorizing*. "Politicizing" here does not simply mean that Documenta 11 saw itself as a political intervention on the level of cultural symbolic production; above all, it means that analytical, political practices moved to its center, and the exhibition became an instrument of political analysis that also caused or continued certain shifts in the canon of the art field. Decentering the West means not only shedding light on European art's involvement in colonial history, but also displacing the West from the center (this occurred through a series of what were called "platforms," held in New Delhi, Saint Lucia, and Lagos, among other places) so that the "non-West" could become the focus. Documenta 11, as Enwezor put it, was only about the "attempt to expand the dimension of Documenta with regard to what is understood as public space" in a qualified sense.[9] It was a temporal and spatial deterritorializing of the exhibition to create five platforms, including four "theoretical" ones, that extended the space for confrontation and controversy between Documenta and its audience.[10] Thus, the "theorizing" of the exhibition, as I have advanced here, means not only that the actual history and function of exhibiting were considered more carefully, but also that the intersection of art and theory was emphasized more strongly than ever before.

Ultimately, any antagonism that can be generated by institutions such as Documenta has to be located elsewhere—namely, in its institutional practice proper, which I have characterized, in the sense indicated above, as *anticanonization*. In this case, the power of the institution to define is used and turned—ironically—against its previous hegemonic definition. This strategy aims to produce a conflict not so much with the institution as with the dominant culture from which an institution was wrested in order to help shift the canon. The power of the institution to define and canonize is not attacked; indeed, it is welcomed, because it lends the intended canon shift the necessary symbolic capital and operative infrastructure.

Admittedly, there is a risk associated with this: even biennials with progressive curators can lead to a kind of "normalization" of the political. As early as 1993, on the occasion of the Whitney Biennial—also known as "the politically correct biennial"—James Meyer warned against political art being "normalized" into identity art: "For all its good intentions, the 'multicultural,' 'grunge' Biennial canonized the emergence of the political as a style, the latest trend in high cultural consumption."[11] Meyer himself argued for a strategy combining institutional critique and activism, but one that remained skeptical about the merely metaphorical exhibition of political content. If we consider a more recent example from the post–Documenta 11 phase—the tenth Istanbul Biennial (2007), curated by Hou Hanru—it becomes clear that this normalization of political art even manifests itself in a spatial separation: for example, the explicitly political works were exhibited in Istanbul's somewhat rundown textile market, while the market-oriented works were assembled in the central exhibition location, the Antrepo.[12] Although Hanru was continuing a strategy from the ninth Istanbul Biennial in 2005, curated by Charles Esche and Vasif Kortun with the title *Art, City, and Politics in an Expanding World*, by expanding into urban space, the tenth Istanbul Biennial unintentionally cemented the marginal status of political practices in the arts by exiling marginalized art to peripheral sites while the center—the Antrepo—continued to be reserved for the mainstream. If they had wanted a truly political exhibition, as was ultimately achieved by the eleventh Istanbul Biennial, curated by What, How and for Whom (WHW) in 2009, they could have preceded in precisely the opposite fashion, reserving the center for marginalized art practices (Documenta 11 had tried to achieve precisely that with its strategy of decentering).

This example illustrates that at least some of the problems of representing political practices for art disappear as soon as political art ceases to be understood as a genre and the exhibition concept is considered as a whole. Hence what is relevant is not only whether specific works included are political, but also the extent to which the conception and realization of the exhibition *as such* provide room for art as a form of political analysis or rather depoliticize political works by means of an exhibition apparatus that neutralizes or defuses them. This is precisely what happened at Documenta 12, for which Roger M. Buergel and Ruth Noack were responsible, as a result of a *retransformation* of the political into the bourgeois dominant discourse that characterizes the art field—and not only the art field. It became clear that Buergel and his co-curator Noack pursued a curatorial strategy for Documenta 12 of depoliticizing even the political works that had made it into the exhibition. An analysis of the depoliticizing strategy of that exhibition enables us to break it down into at least three substrategies. Documenta 12 domesticated all politics by *decontextualizing, formalizing,* and *aestheticizing* selected works. Along this tripartite line of domestication, Buergel and Noack presented the proof that it was possible to curate a completely apolitical exhibition despite the presence of a significant number of political works. It is quite sufficient to tear the works out of their original political context, formalize their content (while suppressing all information such as wall texts or an affordable short guide), and aestheticize them through their arrangement and display in the exhibition.

Shortly after Roger M. Buergel was appointed artistic director of Documenta, he announced in a press statement that Documenta would once again return the "beautiful" to its accustomed place. In the interview he stated that not only did he have no problem with the concept of beauty, but beauty would dominate at the new Documenta.[13] This proclaimed return to the beautiful in art was rightly recognized by the press as a paradigm shift in the philosophy of Documenta: a return—after two explicitly political exhibitions—to an exhibition that would offer less theory, less politics, less critique, and more beauty. The beautiful in art should, Buergel postulated, be revealed before the work of art in quiet "contemplation"—only then would the true political potential of art open up.[14] Although very few were willing to believe that it could really go that far, the exhibition opening demonstrated that Buergel had intended his announcement seriously. Finally, politics and beauty joined forces again—the bourgeois German feuilletons expressed pleasure and defended the curator against certain representatives of the specialist publications who could not believe their eyes. It became evident that the aestheticizing of the political has long since ceased to be an exclusive feature of Fascism, as Walter Benjamin believed, and that the bourgeois hegemony itself has appropriated the political *with the proviso that it be aestheticized.* To put it another way, the aestheticizing of the political content of artistic works—that is, their incorporation and commodification for enjoyment—has itself become one of the main strategies of the bourgeois hegemonic project.

This circumstance does not, of course, say anything per se against political art, since the art field is an important site of reproduction for the dominant Western, bourgeois culture, and it should be neither ignored nor dismissed. It does, however, say something against the "aestheticizing" of political art for the sake of decoration: at Documenta 12, it became wallpaper. To do this, of course, it had to be robbed of its original meaning and context by means of a radical de(con)textualization. In their decidedly brief preface to the catalogue, Buergel and Noack make it known that it goes without saying that art always has a local history, but an exhibition is only worth looking at "if we manage to dispense with preordained categories and arrive at a plateau on which art communicates itself and on its own terms."[15] They were postulating that text and context are superfluous, since things always speak for themselves if we allow them to affect us. This explains the extreme formalism that surprised most of the people who visited the exhibition.

Buergel's slogan of the "Migration of Form" legitimized replacing the critical, political approach that had characterized both Documenta 10 and Documenta 11 with superficial formal analogies between works of art that lay far apart both temporally and geographically. These formal analogies arose in allusion to the discourse of a conservative art history (the imaginary principle of representation behind it is the principle of double projection) but without any need to offer scholarly reasons for the curatorial comparisons of form. That means that the scholarly justification of formal comparisons that could be expected of the art historical discourse to which Buergel alluded was replaced at Documenta 12 by the purely voluntarist dictates of taste of a curator who has determined decisionistically and groundlessly what does and does not "go together" formally.[16] There were hardly any cases in which the result could be understood by a reflective audience. As he admitted himself, even the artistic director could not understand it. From one of the few coherent texts in which Buergel articulated his understanding of form, it becomes clear that the exhibition followed the principle of pure association. The audio guide through the Museum Fridericianum that Buergel himself narrated, which occupied a special place not least because it replaced the nonexistent wall texts, is formalistic to the point of self-parody. Buergel guides us through Room 1 of the Fridericianum with the following words:

> *Like all four large rooms in this building, this room is organized thematically—that is to say, formally. That means one sees works by different artists, among which we—Ruth Noack, the curator of the exhibition, and little old me—have discovered correspondences or family resemblances—family resemblances of a formal nature, even though the artists may have nothing to do with one another. Take a look, for example, at the three photographs by Ahlam Shibli on the end wall to the left: there are two interiors of Palestinian homes and a view of a courtyard in which some laundry is covering a person. I do not wish to go into the details of the work but simply ask you to see the hung laundry in relation to the cloths hanging down on the sculpture to the right of the entrance—Cosima von Bonin's lion in the bonsai forest—and to connect the bamboo poles hanging down in the bonsai forest to the hair hanging down out of Hu Xiaoyuan's fragile embroidered frames.*[17]

What do we learn here about the principle of selection in and the organization of Room 1? First of all, we learn that "thematic" means "formal" for Buergel and that correspondences between the works were discovered by Noack and "little old me," Roger Buergel. And of what do these correspondences and family resemblances in Room 1 consist? They consist of the fact that *something is hanging down* in all the works. That is what connects them to one another. That is Noack and Buergel's astonishing curatorial achievement: having found works in which something is hanging down. If we continue to listen to the audio guide, we ultimately learn that the artistic director himself does not know what it is really supposed to be or even if it is supposed to be something at all: "By means of all these correspondences, whose significance we do not know precisely—indeed, about which it is not even clear whether they mean anything at all—we approach the large painting on the built-in partition wall in the back of the room."[18]

This confession in the form of an audio guide was far too often overlooked by critics, probably because most writers from the specialist journals are too good to rely on audio guides at all and therefore never heard it. Buergel's remarks illustrate the rift that separated Documenta 12 from Documentas 10 and 11. Documenta 12 functioned as a depoliticizing machine, reducing even the political works that were included to objects of formal and aesthetic contemplation (fig. 2). The political clichés occasionally strewn through it could not disguise this: the goal of this aestheticizing of politics was nothing other than the conversion, the transformation of political critique of the mere affirmation of the formal—for example, in the form of something hanging down—that had been articulated by Documenta 10 and Documenta 11.

DE- AND RECENTERING THE WEST (THE SECOND SHIFT)

DOCUMENTA 12 turned out to be an unexpected "setback" for the critical sectors of the art field, which wanted to use its institutions to propagate antihegemonic critical discourses—a project that had gained considerable legitimacy with Documenta 10 and Documenta 11. Now this legitimizing background seemed destroyed all at once. Documenta 12 went to great trouble to depoliticize even the more political works presented by means of decontextualization, aestheticization, and formalization. The more conciliatory hegemonic project of Documenta 12, which threatened to put an end to all criticism in favor of the aestheticizing of political works into reauraticized objects of contemplation, threatened the basis for legitimizing created by the Documenta exhibitions that preceded it. This picture should not be painted in overly gloomy colors, since Documenta 12 also faced an altered hegemonic situation that the curators could not undo entirely without appearing ridiculous. Let us therefore turn to the second axis of the shift in the canon embodied above all by Documenta 11. With its strategy of decentering the West, Documenta 11 moved non-Western art to the center of the art field and *institutionally* decentered Kassel as an event venue; it advocated the "de-Kasselizing" of Kassel, so to speak.

The platform structure of Documenta 11 was intended as nothing less than a temporal, spatial, and thematic expansion and deterritorialization of Documenta the institution: Documenta 11 began long before the summer of 2002 and far from Kassel. It started in March and April 2001 in Vienna with the first platform, *Democracy*

Unrealized, which was continued in October of that year at the Haus der Kulturen der Welt in Berlin. The second platform, held in New Delhi and entitled *Experiments with Truth,* was dedicated to the issues of truth, justice, and reconciliation in states that have just emerged from genocide or civil war. The third platform in St. Lucia raised the questions of *créolité* and creolization, while the fourth platform in Lagos was concerned with urban and social problems in the African megacities of Freetown, Johannesburg, Kinshasa, and Lagos. Only the fifth and final platform, the only one to be held in Kassel, corresponded to what is usually associated with Kassel's Documenta. Using this strategy, Enwezor was able to decenter Documenta not only in terms of content but also geographically and temporally.

This strategy can certainly be described as a thorough deconstruction of an institution that has historically laid the groundwork for Eurocentrism and Occidentalism, given that Documenta had been indebted to the dual project of Europe and the West ever since it was founded. This is already evident in the programmatic use of terms such as "Occident" and "freedom" by certain ideologues of the early editions of Documenta. For Werner Haftmann and the first three Documenta exhibitions, abstraction was a "world language," although, because of the particularlist universalism of the West, it had to be clear that world art was nothing other than Western art. Kassel's location near the border between East and West Germany contributed to Documenta's view of itself as an outpost in a competition between systems being carried out on the level of art. The crucial antagonism was between Western, modernist abstraction on one side and Socialist Realism on the other.[19] Despite all of the attempts to break out of this (e.g., Manfred Schneckenburger's integration of East German art at Documenta 6), it would remain this way for some time.

It can therefore be said that the crucial break with the intention of decentering the West along the postcolonial axis began with Documenta 11, despite all the contributions made by Documenta 10. This process is certainly filled with contradictions, turning any curatorial effort in this area into a slalom around diverse pitfalls. On the one hand, the West is not everywhere, which is why it is not so simple to speak without further ado of the West's dominance over the rest of the world. If globalization means anything at all, it means the transformation of *every* local culture—even Western cultures—through contact with a large number of other local cultures to form a hybrid. The Western industrial nations are subject to this process just as much as supposedly traditional cultures are. But that does not resolve the matter, since, on the other hand, the hegemony of the West does not by any means dominate unchallenged. There are clear relationships of dominance between various regions; there are forms of political, economic, and military neocolonialism and forms of resistance, and there continues to be a dialectic of the colonial—that is, exoticizing—gaze, which is difficult to escape. Okwui Enwezor constantly tried to avoid pinning down identities, and that was probably the only practicable strategy he could have employed. At no time did Documenta 11 wish to exhibit the foreign or the Other, which would only have been acting as an accomplice to the Occidental gaze. And yet Documenta 11's declared goal was to decenter the West and recenter what the West had excluded (that is, what I have been calling a canon shift).

In this respect, it differed from most large exhibitions that have sought to offer a central place to non-Western art. Although the Western art world's interest in the "non-Western"—with all the pitfalls of Orientalism, exoticism, and a new primitivism[20]—had begun to increase at the very latest by the time of the *Magiciens de la terre* exhibition at the Centre Georges Pompidou, curated by Jean-Hubert Martin in 1989, the "postcolonial" Documenta 11 of 2002 (thirteen years after *Magiciens*) marked a break in the art field. Naturally, this break was not due entirely to Documenta: the emergence of peripheral biennials in Havana, Dakar, Johannesburg, Istanbul, and elsewhere played its part, as did the hunger of the Western art system for input that could be reevaluated. However, Documenta 11 took a canon shift that was already underway at the margins of the field and moved it precisely to the (imaginary) center of the Western art world.

Documenta 12, by contrast, was characterized by a dreamy aestheticism even in its approach to the postcolonial constellation. This does not mean that Documenta 12 had simply set off on the path back to *Magiciens de la terre,* since, as noted above, there is no going back to square one in hegemonic debates, only an institutional reintegration of the breaks. Reintegration does not mean complete absorption. The breaks continue to exist even when their meaning is supposed to be inverted. After Documenta 11, therefore, Documenta 12 also had to integrate non-Western art, and it did so, among other ways, with a gesture of outdoing its predecessors, by not mentioning the city or country of birth of the participating artists on the exhibition signage. This antinational gesture of outdoing was, however, undermined elsewhere by the attempt to invert exactly Documenta 11's postcolonial strategy. For Okwui Enwezor, any colonialist pose of the discovery of non-Western art had to be avoided. Indeed, the very idea of a "non-Western artist" was almost a contradiction in terms for

Enwezor—or at least a Western projection, since a significant number of supposedly "non-Western artists" actually live in New York or other Western metropolises. The Western search for an ostensibly authentic non-Western art beyond the circulation system of the Western art market ran the risk of an equally ostensible autochthonous "Other." For this reason, one of the major goals of Documenta 11 was to escape the traps of a new primitivism like the one that characterized *Magiciens de la terre*. The Europeans Buergel and Noack, by contrast, dedicated themselves cheerfully to ostensibly authentic non-Western art: they claimed to have discovered many artists unknown in the West (if not in their own countries).

This return to the gesture of the colonial discoverer continues in many of the catalogue texts, which overflow with discursive tropes from ethnology, culturalism, and authenticism. One of these tropes is that of millennia-old, distant civilizations from time immemorial. For example, we are told that Sakarin Krue-On's rice fields next to Schloss Wilhelmshöhe were an example of European architecture encountering "the millennia-old practice of wet rice cultivation"—as if it were not possible to find rice fields in Italy, just a few hundred kilometers south of Kassel.[21] A similar remark in the catalogue is made of Romuald Hazoumé's work: "If you're part of a four-thousand-year-old African culture, you don't need Western art history."[22] That is not only an insult to Hazoumé, whose work is thus located in the Stone Age, but also symptomatic of Documenta 12's approach to so-called non-Western art, or to Western art that has suddenly adopted this role. Documenta 12 culturalized it, exoticized it, and dressed it up as authentic by dissociating it from the Western discourse on art. To give another example, J. D. 'Okahi Ojeikere's photographs of Nigerian hairstylists are presented in the catalogue as follows: "Hairstyling was long considered an incompatible form of artistic expression. When wigs were introduced in the nineteen-fifties and -sixties it seemed this cultural heritage would be lost, a heritage that was an integral part of Nigerian culture . . . Thanks to his personal passion and insight, 'Okhai Ojeikere's work provides a testament to a culture that is constantly changing." Nor does the author fail to mention that this is "a singular work of great beauty."[23] Such texts offer the nostalgic lament of the Western ethnologist who seeks a "four-thousand-year-old culture" in Africa only to observe with regret that times change even in Africa. And whereas, in keeping with the curators' detextualization strategy, most of the political works in the exhibition had no text, even when the artist had wanted texts, 'Okhai Ojeikere's work was accompanied by a wall text with detailed ethnographic descriptions. From this one can only conclude that political, historical, and social contextualization was unwanted at Documenta 12, but culturalist and exoticist contextualization was always welcome.

But anyone who preaches meditative "immediacy" in dealing with non-Western works and withholds information merely creates projection screens for the primitivist, and perhaps even the racist fantasies of the exhibition visitors. In the absence of any critical discourse on the works, to say nothing of the exhibition as a whole, there is nothing to keep visitors from such projections; Buergel's strategy of decontextualization ensured that. When the work of art is simply allowed to speak for itself, it does not lead to an unprejudiced conversation between the work and the viewer, since there is no neutrality in the hegemonic field. Allowing things to speak for themselves always means providing space for the hegemonic formation to speak. The result is that a Western, Eurocentric, and occasionally racist apparatus is called up and constructed not only in the exhibition but also in the heads of the viewers.

Documenta 12 was thus characterized by the return of primitivism under new hegemonic conditions. While it integrated non-Western art in a seemingly progressive, equal way, it believed it could take the liberty of ignoring the critique of the Western gaze in postcolonial theory (and museum studies). This was most clearly evident from the approach to Kerry James Marshall's works, which were distributed throughout the exhibition; through a process of decontextualization, they were reduced to quasi-primitivist representations of "black faces" and "black bodies," and hence became primitivized themselves. Even in the case of the so-called intervention in the art historical collection of the Schloss Wilhelmshöhe, where Marshall's works were placed beneath two paintings by Karel van Mander, the complete absence of all discourse reduced the pairing to a simple mimetic doubling of "black faces" rather than presenting a serious commentary on the colonial imagination in European art. Viewers learned nothing of the relationship of Marshall's works to the civil rights movement; instead, Buergel's catalogue entry on the artist offered only formal analyses of the "promiscuous patchwork" of this "great painter" (fig. 3).[24]

Whereas Buergel celebrated a formalism that turned into primitivism, Enwezor insisted on conceptualism precisely to escape primitivism. The Conceptual art of Hanne Darboven, Bernd and Hilla Becher, and Maria Eichhorn was brought into a constellation with Latin American political Conceptual art (Luis Camnitzer, Artur Barrio, and Cildo Meireles) and the works of African artists such as Frédéric Bruly

Bouabré. In this way, the primitivist, if not racist, cliché that art elsewhere was less conceptual and instead "more emotional" could be disabused in favor of positioning African art *as conceptual art.*[25] The formalism of Documenta 12, by contrast, led to the exact opposite by formalizing and primitivizing nonformalist African art:

> *After all the discussions of the past twenty years concerning who represents what, the retreat to private interest in formal comparisons takes on a different significance. Buergel's praise of "aesthetic experience" ... becomes problematic in a curatorial attitude that serves the cultural and artistic products of diverse regions and contexts from a culinary metaperspective, like a creative cuisine in which mozzarella is served with blood sausage because they have similarly rounded forms.*[26]

THE INTERSECTION OF ART AND THEORY (THE THIRD SHIFT)

THE political break marked by Documenta 10 and Documenta 11 in relation to previous editions of Documenta was manifested not least in their interest in theory. Three formats were employed by Documenta 10: a series of journals, a series of daily lectures, and a volume of theoretical writings that accompanied the exhibition. The *Documents* series of journals—concerned with, among other things, questions of identity in an era of globalization—preceded the Documenta 10 exhibition proper as a kind of propaedeutic and provided insight into David's Documenta philosophy and approach, which was based on the concept of the montage. Publishing these working papers in advance was intended to record the collage process in the creation of Documenta. Similarly, the "100 Days–100 Guests" program held during the exhibition provided a space for theory that had rarely existed previously with such intensity (fig. 4). Indeed, as a gesture that gave discursivity a central place and insisted that Documenta should not merely be an exhibition in the classical sense, Documenta 10 arguably enacted one of the single most important paradigm shifts for Documenta the institution (or at least could be said to have provided the inspiration for the subsequent "platforms" of Documenta 11 and the journal project of Documenta 12). Finally, the accompanying book *Politics / Poetics*, which was more than 800 pages long, extended the montage principle to the whole postwar period. The book represented, as the editors wrote, an attempt to "indicate a political context for the interpretation of artistic activities at the close of the twentieth century."[27]

David's genre-transcending principle of montage—in comparison to the Documenta 11 principle with which we will contrast it—included several crucial strategic disadvantages that can be demonstrated with examples of its approach to theory. In addition to several original texts (and interviews conducted for the volume) that are printed in full, the accompanying book consists primarily of a large number of theoretical sound bites—"theory bites," as it were—ranging in length from a paragraph to several pages. Theoretical texts by writers such as Édouard Glissant, Jürgen Habermas, Edward Said, Claude Lefort, and James Clifford were printed only in excerpt and were thus subordinated to the logic of the art field rather than having the latter accept the specific logic of the theoretical production of knowledge. At best, the text fragments can be understood as extended footnotes, as indices that serve to point the reader to the full texts. From a less charitable viewpoint, however, they could also be measured by their mere iconic quality, which is in keeping with the logic of an art field in which the symbolic impact of a famous theorist's name always overwrites the actual statements of the theory.

Documenta 11 took another route in its approach to theory. It granted the specific format of the scientific or theoretical production of knowledge and printed the texts of those invited to the symposia in full. The results of the first four platforms were not turned into a collage but instead published in four clearly designed volumes of theory and discourse. The reason for this decision should probably be sought in the fact that Documenta 11 had made providing a set of diagnostic instruments its primary objective. Despite a certain voluntarist prejudice, the instruments of theory do not function if they are arbitrarily taken apart or even demolished. When they are, they turn out wrong or not at all. By contrast, Documenta 11 understood itself as an instrument of cognition that accepted the heterogeneity of various ways of producing knowledge—philosophy, science, and art. The seemingly rigid separation of the first four platforms from the fifth was thus by no means inconsequential.[28] It testified to a knowledge of the fact that an exhibition in Kassel cannot achieve the same thing as a conference in New Delhi on politics or one in Vienna and Berlin on the theory of democracy. And yet all of them were supposed to be components of one project—the project of Documenta 11.

The first four platforms studied various aspects of the postcolonial constellation in series of lectures and in conference and workshop formats. In the process, various perspectives were integrated, not just those of specialists. Take the example of the *Democracy Unrealized* platform in Vienna and Berlin. It included guests from fields such as philosophy, political theory, legal theory, economics, cultural studies, postcolonial studies, and art theory, including Stuart Hall, Bikhu Parek, Immanuel Wallerstein, Chantal Mouffe, Ernesto Laclau, Enrique Dussel, Homi Bhabha, Michael Hardt, and Antonio Negri. At the same time, there was a podium for activist and art-activist practices, including groups such as kein mensch ist illegal and Arquitectos sin fronteras, the Roma activist Sean Nazerali, and the American human rights lawyer Mark Potok. In Vienna a decision was made, in the wake of protests against the inclusion of the Freiheitliche Partei Österreichs (FPÖ, Freedom Party of Austria) in the ruling coalition, to invite the civil society group Demokratische Offensive.[29]

Hence these were *theory* platforms only if the concept of theory is interpreted quite broadly. In reality, the first four platforms should not be understood so much as traditional theory events than as platforms for political debates and controversies relating to a certain predetermined set of themes and taking place in various media, including science and theory among others. In my view, the reason the classic formats of the lecture, the symposium, and finally the symposium volume were chosen is that the focus of Documenta 11's strategy was not the avant-garde transgression of institutional frameworks (as it was for Szeemann's first concept and, as a kind of unintentional parody of that era, as it was in the *Utopia Station* of the fiftieth Venice Biennial) but rather decentering the institution. Just as the exhibition platform deliberately left room for the individual artistic works, the theory platforms offered the invitees a certain degree of *respect*—to use an old-fashioned word—namely, respect for the specifics of the formation of knowledge they represented. The recognition of heterogeneity and specificity—regardless of whether it was the specificity of artistic works or the specific thematic competence of the invitees from the field of science or theory—is precisely what distinguished Documenta 11. This retention of a "classic" format, be it the relatively classic exhibition design in Kassel or the equally classic concept of the symposium, should not be misunderstood as a simple affirmation of institutional conditions. Rather, the classic form of the institution was used to lend symbolic legitimacy to a canon shift with regard to content. On the other hand, the equally necessary deconstruction of the *form* of the institution was not achieved by "exploding" all the institutional boundaries by creating a giant happening (which would have merely turned the event into a spectacle and thus devalued the non-Western works presented) but rather by deterritorializing the institution temporally, spatially, and thematically.

Along the axis of theory, Documenta 12 ultimately furnished a fine example of what we have termed the strategy of *transformatism* in the art field. Rather than rejecting certain antihegemonic shifts outright, a transformist strategy transforms them in a manner that no longer stands in the way of the hegemonic consensus, what we have also termed the "organic ideology" of the art field. In spite of the anti-intellectualism of an artistic director who sought "aesthetic experience," prized immediacy, wished to rehabilitate "beauty," and published a "picture book" with no text at all, it was impossible for any curator who came after Documenta 10 and Documenta 11 to curate a Documenta without a certain minimum of intellectual and theoretical ambition. Certain leitmotifs were chosen: "Is modernity our antiquity?", "What is bare life?", and "What is to be done?"

The answering of these questions, whenever they should have taken place in the medium of theory, was outsourced to an international magazine consortium. This simultaneously followed and did not follow Documenta 11. The idea of linking up with a transnational network of magazines in the art–theory–politics nexus was without a doubt the most interesting idea of Documenta 12, and was in continuity—even if it was an unspoken continuity—with the philosophy of Documenta 11. The project proved problematic in its realization, however, for it legitimated the complete "outsourcing" of theory, and even of intellectuality. The links Documenta 11 sought to produce between art, theory, and politics were cut back, and the theoretical involvement with political problem areas was allotted to worldwide subcontractors. They were the ones who had to take on all of the text, theory, and program production that the artistic director and the curator were not willing or able to do. Documenta's leadership was relieved of the work of providing their vague leitmotifs with contents beyond bare associations and analogies. This made it possible to bring in intellectuals from across the globe to compensate for the lack of intelligence on site—and all of this without wanting, or being able, to make available anything at all in exchange (money, resources, etc.). It is no wonder that many of the participating magazines were reminded of neoliberal outsourcing models and ultimately felt that they had been taken in.[30] The results were three issues of *Documenta* magazine, which made an upstanding effort to extract some kind of relevant meaning from the curators' mental musings and thereby provide the intellectual fig leaf for an out-and-out anti-intellectual exhibition.

The anti-intellectualism of Documenta 12 was manifested, finally, in one other peculiarity. For behind all the talk of form and beauty, there was a more fundamental discourse that seemed to organize Documenta 12: the return of *the esoteric*. Buergelian esotericism was exemplified by Poul Gerne's psychedelic decorative art from the sixties and by John McCracken's Mandala Paintings from the early seventies (as well as his metaphysical sculptures) (fig. 5). Here, art returned to its roots in religion and neopaganism. Buergel enlightened us as follows:

> *In his mandalas, all created in the autumn after the "summer of love", McCracken touches base with the spiritual font of artistic creation. Mandalas, with their two axes of symmetry, are representatives of holistic notions, but they are not solely images to gaze at in wonderment or when getting high . . . [They are] also forms stemming from an ancient religious practice found, for example, in Tibetan Buddhism: painting as meditation. Enough ink has been spilt on the subject of the esoteric currents in the anti-Vietnam movement. However these esoteric currents, from the French Symbolists to anthroposophy, have always also been an integral part of modern abstraction. They admonish the re-enchantment of that world so thoroughly stripped of magic by the capitalist rationality of the Industrial Revolution.*[31]

The last sentence reveals that Buergel really wants to identify in esotericism a form of antirational "critique" that he latches onto curatorially with his exhibition. In other words, the passage above should not be understood as merely a description of the esoteric program of modernism in general or of the Mandala Paintings in particular, but also as Buergel and Noack's "own program." Documenta seems to have given Buergel the stage on which he could fantasize about holism (thus the bare associations, for in a holistic universe everything is connected to everything else), "ancient forms" (thus the many premodern objects in the exhibition), magic and the quasi-religious "reenchantment" of the world—thus the return of the mandalas (John McCracken) and, as Robert Fleck noted, crosses (Churchill Madikida) at Documenta 12. And all of this was dipped in the regressive discourse of "the beautiful." At last, peeping through Buergel's formalism and aestheticism, a spiritualistic and esoteric irrationality that allows him to shake off every text, every real criticism, and every politics in the art field emerged. The transformations to be achieved by Documenta 12 in the hegemonic structure of the art field—on the basis of the strategies of decontextualization, formalization, and aestheticization (to which may now be added spiritualization)—add up, in sum, to the project of a curatorial counter-Enlightenment.

With art exhibitions, as with politics, it is never possible to revoke or cancel everything at once, for hegemonic shifts necessitate compromises and tactical retreats.

CONCLUSION

ANY concept of "rollback" or "backlash" is misleading in the field of hegemony for this reason. Every "going back" is ultimately a "moving forward," if perhaps forward into the reactionary: a *forward back!* Therefore, a hegemonic power reacts to antihegemonic attacks when the latter have achieved a temporary partial victory, and not through a simple return to a status quo ante. Instead, the hegemonic power develops further by seeking to make criticism productive for itself, even to make it into an argument for its own position. This can be discerned in the example of Documenta 12. The field has shifted, and this shift cannot simply be *undone.* Only through *a further shift* can the shift be captured, played down, or covered up. It would appear that precisely this was the project of Documenta 12 in relation to Documenta 10 and Documenta 11. Yet there is a glimmer of hope. For it has been seen here, as everywhere in politics, that no antihegemonic gain of territory, however small or fleeting, is futile. It always impels the dominant discourses to work on their own hegemony, and it forces them to redefine themselves to maintain this hegemony and shore it up against further attacks. All of this makes politics into an objectively ironic business with an open outcome. The hegemony-theory analysis of the art field, which has been attempted here to some extent through the example of biennials and the example of Documenta in particular, can show not only how a progressive canon shift is altogether possible at the "center" of the art field, but also how the bourgeois dominant culture will at once seek to neutralize it. ●

This essay is an abridged and translated version of: Oliver Marchart's *Hegemonie im Kunstfeld: Die Documenta-Ausstellungen dX, D11, d12 und die Politik der Biennalisierung* (Cologne, 2008).

Translation by Steven Lindberg.

1 I use the term "biennial" here—as is often done by critics, curators, and the press today—to refer to the perennial, large-scale exhibition of contemporary art at large, including even, in this case, Documenta (which, occurring every five years would, properly speaking, be a quinquennial), and not merely those that recur biannually, as the term was initially meant to imply.

2 The biennial boom can largely be explained by the coincidence of the global and the local: a globalized art field and the local marketing of cities.

3 See Okwui Enwezor, *Grossausstellungen und die Antinomien einer transnationalen globalen Form* (Munich, 2002), p. 46. An English translation of the text entitled "Mega-Exhibitions and the Antinomies of a Transnational Global Form" has been included in the present volume. Enwezor added that "the recent phenomenon of biennales in the periphery should not be bemoaned as a readymade example of the biennale syndrome. Instead, there is a need to see in the biennale phenomenon the possibility of a paradigm shift in which we as spectators are able to encounter many experimental cultures, without wholly possessing them." (Ibid., p. 55).

4 Walter Benjamin, *The Arcades Project,* trans. Howard Eiland and Kevin McLaughlin (Cambridge [MA], 1999), p. 7.

5 Ibid., p. 8.

6 On "New Institutionalism," see, among others, Nina Möntmann (ed.), *Art and Its Institutions* (London, 2006). Art institutions in the Netherlands and the Scandinavian countries are often cited as examples of the New Institutionalism, above all the Rooseum in Malmö, under the direction of Charles Esche; the Office for Contemporary

NOTES

Art Norway, under the direction of Uta Meta Bauer; Museet for samtidskunst in Oslo; the Contemporary Art Center in Vilnius; the Kunsthalle Helsinki; x-room in Copenhagen and the NIFCA; also mentioned are the Münchner Kunstverein, with Maria Lind as artistic director; the MACBA in Barcelona; and the Palais de Tokyo in Paris, under the direction of Nicolas Bourriaud and Jérôme Sans, but the work of less visible arts societies could also be subsumed under the concept of New Institutionalism. Many of these experiments have not been continued, however; see Nina Möntmann, "Aufstieg und Fall des *New Institutionalism*: Perspektiven einer möglichen Zukunft," http://transform.eipcp.net/transversal/0407/moentmann/de.

7 See Antonio Gramsci, *Selections from the Prison Notebook* (London, 1971), and Ernst Laclau and Chantal Mouffe, *Hegemony and Socialist Strategy* (London, 1985).

8 Okwui Enwezor outlined the concept of the postcolonial constellation as follows: "It is a name that echoes itself in a series of structural, political and cultural entanglements from the postwar movements of decolonization, to Civil Rights, feminist, gay/lesbian, anti-racist, anti-essentialist, counter-hegemonic politics of a new global community." Okwui Enwezor, "The Postcolonial Constellation: Contemporary Art in a State of Permanent Transition," in Gilane Tawadros and Sarah Campbell (eds.), *Fault Lines: Contemporary African Art and Shifting Landscapes* (London, 2003), p. 77.

9 Okwui Enwezor, "Reflexionen zur d5: Eine neue Auffassung kuratorischer Praxis," in Roland Nachtigäller, Friedhelm Scharf, and Karin Stengel (eds.), *Wiedervorlage d5: Eine Befragung des Archivs zur Documenta 1972* (Ostfildern, 2001), p. 43.

10 Ibid., p. 43.

11 James Meyer, "The Whitney Biennial: Generalization of the Political," in idem and Gregg Bordowitz, *What Happened to the Institutional Critique?* (New York, 1993), p. 8.

12 To a lesser extent, Documenta 11 also fell into the trap of spatial separation of works that were more activist and process-oriented, which were located only in the Documenta hall, from the Documentary works in the Museum Fridericianum and the Binding-Brauerei.

13 Interview with Roger M. Buergel, "Genuss wie im Restaurant," *Der Spiegel*, April 26, 2004.

14 Ibid.

15 Roger M. Buergel and Ruth Noack, "Preface," in idem (eds.), *Documenta 12 Katalog* (Cologne, 2007), pp. 11–12.

16 At the same time, Buergel's defended claim (in part in response to an earlier formulation of my critique of him, published in *Texte zur Kunst*) that politics was somehow sedimented in every "form" explains why criticism runs aground on a traditional dualism of form and content. The claim is complete nonsense, for if the assertion is that politics is sedimented in the formal (which is perfectly possible), then it would have been up to Documenta 12 to excavate and expose this politics, which is exactly what was *not* done. On the contrary, politics, where it was present in certain works, was formalized by Buergel's concept.

17 See Roger M. Buergel, "Ist die Moderne unsere Antike?" (2007), audio guide, previously available at http://Documenta12.de.

18 Ibid.

19 Harald Kimpel, *Documenta: Mythos und Wirklichkeit* (Cologne, 1997).

20 Simon Njami sums up the problem of *Magiciens de la terre* as follows: "In the late '80s, the art scene found itself divided into two categories of actors: magicians, descended from the non-Western world, and men." See Njami, "The Curator as Naked King: Contextualisation and Decontextualisation," in *South Meets West*, exh. cat. Accra, National Museum of Ghana (Bern, 2000), p. 54.

21 Buergel and Noack 2007 (see note 15), p. 274.

22 Ibid., p. 142.

23 Ibid., p. 96.

24 Ibid., p. 134.

25 See Eriberto Eulisse (ed.), *Afriche, diaspore, ibridi: Il concettualismo come strategia dell'arte africana contemporanea* (San Marino, 2003).

26 Christian Kravagna, in "Betrachter- und Formschicksale in Kassel: Berichte von der Documenta 12," *Texte zur Kunst* 17, no. 67 (September 2007), pp. 197–211, esp. 205–6. And he added "all premodern works of art and all cultural artifacts from Asia and Africa but not—as in any museum of ethnology—Europe as well. Complementarily, the numerous looks back at the history of the avant-garde focused exclusively on Europe and America." Ibid., p. 206.

27 Catherine David and Jean-François Chevrier, *documenta X: the book*, ed. Documenta and Museum Fridericianum Veranstaltungs-GmbH (Ostfildern, 1997), p. 24.

28 Although a few workshops were offered during the Documenta summer—for example, with Fareed Armaly, Walid Ra'ad, Joan Jonas, and Andreja Kuluncic—as well as discussions with Okwui Enwezor and specific artists, the theory program of Documenta 11 essentially consisted of the first four platforms.

29 All these contributions can be found in Okwui Enwezor et al. (eds.), *Democracy Unrealized* (Ostfildern, 2002).

30 See Kati Morawek and Beat Weber, "Die Akte Documenta," *Malmoe* 38 (2008), http://www.malmoe.org/artikel/regieren/1438.

31 Buergel and Noack 2007 (see note 15), p. 88.

BIOGRAPHIES
BIBLIOGRAPHY
ACKNOWLEDGMENTS
INDEX

BIOGRAPHIES

Lawrence Alloway (1926–1990) was an English art critic and a leading member of the Independent Group in the nineteen-fifties in the UK. From 1955 to 1960 he was Assistant Director of the Institute of Contemporary Arts in London, organizing several landmark exhibitions. In 1956 he contributed to the organization of the exhibition *This Is Tomorrow,* and from the sixties onward he remained an influential writer and curator in the U.S., holding positions including Senior Curator at the Solomon R. Guggenheim Museum (1961–66), where he curated such shows as *Six Painters and the Object* (1963) and the highly influential *Systemic Painting* (1963). In 1967 he joined the Art Department at Southern Illinois University Carbondale as a lecturer, and in the seventies he wrote for *The Nation* and *Artforum* and lectured at the State University of New York.

George Baker is Associate Professor of Modern and Contemporary Art and Vice-Chair of the Department of Art History at UCLA. He is also co-editor of the journal *October* and the series *October Books*, has been a critic for *Artforum* since the nineties, and is the author of *The Artwork Caught by the Tail: Francis Picabia and Dada in Paris* (Cambridge [MA], 2007), whose first paperback edition will be issued later this year.

Carlos Basualdo is the Keith L. and Katherine Sachs Curator of Contemporary Art at the Philadelphia Museum of Art and Curator at Large at MAXXI (Museo nazionale delle arti del XXI secolo) in Rome. He was a part of the curatorial teams for Documenta 11 and the fiftieth Venice Biennial, and he conceived and curated *Tropicalia: A Revolution in Brazilian Culture*, which traveled from the Museum of Contemporary Art, Chicago, to the Barbican Gallery in London (2004–05) as well as the Bronx Museum in New York and the Museu de Arte Moderna in Rio de Janeiro (2006–07). He was also the lead organizer of *Bruce Nauman: Topological Gardens,* which represented the U.S. at the 2007 Venice Biennial, where it was awarded the Golden Lion for Best National Participation. He is currently organizing a survey exhibition of the work of the Italian artist Michelangelo Pistoletto scheduled to open in Philadelphia in the autumn of 2010 and then travel to Rome in the spring of 2011.

Michael Brenson is a critic, scholar, and teacher. He received a doctorate in art history and a Master's degree in creative writing from The Johns

Hopkins University. From 1982 to 1991 he was an art critic for *The New York Times*. His publications include *Visionaries and Outcasts: The NEA, Congress, and the Place of the Visual Artist in America* (New York, 2001), *Sol LeWitt: Concrete Block Structures* (Milan, 2002), and *Acts of Engagement: Writings on Art, Criticism, and Institutions, 1993–2002* (Lanham [MD], 2004); he has also edited *Conversations at the Castle: Changing Audiences and Contemporary Art* (with Mary Jane Jacob; Cambridge [MA], 1998), *Witness to Her Art: Art and Writings by Adrian Piper, Mona Hatoum, Cady Noland, Jenny Holzer, Kara Walker, Daniela Rossell and Eau de Cologne* (with Rhea Anastas; Annandale-on-Hudson, 2006). He is a Getty Scholar and Guggenheim Fellow. He is currently a Visiting Senior Critic in the University of Pennsylvania's School of Design's Department of Fine Arts and a member of the sculpture faculty at Bard's Milton Avery Graduate School of the Arts. He is currently working on a biography of David Smith.

Daniel Buren was born in 1938 in Boulogne-Billancourt. He lives and works in situ.

Charlotte Bydler is a writer, art critic, and lecturer in the Department of Art History of the School of Culture and Communication of Södertörn University College in Sweden. She received her doctorate from the Department of Art History at Uppsala University and published her thesis, *The Global Art World, Inc.: On the Globalization of Contemporary Art*, in 2004. As one of the first serious publications on biennials in relation to globalization, her book's source material came from the study of a number of biennials from around the world.

John Clark is Professor of Asian Art History at the University of Sydney. He is working under an ARC Professorial Fellowship on a new comparative study of *The Asian Modern* that focuses on twenty-five artists in five generational cohorts across Asia (including Australia) from the 1850s to the 1980s. His books include *Modern Asian Art* (Honolulu, 1998), the co-edited *Eye of the Beholder* (Sydney, 2006), *Modernities of Chinese Art* (Leiden, 2010), and *Asian Modernities: Chinese and Thai Art in the 1980s and 1990s* (Sydney, 2010).

Okwui Enwezor is a curator, writer, and critic. He was Dean of Academic Affairs at the San Francisco Art Institute and has served as artistic director for a number of international exhibitions, including the second Johannesburg Biennial, the seventh Gwangju Biennial, and Documenta 11. He is currently an adjunct curator at the International Center of Photography, New York, and is founder and editor of *Nka: Journal of Contemporary African Art.* He is also co-author of *Contemporary African Art Since 1980* (with Chika Okeke-Agulu; New York, 2009).

Bruce W. Ferguson is a curator, critic, and academic who has organized many exhibitions and written numerous essays on artists and the cultural sector for catalogues and journals. Among his publications, he co-edited *Thinking about Exhibitions* (with Reesa Greenberg and Sandy Nairne; London, 1996). He is currently Director of Future Arts Research at Arizona State University and in September 2010 will become Dean of the School of Humanities and Social Sciences at the American University in Cairo, Egypt, while maintaining a consulting relationship with ASU on the Desert Initiative. His most recent academic interests include the infrastructure of arts organizations—with an emphasis on biennials—and the historical and contemporary aesthetics emerging from "deserts" around the world.

Elena Filipovic is a curator at Wiels Contemporary Art Centre in Brussels. In 2008, she co-curated the fifth Berlin Biennial, *When Things Cast No Shadow* (2008), with Adam Szymczyk and is co-editor of *The Manifesta Decade: Debates on Contemporary Art Exhibitions and Biennials in Post-Wall Europe* (with Barbara Vanderlinden; Brussels and Cambridge [MA], 2006). Her recent curatorial projects include *Marcel Duchamp: A work that is not a work "of art"* at the Museu de Arte Moderna in São Paulo and the Fundación Proa in Buenos Aires (2008–09), and *Felix Gonzalez-Torres: Specific Objects without Specific Form* at Wiels, the Fondation Beyeler, Basel, and the Museum für Moderne Kunst, Frankfurt am Main (2010–11). She is a tutor of theory/exhibition history for the De Appel postgraduate curatorial training program, an advisor at the Rijksakademie, both in Amsterdam, and is currently also guest curator of the Satellite Program for emerging artists at the Jeu de Paume, Paris (2009–11). Together with Marieke van Hal and Solveig Øvstebø, she co-organized the 2009 Bergen Biennial Conference and co-edited the present volume.

Marieke van Hal is an art historian and Director of the Biennial Foundation. From 1997 to 2001 she worked as a curator at Montevideo/TBA, the Netherlands Media Art Institute, and then became General Coordinator of International Foundation Manifesta and managing editor of *MJ–Manifesta Journal* (2001–06). In 2007 she was director of the first Athens Biennial and subsequently founded the Biennial Foundation. Since 2008 she has been a research candidate in the Curating Contemporary Art Department of the Royal College of Art, London. She has lectured extensively on the topic of biennials, and together with Elena Filipovic and Solveig Øvstebø she co-organized the 2009 Bergen Biennial Conference and co-edited the present volume. She lives and works in Athens, Greece.

Maria Hlavajova has been the artistic director of BAK, basis voor actuele kunst, Utrecht, since she founded it in 2000. She is also the initiator and artistic director of Former West (2008–13), a research, education, publication, and exhibition project. In 2008 she co-curated *Once is Nothing* (with Charles Esche), a joint contribution of BAK and the Van Abbemuseum, Eindhoven, to the first Brussels Biennial. She also curated the three-part project *Citizens and Subjects,* the Dutch contribution to the fifty-second Venice Biennial in 2007. Apart from the numerous exhibitions and projects she has organized at BAK, she also regularly edits and contributes to numerous critical readers and catalogues. In 2004, she curated *Who if not we should at least try to imagine the future of all this?* She is a founding board member of the Július Koller Society, and founding director of the tranzit network (with Kathrin Rhomberg). Hlavajova also is a fellow of the Centre for the Humanities at Utrecht University and teaches at both Utrecht University and the Rietveld Academy in Amsterdam. In the past, she has been a faculty member at the Center for Curatorial Studies, Bard College, New York (1998–2002), co-curator of Manifesta 3, Ljubljana (2000), and director of the Soros Center for Contemporary Arts in Bratislava (1994–99). She lives and works in Amsterdam and Utrecht.

Milena M. Hoegsberg is a New York–based freelance curator who works on exhibitions, research, and arts-related projects. She earned her Bachelor's degree in art history at Columbia University and her Master's degree at the Center for Curatorial Studies, Bard College. She recently curated the solo exhibitions *Nanna Debois Buhl: Looking for Donkeys* (2010) at the Southern Alberta Art Gallery in Canada and *Lucy Raven: China Town* (2010) in Overgaden, Denmark.

BIOGRAPHIES

Ranjit Hoskote is a poet, cultural theorist, and freelance curator. He is the author of nineteen books, including five volumes of poetry, nine monographs on art and artists, a critical history of cultural confluence entitled *Kampfabsage* (Munich, 2007), which he co-authored with the German novelist and essayist Ilija Trojanow, and an artist's book he collaborated on with Atul Dodiya, *Pale Ancestors* (Bombay, 2008). His essays have appeared in numerous books and anthologies. In 2008 he co-curated the Gwangju Biennial in Korea with Hyunjin Kim and Artistic Director Okwui Enwezor. He was also co-curator of the trans-Asian collaborative curatorial project *Under Construction* (Japan Foundation, Tokyo, and other Asian venues, 2001–02). Hoskote has curated 21 exhibitions of contemporary Indian and international art, including a mid-career survey of the work of Atul Dodiya (Japan Foundation, Tokyo, 2001), a lifetime retrospective of Jehangir Sabavala (National Gallery of Modern Art, Bombay and New Delhi, 2005–06), and *Detour,* a critical homage in the centennial of Gandhi's foundational 1909 text, *Hind Swaraj,* through the work of five contemporary photographers, filmmakers, and activists: Dayanita Singh, Ravi Agarwal, Ram Rahman, Sonia Jabbar, and Samar Jodha (Chemould Prescott Road, Bombay, 2009).

Caroline A. Jones is Professor of Art History and Director of the History, Theory, Criticism Program in the Department of Architecture at MIT. She studies modern and contemporary art, with a particular focus on its technological modes of production, distribution, and reception. She has also worked as an essayist and curator, most recently at MIT's List Visual Art Center on *Sensorium* (2006), *Video Trajectories* (2007), and the upcoming *Hans Haacke 1967* (2011). She has held positions at the Museum of Modern Art in New York and the Harvard University Art Museums. Her exhibitions and/or films have been shown at MoMA as well as the San Francisco Museum of Modern Art, the Hirshhorn Museum and Sculpture Garden in Washington, D.C., and the Hara Museum in Tokyo, among other venues. Her publications include *Sensorium* (as editor; Cambridge [MA], 2006), *Eyesight Alone* (Chicago, 2005), *Machine in the Studio* (Chicago, 1996), and the co-edited volume *Picturing Science, Producing Art* (New York, 1998). A frequent contributor to *Artforum,* her current research will be published as *Desires for the World Picture: The Global Work of Art*, which examines how art functions in world's fairs, national pavilions, and biennial culture.

Yacouba Konaté is a curator and Professor of Philosophy at the University of Cocody in Abidjan, Ivory Coast. In 2008 he was elected president of the International Association of Art Critics (AICA). Konaté is a member of l'Académie des Arts, des Sciences et des Cultures d'Afrique et des Diasporas in Abidjan and was Artistic Director of Dak'Art in 2006, the seventh Biennial of Contemporary African Art. He has been a Fulbright Professor at Stanford University (1998), taught at l'École des hautes études en sciences sociales in France (2004–08) and at The University of Laval (2007), and been a Carter Fellow at the University of Florida, Gainesville (2007). He has written several books and articles, including: *La Biennale de Dakar: Pour une esthétique de la création africaine contemporaine: Tête à tête avec Adorno* (Paris, 2009), *Croquis de frontières, profils de passeurs: L'art contemporain en perspective* (Bâle, 2009), *Christian Lattier: Le sculpteur aux mains nues, Saint-Maur* (Saint-Maur, 1993), and *Alpha Blondy: Reggae et société en Afrique Noire* (Paris, 1987).

Oliver Marchart is a professor in the Department of Sociology at the University of Lucerne, Switzerland. He works in the fields of political theory, art theory, and discourse analysis. His books include *Die politische Differenz: Zum Denken des Politischen bei Nancy, Lefort, Badiou, Laclau and Agamben* (Berlin, 2010), *Hegemonie im Kunstfeld: Die documenta-Ausstellung dX, D11, d12 und die Politik der Biennalisierung* (Cologne, 2008), *Cultural Studies* (Constance, 2008), *Post-Foundational Political Thought: Political Difference in Nancy, Lefort, Badiou, Laclau* (Edinburgh, 2007), *Neu beginnen: Hannah Arendt, die Revolution und die Globalisierung* (Vienna, 2005), and *Laclau: A Critical Reader* (co-edited with Simon Critchley; London, 2004).

Sabine Marschall received her doctorate in art history from Eberhardt-Karls Universität in Tübingen. She has been residing permanently in South Africa since 1995 and is currently Associate Professor and Programme Director for Cultural and Heritage Tourism at the University of KwaZulu-Natal. She has published on South African art and architecture, with a special focus on community mural art. During the past decade her research has focused on postapartheid heritage and memorialization.

Federica Martini is an art historian and curator. After having studied American literature and contemporary art at the University of Turin, in

2007 she completed a doctoral degree focusing on the evolution of the biennial exhibition format in the nineteen-nineties. From 2003 to 2007, she collaborated with the curatorial department of the Castello di Rivoli Museum of Contemporary Art, Rivoli-Turin. In 2009, she curated the visual arts section of the Festival des Urbaines, Lausanne. She is currently a curatorial associate at the Musée cantonal des Beaux-Arts, Lausanne, and serves as a teacher and coordinator of MAPS, the "Arts in Public Spheres" Master's degree program at the École Cantonal d'Art du Valais, Sierre.

Vittoria Martini is an art historian. Her doctoral dissertation, which is currently in progress, is entitled "The Unattainable Revolution: The Venice Biennale, 1968–1978" and focuses on the history of the Venice Biennial during the nineteen-seventies. In 2005 she did the historical research for the art project by Muntadas entitled "On Translation: I Giardini," which was presented in the Spanish Pavilion at the fifty-first Venice Biennial. From 2005 to 2007 she was assistant curator at the Fondazione Sandretto Re Rebaudengo in Turin and in the spring of 2009 she worked as "ambassador" at The Bijlmer Spinoza-Festival, Thomas Hirschhorn's new public space project.

Thomas McEvilley is a scholar, critic, philosopher, and poet who lives in New York. He has written hundreds of books, catalogues, and essays on ancient and modern art, literature, and culture. His most recent books are *Art, Love, Friendship: Marina Abramović and Ulay, Together and Apart* (Kingston [NY], 2010) and *Yves the Provocateur: Yves Klein and Twentieth Century Art* (Kingston [NY], 2010).

Gerardo Mosquera is a freelance curator and art critic based in Havana, Cuba. He is an advisor at the Rijksakademie van Beeldende Kunsten, Amsterdam, and a member of the advisory boards of several art journals. He is one of the founders of the Havana Biennial. He has curated many international exhibitions and is currently a curator at the New Museum of Contemporary Art, New York. He has published numerous essays and books on contemporary art and art theory, including *Over Here: International Perspectives on Art and Culture* (Cambridge [MA], 2004), which he co-edited with Jean Fisher, and *Beyond the Fantastic: Contemporary Art Criticism from Latin America* (London and Cambridge [MA], 1995).

Rafal Niemojewski is an art historian, curator, and critic. In 2004, he graduated in the history of art and curatorial studies from La Sorbonne and in 2010 he received his doctorate for his research on the proliferation of biennials from the Royal College of Art in London. Since 2007 he has been working as Curator of Public Programmes at the Hayward Gallery, Southbank Centre, where he recently organized *Deschooling Society,* an international conference focusing on the changing relationship between art and education. Prior to that he worked as the curator-in-residence at LBi and managed the office of *point d'ironie* for agnès b and Hans Ulrich Obrist. He has also contributed to *Artforum, Artvehicle,* and *MJ–Manifesta Journal,* among other periodicals.

Paul O'Neill is a curator, artist, and writer based in Bristol. He is the Great Western Research Alliance (GWR) Research Fellow in Commissioning Contemporary Art with Situations at the University of the West of England, Bristol, where he is leading the international research project *Locating the Producers.* From 2001 to 2003, he was gallery curator at the London Print Studio Gallery and previous to that was Artistic Director of MultiplesX from 1997 to 2006. In all, he has curated or co-curated over fifty exhibition projects. As an artist, he has exhibited widely. Among other places, his work has been shown at: Zaçheta Gallery of Contemporary Art, Warsaw; the Irish Museum of Modern Art, Dublin; temporarycontemporary, London; Andrew Kreps Gallery, New York; Villa Arson, Nice; South London Gallery; Cell, London; Hugh Lane Gallery, Dublin; and Temple Bar Gallery, Dublin. He is an associate lecturer in the curatorial training programmes at Goldsmiths in London and De Appel in Amsterdam. His writing has been published in many books, catalogues, journals, and magazines, including *Art Monthly, Space & Culture, Everything, Contemporary, The Internationaler,* and *CIRCA*. He edited the anthology *Curating Subjects* (Amsterdam and London, 2007) and co-edited *Curating and the Educational Turn* (with Mick Wilson; Amsterdam and London, 2010). He is currently working on an authored book with MIT Press entitled *The Culture of Curating, Curating Culture(s).*

Solveig Øvstebø is an art historian and has been Director of the Bergen Kunsthall since 2003. She has curated and co-curated numerous exhibitions, including *Christopher Williams* (2010), *Looking Is Political: Nairy Baghramian, Bojan Šarčević, Ane Hjort Guttu* (2009), *Sergej Jenssen*

(2008), *Leibhaftige Malerei Jxxxa: Jutta Koether* (2008), *The Absence of Mark Manders* (2007), *Center of Gravity: Runa Islam* (2007), *Awakenings: Rodney Graham* (2006), *Shifting Shifting: Aernout Mik* (2006), and *The Welfare Show: Elmgreen & Dragset* (2005). She is a board member of Arts Council Norway. She has taught theory and art history at the art academies of Helsinki and Bergen and has written and lectured extensively on contemporary art. In 2009, she initiated and co-organized the Bergen Biennial Conference together with Elena Filipovic and Marieke van Hal, with whom she co-edited the present volume. She lives and works in Bergen, Norway.

Marian Pastor Roces is a cultural critic and independent curator whose research interests include cities, museums, identity politics, and international contemporary art events in relation to nineteenth-century expositions. She is presently working on a doctoral thesis on the accelerated urbanization of Perth, Western Australia, developing a critique of identity politics by exploring discordant temporalities. She also heads TAO INC, a museum development corporation based in the Philippines.

Donald Preziosi is Emeritus Professor of Art History at UCLA and a former Slade Professor of Fine Art at Oxford. He was educated at Harvard, where he received a doctorate in art history, and he has taught at Yale, MIT, SUNY, and UCLA. The author of twelve books on art history, critical theory, and the historiography of cultural institutions, his book *The Art of Art History* (Oxford, 1998; 2nd ed., 2009) is the most widely used introduction to the field in English. He is also co-author and co-editor with Claire Farago of *Grasping the World: The Idea of the Museum* (2004). His newest book, *Enchanted Credulities: Art, Religion, and Amnesia,* is forthcoming from Routledge in 2011.

Raqs Media Collective was formed in 1992 by Jeebesh Bagchi, Monica Narula, and Shuddhabrata Sengupta. The Collective is based at Sarai, an offshoot of the Centre for the Study of Developing Societies in Delhi that they co-founded in 2000. Their work takes the form of installations, video, photography, image-text collages, on- and off-line media objects, performances, and encounters. They also work as curators. The Collective has been exhibited widely at major international events, including Documenta 11 (2002), the Venice Biennial (2003, 2005), the Guangzhou Triennial (2005), the Sydney

Biennial (2006), and the International Istanbul Biennial (2007), among others. For Manifesta 7, the Collective curated *The Rest of Now* and co-curated *Scenarios with Anselm Franke & Hila Peleg and Adam Budak.*

Simon Sheikh is a freelance curator and critic based in Berlin and Copenhagen. He is a correspondent for *Springerin,* Vienna, and a columnist for e-flux journal, New York. He is a researcher for the on-going Former West project, initiated by BAK, Utrecht. He has been Coordinator of the Critical Studies Program at the Malmö Art Academy in Sweden (2002–09), a curator at NIFCA in Helsinki (2003–04), and director of the Overgaden Institute of Contemporary Art in Copenhagen (1999–2002). From 1996 to 2000 he was editor of the magazine *Øjeblikket,* and from 1993 to 2000 he was a member of the project group GLOBE. His most recent curatorial work includes *Capital (It Fails Us Now)* at UKS, Oslo (2005), and Kunstihoone, Tallinn (2006), and *Vectors of Possibility,* BAK, Utrecht (2010). Recent publications are *We Are All Normal* (with Katya Sander; London, 2001), *Knut Åsdam* (Zug, 2004), *In the Place of the Public Sphere?* (Berlin, 2005), and *Capital (It Fails Us Now)* (Berlin, 2006). A collection of his essays from the journals *Afterall, AnArchitectur, Open,* and *Texte zur Kunst,* among others, is forthcoming from b_books in Berlin.

Vinicius Spricigo received his doctorate from the School of Communication and Art at the University of São Paulo, and his doctoral dissertation focused on the history of the São Paulo Biennial. He has been the editor of *Permanent Forum: Art Museums: Between the Public and Private Domain* (2006–08) and a Visiting Research Fellow in the Curating Contemporary Art Department of London's Royal College of Art (2007). One of his latest articles appeared in *Global Art and the Museum,* an online project of the ZKM–Centre for Art and Media in Karlsruhe, and he recently gave a lecture at "Transnational Latin American Art," the 1st International Research Forum for Graduate Students and Emerging Scholars, which was held in Texas in November 2009.

Jan Verwoert is a critic who writes for numerous publications. He is a contributing editor of the journal *Frieze,* teaches at the Piet Zwart Institute in Rotterdam and in the De Appel curatorial program, and co-curated the biennial exhibition *Yes, No and Other Options* for Art Sheffield in 2008.

BIBLIOGRAPHY

Alloway, Lawrence. *The Venice Biennale, 1895–1968: From Salon to Goldfish Bowl.* London: Faber and Faber, 1969. [Reprinted in the present volume.]

Allwood, John. *The Great Exhibitions.* London: Studio Vista, 1977.

Altshuler, Bruce. *The Avant-Garde in Exhibition: New Art in the 20th Century.* New York: Harry N. Abrams, 1994.

Altshuler, Bruce. *Salon to Biennial: Exhibitions that Made Art History, Volume I: 1863–1959.* London: Phaidon Press, 2008.

Appadurai, Arjun. *Modernity at Large: Cultural Dimensions of Globalization.* Minneapolis: University of Minnesota Press, 1996.

Ardenne, Paul. "From Biennale to Banal? Schmooze and Globalization." *Art Press* 291 (June 2003): 40–43.

Arrhenius, Sara. "Independent Curating Within Institutions Without Walls." In *Cautionary Tales: Critical Curating,* edited by Steven Rand and Heather Kouris. New York: Apexart, 2007.

Asia Art Archive. Online resource: http://www.aaa.org.hk/onlineprojects/bitri/en/index.aspx.

Aus dem Moore, Elke, Ursula Zeller, and Katia Reich, eds. *Germany's Contributions to the Venice Biennale 1895-2007.* Cologne: DuMont Buchverlag, 2009.

Babius, Marius, ed. *Im Zentrum der Peripherie: Kunstvermittlung und Vermittlungskunst in den 90er Jahren.* Dresden: Verlag der Kunst, 1995.

Baker, George. "The Globalization of the False: A Response to Okwui Enwezor." *Documents* 23 (Spring 2004): 20–25. [Reprinted in the present volume.]

Baker, George, Rosalind Krauss, Benjamin H. D. Buchloh, Andrea Fraser, David Joselit, James Meyer, Robert Storr, Hal Foster, John Miller, and Helen Molesworth. "Round Table: Present Conditions of Art Criticism." *October* 100 (Spring 2002): 200–228.

Balibar, Étienne. "Critical Reflections." Translated by Jeanine Herman. *Artforum* 36, no. 3 (November 1997): 101, 130.

Barker, Emma, ed. *Contemporary Cultures of Display.* New Haven: Yale University Press, 1999.

Basualdo, Carlos. "The Unstable Institution." In *Questions of Practice: What Makes a Great Exhibition?,* edited by Paula Marincola. Philadelphia: Philadelphia Exhibitions Initiative, 2006. Reprinted in: Hal, Marieke van, Viktor Misiano, and Igor Zabel, eds. "Biennials," special issue, *MJ–Manifesta Journal* 2 (Winter 2003–Spring 2004). [Reprinted in the present volume.]

Basualdo, Carlos, and Reinaldo Laddaga. "Rules of Engagement: Art and Experimental Communities." *Artforum* 42, no. 7 (March 2004): 166.

Becker, Carol. "The Romance of Nomadism: A Series of Reflections." *Art Journal* 58, no. 2 (Summer 1999): 22–29.

Belting, Hans. "Contemporary Art as Global Art." In *The Global Art World: Audiences, Markets and Museums,* edited by Hans Belting and Andrea Buddensieg. Ostfildern: Hatje Cantz, 2009.

Bennett, Tony. *The Birth of the Museum: History, Theory, Politics.* London: Routledge, 1995.

Bergen Biennial Conference, 2009. Online resource: http://www.bbc.2009.no.

Bhabha, Homi K. *The Location of Culture.* New York: Routledge, 1994.

Bianchi, Paolo. "Dialogkultur, Retrovision, neue Urbanitt und das Dazwischen." *Kunstforum* 118 (1992): 76–107, 466–467.

Biennial Foundation. Online resource: http://www.biennialfoundation.org.

Bonami, Francesco. "Debate: Biennials." *Frieze,* no. 92 (July–September 2005): 104–5.

Bourriaud, Nicolas. "Altermodern." In *Altermodern: Tate Triennial.* Exh. cat. London, Tate Modern, 2009.

Bradley, Jessica. "International Exhibitions: A Distribution System for a New World Order." In *Beyond the Box: Diverging Curatorial Practices,* edited by Melanie Townsend. Banff: Banff Centre Press, 2003.

Brenson, Michael. "The Curator's Moment: Trends in the Field of International Contemporary Art Exhibitions." *Art Journal* 57, no. 4 (Winter 1998): 16–27. [Reprinted in the present volume.]

Brett, Guy. "Venice, Paris, Kassel, São Paulo and Havana." *Third Text,* no. 20 (Autumn 1992): 13–22.

Buergel, Roger M. "The Origins." *Documenta Magazine Reader,* nos. 1–3 (2007): 25–39.

Buren, Daniel. "Exhibition of an Exhibition." In: *Exhibition of an Exhibition: Documenta 5.* Exh. cat. Kassel, Museum Fridericianum, 1972. Reprinted in: *The Next Documenta Should Be Curated by an Artist,* edited by Jens Hoffman. New York and Frankfurt: E-Flux and Revolver Archiv für Actuelle Kunst, 2004. [Reprinted in the present volume.]

Buren, Daniel. "Where Are the Artists?" In *The Next Documenta Should Be Curated by an Artist,* edited by Jens Hoffman. New York and Frankfurt: E-Flux and Revolver Archiv für Actuelle Kunst, 2004. [Reprinted in the present volume.]

Bydler, Charlotte. *The Global Art World, Inc.: On the Globalization of Contemporary Art.* Uppsala: Acta Universitatis Upsaliensis, 2004. [An abridged version appears in the present volume.]

Choy, Lee Weng. "Biennale Time and the Specters of Exhibition." *FOCAS: Forum on Contemporary Art and Society,* no. 3 (January 2002): 57–61.

Clark, John. *Biennales and Contemporary Asian Art: Histories of the Asian "New"* (forthcoming). [A slightly revised version of Chapter 1 of this book appears in the present volume.]

Coles, Alex. "Curating: Then and Now." *Art Monthly,* no. 275 (April 2004): 1–4.

Coombes, Annie E. "Inventing the 'Postcolonial': Hybridity and Constituency in Contemporary Curating." In *The Art of Art History: A Critical Anthology,* edited by Donald Preziosi. Oxford: Oxford University Press, 1998.

Crimp, Douglas. *On the Museum's Ruins.* Cambridge, MA: MIT Press, 1993.

David, Catherine. "Undurchsichtige Räume: Oder die Prozesse kultureller Konstruktion." In "Das Marco Polo Syndrom," special issue, *neue bildende kunst,* nos. 4–5 (1995): 19–21.

De Baere, Bart. "Joining the Present to the Now." *Kunst and Museumjournaal* 6 (1994–95): 59–70.

De Duve, Thierry. "The Glocal and the Singuniversal: Reflections on Art and Culture in the Global World." In "The Art Biennial as a Global Phenomenon: Strategies in Neo-Political Times," edited by Jorinde Seijdel and Liesbeth Melis, special issue, *Open* 16 (March 2009): 56–65.

Derieux, Florence, ed. *Harald Szeemann: Individual Methodology.* Zurich: JRP|Ringier, 2007.

Doherty, Claire, ed. *Contemporary Art: From Studio to Situation.* London: Black Dog Publishing, 2004.

Doherty, Claire. "Location, Location." *Art Monthly,* no. 281 (November 2004): 7–10.

Domela, Paul, ed. *Manifesta Coffee Break.* Exh. cat. Liverpool, Liverpool Biennial of Contemporary Art, 2005.

Drabble, Barnaby, and Dorothee Richter, eds. *Curating Critique.* Frankfurt am Main: Revolver, 2007.

Drabble, Barnaby, Dorothee Richter, and Eva Schmidt, eds. *Curating Degree Zero: An International Curating Symposium.* Nuremberg: Verlag für Moderne Kunst, 1999.

Ekeberg, Jonas, ed. "New Institutionalism," special issue, *Verksted,* no. 1 (2003).

Elkins, James. *Is Art History Global?* New York: Routledge, 2006.

Enwezor, Okwui. "Between Localism and Worldliness." *Art Journal* 57, no. 4 (1998): 32–36.

Enwezor, Okwui. "Curating beyond the Canon, interviewed by Paul O'Neill." In *Curating Subjects,* edited by Paul O'Neill. Amsterdam and London: De Appel and Open Editions, 2007.

Enwezor, Okwui. "Grossausstellungen und die Antinomien einer transnationalen globalen Form." In *Berliner Thyssen Vorlesung zur Ikonologie der Gegenwart,* edited by Gottfried Boehm and Horst Bredekamp. Munich: Wilhelm Fink Verlag, 2002. Reprinted in translation as: "Mega-Exhibitions and the Antinomies of a Transnational Global Form." In "Biennials," edited by Marieke van Hal, Viktor Misiano, and Igor Zabel, special issue, *MJ–Manifesta Journal* 2 (Winter 2003–Spring 2004): 6–31. [Reprinted in the present volume.]

Enwezor, Okwui, and Olu Oguibe, eds. *Reading the Contemporary: African Art from Theory to the Market Place.* London: Institute of International Visual Arts, 1999.

Esche, Charles. "Debate: Biennials." *Frieze,* no. 92 (July–September 2005): 105.

Farias, Agnaldo, ed. *Bienal: 50 Anos Bienal de São Paolo: 1951–2001.* São Paulo: Fundação Bienal de São Paulo, 2001.

Farquharson, Alex. "Bureau de Change." *Frieze,* no. 101 (September 2006): 156–59.

Farquharson, Alex. "Curator and Artist: Part 2." *Art Monthly,* no. 270 (October 2003): 13.

Farquharson, Alex. "I Curate, You Curate, We Curate: Feature on Curating, Part 1." *Art Monthly,* no. 269 (September 2003): 7–10.

Ferguson, Bruce W., Reesa Greenberg, and Sandy Nairne. "Mapping International Exhibitions." In *Thinking about Exhibitions,* edited by Reesa Greenberg, Bruce W. Ferguson, and Sandy Nairne. London and New York: Routledge, 1996.

Fidelis, Gaudêncio. "The Behavior of Biennials: Notes for a Psychology of Institutional Profile." In *Rosa-dos-Ventos: Posições e Direções na Arte Contemporânea, Histórias da Arte e doEspaço,* edited by Paulo Sergio Duarte. Porto Alegre: Fundação Bienal de Artes Visuais do Mercosul, 2005.

Filipovic, Elena. "The Global White Cube." In *The Manifesta Decade: Debates on Contemporary Art Exhibitions and Biennials in Post-Wall Europe,* edited by Barbara Vanderlinden and Elena Filipovic. Brussels and Cambridge, MA: Roomade and MIT Press, 2005. [Reprinted in the present volume.]

Filipovic, Elena, Rafal Niemojewski, and Barbara Vanderlinden. "One Day Every Wall Will Fall: Chronology of Art and Politics after 1989." In *The Manifesta Decade: Debates on Contemporary Art Exhibitions and Biennials in Post-Wall Europe,* edited by Barbara Vanderlinden and Elena Filipovic. Brussels and Cambridge, MA: Roomade and MIT Press, 2005.

Fisher, Jean, ed. *Global Visions: Towards a New Internationalism in the Visual Arts.* London: Kala Press and Institute of International Visual Arts, 1994.

Gielen, Pascal. "The Biennale: A Post-Institution for Immaterial Labor." In "The Art Biennial as a Global Phenomenon: Strategies in Neo-Political Times," edited by Jorinde Seijdel and Liesbeth Melis, special issue, *Open* 16 (March 2009): 8–17.

Gielen, Pascal. *The Murmuring of the Artistic Multitude.* Antennae Series, no. 3. Amsterdam: Valiz, 2009.

Gillick, Liam, and Maria Lind, eds. *Curating with Light Luggage.* Frankfurt: Revolver Archiv für Aktuelle Kunst, 2005.

Grasskamp, Walter. *Art and the City: Contemporary Sculpture: Projects in Münster.* Ostfildern: Hatje Cantz, 1997.

Grasskamp, Walter. "To Be Continued: Periodic Exhibitions (Documenta, for Example)." In "Landmark Exhibitions," special issue, *Tate Papers* 12 (Autumn 2009). Online at: http://www.tate.org.uk/research/tateresearch/tatepapers/09autumn/.

Greenberg, Reesa. "Identity Exhibitions: From *Magiciens de la Terre* to Documenta 11." *Art Journal* 64, no. 1 (2005): 90–94.

Greenberg, Reesa, Bruce W. Ferguson, and Sandy Nairne, eds. *Thinking about Exhibitions.* London and New York: Routledge, 1996.

Griffin, Tim, James Meyer, Francesco Bonami, Catherine David, Okwui Enwezor, Hans Ulrich Obrist, Martha Rosler, and Yinka Shonibare. "Global Tendencies: Globalism and the Large-Scale Exhibition." *Artforum* 42, no. 3 (November 2003): 152–63, 206, 212.

Groys, Boris. "From Medium to Message: The Art Exhibition as Model of a New World Order." In "The Art Biennial as a Global Phenomenon: Strategies in Neo-Political Times," edited by Jorinde Seijdel and Liesbeth Melis, special issue, *Open* 16 (March 2009): 56–65.

Grzinic, Marina. "Global Capitalism and the Genetic Paradigm of Culture." *Seijo Journal of Aesthetics and Art History* 16 (2004): 91–104.

Haacke, Hans. "Gondola! Gondola!" In Pierre Bourdieu and Hans Haacke, *Free Exchange.* Cambridge: Polity Press, 1995.

Haacke, Hans. "Lessons Learned." In "Landmark Exhibitions," special issue, *Tate Papers* 12 (Autumn 2009). Online at: http://www.tate.org.uk/research/tateresearch/tatepapers/09autumn/.

Hal, Marieke van, Viktor Misiano, and Igor Zabel, eds. "Biennials." Special issue, *MJ–Manifesta Journal* 2 (Winter 2003–Spring 2004).

BIBLIOGRAPHY

Hall, Stuart. "Museums of Modern Art and the End of History." In *Modernity and Difference,* edited by Stuart Hall and Sarat Maharaj. Vol. 6 of *inIVA Annotations,* edited by Sarah Campbell and Gilane Tawadros. London: Institute of International Visual Arts, 2001.

Hannula, Mika, ed. *Stopping the Process? Contemporary Views on Art and Exhibitions.* Helsinki: Nordic Institute for Contemporary Art, 1998.

Hanru, Hou. "Towards a New Locality: Biennials and Global Art." In *The Manifesta Decade: Debates on Contemporary Art Exhibitions and Biennials in Post-Wall Europe,* edited by Barbara Vanderlinden and Elena Filipovic. Brussels and Cambridge, MA: Roomade and MIT Press, 2005.

Harding, Anna, ed. *Curating: The Contemporary Art Museum and Beyond.* London: Academy Group, 1997.

Hasagawa, Yuko, and Isabel Carlos. "Last Words on Biennials." *Flash Art* 28, no. 185 (November–December 1995): 74.

Haupt, Gerhard, and Pat Binder, eds. "Universes in Universe." Online resource: http://universes-in-universe.org.

Haye, Christian. "Spin City." *Frieze,* no. 38 (January–February 1998): 48–51.

Heartney, Eleanor. "Into the International Arena." *Art in America* 84, no. 4 (April 1996): 50–54.

Heinrich, Barbara, ed. *Das Lied von der Erde / The Song of the Earth.* Exh. cat. Kassel, Museum Fridericianum, 2000.

Held, David, ed. *A Globalizing World? Culture, Economics, Politics.* London: Routledge, 2004.

Hill, Joe Martin. "The Burden of (Mis) representation and other ______s of the Biennial Spectacle." *Yishu: Journal of Contemporary Chinese Art* 4, no. 3 (Autumn 2005): 11–17.

Hill, Joe Martin. "Developing a Consequential Biennials Dialogue." *Asia Art Archive Newsletter* (January 2006).

Hill, Joe Martin. "Reflections on Venice and the Proliferation of Cultural Festivals in Recent Decades." *Platform* 2, no. 2 (October 2001).

Hiller, Susan, and Sarah Martin, eds. *The Producers: Contemporary Curators in Conversation.* B.Read, vols. 2, 4, and 5. Gateshead: BALTIC, 2000–03.

Hobhouse, Hermione. *The Crystal Palace and the Great Exhibition: Science, Art and Productive Industry: The History of the Royal Commission for the Exhibition of 1851.* London: Continuum International Publishing Group, 2002.

Hoffmann, Jens, ed. *The Next Documenta Should Be Curated by an Artist.* Frankfurt: Revolver, 2004.

Hoffman, Jens. "Running on Empty: The Biennial is Dead! Long Live the Biennial." *nu-e* 1 (September 2003). Online at: http://www.nu-e.nu.

Hutchinson, Michael. "The New Curation." *Art Monthly,* no. 277 (June 2004): 44.

IFA–Institut für Auslandsbeziehungen: Biennalen Datenbank. Online at: http://www.ifa.de/info/biennalen-datenbank/.

Jacob, Mary Jane, and Michael Brenson. *Conversations at the Castle: Changing Audiences and Contemporary Art.* Cambridge, MA: MIT Press, 1998.

Jones, Caroline A. "Troubled Waters: On Globalism and the Venice Biennale." *Artforum* (February 2006): 91–92.

Kapur, Geeta. "Contemporary Cultural Practice: Some Polemical Categories." *Third Text,* no. 11 (Summer 1990): 109–17.

Kapur, Geeta. "Globalisation and Culture." *Third Text,* no. 39 (Summer 1997): 21–38.

Karlsen, Anne Szefer, Morten Kvamme, and Arne Skaug Olsen, eds. *Lokalisert / Localised.* Bergen: City of Bergen and Bergen Kunsthall, 2009.

Karp, Ivan, and Steven Levine, eds. *Exhibiting Cultures: The Poetics and Politics of Public Display.* Washington, D. C.: Smithsonian Institute Press, 1992.

Kleeblatt, Norman L. "Identity Roller Coaster." *Art Journal* 64, no. 1 (2005): 61–63.

Konaté, Yacouba. *La Biennale de Dakar: Pour une esthétique de la création africaine contemporaine: Tête à tête avec Adorno.* Paris: L'Harmattan, 2009. [An abridged and translated version of several chapters of this book appears in the present volume.]

Krauss, Rosalind, Hal Foster, Silvia Kolbawski, Miwon Kwon, and Benjamin H. D. Buchloh. "The Politics of the Signifier: A Conversation on the Whitney Biennial." *October* 66 (Autumn 1993): 3–27.

Kravagna, Christian. "Dr. Livingston, I Presume . . . Some Problems with Transcultural Curating." *Art Planet: A Global View of Art Criticism* 1, no. 0 (1999): 58–67.

Kwon, Miwon. *One Place After Another: Site-Specific Art and Locational Identity.* Cambridge, MA: MIT Press, 2002.

Lamoureux, Johanne. "From Form to Platform: The Politics of Representation and the Representation of Politics." *Art Journal* 64, no. 1 (2005): 64–73.

Lee, Pamela M. "Boundary Issues: The Art World Under the Sign of Globalism." *Artforum* 42, no. 3 (November 2003): 164–67.

Leggewie, Claus. "Europa in den 'United Colors of Benetton: Ein Multikultur-Marktbericht.'" *Kunstforum* 118 (1992): 147–57.

Leon, Dermis P. "Havana, Biennial, Tourism: The Spectacle of Utopia." *Art Journal* 60, no. 4 (Winter 2001): 17–23.

Lesage, Dieter. *Vertoog over verzet: Politiek in tijden van globalisering.* Amsterdam: Meulenhoff, 2004.

Lippard, Lucy. "Alles neu benennen! Unser Afro-Asian-Hispano-Amerika." *Kunstforum* 118 (1992): 158–75, 471.

Lippard, Lucy. *The Lure of the Local: Sense of Place in a Multicultural Society.* New York: New Press, 1997.

Llanes, Lilian. "La Bienal de la Habana." *Third Text,* no. 20 (Autumn 1992): 5–12.

Mackay, Hugh. "The Globalisation of Culture?" In *A Globalizing World? Culture, Economics, Politics,* edited by David Held. London: Routledge, 2004.

Maravillas, Francis. "Cartographies of the Future: The Asia-Pacific Triennials and the Curatorial Imaginary." In *In the Eye of the Beholder: Reception and Audience for Modern Asian Art Sydney,* edited by John Clark et al. Sydney: Wild Peony Press, 2006.

Marchart, Olivier. *Hegemonie im Kunstfeld: Die documenta-Ausstellungen dX, D11, d12 und die Politik der Biennalisierung.* Cologne: Walter König, 2008. [An abridged and translated version appears in the present volume.]

Marincola, Paula. *Curating Now: Imaginative Practice / Public Responsibility.* Philadelphia: Philadelphia Exhibitions Initiative, 2001.

Marschall, Sabine. "The Impact of the Two Johannesburg Biennales (1995 and 1997) on the Formation of a 'New South African Art.'" *Social Dynamics, 1940-7874* 25, no. 2 (1999): 119–37. [Reprinted in the present volume.]

Martin, Stewart. "A New World Art? Documenting Documenta 11." *Radical Philosophy* 122 (November–December 2003): 7–19.

Martino, Enzo Di. *The History of the Venice Biennale.* Venice: Papiro Arte, 2007.

McDonald, Sharon, ed. *The Politics of Display: Museums, Science, Culture.* London: Routledge, 1997.

McEvilley, Thomas. "Arrivederci, Venice: The 'Third World' Biennials." *Artforum* 32, no. 3 (November 1993): 114–16. [Reprinted in the present volume.]

McEvilley, Thomas. "Marginialia: Thomas McEvilley on the Global Issue." *Artforum* 28, no. 7 (March 1990): 19–21.

McEvilley, Thomas, and Roger G. Denson. *Capacity: History, The World, and the Self in Contemporary Art and Criticism.* Critical Voices in Art, Theory, & Culture Series, Vol. 1. London and New York: Routledge, 1996.

McLean, Ian. "Documenta X and Australians at Oxford: Thinking Globally from Europe." *Third Text,* no. 42 (Spring 1998): 57–70.

McLean, Ian. "On the Edge of Change? Art, Globalisation and Cultural Difference." *Third Text* 18, no. 3 (2004): 293–304.

Mercer, Koberna. "Intermezzo Worlds." *Art Journal* 57, no. 4 (Winter 1998): 43–45.

Mesquita, Ivo. "Biennials, Biennials, Biennials." In *Beyond the Box: Diverging Curatorial Practices,* edited by Melanie Townsend. Banff: Banff Centre Publishing, 2003.

Miller, John. "The Show You Love to Hate: A Psychology of the Mega-Exhibition." In *Thinking about Exhibitions,* edited by Reesa Greenberg, Bruce W. Ferguson, and Sandy Nairne. London and New York: Routledge, 1996.

Minglu, Gao. "Extensionality and Intentionality in a Transnational Cultural System." *Art Journal* 57, no. 4 (1998): 36–39.

Misiano, Viktor, Filipa Ramos, and Nathalie Zonnenberg, eds. *The Grammar of the Exhibition.* Vol. 7 of *MJ–Manifesta Journal.* Milan and Amsterdam: Silvana Editoriale and International Foundation Manifesta, 2009.

Misiano, Viktor, Filipa Ramos, and Nathalie Zonnenberg, eds. *Collective Curating.* Vol. 8 of *MJ–Manifesta Journal.* Milan and Amsterdam: Silvana Editoriale and International Foundation Manifesta, 2010.

Möntmann, Nina, ed. *Art and Its Institutions.* London: Black Dog Publishing, 2006.

Mosquera, Gerardo. "The Marco Polo Syndrome: Some Problems around Art and Eurocentrism." *Third Text* 21 (Winter 1992): 35–41. [Reprinted in the present volume.]

Mosquera, Gerardo. "The World of Differences: Notes about Art, Globalization, and Periphery." In "Das Marco Polo Syndrom," special issue, *neue bildende kunst,* nos. 4–5 (1995): 19–21.

Mosquera, Gerardo, and Jean Fisher, eds. *Over Here: International Perspectives on Art and Culture.* Cambridge, MA: MIT Press, 2005.

Müller, Hans-Joachim. *Harald Szeemann: Ausstellungsmacher.* Ostfildern: Hatje Cantz, 2006.

Müller, Vanessa Joan, and Nicolaus Schafhausen, eds. *Under Construction: Perspectives on Institutional Practice.* Cologne: Walther König, 2006.

Obrist, Hans Ulrich. "Biennial Manifesto." *Flash Art,* no. 268 (October 2009): 42.

Obrist, Hans Ulrich. *A Brief History of Curating.* Zurich and Dijon: JRP|Ringier and Les Presses du réel, 2009.

Ogbechie, Sylvester Okwunodu. "Ordering the Universe: Documenta 11 and the Apotheosis of the Occidental Gaze." *Art Journal* 64, no. 1 (2005): 80–89.

Oguibe, Ole. *The Culture Game.* Minneapolis: University of Minnesota Press, 2004.

O'Neill, Paul, ed. *Curating Subjects.* Amsterdam and London: De Appel and Open Editions, 2007.

O'Neill, Paul. "Curating U-Topics." *Art Monthly,* no. 272 (December 2003–January 2004): 7.

O'Neill, Paul. "The Curatorial Turn: From Practice to Discourse." In *Issues in Curating Contemporary Art and Performance,* edited by Judith Rugg and Michele Sedgwick. London: Intellect Books, 2007. [Reprinted in the present volume.]

O'Neill, Paul, and Mick Wilson, eds. *Curating and the Educational Turn.* Amsterdam and London: De Appel and Open Editions, 2010.

Osborne, Peter. "Art as Displaced Urbanism: Notes on a New Constructivism of the Exhibition Form." In *Manifesta 5: With All Due Intent,* edited by Massimiliano Gioni and Marta Kuzma. Exh. cat. Manifesta 5, 2004.

Osborne, Peter."Non-Spaces and the Places of Art." *Journal of Architecture* 6 (Summer 2001): 183–94.

Pastor Roces, Marian. "Crystal Palace Exhibitions." In *Over Here: International Perspectives on Art and Culture,* edited by Gerardo Mosquera and Jean Fisher. Cambridge, MA: MIT Press, 2005. [Reprinted in the present volume.]

Piotrowski, Piotr. "Central Europe in the Face of Unification." Online at: http://www.artmargins.com/content/feature/piotrowski2.html. Reprinted in *Who if Not We Should at Least Try to Imagine the Future of All This?,* edited by Maria Hlavajova and Jill Winder. Amsterdam: Artimo, 2004.

Piotrowski, Piotr. "Framing Central Europe." *Moscow Art Magazine,* no. 22 (October 1998). Online at: http://www.guelman.ru/xz/english/XX22/X2210.htm.

Poshyananda, Apinan. "Positioning Contemporary Asian Art." *Art Journal* 59, no. 1 (2000): 10–13.

Preziosi, Donald. "The Crystalline Veil and the Phallomorphic Imaginary." In idem, *Brain of the Earth's Body: Art, Museums, and the Phantasms of Modernity.* Minneapolis and London: University of Minnesota Press, 2003. [Reprinted in the present volume.]

Ramírez, Mari Carmen. "Constellations: Toward a Radical Questioning of Dominant Curatorial Models." *Art Journal* 59, no. 1 (2000): 14–16.

BIBLIOGRAPHY

Rand, Steven, and Heather Kouris, eds. *Cautionary Tales: Critical Curating.* New York: Apexart, 2007.

Ratnam, Niru. "Art and Globalisation." In *Themes in Contemporary Art,* edited by Gill Perry and Paul Wood. New Haven: Yale University Press, 2004.

Ray, Gene. "Another (Art) World is Possible: Theorising Oppositional Convergence." *Third Text* 18, no. 3 (2004): 565–72.

Rogoff, Irit. "Geo-Cultures: Circuits of Arts and Globalizations." In "The Art Biennial as a Global Phenomenon: Strategies in Neo-Political Times," edited by Jorinde Seijdel and Liesbeth Melis, special issue, *Open* 16 (March 2009): 8–17.

Rogoff, Irit. *Terra Infirma: Geography's Visual Culture.* London: Routledge, 2000.

Rogoff, Irit. "Twenty Years On . . . Inside, Out." *Art Journal* 57, no. 4 (1998): 46–49.

Rugg, Judith, and Michele Sedgwick, eds. *Issues in Curating Contemporary Art and Performance.* London: Intellect Books, 2007.

Rugoff, Ralph. "Rules of the Game." *Frieze,* no. 44 (January–February 1999): 46–49.

Seijdel, Jorinde, and Liesbeth Melis, eds. "The Art Biennial as a Global Phenomenon: Strategies in Neo-Political Times." Special issue, *Open* 16 (March 2009).

Sassen, Saskia. *The Global City.* Princeton, NJ: Princeton University Press, 1991.

Sassen, Saskia. *Global Networks, Linked Cities.* New York: Routledge, 2002.

Schneckenburger, Manfred. *Documenta: Idee und Institution.* Munich: Bruckmann, 1983.

Sheikh, Simon. "Constitutive Effects: The Techniques of the Curator." In *Curating Subjects,* edited by Paul O'Neill. Amsterdam and London: De Appel and Open Editions, 2007.

Sheikh, Simon. "Marks of Distinction, Vectors of Possibility: Questions for the Biennial." In "The Art Biennial as a Global Phenomenon: Strategies in Neo-Political Times," edited by Jorinde Seijdel and Liesbeth Melis, special issue, *Open* 16 (March 2009): 68–79. [Reprinted in the present volume.]

Sinnreich, Ursula, Cay Sophie Rabinowitz, and Ali Subotnick, eds. "Inquiry: Learning from Documenta." *Parkett* 64 (2002): 1–22.

Smiers, Joost. *Arts under Pressure: Promoting Cultural Diversity in the Age of Globalisation.* London: Zed, 2003.

Smith, Royce. W. "Cultural Development? Cultural Unilateralism? An Analysis of Contemporary Festival and Biennale Programs." *The Journal of Arts Management, Law, and Society* 36, no. 4 (Winter 2007): 259–72.

Smith, Terry. "Biennials: In the Conditions of Contemporanity." *Art and Australia* 42, no. 3 (Autumn 2005): 406–15.

Stamenkovic, Marko. "Curating the Invisible: Contemporary Art Practices and the Production of Meaning in Eastern Europe." *Inferno,* no. 9 (2004): 53–61.

Staniszewski, Mary Anne. *The Power of Display: A History of Exhibition Installation at the Museum of Modern Art.* Cambridge, MA: MIT Press, 1998.

Šuvaković, Miško. "The Ideology of Exhibition: On the Ideologies of Manifesta." *PlatformaSCCA,* no. 3 (January 2002): 11.

Tannert, Christoph, and Ute Titchler. *MIB–Men in Black: Handbook of Curatorial Practice.* Berlin: Kunstlerhaus Bethanian, 2004.

Tawadros, Gilane, ed. *Changing States: Art and Ideas in an Era of Globalisation.* London: Institute of International Visual Arts, 2004.

Thea, Carolee, ed. *Foci: Interviews with Ten International Curators.* New York: Apexart, 2001.

Tomlinson, John. *Cultural Imperialism.* Baltimore and London: Johns Hopkins University Press, 1991.

Townsend, Melanie, ed. *Beyond the Box: Diverging Curatorial Practices.* Banff: Banff Centre Publishing, 2003.

Troncy, Eric. "A Future One Would Like to Be Able to Defer." *Parkett* 69 (2003): 194–96.

Vanderlinden, Barbara, and Elena Filipovic, eds. *The Manifesta Decade: Debates on Contemporary Art Exhibitions and Biennials in Post-Wall Europe.* Brussels and Cambridge, MA: Roomade and MIT Press, 2005.

Verwoert, Jan. "'Forget the National: Perform the International in the Key of the Local (and Vice Versa)!' On the Experience of International Art Shows." In *Research Paper: Biennials and City-Wide Events,* edited by Steve Dutton and Jeanine Griffin. Supplement published with *a–n* (December 2007): 10–11.

Vidokle, Anton. "Art without Artists?" *e-flux journal,* no. 16 (May 2010). Online at: http://www.e-flux.com/journal/view/136.

Vine, Richard. "Asian Futures." *Art in America* 86, no. 7 (July 1998): 34–41.

Vine, Richard. "Beyond the Biennale." *Art in America* 86, no. 7 (July 1998): 38–40.

Wade, Gavin, ed. *Curating in the Twenty-First Century.* Walsall: New Art Gallery, 2000.

Wallenstein, Sven-Olov. "The Site of the Work of Art." German issue, *MLN* 109, no. 3 (April 1994): 478–94.

White, Peter, ed. *Naming a Practice: Curatorial Strategies for the Future.* Banff: Banff Centre Press, 1996.

Wilson, Mick. "Curatorial Moments and Discursive Turns." In *Curating Subjects,* edited by Paul O'Neill. Amsterdam and London: De Appel and Open Editions, 2007.

Wimmer, Franz. "Globalkultur: Der Mensch in einer global sich vereinheitlichenden Kultur." *Kunstforum* 118 (1992): 108–21, 467–70.

Wu, Chin-Tao. "Biennials Without Borders?" *New Left Review,* no. 57 (May/June 2009): 107–55. Reprinted in: "Landmark Exhibitions," special issue, *Tate Papers* 12 (Autumn 2009). Online at: http://www.tate.org.uk/research/tateresearch/tatepapers/09autumn/.

ACKNOWLEDGMENTS

The making of such a volume necessarily incurs many debts, as it is the result of years of discussion and learning from others. Our reflections in shaping this collection have therefore been inspired by and benefited from many people, including those who so generously allowed us to reprint their previously published texts in this volume, those who responded to our "Call for Biennial Knowledge," and all of the lecturers, reviewers, and moderators who participated in the 2009 Bergen Biennial Conference: Carlos Basualdo, Ute Meta Bauer, Ina Blom, Charlotte Bydler, John Clark, Ann Demeester, Ingar Dragset, Per Gunnar Eeg-Tverbakk, Jonas Ekeberg, Mahita El Bacha Urieta, Bruce W. Ferguson, Gridthiya Gaweewong, Maria Hlavajova, Milena M. Hoegsberg, Ranjit Hoskote, Chrissie Iles, Caroline A. Jones, Yacouba Konaté, Meredith Martin, Vittoria Martini, Sarat Maharaj, Gerardo Mosquera, Rafal Niemojewski, Hans Ulrich Obrist, Tommy Olsson, Paul O'Neill, Marit Paasche, Nikos Papastergiadis, Anri Sala, Shuddhabrata Sengupta, Vinicius Spricigo, Monika Szewczyk, and Sabine B. Vogel.

We would like to thank all of those who provided illustrations for *The Biennial Reader:* Andreas Huber Gallery, Vienna; Archivio Storico delle Arti Contemporanee, Venice; Arquivo Histórico Wanda Svevo; BAK, Utrecht; Biblioteca Querini Stampalia, Venice; Thor Brødreskift; Fernando Chaves; John Clark; Florence Derieux; Documenta Archive; ExpoUni; family of Harald Szeemann; Fundação Bienal de São Paulo; Gwangju Biennial Foundation, Gwangju, Korea; Ryszard Kasiewicz; Lacaton & Vassal Architectes; Lalit Kala Akademi (National Fine Arts Academy), New Delhi, India; Ben Langlands and Nikki Bell, Gavin Brown's enterprise, New York; Eirik Lande; Werner Maschmann; Regents of the University of Minnesota; University of South Florida; VG Bild-Kunst; Rachel Weiss.

We also extend our thanks to: The City of Bergen, Department of Culture, Church Affairs, and Sports: Evelyn Holm, Monica Maeland, Harald Victor Hove, Bjørn F. Holmvik, and Øyvor Johnson; Board of the Bergen Kunsthall and Kari Wiik; Hatje Cantz: Annette Kulenkampff, Tas Skorupa, Angelika Hartmann, and Krystina Stermole; Grandpeople: Magnus Helgesen, Jørgen Eidem, Gaute Aase; Translators: Steven Lindberg, Rodrigo Nunes, Vanessa Mary Palomba, and Charles Penwarden; Dominic Eichler; T. J. Demos; Miško Šuvaković; Gaudencio Fidelis; Roger Conover; Bjørnar Vasenden; Manifesta: Hedwig Fijen; Kunst-Werke Berlin and the Berlin Biennial: Gabriele Horn; Renate Wagner; Rhea Dall; Dirk Snauwaert; Adam Szymczyk; Bojan Šarčević; The Biennial Foundation; Bergen Kunsthall staff: David Alomia, Stein-Inge Århus, Gunvor Bakke Kvinlog, Gustav Birkeland, Frank Christensen, Ingrid Erstad, Ramona Horn, Susanna Kajermo, Morten Kvamme, Mai Lahn-Johannessen, Landmark Kafé, Andrea Rudi Lorås, Åse Løvgren, Mia Øquist, Solfrid Otterholm, Hilde Marie Pedersen, Yngve Pedersen, Hector Pina-Barrios, Tom Rosson, Lillian Samdal, Iver Sandøy, Steinar Sekkingstad, Jonas Skarmark, Karen Skog, Daniel Stockhaus, Arild Thomassen, Einride Torvik, Borghild Unneland, Sveinung Unneland, Vegard Urne, Knud Young Lunde, and all of the volunteers who assisted with the 2009 Bergen Biennial Conference.

The Biennial Reader and the 2009 Bergen Biennial Conference enjoyed the generous support of: the Norwegian Ministry of Culture; the Norwegian Association of Art Societies; Sparebanken Vest; Bergens Tidende; Norwegian Hull Club; BKK; Sinco A/S; Stadsporten, as represented by Stein Olaf Onarheim; the Mondriaan Foundation; Fritt Ord; the Royal Norwegian Embassies in London, Berlin, Bern, and Vienna; the Royal Norwegian Consulate General, New York; The City of Bergen, Department of Culture, Church Affairs, and Sports; the Hordaland County Council; and Arts Council Norway.

Special thanks go to Henning Warloe, who proposed the idea of launching a biennial in Bergen, and to our editorial assistant, Helene A. Lazaridis.

INDEX

INDEX

IMAGE CREDITS

P. 25, fig. 1: Hans Haacke, courtesy of the artist / © VG Bild-Kunst, photo by Roman Mensing / artdoc.de; pp. 46, 47, figs. 1–4: © Regents of the University of Minnesota; p. 56, fig. 1: courtesy of the Florida Center for Instructional Technology; p. 56, fig. 2: courtesy of the Library of Congress, Prints and Photographs Division, Washington, D. C.; p. 84, fig. 1: image is in the public domain; p. 84, fig. 2: courtesy of the Archivio Storico della Arti Contemporanee, Venice; p. 84, fig. 3: courtesy of John Clark, photo by John Clark; p. 84, fig. 4: image is in the public domain; p. 85, fig. 5: courtesy of the Biblioteca Querini Stampalia, Venice; p. 85, fig. 6: courtesy of ExpoUni, Lacaton & Vassal Architectes; p. 170, figs. 1, 2: courtesy of the artist and Gavin Brown's enterprise, New York; p. 171, fig. 3–5: courtesy of the artist and John Clark, photo by John Clark; p. 201, fig. 1: courtesy of Rachel Weiss, photo by Rachel Weiss; p. 201, fig. 2: courtesy of the artist, photo by Eduardo Ruben; p. 215, fig. 1: courtesy of the Archive Harald Szeemann; p. 301, figs. 1, 2: courtesy of the Andreas Huber Gallery, Vienna, photo by Josef Dabernig; p. 305, fig. 1: courtesy of the Andreas Huber Gallery, Vienna, photo by Josef Dabernig; p. 311, figs. 1, 2: courtesy of Lalit Kala Akademi (National Fine Arts Academy), New Delhi, India; p. 311, fig. 3, 4: courtesy of the artists and The Gwangju Biennial Foundation, Gwangju, Korea; p. 348, figs. 1, 2: courtesy of the artist and Marieke van Hal, photo by Marieke van Hal; p. 356, fig. 3: courtesy of the artist and the Arquivo Histórico Wanda Svevo / Fundação Bienal de São Paulo, photo by Gal Oppido; p. 356, fig. 4: courtesy of the artist and the Arquivo Histórico Wanda Svevo / Fundação Bienal de São Paulo, photo by Fernando Chaves; p. 356, fig. 5: courtesy of the artist and Fernando Chaves, photo by Fernando Chaves; p. 380–381, fig. 1: courtesy of Ben Langlands and Nikki Bell; p. 423, figs. 1, 2: courtesy of Rachel Weiss, photo by Rachel Weiss; p. 470, fig. 1: © documenta Archiv, photo by Werner Maschmann; p. 470, figs. 2–5: © documenta Archiv, photo by Ryszard Kasiewicz.